INDUSTRIAL ADMINISTRATION AND MANAGEMENT

INDUSTRIAL ADMINISTRATION AND MANAGEMENT

by

J. BATTY

D.Comm.(S.A.), M.Com.(Dunelm), A.C.W.A.,
M.I.O.M., M.B.I.M.

*Head of School of Business Management
Studies
Robert Gordon's Institute of Technology, Aberdeen*

Assisted by Specialist Contributors

SECOND EDITION

MACDONALD AND EVANS LTD

8 John Street, London, W.C.1

1969

First published October 1966
Second Edition September 1969

© MACDONALD & EVANS LTD
1969

S.B.N.: 7121 0923 4

By the same author:

STANDARD COSTING

MANAGEMENT ACCOUNTANCY

CORPORATE PLANNING AND BUDGETARY CONTROL

Printed in Great Britain by Richard Clay (The Chaucer Press), Ltd.,
Bungay, Suffolk

PREFACE TO FIRST EDITION

In writing a book on industrial administration and management an author is faced with an extremely difficult task. There is the problem of knowing all about such diverse subjects as economic history, economics, law, accountancy and management. In addition, the subject as a whole is so vast that to include every possible facet would involve running into many volumes.

As regards the individual subjects I have been very fortunate in having at my disposal a number of experts who have had experience in both industry or commerce and education. They have been responsible for writing the relevant chapters on the subjects indicated below:

C. A. Inglett, B.A.—Economic history
D. P. Whiting, B.Sc.(Econ.), A.I.B.—Economics
D. A. Whitmore, B.Sc., A.M.I.E.E., A.M.I.E.R.E., A.M.B.I.M.—Production management and statistical method
W. I. Williams, M.Sc.(Econ.), B.A., B.Com., F.C.I.S., F.S.S., BARRISTER-AT-LAW—Legal aspects of business.

They have also been available for advice on related matters.

The aim of the book is to present a concise coverage of the subject *industrial administration*. Careful selection of the topics has enabled the book to be kept to a reasonable size. Special emphasis has been placed on the coverage of all the latest ideas and techniques in the management field. Such techniques as ergonomics, value analysis, work study, marginal costing, budgetary control, the seven-point plan and job evaluation are all explained in brief yet adequate terms.

Because of its practical slant the book should be very useful to practising managers. However, the main concern is with students and, therefore, in determining the scope of the work reference has been made to the appropriate examination syllabuses of the following bodies:

Institute of Mechanical Engineers—Industrial administration
Institution of Production Engineers—Industrial administration
Institute of Personnel Management—Business economics with business administration
Institution of Works Managers—Fundamentals of management
Institute of Work Study Practitioners—Social and economic aspects.

Students of accountancy, and similar subjects, will also find that there is much of value in the book, especially on business administration and the principles and practice of management.

I would like to offer my thanks to all who have assisted in getting the book into print: a list of acknowledgments is given on page ix. Special mention is due to the associate authors mentioned earlier. In addition I am very grateful to colleagues mentioned below:

P. W. Betts, M.I.O.M., A.M.B.I.M., A.M.I.W.M., A.INST.M.S.M., who freely gave advice and read the typescript.

Mrs J. Martin, B.A., A.M.I.P.M., who provided material and advice on interviewing techniques.

S. H. Downs, A.M.B.I.M., M.I.O.M., who supplied some of the information on personnel management.

J. R. M. Aslett, M.A. (CANTAB), M.INST.M.S.M., who made available details on marketing organisations.

My wife's contribution in the form of typing, checking and general assistance made the book possible. Without her sacrifices and patience the work would still be in the planning stage.

London J. BATTY

PREFACE TO SECOND EDITION

A NUMBER of changes and developments have taken place since the first edition, and therefore an opportunity has been taken to revise and enlarge the text.

Additions include modern theory of organisation, the administrative function and, because of the role of Government in industry, a chapter has been added to show how statutes are made and the areas in which the State is now taking an active part.

For the first edition I was fortunate in having the assistance of the experts named in the original Preface. In this new edition I have received help from my colleagues at the Robert Gordon's Institute of Technology, Aberdeen. In particular, I offer my thanks to Hugh Stirrat, B.SC.(ECON.), A.I.B.(SCOT.), D. H. F. Gourlay, B.Phil., M.A., DIP.ED., A.M.B.I.M., A.M.I.P.M., and Mrs D. Morgan, M.A. Revision has been necessary in a number of chapters, and those dealing with the legal aspects have had to be amended quite substantially.

Any views expressed are, of course, my own. Letters from lecturers who have ideas for improvement of the text will always be welcome. I can only hope that this revised impression will continue to meet the need which has been clearly indicated by the success of the first edition.

Aberdeen   J. BATTY

ACKNOWLEDGMENTS

I WOULD like to acknowledge the assistance given by a number of people and organisations in making this book more useful. The following are offered my grateful thanks:

"*The Times*" *Review of Industry* for permission to use the chart on mergers.

WOFAC Corporation for details of their work factor scheme and permission to reproduce Work Factor Tables.

International Time Recording Co Ltd, for permission to reproduce the job timing card.

BP Ltd, for information on their central staff department.

The Daily Telegraph for permission to use advertisements.

The Institute of Cost and Works Accountants for permission to use past examination questions. All questions used have been taken from the Institute's past papers.

Professor Alec Rodger and the National Institute of Industrial Psychology for details of the Seven-Point plan.

The Editor of *The Manager* and the British Institute of Management for permission to reproduce charts from *Problems of Growth in Industrial Undertakings* and to draw on material available in articles in *The Manager*.

Professor Frederick Herzberg and John Wiley and Sons Ltd, for permission to use the chart on page 195 from the book *The Motivation to Work*.

Sir Isaac Pitman & Sons Ltd, for permission to use items from the book *Time Study and Ratefixing*.

The Institute of Office Management for details of their salary grading scheme.

CONTENTS

LIST OF ILLUSTRATIONS

CHAPTER I

GENERAL FRAMEWORK

"INDUSTRIAL administration" is a very wide and comprehensive subject. In effect, it is a combination of a number of *related* subjects, which together help to give an understanding of the operation of the economy. Within the latter are companies and other forms of business upon which the wealth of individuals and nations must depend. Managers should understand the general framework so that they can make the most effective use of the labour and assets under their control.

The subjects developed since civilisation began are too numerous to mention. Some, such as Logic and Ethics, could be included as part of the studies required by managers: generally though these are regarded as purely academic disciplines. There is always some difficulty in deciding which subjects are *practical enough* for study by managers or would-be managers and those which are included should be capable of justification. They should be those which make better managers not only for individual companies, but also for the country as a whole.

In summary form, the subjects which are usually included in *industrial administration* are as follows:

1. Historical development of management and the work of the early writers on management thought.
2. Business organisation and *current* principles and practice relating to production, selling, administration, finance and other functional areas.
3. Historical background to industrial growth.
4. The economic and financial system which influences the operation of the business.
5. The banking and legal framework.

These are explained below. More details are included throughout the book.

HISTORICAL BACKGROUND

The present state of the British economy has been achieved gradually. Some companies have grown, whereas others have stagnated or even been eliminated. A study of the history of industrial growth shows what has happened in the past, and the likely developments in the future. This is not to suggest that *the past* is likely to be an *accurate indication* of the *future,* but lessons can be learnt and used with profit.

1

The plan of the book follows the sequence indicated in the preceding section. In more detail, this is as follows:

1. Development of management

Management thought has developed very slowly. Yet managers have been required and used for centuries. In the western world, which includes the U.S.A. and Great Britain, the interest in management has only developed in the past sixty years. The work of F. W. Taylor and other pioneers triggered off an upsurge of interest in the subject. This has continued, at times intermittently, until there is now general recognition that management is a distinct process worthy of academic and practical study. In Chapter II the work of the principal pioneers is explained.

2. Current management principles and practice

The functions of management are used in the operation of any business, no matter how small or large. Whether they are consciously recognised or not is not absolutely essential, but such an understanding can make managers more effective and can lead to improvements in the methods and techniques employed. Management is very much an *art* in that it is concerned with dealing with people so as to obtain maximum co-operation. The suggestion that managers cannot be made is wrong and misleading.

Provided a man has the appropriate background in education, and he has the correct personality, there is much that can be done to make a manager a *better* manager. The art can be improved and the new techniques of management can be learnt; above all, skills can be developed to cover many of the functions of management.

The old-fashioned idea of learning from someone else ("Sitting with Nellie") *without* any education and training in principles can be both damaging and unprofitable. If the "someone else" has all the knowledge required then all may be well. However, how many managers have the ability or time to train their successors? Unfortunately, a manager training his successor may do the task unwillingly or he may not even bother to mention some matters at all.

Training in the *practical aspects* of management is vital; there is no doubt regarding this fact. However, this practical training should be preceded by education and training in the subjects likely to be required. The potential manager can then use his knowledge and skill to learn more effectively, and, where necessary, to improve on the practices which are followed.

Management is concerned with getting the best out of people in the achievement of the objectives of a business. The recruitment of the necessary personnel and their control and motivation are the subject matter of Part Three. What is often overlooked is that personnel management is *not* simply the term given to the functions of the personnel department. Good personnel relations should permeate the whole organisation, and should be the concern of all managers.

The personnel aspect enters into every facet of management. The new techniques which have been developed do not eliminate the need for good personnel relations; in fact, they often intensify the need for tact and understanding. If a computer is to be introduced then staff should be educated so that they understand the implications and, particularly, how they are to be affected by the change. The latter, in any form, is usually viewed with suspicion and the necessary steps to dispel fears should be taken as soon as possible.

Parts Two and Four are concerned with the management techniques and services used in producing, selling and administration. Tremendous improvements have been made to increase the effectiveness of managers through the employment of techniques such as work study, value analysis, management accountancy, ergonomics and job evaluation. Whether he has to use the techniques himself, or deal with people that use them, a manager who is intent upon giving the best service possible will make sure that he keeps himself up to date.

3. The industrial environment

Part Five of the book outlines the major developments which have taken place in British industry. This evolution has been based primarily on free enterprise, but in recent years there has been considerable Government intervention in the operation of industry.

4. The economic system

Study of the economic environment and the way prices behave with changes in supply and demand is an essential requirement for all who have to work in the commercial field. Unless there is a clear understanding of how markets operate, it is unlikely that a reasonable profit will be earned. The continuing existence of companies also requires the same knowledge.

5. The legal system

Businesses operate in a world of contracts. They may be simple, gentlemen's agreements, written contracts or even deeds. Irrespective of the type, a good manager should appreciate the essentials of a legal contract. Whether buying goods or engaging employees it is necessary for all businesses to operate within the law.

COMPLEXITY OF MANAGEMENT

Another factor which has emphasised the need for more efficient managers and, therefore, the need for management education is the growth and size of business organisations. There is a tendency for companies to grow larger and larger, either by ploughing back profits

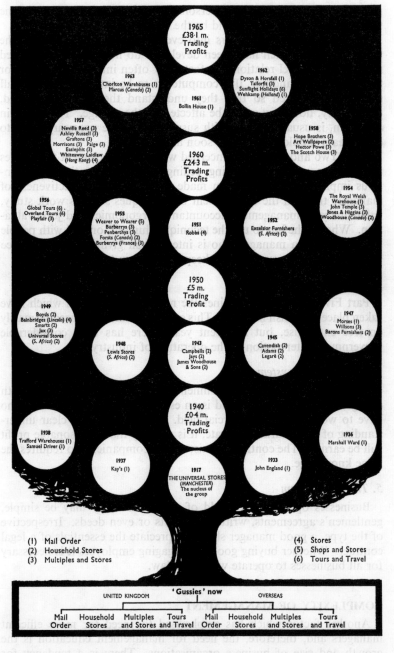

Fig. 1.—*How a giant grows: companies forming the Great Universal Stores*
Reproduced from The Times Review of Industry, *August 1965, by kind permission of the publishers.*

or by merging with other businesses. Often the mergers result from take-over bids, which have as their objective economies in administrative, research, advertising and other costs.

Irrespective of the reasons for mergers it does mean that managers, particularly those at or near the top, have heavy responsibilities. In theory, the span of control can be limited; in practice, a board of directors wishes to keep its finger on the pulse of the whole organisation, not just a fraction of it. An example of "how a giant grows" is shown in Fig. 1. This is in respect of the Great Universal Stores, but is typical of the way very successful businesses tend to grow by merging with others. In the illustration it will be seen that the growth has been "horizontal"; *i.e.* with businesses of the same type; in this case, distribution. Many companies expand vertically so that they can control the supply of raw materials, manufacturing and distribution.

Another factor which increases the complexity of management functions is linked with mergers; the need to reduce costs. Great Britain must export to survive and this means that prices charged abroad should be not more, and, if possible should be less, than those of manufacturers in the importing countries. The growth of such areas as the Common Market and the European Free Trade Area has tended to put Britain in an unfavourable position. Tariff barriers have been erected and this fact has accentuated the need to reduce costs.

The increase in size of a company can give the economies of large-scale production, but this is not enough. Fullest use should be made of the latest techniques in management, not just as "gimmicks," but as methods of increasing efficiency and thereby reducing costs. Unless a manager is trained to know when and where to employ the appropriate methods, he is like an unarmed man who is fighting an armed-to-the-teeth adversary. Only his skill at ducking will save him from immediate death.

PART ONE

GENERAL PRINCIPLES AND THE GROWTH OF MANAGEMENT THOUGHT

CHAPTER II

GROWTH OF MANAGEMENT THOUGHT

THERE is difficulty in writing a detailed description of the growth of management thought in Great Britain because much work has gone unnoticed and unrecorded. In addition, writers on management have been very few, no doubt because of the reluctance of businesses, or those who managed them, to undertake such work, being somewhat sceptical of the value of formal training and education in this field.

The earlier writers on management tended to be economists rather than managers. Worthy of special mention are Adam Smith who wrote his *Wealth of Nations* in 1776 (*see* p. 35) and Alfred Marshall who produced a book on *Principles of Economics* and an *Economics of Industry* (1890). They were more concerned with management in a general way and made observations on such matters as the structure of industries, specialisation, training, prices, wages and profits.

Except for relatively small contributions from British writers, management thought has tended to follow the pattern developed in the United States of America. Admittedly, what ideas have developed have been significant, but there has been no growth of any movement such as the "scientific management" idea developed by F. W. Taylor in the U.S.A.

Fig. 2 illustrates the development of management thought by its pioneers. This is not a *complete* coverage, but a brief survey. Similarly, the descriptions are kept as concise as possible and only the most important pioneers are covered. Where appropriate, reference is made in the text throughout the book to those who have made significant contributions to the subject. All the men listed and the two women (Mary Parker Follett and Lilian Gilbreth) have written books and/or articles, as well as being responsible for original thought. Present-day principles and practice owe much to their ideas and perseverance, often in the face of adverse criticism.

THE PIONEERS

A brief coverage of the work of some of the pioneers is given below.

ROBERT OWEN (1771–1858)

Robert Owen was a social reformer who is noted for the part he played in assisting in the development of the following:

1. Personnel relations: he believed, and practised, the idea that workers should be treated as human beings. He aimed at obtaining

results through what is now known as "positive motivation" (*see* p. 24).

2. Improved conditions of employment. He was largely responsible for the introduction of the *Factory Act* of 1819.

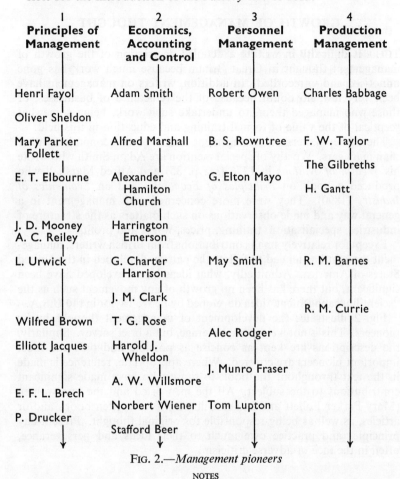

1 Principles of Management	2 Economics, Accounting and Control	3 Personnel Management	4 Production Management
Henri Fayol	Adam Smith	Robert Owen	Charles Babbage
Oliver Sheldon			
Mary Parker Follett	Alfred Marshall	B. S. Rowntree	F. W. Taylor
			The Gilbreths
E. T. Elbourne	Alexander Hamilton Church	G. Elton Mayo	H. Gantt
J. D. Mooney A. C. Reiley	Harrington Emerson		
L. Urwick	G. Charter Harrison	May Smith	R. M. Barnes
	J. M. Clark		R. M. Currie
Wilfred Brown	T. G. Rose	Alec Rodger	
Elliott Jacques	Harold J. Wheldon	J. Munro Fraser	
	A. W. Willsmore		
E. F. L. Brech	Norbert Wiener	Tom Lupton	
P. Drucker	Stafford Beer		

FIG. 2.—*Management pioneers*

NOTES

1. The vertical columns indicate the broad divisions, but many of the disciplines overlap. Moreover, some of the pioneers of management made contributions in more than one field (*e.g.* Taylor could well appear under columns 1, 2 and possibly 3).

2. Not all the important names have been included; space does not allow a full coverage.

3. The order of each name on a line is not intended to show the precise order in which each person developed his or her work.

4. Wilfred Brown (now Lord Brown) and Elliott Jacques have collaborated on what is termed the *Glacier Project*. This was the application of new ideas and concepts in the actual management of an engineering company (The Glacier Metal Co Ltd). A number of publications are available on the work carried out.

3. Co-operative movement and the reform of working conditions for children.

His experiments were not all successful and he lost many thousands of pounds in schemes that were quite impracticable. Nevertheless, he certainly deserves his place in the history of the growth of management thought.

CHARLES BABBAGE (1792–1871)

Charles Babbage was the Lucasian Professor of Mathematics at Cambridge University, a post he held from 1828 to 1839. Although he did not develop his ideas into what would now be regarded as "tools of management," he certainly indicated what could be done. The contributions worthy of special mention are as follows:

1. Cost accounting: he recognised the necessity for detailed costs.
2. Invented the Babbage calculating machine.
3. Attempted to show how the various disciplines were interrelated and pointed the way to the development of a separate subject of management science.

Unfortunately, little notice was taken of his writings by his contemporaries. He shared the fate of other brilliant men who had ideas which were ahead of the times.

HENRI FAYOL (1841–1925)

Without doubt, Henri Fayol was one of the first writers to introduce concepts which are still part of current management thought. These are discussed in detail in Chapter IV, in so far as they affect organisation. He was a Frenchman who had spent many years in industry as a very successful manager. Some of the concepts developed by Fayol are mentioned below:

1. Principles of organisation (*see* p. 35).
2. Functions of the business and functions of management. The latter are discussed in Chapter III. He named the main functions as planning, forecasting, organising, commanding, controlling and co-ordinating.
3. Analysis of the work of a manager according to the nature of the responsibilities (*see* p. 49).

This brief list hardly does justice to the importance of the work of Fayol. However, much more is stated in other parts of the book and students are advised to study the appropriate sections.

OLIVER SHELDON (1894–1951)

Oliver Sheldon, like Mary Parker Follett, was interested in the philosophy of management. In fact, his book had these words as the title.*

* *The Philosophy of Management*, Pitman, London, 1923.

He was a director with Rowntree and Co Ltd, York, and, therefore, was able to work in the appropriate environment with a company that was a leader in the development of sound personnel practices.

He recognised that a company should play an important part in society and not simply be a means of earning profit for shareholders. Better working conditions, a shorter working week and more efficient management were included in his ideas.

His main contribution was the bringing together of the scientific method (Taylor's scientific management) and the human problems of business and society into a co-ordinated philosophy. Many regard Sheldon as one who changed the ideas on the role of the manager and thereby gave him status. Viewed from this aspect, he was one of the first to put management into its true place as recognised by modern society.

MARY PARKER FOLLETT (1868–1933)

The best-known fact regarding Mary Parker Follett, an American business philosopher, is that she invented the *Law of the Situation*; or, at least, she gave formal recognition to its existence. She showed that orders came from following the system and not from the personal wishes or whims of supervisors or other managers. Had she been writing today she would no doubt have linked her concept with the law known as the *Parity of Objectives*.

In addition, she believed in joint consultation so that any grievance or dispute could be settled by peaceful means.

FREDERICK WINSLOW TAYLOR (1856–1915)

There seems little doubt that Frederick Winslow Taylor stands out as the most significant figure in the history of management thought. Much of the vast field of what is now termed "management services" received some attention from Taylor. His work had a very mixed reception: by some he was hailed as a creator of efficiency; at the other end of the scale he was viewed as a menace to the whole of the labour force engaged in industry. Today he is acknowledged as the founder of "scientific management." This term is unfortunate because it implies a precision which cannot always be present when dealing with human beings. A more accurate description is the "application of scientific method to the problems of management."

Space does not permit a full coverage of all the achievements which Taylor packed into his lifetime. However, some of the most significant are listed below:

1. Work study

Work study in its basic form consists two elements: time study and method study. There is universal acceptance that time study was invented by Taylor in 1881, while he was employed at the Midvale Steel Company, in the United States of America.

It was at a later date that F. B. Gilbreth (*see below*) began investigations into method study so that he could find the "one best way." If the impression is given that Taylor ignored motion study altogether, then this is incorrect. In fact, he recognised its existence and employed it, but only to a limited extent.

For a description of work study, which *fundamentally* has changed very little since Taylor's day, the reader is advised to turn to page 115. What is now recognised is that the technique is capable of being applied in some form to all types of industrial or commercial work.

2. Application of scientific method

Taylor recognised that scientific method could be applied to industrial problems. He observed, recorded the facts and then applied the knowledge to the solving of problems. In this way he was able to select the best methods and avoid mistakes made previously.

He was able to apply this approach to improving the efficiency of workers and, with increased productivity, higher wages were possible.

3. Incentive methods

The Taylor Differential Piece Rate Scheme provided a tremendous incentive for a worker to achieve a high level of output. Critics of the scheme thought that it was too harsh on many workers. Even if there is some truth in this statement—and the fact that the system is very rarely used now shows this to be so—the importance of the scheme cannot be ignored. It provided a basis for showing how productivity could be increased with the right incentive.

4. Principles of management

If the reader turns to pages 60 and 61 he will see a description of Taylor's ideas on functional management. Although it is possible to criticise the system, many of the ideas are found in present-day organisations.

5. Experiments

Many of the experiments carried out by Taylor are now known throughout the world. Examples of these are:

(*a*) *Shovelling.*—At the works of the Bethlehem Steel Corporation in 1898, Taylor gave his attention to the best methods of shovelling different types of material. He selected $21\frac{1}{2}$ lb as being the optimum shovel-load and then designed shovels big enough to hold this amount. For handling ore he designed a small shovel and for lighter material a much larger shovel. The result was that each man lifted $21\frac{1}{2}$ lb and could maintain an optimum level of output.

(*b*) *Machine tools.*—His work led to much more effective utilisation of machine tools.

(*c*) *Cutting metals.*—Taylor had a paper published on the "Art of Cutting Metals." His experiments revealed how to keep metal cool when being cut and the depth of cut which could be made.

6. Standards and standard costs

Although Taylor did not invent the first standard costing system, he did pave the way by his methods of setting standard times. In addition, he introduced and operated costing systems of various types.

7. Backing of workers and top management

When the scientific management ideas were introduced there was a great deal of suspicion and opposition. Taylor showed himself to be an excellent tactician; he introduced his methods by gradual stages. For example, one or two men were shown how to work the Taylor way and then others were willingly brought into the scheme when they saw the wages that could be earned.

One of the basic principles of management is that any new scheme should have the backing of top management and the co-operation of workers. Taylor acknowledged this fact just as he did many others.

CRITICISMS OF TAYLOR

There were many who criticised Taylor. Certainly, his attitude to some matters seems harsh by present-day standards, but it should be remembered that he was an early pioneer working in conditions which were far different from those prevailing in modern society.

The use of the word "scientific" gave the impression that there was no need to consider people. Taylor himself did not make this mistake, but many other managers who introduced his ideas thought they could ride roughshod over the workers and that scientific methods would correct any wrongs. All the essential requirements such as work load, method of carrying out the work and the pay earned were carried out scientifically so it was felt that the workers could have no complaint. In effect, they tried to treat the workers just like the other factors of production.

In the hands of unscrupulous managers who "fixed" the rates to suit themselves, and resented paying very high wages, scientific management became scientific exploitation. There are those who argue that systems worthy of recognition should be capable of being employed by all types of managers. They conclude by observing an inherent weakness in scientific management: the failure to understand that human beings have problems which must be recognised and dealt with. Instead of the system being the driving force, there should be co-operation and motivation.

Even after allowing for the harshness of some of Taylor's ideas, credit must be given for his creativeness and ingenuity. He gave recognition to the detailed planning necessary for successful production.

FRANK B. GILBRETH AND LILIAN M. GILBRETH

The combined efforts of Frank Bunker Gilbreth (1868–1924) and his wife Lilian did much to bring motion study to its present high state of perfection. Indeed, some work study engineers think that Frank Gilbreth went too far when analysing work into its fundamental motions.

Being Americans, as was Taylor, they were concerned with the conditions which existed in the U.S.A. at that time. Gilbreth served an apprenticeship as a bricklayer and subsequently owned his own contracting business. His wife was a trained psychologist who was able to contribute in a substantial way to the work which was done, especially on such matters as fatigue and monotony.

Very briefly, then, some of the most important work done by the Gilbreths was as follows:

1. Development of motion study

As noted earlier, in connection with F. W. Taylor, Gilbreth was responsible for the development of the motion study side of work study.

2. Improvement of the building industry

From his study of bricklaying Gilbreth was able to reduce the number of motions required to lay a brick and also to increase the number of bricks laid per hour by as much as three times. Unfortunately, the British building industry does not achieve such high standards even today!

3. Invention of a number of new techniques

The principles of these are as follows:

(a) *Micromotion study.*—The use of cine cameras to show the breakdown of work into its fundamental elements and their timing.

(b) *Chronocyclegraph.*—A record used in connection with a cyclegraph (*see* p. 124).

(c) *Process charts* (*see* p. 123).

(d) *Therbligs* (Gilbreth spelt backwards).—A representation of the seventeen elementary motions used in method study.

4. Study of fatigue

This was an attempt to reduce the effects of fatigue by allowing rest periods, and planning seating and working conditions (*see* ergonomics, p. 124).

His search for the "one best way" took up the whole of his life. He had his critics, but they never seem to have been as harsh to him as they were to Taylor. Psychologists have pointed out that the *one best way* for one man may not necessarily be the best for another. In short, rigid adherence to the assumption that there is one way to suit everyone, without modifications, is quite wrong.

THOMAS GERALD ROSE (1887–1963)*

Thomas Gerald Rose was a British engineer who served in various capacities, including periods as works manager and general works manager. In 1926 he set up as a management consultant.

Throughout his life Rose showed a fascinated interest in accounting, especially what he called "higher business control." As an engineer he wanted to see facts relating to profit and loss presented clearly and without ambiguity. As Harold Norcross so ably summed up the position:

"His fame as a consultant—and also his fame as an author—owes much to his work of introducing what he termed 'higher management control.' He showed a grasp of the financial problems of business undertakings—and particularly of the inter-relationship between the problems of management and those of finance—which put him years ahead of his time. His work in the lucid interpretation of accounting figures to the men responsible for managing a business was, indeed, one of the foundations on which some of the best management accounting systems of the present day have been built. Here was an engineer who taught accountants much about accounting, and in the books he wrote much of his teaching can still profitably be absorbed today."

In brief terms, the work of T. G. Rose for which he is best known in the management field is as follows:

1. Development of management accountancy

There is no doubt that Rose played a major part in developing an interest in what is now termed *management accountancy*. This is especially true of his work on the analysis and interpretation of financial accounts, including balance sheets. His book *Higher Control in Management* is still used today very much in its original form. Besides analysing figures he showed how they should be presented to management in the form of business charts and other statistical aids.

2. Pioneer of management education

He worked unsparingly to raise the standards of management education in this country. The Institute of Industrial Administration owed

---

* Details have been taken from "T. G. Rose": a tribute by Harold Norcross, published in *The Manager*, December 1963. Permission of the Editor to use the source is gratefully acknowledged.

much to his efforts and he served as chairman from 1938 to 1943. From the I.I.A. developed the present British Institute of Management, and there is no doubt that without the leadership of such men as T. G. Rose this would never have occurred.

EDWARD TREGASKISS ELBOURNE (1875–1935)

In Great Britain, management as a subject for study was for a long time disregarded by industry and educational institutions alike. You were either a manager or were not: *very few* believed that management could be taught and that existing management practices could be improved by formal learning. Edward Elbourne belonged to that "few" and he had the vision to see the need for a body which would further the interests of management as a profession.

Edward Elbourne was an engineer who developed his capacities by employment in industrial accountancy and other fields. He was Assistant General Manager at one of the factories of John I. Thorneycroft & Co Ltd, before becoming a consultant. In the field of management he is well known for two related aspects which are as follows:

1. Founder of the Institute of Industrial Administration in 1920

Against apathy and opposition Elbourne established the Institute and continued to share in its development until his death. Undoubtedly, he should be given due recognition for his work in raising the professional standards in business. Without the start he made, education for management would be in a very sorry state indeed.

2. Writer and lecturer

His books on administration, management and cost accounting helped to establish a field of knowledge which was so vital for the training of engineers and others in the fundamentals of industrial administration. Indeed, his books are still used and quoted, even though some of the techniques explained are now outdated.

As a lecturer, he spread the gospel on the need for management education and for qualifications in management philosophy and techniques. Before he died his endeavours began to show results: professional bodies included industrial administration and management in their syllabuses. Today, without exception, all bodies which have some connection with the running of firms in industry and commerce include management in some form or other as part of their training.

THE OTHER PIONEERS

Space does not permit a full coverage of all the pioneers, but readers who are interested can study such books as *The Making of Scientific*

B

Management, Thirteen Pioneers by L. Urwick and E. F. L. Brech or *The Golden Book of Management* edited by L. Urwick (London, Newman Neame Ltd, 1956).

In the field of cost accounting, men like Alexander Hamilton Church, Harrington Emerson, G. Charter Harrison and Harold J. Wheldon were responsible for the development of many of the ideas used today. Charter Harrison may be regarded as the inventor of the first complete system of standard costing, including variance analysis. A. W. Willsmore, who is still writing, may rightly be regarded as a pioneer in the field of budgetary control. His book *Business Budgets and Budgetary Control* was first published by Sir Isaac Pitman & Sons Ltd in 1932. The principles employed still apply today, although a different philosophy is now being used.

B. S. Rowntree and G. Elton Mayo will long be remembered for their efforts to improve human relations in industry. Seebohm Rowntree of the firm of Rowntree & Co Ltd, York, carried out investigations into poverty and developed ideas on joint consultation and welfare work in industry. Elton Mayo is regarded by many as the creator of the modern ideas on human relations. He led a team from Harvard University which co-operated with the Western Electric Company of Chicago in the period from 1927 to 1936. This research is now known as the *Hawthorne Experiments* because of the fact that they were conducted in the Hawthorne Works of the company. The experiments revealed that the attitude of mind of the workers was one of the most crucial factors in obtaining a high level of output. It was found that any change to be made should be explained, and in particular the *meaning* of the change should be made quite clear. The fact that a change is logical is not enough, because the workers may not appreciate the logic. Much of the information on group behaviour also came from these experiments.

Henry Gantt was a follower of F. W. Taylor and was responsible for many improvements in production planning and control. He is probably best remembered for the production control chart which he invented and is appropriately named the Gantt Chart. His work on incentive schemes is also very noteworthy.

The majority of the pioneers not covered in this chapter, but included in the chart (Fig. 2), are mentioned in various places throughout the book. Messrs Urwick, Brech, Drucker, Rodger, Munro Fraser and Lupton could really be included in the "current management thought" for they are still active and writing. May Smith and R. M. Barnes are well known for their contributions to industrial psychology and work study respectively.

The newer quantitative techniques of management, many using mathematical models, have been developed by a number of writers. The subjects include operational research, linear programming, electronic data processing and cybernetics. For the latter Norbert Wiener in the U.S.A. and Stafford Beer in Britain are worthy of mention. Since operational research is still in its infancy, there is difficulty in naming any one person who has yet made a significant contribution. In the field of computers and automation John Diebold is probably the best known. In a few years when these new developments have stood the test of time and validation after application to problems it should be possible to be m ore definite.

EXAMINATION QUESTIONS

1. Write brief notes on the contribution to industrial development made by the following:

    (a) Robert Owen.

    (b) F. W. Taylor.

2. Discuss the contribution to the subject of management made by any *two* of the following:

    (a) Fayol,   (c) Gilbreth,

    (b) Taylor,   (d) Rowntree.

3. State briefly what you consider to be the main contribution to industrial management by:

    (a) F. W. Taylor.   (c) Urwick.

    (b) Gilbreth.   (d) B. S. Rowntree.

4. Write an account of the contribution to technical or managerial development in industry of *two* of the following:

    (a) Robert Owen,

    (b) B. S. Rowntree,

    (c) F. W. Taylor.

CHAPTER III

OUTLINE OF MANAGEMENT THEORY

THERE is no generally accepted definition of "management." Much depends upon the point of view of the person who is attempting to define the term. Some writers stress the directing of human activities; others the earning of maximum profits or the making of the correct decisions for maximising profits. These and other variations in emphasis exist not only because of differences of opinion, but also because of the complex nature of business enterprise. There is no doubt that the control of personnel is very important, but can it be said that a manager is not a manager because he is responsible for an automated factory with very few staff under him? Similarly, if a business is not earning a profit does this mean that there are no managers or, if they do exist, that they are inefficient? The answer to the latter depends upon the circumstances: not all organisations aim to earn a profit and at certain stages in the life of an enterprise (*e.g.* early development or trade depression), the efficient manager is one who is able to carry out his functions in such a way that he minimises losses and retains the goodwill of customers and employees.

These differences of opinion have tended to give the impression that there are at least two distinct theories of management. On the one hand, there is what might be described as the *sociological* approach and, on the other, the *quantitative* approach. The former is distinguished by the special attention paid to motivation, the establishment of the correct social relationships; the development of social groups and the creation of an organisation within which there will be a high level of morale. As implied, the quantitative approach is concerned with results as shown by statistics on productivity and efficiency. There is an extension of the scientific management principles of F. W. Taylor; widespread use is made of a systematic method for planning and carrying out the work to be done. In addition, the modern approach *recognises* that management must concern itself with human problems and conflicts. Accordingly, full employment of work study, operational research, management accountancy and other techniques is possible without the rigid adherence to the inflexible rules propounded by Taylor. Any rules that are necessary are observed within the framework of a sound policy which includes full recognition of a satisfactory manager–employee relationship.

When either approach gives a biassed impression of what management is all about, then there is nothing but disservice to all those concerned with learning or teaching the subject. Any explanation or definition of management should not give undue emphasis to any function. Rather there should be an adequate coverage, and balanced account, of all the functions which combine together to make a complex subject intelligible and useful. A list of these functions, with an explanation of each, is given in the next section but one.

DEFINITION OF MANAGEMENT

A manager is a person who attempts to achieve stated objectives by directing human activities in the production of goods or services. He utilises the land, factory, offices, machinery and other facilities at his disposal in the most effective manner. The act of carrying out the *functions* which go to make up his job is described as "management." This term is also used to denote a group of managers, but here the concern is with the actual *process of management*.

There is reference to the "functions" and when defining management it is usual and proper to list these and explain them in turn. All managers perform these functions, but the extent to which each is performed depends upon the nature and responsibilities of the manager concerned. Many attempts have been made to divide a manager's total time according to the approximate time spent on each principal function, but although this is possible in theory, in practice the division is very difficult to achieve with any certainty. In any event, a General Manager of one business may have quite different responsibilities and authority from those held by the same executive in another, similar business. Nevertheless, the time allocation of functions can serve a very useful purpose in showing how the *nature* of managements can vary.

THE FUNCTIONS OF MANAGEMENT

The functions of management may be classified in many ways. One possible list is as shown below:

Forecasting	Controlling
Planning	Communication
Organising	Leadership
Motivating	Decision making
Co-ordinating	

Which of these should be regarded as *principal* or *organic* functions is again a subject of disagreement. However, planning, organising, and controlling can be extended to embrace all the functions and may accordingly be regarded as the principal functions. They are to be found in management irrespective of the title given to the manager who is carrying them out. Provided these three principal functions are being performed by a person who is controlling the work of others, whether these be workers, supervisors or other managers, that person may rightly be termed a "manager." In this explanation a separation is made between supervisor and manager, but it should be clear at the outset that the supervisor carries out management just as much as one who is given the title of "manager." What is important is that those who are regarded as *managing* do actually carry out the functions enumerated above and explained in the subsequent sections.

FORECASTING

Forecasting is inevitable in all aspects of business activities. From the moment an idea is conceived, whether it is to buy and sell, manufacture or offer a service, there is consciously or subconsciously an attempt made to assess probable quantities, prices, costs and related details.

When forecasting is given formal recognition, then it is usual to prepare statements in terms of quantities and values. Either the sales forecast or production forecast is generally the starting point and this would be followed by forecasts for costs, finance, purchases, capital expenditure and profit and loss. The system employed is known as "budgetary control" and this is discussed further in Chapter XXI.

The important fact to note is that forecasting involves estimating, and then considering alternative courses of action. When the most profitable set of forecasts has been found, these form the basis for the plans to be carried out and are, in fact, incorporated into budgets.

Where forecasting ends and planning begins is difficult to say with exactness. Indeed, some writers regard forecasting as part of the planning function. There is no doubt that forecasting can assist materially in determination of what should be done; in other words, the *contents* of the plans. For this reason, forecasting can be regarded as a necessary preliminary to planning. Possibly, for all practical purposes, there is little to be gained from attempting to separate forecasting and planning.

PLANNING

Planning is one of the most important functions of management. The most significant change in management thinking in modern times has been the emphasis given to *pre*-planning. Instead of "hoping for the best" and making corrective changes each time difficulties are experienced, all aspects of production, selling and other activities are planned so that intangibles are reduced to a minimum.

From the moment a commercial idea is conceived there must be decision making. This involves the consideration of alternative courses of action and then selecting that which is likely to achieve the desired result. After this, the way and manner in which the decision is to be put into practical reality has to be determined. If a sales forecast shows that 100 typewriters per month can be sold, then a decision has to be made on whether to go ahead. If the decision is "yes," then the detailed means of carrying out the production and selling must be worked out. This is a very simple example, but it should show what is involved in planning.

In its widest sense, the function involves all decision making and the determination of how the objectives are to be carried out. The broad objectives of a business, the products to be manufactured, fixed assets to be purchased or leased, profits to be earned and the social obligations to employees and consumers are all matters which should receive attention. Once these have been settled, there is the planning of the organisation and the manner in which the other functions—motivating, co-ordinating, controlling, communicating and leadership—are to be achieved in accordance with the policy laid down. Planning should be comprehensive and all-embracing.

There has been reference to "policy." Management theorists have tried to distinguish between policy-making and management. The former is sometimes termed "administration," but this word is also used as being synonymous with management and, therefore, cannot be regarded as being a generally accepted description. Whether *policy-making* and management should be separated as two distinct sub-functions is a matter for debate.

In a limited liability company the objectives are stipulated in a document known as the Memorandum of Association. This sets out at length the objects, *i.e.* the purpose of the company. This may be to manufacture and sell motor cars, to carry on as a general engineering business or to provide some form of service. These are given as alternative examples; legally the prime purpose is known as the *main object* and the policy of the company should be based on this object. Because of the existence of the Memorandum, it follows that the basic policy decisions have already been made. Accordingly, an argument can be advanced that any further decisions should be regarded as coming within the total concept of management.

The titles of *director* and *manager* do not really help to settle the dispute. Although directors have often more influence on policy than some managers they cannot be regarded as playing a different role to that of other executives who are described as managers. A further complication is the *executive director* who has a responsibility for a specific function. Titles are only indicative of a degree of responsibility; they do not reveal the *extent* of the authority vested in a particular person.

This is not to suggest that all managers carry out exactly the same functions to an identical degree. As a general rule, only senior managers have a positive influence on policy-making. However, this is not to say that middle management, including foremen, have no interest in the function. Modern techniques are usually operated only after all interested parties are consulted. For example, when compiling departmental forecasts and budgets it is usual to bring in departmental managers for discussion. Only when agreement has been reached on essential matters are the budgets finalised. In this way, the departmental managers affect planning in an indirect manner.

Whether there is any real reason to distinguish between administration and management is clearly open to doubt. However, because the two terms are employed by many writers it is desirable to explain them without coming to any definite conclusion regarding their use.

In the field of planning there have been developed many new techniques. In the main they are of a quantitative or statistical nature. Where necessary, the use of these techniques has been explained in later chapters. They include operational research, simulation and model building, linear programming, and forecasting by means of sophisticated statistical analyses. Often these are operated alongside, or as a part of, work study and management accounting. Unfortunately, they are sometimes regarded as being synonymous with "planning"; in fact, they are only tools for assisting managers to arrive at rational decisions.

ORGANISING

Organising means the establishment of a framework in which responsibilities are defined and lines of authority are laid down. Unless there is due thought given to establishing the correct relationships within a business, there are bound to be many managerial problems.

When planning the organisation it is necessary to recognise that this is not simply a "once only" task. As the structure of the business changes then the framework within which it operates may also have to be adjusted or changed. Recognition of this fact is given by the employment of organisation and methods experts, practically unheard of a decade ago, but now regarded as an indispensable aid to management.

More is said on this function in later chapters. Here it is enough to see its relationship with the other functions and to note that there is need for an organisation of some kind in all types of business. This may be *formal* or *informal*; these two terms are also discussed later.

MOTIVATING

The definition of management emphasised the importance of controlling the work of others. This control may be achieved in a variety of ways; modern management theory recognises that employees should be treated in a fair way and that they should *feel* that they are being so treated. The right atmosphere should result in co-operation and maximum production: in short, there should be positive motivation throughout the organisation.

Motivation can come in a variety of ways. At one time, pride in a man's work was often the strongest incentive, but mass-production and standardisation has considerably reduced the importance of craftsmanship. Similarly, when employment was difficult to find, the fear of unemployment was the main motivating power: the present age of full employment has removed this factor.

Undoubtedly, financial incentives can provide the necessary encouragement for employees to work harder and more efficiently. Whether these should be *indirect* or *direct* seems a matter for the individual employers and the unions. The indirect payments are those made to a group, whereas the direct are those paid to individuals. By those in favour it is usually argued that the former lead to more teamwork. On the other hand, those against group schemes argue that a man will respond better when he is paid on the basis of what he produces *personally*, and that he resents sharing with others. The pros and cons of incentive schemes are covered in Chapter XV. Here it is important to note that the question of rewarding employees is vital to all sound management. There are probably more cases of withdrawal of labour (strikes) from disputes over wage rates than from all other causes put together.

The importance of creating an atmosphere which is conducive to efficiency has already been mentioned. This is a vital factor, without which there can be little or no motivation. Within each business there is usually a formal organisation which is depicted by organisation charts. In addition, there is also an informal pattern of relationships, often referred to as an "informal organisation." The latter word implies a positive framework from which it is hoped that efficiency will stem; accordingly it is a debatable matter whether in fact "informal *organisation*" is an appropriate description. The informal pattern may be conducive to efficiency or it may be in entire opposition to the formal organisation. The number of unofficial strikes which have occurred in recent years have indicated the power which can be wielded by individuals or groups who are out to further their own ends.

The efficient manager recognises that the business is composed of distinct social groups, each individual having a loyalty to his own group. If there is an urge to work hard within a group, then generally the individual will respond. Alternatively, if there is conflict against management, other social groups, or even the system itself, then maximum efficiency is unlikely to be achieved.

Sound leadership from the man at the top and all others in the chain of command can also be regarded as a vital factor in motivation. Since this element is regarded by some writers as being a separate management function the matter is discussed below.

CO-ORDINATING

A business should be working towards maximum efficiency. This implies that all the segments should operate in harmony and not in a way which causes conflict. The description employed to indicate the dovetailing and harmonising of all the assets and employees into a coherent whole is known as "co-ordination."

Maximum profit is generally taken as the yardstick against which to measure efficiency. However, in management theory, and practice, this objective has to be achieved with regard to the satisfaction of the consumer and the well-being of employees. There should be satisfaction of all parties concerned with the processes of producing and selling.

In the majority of businesses there are specialists responsible for the main aspects of the work to be done. A typical breakdown is into sales, production and administration, and it is the responsibility of the General Manager to ensure that these main divisions are synchronised. Within each main division there are sections which also have to be woven into an efficient unit. Full recognition of this important factor shows itself in the development of modern management techniques. Production control and management accounting stress the importance of the integration of plans and figures. These are covered in Chapters VIII and XXII.

An efficient organisation can go a long way towards creating effective co-ordination. Provided the framework is appropriate to the particular business, and there is motivation with consequent high morale, co-ordination should not be unduly difficult.

CONTROLLING

Planning, including policy-making, is the beginning of the management process. Control is just as important; without the watchfulness and "feedback" of an efficient control system there is little likelihood that even the best laid plans will ever work out as expected.

Control should be systematic and regular. Systems may be divided into those which are primarily concerned with: (a) physical quantities and (b) financial costs and values. Production control comes into the first type, whereas standard costing and budgetary control belong to the second. Irrespective of the control system used, there should be planning; establishment of standards; comparison of actual results with standards; reports to managers where there are deviations from plans, and taking of appropriate, corrective action.

With the development of computers new techniques of control have emerged. Programme Evaluation and Review Technique (PERT) aids in planning and controlling. The critical paths are identified and detailed schedules are compiled for all the times involved. Subsequently, when the work is being done, the tasks of comparing and taking corrective action are greatly facilitated.

The science of control systems has been named "Cybernetics." Men such as Norbert Wiener in the U.S.A. and Stafford Beer in Britain have developed a theory of cybernetics to show how *automatic regulation* can be introduced into a business. There are different versions of what is covered by the term cybernetics, but generally the following features are included:

1. Construction of a model to represent a business and its operations.—
In the terminology of the writers on quantitative techniques of management this function is the construction of "dynamic system models."

*2. Include in the model functional networks which respond according to
the behaviour of the system.*—This has been compared with the nervous
system of the human body which gives signals to the brain.

*3. Incorporate a servo-mechanism into the system so that any deviations
are corrected.*—"Feedback," the method whereby the control unit is
informed of deviations, is an essential requirement of a control system.
In a truly cybernetic system there should be self-regulating action so
that deviations are corrected before they become significant. Moreover,
provision should also be made for dealing with any necessary adjustments (*i.e.* replanning) quite automatically.

4. The system is so designed that all control becomes quite automatic.—
This is implied by *2* and *3*, but is repeated to stress the importance of the
self-regulating nature of a system.

In practice, where human beings are involved as distinct from an
electronic system the true cybernetic system may be difficult to achieve.
However, with the computer, and the development of management
information systems, the necessary feedback can be quite rapid. This
does not necessarily mean that action will be taken, but at least the
deviations will be available.

A diagram which illustrates a simplified version of the principle is
given below (Fig. 3). The input is put through the control unit, which is

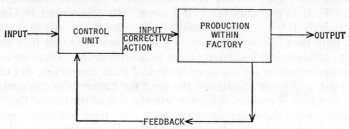

FIG. 3.—*Diagram of Feedback Principle*

made up of Planning, Accounting and various other departments. The
production is then carried out according to plan, and any deviations
are fed back to the control unit so that information can be fed into the
Production Unit for corrective action to be taken. A system which
complies with cybernetic principles would carry out the functions quite
automatically.

More details of the control function are to be found in the
chapters on production control, management accountancy and related
techniques.

COMMUNICATION

This function is the transmitting of instructions and information to all interested parties—employees, customers, suppliers, shareholders and the general public. Fears, anxieties, mistrust and other enemies of efficient management can all arise from a lack of knowledge or a misunderstanding of information that has been given.

All ideas, to be of value, must be accepted by those who are to put them into practical use. If a new production method has been conceived, the reasons for its proposed introduction and its likely effects upon employees should be explained fully *before* any effort is made to put it into effect. Joint consultation, works committees, effective organisation and the appreciation of sound management principles all contribute to sound communication.

This function is elaborated in later chapters, especially Chapter XXI (report writing) and Chapters V and XIII. It is important to notice at this stage that some writers group co-ordination and communication together. In order to obtain effective co-ordination there must be reporting back so that everyone is informed of what is taking place.

LEADERSHIP

"Leadership" covers a variety of meanings or shades of meanings. Fundamentally, the term means to inspire confidence and trust so that there is maximum co-operation from the employees within the control of a manager.

In the U.S.A. there have been many great industrial leaders, but Henry Ford is probably the best known. His counterpart in Great Britain is the late Viscount Nuffield who founded the Morris Motor Co Ltd; both men had vision, drive and inventiveness so that they were able to create industrial empires from virtually nothing. There are now fewer opportunities for the development of giant enterprises, but they still exist, and there is certainly the need for leaders who can control large numbers of people. Since the introduction of the limited liability company, from the successive *Companies Acts*, there has been a rapid growth in the number of public companies. This trend has been facilitated by the changing pattern of the ownership of companies: today there are thousands of shareholders who own only a very small stake, but who nevertheless have made possible the raising of large sums of capital.

The possession of the quality of leadership is desirable in all managers. Reference has been made to *the* leader of a company. In fact, any business which is run efficiently is composed of many leaders at different levels. Each is responsible for his own group and to the leader above him. The qualities required for a General Manager cannot be said to be the same as those required for a foreman but there are similarities.

Both have to be leaders and have to make decisions. The differences between them are explained in Chapter V.

DECISION MAKING

Decision making in business is the prerogative of managers; indeed, what is surprising is that so little attention has been paid to this function in defining the functions of management. Whether the latter is looked upon primarily as dealing with people, earning a profit or simply ensuring that work is carried out, there has to be decision making in some form.

Managers are given different levels of responsibility along the lines indicated in Chapters IV, V and VI, which deal with organisation. At director and senior management level *corporate planning* decisions have to be made. Below this there have to be *operational decisions* by the middle-level functional and line managers, but within the plans already made. At the lower levels of supervisors and charge-hands the decisions should be of a relatively simple nature and within the well-defined areas indicated by the instructions given to the appropriate departments, and by the general regulations or management conventions. In an emergency, then, all managers are expected to act in a rational manner so as to safeguard persons and property.

From this principle, that managers operate within their responsibilities, it follows that any decisions which can be made by a particular manager should be left to him. A foreman should make decisions on how best to get the work done within the framework of his defined area of responsibilities. However, he should *not* change the methods of operation or other procedure without obtaining the necessary authority. The most efficient methods are often determined by the employment of work study techniques, and therefore a foreman who wishes to make improvements should communicate his suggestions via his own line manager. Permitting arbitrary changes would bring about chaos and a lack of respect for any systems being employed.

The concept of making decisions within the area of responsibilities is really a part of the management law the *Principle of Exceptions* (*see* p. 355). Only matters which cannot be dealt with by a manager should be referred to higher authority. Otherwise senior managers would find themselves being inundated with operational problems and there would be little time for broader issues.

Many theories of decision making have been put forward by writers on management. Quite naturally, since decisions are often made on the basis of personal judgment, there is difficulty in stating what rules should be followed. One manager can get very good results from employing ideas, hunches or methods which would be regarded by another manager as being quite "suicidal." Results may be obtained which are quite satisfactory, but which were obtained from applying the wrong decisions when viewed logically after considering all alternatives. It is against this background that a decision theory has to stand (or fall!).

Basically there are two approaches:

1. *Rational decisions*

With the emphasis on *quantitative techniques* of management this approach is often given recognition as the "ideal method." All facts are considered, a logical approach is made and the optimum solution is found.

This approach recognises that the more information available on a project, the lower the risk. A decision based on a knowledge of all relevant facts is likely to be rational and more acceptable than one based on "hunch." Even accepting these facts, the following factors should be considered:

(*a*) Information available is often based on estimates and forecasts which are wrong if assumptions made are invalid.

(*b*) In practice, "political" reasons may influence a decision; *e.g.* the desire to keep a customer even to the extent of selling temporarily at a loss.

(*c*) Many managers prefer the methods already employed rather than introducing new ideas which do not give better results than those already being obtained. This was the experience of a large construction and civil engineering company known by the author. They changed over from their programming method of planning to network analysis only to find that the old method could produce better results. This was a case where an efficient method was already in operation, so this reasoning would not necessarily apply to a company employing haphazard methods.

What should be added is that decisions would still have to be made irrespective of the techniques employed. However, they may not warrant appearance under the heading of a rational decision.

2. *Reacting to the situation*

This approach to decision making assumes that, once corporate plans have been made, the decisions follow as a *natural consequence* of the operation of the business. The organisation structure, the systems employed and personnel all interact, one with the other, both within the business and in dealing with external bodies.

In effect, decision making is regarded as part of the continuous process of carrying out the company objectives. A decision is made; as a result there are occurrences, which will call for further decisions to continue to pursue the policy being adopted. A decision is not made for all time, but is a link in a chain which will have to be strengthened by further links when circumstances or events call for action.

Integrated approach

In practice, decisions will tend to be made on the basis of facts, figures, judgment and intuition. Both rational and reaction-to-situation approaches will have to be employed, usually in a combined form.

There should be recognition that the so-called *optimum* solution is often the *attainable* solution for a combination of factors. There has to be technical and commercial balance between the different sectors of a business. The improvement of one function, such as output from a machine shop, may be possible with little capital outlay. However, if there is no way of dealing with the additional units produced because the stores facilities are limited, or assembly are operating to full capacity, then sub-optimisation for the function should be continued.

Getting the correct balance and full integration of the resources is a vital requirement of the management process.

Effects of decisions

Just as with law making, once a decision is made a *precedent* has been established which may have to be followed in the future. This is not an invariable principle, but it would often apply. The interpretation of an instruction would be followed in the same manner once a decision had been made; similarly, when delivery of products had been established for a certain time or in a specific manner the rule laid down would tend to be followed. All concerned would know what to do and the consequences of doing it in that way.

Some decisions may be of the "one-off" category, such as a major decision to cope with a particular situation; *e.g.* the reduction of prices to offset a falling off in trade. These do not necessarily establish a precedent, but they will influence future behaviour and decisions.

Any decisions made should be capable of implementation. If a new system is to be introduced, but the practical difficulties of control are immense, then a less sophisticated method may be more appropriate. For example, an attempt may be made to reduce all cost variances to within two per cent of standard costs. This may be possible by a very detailed system of standard costing with methods of revising standards at least once a month. On the other hand, a system which revises the standard costs once a year and costs much less to operate may be found to obtain control within five per cent. If this is the case there may be justification for adopting the cheaper system.

In other circumstances the control aspect may be outside the jurisdiction of the particular business; *e.g.* delivery of a fixed asset. However, some form of safeguard, such as a penalties clause in a contract, may be possible in these circumstances.

Once a decision is made, the machinery for carrying out the work should be put into operation. This will take the form of systems, procedures, briefings, meetings and delegation of responsibility. A decision may never reach fruition because the steps taken are inadequate.

If decisions are to produce results or consequences there should be provision for testing the *effectiveness* of what has been done. For example, a fixed asset is usually purchased to earn a profit, and a check should be made on the outcome to ensure that the expectations are being realised. There should be *validation* of projects and systems to ensure that managers are acting in an appropriate manner. In addition, there should be regular *feedback* so that any deviations from plans are quickly brought to the notice of those concerned.

Basis of decisions

Normal commercial decisions should be based on the selection of the course of action which is likely to lead to the achievement of the company objectives. Put another way, any decision should be in furtherance of the company policy and strategy.

This is a general statement, but measures related to the overall aim may be stated as follows:

1. Earning an adequate return on capital employed.
2. Increasing profit.
3. Obtaining a greater "contribution" (*i.e.* difference between sales revenue and marginal costs).
4. Reducing total costs.
5. Improving methods.
6. Carrying out policy in relation to a specific function; *e.g.* personnel.
7. Increasing sales revenues.

These are the main yardsticks, but others may also be employed; for example, a medical centre may be built because the directors feel that this would give benefit to employees and, in the long run, would reduce absenteeism. Economists have attempted to develop this method in relation to capital projects, such as the building of roads. The technique is known as *Cost Benefit Analysis*. However, as applied to business, C.B.A. cannot be viewed purely from the point of view of social benefit or common good. There has to be an expectation that profits will be increased indirectly. Profit-earning projects will have to cover the costs of welfare and similar proposals.

(As will be shown in the chapters on management accountancy, sales revenues may be discounted to present values.)

EXAMINATION QUESTIONS

1. Discuss the importance of leadership and authority in an organisation.
2. What are the responsibilities normally undertaken by a board of directors? State the particular functions of the managing director and his relationship to the rest of the board. What are executive directors?

3. Explain what is meant by the term *policy* as it is used in the discussion of management.

State *four* items that might be included in a statement of the production policy of a company.

4. "Management is the art of directing human activities."

(*a*) Why is it an art?

(*b*) Name *three* pre-requisites of directing activity (that is, conditions necessary before one can begin to direct).

5. Define *management*. What do you consider to be the functions of management?

CHAPTER IV

BUSINESS ORGANISATION

WITH the growth in size of a business there is a need to establish the framework around which the principles of management can be operated. Otherwise, there will be chaos and inefficiency with the resultant bad effect upon the earning of profit.

There are different interpretations of the word "organisation," but in simple terms it means paying attention to the following aspects:

1. Determination of the functions to be performed to achieve the stated objectives.
2. Selection of the machines and other fixed assets and the personnel necessary to carry out the work.
3. Establishment of the relationships which are to exist.
   For example:

   (*a*) Managers: their responsibilities and authority.
   (*b*) Chain of command.
   (*c*) Division of the business into functional departments or sections.

4. Communications systems and methods.
5. Centralised or decentralised planning and control.

These and related matters should be given attention when planning the organisation of a business. Most of the discussions in the past have been upon the ideal, *formal* organisation. Recently, more attention has been paid to the *informal* patterns which may operate in a business. It is now realised that formal organisation planning is quite ineffective unless there is also recognition of the informal "organisation." There is little point in stating that a certain manager has authority and responsibility for a specific function when, in fact, in practice he is not called upon to carry out the work involved. Similarly, it would be foolish to rely solely upon the formal communication network, assuming that the "grapevine" does not exist.

If everyone knew the organisation and the policy, there would be no need for the relevant matters to be put into written form. But the complexity of modern business, and the fact that personnel changes are taking place constantly, create the need for organisation charts and manuals. Moreover, the existence of job specifications and other descriptions of responsibilities tends to remove the danger of conflict, especially where there is a possibility of overlapping duties. Each employee in the organisation is able to see what is expected from him and what behaviour he can expect from other employees. This fact alone should have a stabilising effect upon all that is done, and should achieve an orderly state.

If the organisation is badly conceived then there are likely to be misunderstandings, discontent and friction. Only by paying attention to the matters outlined above can the highest level of efficiency be achieved.

SCIENTIFIC ORGANISATION*

FAYOL'S PRINCIPLES

Claims have been made that, provided the organisation is based on scientific principles, management is made much easier. Henri Fayol, a Frenchman, is regarded as the founder of the movement for better organisation. He recognised that haphazard muddling along could only lead to inefficiency. In 1916 he examined the principles of organisation, which are summarised below. Additional comments have been added so that the principles reflect *current* thought:

1. The division of labour

Fayol was not the first to recognise the importance of the division of labour. Adam Smith, the great Scottish economist, had the following to say as long ago as 1776 (*see* p. 7, *The Wealth of Nations*):

> "This great increase of the quantity of work which, in consequence of the division of labour, the same number of people are capable of performing, is owing to three different circumstances; first, to the increase of dexterity in every particular workman; secondly, to the saving of the time which is commonly lost in passing from one species of work to another; and lastly, to the invention of a great number of machines which facilitate and abridge labour, and enable one man to do the work of many."

There is no doubt that specialisation tends to improve efficiency, and the great increases in productivity which have taken place in modern times have been largely due to this fact receiving its due recognition. On the other hand, if carried too far there is a loss of skill and craftsmanship with the result that employees become machine minders and no more. The problem is to generate a sense of pride in the work so that there is a feeling of belonging to a worthwhile venture. The importance of motivation, leadership and communication is very evident when considering how to achieve a high standard of morale, when there is full-scale specialisation.

2. Authority and responsibility

That authority and responsibility should go together was recognised by Fayol, and is now regarded as a management law—the *Parity of Authority and Responsibility*.

* *See* Chapter VI for a comparison of traditional and modern theories.

Authority is the right to give orders and expect to see them obeyed. If a machine-shop foreman instructs an operator to drill holes in a component then he expects to see the work done. Along with the authority is the *responsibility* for the consequences of any orders given. If the holes should not have been drilled then the foreman will bear the blame.

Today the principle is still followed, but there is also recognition that there are occurrences over which a manager can have no control and, therefore, cannot be held responsible. This is recognised in cost accounting by the separation of variances into "controllable" and "uncontrollable."

If the foreman quoted in the example had been given his orders by the use of an inaccurate production order, can he be said to be responsible for the error? Obviously, there is difficulty here. If there has been no carelessness on the part of the foreman, then the blame should be placed at the door of the production planning department.

3. Discipline

There should be recognition that discipline is necessary in all efficient organisations.

What is important to notice is that discipline can take many forms. The "whip" has now disappeared and has been replaced by motivation. Reprimands are still necessary, but the approach tends to be flavoured with reasonableness. There is no doubt that the growth in the strength of the trade unions and new ideas on management theory and practice have done much to foster this approach.

Mary Parker Follett recognised that orders should come from the authority of the system and, therefore, should not be regarded as being personal instructions from one to another. Rather, all employees, irrespective of status, are working towards a common goal and obeying the *Law of the Situation*.

4. Unity of command

Orders and instructions to an employee should be given by one manager. Otherwise, if there is division of authority, there will tend to be confusion, mistakes and delays. There is nothing more demoralising than being instructed by one man, then having the orders changed by another, without any apparent good reason.

This management law, like the others, should not be regarded as being absolutely inflexible. There is no doubt that an employee should only have one *regular* supervisor. However, if full use is to be made of specialists, then a certain relaxing of the law is inevitable. For example, an inspector may be responsible for ensuring that products are inspected in the course of production, one operation being checked before going on to the next. If defects are found in the products then contact with operators is essential and this should be immediate. The process of going through foreman and supervisors would be obeying the unity of command concept, but is not really practicable. A short cut is likely to lead to greater efficiency, the inspector making a direct contact with the operator concerned. This can apply to other specialists in *appropriate circumstances*.

The unity of command is still observed on a *regular* basis, but there are exceptions. The latter can safely be incorporated into the management structure, provided the foreman and operators understand the role of each functional specialist. Generally the delegation of authority given to a functional specialist will be of a very limited nature and, therefore, there should be no serious violation of the unity law.

5. Unity of management objectives

"Unity of management" means that there is a specific objective and that all the necessary efforts are co-ordinated under one authority.

The term *unity of objectives* is a more precise description of this management law. The idea that there should be one manager and one set of objectives is sometimes put forward as being unity of management. Obviously, this is misleading, for the principle is concerned with ensuring that *all* activity is geared towards attaining the objectives with maximum efficiency. All functions of management should be organised towards this end, and thereby serve all the social groups.*

6. Harmony of personal interests and the common good

This principle is linked with the *unity of objectives* (*see* 5 above). It recognises that the common good of the business should come first.

One of the difficulties associated with this principle is what is meant by the "common good." Is it maximum profit, or high dividends, or fair wages, or some other criterion?

Some modern writers have distinguished between the interests of the business and those of the individual. The former are called the *primary* objectives and the latter the *collateral* objectives. The problem which confronts management theorists is how to harmonise the two goals; the manager has to put the theory into practice.

The producing and selling of products or services are the primary objectives; whereas the financial rewards and job satisfaction are the collateral objectives. There is no doubt that financial rewards are of the utmost importance, but in a period of full employment there is a tendency for the non-monetary incentives to be emphasised. Included in these are the status of the individual, social activities, satisfaction in the work done, pride in belonging to a particular company, and the feeling that there will be fair play in any matters affecting managers and employees. In short, there should be a positive link between the primary and collateral objectives.

* See p. 299 on the social obligations of management.

Unfortunately, this is not an easy task because personal goals tend to differ from one individual to another. One man will receive great satisfaction from being recognised as worthy to go on a training course or to be promoted to a more senior position; another man may resent being sent on a course and would not wish to undertake further responsibilities such as those involved in promotion. It is in this field that often the difference between the efficient and inefficient manager is revealed. The efficient manager tries to *understand* the requirements of each individual and the group as a whole. He then sets about achieving the primary objectives with the collateral objectives always present and under consideration. Each manager is a personnel manager as well as a manager on some technical aspect. The management law which sums up this matter is given recognition by modern writers under the term *Principle of Harmony of Objectives.*

7. Fair rewards for work done

This principle is concerned with ensuring that the remuneration of all members of an organisation is satisfactory. Managers have to decide the most equitable method of calculating wages and what fringe benefits should be awarded. These matters are discussed further in Chapter XV. Here it is important to notice that many authorities are now against incentive schemes, which were regarded by Taylor and some of the other pioneers of management thought as being absolutely essential. There is no doubt that many schemes acquired a bad reputation for themselves, and that the increase in mechanisation with machines setting the pace has done much to cause the rethinking which has taken place. However, to say that all financial incentive schemes are wrong and that non-financial incentives are correct would be very far from the mark.

There is a story told of a well-known company which experimented with paying a straight time rate and decided to discontinue all incentive schemes. This worked extremely well and the example was later followed by other companies. The story continues that after some years the first company decided that an incentive scheme would now result in greater productivity. Accordingly, steps were taken to change back to the original policy. The moral seems to be that schemes may work for a time then new managers, altered conditions, and even the desire for a change, may dictate the need for fresh thinking.

8. Effective centralisation

Some degree of centralisation is essential in all business organisations. The question to be answered is which functions should be centralised and which could be safely decentralised.

There is no hard and fast rule on this matter. Much depends upon the size and complexity of the business concerned. What is known is that complete centralisation can throw a tremendous burden on to the managers at head office. Communication becomes difficult, and there is a danger that the managers at the centre are so busy dealing with problems that they have no time to deal with improvements or to assist with policy.

9. Hierarchy (*the Scalar Principle*)

Fayol recognised the need for a *hierarchic channel* so that there could be unity of command and efficient communication.

The modern term, the *Scalar Principle*, states that there should be an unbroken line of authority and command through all levels, from the General Manager to the lowest employee.

The importance of this principle is that there is due recognition given to the fact that *formal* authority is necessary in all organisations. Employees are expected to obey orders or to suffer penalties; dismissal, reprimand or loss of promotion are examples. There is no compulsion for a man to obey every order he is given, although legally an employer can dismiss for disobedience of an order entitled to be given in the contract of employment. Obviously, though, a good manager will not be interested in invoking the help of the law when he is not obeyed. Rather, there should be firm and fair management so that orders are obeyed willingly.

10. Justice and fair play

This principle was an important one in the early days of scientific management when the "boss" was an integral part of the system. A softening of the concepts became inevitable and Fayol recognised this fact. Oliver Sheldon in England and G. Elton Mayo in the U.S.A. also held similar points of view.

Today there is no compulsion to stress the need for justice and fair play; it is universally accepted in all democratic countries.

11. Reasonable labour turnover

If employees do not stay with a business very long, there tends to be a feeling of instability. A very high rate of turnover means excessive training and recruitment costs. Moreover, since each new employee will take some time to adjust himself, this means that maximum efficiency is never achieved.

When the problem of replacement is applied to managers many thousands of pounds may be spent in obtaining the services of the right men. The shortage of specialists has resulted in the widespread use of display advertisements in national newspapers and in the growth of professional organisations which deal with getting the right man for the job. This may or may not be the correct way to recruit, but the fact remains that a high managerial turnover can be extremely costly.

12. Good morale

Good morale is vital to all organisations. Accordingly, there should be a constant effort to ensure harmony and team spirit. This principle is related to (6) above.

Managers should recognise the need for harmonising the primary objectives and the collateral objectives, explained earlier.

Additional principles

In addition to the principles given above, there are others which are vital to efficient organisation planning. In Great Britain Oliver Sheldon, L. F. Urwick and E. F. L. Brech, and other writers, have paid attention— to explaining organisation and its importance; they have also played a major role in developing the concepts.

THE SPAN OF CONTROL

This is one of the most quoted principles of management. As a *general* rule, it is stated, no manager should directly supervise more than six subordinates. However, this rule is subject to the remarks made below.

In the early 1930s V. A. Graicunas developed the concept that the relationships of management multiplied in geometric progression— the "Graicunas Theorem." The statement which follows should not be regarded as a precise description of the theorem: it is a simplified version. By means of a mathematical formula he showed that the following relationships apply:

Subordinates	Relationships
2	6
4	44
6	222
8	1,080

Graicunas suggested many types of relationships which might exist. Examples are:

1. Superior *dealing with* direct subordinates.
2. Superior *dealing with* other superiors.
3. Superior *dealing with* different groups under his control.
4. Combinations of 1, 2 and 3.

"Permutations" and combinations are understood by most people nowadays, possibly due to the publicity given to such matters in connection with football pools. There are many "permutations" of direct relationships, of the relationships with different groupings and the many cross-relationships between the different subordinates. Graicunas's main concern was apparently with managers dealing with managers, including supervisors.

The *Graicunas Theorem* is important because it shows, in positive terms, the possible increase in complexities which may result from increasing the span of control. Some authorities have pointed out that Graicunas was not absolutely accurate in his analysis of the possible relationships. This may be true, but the principle is still substantially accurate as outlined earlier in this section.

Modern management writers recognise the importance of the span of control, but qualify the law by the statement that: *a manager should not directly supervise an excessive number of subordinates whose work interlocks, having regard to the nature of the type of organisation and the complexity of the work involved.*

There is now recognition that the span of control may be any number from, say, two to twenty. For each business, or division of a business, the optimum number should be determined. If the span is very narrow (*e.g.* two or three) the business tends to be "top heavy" with excessive administration overhead costs. Conversely, if there is a large number of subordinates to each manager, then employees may feel that they are too remote from the point of control and that they are an impersonal, unimportant part of an organisational machine. Undoubtedly, the answer is to take each case on its merits and work out the solution. Some of the factors which should be considered are as follows:

1. Nature of the work

The more complex the work being done, then the fewer should be the subordinates. This is on the basis that there will be more problems for the manager to deal with.

2. Capacity of the manager

Some managers may be capable of controlling ten subordinates, whereas others may only be able to deal effectively with six, even though the nature of the work is the same.

3. Efficiency of the system employed

The efficiency of the organisation and the control system employed will affect the optimum size of the span of control. Both the physical controls (inspection, progressing and production control) and the financial controls (budgeting, standard costing, management statements) are important. Communication will also have a direct bearing on the matter. Of vital significance is the efficiency of all managers in the organisation. When considering the span of control for one manager, the extent to which he can be supported by other managers should be taken into account.

4. Use of personal assistants

The personal assistant (the "P.A.") is a fairly common device to offset the burdens associated with a wide span of control. Many young executives are appointed to the board of directors after acting as P.A. to the managing director of a company.

A personal assistant can often deal with day-to-day problems without recourse to his immediate superior. This has the effect of cutting down the number of contacts by subordinates with the manager concerned. He is thus able to control a larger span.

Even where there is no official personal assistant, in practice there is often someone who acts the part. Within the formal or informal groups there is usually one person who carries out part of the management function. There is also the influence of the functional managers and departments on the efficiency of the producing departments. For example, the costing department may require certain tasks to be carried out as part of the routine and where these are not done a clerk may check on the employees responsible, thereby ensuring that the work is carried out. In this way the line manager is relieved of some of his work.

Span of control in practice

From the text given above it will be apparent that there can be no hard and fast rule regarding the normal span of control. The concept is subject to so many variable factors that a generalisation would be dangerous.

Even within the same business there can be no standardisation. In a production department the span may be, say, eight, whereas in the invoicing section in the office where routine repetitive work is being done the number may be twelve or more.

Study of actual practice will show the differences which exist. Examples taken from companies known by the author are given below.

Examples

Company A.—Divided into a head office and five area offices. Each area has a General Manager and, reporting to him, a technical manager, a sales manager and an accountant. Under each senior manager are departmental managers, the number varying from one area to another. A typical example is shown on the organisation chart given opposite (Fig. 4).

Company B.—A subsidiary, run independently of the parent company. The General Manager is responsible for the efficient operation of the business and is on the parent board. Executives reporting to the General Manager are: chief chemist/metallurgist, production manager, purchasing officer, accountant. The span of control for each of these managers is as follows:

Chief chemist: two direct subordinates.
Production manager: nine direct subordinates.
Purchasing officer: three direct subordinates.
Accountant: six direct subordinates.

These examples show the differences which may arise in the spans of control from one company to another and within the same company. An excellent way of learning about the span of control is for the reader to study the organisation of the business in which he is employed.

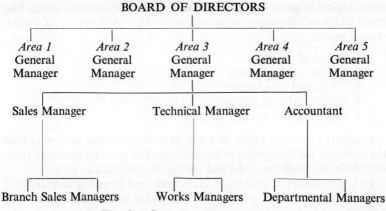

FIG. 4.—*Company organisation chart*

1. Area 3 is extended to show the responsibilities of the senior managers in that area. This would be done for each area.

2. The Area Accountant has the largest number of subordinates reporting to him, but they are all in the same office, whereas there is geographic separation for the sales and works managers.

THE DIVISIONS OF MANAGEMENT

The three main types of business organisation are as shown below:

1. One-man business.
2. Partnership.
3. Company.

From an industrial and commercial point of view all these are important. However, the size and complexity of *companies*, both private and public, makes them the most important type so far as management is concerned. With the one-man business and the partnership, management is still necessary, but the problems faced are relatively simple. Because of this the decisions made in either of these types of business do not tend to have the far-reaching effects they have in a company.

In the sections which follow is given an outline of the pattern which usually develops in a company so far as the management strata are concerned. There is no standardised pattern which may be taken as the "ideal": accordingly, the description should be looked upon as a possibility and not a blueprint to be copied without discrimination.

THE MANAGEMENT STRATA

For a limited company there are many different types of managers. A detailed description of each could be given, but this would not be very meaningful because titles vary from one company to another. A more logical approach is to break down the management strata into levels which reflect management responsibilities. A summary of these is shown below.

1. Board of directors.*
2. General management.
3. Divisional management.
4. Functional management.
5. Departmental management.

Category (3) would apply in a company divided into divisions: with the tendency for companies to integrate, and to grow by means of take-over bids, the need for divisional managers continues to grow.

In appropriate circumstances there may be a board of directors for each company within a group. There may also be need for a number of general managers.

The first two categories listed are now examined in turn. Appropriate explanations on line and functional managers are included in the other chapters which deal with organisation.

BOARD OF DIRECTORS

The board of directors represents the top level of management. Legally a public company must have at least two directors. On the one hand they are trustees of the company, and on the other they are agents. They are expected to safeguard the company's assets over which they have control.

Some directors are employed in a part-time capacity attending only for board meetings to give advice and counsel. Others are full-time and have management responsibilities as well as acting as directors. Irrespective of the type of director, he should pay attention to all matters affecting policy. In summary form, the matters which should be covered by the board of directors are as follows:

1. To make policy and approve general plans.

The objectives of a company in terms of *what* is to be produced and *how* this is to be done should be determined by the board of directors. References to policies are made in various chapters throughout the book. Thus, for example, in Chapter XIII personnel policy is dealt with.

Wherever feasible, any matter which results from a policy decision should be put into written form. Examples of these are all those matters covered in a personnel policy, organisation structure, accounting principles and practice to be employed, and any similar matter which forms the basis of the management framework. Unless written manuals are produced there is likely to be confusion and trouble.

* Readers should also refer to the work of the Company Secretary in Chapter XI.

2. To authorise expenditure or engagement of senior personnel.

Major items of capital expenditure (*e.g.* over £2000) should have the approval of the board of directors. Since acquisitions of this type should be very much part of the policy being followed it is only right and proper that the directors should give approval. In very large companies the figure requiring sanction from the Board may be as high as £10,000 or above.

When senior staff are being appointed the board of directors should see applicants and select who is to be appointed. Positions which would come into this category would be general manager, chief accountant, production engineer, works manager and office manager. They may be required to report to one or more directors as part of their duties and, therefore, those directors should approve the appointments.

3. To provide leadership, inspiration and advice to the management of the company.

4. To ensure that shareholders are dealt with fairly and determine the policy to be followed regarding dividends and the appropriation of profits.

The size of the Board varies from one company to another. Some have only a few directors whereas others have ten or even more. Much depends upon the size and nature of the organisation. There should certainly be representation on a board of directors for the major functional divisions of production, selling and finance. In addition, research, development and distribution may also be represented. The nature of the company's operations will very much influence the composition of the Board. The leader of the board is known as a "Chairman," whereas the person who ensures that policy is understood and carried out is called the "Managing Director."

GENERAL MANAGEMENT

The duties of the directors are outlined in the preceding section. Quite often a general manager performs much the same work as a director, especially an executive director who works on a full-time basis.

Strictly speaking, the directors should formulate policy and the general manager should ensure that all necessary plans are made and put into practice. He should have a broad and comprehensive approach to dealing with problems: in particular, he should be a good leader who is able to co-ordinate the work of others.

Quite often general managers are selected from line or functional management. If so, there is a need for the general manager to broaden his outlook: he will be concerned with the business as a whole and not simply one department or function. The technical content of his job becomes smaller and the management proportion becomes more important.

FUNCTION		Owner—General Manager	General Works Manager	Sales Manager	Controller
CENTRAL OR GENERAL MANAGEMENT	Overall Planning, including Forecasting, Broad Allocation of Resources and General Development	Assistant (Development)			
	Organisation and Methods, including Publication, Clerical Management and Accommodation				Assistant (Clerical Methods) Chief Typist
	PERSONNEL MANAGEMENT	Assistant (Staff and Labour Questions) Welfare Supervisor	Training Section		Canteen
DISTRIBUTION MANAGEMENT	SELLING			Sales Manager (N) Sales Manager (S) Sales Office	
	ADVERTISING			Assistant (Advertising)	
	MARKETING	Assistant (Markets Research)			
DEVELOPMENT	TECHNICAL RESEARCH		Experimental Plant		
	PROCESS AND PRODUCT DEVELOPMENT		A/Engineer, Process Research		
	MANUFACTURING METHODS DEVELOPMENT		Development Engineer A/Engineer, Methods Research		
PRODUCTION MANAGEMENT	PLANNING INCLUDING PREPARATION AND SCHEDULING		Production Office Assistant i/c Planning		
	PRODUCTION		Superintendent of Manufacture Department A Department B Department C		
	INSPECTION				
CONTROL	ACCOUNTING, INCLUDING BUDGETING AND COSTING		Chief Cost Clerk		Accountant Cashier
	STATISTICS		Assistant i/c Wages and Labour Statistics		Statistical Clerk
TRANSPORT	CONVEYANCE OF GOODS OR MATERIALS BY AIR, SEA, ROAD OR RAIL			Transport Clerk	
	WAREHOUSING, ASSEMBLING and PACKING		Assistant i/c Warehouse		
PURCHASING	BUYING GOODS, MATERIALS, EQUIPMENT, ETC.				Chief Purchasing Clerk Bought Ledger
	STORES CONTROL		Assistant i/c Material Control		Stores Ledger
MAINTENANCE OF PROPERTIES, BUILDINGS AND EQUIPMENT			Maintenance Engineer		

FIG. 5.—*Functional analysis of management*
Courtesy of the British Institute of Management.

FUNCTIONAL ANALYSIS

The chart shown in Fig. 5 illustrates the breakdown of an organisation into functions.

EXAMINATION QUESTIONS

1. Apart from the legal obligations, discuss the nature of the responsibility which a board of directors has towards:

(a) customers;
(b) employees;
(c) shareholders; and
(d) the community.

2. What do you understand by the "span of control of management"? Discuss the factors influencing it.

3. "Every manager is concerned with the quality of discipline and morale that characterises his subordinates, for these factors have an important bearing upon the productivity of his department." Discuss this statement, showing any evidence you have of the relationship between discipline and morale on the one hand and productivity on the other.

4. Define *control* as the word is used by Fayol in "To manage is to forecast and plan, to organise, to command, to co-ordinate and to control."

Similarly, briefly define quality control, credit control, financial control, cost control, stores control.

5. Henri Fayol said that management consisted of six main activities: forecasting, planning, organising, commanding, co-ordinating and controlling. Comment briefly on the nature of each of these functions.

CHAPTER V

GROWTH OF ORGANISATION

ORGANISATION may be simple or complex; efficient or inefficient; appropriate or inappropriate; personal or impersonal; costly or inexpensive. These are all relative terms and will have different meanings from one business to another or from one year to another. Because of the dynamic state of business enterprise an organisation may be efficient in *a particular form* only for a fairly short period. Change of some kind is usual and, therefore, the organisation should be under constant review. An appreciation of the problems which may be involved in determining the best type of organisation should become apparent from the descriptions given in this chapter.

STAGES OF GROWTH

The main functional divisions of a business are as follows:

1. Production.
2. Sales.

These two divisions are all that are necessary for any simple, manufacturing business. The purchasing and storage would come under the production function.

For both production and selling there is one essential, common element: this is "finance," the money, including credit, which is needed to pay for purchases, manufacturing and selling costs. Without financial backing of an adequate dimension a business cannot survive. For this reason it is necessary to remember throughout any study of management that all three functions—production, sales and finance—should receive attention.

The size of the business affects the abilities necessary for managing effectively. One very important factor is the use made of specialists. In the very small concern the owner–manager will require a thorough knowledge of all the technical skills; in the large companies experts will be available to give advice on production, selling, finance and various sub-divisions of these.

A possible division on size is as follows:

1. One-man business.
2. Small business controlled by two or more partners or directors.
3. Medium-sized business.
4. Large business.

48

These definitions are by no means precise. Category 2 could include both medium and large companies. A possible way of overcoming this difficulty is to classify on the basis of capital employed; that is, the total value of the assets employed in the business.* The medium-sized concern may be regarded as having a capital employed of between, say, £50,000 and £500,000. A company with a higher figure than this would be treated as a large business. However, these are only rough guides and cannot be regarded as exact measures. For example a company which provides services, whether distribution, consultancy or some other type, will tend to have a much smaller volume of assets employed than the highly mechanised, manufacturing company.

The abilities required by personnel have been analysed by writers in different ways. Fayol used the following classification:

1. Managerial.
2. Technical.
3. Commercial.
4. Financial.
5. Security.
6. Accounting.

Together these were taken to represent 100%. For the one-man business Fayol estimated that 15% would be absorbed by managerial skill and 40% by technical ability. On the other hand, for the very large business he assessed managerial skill at 50% and technical skill at 10%. For abilities 4–6 the proportions were taken as around 10% for all sizes of business, but commercial ability varied from 20% for the small business to 10% for the very large concern.

Present-day authorities take a similar view, but there is now recognition that there can be no absolutely clear demarcation between the different abilities. There is no doubt that, in the small industrial business, technical ability is the most important aspect. However, if the many functions of management which go to make up the "managerial ability" are considered (p. 21) it will be evident that they are very much linked with the technical, commercial, financial and other necessary attributes. For example, how can planning be carried out without technical ability? Similarly, control would be impossible without a knowledge of accounting.

An alternative approach is to consider the functions of management in relation to the responsibilities of a manager. A general manager will be involved for much of his time with planning, organising, co-ordinating and leadership. In contrast, a foreman or supervisor will tend to be concerned primarily with motivating, controlling, communicating and leadership, but will have very little concern with planning and organising. However, as will be shown in connection with budgetary control

* *See* Chapter XXII for the definition of capital employed.

C

(Chapter XXI), a foreman should be a party to determining the goals or targets which he is expected to achieve; this principle is one of the foundation stones of responsibility accounting.

As a business grows in size the problems multiply, both in number and complexity. It becomes a necessity to plan the organisation and to employ specialists for the main functions—production, selling and finance—and for the departments within each functional division. The principles followed in developing an appropriate organisation were explained in the previous chapter. Here the concern is with the devices employed for *communicating* details of the organisation within a business. The organisation chart and organisation manual are explained below.

ORGANISATION CHARTS

CONTENT AND PURPOSES

An organisation chart is a diagrammatic representation of the framework or structure of a business. Some of the matters which may be shown are as follows:

1. *Head of the organisation or chief executive.*—It is sometimes suggested that an organisation chart resembles a human body. The "head" or top of the chart indicates the most important manager; the one who controls the whole nervous and circulatory systems. Similarly, the lines of command may be regarded as showing the mode of operation of these systems.

2. *Authority and responsibility.*—The lines of command are shown much more clearly than is possible by lengthy written descriptions.

3. *Relationships between different managers.*—Managers on the same horizontal line are regarded as having similar status. As a corollary, each manager reports to his superior on the horizontal line immediately above. These statements are general in nature and are subject to the disadvantages associated with organisation charts, outlined below.

4. *Kinds of relationships which exist.*—In the modern, complex business there are many kinds of managerial relationships. There are line, staff and functional relationships which may be grouped into divisions, departments and cost centres. In addition, the grouping may be on a lateral and/or vertical basis. These terms are described below.

5. *Names of managers and titles.*—Not all charts give this information although desirably they should. One of the problems is that inclusion of names may give a chart a very short life. Only one man has to change his position for the chart to be out of date. Although not giving the same detail, the title of the manager—*e.g.* production controller—or the name of the department—*e.g.* production control—may be employed.

The definition and importance of the span of control were covered in Chapter IV.

Advantages of organisation charts

The principal advantages claimed for organisation charts are summarised below:

1. Rationalisation.—Preparation of an organisation chart means that a preliminary study of the organisation structure is essential. This in itself can lead to greater efficiency; responsibilities are clearly defined; lines of authority are shown and each manager knows where he stands in relation to other managers.

2. The chart acts as a blueprint.—It is therefore useful for showing existing staff and newcomers the nature of the organisation. In addition, it may be used as a basis for reorganising or making any modifications in the structure of the business.

3. Relationships.—Segments of a business can be conveniently grouped either in relation to other parts or separately. This means that the relationships between divisions or departments can be clearly shown for the business as a whole or other suitable grouping. Alternatively, a detailed breakdown of a single division may be carried out.

4. Reference.—An organisation chart lends itself to easy reference. It can be displayed in an office or on a notice board in a corridor or other suitable place so that all staff may see the structure and note any changes which take place.

5. Information.—It gives additional information which supplements the details available in an organisation manual or which is known by convention as being part of the *informal* structure of the business.

Disadvantages of organisation charts

Organisation charts have imperfections; the biggest are as follows:

1. Quickly become out of date.—However, only slight ingenuity is needed to devise a method for revising with little trouble or effort: magnetised boards, frames for holding strips of paper and pin boards on which discs can be hung are examples of devices which can be employed.

2. May encourage red tape.—A chart shows definite channels through which information must flow. In practice, short cuts are often taken which can result in improved efficiency.

3. Show a static picture, whereas a business is a dynamic organism for- ever changing its form.—This is true, but this does not entirely invalidate the use of organisation charts.

4. Human relationships are very difficult to portray on a chart.—There is some truth in this statement, but nobody pretends that charts are perfect representations of the many complex relationships which exist in a modern business.

5. Responsibilities cannot be clearly defined as shown on an organisa- tion chart.—One of the assumptions made is that managers on the same horizontal line are of equal status. In practice, this is very rarely the case. The manager of one key department may be much more important than his fellow departmental heads.

6. *The drafting of the organisation chart is left to the ill-informed with disastrous results.*—This is often the case, but the fault here lies with the manager responsible for drafting the chart and not with the chart itself.

Conclusion

Although organisation charts do suffer from certain weaknesses they do, nevertheless, serve a very useful purpose. Their maximum utility is likely to be achieved when they are drafted by a person who knows how they should be prepared. He should be assisted by top management supplying all the information necessary for the task. Once compiled they should be kept up to date and for this purpose an organisation audit will be found extremely valuable.

FORM OF ORGANISATION CHART

An organisation chart may be drawn in a variety of ways. Generally, it consists of horizontal and vertical lines with rectangular boxes in which the names or titles of managers are shown, as in Fig. 6.

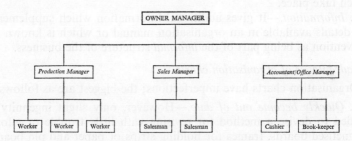

FIG. 6.—*Simple organisation chart*

When preparing an organisation chart which portrays different relationships it is usual to include a "key." In this way, the line, staff and functional relationships can be shown clearly and unmistakably. How this is accomplished is indicated by the chart in Fig. 7.

ORGANISATIONAL RELATIONSHIPS

The formal relationships which may appear on a chart are described in the subsequent sections; these are primarily the line, staff and functional relationships, to which may be added inter-relationships and informal connections. All the *main* details should be shown in an Organisation Manual which becomes a reference book for all managers.

LINE RELATIONSHIPS

Within any manufacturing business there will be two basic functions —production and sales. The managers who are *directly* concerned with the producing and/or selling of the commodities are known as "line managers." However, this is by no means an all-embracing definition and reference should be made to p. 58 *below*.

In its basic form the line organisation is made up of "all-round men." They all carry out a multitude of functions and do not specialise to any large degree. For example, a manager may be responsible for designing, producing, buying, and possibly even selling, within his own department.

Later, as the organisation becomes larger and more complex, the line managers become those who are *directly* concerned with those aspects of producing and selling which are not the responsibility of the functional specialists (*see under* Functional Relationships *below*).

What should be made clear is that in practice there may be difficulty in distinguishing between line and functional managers. Moreover, there are staff relationships (also described later) which grow from the line type of organisation. Another factor to be remembered is that an organisation is necessarily dynamic in nature, and, therefore, the relationships which exist in one business are not always the same as those in other, similar businesses. In addition, with the inevitable changes which take place in a dynamic business the relationships tend to vary in breadth of responsibility and in the way each manager's responsibilities are affected by the work of other managers and departments.

The complexities of modern, large-scale business make a purely line organisation an unrealistic proposition. A corollary of specialisation is the employment of experts, each one of whom can devote his time fully to a limited field of activity. No single man can hope to become conversant with the accountancy, legal and other complex requirements. The line organisation ignores the necessity of employing functional managers and, therefore, cannot ever hope to achieve maximum efficiency *unless* it is applied in a small business.

Personal assistants

One way to avoid over-burdening senior line managers with the detailed complexities of particular aspects such as accountancy, personnel management, research and development, and marketing is the employment of Personal Assistants. These can take over the day-to-day running of a particular facet of the business and act as intermediaries between a manager and his subordinates: when a P.A. becomes an adviser on a specific function he then becomes a "staff manager." This function is considered in more detail later in this chapter. Here it is important to notice that the growth of staff relationships may come about by the line organisation growing to a point where

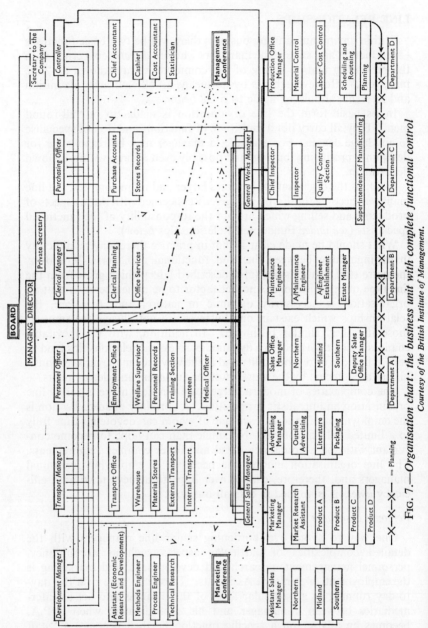

FIG. 7.—Organisation chart: the business unit with complete functional control
Courtesy of the British Institute of Management.

Note that the managing director has eight persons directly responsible to him. This may be too wide a span of control, and he may be overwhelmed with problems of co-ordination and have insufficient time for personal leadership.

(Key as given in Fig. 8.)

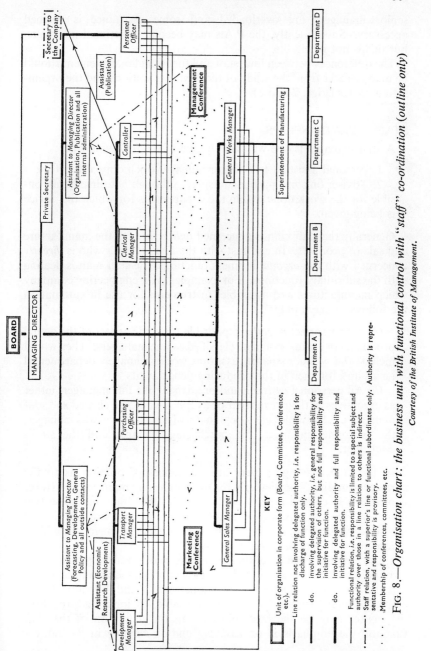

FIG. 8.—*Organisation chart: the business unit with functional control with "staff" co-ordination (outline only)*

Courtesy of the British Institute of Management.

Note that the functional managers retain their right of access to the managing director on important matters, but normally and on all questions of routine deal with his assistants ("staff" officers) who are thus able to relieve him of much of the detail of co-ordination. The personnel officer remains directly responsible to the managing director: much of his normal work involves "staff" relationships.

senior managers are overloaded and some assistance is deemed
necessary. Subsequently, the P.A.s may become functional managers,
but this is not inevitable.

The differences between line, staff and functional management should
be made clearer from the study of the next two sections and the organisation charts (Figs. 7 and 8).

STAFF RELATIONSHIPS

A staff manager is one who acts in one of the following roles:

1. Personal assistant to a senior manager (including a director).
2. Adviser on some particular aspect, although not directly responsible for the work done within the departments for which the advice
is being given.

Generally the staff man is concerned *indirectly* with the manufacture
and sale of products. In contrast with the line manager who is *directly*
concerned with the *organic* business functions, the staff man is dealing
with the subsidiary functions. For example, in an engineering company
which manufactures and assembles instruments for use in automation
the following may apply:

(*a*) All personnel *directly* responsible for some aspect of the actual
producing or selling would be classified as line managers. They would
include the works manager, assistant works manager, departmental
heads and foremen in the producing departments.

(*b*) All personnel *assisting* and/or advising the line managers either
as executives in their own right or as P.A.s would be classed as "staff
managers." Examples are a personal assistant to the works manager,
the personnel manager, the purchasing manager and the stores
controller.

In the latter examples there are differences of opinion as to the
correct "grouping," particularly for the purchasing manager and stores
controller. It can be argued, with some justification, that these two
managers are responsible for specific functions and are not simply
advisers. Accordingly, so the argument runs, these managers should be
regarded as "functional" and not "staff."*

Unfortunately, because of the non-existence of standard management
terminology, the example quoted is not the only misunderstanding which
can and does arise. Sometimes, the terms "staff" and "functional" are
employed as if they are quite interchangeable. A logical approach to
the matter may be the best solution. In the definition of the staff
function the emphasis is on *assisting* and/or *advising* in an indirect

* This misunderstanding appears to arise from the loose use of the term "line and
staff," as meaning "line and functional." Modern usage tends to limit staff to P.A.s
and personnel managers.

manner on the basic functions of producing or selling. If the manager is primarily concerned with assisting or advising, and does not have responsibility for the work of those he is advising, then he is a staff manager. When a manager spends most of his time on carrying out a particular function then he can be regarded as a functional manager. The distinction is one of degree and, therefore, no dogmatic rule can be propounded. Undoubtedly the P.A. is a staff man and there is little doubt regarding the personnel manager *as regards the business as a whole*, since he is primarily an adviser.

Even when a definition has been decided upon there is still no finality. Within his own department the staff or functional manager has a line function in the sense that he has subordinates in a direct line of command. This is an alternative definition of a line relationship. It differs from that given above in that the line manager was defined as being *directly* responsible for some aspect of the actual producing or selling. An advantage of the earlier definition is the clear-cut separation which is given between the line manager and the "staff" and "functional." There is no question of having a hybrid species, a manager falling partly into one category and partly into the other. This avoidance of dual relationships for the same manager can lead to more precise definitions. However, not all exponents would agree with this view so it is safer to regard the alternative as a second definition. In any case, if the origin of the term "line" is to be taken as being in the direct line or chain of command then this broader definition may be more logical.

Whether a staff relationship even warrants separate consideration is open to doubt. If the person in question is a personal assistant to a manager he generally carries out the instructions of his superior and, *in theory at least*, he has no authority over his subordinates. In practice, he may of course, especially after a time, assume responsibility and thereby become a line or functional manager. However, if he is purely an assistant there is doubt whether he is a manager at all; a requisite of this title is that the person must control the work of others and have authority over them. As regards the personnel manager a solution here would be to classify him as a functional manager.

A point in favour of the use of the term "staff relationship" is the fact that the persons involved are given a special category which tends to emphasise their relationships with other managers. Properly trained, they can assist co-ordination and can relieve a busy manager of the burden of routine work.

There are dangers: a strong personal assistant may soon take over responsibility and become the "power behind the throne." There have been cases where the manager has become so dependent on his P.A. that he has been nothing more than a figurehead. A further possible disadvantage is the above process in reverse. If the senior manager is the type who finds delegation very difficult he may cling to his excessive responsibilities by the employment of personal assistants instead of making full use of the functional specialists. This will probably result in duplication of the work and a loss in efficiency.

FUNCTIONAL RELATIONSHIPS

A functional relationship exists when a specialist manager is responsible for a specific function within a number of departments. Thus, for example, the works accountant may be responsible for all accounting matters throughout a works. He is thus a functional manager for this particular aspect of work.

The need for functional managers arises because of (a) the complexity of modern, large-scale organisations, (b) the need to make the fullest use of specialists and (c) the necessity to avoid burdening line managers with complex problems and making decisions on matters which are outside the *direct* process of producing and selling.

Here it is first as well to observe the difficulties which exist as regards definitions. Generally, a line manager is taken to be on the technical or production side. However, this is a very limited definition and when analysed closely it will be apparent that the production manager does not differ very much from the sales manager who is just as important as the production man; indeed, in the agency type of concern he will be more important. Similarly, the accountant is absolutely essential for the provision of finance and the control aspect, without which there may be no profit. Accordingly, it can be argued that all managers are line managers. Conversely, because of the specialised knowledge that is required on production, sales, accounting and other necessary sub-divisions a case could be made for calling all managers "functional." A production manager would have specialised knowledge of production techniques and would be required to deal with any problems which arose; this would apply whether they originated in the production, sales or accounting divisions.

This reasoning would tend to apply to senior men and not to middle or lower level managers who would have little or no say outside a relatively narrow field of responsibility. Nevertheless, this difficulty of defining with preciseness is always present.

The functional manager is required because of the existence of a field of specialised knowledge. He becomes necessary because of the technicalities inherent in his own field of responsibility. If care is not exercised in using the knowledge, then there is a danger that fear, suspicion and misunderstanding may arise. The use of technical jargon and mathematical formulae all tend to complicate the management processes, particularly communication. In addition, if specialisation is carried too far, there is a tendency for the primary objectives to be overlooked and techniques are developed for their own sake rather than as a means to an end.

A further difficulty which may arise is that the number of managers tends to increase so that line employees are not sure of how many superiors exist. The method employed to overcome this problem is to insist that all matters must go through the line managers. This is known as the *Law of Functional Authority*; the exceptions to this principle were discussed earlier. This states that as the volume of work grows in an arithmetical ratio, there will be a tendency for the functional relationships to multiply in geometric ratio. This law, like many others, indicates a tendency and, therefore, the use of the terms "arithmetical" and "geometric," which indicate *preciseness*, is perhaps unfortunate. There are, nevertheless, still complications which may arise; for example, even when responsibilities appear to be defined quite clearly there will inevitably be a certain amount of overlap. If, for example, employees are not utilising the time recorders correctly, the accountant will be concerned and at the same time any disciplinary action should come from the line manager. If dealt with otherwise, there is a breach of the *Law of Unity of Command*.

There is recognition that despite the difficulties which *may* occur, the role of the functional manager tends to grow in importance. Moreover, this has resulted in a larger number of specialists being employed. A number of generalised theories have been put forward: a law ascribed to Professor C. Northcote Parkinson and not unnaturally called *Parkinson's Law* states that *work tends to expand to fill the time available for its completion*. This would appear to have particular application to the increase in the number of functional managers and their staffs. This matter is covered further in the next paragraph. Chapter XI examines the functions involved in administrative management in which excessive costs can occur.

Growth of management services

Coming to the specific rather than the general reasons for the growth of functional relationships, the size of business units plays an important part. With a very large business a percentage saving of, say, 5% in manufacturing costs may involve as much as £1 million or even more. The opportunities to eliminate waste (or, conversely, for waste to multiply) are forever present on a massive scale in a large organisation. In addition, a period of full employment has brought about the realisation that labour turnover or strike action can be extremely costly. Accordingly, working facilities, social amenities, communications, improved industrial relations and other factors have increased the need for more experts to be employed. Finally, there has been an upsurge in interest in management education and in new techniques such as work study, management accounting, operational research and data processing. This growing interest has resulted in the establishment of Management Services Units which are a form of internal consultancy service. Large businesses with many operating subsidiaries are making use of management services units to standardise procedures and improve efficiency throughout the company as a whole. Provided these are used effectively there is no doubt that much good can come from their employment.

Taylor's functional authority

No discussion of functional relationships would be adequate without some mention of the part played by Frederick W. Taylor who introduced the idea of functional authority into industry. He recognised that there could be greater productivity and improved efficiency through the use of specialised knowledge and skill. He saw that one man, concentrating on a limited number of tasks, could become highly skilled. As part of his scientific management, he broke down the work of a single foreman into eight separate functions with a man in charge of each as follows:

1. *Executive functional bosses.*—These were concerned with the supervision of the work on the shop floor. The titles given were:

(a) Gang boss—getting the job to the worker and providing the tools, drawings and materials.

(b) Speed boss—instructing workers and seeing that the job is done correctly and at the right speed.

(c) Inspector—inspection and guidance on drawings.

(d) Repair boss—repairs and maintenance.

2. *Functional bosses.*—These were concerned with planning and control, and were given as:

(a) Order of work clerk—determination of how the job was to be done and completion of the production orders.

(b) Instruction card clerk—making out instruction cards.

(c) Time and cost clerk—predetermination of times and costs and recording.

(d) Shop disciplinarian—responsible for discipline throughout the works.

These four were located in the planning room.

Taylor sought to define the responsibilities of his functional bosses, but to do this with exactness was a virtual impossibility. There was the close relationship between the duties performed by the eight foremen and the inevitable overlap of some of them. The worker had eight bosses so it leaves little to the imagination as to what was felt on the shop floor.

There is a place for a form of functional authority in modern business, but the following matters should receive attention:

1. The principle of unity of command should be followed, except where special circumstances exist (*see* p. 36).

2. Discipline should be exercised through the line manager.

3. The organisational principle of *parity of authority and respon-sibility* should be observed.

Unless a foreman can be shown the area of responsibility he can hardly be expected to be taken to task for anything which goes wrong. All modern control techniques now give recognition to the establishment of standards of performance: budgetary control and standard costing (defined in Chapter XXI) employ the concepts of budget centres and standard costs.

From what has been said it should be apparent that F. W. Taylor carried the functional idea too far, breaking the work of the foreman into segments which overlapped and violated the principles of sound organisation. However, the concept was *not* basically unsound, and if a study is made of a modern business it will be observed that a refined version of the Taylor system is employed. For example, the following functional specialists may be employed in a works:

Inspector
Maintenance engineer
Cost accountant
Planning engineer
Work study engineer
Storekeeper

These, and others, are in addition to the supervisors and foremen. The main differences are that each specialist generally assumes respon-sibility for his work in *all* departments and any contact with the workers is usually made through the line managers; *i.e.* the foremen.

INTER-RELATIONSHIPS

From what has been said in the sections on line, staff and functional relationships it should be apparent that the three are closer than distant cousins. Indeed, the line relationships may be regarded as the parent stock from which, with the growth of the organisation, there emerge the staff and functional species. These two are providing nothing new; rather they should enable a complex business to be run more efficiently by the use of assistants or managers with highly specialised knowledge.

Provided the organisation does not become stifled by the use of too many experts then there is much to be said for their employment. Similarly, adopting a purely line organisation structure can retard growth and efficiency. Unfortunately, there is no standard formula for achiev-ing the correct balance. Bearing in mind the organisation principles outlined earlier, an optimum solution has to be found. An integrated approach is essential: production, sales and finance should be con-sidered along with all the basic functions of management discussed on pp. 11–32.

Besides the formal relationships which exist there are also informal patterns which affect authority, communication and morale. In addition, there are the complexities brought about by the growth of a business through integration or merger. There is also the problem of whether to centralise or decentralise many of the managerial activities. These matters are discussed below and in subsequent chapters.

INFORMAL RELATIONSHIPS

The *formal relationships* which exist are those shown by the organisation charts and manuals. They include responsibility, authority, channels of communication and related factors. By the adoption of the most efficient organisation structure, it is hoped that the objectives of the business will be achieved in a manner which will maximise profits.

Within each business exist *informal relationships* which operate concurrently with those which are formal. They may make the latter more or less efficient, and, quite clearly, management theory and practice should recognise their existence. Indeed, some writers have insisted that informal relationships can negate the effects of the formal structure.

Each business is broken down into departments and sections within which are the primary working groups. The formal organisation chart often *ignores* each group which is made up of a small number of workers all working on similar tasks. On the other hand, recognition is often given by the employment of a supervisor who looks after the work of a reasonable number of subordinates.

The larger the formal group, the more danger there is of unofficial groups being formed and this is aggravated if a departmental manager is weak and inefficient. Unofficial leaders may also emerge, sometimes undermining the formal authority. Shop stewards may also affect the leadership and the functioning of the organisation.

There is no doubt that full recognition should be given to both formal *and* informal relationships. Unless this is done communication, authority and leadership are unlikely to be effective. Reconciliation of the objectives of the business with the goals of employees is essential. Only in this way will it be possible for the formal and informal relationships to interact in sympathy. Whether financial incentives, social benefits, good working conditions, sense of purpose or other rewards should form the basis of employees' goals is a decision to be made by the board of directors. Some of these problems are discussed further in Chapters XIII to XVII.

Examination Questions on Chapter V are given at the end of Chapter VI.

ORGANISATION PROBLEMS

CORPORATE PLANNING

THE fact that the establishment of company objectives is the prerogative of the board of directors is stressed in an earlier chapter. This involves decisions on a number of key factors which are all part of the *planning process*.

Producing goods and services at a price which will yield a satisfactory return on capital employed (*see* p. 381) is the prime requirement. However, there is more to the matter than simply earning an adequate profit, although this must be the ultimate criterion. Some of the problems which must be resolved are discussed later in this chapter. They are technical and financial in nature—a specific plant has to be utilised to the best advantage and there has to be adequate finance to meet all bills as they become due.

Looked at from the point of view of employees, there is necessity to define the objectives and then show how they can be achieved by the motivation of all personnel. This linking together of the motives of the directors (the company objectives) and those of the individual employees is an extremely difficult task. One of the main problems is to define this state, referred to later as the *harmony of objectives*.

Economists speak of "optimisation" of the business resources in a way that implies that maximum efficiency is achieved. Applied to management the concept requires the following:

1. Evaluation of all alternative company objectives.
2. Evaluation of all the various ways of achieving these objectives.
3. An adequate knowledge of the future to be able to select the best combined solution from 1 and 2 so that profit is maximised, all the social groups are given satisfactory treatment (*see* p. 299) and there is financial stability.

In practice, optimisation in its pure form is rarely found. The development of management information systems in the future may improve the state of knowledge, but even so, when dealing with a complex business uncertainty will always be present. Multiproduct companies, which tend to be the type in existence, have many problems, including the selection of the *product mix* which earns the planned profit.

Moreover, when discussing organisation there comes the inevitable question of how a business is to be divided up so as best to achieve the company objectives. Whilst this is impersonal up to a point—the division into profit, responsibility and cost centres—at all times *personal* relationships have to be considered. For this reason a high level of motivation should be sought, at the same time extending as far a possible the capabilities of individuals so that they assume responsibilities for the benefit of the company.

Since individuals do not belong to a species which is standardised in terms of behaviour patterns or motivation requirements, it follows that optimisation cannot be achieved. Rather there has to be a compromise which may be termed "sub-optimisation" or "attainable optimisation," thus recognising the practical difficulties which exist.

This does not mean that a high level of efficiency should not be the aim. If this aspect is ignored, then the *target profit*, *i.e.* the profit planned by selection of the relevant company objectives, is unlikely to be achieved or, at any rate, will be much lower than is possible with a more effective utilisation of resources. What is required is a recognition of the problems and limiting factors which exist within a business so that the resources can be used as effectively as possible. Some of the difficulties are now considered.

ESTABLISHING THE TARGETS

Theoretically the aim should be to establish targets for all levels of personnel; these should represent a high level of attainment. Without delving too deeply into complex issues, the following aspects should be considered:

1. At company objectives level

What is to be produced and *how* are rarely simple matters. Many varied and complex questions, some apparently quite unrelated, have to be answered before *policy* can be determined.

Traditional organisation theory has stressed the *internal* organisation of the business. However, when viewed at director level there is a need to consider the *external* requirements and to adapt the organisation structure to cover these needs as well as those within the business. In recent times, with this looking outwards there has been an attempt made to develop fully integrated *management information systems*. The basic idea is to centralise the point at which information is collected and then communicated to others. In effect, a business is looked upon as a collection of sub-systems which are co-ordinated at a central point. When the volume of work justifies a computer the integrated system should be computerised.

Considering the internal structure alone is not enough. The consumers' preferences, the financial situation, political and economic stability, changes in prices and other external factors must be taken into account when the company objectives are established. A summary of these external factors is given below:

1. Financial policy being pursued by the Government, *e.g.* heavy taxes, credit control.

2. The degree of control being exercised by the Government. This category covers many aspects, from safety and other regulations (*e.g.* safety belts on cars) to direct or indirect control on prices, incomes and other factors.

3. Price levels operating at a particular time.

4. Population growth and its composition—the proportions of the different age groups.

5. The strength of the political party in power. This may not be of vital importance in a country such as Britain. However, political stability can affect sales overseas and even the ownership of foreign subsidiaries.

6. Levels of employment and productivity within a country. These will also affect the income available for spending on the products being made.

7. Total expected demand for the industry as a whole.

8. Share of the market which can be expected for the business concerned.

The state of *confidence* which exists will affect the business world. If expectations are at a high level businessmen will be prepared to invest more money in expanding their companies. Conversely, when trade conditions are depressed there will tend to be great difficulty in maintaining the supply of products at a reasonable level.

The personalities of the directors will influence the policy decisions. If a business is in a field where rapid technological developments are taking place, then unless the directors are willing to accept the advice of senior managers and functional specialists, they are likely to make serious mistakes. In a large, complex business the leaders have to keep abreast with developments or there is likely to be stagnation.

A further problem is the reluctance of some directors and senior managers to delegate duties to others. Clearly, they have to retain the *final* and overall responsibility, but to some extent this can be shared.

2. At line manager level

Once the company objectives have been established they have to be transformed into practical realities. It is not enough to state what is to be done; the precise details have to be worked out so that all levels of employee know what is expected. Establishing rules to follow in realising the company objectives and the application of these rules is known as "company strategy."

When looked at from the point of view of individual managers the question is, how can the strategy be communicated? As conditions change, the methods employed for achieving the policy (the company objectives) must also be modified.

This is the day of the functional specialist, and therefore company goals may be viewed in a different light, depending upon the manager concerned. A sales manager will think in terms of the volume of products sold and will expect high quality for a relatively low price. On the other hand, a production manager will be concerned with a large volume of output at the lowest possible cost—at times he may prefer to sacrifice quality to some extent in order to achieve his targets. How are the company goals to be achieved so that all pull in the same direction? The common purpose of the business has to be spelled out by the board of directors. Modern ideas stress the establishment of a broadly based policy—we are "in the hotel business" becomes we are "suppliers of food, drink and related activities." In this way full advantage can be taken of activities which impinge upon the main objectives. There may be links established with catering, food manufacturing, holiday package deals and other possible services.

Linked with this broad statement are the key aims for the business. Examples are as follows:

1. Growth rate.—At what rate is the company to grow? A percentage should be established in terms of return on capital employed and/or other measures such as investment in the business, turnover achieved or personnel employed.

2. Type of growth.—Whether to grow horizontally (making the same products) or vertically (expanding into all related fields) is a question to be resolved. Each has its own advantages and problems.

There is also the possibility of "conglomerate diversification," which means moving into wide and varied fields of activity. This could be horizontal or vertical growth, but usually there is a move to broaden the range of product and services provided.

If a business moves into related activities this is known as "concentric growth"; *e.g.* a garage company obtaining a tyre-servicing organisation. When the diversification is in an unrelated field this is known as "profit-motivated growth"; *e.g.* a garage company acquiring a clothing company.

Usually the purpose of conglomerate growth is to use up finance which is available and thereby earn more profit as well as spreading the risks. If the move is *concentric growth* the aim may be to make full use of available "know-how."

3. Financial stability in terms of a steady cash flow.—Having adequate working capital is important at all times. When a company is growing very rapidly great care has to be taken to avoid *overtrading*; that is, spending in excess of money being received. Since expansion tends to require more money as a natural consequence of development, it follows that a financial strategy will be necessary for dealing with the situation.

4. Personnel policy being pursued.—Good personnel relations are essential. There should be a clearly defined *policy* on how the employees are to be treated and a *strategy* to deal with situations as they arise.

In effect, there has to be a *management philosophy* consisting of the policy and strategy, and this has to be communicated to all managers and other employees. What is a sound philosophy for one company may not work for another. The leadership and attitudes of senior managers can have a considerable influence on the actual philosophy as opposed to the policy and strategy statements. For success the actions of managers should not be in conflict with the written statements.

How are these objectives to be subdivided into realistic targets for individual managers? Some of the possibilities are summarised below:

(*a*) Have policy and strategy statements which summarise the management philosophy being adopted.

(*b*) Make full use of all tools of management which encourage participative management. These include—

(*i*) Budgetary control.
(*ii*) Standard costing.
(*iii*) Management by objectives.

These all establish targets and, when properly organised, obtain the views of managers when budgets are set. *Management by objectives* places great importance on the defining of responsibilities and thereby establishing targets. Included in the technique is a comprehensive set of job descriptions which cover all key managerial posts. The importance of participation is considered further, later in this chapter or elsewhere in the book.

(*c*) Use accounting, budgeting and other procedural *manuals* for describing the procedures to be followed.

(*d*) Divide the business into profit, responsibility and cost centres.

One of the main problems encountered in practice is to establish realistic targets which are capable of being attained and yet represent a high level of efficiency. If set too high workers become frustrated at never being able to achieve them; if too low they are meaningless and serve no useful purpose. A real attempt has to be made to establish performances which do represent a reasonable efficiency when all are striving to achieve this level. Management accountants and work study practitioners know full well what is meant by using the best methods and eliminating waste. Unfortunately, communication and translating the ideas into practical terms are far from easy, and there are many managers who believe that they are operating at a level which cannot be improved upon. In fact, in the majority of cases efficiency can be improved with very little effort on the part of those concerned. The complication is getting the managers to adapt themselves to new ideas.

TRADITIONAL AND MODERN ORGANISATION THEORY

In recent years there has been a movement started which has questioned many of the basic concepts of organisation theory. There is no precise date when this commenced, but around the mid 1950s is probably correct. At this time many of the assumptions or principles advanced by Fayol, Follett and Urwick began to be questioned. In more recent times new thought has been added to cover the developments in electronic data processing and management information systems and their impact on the organisation.

THE TRADITIONAL APPROACH

Before turning to the criticisms of the traditional theories of organisation it is as well to consider the conditions which existed when the earlier writers were expressing their ideas. In the case of Fayol, he was writing in 1916 at a time when most of the world was at war, and the present-day ideas on motivation and joint consultation were very much in their infancy—some were not even conceived. The *scientific management* movement was expanding and the stress was on efficiency, irrespective of the conditions under which employees worked. A number of statutes were in force, but these were not fully comprehensive and, as shown in the chapters which deal with business history, "sweat shops" still existed. In these circumstances it is hardly surprising that many aspects, especially those concerned with human relations, appeared to be neglected by present-day standards.

Reference to the preceding chapter will show that the traditional theory stressed the following aspects of organisation:

1. There is an assumption made that the same principles will apply to all types of business. Yet the one ideal organisation structure is simply not a practical proposition. The technical processes involved in manufacture must affect the development of the organisation. Similarly, the methods used for selling and the marketing philosophy adopted should have a considerable influence on the allocation of responsibilities.

The development of management information systems is also having some effect. However, this should not be stressed too much until more experience is gained in what management writers have called *total* or fully *integrated* system. If the latter is in existence—so the argument runs—there should be much more centralisation of decision making. This should mean that the conventional organisational boundaries should not apply at the broad planning stages, although they will still apply when considering the detailed planning and control. Unfortunately, even the *modern theory* does not provide all the answers on this matter.

2. The design of the *formal* organisation is regarded as an essential requirement for efficient management.

3. The management structure is shown as a series of steps, and therefore there are vertical and horizontal relationships and "rules" regarding the approaches to the various levels. This also applies to the employees under the various line managers. As shown in Chapter IV, relaxation of the principle of the *unity of command* is permitted. This matter is considered further below.

4. Too much emphasis is placed on the *internal* relationships without considering the *external* factors, and in particular the importance of the consumer and the role of the Government and trade unions in operating a business.

5. Normative rules are laid down for behaviour within a business. This approach is acceptable provided there is *flexibility*. Indeed, *modern* theory stresses the need for a strategic and tactical approach to management.

MAIN FACTORS IN MODERN THEORY

What are the main deviations from the traditional approach? In other words, which factors are stressed in the modern theory? Different writers would not be in complete agreement on this matter. A complete coverage of all the theories which now make the so-called modern theory would require much more space than is available in this book. However, it is possible to indicate the main factors which are as follows:

1. Company objectives

Establishment of the company objectives (*i.e.* the policy) and the means of achieving them, including the "rules" to follow (*i.e.* the strategy), is regarded as an essential prerequisite to organisation planning.

2. Achievement of objectives

The organisation, and the sub-systems which operate within a business, should be designed to achieve the objectives.

3. The motivation

There has to be recognition that employees other than managers can affect the fortunes of a company. This is possibly one of the main criticisms of the traditional theory. There was not enough recognition of the need to motivate employees.

4. Authority and responsibility

Traditional theory states that these must go together. The present-day writers stress that authority can be delegated, but there is difficulty in doing the same for responsibility to the *same degree*. A general manager can delegate authority to, say, his production manager. The latter will be expected to take on responsibility for the matters under his control, but the general manager must still accept the *ultimate* responsibility.

5. Defining responsibilities

Some modern writers have argued that the traditional theorists put responsibilities into neat compartments. There is no denying this fact, but it should not be forgotten that modern concepts of management require the use of job descriptions and other methods of defining a manager's job. Strict demarcation of duties may stifle initiative, and therefore some flexibility is desirable.

6. Applying responsibilities

A manager can be given authority and responsibility, but within prescribed limits how he uses them is in his own hands. They can be applied wisely for the benefit of the company or in a fashion which gives the greatest benefit to the individual. Those seeking rapid promotion may "go all out" to impress, using methods which may not benefit the long-term stability of the business.

If management is to be regarded as a profession, then there should be codes of conduct developed, within which managers operate. Unfortunately, business ethics have received little attention from management writers.

7. Status

Status is of considerable importance. Certain positions carry with them recognised privileges and benefits. In a sense, status symbols provide an incentive for employees to strive towards more senior positions. What is not always recognised is that status also carries influence, and this varies *not* according to the formal organisation chart but with the personality or other attribute of the person concerned. The latter does not necessarily have to be a manager. A personal assistant may exercise considerable influence on a managing director. Similarly, managers at the same level in the hierarchy may have quite different impacts on the efficiency of the business. One company may be "accountancy-oriented," whereas another may be "marketing-oriented," simply because of the influence of chief accountant or marketing manager respectively. When possessed to a high degree the influence becomes *power* and is of considerable importance to the way a company is operated.

8. Loyalty

The loyalties which exist will affect the co-operative spirit of the enterprise. In particular, there will tend to be loyalty towards the working group to which an employee belongs. The traditional theory pays little attention to this aspect, yet the efforts of each working group will affect the total output. Reconciliation is essential, so that the working group's loyalties are the same as company loyalties.

At managerial level a high degree of loyalty is very essential. The giving and receiving of orders and commands can be affected by the enthusiasm and general attitude of those concerned. Without loyalty there can be no expectation that commands will always be obeyed.

Modern writers quite rightly stress the importance of developing loyalties. Many factors should receive attention. Treating employees fairly, providing good working conditions and paying adequate remuneration and fringe benefits are all essential requirements. Sound leadership is vital and, unfortunately, when this is *not* present very little can be done to change the position, at least in the short term. Failure to delegate and the existence of pseudo-participation are possible weaknesses; "participative management" is considered below.

9. Conflict

Conflict in some form is inevitable, and this fact has to be recognised in any sound organisation theory. The very fact that responsibilities have to be divided on the basis of divisions, profit centres and cost centres means that to some extent each area is self-contained. At the same time there has to be reliance on the work of others, both service centres and producing centres.

The main problem is to ensure that maximum co-operation is obtained. Whenever there are overlapping duties or services required, including the transfer of products from one department to another, frictions may arise. A static theory of organisation fails to recognise these conflicts.

10. Participative management

Newer ideas on management include *active participation* by all key personnel in the setting of targets. This principle is best seen in such techniques as Management by Objectives and Budgetary Control. The underlying motives of the concept of participative management are as follows:

(*a*) Allowing supervisors and line managers to take an active part in management develops a sense of responsibility in all concerned.

(*b*) The knowledge and experience of all managers is used to the fullest possible extent.

(*c*) Targets which have been established after considering the views of those who have to achieve them should be accepted more readily.

(*d*) Communications and motivation should improve because of the very fact that personnel become *involved*.

There are some writers who have criticised this approach on the grounds that the board of directors should be stating what is to be done, not the managers under them. For example, it is argued that if a sales manager is asked to prepare a forecast and budget he will prepare figures which suit his own purpose. Depending upon his optimism (or pessimism), the targets will be too high (or too low). In this way managers are telling the directors what to do, a state of affairs known as *bottom-up* management.

In fact, provided the starting-point of modern management theory is taken as a foundation of business organisation, there is no abdication of authority by the directors. Company objectives have to be established *before* any targets are set. If this is done, then the participation means that the objectives are being converted into practical terms by those who are expected to carry out the work.

There is no question whatsoever that participation is an important factor in establishing the correct environment and atmosphere for a high level of efficiency and good industrial relations.

11. Informal relationships

The development of informal relationships should be recognised, and when they do exist, they should be used to the best advantage. In later chapters the "grapevine" and the emergence of unofficial leaders are considered.

12. Ad hoc *investigations*

The quantitative aspects introduced into management have shown that business problems, and therefore planning, are now very complex issues. Decisions can no longer *safely* be made "off the cuff"—if they could at any time! Capital expenditure on fixed assets can involve many millions of pounds sterling in a year. Only when all external and internal factors have been enumerated and evaluated should any decision be made.

Ad hoc investigations should be a feature of all organisation structures. As special problems arise or important decisions have to be made there should be a collection of all relevant facts and presentation in the appropriate form.

13. Electronic data processing

As computers and the related electronic data processing systems are developed, there has to be new thinking on the conventional organisation structures. The greater volume of information which becomes available can simplify decision making, planning and control. If full centralisation of management is practised there may be difficulty in getting effective participation. Job satisfaction is higher when small groups are involved, so this may suffer with the *total system* approach. The fact remains that management information systems are now being developed, and means have to be found for adapting the organisation so as to optimise the business resources. They have to be combined so that maximum efficiency is achieved without losing the important requirements of a sound personnel policy (*see* Chapter XXIII).

14. Financial stability

The theory which deals specifically with organisation structures, both in the traditional *and* modern forms, tends to neglect the financial aspects of management. With the stress on human relations and motivation there has been neglect of the financial problems—except in general works written to cover all aspects of management or in books for accountants. Yet if organisation is really the *framework of management* full consideration should be given to the use being made of the money supplied by shareholders, lenders and creditors. There is an obligation to ensure that finance is not used in an inefficient manner, and assets, once purchased, should be safeguarded against abnormal losses. In addition, the financial *stability* of a business should receive attention. Unless cash flows into the business at an adequate rate difficulties will be encountered. The organisation structure should ensure that these requirements and related functions are adequately covered.

FUTURE REQUIREMENTS

There is little doubt that organisation theory will be developed still further. What are needed are empirical studies of human behaviour in actual working conditions. Any research that has been carried out tends to be biased towards a particular discipline, *e.g.* sociology, so the conclusions drawn from the facts do not give a balanced view. While the personnel aspects should be given great emphasis, there should also be the fullest attention paid to the earning of profit. Without the latter there is unlikely to be the necessary finance to carry out a sound personnel policy.

EXAMINATION QUESTIONS
Also includes Questions on Chapter V

1. There has been for some time a conflict of views as to whether an organisation should be formulated according to deductive principles and in the abstract without any reference to personalities, or whether the group of responsibilities should be built around the available personalities. Discuss this problem, setting out your own recommended line of procedure.

2. The Board of a company having eleven manufacturing units have decided on a policy of decentralisation of authority and responsibility. Enumerate the steps necessary to implement such a policy and illustrate with an organisation chart.

3. Describe the line and staff system of organisation. Give two examples of functional executives and the general nature of the duties they perform in relation to line staff.

4. State the essentials of good company–employee relationship and welfare services.

5. What are the responsibilities normally undertaken by a board of directors? State the particular functions of the managing director and his relationship to the rest of the board. What are executive directors?

6. The Managing Director of the Omega Company has in his office an organisation chart on which are entered the titles of all positions down to first line supervisor, and the names of the persons occupying those positions. Explain:

(*a*) what such a chart reveals of the organisation of the business;

(*b*) what important aspects of the organisation it does not reveal;

(*c*) what other information is needed to give a complete picture of the organisation of the company.

7. What is an organisation chart? Discuss its significance.

8. You are asked to draw up an organisation chart for a large business. What are the main factors to be considered? State the purpose of producing this chart and its advantages and disadvantages.

PART TWO

PRODUCTION, MARKETING
AND ADMINISTRATION

CHAPTER VII

ORGANISATION AND THE MANUFACTURING FUNCTION

PRODUCTION is the word used to describe the process of producing goods from raw materials. A look through the stores of a factory will show that these raw materials can be anything from sheet metal or cotton to nuts and bolts, electric motors or instruments as these items are often referred to as "raw material" by the firm using them.

Whether this production takes place in a plant employing 3000 people or in a back-yard where a dozen craftsmen are engaged on precision engineering, the business must be organised to *produce effectively*. The activities involved in production are almost independent of the size of the undertaking. In the smaller concern one person may carry out several functions, while in the larger one each function may be carried out by separate individuals or teams.

This chapter and the two which follow cover three aspects of production, namely:

1. Manufacturing—concerned with making the product.
2. Ancillary functions—these include activities necessary to support production, but not directly engaged on manufacturing the products of the firm.
3. Advisory functions—including those which do not provide materials or direct production, but act in an advisory capacity, such as work study, operational research, and inspection.

The production departments are usually arranged as shown in Fig. 9. It is almost impossible to set out a "typical" arrangement as organisation depends on such factors as the type of product and the type of production.

This chart sets out the functions rather than the titles of the persons carrying out the activities. In a small firm the manager may carry out supervisory duties, planning, control and buying himself, but whoever actually does the work the functions shown will usually be present in some form or other.

In some respects the organisation will vary with the size of the business. Most small firms will not employ work study technicians and only the very large firms will undertake operational research or employ ergonomists.

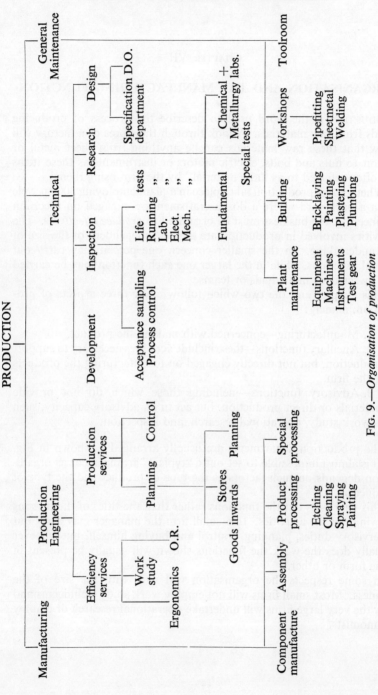

FIG. 9.—*Organisation of production*

1. The emphasis is on functions not managers.
2. O.R. = Operational Research; D.O. = Drawing Office.

STAGES IN PRODUCTION

The following outline plan shows the steps taken before the marketing of a product:

1. Market research probes the market in an attempt to ascertain the need for a new product. (*See* p. 144.)

2. Research is carried out to provide information on which to base a design for a prototype.

3. Design work is started which should produce a basic product.

4. Development work is carried out to develop the design.

5. Prototype production.—This stage goes hand in hand with design and is the production of a few products, often made with parts fashioned by hand. These are used for experimental and test purposes.

6. Pre-production.—The next step is to produce a number of items as nearly as possible under factory conditions using, where possible, the tools and equipment which will be used on the production line. These samples are tested and may also be supplied to customers for their consideration. Some manufacturers supply pre-production models to regular or selected customers and invite their comments and criticisms. Market research can also assist here.

7. Manufacture.—The product is then put into full production after an initial build-up to the final figure. This build-up allows time for the operatives to learn the new assembly cycles, etc., and ensures that the initial programmes will be met in spite of the high level of rejects which may occur at the start of production. Even the pre-production stage does not iron out all the "bugs" and it is hoped that the initial low level will allow for this.

The goods then leave for the warehouse and become the responsibility of the sales organisation.

THE FACTORY

When a manufacturing concern is launched or an existing business is expanding into other premises, the problems of placing departments and of "laying out" the equipment within these departments fall into two categories: (*a*) layout of previously inhabited buildings, and (*b*) planning of new factories built to the firm's own specification. The problems existing in the first case are basically concerned with making the best use of existing buildings. As these would not have been "tailor made" for the new products, the difficulties encountered when planning short flow-lines and an "ideal layout" are obviously great.

FACTORY LOCATION AND DESIGN

In selecting a site for a new factory or selecting a suitable vacant factory there are obviously certain factors to be considered. Some of the most important are as follows:

1. Availability of labour of the right type. Some areas specialise in certain crafts.

2. Transport facilities by road, rail and water, to get the personnel and materials to the factory and finished goods away.

3. Availability of material. An oil refinery may be near a port, and a car-body factory near a steel-rolling mill. (In whaling the factory actually chases the whales.)

4. Availability of services such as water, gas, electricity and waste disposal.

5. Room for expansion and also for car parking and recreational facilities.

6. Suitability and cost of land.

7. Suitability of climate for the particular product.

8. Local bye-laws, restrictions and regulations.

9. Government grants, such as those for north-east England, offered as an incentive to firms to expand in *development* areas.

When designing the buildings, it is also necessary to decide on the height of buildings; that is, whether to use single- or multi-storey construction. There are many factors which may affect the choice and it is necessary to weigh up the relative advantages and disadvantages of each. This is done below:

Single storey

1. Buildings and building maintenance costs are usually lower.

2. Floors may be illuminated by natural light.

3. Internal transport quicker and easier.

4. Virtually no restrictions on the placing of large presses and other heavy machinery.

5. General circulation easier—no lifts or stairs required.

Multi-storey

1. Shorter service runs—cables, pipes, vent shafts, etc., can run vertically to feed the floors in turn.

2. Gravity can be used for transporting, sorting and stacking.

3. Heat is not lost through the roof (except on the top storey), each floor helping to insulate the other floors.

4. Smaller site area, important where site cost is high or space restricted.

Once the requirements of the firm have been made known to the architect he can be left to perform his specialist function regarding the design of the building itself. But due regard must be paid by the architect to the human side. Very careful thought must be put into the planning of the offices, workshops, canteen and external environment. The human element is the life blood of the organisation and therefore must be a major consideration. Recent research has shown the importance of the working group and departments should be designed to encourage the informal groups to achieve the company's objectives, discussed earlier.

FACTORY LAYOUT

In some plants full-time works layout departments are formed, consisting of two or three experts, usually with work study background, and experienced personnel drawn from various departments such as electrical, plumbing, maintenance and safety, and from the production floor. These works layout departments are employed to allocate the space in a new factory and then to re-plan to accommodate expansions and contractions. They tailor the wishes and requirements of production management to suit the actual availability of space and services such as water, electricity, gas, drainage, and to satisfy lighting, ventilation, safety and other regulations.

Services

During the planning, an important feature for consideration is the running of services. Layouts are continually being altered to suit changing conditions, and services must be capable of easy modification. Some concerns favour the overhead system of services where all pipes and cables are fed along the ceiling and machines are connected by "drops" from these service lines. Others install services under the floor, which avoids the "cluttered up" look of the vertical drops. A third system, sometimes known as "island services," uses a system of supports running in straight parallel lines at intervals across the floor, usually about 18 in. above it. To these supports are attached the gas, water, air and electrical services so that the machines positioned along these runs can be tapped into the lines. This latter scheme restricts the movement of personnel between the lines of machines to the side gangways. Also, on re-arrangement of machines, they are restricted to the lines unless the supports and runs are bodily dismantled and moved. The advantage of this scheme, however, is that all service work is at a convenient level and ladders are not required.

The magnitude of the problems connected with service runs can be appreciated when considering the list of supplies which could be required for certain products. In just one department manufacturing radio valves, for example, it is necessary to supply low-pressure air, compressed air, oxygen, town gas, nitrogen, hydrogen, low vacuum, high vacuum, water, single-phase and three-phase electricity, water drains, acid drains and fume extraction vents, and most of these in fact to each machine!

Individual machines are powered either by mechanical transmission through overhead shafting driven by a prime mover, or by individual electric motors attached to the machines. The prime mover can be a steam engine, or gas, oil or electric motor. Although the overhead

D

counter-shafting can be installed in an easily interchangeable form, the individual motor offers considerably more flexibility.

Heating, lighting and ventilation

The *Factories Act* requires that in all workrooms a reasonable temperature must be maintained and where most of the work is sedentary the temperature must be at least 60° F (15° C). This Act also states that adequate ventilation by circulation of fresh air must be provided. This is usually taken as about three changes of air per hour. Local exhaust must be provided where dust and fumes are present.

Forced ventilation is usually accomplished by the use of fans which either blow air into, or extract air from, the room. Vents are situated in or on the ceiling and air is carried to or from these vents through trunking. Care must be taken not to "short circuit" the flow by opening windows directly under the vents. Fans which force air into the building are usually equipped with filters which clean the air. Spraying booths, acid etching plants, "tricho" cleaning plant and other processes containing fumes and dust are fitted with hoods over the position, the hoods being connected to the exhaust trunking. In these cases the trunking and fans should be made from non-corrosive material.

For some special processes air-conditioned rooms are required. Before entering the room the air is filtered, pre-heated, sprayed with water and chilled to remove the moisture. It is then warmed and distributed about the room.

In order to satisfy temperature requirements various methods of heating are available. One method, where forced ventilation is used, is to combine this with the heating system. A more effective method as far as emission of heat per square foot of radiating surface is concerned is the high-pressure hot water system which uses water above the normal boiling point: this is possible due to the fact that the boiling point of water is raised when it is under pressure. The cheapest installation is low-pressure steam heating: low-pressure steam at about 4 lb/in^2 is circulated in the pipes. High-pressure steam can be used at about 20 lb/in^2. The advantage of steam heating is that the radiating surfaces can be less than those for normal hot-water radiators as the steam is at a temperature above 212° F (100° C). Coke or oil-fired boilers are used in most systems.

Again, under the *Factories Act*, adequate lighting must be provided in workshops and passages. The usual artificial lighting in larger plants and in offices is provided by fluorescent tubes. As these lamps rely for their operation on the energy released by electron bombardment rather than on the heating of a metal filament, the consumption of power is less than with the normal tungsten lamp for the same illumination. Industrial installations are supplied in 4-, 5- and 6-ft lengths, and are arranged to spread the light in such a way as to reduce shadows and glare which can result from the use of point sources, such as the tungsten lamp. For fine assembly work and inspection, which require a light intensity of 100–200 l/ft^2, individual tungsten angle-lamps or small fluorescent strips may be needed to supplement the main lighting which, for general work, will give 30 or 40 l/ft^2.

Although the minima may be just acceptable, and within the legal requirements, it is in the organisation's own interest to provide adequate lighting: the operators must be able to see clearly without eye strain in order to carry out their duties properly. Also quantity and quality of production will definitely suffer through low operator morale arising from bad lighting and heating conditions. These two factors together with ventilation and draughts are often used as scapegoats and reason for complaints on joint consultative committees and works councils; in a number of cases the criticisms are well founded and really do affect the general morale of the shop.

PRODUCT DESIGN

When creating a new product the designer must consider the functional requirements and the aesthetic qualities, and also keep his eye on the cost of manufacturing the finished design. He must view the product in its proper perspective and when this is done he will attach varying degrees of importance to each of these considerations. For example, the petrol pump on a car must be functional and must be fairly cheap to produce: these factors are more important than its appearance although it should not be too offensive to the eye. On the other hand when designing the facia or instrument panel appearance is as important as layout. Ergonomics (discussed later) can assist the designer in this respect.

Functional aspect

A handsome product which does not function to the satisfaction of the customer is of no use to anyone, so the first consideration must be the functional requirements. On flexible layouts such as electrical circuits, the first design which is required to investigate the electrical properties is just a prototype or "mock-up" and looks such a mess to anyone other than the designer that it is often called a "bird's nest." The second stage is to lay out the circuit as neatly as possible. Technical restrictions such as high-frequency operation often impose limitations on the neatness of the final design. On other layouts, controls and switches most frequently used must be positioned within easy reach subject to technical restrictions—ergonomics once again.

Due consideration should be paid to accessibility of the various parts both during use and for servicing. Motor cars have in the past lagged behind electrical equipment in this respect. On most modern radio and television sets the removal of the back-plate reveals the business side of the circuit, thus avoiding the removal of too many screws and other parts.

Aesthetic considerations

At the other end of the scale are the products in which the aesthetic factor is paramount. These are the decorative items and range from pictures and ornaments whose only function is perhaps to fill a bare spot in a room, to buildings, cars and clothes which are essentially useful but must also be attractive to the eye.

Industrial design

In 1944 the Board of Trade set up a Council of Industrial Design with the object of raising the standard of design in British Industry. Some of the main functions of the Council are:

1. To assist in the establishment of Design Centres.
2. To hold exhibitions of good design.
3. To advise and provide information on industrial art.
4. To co-operate with educational authorities on the training of designers.

DRAWINGS AND SPECIFICATIONS

Drawings are pictorial representations of the parts to be manufactured and as such must show enough detail and different views (elevation, plan, side and perspective) to enable the production staff to reproduce the part exactly.

A *specification* is also added to include descriptions and processing instructions together with a *parts list*.

TOLERANCES

Mass production techniques introduce their own machine and human variations and even the craftsman has his accuracy limitations. Therefore all dimensions must have working limits within which the products must comply. These limits should be a compromise between the maximum the designer can tolerate and the minimum the production can accept consistent with efficient manufacture. Designers usually like their creations to be made as accurately as possible and often tend to make their tolerances too tight for efficient manufacture. Obviously, mating parts must be controlled fairly closely, but too tight a control will produce unnecessarily high levels of rejects, inspection, machine setting and control generally. Another cause of tight limits can be the indiscriminate use of standard tolerances without prior or due consideration. Thus if the general tolerance for "Perspex" parts is, say, $\pm \frac{1}{8}$ in. the smaller parts carry limits of the order of 1%. Should this tolerance be applied generally and indiscriminately, it will appear unrealistic when applied to such things as 6 ft rods, which are flexible anyway.

COST CONTROL

The design stage is one place where cost can be minimised. Cost can be attacked far more easily in design than later on when the product is actually being manufactured. Economies can be built into the design, whereas later improvements must be more expensive in tool modifications. When considering cost reductions in designs care must be taken to avoid making savings which will interfere with the efficient functioning or working life of the product. Some of the areas in which savings can be made are discussed below:

Materials.—The choice of correct materials is most important. Sometimes the choice is limited by technical considerations such as electrical conductivity. Copper is expensive, but an excellent conductor when compared with iron. Thus copper must be used in making wires and flex. It may be possible to use plastic instead of metal when making pulleys. Terminal blocks and connectors are made from plastic in preference to the more expensive porcelain. In the radio valve industry many parts made from expensive nickel can be manufactured in nickel-plated mild steel; often copper-plated mild steel is used in place of pure copper. Machinability must also be taken into consideration: cheaper materials are often easier to machine, thus allowing faster cutting speeds and less tool wear and breakage. Stainless steel is an instance of a material which is expensive and tricky to machine.

Assembly.—When a product is to be mass produced it is designed in such a way that components can be manufactured and assembled by mass production methods. Method study strives to reduce assembly movements so the designer can assist in achieving this end by cutting down assembly operations. This can be done by combining parts and components either by machining, casting or moulding them all in one piece.

Blanking and forming.—When blanking out components from strip, material can frequently be saved by a slight modification in the shape to be blanked. Modern processes allow complex shapes to be formed which can eliminate the welding or bolting together of a number of parts.

PRODUCT MANUFACTURE

SIMPLIFICATION AND STANDARDISATION

Any concern which desires to remain competitive must ensure that it has an efficient system of cost control. Important in the reduction of costs are the factors of simplification and standardisation.

Standardisation is the agreement upon certain factors affecting an item such as its performance, quality and various dimensions. Certain components in a range of models may be standardised and made interchangeable. For example, all the different cars turned out by an automobile group may have the same door handles, instruments and so on.

Simplification is the deliberate reduction in the variety of components or end products. A manufacturer may reduce the number of different types of radio sets from a dozen to three or four to simplify his range.

The manufacturing side of industry is often under pressure from the sales group to provide exactly what all their customers require. This is obviously uneconomical and impossible under mass production conditions and managements are torn between satisfying the sales organisation and customer, and variety reduction with its attendant low costs but reduced choice. Often the range is artificially enlarged by external or slight internal variations on the basic model. In the example of the radio sets given above, the same chassis can be used in two or three different cabinets, or by altering just the output stage in the circuit; alternatives of single ended or "push–pull" output can be offered. Thus two slightly different chassis and three cabinets can be offered as six different models.

There are obvious advantages and disadvantages in simplification and standardisation. The *advantages* to be gained are:

1. Longer production runs are possible with fewer changeovers and wider use of automation and mechanisation.

2. Operators become familiar with the work and produce at consistent quality and speeds.

3. It is possible to analyse and break down the operations into short repetitive cycles which are easily learned.

4. Variety reduction cuts down the indirect labour force including designers, inspectors, supervisors and stores personnel.

The most obvious *disadvantage* is in the reduction in choice and consequent loss of custom. A second disadvantage is that the customers must be persuaded to buy the same basic model for a number of years as re-tooling for the more expensive products is a costly business. This can be assisted by providing periodic "gimmicks" or by slightly modernising the lines. In the car industry the Ford Anglia and the Morris Minor ran for many years, virtually unchanged, at a very high level of sales.

PREFERRED SIZES

While on the subject of standardisation the question of preferred sizes may be considered. An example of this is found in the manufacture of shoes which are only made in steps of half-sizes. In the communication industry, the standard resistors are made in preferred values such as 47, 470, 4700, 47,000 ohms, 56, 560, 5600, 56,000 ohms and so on. Designers can build these preferred sizes into their new product, thus contributing to the reduction of costs.

THE BRITISH STANDARDS INSTITUTION

This non-profit-making institution was found in 1901 with the object of setting up standards for quality, performance, sizes and dimensions for the engineering, textile, building and chemical industries. The Institution prepares specifications under B.S. numbers and the acceptance of these standards by producers, while not compulsory, is desirable. Firms whose products conform to these specifications may affix the familiar kite-mark to those products. Standards for definitions are also prepared. One example of this is the *Glossary of Terms in Work Study* B.S. 3138:1959.

RESEARCH AND DEVELOPMENT

When an industry is engaged in a technological field which is expanding very rapidly, research and development are essential. There has to be response to the changes which take place viewed from two aspects:

(*a*) *Consumers*—this is *market research*, covered briefly in the chapter on marketing.

(*b*) *Products*—so that they comply with the latest ideas in terms of current technology, including the best aesthetic and functional standards.

Stages in research and development

There are many stages involved in the research and development function. An indication of their nature is given below:

1. Corporate policy.—There has to be recognition of how far a company is to commit itself on research and development. Without backing from the top, corporate planning is quite meaningless.

2. Integration with company objectives.—The products being developed should be of the type which can be fitted into the company structure and which are in line with company objectives. This is not to say that remotely connected products should not be considered. Many new inventions have opened up entirely new marketing possibilities for companies.

3. Opportunities have to be exploited.—A watch has to be maintained on all factors which affect a company's fortunes. This would include:

(*a*) New developments in related technologies.

(*b*) Legal requirements which affect products, *e.g.* tyre-tread specifications and safety-belt regulations as affecting car-accessory sales.

(*c*) Improving the performance or suitability of the existing products.

(*d*) Developing by-products from the waste materials which are left after the main products are made.

(*e*) Improving the product mix so that the average contribution earned is increased. The following situation may apply:

Product A	100,000 units
Product B	40,000 units
Product C	60,000 units

If the *contribution* on "C" is quite small, the company may attempt to develop a new product to take its place. (The contribution is the difference between the price and variable costs.)

(*f*) All ideas have to be "screened," and if there are possible commercial developments these should be investigated.

Balancing the work load

Research and development should pay for itself in terms of improved products or processes. Yet *all* the work done cannot possibly yield a profit. *Fundamental* research is concerned with general principles or problems, but has no specific aim. On the other hand, *applied* research attempts to solve specific problems or produce improvements in a certain area.

Once research has reached a certain stage the *development* function commences. This covers all the work connected with building prototypes, making tests, adjusting or adapting where necessary, and generally making the product fit for manufacturing on the scale required.

ORGANISATION OF PRODUCTION

The way in which production is organised to manufacture a product depends on the quantity required and on the type of product. It is usual to classify types of production under three main headings, namely, job production, flow production and an intermediate type called batch production.

JOB PRODUCTION (JOBBING)

This is the "special order" or "one off" type. It is usually carried out by firms engaged on sub-contract work such as toolmaking, machining, sheet-metal work and sub-assembly for larger firms concentrating on mass production, or for customers requiring special equipment. Jobs are carried out to the customers' special requirements or specifications. Owing to the small number required and the length of the "run" the manager usually is not too concerned with work measurement or method study. This, together with the fact that the labour and the equipment must be flexible to accommodate the continually changing production, often leads to inefficient utilisation of labour and plant. The selling price is usually based on past experience. Costing and estimating are covered in Part Four of this book.

BATCH PRODUCTION

When items are required in larger numbers it may be possible to tool up for repetitive production. However, a fixed quantity or batch may still be required rather than a continuous supply. If a batch is required to fulfil a special order the items are usually completed in one run. A form of batch production is also used when certain machines and processes supply a variety of products to various departments or lines. In this case a batch of, say, two months' work is made on product "A" and then the machine is changed over to product "B" to build up the stock of "B" and so on. This is described in the section below, dealing with determination of the economic batch size. Often "mass" production is organised on a batch production basis, the batches following each other continuously. The reason for this is to break up the flow of products into convenient lots for checking, costing, handling, inspection, operator payment and other purposes.

FLOW PRODUCTION (OR CONTINUOUS PRODUCTION)

Where the products are required in a continuous supply the production can be arranged to "flow" from one operation to the next. The same requirements are analysed and the production planning department will load the manufacturing department to an optimum level to be reached after an initial build-up. This build-up is required to allow the operatives to reach the budget speeds for the department and to allow time to cure the teething troubles not ironed out in the pre-production period. The programme, as this loading is usually called, provides the manufacturing department with its instructions regarding levels of production. The repetitive nature of the processes greatly simplifies the production control problems.

Although one day is much the same as any other and the products almost identical, problems of quality, quantity, labour and materials are still very much in evidence.

The choice of an economic batch size

Where components are manufactured to supply a unit engaged on flow production, in order to keep the machine utilisation high the machines may be run to provide several weeks' supply as a "buffer stock" and then broken down and re-tooled to produce a batch of different components. When the stock of one component has fallen to a low level, the machine will be re-set for this component and another batch produced.

The frequency of changeover will be determined by several factors, including the tendency of the stock to deteriorate or become obsolete, the cost of storing large quantities, the cost of changeover and loss of production time during changeover. The first two factors will encourage more frequent changeovers, while the third will tend to lengthen the time between them.

The build-up and run-down of stock with time can be shown graphically as in Fig. 10. This graph shows the position when the stocks are

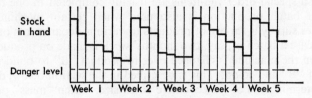

FIG. 10.—*State of stock graph*

replenished at the *correct frequency*. If the frequency is too high the stock level will gradually rise, but if too low the stock will run out. Examples of what may happen if stocks are not replenished at correct intervals are shown in Figs. 11 and 12.

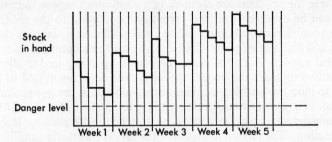

FIG. 11.—*Re-ordering at five-day intervals: stock rises*

The factors determining the frequency also affect the batch size and several formulae of varying complexity have been derived to determine the economic batch size.

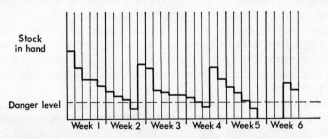

FIG. 12.—*Re-ordering at nine-day intervals: stock runs out*

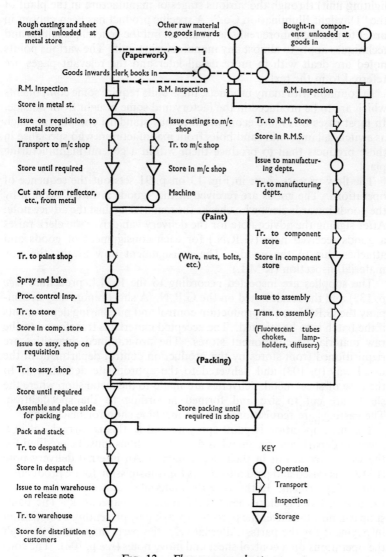

FLOW CHART OF THE PROGRESS OF MATERIAL THROUGH
FACTORY OF "DAYLIGHT" ILLUMINATION CO.

Manufacturers of fluorescent lighting

FIG. 13.—*Flow process chart*

THE MANUFACTURING FUNCTION

In order to obtain a clearer picture of the over-all manufacturing function it is proposed to follow an imaginary product (a fluorescent lighting unit) through the various stages of manufacture in the plant of the "Daylight Illumination Co." A specific product has been chosen in order to present a more realistic situation, but the general principles and techniques apply to almost any manufacturing unit. The various points noted are dealt with in more detail later and the relevant pages are referred to in the text.

In common with many products, these units require some components which are to be produced in the factory and some bought from outside. In most cases it is more economical to buy standard components such as switches, lamps, nuts and bolts from manufacturers who specialise in these products than to produce them within a general manufacturing plant.

The flow process chart in Fig. 13 on p. 91 sets out the sequence of operations. The goods are received at the "goods inwards" section by the goods inwards clerk who checks the material against the advice note. After signing the advice note for the delivery van driver the clerk raises a goods received note (G.R.N.) for each consignment of goods and attaches this to the goods. The consignment now awaits the raw material inspection (R.M.I.)

The supplies are inspected according to the R.M.I. procedure (*see* p. 133) and the result noted on the G.R.N. A short report may accompany the G.R.N. to the production control and purchasing departments if the batch is to be rejected. The accepted material is transferred to the raw material or component stores. The programmed quantities are requisitioned from stores by the production control department in the usual way (p. 103) and delivered to the appropriate department. In the case of sheet metal, deliveries are made to the metal shop where the sheets are cut to size and formed according to the specification. The castings are requisitioned by the machine shop for machining.

The next operation is paint spraying and as this is carried out in a separate department the metal and machine shops must be credited for the work carried out in their departments. An internal delivery note (I.D.N.) is raised and paid into stores for transmission to the production control department. In this case the material does not actually go into the stores, but the stores may still handle the paperwork. The paint shop can now take over the parts for spraying by presenting a requisition in payment for the parts. Alternatively, the parts may travel through the operations on a control sheet and move notes (*see* p. 104). The control note travels with the material, recording its progress while move notes are raised after each operation and passed to production control for their information.

After spraying, the parts are inspected by a process control inspector and the good batches are passed into the component store with the relevant paperwork. Rejects may be cleaned off and re-sprayed.

The production control department will now issue all the necessary parts to the assembly department on a bulk requisition or on separate demand notes. The various parts are assembled on the production lines and finally packed into cartons ready for dispatch to the main warehouse. Before dispatch they may be subject to a final acceptance sampling inspection.

EXAMINATION QUESTIONS

1. What advantages are to be derived from improving the layout of plant and machinery?

2. There is always the possibility of error in product design. The product may appear correct from one point of view and yet be quite wrong from another. List the possible areas and sources of error, illustrating fully to show your understanding and to indicate how such errors can be detected.

3. During an investigation it is discovered that the volume of work in process in a factory is excessive. What short-term and long-term action would you propose to correct this situation? To achieve control in the future what measurement would you apply to work in process?

4. What do you understand by the term automation? Trace its effect on:

   (a) product design;

   (b) employment policy;

   (c) wages structure;

   (d) management organisation;

   (e) sales planning.

5. In a manufacturing company which is so organised as to make a clear separation between functions, what should the manager of a manufacturing department know about the firm's policy in relation to selling, design, quality and capital expenditure?

6. To maintain their sales a firm has decided to introduce an entirely new range of products. What action should be taken to ensure the least possible interference with manufacture of existing products?

7. What influence has the design of a product upon the processes of manufacture? Give instances from factories you know and give one example of how manufacture has been simplified by change of design.

8. Since product design must take into consideration a large number of factors there is always the possibility of error. Draw up a check list which could give a logical approach to checking for design errors.

9. The degree to which production control requires to be developed varies with different industries. What are the principal variants in classification of manufacture which determine this degree?

What factors tend:

   (a) to a complex control system;

   (b) to a simple control system?

10. In many businesses the prototype or mock-up of a new product is constructed. Set out the objectives of this procedure.

11. What factors would affect the decision of the size of batches to be put into production?

12. When laying out a factory, what points would you take into consideration in order to ensure maximum production and that the supporting services are conveniently located?

CHAPTER VIII

PRODUCTION—THE ANCILLARY FUNCTIONS

MAINTENANCE

A VERY important branch in the organisational tree is the maintenance function. Equipment, whether it be a half-million-pound computer or a tenpenny light bulb, a lathe or a chisel, needs periodic attention, as anyone with a car or television set knows: the latter usually receives attention when it ceases to function correctly. The car is in a slightly different position, receiving planned periodic attention after so many miles.

The maintenance department is the responsibility of the plant engineer, and he employs millwrights, carpenters, painters, pipe-fitters and plumbers, electricians and cleaners. Smaller firms employ more general personnel. A further asset to the maintenance department is the "heavy gang." These brawny individuals move the heavy equipment during reorganisations and for purposes of repair and maintenance.

The more enlightened managements now employ planned *preventive maintenance* schemes. Regular servicing of a motor car was an instance quoted above: this is preventive maintenance to a certain degree, but in factories the practice goes further than this—to the point of replacing seemingly perfect parts *before* they fail. A carefully devised scheme, calculated from probability and past records, will eliminate most break-downs, but obviously not accidents or mis-use. One advantage of this scheme is that inspection and replacement can be performed during normal shutdown periods, whereas breakdowns occur during working hours when the machine is most required. It is essential to keep proper records of breakdowns in order to modify the scheme where necessary.

OPERATIONAL RESEARCH (O.R.) AND MAINTENANCE

In order to assist themselves in problems of optimum replacement policy, managements can call on the techniques of operational research replacement or renewal theory. This covers balancing the following factors:

(*a*) the certain cost of inspection labour and throwing away seemingly good components, against

(*b*) the probability of greater cost in damage and loss of production should the machine break down later.

The application of O.R. techniques to such problems is steadily gaining ground.

PRODUCTION PLANNING AND CONTROL

When a product is to be manufactured, the production must be carefully *planned* in order that the manufacturing departments are loaded efficiently and within their capacities. While the product is being manufactured, the production must be *controlled* to ensure that the programmed output is constantly maintained. These functions are known as Production Planning and Production Control respectively.

In the large number of small concerns, these functions are carried out by the manager, superintendent or foreman who will rely on his experience to guide him in his simplified form of planning. He will also control the production by means of his constant "on the spot" supervision.

Larger establishments cannot afford to rely on memory and personal supervision of all operations, due to the quantity of items produced and the complexity of the processes. These concerns require some aids to memory and routines which ensure that nothing is overlooked or forgotten. This is usually achieved by some sort of paperwork control. Even when mass producing articles by flow production methods, a manager cannot expect the plant to run without constant control. Production planning and control relieves managers and supervisors of the burdens of ordering, chasing and detailed paperwork and allows them to concentrate on the technical and managerial aspects of their jobs.

The actual systems used in production planning and control vary with the product, types of processing and size of organisation, but the principles behind the functions are similar in most respects. The direct elements of planning and control can be classified under four headings:

1. Planning

The term "planning" is used to indicate all the issues concerned with deciding how the production should be carried out. Sometimes it is referred to as "programming," acknowledging the fact that detailed schedules and programmes have to be prepared.

2. Scheduling

The scheduling process covers all aspects of the *timetabling* of production. Precisely when each operation or process has to be carried out is determined.

3. Dispatching

Dispatching deals with all aspects of giving the *necessary authority* to start the work and to obtain tools, materials and other requirements.

4. Progressing

Ensuring that the work is carried out as planned is the responsibility of the progress department. The timetable prepared by the scheduling section has to be complied with; *i.e. the planned dates have to be met.*

These are explained below, and their relation with other functions is also considered. Other departments which often come under the control of the production planning and control department are stores, goods inwards, inspection and dispatch.

PLANNING

The planning section of the production planning and control department is responsible for planning the products through the manufacturing stages, which include the manufacture of components, assembly, finishing and packing. Some of the responsibilities of the planning section are:

1. Transforming the requirements of the sales organisation into instructions to the producing departments. On job and batch production these are works orders and on flow production are usually in the form of programmes.

2. Preparation of programmes, or schedules of production such as Gantt charts, in order to provide the producing departments with target levels of production.

3. Keeping these schedules up to date to show the actual progress against the planned output to highlight deficiencies and deviations from the programme.

4. To act as a liaison department between the sales organisation and production departments to keep both sides supplied with up-to-date information, and to re-schedule when planned output cannot be maintained or when increased output is required.

5. Maintenance of stock records. These should be kept by the planning production and control department rather than by the storekeeper in order that the former has all the information associated with production, progress and stocks of materials in one central place.

6. Placing of orders on the purchasing department and keeping records of these orders and delivery dates.

SCHEDULING

On batch and flow production the programme is usually drawn up by the production planning and control department from levels mutually agreed by, and in collaboration with, the sales organisation and producing departments. The sales department usually requires certain quantities of products to be delivered within specified periods and these figures must be adjusted to suit the labour, material and machine availabilities. The revised figures are then spread over the available periods and weekly totals calculated and issued. When a type changeover occurs in a department the operatives must be allowed time to adjust themselves to the new motion patterns and component handling. Furthermore, time must be allowed for the inevitable technical and production problems which arise during the period immediately following the changeover. Thus the programme must show a gradual build-up from the initial low level to a final level which will be sufficiently high to ensure completion of the required quantity in the planned time.

The actual information issued to the departments concerned is usually in the form of a sheet set out in weeks or months and containing the requirements for each component or product under the corresponding periods. Alternatively, it may be set out in a graphical form such as a bar chart plotted against a fixed quantity scale or a Gantt chart to a time scale. Most scheduling is carried out with reference to time: "8000 parts in arrears" may not mean very much unless the statement is referred to the programme level, but "2 days behind" conveys much more information to everyone concerned as does "2 days' stock left." As with percentages, a person does not require to know the reference or absolute level against which to weigh up the relative values. It takes time to re-order or time to produce so what is required is a knowledge not of the *number* of items in arrears (or in stock) but of the *days'* production in arrears (or days' stock remaining). An example of a schedule of the Gantt type and of a programme are given in Figs. 14 and 15 respectively.

PRODUCTION PLANNING DEPARTMENT
PROGRESS SCHEDULE

Dept.: 8D
Product: C 200 Range

Date of issue: 14/4/66
Schedule no.: B 16/B
Cancels: B 16/A of 23/3/66

TYPE	LINE	Required for week ending:									
		4/3/66	11/3/66	18/3/66	25/3/66	1/4/66	8/4/66	15/4/66	22/4/66	29/4/66	6/5/66
C 209	A	3 2·8	3	3	3 3·2	3 3·5	3 2·8	1·5 1·6			
C 210	B	4·8 5	4·8 5	2 2·2	2 1·6	2 1·5					
C 213	B			·5 0	·8 ·3	1 ·5	1·4 ·9	1·8	2·4	2·4	2·4
C 220	A					·2 ·2	·6 ·9	1	1·4	2	2·5

FIG. 14.—*Gantt chart—progress schedule*

A more detailed description of the Gantt chart is given in the statistics section of this book. More elaborate systems based on bar charts may be obtained commercially which have the advantage of being easily

adjusted and are neat in appearance. When the components manufacturing department lags behind the programme on certain items the
Progress Section will pick this up and the items concerned will appear

PRODUCTION PLANNING DEPARTMENT											
PROGRAMME											

Dept.: 8 D   Date of issue: 14/4/66
Product: C 200 Range   Programme no.: 14/8D
                                       Cancels: 13/8D   of 20/3/66

TYPE	LINE	Number required for week ending:									
		4/3/66	11/3/66	18/3/66	25/3/66	1/4/66	8/4/66	15/4/66	22/4/66	29/4/66	6/5/66
C 209	A	3,000	3,000	3,000	3,000	3,000	1,500	–	–	–	–
C 210	B	4,800	4,800	2,000	2,000	2,000	–	–	–	–	–
C 213	B			500	800	1,000	1,400	1,800	2,400	2,400	2,400
C 220	A					200	600	1,000	1,400	2,000	2,500
TOTAL		7,800	7,800	5,500	5,800	6,200	3,500	2,800	3,800	4,400	4,900

FIG. 15.—*Programme form of the data shown in Fig. 14*

on a *shortage list* compiled by the progress chaser. The department will
then concentrate its resources on these areas to relieve the shortage.

Critical path analysis approach to planning

The planning of a product may be carried out more efficiently in some
cases by employing one of the critical path techniques, especially when
dealing with large, complicated, "one-off" jobs. These techniques are
particularly suited to solution by computer. The job is first broken
down into its basic elements. A network is then constructed from this
list and times for each activity noted on the diagram. The network is
then analysed to obtain the earliest and latest starting and finishing
times for each element. A simplified example of such a project is outlined for the manufacture of an electronic desk calculator on p. 129
where the subject is dealt with in more detail.

Stock records

For a number of reasons it is very important that some form of
continuous check be kept on the stocks held by the stores. This control
can be a physical check in the form of a safety stock which must only be
issued when the normal stock has been used up and which serves to

indicate that further orders must be placed with the supplier to replenish the stock. With larger firms, using perhaps thousands of different items, it becomes necessary to use a form of paperwork or clerical record such as *stock cards* which are kept in the production control office and maintained by this department. Whatever system is used it is essential

STOCK RECORD CARD

Supplier: E. Smith & Co.	Part I. Specification		Description: "K" bracket
Alternative supplier: V. P. Wilkinson			Code number: EP/682/47
			Price: 23/- per 100

Required for component:	P 38	L663/7	F111/3			
Quantity per wk.:	3,000	2,600	365			5,965

Part 2. Stock   Danger level

	Receipts		BALANCE		Issues			
			b/f 16,000		Dept. no.			Req. no.
Date	Order	G.R. No.		P	L	F		
7/1/66	10,000	18269	26,000					
			23,000	3,000				12879
			20,000		3,000			23110
			19,500			500		09094
14/1/66	8,000	18378	27,500					
17/1/66	2,000	18387	29,500					
			c/f =					
			Total iss. to dept.					

Part 3

ORDERING			RECEIPTS					
Order date	Order number	Quantity	Advice note	G.R.	Date	Quantity	Rej.	Outstdg
15/12/65	B 6387	10,000	PJ 276	18269	7/1/66	10,000	–	–
6/1/66	B 6399	10,000	PJ 334	18378	14/1/66	8,000	–	2,000
–	–	–	PJ 349	18387	17/1/66	2,000	–	–

FIG. 16.—*Stock record card*

that the records are accurately kept: inaccurate information is worse than none at all—it can create a false sense of security regarding stock levels. The main reasons for keeping such records are:

1. To warn the controller when re-ordering becomes necessary.
2. To act as a check against pilfering.
3. To provide information which will enable the controller to make a decision, when faced with a request for material required for a use other than that for which the material was purchased.

It is obviously important that material is not issued from stores as in 3 above without the authorisation of the controller. What sometimes happens is that the departmental manager decides to use a different component in order to improve the assembly or to overcome some production difficulty and, on discovering that this component is already used by another department in the factory, requisitions the new component from stores. If undetected this practice soon uses up the stock and *both* departments stop producing the particular products affected. In ordering components, requirements for each product are totalled and orders placed with suppliers for this quantity. The requirements are obtained from stock record cards and any alterations to the requirements are picked up from specification changes and recorded on the "fixed heading" portion of the card. The orders placed with suppliers are accordingly amended. Thus the manager who wishes to use a different component or change the material should initiate a specification change and at least, as a temporary measure, send a memorandum to the production controller requesting that more material be ordered pending the change of the specification.

A typical stock record card is illustrated in Fig. 16. A suitable card for this purpose should contain the following information:

1. Specification of the material

(*a*) description;
(*b*) code number;
(*c*) price of the material;
(*d*) supplier's name;
(*e*) products in which it is used and their code numbers.

2. Bin balance

(*a*) receipts with amount, date and goods returned note number;
(*b*) issues with amount, receiving department and requisition number;
(*c*) balance in stock. Each time goods are received the quantity is added to the balance to obtain the new figure and similarly issues are deducted from the balance;
(*d*) replacement level and/or danger level corresponding to the safety stock.

3. Ordering record

(*a*) (i) date ordered;
(ii) order number and quantity;

(b) (i)   actual amount received;
   (ii) date received;
   (iii) inspection result;
   (iv) net passed into stores;
   (v)   outstanding amount (*i.e.* amount ordered—actual receipts *less* amount rejected).

DISPATCHING

Documents required in production control

1. Works order.—In order to authorise the factory to commence production on a batch, a works order is issued. This document usually contains information such as code number and description of the product, quantity, job number and material required, and then a list of operations and processes through which the product is routed, together

MANUFACTURING ORDER							
SPECIFICATION							
Date:				Department:			
Description:				Material:			
Code number:				Drawing no. Price:			
PROCESS							
Process	Code	Dept.	Charge to	Equipt.	Charges		
					labr.	matl.	m/c
Special instructions:							
Inspection details:							
Special treatment or processes:							

Fig. 17.—*Works manufacturing order* (*route card*)

with the allowed times for each of these. As it lays out the sequence of operations or route taken by the product it is often referred to as a route card (Fig. 17).

2. *Material requisition.*—This document (Fig. 18) is required when drawing material from stores. It acts as a "cheque" with which to "pay" for the goods. Usually two copies of the requisition are presented to the stores and one copy remains in the book. Often the storekeeper cannot

MATERIAL REQUISITION		
Quantity required	Quantity issued	Sig. of Storekeeper
Description		Code number
Required by dept.	Job number	Date	Sig. of foreman

FIG. 18.—*Material requisition or demand note*

supply the exact amount demanded; it may be in short supply or the material may be made up in fixed quantities, such as reels of wire, from which lesser quantities cannot be supplied. Provision must therefore be made on the requisition for the actual amount supplied as well as quantity demanded. The storekeeper enters the actual amount issued in the appropriate column and returns one copy to the person requisitioning the goods. The requisition is passed from the stores to production planning and control to inform this department of a withdrawal and to enable the stock records to be adjusted accordingly.

CONTROL SHEET								
	1	2	3	4	5	6	7	8
Clock number								
Operation code								
Quantity received								
Quantity scrapped								
Quantity delivered								
Description				Job. no.				Del. to Stores
				Part no.				

FIG. 19.—*Control sheet*

3. Control sheet.—This sheet (Fig. 19) is raised for each new batch of work. Even on flow production it is sometimes more convenient to batch the products into 100 or 1000 lots when they are small in size. The control note proceeds through each process with the batch of work and provides a record of the scrap produced by each operation as well as the good work forwarded for the next operation. At the final process it is used as an internal delivery note on which the finished parts are paid into stores.

4. Internal delivery note (I.D.N.).—Sometimes a separate note (Fig. 20) is used to deliver finished products, finished components or even excess material into stores. It can be regarded as having a function opposite to that of the requisition. It is also known as a *returns to stores note*.

5. Progress note or move note.—A progress note (Fig. 21) is raised after the completion of each operation on a batch of work, and when forwarded to the production planning and control department informs them that the batch has progressed to the next operation. It also states the number of rejects and the number of good items forwarded. As with the control note, this note may be used as an I.D.N. at the final operation.

Special Note: Students are also advised to study the alternative forms which are given in Chapter XX, which deals with costing.

INTERNAL DELIVERY NOTE		395
Code number	Order number	G.R.
Description		Requested by:
Supplier		Advice note
Number advised	Received	Received by	Date
INSPECTION			
Received	Rejected	Passed to stores	Date
Signature:			

FIG. 20.—*Internal delivery note (I.D.N.)*

PROGRESSING

The programme or schedule is supplied to the manufacturing departments for their information, but, as with other similar devices, they do not in themselves ensure that the producing departments meet the required outputs. Some form of continual follow-up procedure is required which will "chase up" those erring departments who fall behind

PROGRESS NOTE			
Date		Dept.	
Description		Code number	
Quantity received	Operation		Op. No.
Operator's name		Clock number	Class
INSPECTION			
Number inspected	Rejected	Passed forward	Allow pay for
Reason for scrap:		PART BATCHES	
		Passed forward	Remaining for process
Sig. of inspector			
Date			

FIG. 21.—*Progress note*

schedule. Thus the function of progress chasing is to be found in most plants and its object is to control the deviations and variations from the programmed level.

The watchdogs of progress, known as *progress chasers*, are usually weekly staff members of the production planning and control department with a status equivalent probably to chargehand or assistant foreman on the production floor. There is usually one progress chaser to each department, dealing with similar processes on many products, or perhaps one chaser to a product if this proves more convenient from the organisational aspect. Their duties can be summarised as follows:

1. To determine the causes of deviations from programme in order that the production planning and control department may report back to the sales organisation.

2. To assist in removing the difficulties causing the deviations.

3. To liaise with other departments supplying material and components to the particular chaser's department.

4. To authorise and sign requisitions.

5. To prepare a shortage list. The shortage list is prepared by the chaser from information obtained from the returns made by the

producing departments. A list of components and materials in short supply is made and this list is circulated daily to all departments. The list includes all material which has a stock in hand of less than the minimum allowed (often three days' supply) and indicates the actual number of days' stock remaining. It serves as a warning to the departments concerned to concentrate their resources on these shortages if possible.

Machine loading

Machine loading is the allocating of jobs to machines (and processes) with due regard to priorities and to labour and machine utilisation. If the standard times for operations are known it is a simple matter to calculate the time required for each job and hence to allocate the available work to the machines in a planned and methodical way.

STOREKEEPING

The organisation of the stores is dependent on the nature of: (a) the product; (b) the materials used; (c) the way in which the flow of production is organised.

Stores can be divided into "direct materials" and "indirect materials." (*See* p. 312 *et seq.* for definitions.) Direct materials stores are:

1. Raw material store.   3. Finished parts store.
2. Component store.   4. Warehouse.

Indirect stores are:

1. Tool store.
2. Sundry materials store.
3. Maintenance store.

There may also be special stores such as inflammable store and chemical store.

Stores are sometimes built to suit special materials, such as grain, oil, beer or gas, but the term storekeeping is usually applied to stores in manufacturing industries rather than processing plants.

The stores collectively hold a very large portion of the products and materials, which may be worth thousands or millions of pounds. Therefore they should be guarded against unauthorised entry and only storemen allowed behind the counter. The usual method is to serve customers through a hatchway. Many of the items, such as light bulbs, paint, cleaning materials and even nuts and bolts, are a great temptation to the "do-it-yourself" enthusiast and, of course, the final product may be just the thing for the kitchen. Most managers and supervisors are required to account for their scrap and losses and an unguarded store may "lose" items needed to cover these losses. Unfortunately, many stores are regarded as non-productive necessary evils and are tucked away in the odd corners nobody wants.

No goods then should leave the stores without "payment" being made. There are three basic methods of payment:

(a) Material requisition:
(i) single items;
(ii) bulk requisition.

(b) Material feed lists, which are standing orders for parts.
(c) Deposit checks, where items are loaned, such as tools.

DIRECT MATERIALS STORES

1. Raw materials store

(a) *Bulk.*—These are of special design to suit the individual industry, such as silos for grain, gasometers, oil storage.

(b) *Bulk solid.*—Separate stores are usually maintained for material such as sheet metal, pig iron, packing material and cartons, and timber.

(c) *Engineering production.*—The smaller items are kept in bins placed in racks. The racks themselves should be in neat lines with adequate aisles between them to permit the use of handling trucks. While a neat layout is all important, an efficient system of locating items is absolutely essential. Where code numbers are used for parts and material, the bins may be arranged in code number order, provided that the coding system collects similar items together under the same numerical group. Where the coding is haphazard the bins may be numbered and a cross reference made with the description or code number.

The bins may also carry a "bin card" which indicates the balance remaining in the bin. This must be amended each time issues are made from, or deliveries made to, the bin. The bin card *should not* be used as the stock control but as an indication to the storeman. The control records should be kept only by production control.

2. Component store

This type of store carries the piece parts which are (a) manufactured in the factory or (b) purchased from outside sources, which may include special castings, switches and plugs, resistors, capacitors and ball races.

Frequently there is no clear distinction between components and raw materials. Some firms will class nuts and bolts as components while to others they will be raw material. Thus the division may be that all purchased material and items will be "raw material and components" and items made within the plant "finished parts."

3. Finished part store

Where the concern is not using automation or transfer machines, finished parts need to be stored in readiness for the assembly or sub-assembly stages. Items are "paid into" the stores on paperwork which may be an internal delivery note (I.D.N.) and then requisitioned out in the usual way. As stated above, it may be that *all* items made within the plant are kept in this store.

4. Warehouse

In this store the finished goods are kept prior to dispatch to customers. The general principles of stores control described below apply here also.

INDIRECT STORES

1. Tool store

Items issued by the tool store may be classified into two categories.

(*a*) *Returnable tools.*—Taps and drills, cutters for milling machines, lathe tools, spanners and screwdrivers are included under this heading. These tools are issued in exchange for a metal or plastic tool check bearing the operator's name or number. The check is held against the return of the tool.

(*b*) *Consumable tools.*—Tools which are consumed by the work such as files, glass paper, emery cloth can be obtained on a requisition as they are non-returnable.

2. Indirect materials store

Indirect materials including cleaning materials, rags, lubricating oil, paint and grease are kept apart from the other goods.

3. Maintenance store

All materials and parts required for routine and preventive maintenance are kept in this store.

RECEIPTS AND ISSUES

Goods may be delivered to or withdrawn from the stores on completion of the necessary paperwork. It is not always desirable or possible for the goods to go physically through the stores, but whether they do or not the paperwork must be in order to maintain accuracy in the records.

Issues may be made on a requisition for items of one type or, if a number of different components are required, a bulk requisition may be used. Materials which are required for a batch or flow production line on a reasonably regular basis may be issued on a "feed list." This is a pre-printed list bearing the description, code number and quantity required of each item to complete, say, a batch of twenty assemblies, or a day's work, or some other convenient amount. The amount issued is also noted on the list as some items may be in short supply.

STOREKEEPERS' INCENTIVE SCHEMES

The storeman is usually poorly paid in comparison with production staff and, perhaps because of this, tends to put comparatively less effort into his work. Obviously normal time study methods are not suitable for the type of variable work, but storemen *can* be employed under incentive schemes based on the standard times for the activities, obtained by analytical estimating as described in another part of this book (p. 122). As the utilisation of store personnel is often well below 50% there is enormous scope for savings in labour costs in these areas.

PURCHASING

Materials, including the raw material from which the products are manufactured, must be continually fed into the organisation in order to ensure smooth and efficient production. Suppliers must be found and prices agreed, and in the larger concerns a separate organisation exists to carry out these functions: this is the Purchasing or Buying Department. In small firms the responsibility for buying often rests with the owner or manager. It is obviously an important function as economies made during design, planning, manufacturing and other stages can be completely cancelled out if the buying is not performed skilfully.

POLICY

Probably the most usual method of purchasing is buying in minimum quantities to replace stock, or buying as current prices and conditions indicate. This is sometimes referred to as "current price buying" or "market conditions buying." The buyer has a free hand, more or less, to decide the right time to place the order, or to obtain alternative quotations to enable comparisons to be made.

A second policy is "contract buying." In order to avoid the carrying of large stocks by the user, the supplier undertakes to deliver agreed quantities at intervals over the period specified in the contract. This method of buying guarantees a market for the supplier and regular supplies for the customer, subject of course to modification or cancellation of the contract preceded by reasonable period of notice.

"Bargain buying" is a policy which should be pursued with utmost caution. Purchases made in bulk at "bargain prices" may result in surplus material should the programme for the product be curtailed or terminated: the buyer should therefore be "in the know" as far as the firm's future policies are concerned. But demand may fall off, or consumers' tastes may change, either resulting in programme cuts. Thus the risks involved in pursuance of this policy are great. However, the fruits of "bargain buying" when the gamble comes off are greatly reduced material costs with consequently higher profits.

PROCEDURE

The usual procedure is for the purchasing department to handle all purchasing from outside sources. This usually covers requirements of individuals who may wish to obtain special items for their inspection, research, production or other activities. Thus the only members of the firm who have any contact with suppliers are the buyers, and other members of staff order through the central purchasing organisation. To assist them in carrying out this function the purchasing department usually carries a comprehensive library of catalogues, and where the necessary information is not available the buyer may request the services of suppliers' representatives. The forms used and procedures followed are covered later.

HANDLING OF MATERIALS

The whole history of the raw material or component through the factory from its reception at "goods inwards" to the dispatch of the assembled product is one of handling and storage. It has been estimated that 15% to as much as 85% of the total cost of production is in materials handling. This, then, should prove to be a profitable area for investigations into cost reduction.

This reduction of costs can be achieved by:

1. The elimination of all unnecessary handling.
2. The reduction of all handling by proper plant layout, by combining jobs and processes to reduce "putting down" and "picking up."
3. The use of handling aids and mechanical handling equipment from which can come:

(a) The introduction of the "unit load" and palletisation.

(b) Reduction of indirect labour resulting from reorganisation of duties of handling personnel, together with the above items.

(c) Reductions in floor space taken up by storage, by using height and storing upwards (stacking) and by using operational research techniques of stock control.

4. Combining transportation and processes; for example, a product which must be sprayed and baked as the last operation before packing can be processed while still hanging from the conveyor which is carrying it between assembly and packing departments.

Investigations into problems of handling are usually the responsibility of the work study department who will chart the flow of materials, or the layout of the assembly shop or stores in order to analyse the flow or layout and then install improved methods.

MECHANICAL HANDLING AIDS AND EQUIPMENT

As mentioned above, the use of mechanical handling equipment can result in great reductions in handling leading to financial savings. However, it is obvious that the savings are not immediate as the capital outlay for such equipment is quite high. These costs must be weighed against the rate at which the savings will be made, *i.e.* how long it will take for the aids to pay for themselves. This rate is reduced when running costs, depreciation, etc., of the equipment are taken into account.

Besides the purely financial considerations there is also the human aspect. There is a definite rise in morale with the introduction of mechanical aids probably due to such factors as easier and cleaner handling and "Hawthorne effect."* The natural fear of redundancy which these aids may bring is another matter, and the extent of this depends on the way in which the aids are introduced.

Only the most usual equipment can be mentioned as most aids are "tailor made" to suit the site, process and material, and this is especially true of conveyor systems.

Any attempt to classify the equipment would probably result in the grouping which is given below:

Bulk material handling equipment

Under this heading would be the suction pipes for unloading or moving grain, fish and sand from the holds of ships. Oil pipelines could also be included.

Trucks

Trucks come in a variety of forms and sizes and include: (1) fork lift trucks, (2) pallet trucks, (3) hand trucks and barrows. The first two are explained below, before describing the palletisation scheme in which they are used; the third type is self-explanatory.

1. Fork lift trucks.—These are normally four-wheeled vehicles equipped with two arms or forks which can be positioned under crates, boxes or any large object in order to transport or stack them. The forks are attached to a column on the truck and at the touch of a lever they travel up the column, carrying their load to any desired height for stacking. These trucks are classified in two ways: as normal or "reach," or as "driver" or "pedestrian."

The reach truck has the added facility of being capable of reaching out to the load, which enables it to move loads in obstructed or awkward situations.

With the driver truck, the operator is seated behind the forks at a car-type steering wheel. The pedestrian type is manipulated by an operator

* *See* p. 18 on the Hawthorne Experiments.

who walks behind the truck. These mechanical devices are powered by many different means. These include:

(*a*) "Manpower"—the operator being seated at a bicycle-type chain-and-pedal mechanism which supplies the motive power.

(*b*) Petrol or diesel engine which produces enough power to raise 25 or 30 tons weight, but also unfortunately produces toxic fumes. It is very useful for outside work and for prolonged use.

(*c*) Gas engine powered by, for example, Calor gas. Remarks in (*b*) above may apply.

(*d*) Electric motor, battery powered. This type is very common especially for indoor work, as no fumes are produced. Will only lift up to 4 tons usually, and its periods of duty are restricted by the battery capacity. Batteries are recharged at night or may be interchangeable.

2. *Pallet trucks.*—These are types of fork lift truck but their lift is only sufficient to raise the load off the ground for transportation (about 4 in.). These too can be "driver" or "pedestrian" and tractive power can be as for fork lift trucks. One addition to the range, which reduces the cost considerably, is the "non-powered" type which is pushed by hand and is fitted with a hydraulic lift operated by a hand pump.

The pallet truck is so named because, like the fork truck, it fits nicely into the palletisation scheme.

Palletisation

This system is based on the pallet, a flat platform usually in standard sizes of 40 × 40 in. or 40 × 48 in. The pallets can be loaded with the boxes, cartons, sacks, etc., ready to be picked up by the fork or pallet truck. These are known as "unit loads."

The boxes are built up on the pallet and "bonded" like bricks in a wall to make the stack more stable. These unit loads can be stacked vertically.

As the pallets are made to standard sizes the floors of stores, warehouses and loading bays can be marked out for ease of positioning. The unit load concept is rapidly spreading and many firms have designed their lorries and buildings to accommodate exact numbers of unit loads. British Rail have standard wagons specially designed around the unit load, and freight charges are lower for these consignments. Shipping and aircraft companies are also adopting the idea.

Once the unit loads have been made up at the factory they can be loaded by fork lift truck on to lorries, unloaded at the station and shipped into the rail car, unloaded at the station and then taken to the final destination by lorry. This method obviously eliminates the manhandling of all the separate cartons.

Conveyors

Instead of the operator placing the material aside ready for separate collection later, handling is reduced if he places directly on to a moving conveyor which transports the material immediately to the next stage. Conveyors can be mechanically driven "belts" or channels containing, for example, parallel rollers over which the material slides under gravity or merely by being given a push. Conveyors are used on production lines to move the products from one process to the next, or in unloading bays running from vehicle to stores—in fact anywhere where it is necessary to get things out of the way quickly. Some lorries are fitted with rollers to facilitate loading at the front.

Overhead conveyors and cranes.—These are useful for conveying heavy goods such as car engines and bodies. They are also used where material must be lowered into tanks or vats, such as in degreasing operations.

Tractors

A further accessory to internal transport is the tractor which can be used for pulling a train of trucks which might normally be operated separately. This type of transport may be seen in the larger railway stations and termini and at airports as well as in factories.

EXAMINATION QUESTIONS

1. Set out a specimen standard practice instruction for the ordering of materials, supplies and outside services through the buyer, using the minimum possible forms for control.

2. The maximum and minimum method provides a means of control for items which are ordered over and over again. State the general objective behind the use of this method. Define the four important quantity levels:

(*a*) maximum;
(*b*) minimum;
(*c*) standard order;
(*d*) ordering point.

Give an example which demonstrates the use of all these four levels.

3. What are the purposes of standardisation? In what fields of industrial activity can it be applied? What are its advantages:

(*a*) to the producer,
(*b*) to the user?

What disadvantages could arise?

4. Your company proposes to extend its output and for this purpose to build a new factory. From investigations you have made you have come to the conclusion that a small extension to the factory, combined with improved methods of manufacture, will suffice to provide the extra output required. Write a report to the Directors submitting your own plan.

E

5. What influence has the design of a product upon the processes of manufacture? Give instances from factories you know and give one example of how manufacture has been simplified by change of design.

6. What are the purposes of industrial research and development? Give *four* measures of effectiveness which can be applied in this particular field and trace the organisational relationship in a company between its research laboratory, the line management and the several production staff specialists such as the plant engineer and the work study engineer.

7. A company is considering manufacturing a product which other makers have been producing for some time. What information would help in determining the quantities of the new product to be manufactured, and how would it be obtained?

8. In the design of a new factory you are considering the layout of the store-room(s). What functional requirements would you take into consideration and what factors would influence the amount of space required?

9. Describe the duties of the factory maintenance engineer and indicate the ways in which he can contribute to the economic and efficient operation of a large works.

10. Describe a simple system for planning and controlling the shop loading in a factory. How would you deal with variations and other contingencies which affect the demand on the shop's capacity?

11. Give a short description of each of the following production terms, but in sufficient detail to explain its purpose:

(*a*) production planning;
(*b*) capacity;
(*c*) loading;
(*d*) material scheduling;
(*e*) route sheet.

12. Material handling is usually a heavy industrial cost. Suggest means by which it may be reduced. You are asked to answer in relation to the broad concept of factories and not one particular industry.

13. State the actions to be taken by a stores superintendent in order to ensure economic administration of his department and the maintenance of minimum stock levels.

14. (*a*) Explain the meaning of labour and machine utilisation.
(*b*) What factors must be taken into consideration when setting levels of utilisation?
(*c*) What factors affect achievement and how would you measure and report variations?

15. State what steps you would take to ensure the efficient use of power and fuel supplies in a factory.

16. The management have noted a significant increase in the level of stocks held and ask you to carry out an investigation. Set out the possible reasons to which you consider this increase might be attributed.

17. What are the advantages of standardisation to:

· (*a*) the manufacturer; and
(*b*) the consumer?

CHAPTER IX

PRODUCTION—THE ADVISORY FUNCTIONS

INDIVIDUAL concerns organise their advisory services to suit their own particular requirements. The best approach, therefore, is to detail the purpose and scope of each of these advisory departments rather than to fit them into an organisational "tree."

WORK STUDY

When the phrase "improvement in performance" is heard, the function which usually springs to mind is work study.

Work study has probably a higher saving: expenditure ratio than any other single management tool. And yet how many firms give it the support it deserves? Most organisations insist on their "rate fixers" who will squeeze the last drop of sweat out of the operative and hourly worker while hundreds of "indirects" (office staff, supervisors, storemen, inspectors and draughtsmen) plod along unmolested. Again, sometimes small changes in the product itself or in the methods used can result in enormous savings over a year. The same effort used in saving pennies by time study could probably save pounds by applying the wider techniques of work study.

These techniques vary in scope and application with the nature of the business, outlook and history of different firms. Some of the most important techniques used are: (a) method study; (b) time study; (c) synthesis; (d) predetermined motion time systems; (e) analytical estimating. With the *exception* of method study (which includes workplace layout, factory layout and improvement of methods generally) the techniques mentioned are known collectively as "work measurement." Each will now be considered separately in turn.

TIME STUDY

From early beginnings in the eighteenth century, with the secret time studies of such people as Jean Perronet in France and other observers in England, time study had a stormy passage right up to recent years but now the system is generally accepted. In some areas, time study is still a "dirty word" carried over from the days of Charles Bedaux in the late 1920s and early 1930s when the introduction of Bedaux's systems coincided with the depression.

Time studies are carried out by trained engineers using a stop-watch as the instrument for timing. They are applied to relatively short-cycle

115

jobs; that is, those where the cycle of operations occupies a few seconds to a few minutes. Long-cycle jobs are timed by other methods.

The job is broken down into "elements" of about 8 to 16 sec duration. The engineer then proceeds to time, say, 20 cycles noting the time for each. It will be appreciated that the operator under observation can regulate the rate of working to suit his own ends and this factor must be taken into account. Besides the time for the cycle, the engineer must also make an estimate of the "rate of working" judged against a "rating scale." The British Standards Institution has recommended that the normal rate at which piece-workers perform shall be 100 rating (known as "standard rating") so that an operator working at, say, half this speed is working at a 50 rating. 100 corresponds to the old "incentive speed" and is equivalent to a walking speed of about 4 m.p.h.

The calculations can now be made and the first step is to multiply the observed times by the corresponding ratings. The products obtained should be reasonably constant; for example:

Rating (a)	Observed cycle time (b)	(a) × (b)
80	10 sec	800
90	9 sec	810
90	8·8 sec	792
75	11·0 sec	825

and so on.

When all calculations have been made, the average may be 810. This is then divided by the Standard Rating (100) to give the *basic time* required for the job. In this example it would be 8·1 sec. The preceding calculation is known as "extension" or "normalising."

Operators are given allowances for personal needs, relaxation and rest, contingencies and other factors in the form of a percentage of their total hours. This percentage can be 5–20%, or even more, and is not given in lump sums but is added to the basic time. In the example given, if a 15% allowance was made, the basic time would be increased by 15% or a factor of 1·15. Thus the 8·1 sec is increased to 8·1 sec + 15% of 8·1 = 9·3 sec. This is the allowed time. The times are usually recorded in decimal minutes or decimal hours.

An operator completing all the day's cycles at an average time equal to the allowed time would be averaging 100 or making *standard performance*. The example below shows how the operator's performance can be calculated and Fig. 22 illustrates the type of form which could be used for this study.

Example

The job is to pack fountain pens in presentation boxes.

Time allowed = 0·4 standard min each.

Working time per day = 8 h (or 480 min).

Operator packs 1080 on this day. What is her performance on this particular day?

Calculation

For each one she packs, she is credited with 0·4 min work.
Therefore, if she packs 1080 pens she has earned:

$$1080 \times 0\cdot4 = 432 \text{ min work.}$$

Now there are 480 min available for work and 480 min constitute a day's work at 100 performance.

So 432 min constitute $\frac{432}{480}$ths of a day's work

$$= 90\% \text{ of a day's work}$$
$$= 90 \text{ out of 100 performance}$$
$$= 90 \text{ performance.}$$

From pre-calculated tables the wages for that day could be determined for this 90 performance.

This example shows how time study can be used to operate incentive schemes. The allowed times can also be used for machine loading and determining the number of operators required in a department. Of course, an average level of working must be assumed for the purposes of calculation and this level is usually taken as 100 performance or predicted from past records.

Human factors

The human element must be considered on both sides during a time study. From the beginning, the engineer must avoid any suspicion of secrecy. He may even decide to discuss his findings with the operator. The first step, however, is to discuss every detail with the floor supervisor and even, in some cases, with the shop steward, underlining the most important consideration: *consultation*. Once the supervisors are on the side of the engineer, the next task is to gain the confidence of the operator and then to proceed with his study. As a management representative he must behave as such, pursuing the management policy with determination, while remembering he is performing a service and often has no executive authority.

The human element on the engineer's part is apparent in the rating stage. Rating is an estimate on the part of the engineer and this may be subject to inaccuracies. To counteract this some firms use films, or hold rating sessions with groups of engineers in order to maintain a standard of rating.

Recording the study

The observed times and ratings must be recorded and various calculations made and these should all be done on a suitable form. These forms are designed to suit the requirements of individual firms: one type which could be used is shown in Fig. 22.

Study code No. *131*	**TIME STUDY RECORD**	Study made by *D. Ford*
Date *20/1/66*		Part No. *ES 62742*
Cancels Study *130*	Dept. *Assembly*	*Pack fountain pens*

Operation *P.U. pen L.H.   P.U. paper R.H. simultaneously. Wrap pen. Release L.H. P.U. box L.H. Insert pen. Hold box L.H. P.U. lid R.H. Place on box. Place aside in carton.*

Details (Equipment, materials, machine speeds, etc.)
Cartons — paper.

Basic time	O/LR A%	Allowances	ALLOWED TIME + Policy Al.
8·1	*15%*	*—*	*9·3S.U. + 0*

Element 1.
As above

Remarks I.T	(b) Rt.	(c) OT	(d) Pr	Remarks I.T	(b) Rt.	(c) OT	(d) Pr	Remarks I.T	(b) Rt.	(c) OT	(d) Pr
	80	10	800								
	90	9	810								
	90	8·8	792								
	75	11	825								
	15										
Total			9720	Total				Total			
Av.			810	Av.				Av.			

Ancillary tasks
1. Cleaning bench, etc.   *l* per *day* = *5* mins.   ⎱ *Not done by*
2. *Change cartons*   *l* per *100* = *$\frac{12}{100}$ seconds* ⎰ *this operator.*
3.   per   =

FIG. 22.—*A time study record sheet*

O/LR A% is the overall relaxation allowance made; *Rt.* is the rating; *OT* is the observed time; and *Pr* is the product of (b) × (c).

PREDETERMINED MOTION TIME SYSTEMS (P.M.T.S.)

Time standards are issued at the standard rating which is a fixed rate of working. As this rate is independent of any particular operator, the individual times obtained from observing a number of operators independently engaged on the same task should be almost identical (after normalising or extending the times). It should be possible, therefore, to break down activities into their basic elements and then to set time standards on these elements. Many years ago Gilbreth attempted to do this with his "therbligs."

TABLE I.—WORK-FACTOR MOTION TIME TABLE FOR DETAILED ANALYSIS

(Time in Work-Factor Units)

Copyright The WOFAC Corporation

(A) ARM—Measured at knuckles / (L) LEG—Measured at ankle

DISTANCE MOVED (in.)	BASIC	1	2	3	4	DISTANCE MOVED (in.)	BASIC	1	2	3	4
1	18	26	34	40	46	1	21	30	39	46	53
2	20	29	37	44	50	2	23	33	42	51	58
3	22	32	41	50	57	3	26	37	48	57	65
4	26	38	48	58	66	4	30	43	55	66	76
5	29	43	55	65	75	5	34	49	63	75	86
6	32	47	60	72	83	6	37	54	69	83	95
7	35	51	65	78	90	7	40	59	75	90	103
8	38	54	70	84	96	8	43	63	80	96	110
9	40	58	74	89	102	9	46	66	85	102	117
10	42	61	78	93	107	10	48	70	89	107	123
11	44	63	81	98	112	11	50	72	94	112	129
12	46	65	85	102	117	12	52	75	97	117	134
13	47	67	88	105	121	13	54	77	101	121	139
14	49	69	90	109	125	14	56	80	103	125	144
15	51	71	92	113	129	15	58	82	106	130	149
16	52	73	94	115	133	16	60	84	108	133	153
17	54	75	96	118	137	17	62	86	111	135	158
18	55	76	98	120	140	18	63	88	113	137	161
19	56	78	100	122	142	19	65	90	115	140	164
20	58	80	102	124	144	20	67	92	117	142	166
22	61	83	106	128	148	22	70	96	121	147	171
24	63	86	109	131	152	24	73	99	126	151	175
26	66	90	113	135	156	26	75	103	130	155	179
28	68	93	116	139	159	28	78	107	134	159	183
30	70	96	119	142	163	30	81	110	137	163	187
35	76	103	128	151	171	35	87	118	147	173	197
40	81	109	135	159	179	40	93	126	155	182	206
Weight Male / Female in lb.	2 / 1	7 / 3½	13 / 6½	20 / 10	UP / UP	Weight Male / Female in lb.	8 / 4	42 / 21	UP / UP	—	—

(T) TRUNK—Measured at Shoulder / (F, H) FINGER-HAND—Measured at Finger Tip

DISTANCE MOVED (in.)	BASIC	1	2	3	4	DISTANCE MOVED (in.)	BASIC	1	2	3	4
1	26	38	49	58	67	1	16	23	29	35	40
2	29	42	53	64	73	2	17	25	32	38	44
3	32	47	60	72	82	3	19	28	36	43	49
4	38	55	70	84	96	4	23	33	42	50	58
5	43	62	79	95	109	Weight Male / Female in lb.	⅔ / ⅓	2½ / 1¼	4 / 2	UP / UP	
6	47	68	87	105	120	**(FT) FOOT—Measured at Toe**					
7	51	74	95	114	130	1	20	29	37	44	51
8	54	79	101	121	139	2	22	32	40	48	55
9	58	84	107	128	147	3	24	35	45	55	63
10	61	88	113	135	155	4	29	41	53	64	73
11	63	91	118	141	162	Weight Male / Female in lb.	5 / 2½	22 / 11	UP / UP	—	—
12	66	94	123	147	169	**(FS) FOREARM SWIVEL—Measured at Knuckles**					
13	68	97	127	153	175	45°	17	22	28	32	37
14	71	100	130	158	182	90°	23	30	37	43	49
15	73	103	133	163	188	135°	28	36	44	52	58
16	75	105	136	167	193	180°	31	40	49	57	65
17	78	108	139	170	199						
18	80	111	142	173	203						
19	82	113	145	176	206						
20	84	116	148	179	209						
Weight Male / Female in lb.	11 / 5½	58 / 29	UP / UP	—	—	Torque Male / Female lb. in.	3 / 1½	13 / 6½	UP / UP	—	—

Work-Factor SYMBOLS

W—Weight or resistance
S—Directional control (Steer)
P—Care (Precaution)
U—Change direction
D—Definite stop

WALKING TIME (30-in. paces)

TYPE	1	2	OVER 2
General restricted	Analyse from table	260	120 + 80/pace
		300	120 + 100/pace

Add 100 for 120°–180°   Up steps (8 in. Rise—10 in. Flat) 126
Turn at start or finish   Down steps 100

VISUAL INSPECTION

Focus	20
Inspect	30/point
React	20
Head turn	45° 40, 90° 60

1 time unit = 0·006 second
= 0·0001 minute
= 0·00000167 hour

Today such systems as Methods-Time Measurements (M.T.M.) and Work-Factor can be installed by consultants from the respective organisations. These systems rely on manuals which give times for different elements such as arm, leg and finger movements, grasps, eye focus, reaction times, assembly elements and so on. These times are computed from high-speed films of basic operations and are made up to the nearest 6/10,000 min or even 1/10,000 min. Allowance is also made for such factors as weight, resistance to motion, care and related matters.

To set operation times with these systems the engineer analyses the job into individual movements and then determines the times required for these motions from the appropriate tables. The sum of all these times gives the time for the operation before allowances. To this time may be added the allowances as shown earlier.

TABLE II.—GRASP TABLE
(Complex Grasps from random piles)
Copyright The WOFAC Corporation

SIZE (Major dimension or length) (in.)		SOLIDS AND BRACKETS THICKNESS (in.) (over 3/64) 0·0469 — Blind Simo	THIN FLAT OBJECTS — THICKNESS (Less than 1/64) 0·0156 — Blind Simo Visual Simo	THIN FLAT OBJECTS — THICKNESS (1/64–3/64) 0·0156–0·0469 — Blind Simo Visual Simo	CYLINDERS AND REGULAR CROSS-SECTIONED SOLIDS — DIAMETER (in.) [0–0·0625 (1/16) / 0·0626–0·125 (1/8) / 0·1251–0·1875 (3/16) / 0·1876–0·5000 (1/2) Blind Simo Visual Simo / 0·5001 and up (Over 1/2) Blind Simo Visual Simo]	Add for entangled nested or slippery objects* — Simo
0·0000–0·0625	1/16 and less	120 172	B B — —	108 154 B B	131 189 | B B | 85 120 | S S | S S | S S | S S	17 26
0·0626–0·1250	Over 1/16–1/8	79 111	B B — —	108 154 B B	85 120 | B B | 85 120 | S S | S S | S S | S S	12 18
0·1251–0·1875	Over 1/8–3/16	64 88	B B 102 145	B B 74 103	B B | 79 111 | 74 103 | S S | S S | S S | S S	12 18
0·1876–0·2500	Over 3/16–1/4	48 64	B B 72 100	B B 56 76	B B | 79 111 | 69 94 | 64 88 | S S | S S | S S	12 18'
0·2501–0·5000	Over 1/4–1/2	40 52	B B 64 88	B B 48 64	62 85 | 56 76 | 56 76 | 44 58 | B B | S S | S S	B 12
0·5001–1·0000	Over 1/2–1	40 52	32 40 64 88	60 82 48 64	44 58 | 62 85 | 56 76 | 48 64 | 44 58 | 40 52 | 32 40	B 12
1·0001–4·0000	Over 1–4	37 48	20 22 53 72	36 46 45 60	28 34 | 56 76 | 48 64 | 40 52 | 40 52 | 36 46 | 37 48 | 20 22	B 12
4·0001 and up	Over 4	46 61	20 22 70 97	44 58 62 85	36 46 | 56 76 | 48 64 | 40 52 | 40 52 | 36 46 | 37 48 | 20 22	B 14

B = Use Blind column, since visual grasp offers no advantage. S = Use Solid Table.

* Add the indicated allowances when objects: (a) are entangled (not requiring two hands to separate); (b) are nested together because of shape or film; (c) are slippery (as from oil or polished surface). When objects both entangle and are slippery, or both nest and are slippery, use double the value in the Table.

Note: Special grasp conditions should be analysed in detail.

Apart from the obvious, one big advantage in using this system is that the engineer *must* analyse the job in detail and this automatically helps him to discover any bad methods which may exist in the activity. It would appear that some basic times can be set without the engineer even seeing the operator and, in fact, this is sometimes done, but psychologically this is bad; the operator usually likes to see what is going on!

One reliable system widely used in Britain, America and many other countries is the *Detailed Work-Factor System* and the charts containing the standards or Work-Factor Time Units are shown in Tables I, II and III. The WOFAC Corporation (who kindly permitted reproduction of these copyright Tables) also publish other Work-Factor Systems, which are far less detailed, but which lose comparatively very little in accuracy.

Use of Work-Factor Tables.—To illustrate the use of the Tables a very simple example of picking up a screwdriver weighing less than 1 lb and situated 10 in. from the operator's hand is analysed below.

Table III.—Assembly Tables

(Average no. of Alignments. A.I.S. Motions)

Copyright The WOFAC Corporation

TARGET DIAMETER (in.)	CLOSED TARGETS — Ratio of plug dia ÷ Target dia. To 0·224	0·225–0·289	0·290–0·414	0·415–0·899	0·900–0·934	0·935–1·000	OPEN TARGETS — Ratio of plug dia. ÷ Target dia. To 0·224	0·225–0·289	0·290–0·414	0·415–0·899	0·900–0·934	0·935–1·000
0·875 and up	(D*) 18	(D*) 18	(D*) 18	(¼) 25	(¼†) 51	(¼‡) 59	(D*) 18	(D*) 18	(D*) 18	(D*) 18	(¼†) 51	(¼‡) 59
0·825–0·874	(D*) 18	(D*) 18	(SD*) 18	(¼) 25	(¼†) 51	(¼‡) 59	(D*) 18	(D*) 18	(D*) 18	(SD*) 18	(¼†) 51	(¼‡) 59
0·375–0·624	(SD*) 18	(SD*) 18	(¼) 25	(½) 31	(½†) 57	(½‡) 65	(SD*) 18	(SD*) 18	(SD*) 18	(½) 31	(½†) 57	(½‡) 65
0·225–0·374	(½) 31	(1) 44	(1) 44	(1½) 57	(1½†) 83	(1½‡) 91	(¼) 25	(½) 31	(½) 31	(¾) 38	(¾†) 64	(¾‡) 72
0·175–0·224	(1) 44	(1) 44	(1) 44	(1½) 57	(1½†) 83	(1½‡) 91	(½) 31	(½) 31	(½) 31	(¾) 38	(¾†) 64	(¾‡) 72
0·125–0·174	(1) 44	(1¼) 51	(1½) 57	(1½) 57	(1½†) 83	(1½‡) 91	(¾) 38	(1) 44	(1) 44	(1) 44	(1†) 70	(1‡) 78
0·075–0·124	(2½) 83	(2½) 83	(2½) 83	(2½) 83	(2½†) 109	(2½‡) 117	(1¼) 51	(1¼) 51	(1¼) 51	(1¼) 51	(1¼†) 77	(1¼‡) 85
0·025–0·074	(3) 96	(3) 95	(3) 96	(3) 96	(3†) 122	(3‡) 130	(1½) 57	(1½) 57	(1½) 57	(1½) 57	(1½†) 83	(1½‡) 91

* Letters indicate Work Factors in move preceding Assembly.

† Requires A(X)S Upright for all ratios of 0·900 and greater (Table value includes AIS Upright).

‡ Requires A(Y)S Upright and A(Z)P Insert for all ratios of 0·935 and greater (Table value includes AIS Upright and AIP Insert).

DISTANCE BETWEEN TARGETS

Distance between targets (in.)	% Addition to Alignments	Method of alignment
0–0·99	Neg	Simo
1–1·99	10	Simo
2–2·99	30	Simo
3–4·99	50	Simo
5–6·99	70	Simo
7–14·99	Align 1st, Insert 1st, Align 2nd (1), Insert 2nd	
15 and up	Align 1st, Insert 1st, Focus and Inspect, Align 2nd (1), Insert 2nd	

(1) If connected, treat 2nd Assembly as open target with no upright

BLIND TARGETS

Distance from target to visible area (in.)	% Addition to alignments — Permanent (Blind at all times)	Temporary (Blind during assembly)
0·0–0·49	20	0
0·5–0·99	30	10
1·0–1·99	40	20
2·0–2·99	70	30
3·0–4·99	130	50
5·0–6·99	250	70
7·0–10·00	380	120

GRIPPING DISTANCE

Distance from gripping point of alignment point (in.)	% Addition to alignments	Length of upright motion (in.)
0–1·99	Neg.	1
2–2·99	10	1
3–4·99	20	2
5–6·99	30	2
7–9·99	40	3
10–14·99	60	5
15–19·99	80	6
20 and up	100	7 and up

GENERAL RULES FOR ASSEMBLY

1. When required add W and P Work Factors to all Assembly Motions according to rules for Transports.
2. Reduce number of Alignments by 50% when hand is rigidly supported.
3. Where Gripping Distance, Two Targets and Blind Targets are involved, add each percentage to Original Alignment. Don't pyramid percentages.
4. Alignments for Surface Assembly are taken from 0·224 column and are AISD Motions.
5. Index is FIS, AIS or FS45°S

Example

This operation is split into three motions, *i.e.* a Reach, a Grasp and a Transport (or "Move" as it is called).

1. Reach to grasp screwdriver: 10 in.

The analysis is A10D. In this analysis the "A" indicates that it is an Arm Motion. The "D" shows a "Definite Stop" because the hand must stop over a definite location; *i.e.* above the screwdriver handle. The addition of this Definite Stop adds 1 Work-Factor Time Unit to the Basic Arm Motion. Thus from the Table in the section headed "Arm," an Arm Motion of 10 in. in the column under "Work-Factors—1" earns a time of 61 W.-F. Time Units.

2. Grasp screwdriver.

The analysis is ½F1. To grasp the screwdriver the fingers (F) move 1 in. (approx) together to pinch the handle. A 1-in. Finger Motion is allowed 16 W.-F. Time Units. As the fingers start the pinching motion before the hand actually stops moving during the "Reach," only half of this time is actually allowed—hence ½F1 which carries a time of ½ × 16 = 8 W.-F. Time Units.

3. Move screwdriver 10 in. to screw head.

Analysis A10SD. This time the arm (A) moves the screwdriver 10 in., comes to a Definite Stop (D) but, as the screw slot is so small, the arm also Steers (S) the blade to the slot. The "D" and the "S" add 2 Work-Factor Time Units, so under the "arm" tables in the column for "Work Factor —2" it can be seen that 78 W.-F. Time Units are allowed.

Thus the final analysis is:

Description	Analysis	Work-Factor Time Units
1. Reach to grasp screwdriver	A10D	61
2. Grasp screwdriver	½F1	8
3. Move screwdriver to screw head	A10SD	78
Total		147

Thus as each W.-F. Time Unit is worth 0·0001 min, the time to pick up the screwdriver is 0·0147 min or 0·882 sec.

SYNTHETICS

The setting of times by synthetics is similar to P.M.T.S., but here the times are those obtained from the firm's own past studies. The study engineer, after making studies, will file certain elements which may be common to other jobs so that he may use these times when studying the other jobs. These times are not set on elements as basic as those detailed under P.M.T.S., but are for whole parts of cycles of perhaps 3–4 sec duration.

ANALYTICAL ESTIMATING

This technique is used mainly for longer-cycle jobs and for jobs containing variable elements. Examples of these are office routines, stores duties and maintenance where the jobs are seldom repeated exactly. A typist will probably never type the same letter twice, or a fitter will remove one nut easily in 1 min, but the next may be rusted in and take 20 min. One way of measuring the typist's output would be to determine the time taken to type a character, add up the number of characters in the memorandum or letter, allow for inserting the paper and its removal, and allow for relaxation. This method would obviously be more trouble and take more time than it is worth. It is better, therefore, to set a standard time for an average letter or page of typing than one for each character. As the jobs are usually long cycles, and so variable in content, there is nothing to be gained by making accurate timings; in fact, a wall clock is the usual instrument.

Examples of time standards

Remove "B" type flange   easy = 2 min
    tight = 4 min
    rusty = 17 min

This type of standard could be used by a maintenance fitter.

ACTIVITY SAMPLING

As the name suggests, this is statistical sampling applied to jobs or activities. It may not be possible for the engineer to make a week's full-time study of an operation to obtain information such as how often the machine is shut down for various reasons. In any case, on a project such as this there is no point when, by observing the machine at random intervals, an accuracy of, say, $\pm 2\%$ can be obtained by spending only $\frac{1}{20}$ of the time of a full study at the machine.

A pilot study is first made on the operation and from this, and the use of a formula, the number of observations or "samples" can be determined. The observer then compiles a table of random times (by drawing out of a hat or from random number tables) at which visits to the process must be made and observations taken.

Armed with these times and a suitable chart the observer can carry on with his normal duties, stopping only to visit the process under examination at the chosen random times. A trained observer is not always necessary, especially on projects requiring just two observations: "working" and "idle." This type can be carried out by a supervisor or a work study trainee.

METHOD STUDY

The above techniques have all been concerned with work measurement. The other main division of work study is method study. This is the methodical analysis, criticism and revision of existing or new methods and of the flow of materials in relation to men, machines and processes.

Method studies are carried out in a planned, methodical manner and for convenience can be divided into five parts or steps:

Step 1.—The first step is to select the job to be studied and a study can materialise in many ways. For example, the engineer may be asked to carry out a time study and may wish to conduct a method study first in order to establish a correct working pattern. Projects may also result from complaints of high costs or from the findings of cost-reduction committees.

Step 2.—When the task has been defined it is broken down and the facts recorded in a suitable form. Many recording aids have been developed to suit particular conditions and requirements and some of these are:

(*a*) Flow-process charts for recording activities of men, materials or processes. An example of this chart was given in Fig. 13. This chart also shows the symbols which are used to indicate the various functions.

(*b*) Two-handed process and "simo" charts for movements of the operator's body members; the latter chart also carrying a time scale.

(c) Multiple activity chart used to log the simultaneous activities of men and machines (also man–machine charts).

(d) String diagrams where string is used to indicate the paths taken by men and materials on a plan or layout.

(e) Scale models to assist in planning layouts. The models are usually made to scales of $\frac{1}{4}$ or $\frac{3}{8}$ in. to the foot.

(f) Memo-motion films in which a day's work can be photographed on cine film at a speed of one or two frames per second which when projected at the silent speed (16 frames/sec) appear greatly speeded up. Thus a day's activities in a department can be condensed into half an hour or so.

(g) Cyclegraphs, pioneered by Gilbreth, add to the range of photographic aids. Small electric bulbs are attached to the fingers of the operator and a photographic plate is exposed to the scene for a period of one cycle. The spots of light trace out the movement of the hands on the exposed plate. A variation of this is the chronocyclegraph, a technique which uses interrupted light in the form of regular flashes so that speed can also be estimated from the pear-shaped spots of light on the photograph.

Step 3.—When the job has been correctly recorded the elements are examined critically to see whether they can be eliminated, combined with other elements, or simplified by the use of aids or jigs.

Step 4.—The new method is developed. This revised method may be the result of an hour's effort on the part of the methods engineer and costs nothing apart from his labour, or it may involve the purchase of new plant which may cost thousands of pounds. It is essential that the savings are calculated in order that the outlay involved may be restricted to a comparatively reasonable amount. On long-term or long-run production it is usual to expect the initial costs to be recovered in about two years.

Step 5.— The revised method is installed, where possible, with the full co-operation of supervisor and operator. The operator is trained in the new method and a follow-up of periodic visits is made to iron out any teething troubles.

The aim of method study is to minimise the effort and time in order to achieve higher productivity for the same effort and in the same time, and thus provides a very important service to management.

ERGONOMICS

Method study seeks to arrive at the best possible arrangement of the workplace in order to obtain economy of movement. The technique has often been criticised for concentrating on this physical economy of movement and for its inability to allow adequately for such factors as fatigue, muscular effort, eyestrain and mental effort. The same is true of work measurement, although here some effort is made to allow for fatigue and, especially in P.M.T.S., for mental effort. A man weighing 220 lb expends more energy than a man of 150 lb engaged on the same job of, say, carrying crates up an incline. However, both are given the same fatigue allowance as, according to usual work measurement practice, the allowance is set with regard to the type of job, and not the type of person doing the job. Ergonomics combines the knowledge obtained from the study of anatomy, physiology, psychology and anthropometry to reduce the stresses on the worker in his work area. It has been defined as "fitting the job to the worker." The word itself is derived from the Greek *ergon* (work) and *nomos* (law).

In order to design machines and equipment so as to reduce physical and mental strain it is necessary to study the human machine. Thus the ergonomics team can consist of engineers, designers, anatomists, physiologists and psychologists. In relatively small firms the ergonomics function can be performed by the work study team.

The areas covered by ergonomics can be defined as follows:

The workplace.—These areas include layout of equipment, displays of information and controls, and design of displays and controls.

General environment.—Under this heading come the effects of heat, lighting, noise, vibration and other conditions affecting the health and well-being of the individual.

Other factors.—These may include fatigue, vigilance and inspection. The problems of older workers and disabled workers also qualify for consideration by the ergonomist.

Where a worker operates or uses a machine, instrument or tool it is essential that man and machine blend into a single working unit. The placing and design of controls and the positioning of information displays, together with the mental and physical stresses to which he may be exposed, will all affect the operator's accuracy, concentration, efficiency and reliability. The obvious place to start is at the equipment design stage. Unfortunately, most designers in producing variations of existing machines still follow the traditional lines of those machines, building the same back-aching, neck-stiffening, eye-straining characteristics into the new machine. The classic example often quoted for its bad design is the centre-lathe. With the new machine, prospective purchasers frequently go for aesthetic value: symmetrical layout and equipment based on ergonomic considerations will often not look as pretty. For example, that beautifully shiny chrome bezel which blinds the operator, unless he crouches out of range of its reflection, will not appear on the ergonomic design.

The subject of ergonomics cannot be adequately covered in a book dealing with general subjects, but it is possible to touch on some of the most important considerations. A more detailed study may be made from the works listed in the bibliography.

THE WORKPLACE

The chair in any type of sedentary work is the item which can be the most obvious source of discomfort as it supports the whole body. Even so, quite often it is the first chair which comes to hand which finds itself at the bench or the typist's table. The writer once collected twenty different chairs (including two old arm-chairs) from a department engaged on identical assembly work. The chair should be adjustable to provide opportunity for adoption of different postures. The seat height should be adjustable (16–20 in. above ground or foot-rest level). It should also be provided with an adjustable back-rest. A foot-rest should be provided where chairs are higher than the recommended height or where the feet would be rested on a bar of the strengthening bracket of a bench.

When the arm is not supported and is involved in such activities as, say, assembly work, a flat arm-rest will take the weight off the arm and reduce "static work" and fatigue caused by continual contraction of the muscle and restriction of the blood supply to the muscle.

When choosing a dial for a particular application the most appropriate one for the job should be used. Where a quantitative reading is important the *counter* should be used and for check readings or assessments the moving pointer dial is superior.

Controls such as levers, pedals, handwheels, knobs and buttons should be positioned close to the body member concerned. Where accuracy or close control is required the hands are used, but the feet can exert more force. Foot pedals should be capable of returning under their own springs.

The sense of touch can be used to identify knobs if each knob has a different shape and the shapes can be identified with a specific function.

There must be a logical connection between the movement of the control and the particular operation (compatibility). Thus switches should be moved up for on, or increase, and down for off or decrease, right for increase and vice versa. For rotary controls clockwise rotation should produce an increase.

ENVIRONMENT

In lighting, daylight, considered important for morale, should be supplemented by artificial lighting where necessary. Care should be taken to avoid glare from chromium plating, polished surfaces of tables, machines and even books, and from glass in front of gauges and dials. Excessive contrast should be avoided. This can occur when gauges or charts are placed in front of brightly lit windows.

When dealing with problems of noise it is necessary to take into account the frequency as well as the intensity. High-pitched sounds are more disturbing than low-frequency hums. The main danger is permanent damage to the ear which may result from prolonged exposure.

OTHER FACTORS

Other factors considered under the heading of ergonomics are problems associated with shift work and with age.

People accumulate knowledge and experience upon which they can call when faced with the everyday problems of working life. Consequently, older workers are often given jobs carrying higher responsibility and requiring decisions based on accurately made measurements or readings, which while they satisfy the desire of the older workers to maintain their status, may be carried out more efficiently by younger people whose lack of experience may be outweighed by such factors as better eyesight and hearing, and faster reaction time. Status is often in conflict with suitability.

OPERATIONAL RESEARCH

A more recent service to management is that which operational research provides. The work study engineer aims to achieve maximum production in the minimum time, with minimum effort and by the use of improvements, whereas the operational research worker is seeking the *optimum* state in all spheres.

Operational research is very difficult to define formally. A manager or executive is continually being called upon to make decisions. Usually there are a number of alternatives and, by using O.R. techniques, data can be processed and the result used to aid the making of these decisions.

The origins of O.R. are vague, but probably the first organised group to be formed was the team doing research into operations of war just prior to the Second World War, hence the name. After the war many firms started their own groups, using the various techniques of O.R. Some of these techniques and areas of application are: linear programming, queueing, stock control, network analysis, replacement theory. Most of the techniques are based on probability theory, and mathematics and statistical method are very much in evidence.

LINEAR PROGRAMMING

This technique is used to solve such problems as allocation, transportation and work loading of machines. Linear inequalities are formed from the variables which are present in the problem. These inequalities can be analysed, and from the solutions obtained deductions can be made. The programmer may be faced with hundreds of linear inequalities and restrictions, whose solution requires the use of a computer.

QUEUEING THEORY

Queueing theory is applied wherever congestion occurs. Examples appear in ports, telephone switchboards, supermarkets and toll houses.

"Customers" appear at random intervals usually, but sometimes also to a pattern giving peak and slack periods. In the case of a supermarket several alternatives must be faced. For example, is it better to cater for the rush hours of lunchtime and evening and install eight cash positions, or allow only for the slack times and position just two registers? The first alternative means idle staff and equipment, whereas the second may result in loss of custom due to the long queues which would inevitably form during peak periods. O.R.'s task in such problems is to find the optimum amount of equipment, plant and personnel required and this will obviously be a compromise.

STOCK CONTROL

The role of the operational research department in stock control is to balance (a) the costs of keeping high buffer stocks, against (b) reduced costs of low stocks, but with the added risk of running out of material.

NETWORK ANALYSIS OR CRITICAL PATH SCHEDULING

Critical path scheduling is used for planning complex undertakings which may involve several thousand activities. Branches of industry which use critical path techniques are civil engineering, on road building, bridge and tunnel construction, the shipbuilding industry and the manufacturing industry engaged on large projects.

When the project to be planned is a simple one in which the various activities follow each other consecutively, the total time to complete the project is obtained simply by adding the separate activity times. Difficulties arise when several activities are to be carried out simultaneously and the times to complete these activities are all different. The planning now becomes more complex. It is advisable in this case to resort to graphical methods and critical path scheduling is a convenient one to use.

Basically, a network is constructed from an activity list and the network is analysed to determine the *longest* path through the network (in terms of time). This is the critical path as all the activities which lie on this path are critical in that they must be completed within the stated time. Other paths are made up of activities which have more time allowed than is actually required. This is amplified below.

When the project is such that the activities forming the project number a few hundred, the analysis may be carried out by hand, but when several thousand activities are involved a computer is essential. In carrying out a project the procedure described below is typical. To illustrate the description the design and construction of a "one off" desk calculator has been used (Fig. 23).

The first step is to break down the project into its components, known as activities. A list of activities is compiled from information obtained from the personnel engaged on the project and care must be taken to ensure that no activities are omitted from the list. From this list the network is constructed, each activity being represented by an arrow. The length of the arrow is *not* proportional to the time taken by the activity. The arrows join *events* (indicated by circles on the diagram) and all activities start at a *preceding event* and finish at a *succeeding event*. No activity can be started until the preceding activity has been completed (*e.g.* don't put on the roof until the supports have been built!). The events are numbered in order to code the data for the computer. The personnel engaged on the project are then invited to submit time estimates for each activity and these are entered on the network. The activities are then coded by using the numbers of the preceding and succeeding events. For example, in the case illustrated,

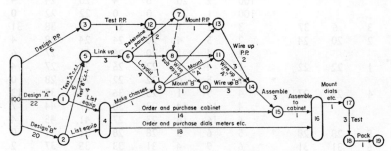

FIG. 23.—*A critical path network*

"Design A" would be coded (100 1) and "Test A" would be (1 5). The next step in the procedure is to punch the information on to cards or on to tape and to verify the key punching. The computer is programmed for critical path analysis and the cards or tape fed into the computer. The result is obtained in a matter of seconds or minutes (depending on the number of activities) and the cards or tape placed into the printout machine. The printout (Fig. 24) gives the full analysis including earliest and latest starting and finishing times for each activity, the various *floats* (which can be regarded as time in hand), and also marks the activities forming the critical path. In the example the descriptions have been abbreviated and a few have been omitted. In practice, the full details would be required.

From the network and the times obtained a bar chart can be constructed to a time scale which can be used as a schedule of work.

By using the various critical path techniques firms are able to ensure that the materials and other supplies are ordered at the correct times and, by using the appropriate technique, can allocate their resources (manpower and machinery) and allocate their money correctly and efficiently.

INSPECTION

The growth of mass production methods and the introduction of incentives have brought with them attitudes of more detached interest between the operator and the product. Familiarity does breed contempt: as, for example, making a couple of hundred chair legs each day

DESK CALCULATOR F22

CRITICAL PATH ANALYSIS

E.T.   Earliest time S.E.   Succeeding event
L.T.   Latest time *   Critical path
P.E.   Preceding event

Event	E.T.	L.T.		Activity duration		Start		Finish		Total
				P.E.	S.E.	E.T.	L.T.	E.T.	L.T.	Float
100	0	0		100	3	6	0	31	6	37	31
				100	2	20	0	4	20	24	4
			*	100	1	22	0	0	22	22	0
3	6	37		3	12	1	6	37	7	38	31
2	20	24		2	5	4	20	24	24	28	4
				2	4	1	20	26	21	27	6
1	22	22		1	4	1	22	26	23	27	4
			*	1	5	6	22	22	28	28	0
4	23	27		4	9	1	23	36	24	37	13
				4	15	14	23	30	37	44	7
				4	16	18	23	27	41	45	4
5	28	28	*	5	6	3	28	28	31	31	0
6	31	31		6	9	4	31	33	35	37	2
			*	6	8	3	31	31	34	34	0
				6	7	2	31	32	33	34	1
9	35	37		9	10	1	35	37	36	38	2
				9	12	0	35	38	35	38	3
				9	11	1	35	37	36	38	2
7	33	34		7	8	0	33	34	33	34	1
8	34	34	*	8	10	4	34	34	38	38	0
				8	11	3	34	35	37	38	1
10	38	38	*	10	14	3	38	38	41	41	0
12	35	38		12	13	1	35	38	36	39	3
13	36	39		13	14	2	36	39	38	41	3
11	37	38		11	14	3	37	38	40	41	1
14	41	41	*	14	15	3	41	41	44	44	0
15	44	44	*	15	16	1	44	44	45	46	0
16	45	45	*	16	17	1	45	45	46	46	0
17	46	46	*	17	18	3	46	46	49	49	0
18	49	49	*	18	19	1	49	49	50	50	0
19	50	50	*								

FIG. 24.—*Typical printout of a project from data in Fig. 23*
The activities between events marked with an asterisk have no "float time," and thus form the critical path.

instead of fashioning and assembling an individual piece of furniture by hand. The old craftsman would treat each piece as his own individual creation, checking and measuring as he went, and it was not so important that legs, seats and backs were interchangeable. With mass production, where parts are taken at random, it is essential that any two parts will mate reasonably accurately. Again, if an operator is minding three or four machines it is inevitable that rejects will be caused (if only through variations inherent in the operation) and these will not be seen. In view of this, it is obvious that some form of inspection is necessary.

Nowadays inspection is commonplace, but even today when the question of more thorough inspection is raised there is an outcry. There is still confusion between *more* inspection and *more thorough* inspection. The latter can be achieved by the use of statistical method without additional cost or time. This control of quality by statistical method is known as statistical quality control.

Incentives will tend to reduce quality when the emphasis is on quantity of output. Speed does not in itself cause bad quality, but *hurry* in a less experienced operator who is trying to surpass his existing limit can do so. Some years ago, inspectors known as penalisers would pick out operators' rejects and penalise them through their wage packets.

Modern managements are moving away from the system of sitting inspectors on the end of the line to catch the rejects before they go out to the customer, to the techniques of spotting and rectifying the causes at source. By these methods not only are the defects noticed well before two or three hours' worth of rejects have been produced, but also all the work subsequently performed on these rejects is saved. As in police work, prevention is better than detection.

STATISTICAL QUALITY CONTROL

Statistical quality control (S.Q.C.) is quite an important management tool. The operative word is "tool" as S.Q.C. will not control quality by just being there. Like any tool it must be *used*, and like any tool, results are only as good as the person using the tool. A manager cannot sit back and let S.Q.C. magically cure or prevent trouble as the sorcerer's apprentice used the broom to fetch his water.

There are basically two areas of quality control:

1. Inspection of batches of work, such as raw materials, finished goods, etc., by taking samples of the work: this is known as "acceptance sampling."

2. Inspection of parts from a running process as soon as they are produced, in order to detect any variations in that process which may be "out of control": this is usually called "process control."

Secondly there are two ways of checking parts:

1. By measurements, such as diameters, lengths, resistance, angles, in fact anything which can be read on a dial or gauge. This is checking by variables.

2. By attributing qualities to the parts or processes such as "discoloured," "damaged," "good" and "reject." This is checking by attributes.

Thus a micrometer will tell the inspector that the diameter is 0·66 in. (checking by variables) while a "go–no-go" gauge will tell him "good part" or "reject" (attributes).

SAMPLING

By inspecting every item in a batch or in a process (100% inspection as it is called) it is generally held that an inspector can find all the rejects. However, this is not always the case. Even the most conscientious inspector becomes fatigued or bored, especially when faced with a few thousand measurements to carry out on parts all identical in appearance. Managements who pretend that they have 100% inspection are hiding from the fact that it is well known for inspectors to sample during their "100% inspection" by testing a number of items and, if few rejects are found, passing the remainder through untested. It is not uncommon for unscrupulous inspectors when engaged on sampling to sample the sample, especially when the sample looks good!

On destructive tests, it is obvious that sampling must be used. By taking properly defined samples a picture of the whole can be obtained and the "goodness" of the whole batch estimated nearly as accurately as with 100% inspection.

The size of the sample can be determined from pre-calculated tables and depends on the degree of certainty required and not on the size of the population or batch size. Obviously, larger batches would require larger samples due to the consequences of passing a large bad batch or failing a large good batch. It appears, then, that there exists the chance of making a wrong decision. In fact, sampling depends on statistical probability and, because of this, samples must be taken scientifically and completely at random with precautions against bias.

Acceptance sampling

When a firm samples batches of raw material (the firm being the customer) or is supplying finished articles to a customer (the firm in this case being the supplier) there must be in both cases an agreement between supplier and customer on the acceptable quality level (A.Q.L.). The A.Q.L. is the highest percentage of rejects that is acceptable, such that this percentage is only exceeded in one batch in twenty. The customer obviously would like no rejects, but he knows that this is economically not possible. On the other hand, the supplier hopes for a high reject acceptance.

Sampling plans are introduced which lay down a sample size and maximum number of rejects which can be accepted in a sample. If the rejects in the sample exceed the acceptance number the batch is rejected.

Examples

(a) If the customer can accept up to 1% rejects in the majority of batches a sample size of 200 may have up to 4 rejects in it.

(b) If, however, he can tolerate 3% then on a 200 sample 10 rejects may be accepted.

Process control

As previously stated, it is not enough to stop bad batches and weed out the rejects. The cause of the rejects must be spotted quickly and the trouble put right.

If a machine is subject to a routine quality control check of, say, a sample of ten consecutive parts per hour, the required dimensions will be measured and plotted on a chart. This chart can show individual items plotted as points against a scale of measurements on the y axis, or alternatively the average and range of the readings may be plotted. Control lines are drawn on the chart and as long as the points wander about inside these limits the process is under control, the wanderings being due to variations inherent in the process. Points falling outside these limits indicate that something has definitely altered in the process and that rejects will occur in appreciable quantities.

Charts may be designed for attributes also. The statistical treatment of the subject and a typical chart are given in Chapter XXIII.

AREAS OF INSPECTION

The types of controls at the disposal of management have been discussed and now the application of these controls can be outlined.

Raw material inspection (R.M.I.)

This is a form of acceptance sampling carried out on material reaching the firm from outside suppliers. The material can be in the form of raw material such as sheet-metal, paint, glass and timber, or components such as castings, brackets, switches, packing material, nuts, bolts, etc. The material can be checked for dimensions, chemical composition, hardness, colour, electrical properties, damage, appearance and any other special tests laid down. The acceptance quality level should be agreed between the supplier and the firm and any batches failing this should be returned, or, by prior agreement, 100% inspected and the rejects returned. When articles are in short supply the production management usually insists on the latter course and even, on occasions, over-rule the inspection and use the batch, rejects and all.

Process control

Process control has already been discussed above, and can be installed anywhere in the factory where there is a need. The inspection can be carried out by "patrol inspectors" who are engaged to patrol the section regularly and take their samples from the work turned out by the operators or machines in their section. Their findings can result in bad work being returned to the operator for re-inspection and correction by the operator, or for the correction of the machine when this is at fault.

Alternatively, the operator can carry out his own process control by inspecting the sample and plotting the results on his own chart. Provided that the incentive scheme does not encourage dishonest practice this scheme can work quite successfully. Quite often the chargehand who is looking after the section acts as patrol inspector, combining this function with supervision.

Laboratory tests

Obviously there are some scientific tests which are beyond the means and skill of inspectors on the production floor. These tests must be made in laboratories specially equipped for them to be carried out. Examples of these are analyses in food production plants, in paint or chemical works; tests on electrical equipment, such as television and radio receivers; and tests on parameters of radio valves, transistors and television tubes.

Life tests and running tests

Besides the checks necessary to ensure that equipment leaves the factory in working order it is also important for management to know how long the product will last in service outside the factory. Samples of the products are therefore taken at intervals and given "running" or "life" tests. Sometimes these are accelerated in order to obtain the information in a shorter time than would normally be possible. This acceleration can take the form of an over-run condition which, in the case of electric lamps for example, would be to run them at a higher voltage than normal.

Motor cars can be given severe road tests on which they cover thousands of miles in a few weeks. Switches can be operated every few seconds in order to test their durability during several thousand operations. Fluorescent and tungsten lamps can be run for several weeks with occasional switching on and off as a life test. Thus products can be given the same usage in a relatively short time as they would normally receive during several years of normal duty.

Outgoing quality inspection

This is the final inspection before the product leaves the factory. It is another instance of the use of acceptance sampling, this time on the customer's behalf. The inspection is usually carried out by a central inspection department which is not responsible to the production manager. The outgoing batches are sampled and either accepted for transit to the commercial stores or rejected for re-processing by the production department. In the case of certain Government contracts the inspector is answerable to the Government inspector and sometimes re-processing is not allowed, in which case the rejected batches are scrapped or used as the commercial equivalent if this is permitted.

INSPECTORS

Inspection is not a necessary evil to which position failures are relegated or faithful hands are "pensioned off" before retirement. The function is a very important one requiring a methodical, intelligent and conscientious individual. As previously mentioned, it is the way in which the results of inspection are interpreted which determine the value of the inspection. The inspector must be capable of maintaining a constant vigilance and should therefore be a younger person rather than an older, "more experienced" man. Any "payment-by-results" scheme introduced to inspection must be well designed in order to avoid lax inspection or "sampling of samples." It is usual to impose a top limit on the earnings and this limit is set to give the inspector a reasonable day's work without pushing him. However, it is preferable to pay an inspector as a time worker and ensure reasonable working by adequate supervision or non-financial incentive schemes.

EXAMINATION QUESTIONS

1. What are the main stages in a work study application and what are the principal advantages that may be derived from it? Your answer may take the form of a diagram.

2. Write a schedule of executive responsibilities for a production manager in a large concern. Give the background to this schedule by means of a chart showing the organisation relationships of the production manager with other managers of the concern.

3. What are the purposes of standardisation? In what fields of industrial activity can it be applied? What are its advantages:

(a) to the producer,
(b) to the user?

What disadvantages could arise?

4. In an expanding business the works manager is in complete charge of the manufacture of goods for orders received and for their delivery to customers. He is responsible for all services in the factory. The time has come for him to shed some of his duties in order to concentrate on manufacture. What are the duties that can be shed and what new positions in the company would need to be established? In what sequence should relief be provided?

5. What are the advantages to be gained by using *quality control* in the inspection of mass produced parts? How is satisfactory control achieved?

6. What is motion study? Describe its application to any office job which you think would benefit from it.

7. Describe the method adopted by a company, in which you have been employed, for inspection for the quality of their parts and products.

8. Work study can be divided into two main techniques. What are the techniques and what are the objectives of each? Why is it important that work study engineers and cost accountants should co-operate for the purposes of cost reduction?

9. Define:

(a) standardisation;
(b) simplification;
(c) classification.

What advantages would accrue to manufacturers, distributors and consumers respectively through the diminution of excess variety throughout an entire industry?

10. Define the duties and responsibilities of the chief inspector in a large engineering works engaged on jobbing work. Show by means of an organisation chart the relationship of this function with the other main functions of the firm.

11. What are the fundamental requirements of a successful quality control procedure? What benefits would you expect to arise from its use?

12. What is meant by the terms:

(a) work study;
(b) operational research;
(c) predetermined time standards;
(d) work specification?

13. Define operational research and describe its salient features, with an outline of the procedure used. Show the profitable areas for operational research work in three major aspects of a business, chosen from:

(a) production and stock control;
(b) manufacturing processes and operations;
(c) product design and development;
(d) personnel management;
(e) purchasing;
(f) sales, distribution and marketing.

14. Describe the work carried out in a design and drawing office. What effects can the quality of the department's work have on production and selling?

15. Compare the advantages of a centralised inspection department with the advantages of floor inspection. How would you decide which method to use?

16. Set out the stages necessary in order to carry out a methods study. Give a brief description of each stage.

Note: Some questions are of a general nature, so reference should be made to other chapters on production.

CHAPTER X

MARKETING*

THE term "marketing" is quite broad in meaning and includes the policy, techniques and methods necessary for selling and distribution. Without this function, goods and services cannot be sold; in some businesses marketing is more important than production.

THE MARKETING DIRECTOR

In brief terms the responsibilities of the marketing director are as follows:

1. Determination of marketing policy.—Policy would have to be a matter for the board of directors, but the marketing or sales director would be expected to develop plans so that policy could be formulated.

2. Market research.—A business must know the size of market and the share which may be obtained for itself.

3. Sales promotion.—The pricing of products, the channels of distribution and the methods of achieving the marketing policy should receive constant attention.

4. Sales forecasting and budgeting.—There is a very real need to put the expected sales into terms of quantities and values. The marketing director and his managers should play an active part in the compiling of sales forecasts and budgets.

5. Advertising.—This can create demand so that production can be increased, thereby reducing prices. Unfortunately, some advertising has been regarded as wasteful and there may be some justification for this criticism in some cases.

6. Sales statistics.—Some market research is what is known as "desk research." It involves the use of statistics compiled from many sources, both internal and external. From these figures forecasts are made for use on sales promotion projects.

7. Maintainance of an efficient sales force.—There is need for staff of all grades to cover all the functions. In a large organisation, it is usual to have managers for sales, advertising, distribution and subdivisions of each of these. The employment of representatives is the most common and effective method of selling a firm's products.

* The marketing (including selling) aspects of management are dealt with briefly in this chapter. Much of the material elsewhere in the book on general management, personnel, and accounting also applies to the marketing field. For guidance on *detailed* aspects, the reader is advised to study one of the specialist books contained in the bibliography.

PHILOSOPHY OF MARKETING

Throughout any application of the marketing function, irrespective of the type of business, there should be adherence to the following two principles:

1. Recognition that the consumer is all-important (customer orientation)

There is an adage which asserts that "the customer is always right." Unfortunately, this has been very much ignored in recent times because companies have been able to sell even though the customer was treated with indifference and was often regarded as being *wrong*.

This self-complacency overlooks the fact that a company should not be content just to hold its own. Instead, it should strive to obtain a larger share in the existing market. Only by giving recognition to the importance of the consumer is this possible.

In marketing terminology, a business should be *customer oriented*. Some writers, notably Peter Drucker in the U.S.A., have emphasised that marketing is the most important function carried out by a business: it is this which determines whether a business will be profitable or unprofitable.* Admittedly, there must be an acceptable product, but it is up to the marketing director and his staff to determine what the consumer desires, and then to co-operate with production to ensure that it is produced.

Once a product is made available consumers must be *induced* to buy; there should then be *satisfaction* in the product; finally, consumers should be so satisfied that they buy again and again and *recommend* the product to their friends, relatives and colleagues. This is the truly *customer oriented* business.

2. Production of a sales volume which will give the planned profit

This means producing goods and services at a level which will allow costs to be minimised and yet permits a steady growth without excessive fluctuation. There should be consideration of employees as well as profits: nothing is more unsettling and damaging to a company than intermittent redundancy of workers or short-time working.

Increased sales can bring about substantial reductions in production and selling costs. However, increased production facilities should be obtained only if the demand is likely to be permanent. Any temporary increase can be met by overtime or shift working, or even by subcontracting. Adherence to well-conceived plans, backed by budgetary control, are an essential part of planning for profit.

The marketing function is thus seen as an essential part of business management. It embraces all aspects of selling and distribution. By giving due recognition to the customer there is a definite philosophy

---

* See, for example, *The Practice of Management*, by Peter Drucker, published by Wm. Heinemann Ltd, London.

which, properly communicated, can permeate the whole business organisation and can ensure the continued prosperity of a business.

DETERMINATION OF MARKETING POLICY

Determination of policy involves the *appraisal* of all factors which affect marketing, and then deciding on the broad principles which the company is to follow. Some of the most important matters which would be considered are as follows:

1. Degree of competition from rival companies.
2. Quality of products.
3. Prices being charged.
4. Size of market.
5. Need for new products.
6. Need for increased volume of existing products.
7. Adequacy of sales force.
8. Adequacy of salesroom, warehouse and transport facilities.
9. Satisfaction among salesmen, sales managers and other staff as regards working conditions, incentive payments and salaries.
10. Advertising campaigns.
11. After-sales service.
12. Sales quotas.
13. Training of salesmen.
14. Sales outlets and methods of distribution.
15. Effective sales organisation.

As far as possible these should be compared with the facilities or services offered by competitors. The aim should be to give services at least equal to those given by rivals and, in some aspects, to better them.

When determining policy the matters considered below should be given special consideration.

SELLING PRICE

Reference to the chapters on economics will show that price is determined by supply and demand. The latter is affected by the attitude of consumers to the products.

On the supply side it is necessary to consider costs. How a price can be determined is shown in Chapter XX which deals with costing systems. Here it is important to notice that prices should cover costs and allow for a profit to be earned. Sometimes a price is determined by larger competitors so that the main problem becomes one of keeping costs down to a reasonable level.

Price discrimination may be practised—different prices for different types of customers—and, if so, the formula to be adopted should be clearly defined.

VOLUME TO BE SOLD

Market research should provide the answer as to how much can be sold. A break-even chart can then be compiled to see what volume is required in order to earn a profit.

PRICE MAINTENANCE

The price to be paid by a customer may be determined by a business, but it is left to the channel of distribution to charge that recommended price. This occurs when goods are sold through retailers: the manufacturer recommends a retail price and expects the retailer to comply.

In recent years there has been a move away from price maintenance, but the long-run effects of this are not altogether clear. In the short run there has been a tendency for prices to be reduced. The growth of supermarkets has tended to increase the amount of price cutting which takes place.

CHANNELS OF DISTRIBUTION

An important policy decision is to determine the appropriate channels of distribution. Possibilities are as follows:

Sale direct to customers

This method is known as *direct* distribution. It is a direct line from manufacturer to consumer and, therefore, can be most effectively controlled. If *direct canvassing* is employed—salesmen visiting consumers—the business is fairly certain that the policy is being followed and that the largest possible "punch" is being given to the sales effort. Furthermore, any special instructions on discounts, publicity material, price maintenance and other matters can be supervised by the salesmen. Properly trained salesmen can also ensure that bad debts are minimised. When calling on shops or other channels of distribution an alert salesman can generally "sense" the credit standing of a customer.

For goods which have high profit margins, direct canvassing can be very effective and profitable. This applies to office machinery such as photocopying machines, accounting machines, computers and calculators. There is also a tendency to have salesmen calling on shopkeepers or householders when competition is very keen. If a call is not paid at regular intervals then orders may be lost. In these cases the manufacturer has to rely upon a large volume of sales being obtained by each salesman. In this way the high cost of keeping a man on the road is more than covered.

An alternative to direct canvassing is *direct mail order* or *mail order through advertising*. The former means writing to selected customers, possibly sending catalogues, and waiting for orders to be received. Mail order advertising means that goods are advertised in newspapers, on television, or through club organisers, and goods ordered are sent through the post.

Many businesses do tremendously well by adopting either or both of these methods. The costs of publicity can be very high, but as no salesmen are employed there is a large saving in salaries. When designing letters, catalogues and advertisements there must be an aim to produce a very strong impact which will stimulate sales and, where necessary, overcome resistance.

Even if the method is not used exclusively it can be very useful as a supplementary method. Campaigns can be conducted by direct mail order methods and salesmen can follow up any enquiries received.

A further method of selling direct to consumers is for the manufacturer to own shops. There is a growing tendency for this situation to develop, either by a manufacturer opening shops or by a distributing company forming its own manufacturing units. Examples are to be found in all large towns: Boots the Chemists (Boots Pure Drug Co Ltd), J. Sainsbury Ltd, Montague Burton Ltd the tailors, W. Barratt & Co Ltd the shoe makers, and Marks & Spencer Ltd. Generally there are enough shops to market all the goods produced by the company concerned. If only one product is being produced, without variation in size or colour, the use of a manufacturer's own shop is unlikely to succeed.

Sales via a middleman

Selling via a middleman is known as *indirect distribution*. For many products with a low profit margin this is the only practical proposition. It may take the form of going to: (*a*) a retailer, (*b*) a wholesaler or (*c*) both wholesaler and retailer.

Going through a wholesaler will usually result in larger orders. This can mean that a smaller sales organisation is possible—fewer salesmen, clerks, packers and delivery men. As a result, there may also be a tendency for lower costs associated with marketing, and bad debts may be avoided. Against these advantages must be offset the disadvantages such as having to comply with the whims of wholesalers, receiving lower profit margins, and the loss in the effectiveness of the sale effort. A wholesaler cannot be forced to stock particular goods nor can he be induced to push them unless the terms are made attractive enough. In some cases, television time and other forms of advertising are expected by the wholesalers to strengthen sales.

When the channel of distribution is via a retailer a larger number of orders have to be handled with a resultant high cost of selling and distribution. Much of a salesman's time may be spent waiting for a shop-keeper to give him an order: the control over the sales effort thus becomes a major problem.

There are other methods, such as telephoning customers or selling via agencies, and for details of these the reader is advised to study a textbook on marketing.

ADVERTISING

Advertising is discussed below. There should be a clearly defined policy on the volume of advertising and the media to be employed.

MAINTENANCE OF AN EFFICIENT SALES FORCE

What is meant by a "personnel policy" is discussed in detail in Chapter XIII, Personnel Management. Here it is essential to notice that there should be an adequate sales organisation and sales force to obtain the desired volume of sales. Conditions of service, salaries and incentives should be adequate enough to stimulate a high level of active selling (*see* p. 264).

THE MARKETING ORGANISATION

Earlier in this chapter an outline is given of the aspects which are generally included as part of the marketing function. This section is concerned with explaining some of these aspects within the broad framework of the marketing organisation.

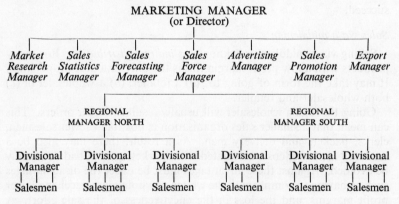

FIG. 25.—*Sales organisation chart*

FORM OF ORGANISATION

The type of organisation to adopt depends very much upon the size of the business, the nature of the products and the policy being followed. Each business should have an organisation which suits its own requirements: there can be no question of a standard type for all sorts of companies.

Bearing these facts in mind, two forms of organisation are illustrated. The first type (Fig. 25 above) illustrates a fairly simple organisation for a medium- to large-size company. This organisation is suitable where a business is concerned with a straightforward, homogeneous line of products to sell over a geographically spread sales force. This implies that a company has a country-wide market which can conveniently be divided. The sales force manager would handle all matters affecting sales staff; the other managers would control the aspects indicated such as market research, sales statistics, advertising, sales promotion, export and forecasting. The marketing manager (or director) would

FIG. 26.—*Sales organisation chart for a company with a variety of sales brands*

co-ordinate the efforts of all the managers. No staff have been shown for the departments, other than the regional and divisional sales force managers, but obviously they would have to be included when considering such a chart in practice. The sales ledger accounting division may also come under the marketing manager, but many organisations prefer this to be the responsibility of the accountant.

A second form of chart emphasises the products being made and sold. It attempts to give more strength to the sales effort by dividing the market according to some distinctive attribute such as channel of distribution or brand (Fig. 26). Examples may be cited as follows:

1. Grouping according to the market. Products may be sold to businesses or to householders. In this case it may be feasible to have an industrial sales manager and a domestic sales manager.

2. Grouping according to the different applications of products. In the case of an oil company there may be separate managers for heating oils, petrols and oils for automative use, and petro-chemicals.

A further application of this principle is seen in the flour milling/ animal feeding-stuffs industry where companies may have the following divisions:

Bakeries flour sales manager.
Retail flour sales manager.
Dog foods sales manager.
Animal foods sales manager.

3. Grouping according to brands. The policy of a company may be to market a number of brands even in such a way that they compete with each other. For example, in the case of Proctor and Gamble Ltd "Daz" and "Tide" are sold as fierce rivals to each other.

As stated earlier, the organisation to be employed should be that which gives maximum efficiency. The marketing manager should ensure that the organisation does not become "top heavy" so that it is both inflexible and too costly.

MARKET RESEARCH

Market research is a combination of methods and techniques employed for answering questions relating to the present and future market potentialities. Data are collected by interviewers or from newspapers, journals and official statistics. These data are then employed to answer questions of the type shown below:

1. Will the price secure the optimum sales volume?
2. Who will buy, or are likely to buy, the products or services?
3. What will give satisfaction to the consumer?
4. What factor influences buyers to select the products?
5. Is the design both aesthetically pleasing and functional?
6. Which methods of advertising are likely to be the most effective?
7. Are there any seasonal demands for the products?
8. Can new products be introduced to fill any slack periods in production?

In effect there is a complete study of the market; products are made to satisfy consumers; any competitors are studied and where necessary prices and products are improved; finally the business makes its plans and produces and sells to that share of the market indicated by market research.

SALES PROMOTION

There is no hard and fast definition of "sales promotion." What is generally agreed is that the technique is intended to raise the demand level for a product very quickly. In other words, the sales effort is directed very firmly in the direction of increased sales.

Sometimes the term is used to describe the total activities involved in selling, including advertising, packaging and the control of salesmen.

However, many sales directors would prefer the narrower definition of applying tactical planning and control of selling techniques in the strategy of marketing operations. This is not to say that other aspects should not be considered. Indeed, sales promotion will require use of advertising and other aids to selling. The difference lies in the fact that sales promotion is generally a short-term technique which is very flexible.

Methods employed

The methods employed may be directed towards:
1. The channels of distribution, which are discussed in this chapter.
2. The consumers.

1. The channels of distribution.—The sales promotion may consist of giving incentives in the form of discounts for display and for quantity or special bonus packs (*e.g.* fourteen for the price of twelve). Alternatively, the trader may be given gifts or may be awarded prizes on the basis of display or volume of sales. A new shop front or van may be offered.

In effect, an attempt is being made to obtain favourable treatment from the distributor. He agrees to stock and display the products for the benefits he is to receive. He is committing his capital and, at the same time, enabling the business concerned to capture a larger share of the market.

2. Consumers.—The methods available for approaching consumers are summarised below:

(*a*) *Premiums*

 (*i*) *Coupons*—put through the door and redeemed when the product is purchased.

 (*ii*) *Box top premiums*—save so many tops or cut-outs and send up for a gift. Useful for a family of products and to retain product loyalty.

 (*iii*) *Self liquidating premiums*—send a box top plus a payment to obtain an article well below market price. Because the company buys in bulk there is, in fact, no loss because the payment covers the cost.

 (*iv*) *Container premiums*—the container is useful—a kilner jar to hold the coffee is valuable in itself, but replaces the usual jar.

 (*v*) *Enclosure premiums*—toys in cornflakes.

 (*vi*) *Direct premiums*—take a plastic container from the shop when you buy a packet of soap.

 (*vii*) *"3d. off"*—bargain packs.

 (*viii*) *Banded packs*—a bar of soap and a tube of toothpaste sold together for a special price. Introduces new products or a slow seller is aided by a good product.

 (*ix*) *Competition premiums.*

There are many other premiums, but apart from the sales stimulus they all aim at the same purpose—they meet price competition without price

F

reductions. This is very important since a price reduction is a permanent measure and the reinstatement of profit requires a price rise which brings sales resistance.

The advantages claimed for premiums are as follows:

1. Names are added to the mailing list.
2. Obtains salesmen contacts.
3. Useful for clearing out old stock for a new line.
4. Increased floor and display space in the shops and the attention and interest of the sales staff.

(b) *Exhibitions and participation in special events and devices such as doorstep prizes for possessing various products.*

(c) *Direct mail advertising* (discussed earlier in this chapter).

(d) *Merchandising.*

Merchandising encompasses a whole range of techniques at the point of sale—displays, in-store promotions, novelties, pamphlets, demonstrations, tastings and samplings. It requires the co-operation of the retailer and this may have to be paid for in one way or another. Its purpose is impulse at the counter.

Benefits from sales promotion

One of the greatest advantages of sales promotion is its flexibility. A scheme can be mounted quickly to curb a declining market or increased competition. Extremely good results may be obtained from a carefully planned scheme.

The technique has, nevertheless, to be employed with caution. A large amount of money can be spent very quickly and this can only be justified by *results*. If people would buy anyway then the sales promotion will serve little purpose. A campaign which has as its basis the issue of £0·025 coupons may be very costly. For example, the redemption of 1 million coupons will cost £25,000. This figure has to be covered by increased sales and, in a competitive market, may be difficult to achieve.

Possibly the safest approach is to allow a cost figure in the sales budget. This allows the sales promotion manager to see how far he can go. He then acts within the limits the company can afford.

SALES FORECASTING AND BUDGETING

Forecasting and budgeting are outlined in Chapter XXI. The sales forecast is a statement which shows the sales in a period in quantities and/or values. The latter may be necessary in engineering when each job is made to customers' specifications and is different from any other. An example of a sales forecast is given in Fig. 27. The precise form it will take depends upon the nature of the product.

Modern management thought now recognises *management by*

participation. An extension of this idea is for salesmen, sales managers and other personnel to participate in the compiling of forecasts and budgets. Some of the methods used are as follows:

 1. Opinions of salesmen and sales managers. Questionnaires or forecast statements are compiled by the salesmen and sales manager. The results are then summarised and adjusted for future trends.

 2. Sales managers are asked for their opinions on future trends. These are used to adjust the previous years' figures.

 3. Market research statistics are used to compile the future sales.

ANNUAL SALES FORECAST

Year ending......................................

	Last Year	Total Year	First Quarter	Second Quarter	Third Quarter	Fourth Quarter
Southern Area						
UNITS of:						
Product A	10,000	11,000	3,000	5,000	1,000	2,000
Product B	12,000	13,200	4,000	4,000	3,000	2,200
Product C	6,000	6,600	1,000	2,000	2,000	1,600
Northern Area						
UNITS OF:						
Product A	4,000	4,400	1,000	1,000	1,000	1,400
Product B	16,000	17,600	5,000	4,000	4,000	4,600
Product C	10,000	11,000	3,000	4,000	2,000	2,000
Southern Area						
VALUE of:	£	£	£	£	£	£
Std. Price						
Product A £0·5	5,000	5,500	1,500	2,500	500	1,000
Product B £1·0	12,000	13,200	4,000	4,000	3,000	2,200
Product C £0·1	600	660	100	200	200	160
	17,600	19,360	5,600	6,700	3,700	3,360
Northern Area						
VALUE of:	£	£	£	£	£	£
Std. Price						
Product A £0·5	2,000	2,200	500	500	500	700
Product B £1·0	16,000	17,600	5,000	4,000	4,000	4,600
Product C £0·1	1,000	1,100	300	400	200	200
	19,000	20,900	5,800	4,900	4,700	5,500
Grand Totals £	36,600	40,260	11,400	11,600	8,400	8,860

Fig. 27.—*Specimen annual sales forecast*

Sometimes a combination of these methods is employed. The object is to select the sales mixture which will give the target profit.

ADVERTISING

Just as communication is vital to good internal management, so is advertising vital to the earning of profit. Put another way, advertising is communication to the outside world; all the qualities of the product must be brought to the notice of consumers.

Advertising can stimulate demand and, where necessary, can even create demand where none exists. By increasing demand a larger volume of output can be produced and this can lead to the economies of large-scale production; in short, lower costs. Study of the chapters on costs will show why this is the case.

The most appropriate methods of advertising have to be selected: those that get the desired message to the consumers. Just as the methods of distribution are classified as "direct" and "indirect," advertising may be treated in the same way.

Direct publicity

Direct mail, circulars and sales literature handed out, inserted in journals or otherwise given to potential consumers come under this heading. These methods do not involve frequent visits by salesmen. If necessary the publicity can be highly selective: for instance a mailing list of people within a certain income bracket can be compiled.

Indirect publicity

All forms of "group" advertising which are addressed generally to customers and potential customers, rather than to individuals. Newspapers and journals are some of the most effective media for advertising. They have varying circulations which can range from national coverage, as in the daily press, to highly selective cover through specialised and technical journals. An important aspect of the advertising manager's work is assessing the suitability of particular newspapers and magazines through which to market his company's products. If Bentley or Rolls-Royce cars are to be advertised then the appropriate paper may be *The Times*; on the other hand, for a cheap family car the appropriate paper may be the *Daily Mirror*. The advertisement becomes a permanent record which may be saved by a potential customer and used in the future.

Posters and bills placed on buses, trains, railway stations, roadside hoardings and other suitable sites are extremely efficient methods for keeping the name of a product before the public.

Other advertising media are the cinema and television screens, package advertising and trade exhibitions and displays. Of the latter the Motor Show is probably the best known. Television advertising for products which are consumed in the home has had tremendous success.

Planned properly, an advertising campaign can be as effective as a visit by a salesman.

Whenever possible, tests should be made to reveal the effectiveness of advertising. This is one of the most difficult aspects of indirect advertising. There is little purpose in continuing to advertise in, for instance, a technical journal that does not "pull its weight," and it is impracticable to restrict advertising to that journal only for long enough to know its true effect on sales. One method of establishing the usefulness of specific advertisements is to include return coupons: the number returned is an indication of the success of the advertisement.

One of the advantages of direct advertising is the fact that response can be accurately and speedily measured and methods adjusted to produce optimum results.

The advertising budget

The advertising manager has to ask for an appropriation for each year. This should be approved by the marketing manager and subsequently by the board of directors. There are different methods employed for fixing the advertising appropriation. None is scientific; often it is just a matter of what a company thinks it can afford. A percentage based on expected sales is a method frequently employed. Theoretically, advertising expenditure should be increased so long as it continues to increase sales enough to more than cover the advertising costs. In practice this is very difficult to measure.

Advertising budgets will usually be prepared to show the likely costs to be involved as well as the most frequently employed advertising media.

MAINTENANCE OF AN EFFICIENT SALES FORCE

For selection of salesmen the Seven-Point Plan described in Chapter XIV should be employed. The job requirements for each salesman would be compiled and then the job and the individual would be "matched" as closely as possible.

A brief outline of possible incentives is given later. Here it is important to notice that a salesman should be paid a good salary *plus* an adequate incentive payment, and any reasonable expenses which are incurred.

THE SALES OFFICE

Considerable reliance has to be placed on the administrative procedures within the office. All aspects of marketing—sales, service and related matters—have to be co-ordinated. The procedures followed are summarised in Chapter XI, which explains the functions carried out by the Sales Office.

The relation of the sales function with other functions is considered in Chapters IV and V.

SELLING ABROAD

Where the business produces to sell abroad, special procedures have to be followed for exporting the products. These depend upon the regulations in force in the particular country concerned. In some cases not only are special procedures to be followed but there are also regulations which affect the product. For example, there may be a law prohibiting colouring in foodstuffs, or the safety regulations for cars or machinery may be much more stringent than in the producing country. This generally means that the products have to be adapted, or produced, specially for export.

The precise procedures will tend to vary from one business to another. However, the following steps should give an understanding of what is involved.

1. Enquiries received from abroad via an associated company or an agency.

2. Quotation prepared, stipulating what is included in the price— FOB (free on board, *i.e.* including the expenses connected with loading on to the ship); FOR (free on rail); CIF (cost, insurance and freight are included in the price); or other variation.

3. Receive order and accept its terms after checking the creditworthiness of the customer, obtaining credit insurance and/or assistance from the Export Credits Guarantee Department.

Publications such as the *Exporter's Year Book* can be helpful. The Export Department handling a substantial amount of business would in any case keep its own records.

Details may also be obtained from banks and such commercial organisations as the Credit Insurance Association Ltd which specialise in the provision of credit insurance to cover overseas transactions.

4. Instruct the Production Department of the special requirements specified by the customer or the regulations of the particular country.

5. Deal with shipping formalities, such as the bill of lading, consular documents, insurance, bill of exchange and other financial documents.

6. Collect the money due from the customers as arranged.

Some of these functions will be carried out by departments other than sales. They are included together to indicate the main responsibilities involved in exporting.

AFTER-SALES SERVICE

After-sales service is a very essential requirement for all companies which produce capital goods, such as washing machines, vacuum cleaners and similar equipment which requires attention over its useful life.

There are two distinct periods for maintenance and service:

1. The guarantee or warranty period. This may cover 6 or 12 months or even longer. During this time any faults will be rectified and adjustments made in accordance with the guarantee issued by the company.

2. General service over the life of the product. Many companies have contracts which provide for annual service of products. A good example is to be found with domestic central heating when the boiler is serviced by an oil company. Typewriters, duplicators and various types of office machines can also be serviced in this way.

With other products, such as cars, the service after the warranty period is covered on request, and the customer is charged on the basis of the work done.

Importance of servicing

Adequate servicing should be provided on a country-wide basis. This is vital for the reputation of the manufacturer. If customers cannot get service, including repairs, the reputation of the products will suffer. There is, in fact, a direct relationship between the efficiency of the servicing facilities and the reliability of the products.

If spare parts cannot be obtained readily and quickly there will be great difficulty in selling the products. This is seen by the mushroom companies which have appeared in the domestic-appliances field. At the first sign of financial instability on the part of a company there is great difficulty in selling the products, and one of the principal reasons is the fear that spare parts and services will no longer be available.

PACKAGES AND SALES

Packaging can play an important part in successful marketing. A colourful package provides the appropriate image to the consumer. However, there is more to the design of packages than giving a pleasing impression.

Many skills are involved in packaging. There is designing, colouring and the selection of the best shapes, sizes and materials. All have to be combined to produce the desired features. Some of the latter are as follows:

1. Functional.—A package has to comply with the functional requirements. It has to hold the product and store it in an appropriate fashion so that adequate protection is given.

2. Sales appeal.—For products which have to be sold in supermarkets and similar forms of "display selling," the package can have a considerable influence on the sales. However, it should not be forgotten that *all* manufacturers pay attention to package appeal, so the advantages are not always obvious. In some cases, such as cosmetics and jewellery, the presentation of the products can play a considerable role in overcoming sales resistance.

PUBLIC RELATIONS

Presenting the appropriate *company image* is vital to the successful marketing of products. In some companies the marketing manager will deal with public relations; in others a special appointment will be made.

The most important function of the Public Relations Officer (the P.R.O.) is to foster good relations with all who deal with the business. Some possible areas of responsibility are as follows:

1. Planning general advertisements which develop the company image.

2. Holding press conferences and issuing information to newspapers in a form which will improve the goodwill of the company.

3. Appearing on television and at exhibitions such as trade fairs, *e.g.* the motor show.

4. Advising on all matters which affect relations with outside bodies.

5. Dealing with trade associations, trade unions and employers' associations.

6. Preparing publications which have, as their primary object, the improvement of public relations. This can cover pamphlets for *external circulation* and for *internal use*, such as a booklet dealing with a company's operations.

These and similar functions should be handled with tact and understanding. A P.R.O. who does not present a good image may cause considerable damage to the reputation of the business. On the other hand, properly handled the public relations function can create a feeling of respect for a company and its operations.

EXAMINATION QUESTIONS

1. Outline the means of advertising, both direct and indirect, available to any industry with which you are familiar, and state how you would attempt to measure the effectiveness of each.

2. What are the purposes of sales forecasting? State the factors influencing the level of sales in any company, distinguishing between controllable factors and uncontrollable factors.

3. You have recently been engaged by a company as sales manager. How would you discover the *policy* of the company in relation to your own duties and responsibilities? Make a list of the headings under which you would be expected to know and understand the policy.

4. Compare the following two channels of distribution available to a manufacturer whose goods are sold through retailers:

(*a*) selling to the retail trade through wholesalers;

(*b*) selling direct to the retail trade.

What factors need to be considered in forming policy in this field?

5. An established manufacturer is considering expansion of his business and in particular the introduction of a new product or products. What factors should be considered before embarking on such a course of action? Illustrate your answer with an example from the household consumer goods field. Outline a programme showing the sequence of events following the decision to embark on the marketing of a new line.

6. Give a job specification for a marketing manager in a company where this position involves responsibility for selling, advertising, sales promotion and market research (*see* Chapter XIV).

7. In what ways can knowledge of the market for a firm's products be obtained? What problems can be investigated by the technique of market research? What is the connection between market research and business forecasting?

8. One of the basic principles of planning is that policies establish the framework upon which planning procedures and programmes are constructed. Discuss what is meant by policies and show how policies are formulated and developed.

One broad classification of policies has to do with the functions of the business—sales, production, finance, etc. Take any one of these functions and give the major policy questions in this area, showing the factors to be considered in making policy decisions thereon.

9. What methods or channels can be used for the distribution of products to users by a manufacturing company?

10. List the information which you consider should appear on the sales department's customer and follow-up records. How would this information be collected and to what uses would it be put?

11. What information would an investigator, employed on market research, seek in order to assess the demand for a new product?

12. Selling methods differ widely according to the type of industry. Describe three of these methods and indicate the industry to which each would apply.

13. Describe the work of a public relations officer, assuming the widest interpretation of this function.

CHAPTER XI

THE ADMINISTRATIVE FUNCTION

INTRODUCTION

THE word "Administration" (with a capital "A") is a noun used to describe the collection of resources under the control of an Administrative Director or a person with a similar title. All *office functions* come under this heading, although there are some areas which are treated separately for particular purposes.

When accountants follow the conventional functional breakdown, certain office functions are included under each main heading. For example, the structure of a business is as follows:

1. Production or manufacturing.
2. Selling and distribution.
3. Research and development.
4. Administration.

The fourth category includes all costs connected with the formulation of policy and management, *excluding* those activities which relate specifically to categories 1, 2 and 3.*

However, when viewed *generally* all clerical, management and director functions come under the heading of the Administrative Function. The next section summarises the main fields included.

MAIN AREAS OF ADMINISTRATION

The main areas which come into the category of Administration or Office Management are as follows:

1. Accounting and Finance—
   (*a*) Financial accounting.
   (*b*) Cost accounting.
   (*c*) Management accountancy.
   (*d*) General financial management, which includes the provision of adequate finance to operate the business.

These aspects are covered in Chapters XVIII to XXII inclusive. However, certain routine functions are considered below, *e.g.* wages.

* See the *Terminology of Cost Accountancy* published by the Institute of Cost and Works Accountants.

2. Company secretariat.
3. Computer and other EDP services.
4. Organisation and Methods.
5. Sales Office.
6. Purchasing Office.
7. Wages.
8. Stock and Stores Control.
9. Production offices:
   (a) Planning and Control;
   (b) Drawing Office;
   (c) Progress.
10. General office services.

These (2 to 10) are considered in turn quite briefly. For further details readers are referred to books in the Bibliography, especially those covering Office Management.

COMPANY SECRETARIAT

The chief official for company secretarial matters is known as the company secretary. Under the *Companies Acts* a company must have a separate officer to act in this capacity. Although he is an employee, he does carry considerable responsibilities. Some company secretaries are also directors, but this is not always the case. However, it is quite usual for a secretary to have considerable powers delegated to him; for example, the signing of contracts along with, say, the managing director.

Whether he is fully responsible for all administrative matters depends upon the organisation structure. Sometimes he is, whereas with some companies he is in charge of a separate department which deals specifically with legal and related matters.

From what has been stated it should be apparent that the precise duties of a company secretary and those under his control will vary from one company to another. Dealing with *basic* functions these may be regarded as follows:

1. Convenes meetings

There are two main types of meeting—those where the directors meet to consider the policy and strategy of the company and those where shareholders are invited.

The *directors' meetings* will be called at regular intervals, possibly once a week, although some companies have regular meetings on a monthly basis. Matters which may be dealt with are as follows:

(a) Corporate planning (policy and strategy).
(b) Approval of senior management appointments and any dismissals at management level.

(c) Sanctioning capital expenditure—usually fixed assets costing above a figure laid down by the Board.

(d) Declaring dividends.

(e) Financial planning of a general nature, such as raising new capital.

(f) Considering special problems, such as labour troubles or a grave shortage of raw materials.

(g) Approval of major contracts.

(h) Approval of transactions relating to company shares or debentures.

(i) Examination of the progress of the company and, where necessary, instructing the managing director, executive directors, and secretary to effect improvements.

The *shareholders' meetings* are usually divided into three classes as follows:

(a) *Statutory Meeting*, which must be called by every public company from 1 to 3 months after incorporation, *i.e.* from the commencement of business. A *statutory report* has to be prepared and sent to shareholders at least 14 days before the meeting. The purpose is to inform shareholders of all the facts relating to the formation of the company.

(b) *Annual General Meeting*, at which any dividends are declared and the Balance Sheet and Profit and Loss Account are presented to shareholders. In practice, it is also usual for a Chairman to make a report on the progress of the company and its future plans and expectations.

(c) *Extraordinary General Meeting*, when special problems are dealt with, often at the request of shareholders. Directors may also call an Extraordinary General Meeting when they require approval of some drastic measure, *e.g.* removal of the Chairman from office.

This is a very brief summary of shareholders' meetings, and since these are given legal status under the *Companies Acts*, readers are advised to consult a book on Company Law for any further details they may require.

2. Prepares documents

Very often a company secretary has legal qualifications, or is qualified as a company secretary by belonging to a professional body such as the Chartered Institute of Secretaries. This is necessary because much of the work is concerned with contracts and legal documents. However, some companies also have legal advisers who can be called upon to deal with complex problems.

3. Complying with legal requirements

A company is required to operate within the law and within the objects laid down in its various regulations, and especially in the following documents:

(a) *Memorandum of Association*, which specifies the nature of the company and its purpose. In other words, it deals with the position in relation to all outside parties who deal with the company.

(b) *Articles of Association*, which stipulate how the business affairs are to be conducted. Examples of matters normally included are as shown below:

(i) dealings with shares;
(ii) meetings;
(iii) voting rights;
(iv) appointment and powers of directors;
(v) accounts, dividends, and audit;
(vi) winding up of the company.

The company secretary should advise the directors if any act is likely to be *ultra vires*, *i.e.* illegal as regards the company.

4. Share transactions

All work connected with the handling of shares is usually the responsibility of the company secretary. Considerable work is involved with the issue and transfer of shares, and again legal requirements have to be observed. With a large company it is usual to have an official called a Registrar, who is responsible to the company secretary. Share certificates have to be prepared to show the details of the shares held and the name of the shareholder.

Dividend warrants have to be prepared by the company secretary for all payments due to shareholders. These are rather like a cheque or *credit transfer* and show the dividend paid by the company.

5. Maintaining registers

Special registers have to be kept, and the company secretary usually has responsibility for these. They include separate registers for the following:

(a) Members, *i.e.* shareholders.
(b) Directors and secretary.
(c) Directors' holdings of shares.

These have to be kept up to date and in accordance with the legal requirements as stated in the *Companies Acts*.

6. Preparing statutory documents

Many statutory documents have to be prepared and distributed to shareholders or sent to the Registrar of Companies. They include an annual return and various other documents which show how the company's affairs are being conducted or what important changes have taken place.

7. Transmission of policy

Any decisions made by the directors have to be put into practice. Usually any policy statements are issued under the signature of the secretary, who acts on behalf of the Board. For example, the conditions of employment are often signed by the secretary.

8. Pensions and superannuation

Where a company has its own pension or superannuation scheme it is usual for the secretary to carry out all the necessary work. He will also be required to invest the funds in accordance with the policy of the company.

9. Approval of certain appointments

With some companies it is a common practice for staff appointments, other than senior managers, to be approved by the company secretary. He may also make arrangements regarding training and education. However, this depends very much upon whether a personnel officer is also employed.

10. Control of accounting function

This applies with some companies, even where there is a chief accountant. In others the accountancy function is kept quite separate from company secretarial work and the two areas are co-ordinated through the managing director or administrative director.

11. Other duties

Trying to give a complete summary of duties is an impossible task. In any case, as indicated, practices vary considerably from one business to another. Moreover, the existence of other executives, such as a company solicitor, accountant, personnel manager, or office manager, can affect the allocation of responsibilities.

Dealing with important correspondence, signing cheques and other routine matters will also come within the company secretary's jurisdiction. He will also be expected to act in an advisory capacity on matters affecting the company, and this will apply for the directors and for managers who require advice on the interpretation of policy.

COMPUTER AND OTHER EDP SERVICES

A computer is a "machine" or group of "machines" which is operated electronically to carry out a number of functions in relation to the collection of vast quantities of figures.

There are two basic types of computer—the *analogue computer*, which is used primarily for scientific work and has limited memory facilities, and the *digital computer*, which has a considerable memory capacity and can store a considerable quantity of data.

The stages involved in computer work (electronic data processing, or in its abbreviated form EDP) are as follows:

1. Programming.—A computer can only operate from detailed instructions showing, step by step, what is required. These instructions are known as a program (or programme).

2. Calculations.—Calculations can be carried out at considerable speed. The registers in the arithmetic unit can multiply, add, subtract and divide.

3. Storage.—Magnetic tapes, drums and cores are employed within a storage unit. In effect, this is a vast memory which holds the information until required.

4. Supplying information.—Information put into the computer by means of the program can be made available through the *output unit*. Paper or magnetic tapes are employed, and these, fed into a printer, produce printed statements, pay rolls, invoices, or other details.

Equipment

The units which are required to carry out the functions described above are as follows:

1. Input unit.
2. Program controller.
3. Arithmetic unit.
4. Storage unit.
5. Output unit.

A diagram which shows the flow of information within a computer is shown below (Fig. 28). This should not be construed to mean that

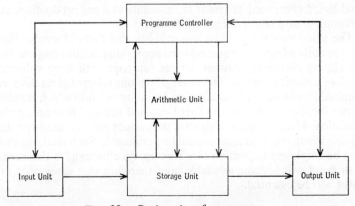

Fig. 28.—*Basic units of a computer*

these units are physically quite separate. With advances in computer design many changes continue to take place. Programs are today greatly simplified from the earlier attempts. The development of more flexible computer "languages" has made this possible—it will be appreciated that figures and code letters have to be employed to summarise the information.

The collective term used to describe the computer equipment explained above is the "hardware." On the other hand, of equal importance, is the "software," which covers all aspects of programming, including the development of suitable languages and "packaged programs," *i.e.* ready-made programs for routine operations.

Justifying a computer

Installation of a computer can be extremely *costly*, not only in terms of money actually spent on planning and acquiring the necessary equipment but in other aspects as well; for example:

1. Obtaining a computer to be in fashion, but not having enough work to justify the acquisition.

2. Limited application on a specific function, with the consequent underemployment of facilities.

3. Inadequate preplanning, so that the installation has many teething troubles.

4. Lack of training and education of personnel to deal with the changes brought about by the installation.

A *feasibility study* should be made to ensure that a computer can be justified in terms of volume of work, cost savings and increased information available for use by managers. Before making a decision the views of all concerned should be obtained. Usually a *steering committee* is established composed of senior representatives from production, sales, accounting, and research and development.

The study may show that a less sophisticated form of mechanisation may be quite adequate. Punched-card accounting, accounting machines, calculating machines or other devices can cope with large volumes of work of a routine nature. Moreover, if the one selected gives the service required there can be no justification for an installation which is unlikely to pay for itself. As shown in Part Four on Financial Management and Statistical Method, quite elaborate techniques may be used for determining whether a fixed asset should be purchased. Such methods should also be employed to justify office machinery, although, in this case, no cash flows will become available, and therefore cost savings or other bases will be essential.

Uses of computers

Computers have been used in many areas of business. They lend themselves to dealing with large volumes of work of a standardised nature. This is why insurance and banking companies have been able to employ computers quite extensively.

As applied to industry, the following have been dealt with by a computer:

1. Wages and payroll procedures.
2. Production planning and control.
3. Stock and stores control.
4. Customers' orders.
5. Sales accounting.
6. Long-term forecasting.
7. Cash forecasting.
8. Capital expenditure forecasting.

The ideal arrangement would be one where all aspects could be fully integrated into a management information and control system. Some companies are moving in this direction. They have a central control from a computer centre and satellite computer terminals at the divisions of the company. In this way there can be a two-way flow of information for planning and control.

ORGANISATION AND METHODS (O and M)

O and M is the application of work study to office procedures and methods. Put another way, the technique attempts to simplify procedures so that they are carried out satisfactorily at reduced cost.

There is a tendency for clerical and other administrative costs to rise because of a number of factors:

1. Increased complexities in manufacturing and selling.
2. Development of new techniques, both technological and managerial.
3. Growth in the size of business units due to normal expansion and mergers.
4. Requests for more information by managers and the establishment of management information systems.
5. Giving customers better and more prompt service.
6. More detailed planning and control of business resources due to automation or a desire for more efficiency.
7. The high costs involved in operating a computer.

These are some of the reasons for larger clerical staffs and increased mechanisation of office procedures. The big question is how they can be kept to a reasonable level. Directly they produce nothing, and therefore administrative costs are a total reduction of profit. However, it should be remembered that, without corporate planning and the use of modern techniques, a business would not survive for very long. The services are very necessary, but they have to be performed at reasonable cost.

Methods of control

Where a separate department can be justified, it is usual to have an O and M manager and staff under him. He can look at the business as a whole and design suitable systems to meet all requirements.

The alternative approach is to have an accountant or other official to investigate a particular area with a view to reducing the costs of carrying out the functions. Such cost-reduction drives can produce *temporary* economies, but since there is usually no attempt made to increase efficiency, costs very quickly rise to the "normal" level. An alternative is for an apparently "unprofitable" section to be eliminated altogether—until it is discovered that vital work is not now being done so that the section has to be reinstated.

The more constructive approach is to employ experts in systems which operate at minimum cost. For details of how *method study* is carried out the reader is advised to turn to Chapter IX.

In addition to establishing methods and procedures which *eliminate* all unnecessary work, attention should be paid to cost control. In collaboration with the office manager or accountant it should be possible to divide office work into distinct categories:

1. Management and similar work of a non-routine nature.
2. Work which can be standardised and for which "work units" can be established:

Functions	Standard Work Unit
Addressing envelopes	Cost per envelope
Book-keeping	Cost per posting or transaction
Calculating	Cost per 100 calculations
Copying	Cost per letter or statement copied
Duplicating	Cost per form or letter duplicated
Filing	Cost per item handled
Invoicing	Cost per invoice prepared
Tabulation	Cost per tabulation prepared
Travelling	Cost per mile or per day
Typing:	

   (*a*) Letter from:

      (*i*) dictating machines⎫
      (*ii*) shorthand   ⎬ Cost per average letter

   (*b*) Invoices   Cost per invoice

Once these work units and unit costs have been determined they may be used to:

(a) Measure efficiency and, possibly, to award a bonus payment to clerical workers.

(b) Aid in amending budgets after the first, when the volume of work in a future period is expected to be reduced or increased.

This approach should be supplemented by a budgetary control system and methods of authorising expenditure so that a watch can be kept on all money spent.

Method of approach

There is no standard method for carrying out O and M work, but usually the following stages are involved:

1. Define the objectives.—There should be a clear understanding of the purpose of the assignment to be carried out, *e.g.* to improve the Stores Control system.

2. Programme the work.—The various stages involved, the people to be employed, timetabling and other related aspects should be included in a written programme.

3. Investigate.—All related areas should be considered and thoroughly examined so that there is full information available.

4. Critical analysis.—The facts should be considered critically. For this purpose it is usual to have a standardised form to show under appropriate headings what is being done and whether any improvements can be made.

Example

The receiving and issue of materials is causing concern because book and physical stocks do not agree. You are required to investigate. Show the main areas you would cover.

Suggested approach

Dealing with the receipt and issue of materials the following aspects should be considered:

Investigation and critical analysis

(a) Are materials entered on Goods Inwards Notes?

(b) Are returns dealt with properly and all documents prepared?

(c) What records are maintained in the Stores, *e.g.* bin cards?

(d) Are all issues and returns covered by material requisitions and stores credit notes?

(e) Are there adequate safeguards against stock movements without the necessary forms?

(f) Is the *perpetual inventory* system employed, whereby the balance on hand of each material is automatically carried down after each entry?

(g) Are stocks checked regularly by means of *continuous stocktaking*, thus ensuring that records and actual stocks held do agree?

Additional procedures that would also be checked would be the purchasing routines and the accounting for payment of invoices. Furthermore, the routes followed, the forms used and the persons receiving them, should receive attention. The purpose served by each copy of every form employed should also be ascertained. Flow charts may be prepared for showing the essential stages.

5. *Recommend new procedures.*—New procedures and forms should be devised so that effective control can be exercised. At the same time the following should be realised:

(*a*) Integration of all procedures so that they work in harmony.
(*b*) No hold-ups in production.
(*c*) A minimum investment in Stores equipment and personnel.
(*d*) No movement of materials without proper documentation.

Why employ a specialist?

The advantage of employing a specialist is that he can give his full attention to problems which arise. In addition, he can view these objectively and in a very broad fashion so that one area is not neglected when others are receiving attention. There is always a danger that the man carrying out the work will see only his side of it and will not appreciate the wider implications.

By his specialist training the O and M expert should be able to see how procedures can be improved. He can also draw on wide experience and his knowledge of similar situations. The outcome should be a considerable improvement in efficiency.

Care has to be taken to ensure that friction does not arise. If changes are being made there is a real danger that the office workers concerned will fear redundancy or, at the least, that their jobs will be altered drastically. For these reasons careful preplanning and preparation are vital. Tact and an acceptable personality are necessary requirements for the O and M specialist, as well as expert knowledge.

SALES OFFICE

"Marketing" is considered in Chapter X, and readers are advised to consider the outline given there to obtain a full appreciation of why a Sales Office is necessary.

As implied earlier in this chapter, the division between Administration and the other functional areas is not always clear and tends to vary from one business to another. With some companies the actual record-keeping will be the responsibility of a Sales Office Manager who comes under the authority of the Marketing Manager. In other cases the Office Manager may be required to supply the necessary information required by the Marketing Manager. The accountant will also be involved, because great care has to be taken to ensure that customers are not given too much credit, thereby incurring an excessive proportion of bad debts.

Bearing these differences in mind, the Sales Office may be regarded as the administrative centre for the marketing organisation. Without full information on the market, individual customers and products, the sales managers and representatives cannot operate successfully.

Some of the most important functions to be covered by the Sales Office are as follows:

1. Liaison between the customers and Production.

2. Receiving orders from salesmen and by post and telephone.

3. Checking the creditworthiness of customers before orders are despatched.

4. Preparing despatching instructions for the Forwarding Department (this may be done by a separate Despatch Office).

In the case of a business manufacturing to customers' specifications there may be considerable work involved in preparing the detailed specification.

5. Ensuring that orders are despatched to comply with the delivery promises.

6. Making arrangements for customers to be charged. Pricing and invoicing are often the responsibility of separate departments, especially when the volume of work is large.

7. Keeping records to show the quantities being purchased, analysed by the following bases:

    (a) Customer.
    (b) Products.
    (c) Size of order.
    (d) Sales area.
    (e) Representative.

8. Following up bad debts and any complaints from customers.

9. Arranging for the receipt of entries for competitions, *i.e.* coupons and other means of encouraging increased sales.

10. General office work connected with representatives, their expenses, car hire, and other acts connected with marketing.

Practical illustration

Although a Sales Office may carry out all the above functions (and a few others as well), in practice many variations are found.

A flow chart showing the departments which exist in a large company known by the author is given in Fig. 29. This has been simplified, but it does show the main stages.

PURCHASING OFFICE

The Purchasing Office is always important, and in some companies plays a major role in reaching a high level of efficiency. For example, in a general engineering company hundreds of orders may be placed weekly and, unless they are received when required, production may be held up.

With some companies the Purchasing Officer (or Buyer as he is also called) is also responsible for the Stores. The alternative is for a Stores Controller to be employed. Irrespective of the precise scope of his responsibilities, the Purchasing Agent deals with a number of matters, which are summarised in Chapter VIII.

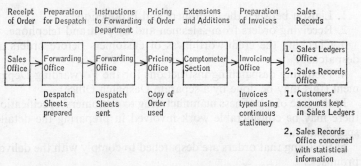

FIG. 29.—*Flow chart showing sales and invoicing procedures*

Purchasing organisation

The organisation will vary from one business to another. This is natural because of the nature and volume of the work. For example, in a flour mill a single man may be able to carry out all the duties listed. On the other hand, in an engineering business a typical organisation is as shown in Fig. 30.

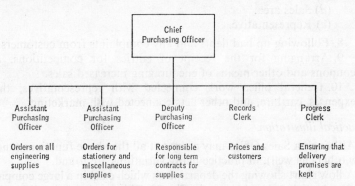

FIG. 30.—*Purchasing office organisation chart*

WAGES OFFICE

The wages and salary administrative procedures for a company have to be planned so that mistakes are kept to a minimum and there is no possibility of fraud taking place. Methods of carrying out the work vary from one business to another. A small business may manage quite well with handwritten records, whereas others with a tremendous volume of work (thousands of employees) may employ a computer. Irrespective of the means employed, the basic principles still apply, which are as follows:

1. Calculate the gross wages or salaries due. In the cases of wages the payment may be computed by reference to a rate per hour (a time rate) or by using an incentive scheme such as piece rates or bonus schemes. Salaries are usually based on a fixed weekly or monthly sum.

2. Make all necessary deductions. These cover deductions required by law and those requested by the employee. In the former category are income tax (P.A.Y.E.) and deductions for graduated pensions and National Insurance.

3. Prepare the pay roll and related pay statements and envelopes.

4. Pay the wages. Usually wages are paid at a certain time each week for the work done in the previous week. Safeguards such as the presence of a supervisor are necessary to ensure that a pay envelope is handed to the correct person.

Salaries are generally paid weekly or monthly into a named banking account. This may also be done for wages, or the payment may be made by cheque, provided the employee agrees to the method. The very obvious advantage of this method is that large volumes of cash do not have to be handled, with the consequent precautions that have to be taken against robbery while transporting the money from the bank. However, many employees are reluctant to turn over to this method.

5. Compile clock cards or other records to show attendance at work. This aspect is covered in the chapter on cost accounting.

6. Compile returns to cover essential facts relating to the labour force:

(a) Wages paid.

(b) Cost analysis sheets to show the division between direct and indirect labour, transfers between departments and other relevant facts.

(c) Absenteeism.

(d) Labour turnover.

7. Co-operate with Government departments and other bodies in supplying information or making payments of income tax, National Insurance, selective employment tax and levies made by training boards.

8. Provide a means of communication whereby important notices can be circulated in pay packets or by other means.

9. Ensure that internal checks and other measures are employed

to prevent the fraudulent payment of wages to fictitious workers and other malpractices, such as improper time recording methods, *e.g.* one man "clocking on" for another employee.

STOCK AND STORES CONTROL

Stock and Stores Control are considered in Chapters VIII and XX. It is important to notice that although this is very much related to Production, the accountancy department is involved, and so is the purchasing function. Great care should be taken to ensure that all aspects are covered in an efficient manner. If not, the whole of the business could be affected.

PRODUCTION OFFICES

The functions covered by the various production offices are given in Part Two of this book. This is a case where responsibility may rest with the Production Manager. However, mention of the main offices is necessary because they are concerned with administrative work; *i.e.* planning and controlling, as opposed to the actual work of producing.

There are four main functions involved in production planning and control—planning, scheduling, despatching and progressing as defined in Chapter VIII. A considerable amount of clerical work is involved in preparing material specifications, parts lists, assembly details, production orders, route cards and other information necessary for carrying out the work in the desired manner and sequence.

"Progressing" can mean the control over planned production and incorporate *feedback*, *i.e.* a system for automatically correcting deviations. Alternatively, the term means the after-the-fact method of chasing orders when they have become overdue. This latter meaning is often the type of progressing employed in general engineering. Usually adequate records and systems are employed to ensure that the work flows through the factory without excessive delays.

The drawing office provides a very necessary link between sales and production. Customers' requirements have to be converted into engineering language by means of drawings. Besides preparation of drawings, means have to be provided for filing copies of drawings and for their reproduction when required.

GENERAL OFFICE SERVICES

The office has to provide a multitude of services to meet the information requirements within the business and also to provide the necessary communication with customers, suppliers, banks, Government organisations and other external bodies. Office machines, methods, systems and procedures have to be provided so that the services are adequate for the business concerned.

There can be no question of invoices, letters and other correspondence being held up for long periods. If this occurs, business may be lost or customers will not pay for goods supplied—some do not settle invoices until the month following their receipt.

Some of the essential services which have to be provided are as follows:

1. Correspondence facilities:

   (a) typing;
   (b) dictation.

2. Duplicating:

   (a) duplicating machines;
   (b) photocopying;
   (c) miscellaneous techniques.

3. Telephones and related services.
4. Office machines:

   (a) accounting machines:

      (i) computers
      (ii) punched card accounting equipment;
      (iii) ledger posting machines.

   (b) calculating machines;
   (c) adding machines.

5. Filing.

These are explained briefly in the sections which follow, except computers, which were covered earlier.

Correspondence facilities

(a) *Typing.* The typewriting services provide an essential means of preparing letters and other vital correspondence. Although some equipment, such as addressing, printing, billing and accounting machines, can produce invoices, statements and standardised circulars, the bulk of the work must still rely on conventional typing.

Different types of machines are available, and they may be operated manually or by electric motor after the appropriate keys have been touched. Various special requirements can be covered, such as an extra-large carriage for typing accounting statements or special type for mathematical formulae. It is also possible to obtain a machine which is capable of producing notices or statements with different sizes or styles of type—known as a vari-typer. Some typewriters can be linked with data-processing equipment or similar arrangement so that details are typed automatically from the information given on punched tape.

For general purposes the best arrangement of typing facilities is a *typing pool,* whereby typists are placed in a central office under a supervisor. There are many advantages claimed for this arrangement:

1. Better planning and execution of work and more flexibility.
2. Higher productivity, because all typists can be given a reasonable work load.
3. Isolation of noise.
4. More effective supervision.
5. Aids the training of junior typists.
6. Centralisation, so that the facilities can be shared by a number of departments.
7. Facilitates the use of dictating equipment.

The main *disadvantages* are the loss of specialised knowledge of a department—one typist attached to a particular department and not being in a "pool" can become an expert on that type of work. There is also the fact that an executive requires a secretary to deal with appointments, type confidential letters, and carry out similar duties which are not of a routine nature.

Many companies adopt a compromise and use a typing pool for all general typing and invoicing but also provide secretaries for senior executives.

(*b*) *Dictation.* Whether dictation should be to a machine or a secretary is a problem similar to whether work should be done in a typing pool. There is little doubt that dictating machines can provide an excellent service at much lower cost. Moreover, there is greater flexibility; if necessary, a portable machine can be used for dictating on-the-spot reports after meetings have taken place or when a function is being carried out.

For routine work, such as commercial correspondence, salesmen's reports, purchase orders, and the summarising of minutes of meetings, dictating machines can be invaluable. Basically, this machine is a recording device which uses discs, belts, tapes, or sheets which are made of a special material. There are two basic processes—the actual *dictating* and the *transcribing* by the typist. In addition, detailed instructions have to be provided for the typist to follow. When the recording has been used the material is erased so that the process can be repeated.

When using dictating machines it is important to provide facilities for transferring the recordings (tapes, etc.) to the typing pool together with any related correspondence or documents. Very often the latter are essential for addresses or other details, so a messenger service must be provided which is quick and efficient. Another problem is when confidential information is involved. Tapes and other recording media can be played back by unauthorised personnel, with the result that there are information leaks which may cause difficulties.

Duplicating

(*a*) *Duplicating machines* are made in various sizes to deal with different volumes of work. Basically there are two main methods:

1. *Stencil duplicator*, which employs a master through which ink is pressed while a drum is rotated.

2. *Spirit duplicator*, which employs a master on which an imprint is made by typing on an hectographic carbon. When the drum is rotated spirit in the machine dissolves the carbon and the image is transferred to the paper fed through the machine.

The stencil duplicator can produce upwards of a 1000 copies from one master. On the other hand, the spirit duplicator is satisfactory only for, say, 100 copies. This depends very much upon the quality of the master and the way the machine is operated—some machines should be able to produce 500 readable copies, but in practice a much smaller number is usually obtained.

There are other machines, such as the *offset lithographic duplicator*, which provide very superior facilities for many thousands of copies from one master.

In addition, refinements are possible on the two basic methods. Different colours can be introduced, and the manufacturers of the machines will produce "electronic stencils" for such matters as letter headings, thus giving a very cheap service for duplicated work.

The spirit duplicator can be operated by an unskilled operator, and the masters can be prepared by hand very easily. For this reason the method offers considerable flexibility for producing instructions, notes and other correspondence within an office or factory.

Mention should also be made of duplicating facilities which are available through *addressing machines* which employ prepared plates. The latter are fed through the machine and automatically print standard information on envelopes, invoices, statements, pay slips, clock cards and other essential forms.

In addition, there are various devices or machines available for completing a number of copies of forms by writing or typing on the top copy. Registers for preparing receipts, delivery notes, despatch notes, and other forms are commonly used in industry. In addition, a type-writer can be adapted to take *continuous stationery*, whereby a number of copies can be produced, special "carbon arrangements" being made so that carbon papers do not have to be handled for each set of forms.

(*b*) *Photocopying machines* may also be used for reproducing a number of copies from an original. There are various methods available, each with its own advantages relating to the quality of the copy and the cost per print. A major advantage is that a copy can be made in seconds without a typist or other person carrying out any work. For this reason a photocopying machine provides a very good method for reproducing when only a few copies are required. Generally, when more than twelve copies are necessary a duplicating machine should be employed.

Since duplicating masters can be prepared by using a photocopying machine, the combination of the two methods is very necessary. A further possibility is the preparation of overhead projector masters, whereby a document or chart can be photocopied and then projected on to a screen by means of an *overhead projector*—rather like the normal film projector, but which has been adapted to make it much more flexible.

Finally, under this heading, the developments in *microfilming* are very important. Records can be reproduced on miniature-size films, around 3000 letters being possible on a hundred feet of 16-mm film.

Telephones and related services

The telephone service provides a vital link with customers and others outside a business. There should be a switchboard manned by a properly trained telephonist. The number of lines and extensions should be adequate for the size and nature of the company concerned.

Quite often the G.P.O. system is inadequate for internal communication and, in any case, care should be taken not to overload the switchboard. A possible additional service is an automatic *internal* telephone system, whereby departments and managers can be contacted simply by dialling the appropriate number and without going through a switchboard.

The telephone systems may be augmented by means of *loudspeaker intercommunication systems* of a suitable type. Transistorised instruments can provide a cheap and yet very effective speaker system with extensions to a number of offices.

Related communication systems include *teleprinters*, which may be supplied by the G.P.O., when it is known as the *Telex* service. A message can be typed on to a machine, and it is then transmitted to a teleprinter in the company to which the message is being sent (each subscriber is given a code number).

An important new development is *close-circuit* television. This is likely to play an important role in production and financial control systems. As yet, full advantage has not been taken of the enormous potential which is offered. Banks, stockbrokers and the Stock Exchange have experimented with the use of the facility.

The *postal system* is one of the most important communication services within a business. Suitable equipment should be provided to deal with incoming mail—opening envelopes, stamping in, and distributing to the appropriate offices; in addition, outgoing mail has to be folded and put in envelopes and then franked by the postal franking machine.

Office machines

In the limited space available little more than an indication of the main types of machines can be shown. However, further details can be found in books which deal specifically with office management. The principal machines are as follows:

1. Punched-card accounting machines.—As indicated, this system uses stiff cards on which information is recorded by punching holes which represent figures. For example, code numbers may be employed to indicate products, where manufactured, costs involved and other information. The cards are divided into sections to cover the facts to be recorded.

The principal stages are as follows:

(*a*) Punching the cards.
(*b*) Verifying the punching by repeating the operation.
(*c*) Sorting.
(*d*) Tabulating and printing statements.

Machines are available for carrying out these operations, and some companies have developed very comprehensive systems for stores control, costing and similar areas. The main problem is the storing of the cards and lack of flexibility when compared with a computer.

2. Ledger-posting machines.—Many types of posting machines are available. They can be used to post a number of documents simultaneously—ledger card, proof or control card, and statement for each customer. With a trained operator, records can be compiled quickly and accurately. The more advanced machines incorporate electronic devices which can carry out many operations very rapidly and quite automatically.

3. Calculating machines.—These range from hand-operated machines, with relatively limited capacities, to automatic machines which can calculate very rapidly. Some machines also print the figures, whereas others give the solutions in dials—the information is transferred on to paper, the dials are then cleared and the new calculation takes place.

4. Adding machines.—Adding machines may be electrically or manually operated. With a little practice a clerk can use a machine quite efficiently. Moreover, a high standard of accuracy can be obtained which is not affected by the degree of concentration being exercised. When estimating, costing, or similar activities are involved, the clerk concerned can often justify his own machine, which is kept on his desk.

Filing

Except by those who operate them, there is a tendency for filing systems to be taken for granted. Only when a letter or other piece of correspondence has gone astray is any interest taken in a system.

The keeping of documents, forms, letters, and copies of all types of correspondence affects efficiency to such an extent that filing should be planned carefully and operated in an efficient manner. A system should be economical in terms of running costs and initial capital costs. Moreover, it should be simple to understand and be quite flexible.

Records, when needed, should be readily available without a great deal of trouble. One of the problems of the fully centralised system is that there may be a delay when a file is required.

The classification employed for records should be appropriate for the subject matter to be kept. Generally, this is a case of deciding the *normal heading under which the correspondence will be considered* by those who will have to refer to it. This should be the guiding factor when selecting the appropriate classification. In addition, the costs of purchase and operation should also be considered.

The main methods of classifying records are as follows:

1. Alphabetical.—Records are kept in strict alphabetical order. Generally suitable for filing by person or place names.

2. Numerical.—Records are placed in numerical sequence—1, 2, 3, 4, etcetera, with suitable divisions and subdivisions being provided by a decimal system—1·112, 1·113. This method is popular when filing accounting records such as cost statements.

3. Geographical.—Records are divided into geographical areas such as North-East, South-East, South-West. They may then be subdivided on the basis of an alphabetical or numerical classification.

4. Subject.—Accounts, Costing, Buying, Engineering and other main headings can be employed. Again, some form of classification, such as alphabetical, will be employed within each main division.

As indicated, a system may employ a combination of two or more of the above methods. In addition, it is quite common for the date to be considered. For example, all correspondence for Mr A. Adams would be put in strict date order within his file which would probably be within an alphabetical classification.

Many types of *equipment* are available, the most popular being the three- or four-drawer filing cabinets. Suspension files with index strips are a very necessary part of a filing system. An index should be available to show how the records are classified, thus making knowledge of the operation of the system available to all concerned.

EXAMINATION QUESTIONS

1. In a medium-sized company the duties of a company secretary may be extensive. Enumerate these duties with reference to external relations, the board of directors and the internal administration of a business.

2. The buyer must obtain all goods and materials for use in the manufacture of the company's products at the cheapest possible price. Comment on this statement.

3. (*a*) What information does the cost accountant require from the manager of the production department in order to produce the budgets?

(*b*) How can the cost accountant help the manager to produce the information?

4. Set out the points which you consider should be included in a company buying policy for the guidance of the purchasing officer.

5. A company receives 3000 invoices per month, covering 5000 items. Each item is allocated to an account code, of which, for invoice analysis purposes, there are 30. Accounting machines are used to determine the totals chargeable to each code.

Give details of the most economical alternative system, not based on accounting machines, which would produce the same, or a similar, analysis.

Adding machines are available, if required. You may ignore the creditor's ledger aspect.

6. Describe what you consider to be the two most economical methods of reproducing about seven copies from originals. (Ignore the possibilities of using carbon paper.)

7. An organisation and methods unit is about to be set up, but it has not yet been decided to whom it should be responsible.

Discuss the relative advantage of making it responsible to: (a) the chief accountant; (b) the managing director.

5. A company receives 1000 invoices per month, covering 5000 items. Each item is allocated to an account code, of which, for invoice analysis purposes, there are 50. Accounting machines are used to determine the total chargeable to each code.

Give details of the most economical alternative system, not based on accounting machines, which would produce the analysis of number of debits. Adding machines are available, if required. You may assume one audit/editing ledger sheet.

6. Describe what you consider to be the two most economical methods of reproducing about seven copies from original. (Ignore the possibilities of using carbon paper.)

7. An organisation and methods unit is about to be set up, but it has not yet been decided to whom it should be responsible.

Discuss the relative advantages of making it responsible to: (a) the chief accountant; (b) the managing director.

PART THREE

PERSONNEL MANAGEMENT AND WAGES ADMINISTRATION

CHAPTER XII

GROWTH OF INDUSTRIAL RELATIONS

THE rapid change-over in Britain from an agricultural to an industrial nation in the late eighteenth and nineteenth centuries, accompanied by the movement into towns and an accelerated growth of population, had a profound effect on the life and social structure of the people. Basic industry expanded greatly, new trades arose and fortunes were made. Conditions in factories and towns were oppressive and overcrowded. Though from the fourteenth to the sixteenth century the State had set out to regulate wages and industrial training and employment generally, the growing complexity of manufacturing techniques made these laws obsolete by the mid-eighteenth century, although they were not in fact repealed until 1813.

In the eagerness of manufacturers to gain wealth and power to supplant the landed aristocracy it is hardly surprising that the fostering of good relations with employees was largely ignored. The development of organisations of workers to negotiate with employers on a more equal footing is an outstanding feature of the Industrial Revolution— so much so that the twentieth century has seen the formation of associations of employers as a balancing factor. Modern industrial relations are based upon this mutual acceptance and general respect.

This chapter outlines the main growth of present-day collective bargaining, commencing with a brief survey of the history of trade unions and employers' associations. For a more comprehensive and authoritative analysis of the whole subject the student is directed to the *Handbook of Industrial Relations*, issued by H.M.S.O.

TRADE UNIONISM

A trade union is a voluntary and continuous organisation of workers in a trade or group of trades for collective bargaining with employers to fix wages and conditions of labour. The modern trade union movement is a product of the factory system and capitalism which divided the industrial population into two main classes—employers and employees.

ORIGINS OF UNIONS

Some historians attempt to trace the beginnings of trade unionism to the mediaeval craft gilds, but these differed almost entirely from trade unions. The gild system included the compulsory membership of all connected with the craft—masters, journeymen and apprentices—and

there was no barrier to prevent apprentices ultimately becoming masters. The system was based on co-operation and integration of interest,
whereas trade unions arose because of the fundamental antagonism of
interests in employer–employee relationships. Even when the gilds
were in their prime there did not exist a large body of permanent wage-
earners as at present, so trade unions in the modern sense could not
arise.

However, when the gild system broke up the masters associated into
livery companies and journeymen formed their own gilds. This more
closely paralleled the (respective) employers' associations and trade
unions of today, especially as the journeymen's gilds strove for similar
objects of improved working conditions and payment. But by the end
of the sixteenth century both forms of organisation had virtually
disappeared.

Between the sixteenth and eighteenth centuries there were occasional
disputes between the merchants and the domestic workers, when local
weavers combined temporarily under the stress of a strong grievance.
However, it was impossible for scattered workers to form lasting
associations and so the beginnings of trade unionism arose in the towns
where the concentration of people enabled groups of workers to unite
for common action.

Early in the eighteenth century there existed in practically every town
various trade clubs (or associations of workmen) in skilled occupations
like printing, weaving and tailoring. They were formed originally to
enforce apprenticeship laws and provide mutual assistance during
unemployment and sickness, rather than to make demands for improved
conditions from the masters. But in the second half of the eighteenth
century these clubs grew bigger and tended to band together in growing
industrial towns to become associations of factory operatives capable
of staging a successful strike to back up the defence of their rights.

COMBINATION ACTS

Until the late eighteenth century any association aiming at any legal
object (such as the enforcement of the *Statute of Artificers and Apprentices, 1563*) was safe from the law courts, and petitions from such
associations were usually received sympathetically by the Government.
The fact that the State fixed wages, in theory at least, made illegal any
attempt on the part of the workers to alter the normal rate; and any
association which aimed at raising wages, reducing hours of work or
improving work conditions generally could be proceeded against as
conspiracy "in restraint of trade." Usually, however, trade clubs and
trade associations of all kinds were tolerated during the eighteenth
century unless they became particularly offensive to employers or the
Government. In fact with the change from domestic to factory labour
the Elizabethan laws fixing wages and enforcing apprenticeships were
repealed.

The effect of the French Revolution in 1789 was to upset this accepted pattern of labour relations for years to come because it alarmed the Government into fearing a similar event in England. During the last decade of the century very stringent measures were taken; in 1794 *Habeas Corpus* was suspended and an arrested man could be held for more than twenty-four hours before being brought to trial; in 1796 seditious meetings (likely to incite revolt and conspiracy) were banned; in 1797 oath-taking other than for the normal working of law was punishable; and in 1799 a *Combination Act* was passed forbidding the establishment of any group of workmen to attempt to decrease hours of work or increase wages. (In 1800 this ban was extended to employers also.)

The main effect of the *Combination Acts* was to leave the workers unprotected. But many unions still existed either underground, perhaps as friendly societies, or more openly, since skilled workers were virtually irreplaceable and not likely to experience severe reprisals at the hands of the justices of the peace (often employers themselves).

Nevertheless, much suffering occurred, especially in the developing industrial towns in the north and particularly in the period of depression and unemployment after the Napoleonic Wars. Trade union organisa-tion would have been a useful outlet for grievances in the bitter years after 1815.

The ultimate repeal of the *Combination Acts* in 1824 was primarily the result of agitation by Francis Place, a Radical leader and a tailor in the Charing Cross Road, London. He spent most of the decade collecting evidence that under the cover of the anti-combination law employers were not infrequently threatening imprisonment if lower wages were not accepted. He argued that a Government which believed in individual liberty was not justified in disallowing workers the liberty to combine.

With the aid of Joseph Hume, chairman of a Parliamentary committee on the subject, the agitation by Place led to the 1824 repeal. Almost at once a host of trade unions arose and strikes occurred so that, in 1825, Parliament passed a qualifying amendment limiting the activities of combinations to peaceful bargaining about hours and wages, without "intimidation, molestation and obstruction" to persuade a workman to join, or to force an employer to change the conduct of his business. Thus, whether or not the use of the strike was ruled to be legal depended on how the judges interpreted these vague words. Unions could now exist, but were unable to take action unless they were prepared for prosecution.

REVOLUTIONARY TRADE UNIONISM

Industrial conditions following the Napoleonic Wars were bad. Industry was dislocated by the transition to peace and slow recovery of markets, while the extension of machinery displaced, or reduced the wages of, thousands of workers. Great social unrest was created and workers were willing to join almost any movement which promised improvement. Strikes, organised by the new unions, failed to halt the downward movement of wages and attempts were made to establish national unions for greater bargaining power—for cotton spinners in 1829 and building craftsmen in 1832.

The particular focus of working-class interest was the short-lived Grand National Consolidated Trades Union of 1834. It arose after the 1832 Reform Bill had extended the franchise only to merchants, businessmen and well-to-do farmers. The main aim was openly revolutionary and was to overthrow the existing order by organising a general strike. Robert Owen, a philanthropic mill-owner, used all his energies and most of his fortune in the movement and within a few weeks its membership was over a half-million. But it soon suffered an equally spectacular decline.

The main reason for its failure was that the Grand National was too ambitious. The mass of workers were illiterate and underpaid, so the union lacked financial stability and co-ordination. (Even the leaders could not agree about aims and methods.) Employers reacted with lock-outs, which usually ended in employees giving in owing to lack of funds, or by compelling workers to sign "The Document" stating that they were not members of the national union.

But perhaps the most famous and demoralising action was the successful prosecution of six Tolpuddle agricultural labourers for taking an illegal oath (under the 1797 Act) in the forming of a local branch of the Grand National Union. In 1834 they were sentenced to seven years transportation to Australia, though they were brought back before completing it as a result of public outcry.

This monolithic union both began and ended the period of revolutionary trade unions and taught two main lessons. The first was that even a huge union could collapse almost overnight if it lacked funds and a strong central organisation. The second was that the function of a union should be simply to look after workmen in their normal employment and not to mix political and industrial demands. After the failure of the Grand National Consolidated Trades Union, working-class interest in the 1840s turned towards smaller labour groupings, but more particularly to the Ten Hours Movement of factory reform and the political agitation of Chartism.

NEW MODEL UNIONISM

During the most outstanding period of Victorian prosperity—the third quarter of the nineteenth century—there was a steady improvement in the condition of the working classes. Wages rose considerably and the trade union movement recovered and grew quite strong. But the "new model unionism" was entirely different from an attempt to overthrow and reconstruct society. The new unionists accepted society as it was and bargained with employers for better wages and working conditions—thus seeking respectability.

It was in this period that the structure of modern trade unionism was built up. The basis was improved organisation, the principal features of this being the creation of a body of full-time officials, continuity of membership and improved financial strength by combining industrial and friendly benefit activities to maintain and attract the membership.

The best example of the "new model" was the Amalgamated Society of Engineers formed in 1851 out of several independent labour-group-ings. Its membership rose to over ten thousand—all skilled engineering craftsmen, the aristocracy of labour in the new industrial age. Each member paid one shilling a week and was entitled to friendly benefits in times of unemployment, sickness and old age. It was a national union, the leaders in the central executive being full-time paid men, moderate and non-revolutionary in outlook, and becoming skilled negotiators. Only the executive of the A.S.E. could call a strike.

Some fifty of these new model unions grew up in a wide range of skilled trades in the 1850s and 1860s. The leaders of the five biggest—engineers, boiler-makers, iron-founders, carpenters, and joiners—formed in London an unofficial "cabinet of labour," the Junta. They met informally and decided matters of trade union policy, though the northern industrial unions were suspicious and critical of the arrangement. The Junta—the forerunner of the T.U.C., founded in 1868—agreed not to spend large sums on unnecessary strikes, but to gain their ends by conciliation and peaceful bargaining. They agitated for political reform, hoping that an extension of the franchise would secure their economic aims and better educational standards generally.

Most important of all the Junta pressed the Government to improve the legal status of unions and workers. They influenced the passing of the *Master and Servant Act* of 1867. This gave the employee breaking his contract fairer treatment since his offence was now considered a civil case and no longer a criminal one, unless injury to life or damage to property were involved.

But in the same year, just at the time when unions were developing their strength, a legal decision and criminal outrage threatened complete disfavour. The Boilermakers' Society (through its secretary, Hornby) tried to prosecute one of its branch treasurers, Close, for absconding with £24 union funds. Both the local magistrate and the Appeals Court judge refused to admit the right of the trade union to sue in the law courts because, though permitted to exist since 1824, it was not pro-tected under the 1855 *Friendly Societies Act* since it had objects "in restraint of trade." As if the realisation that union funds were not legally protected against dishonest officials were not enough, a series of violent outrages against non-striking or "blackleg" Sheffield cutlers in 1866–67 caused Government and public concern about the value of the increasingly powerful labour organisations.

A Royal Commission was set up in 1867 to investigate the trade union movement very thoroughly. The Junta carefully organised its evidence and received a fair hearing, so that the commission's Report published in 1869 generally favoured an existence of unions and legal protection of their funds. A provisional Act to cover the latter point was passed in the same year and in the *Trade Union Act* of 1871 the organisations were given full legal status.

But while the Junta had succeeded in protecting union funds, and showed that the A.S.E. was far more typical of the movement than the murdering cutlers, the 1869 Report created another problem for it by regarding the picketing of non-strikers as "interference in the rights of workers." This resulted in the passing of the *Criminal Law Amendment Act* in 1871—repealing the 1859 Act (which had permitted picketing) and thus making any form of coercion a criminal offence.

The Junta at once organised resistance, especially among householders in towns who had received the vote in the 1867 *Reform Act*. In the 1874 election, union supporters voted against the outgoing Liberal Government under Gladstone and helped to put the Tory Party under Disraeli into power. The new administration passed two important Acts for the movement in 1875; first the *Conspiracy and Protection of Property Act* which legalised strikes and peaceful picketing as well as laying down that no action was illegal when performed by a group of people unless it were illegal when carried out by an individual. The second bill passed was the *Employer and Workman Act* which made employer and employee equal in the eyes of the law.

The Parliamentary activity of the early 1870s greatly encouraged the growth of trade unions and by the middle of the decade they had become an accepted and respected social unit of Victorian Britain. In 1874 the six-year-old T.U.C. claimed to represent over one million workers—but this was only about one-tenth of the labour force, predominantly those in crafts and semi-skilled trades. The scene was now set for the extension of unionism to unskilled workers and on an industrial basis.

INDUSTRIAL UNIONS

The first main attempt to form a combination of all workers in one industry was in 1872 when Joseph Arch inspired the Agricultural Labourers' Union. However, its initial success was ended by the farming depression in the late 1870s and the strong opposition of the propertied classes.

From the 1880s trade unionism did spread among the vast mass of industrial workers, but since wages and subscriptions were generally lower than in the craft trades and unions, friendly benefits were subservient to the pressing needs of better pay and conditions. In 1888 the match-making girls came out on strike and gained higher wages. The following year gas-workers under John Burns obtained a reduction in hours without resorting to a strike. Burns and Tom Mann organised a work-stoppage which immobilised the Port of London for four weeks to back up the dockers' demand for a minimum wage of sixpence an hour. The public was greatly sympathetic and subscribed £48,000 for the striking dock-workers, almost two-thirds of this figure coming from Australia.

As a result of the success of organised action by workers involved in a public utility and overseas trade, the General Railway Workers Union and Miners Federation of Great Britain was formed and helped union-membership to increase to two million by the end of the century. "New unionism" was under way (involving the combination of unskilled workers) and with it the growth of the Labour Party and its intellectual equivalent, Fabian Socialism.

In 1899 the T.U.C. decided to attempt the co-ordination of co-operative and socialist organisations to promote labour representation in the Commons. This was soon to be needed, because in 1901 a final legal judgment in the House of Lords held that the Amalgamated Society of Railway Servants owed the Taff Vale Railway Company £23,000 for loss of income resulting from a strike. A legal principle had been established that even if unions won a strike they were liable to pay financial damages to the employers.

In 1906 the election of twenty-nine Labour M.P.s, together with pledges already made by most Liberal M.P.s, influenced the Liberal Government to pass the *Trade Disputes Act*, which freed unions from financial responsibility for civil actions. But three years later the union movement in general suffered yet another blow, involving the Amalgamated Society of Railway Servants in particular.

The Labour Party was financed by union levies and Mr W. V. Osborne, a railway worker, obtained a House of Lords judgment in 1909 to the effect that such a levy for the purpose of obtaining representation in Parliament was illegal. For four years most of the larger unions were legally restrained from contributing to the Labour Party. Then the *Trade Union Act* of 1913 allowed non-industrial union activities if approved by a majority of members and, if political, financed by a separate levy (from the industrial one) from which any member could "contract-out"—*i.e.* state that he did not wish to contribute.

Just before the First World War there was much industrial discontent and hostility between workers and employers, especially on the railways and in the mines and docks. In 1910 over 30,000 miners in the Rhondda valleys went on strike, involving ten days of rioting when troop movements took place and police reinforcements were sent from London to restore order. In the same year the Port of London was brought to a standstill, but the dockers gained an increase of eightpence an hour. In 1912 the miners again struck, this time for a national minimum wage: in the end the Prime Minister promised legislation, but established a minimum wage by district only. In 1913 the National Union of Railwaymen was formed and the "triple alliance" of miners, railwaymen and transport workers arose to present joint demands to all employers. However, the onset of the First World War postponed such action until the 1920s.

POLITICAL AND ECONOMIC STRENGTH

The First World War and the following boom created stronger unions, arising from amalgamations and a doubled membership, particularly due to the newly-accepted industrial role of women. In 1920 the T.U.C. created a General Council to guide its overall affairs, and one year later the Transport and General Workers Union was formed.

But depression and unemployment were setting in and unions had to struggle more to maintain conditions than try to improve them. A reduction in the wages of miners in 1926 led to a ten-day General Strike in all vital industries, though the miners stayed out for over six months.

The strong feelings of the Government at what was considered to be intimidation by unions led to the passing of the *Trade Disputes and Trade Union Act* in 1927. Strikes and lock-outs which went beyond a trade dispute or intended to coerce the Government or harm the community at large were declared illegal, as was financial and picketing support of them. Members of the Civil Service could not belong to a union with political aims or a union affiliated to one with such aims. Perhaps most far-reaching and unpopular of all, "contracting-out" was replaced by "contracting-in"—union members were now legally assumed not to want to subscribe to political funds unless they signed a specific statement of such an intention. This, of course, reversed the 1913 Act and was most unpopular with the unions and the Labour Party. One of the first actions of the party after coming to power after the Second World War was to repeal the Act (in 1946). Today "contracting-out" is the law.

During the severe inter-war depression total union membership grew, but more so than its strength. A period of unemployment will inevitably give employers the overall whip-hand whereas a boom will tend to reverse the position, since unions have greater financial and membership strength to back their demands. This latter trend has been evident since the Second World War and was perhaps emphasised by six years of Labour rule together with automatic union membership on the boards of nationalised industries.

It has been claimed that trade unions have become too strong in the economy, too inflexible and restrictive in their attitudes, too prone to sectional disputes or domination and have largely outlived their purpose. There may well be an element of truth in some of these assertions but it must be borne in mind that the history of trade unions has been one of a long uphill fight for acceptance and recognition. Yet another House of Lords decision in January 1964 ruled that a former member of the Draughtsmen's and Allied Technicians' Association was entitled to damages, arising from the threat of union officials to BOAC to strike (in contravention of a prior contract) unless the "closed shop" were preserved. This judgment would have limited future rights to strike owing to liability to pay damages, especially in the case of a closed shop or strike-precluding contracts with employers. However, the *Trade Disputes Act, 1965*, provided that an act done in contemplation or furtherance of a trade dispute would not be actionable if it involved only a threat to break a contract of employment or to induce another to break his contract of employment. This restored to trade unions a protection which they had believed the *Trade Disputes Act, 1906*, already provided.

TRADE UNIONS TODAY

The results of the history of trade unionism can be seen in the types of organisations existing today. The earliest development was that of the skilled craft unions associated on an occupational basis; later the general labouring and unskilled classes were organised largely on industrial scales; most recently, associations have arisen of clerical, supervisory, administrative and professional workers.

At the end of 1967 there were 345 *registered* trade unions with 8,472,000 members, which represents 87% of total membership of all unions. This represents a decline of 113,000 during 1967, due mainly to contraction in trade unions representing railway and other transport workers, general workers and miners. Nearly half of the total membership was contained in the six largest unions—the Transport and General Workers Union, the Amalgamated Engineering and Foundryworkers Union, the National Union of General and Municipal Workers, the National Union of Mineworkers, the Union of Shop, Distributive and Allied Workers, and the Electrical Trades Union.

The basic unit of organisation is usually the branch, lodge or chapel, to which all members belong, and based upon locality or work-place. The shop-steward enrols members and acts as their representative if any problem arises. In most large national unions the main problem is to reconcile and combine the efficiency of a strong central administration with the principle of democratic control—to this end regional, district and area committees meet regularly. Smaller unions may affiliate into federations on an industry basis, usually for negotiations with employers.

The overall co-ordinating body and centre of the movement has been the Trade Union Congress, since its inception in 1868. Its basic aim is to promote the interests of its (present) 160 affiliated unions, 8·72 million* members in approximately 175 organisations, and to improve the economic and social conditions of all workers. It thus deals with problems affecting particular trades and general industry at home as well

* Some unions affiliated to the T.U.C. are not registered unions.

as voicing opinions on broader international policy. The T.U.C. is appropriately recognised by the Government as the official means of consultation between its departments and organised employees.

A General Council is elected every year to carry out the decisions of the annual one-week Congress, to which delegates are sent by member-organisations. The Council also watches economic and social trends, provides educational services, mediates in inter-union disputes and broadly represents the T.U.C. during the other 51 weeks of the year. For example, early in 1964 in response to the growing demand for larger industrial unions in modern conditions (arguably to offset possible jealously-guarded parochial differentiations), the General Council invited unions in seven industries, metal-trades, iron and steel, railways, retail distribution, building, the Post Office and part of cotton textiles, to discuss with it means of achieving closer working relations or, preferably, amalgamations. Such rationalisation aimed at one organisation to cover skilled, unskilled and white-collar workers in one industry have made most progress in mining, the railways, agriculture, and iron and steel. It has had less success in the engineering and electrical trades, although in 1968 the Foundry-makers merged with the Engineers to form the Amalgamated Engineering and Foundryworkers Union.

OVERALL ACHIEVEMENTS OF TRADE UNIONISM

The major achievements of the trade union movement have been the reduction of hours and improvement of wages and working conditions for the British labour force as a whole. The principal methods have been collective bargaining, with resort to strikes in cases of strong feeling or deadlock. It has exerted great pressure on Parliament through the Labour Party, which grew from the movement, or through the Trades Union Congress, which is the vigilant and constantly active campaigner for labour interests. It has politically educated the working classes by supporting the Workers Education Association and left-wing newspapers, as well as training trade union officials in responsibility and management. This has led to political careers of outstanding merit, as in the case of Ernest Bevin.

EMPLOYERS' ASSOCIATIONS

Organisations of employers date back to the Middle Ages. They dealt almost entirely with trade, until the late-nineteenth-century growth of the unions made the widening of the employer's sphere of interest and combination necessary. Today there are three main types of association, dealing with customers (on trading matters), employees (on working conditions) or a combination of both functions. They are generally organised on an industrial basis though some are sectional or local. There are at present about 80 National Federations, or combinations of local groups on a national scale.

On the whole there has been less need for, or difficulty in the organisation of, employers' associations as compared with employees' unions. The former are not involved in social benefits, political matters, or early consultations concerning wage alterations. They seem to be generally less concerned with discipline and publicity-seeking, though their representations to the Government and activities on Wages Councils are usually equal to those of the unions. Employers' associations are not really concerned with education, though they may sponsor research and apprenticeship schemes.

In 1919 the National Confederation of Employers' Organisations was formed to co-ordinate actions of local and national Federations dealing with industrial relations. It was later renamed the British Employers' Confederation and should be distinguished from the National Union of Manufacturers (1915) and the Federation of British Industries (1916), which dealt largely with trading matters in secondary industry. In July 1965 the *Confederation of British Industry* (C.B.I.) was incorporated by Royal Charter by amalgamating the B.E.C., the F.B.I. and the National Association of British Manufacturers. The C.B.I. deals with all matters affecting the interests of organised employers and its membership consists of 13,000 individual firms, 280 trade associations and over 50 employers' associations.

The C.B.I. is now virtually the counterpart of the T.U.C., but without the latter's power over constituent members, nor its range of services. The Confederation is the accepted channel of consultation between the Government and employers.

COLLECTIVE BARGAINING AND JOINT NEGOTIATION

Negotiation between representatives of employers and workers to determine conditions of labour is a development of the Industrial Revolution. Its success has lain with the moral strength rather than the legal force of agreements.

During the past 70 years, legislation has been passed to facilitate the peaceful settlement of industrial disputes between employers and unions. The basic principle of Parliamentary action has been to maintain and improve the existing system of voluntary collective bargaining rather than impose a new one—except temporarily in time of war. Though the provisions of the Acts are largely permissive and the decisions of the various independent tribunals which may result are not legally binding, such decisions are normally accepted.

In the *Conciliation Act, 1896*, the Board of Trade was empowered to:

1. Enquire into the causes and circumstances of a dispute.
2. Consider and apply means of bringing the parties together.
3. Appoint a conciliator or conciliation board if either party requests it.
4. Appoint an arbitrator or arbitration board if both parties apply.

These powers were later transferred to the Ministry of Labour (now the Department of Employment and Productivity). The operation of the Act was voluntary and perhaps inadequate at first since larger employers sometimes refused to recognise organisations of workers for negotiation purposes. Nevertheless, the services of appointed conciliators and arbitrators have helped to bring the disputing parties together before the resort to industrial action.

The *Trade Boards Acts*, 1909 and 1918 gave the Ministry of Labour power to establish boards to fix minimum wage-rates in badly-paid or "sweated" trades. This particularly affected the virtual survival of the old domestic industry not covered by the nineteenth-century factory legislation, such as shirt-making and tailoring in London's East End. After the Second World War wages councils with wider powers replaced these boards.

There were many industrial disputes in the First World War, despite the *Munitions of War Act, 1915*, which declared strikes and lock-outs in industries concerned in the war effort illegal and introduced compulsory arbitration. In 1916 the Government set up a committee on the relations between employers and employed under J. H. Whitley, then Deputy Speaker of the House of Commons. The principal terms of reference were, firstly, to consider and make suggestions to improve permanently the relationships between employers and workers and, secondly, to recommend means of securing the systematic review and betterment of industrial conditions influencing these relations.

In 1918 the Whitley Committee's Reports were published, based on its stated opinion that compulsory arbitration was not only unacceptable to the parties in a dispute, but failed to prevent work-stoppages and, thus, that further encouragement of voluntary conciliation and arbitration was desirable. To this end five recommendations were made:

1. That joint industrial councils be set up in well-organised industries.

These are now 300 J.I.C.s or equivalent bodies and they vary greatly in structure from coal mining and engineering to Government service, and in scope from negotiation and bargaining to education, training and research. Each Council has representatives from both sides of the industry and collective agreements rely upon the good faith of each side or, with mutual consent, on the decision of an Industrial Court.

2. That works committees, representative of management and workers, be set up in individual establishments and meet regularly on an equal footing to consider matters of mutual interest in the daily life of workers.

This has been carried out with varying, though general, success. The provision of amenities may not be a major part of management in itself, but it is an important factor in overall human relations.

3. That statutory regulation of wages and conditions occur in trades where workers are badly organised.

This involved an amplification of the *Trade Boards Act* of 1909. Between 1945 and 1959 wages councils took over these functions and now determine a minimum wage by negotiation, which the Minister makes legally binding by issuing an Order.

4. The establishment of a permanent and independent Court of Arbitration; and,

5. That the Secretary for Employment and Productivity be empowered to hold enquiries regarding trade disputes.

These recommendations were embodied in the *Industrial Courts Act, 1919*, which is not usually implemented except in the case of a nationwide dispute. The Court is appointed by the Minister (from representatives of both sides of industry and independent persons including at least one woman) as an alternative method to a single arbitrator or Board of Arbitration, and is used only when the normal methods of negotiation are exhausted. As with the other forms of arbitration both disputing parties must express willingness to participate and usually accept the (not legally binding) award made at the end of the hearing.

The same Act allowed for the Minister to set up Courts of Inquiry, composed of *ad hoc* independent members, to examine in the public interest the circumstances of a trade dispute and to report to Parliament. Again, any recommendation made by the Court at the end of the investigation is not legally enforceable but, until the railwaymen's rejection of one in 1951, the rejection of a recommendation was virtually unknown.

During the strains of the Second World War voluntary negotiation through the usual machinery was maintained, but in July 1940, to safeguard war production after the fall of France, the *Conditions of Employment and National Arbitration Order* (Order 1305) introduced compulsory arbitration, or a legally binding decision by a National Arbitration Tribunal after the normal industrial employer–employee and conciliation channels had been exhausted. Part Two of the same Order prohibited strikes and lock-outs unless disputes had been reported to the Minister and not been referred by him for settlement within 21 days of the report.

Order 1305 was disliked by trade unions and was revoked by the outgoing Labour Government in 1951. But the National Joint Advisory Council, also established at the beginning of the war, but in this case to advise the Government on matters of common interest by equivalently-represented employers and workers, continues to meet quarterly under the Secretary for Employment and Productivity.

In conclusion it must be emphasised that most negotiations are settled at district and factory level. Statistics do not tell the full story on the success or failure of the industrial-relations organisation of a country. However, they do give some indication. In the years 1964–66 the total number of working days lost averaged 2,452,000, and 757,000 workers were involved. Industries which had the worst records were coal-mining, docks, shipbuilding and motor vehicle manufacturing. One of the most serious features has been the very large proportion of strikes which have been *unofficial*; *i.e.* not backed by a trade union.

In the same period 1964–66 the total number of stoppages was 2272, of which only 74 were official. The number and seriousness of unofficial strikes, especially in the four industries mentioned, was a principal reason for the establishment of the Royal Commission on Trade Unions and Employers' Associations which reported in June 1968. The position has not eased since then, and a Government White Paper was published in January 1969, and additional legislation is expected at the time of writing.

In 1968 and early in 1969 the results of the Government legislation began to have its effect on industrial relations. In particular, the additional powers given to the Minister for Employment and Productivity were being exercised. Under the provisions of the *Prices and Incomes Acts, 1966* and *1967*, wage awards can be referred to the National Board for Prices and Incomes. This not only has a delaying effect on wage increases but also enables the Government to keep such increases within a predetermined "ceiling level," thus combating inflation. The notable feature of the new approach has been the personal intervention of the Secretary for Employment and Productivity in the industrial disputes which have occurred.

Not all members of trade unions or employers' associations agree with the regulation of the economy. Some move is necessary to improve industrial relations, and especially to reduce the number of unofficial disputes. This fact is acknowledged by all concerned, but the approach required has not been settled. Many years may have to elapse before the problems have been resolved.

EXAMINATION QUESTIONS

1. State the main features in the development of trade union legislation since 1850.

2. State what you understand by:

    (a) the domestic system of industry;

    (b) the factory system of industry.

What factors brought about the change from (a) to (b)?

3. Compare the position of trade unions in the industrial structure today with the position in 1875.

CHAPTER XIII

PERSONNEL MANAGEMENT

IN simple terms "personnel management" means *dealing with employees*. A fuller definition will emerge from the descriptions given below. Here it is necessary to emphasise that there are two aspects:

1. Personnel management which permeates right through the functions of management.

2. The work of the personnel department.

These are considered below. Inevitably, there is an overlapping of these two aspects. The first is the more important; the second exists to make the other more efficient. In some concerns there is no personnel department, but there are still the problems associated with managing.

This and related chapters contain an explanation of the motives of employees, and the techniques employed for selecting managers and workers.

MOTIVES OF EMPLOYEES

An understanding of the motives which inspire men to work is essential for good management. The objectives of the business and those of employees have to be reconciled so that they both aim for a common goal. It was noted earlier that this concept is known as the *Principle of Harmony of Objectives*. Although an employee may be in his job simply to get all he can from it, the good manager channels his efforts in such a way that the company's needs are satisfied.

One of the great difficulties is that people do not have the same needs and, therefore, the same motives. Some very capable employees are quite content to be in routine positions, whereas others, not so capable, wish to be promoted. The desire for financial rewards is very strong in some workers, but is a matter of indifference to those who only wish to earn enough to keep themselves in food and clothing.

An *understanding* of man's basic needs involves study of industrial psychology. Accordingly, the reader who wishes to go beyond the brief summary given below is advised to study a book which specialises in the subject. A summary is given below:

1. Security.—Fear of being out of work in an economy which boasts an unemployment rate of around 2% is no longer as significant as in the pre-1939 era. Nevertheless, there is still a certain anxiety. Take-overs, mergers, redundancy and similar factors all contribute towards a feeling of uncertainty even if this does tend to be rather remote.

2. Status.—There are many who feel that this is a world of status symbols: keeping up with the neighbours in terms of washing machine, television, car, boat and other indications of material wealth. In order to achieve the status desired a man must work or already be wealthy. If work is the means, then it is often necessary to assume greater responsibilities which may also mean obtaining status in the job. Driving a company car, being paid monthly, having a secretary, eating in the executives' dining-room, and not having to account for time spent at work, are all examples of benefits from a higher position.

3. Creative ability and self-expression.—Most human beings pride themselves on being creative. This may come from being able to paint, write, play games or even grow vegetables. If the desire for creative thinking and self-expression can be harnessed to the job the individual and the company benefit.

4. Development.—Acquiring knowledge and skills is a basic requirement which has been present since the first civilisation was created. In this country, formal learning generally commences at the age of five and goes on through school, college and university. Skills are acquired at various stages including training on the job.

5. Stimulation.—The need for a person to vary his pattern of living is now recognised as being an essential factor in the war against frustration. Whether the variation should come within the realm of employment or in leisure periods is a debatable point. Research has indicated that many employees prefer to keep to routine tasks which do not require positive effort; once the job is learnt the process can be repeated over and over again with little or no thought. Quite often operators listen to music or talk while carrying out the necessary work.

6. Acceptability or recognition.—An individual wants to feel that he belongs to a family, a club or a social group within a business. Being accepted within society is very important: the punishment sometimes inflicted on a fellow worker—ostracism or being "sent to Coventry"— is evidence of the attitude to the importance of acceptability.

All six basic needs have to be satisfied or frustration will result. In extreme cases, this could lead to a revolt against society by crimes being committed. If a person can channel much of his energies and interests into his work then most of the needs may be receiving satisfaction. Skilful management means making the most of these requirements within each employee and harnessing them so that they result in greater efficiency.

RESEARCH ON MOTIVATION

Research on the motivation to work has been conducted by various psychologists. A special project carried out in the United States of America is worthy of serious study. The findings are summarised in a book entitled *The Motivation to Work.**

* By Frederick Herzberg, Bernard Mausner and Barbara Bloch Snyderman, published by John Wiley & Sons, New York, 1959.

A full description of the methods employed for obtaining the information cannot be given here. Nine different companies were taken and a group of people interviewed in each. The companies were specially selected so as to represent a cross-section of industry.

The answers obtained from those interviewed were analysed into:

1. *First-level factors.* Those which resulted in a definite attitude. The example given by the authors is promotion.

2. *Second-level factors.* Those which affected a worker's feelings. The act of feeling good, because of promotion and being recognised, is the example given in this case.

These definitions have been simplified and readers who wish to obtain more details are advised to study the book mentioned. They are mentioned here in order to make Table IV (p. 196) more comprehensible. This Table summarises and compares the attitudes of engineers and accountants to their work.

Comparison of the factors reveals, for example, that there are differences in attitudes of the two groups towards advancement, responsibility and the work itself. The authors of the book explain the possible reasons for these differences.

MOTIVATION OF MANAGEMENT

In other chapters are explanations of the importance of earning an adequate profit. How this is to be achieved has to be determined by the board of directors when policy is formulated. There can be no question of sweated labour nor should there be any hint of coddling the workers. Some writers have attempted to distinguish between different types of policy, and one possible classification is as follows:

1. *Provide the requirements laid down by law and no more* (Autocratic exploitation or despotic management).—Managers and directors who urge this policy look upon an employee just as they would a machine tool. Work is expected for which a wage will be paid; no more, no less. The view taken is that additional benefits can only lead to greater demands, which, in the end, will impose a burden which is too large for the company to carry. Ethically, it is argued, there can be no justification for coddling employees because the consumer has to pay for all benefits given through higher prices.

2. *Give all additional benefits possible regardless of cost* (Paternalistic management).—Some companies have gone to the opposite extreme from policy 1. They regard employees as the responsibility of the business and provide housing, shops, medical centres, social clubs, and many fringe benefits. In some instances the workers all live together on an estate owned by the company.

TABLE IV.—ATTITUDES TO WORK

COMPARISON OF ENGINEERS AND ACCOUNTANTS

	Highs		Lows	
	Engineers	Accountants	Engineers	Accountants
First-Level Factors:				
Recognition	33	34	19	17
Achievement	43	38	10	4
Possible growth	3	9	10	6
Advancement	14	27*	9	15
Salary	15	15	18	16
Interpersonal relationships —superior	5	3	13	18
Interpersonal relationships —subordinate	5	6	1	5
Interpersonal relationships —peers	2	4	10	5
Supervision-technical	3	2	22	18
Responsibility	28	17†	4	7
Company policy and administration	3	2	27	37
Working conditions	2	0	9	13
Work itself	33	17†	14	15
Personal life	2	0	5	7
Status	5	4	3	6
Job security	0	1	1	2
Second-Level Factors:				
Recognition	54	64	24	27
Achievement	58	54	21	17
Possible growth	33	49*	32	35
Advancement	4	1	2	2
Responsibility	35	25	6	11
Group feeling	8	12	4	2
Work itself	37	18†	13	12
Status	18	18	9	12
Security	6	6	6	13
Reactions	4	1	40	35
Pride, guilt, inadequacy	14	3	17	10
Salary	15	25	13	14

* Difference between Engineers and Accountants significant at 0·5 level of confidence.

† Difference between Engineers and Accountants significant at 0·1 level of confidence.

(From: The Motivation to Work. Reproduced by kind permission of John Wiley and Sons and Professor Frederick Herzberg.)

3. Provide the requirements which are part of a realistic policy bearing in mind: (*a*) *the law;* (*b*) *trade unions;* (*c*) *government;* (*d*) *efficient management; and* (*e*) *cost* (Participative, consultative or democratic management).—This policy recognises that the employer–employee relationship is a form of quasi-partnership. There is the hope and expectation that by management providing adequate facilities the employees will co-operate to the maximum. The two-sided bargain of a fair day's work for an adequate reward is given full recognition. Through the adoption of a policy of mutual responsibility it is hoped that the *Principle of Harmony of Objectives* will be fully achieved.

Regulations of all kinds have to be complied with in a modern society. These may take a legal form, such as those contained in the *Factories Acts,* or be implied by the Government of the country through its election manifesto or other policy statements. Subsequently the latter may become law, but until that time a company is free to do as it pleases, although any flagrant violation of a principle could result in a law being made.

There is now full recognition that unions are a very important part of society. This is natural since they represent the interests of millions of employees. Once agreements between employers and unions have been made it is advisable to incorporate these into the personnel policy. Quite often an employer, especially on a small scale, can avoid implementing agreements, but this attitude is very short-sighted and in the end will probably lead to industrial unrest.

Frequent references have been made to efficient management. A personnel policy should recognise that unrest among employees can lead to a high labour turnover and strike action. Avoidance of these very costly occurrences is a vital part of the management function; co-operation, teamwork, high morale are all factors which must be sought and maintained. There should be provision of adequate welfare and other facilities, remembering always the two-sided aspect of the bargain. In recent times there has been a great deal of emphasis given to the employee's part; many wage increases have been given on the understanding that productivity must also increase or that a certain restrictive practice will cease. Workers and unions have had to face up to the fact that there is a limit to demands which can be made; management has had to recognise that wage increases have to be met to keep up with the rising cost of living. Joint consultation—the bringing together of ideas, views and difficulties—has done much to remove the barriers which have existed, and still exist to some extent, in industry. A better understanding of the *common* problems by all levels of employees or their representatives is vital to effective management.

The cost of a personnel policy should not be overlooked. A business produces to sell at a profit and consumers have to pay the prices charged. If welfare facilities are excessive then it is likely that prices are excessive.

In Chapter XXII, which covers return on capital employed and capital expenditure decisions, it is shown that any investment made should result in profit being earned. What the over-zealous personnel manager has to remember is that welfare projects often earn no profit at all. They can result in better personnel relations which, indirectly, can result in higher profits, but directly they earn no revenue. There is a need, therefore, to assess the likely costs of any welfare projects and to authorise them only when they can be afforded.

One of the difficulties likely to be encountered with a general statement relating to welfare projects and costs is that the efficient companies are able to provide the facilities, whereas the others are not. Unfortunately, this is true and is behind that all-important question: do companies become efficient by providing all the necessary facilities *or* are they able to provide the facilities because they are efficient? There is no clear-cut answer to this two-part question, but with efficient management it seems clear that adequate facilities can be provided.

While still talking of costs there is a need to emphasise the fact that once a personnel policy has been formulated and put into practice the expense of upkeeping and running the facilities must be accepted at all times. A company should be capable of carrying the burden imposed both in boom times and depression. There is nothing more demoralising than a call to cut back all welfare expenditure, immediately any trading difficulties are experienced.

A fourth policy, which is adopted by a small minority of businesses, is that of *co-partnership* in which policy is determined by employees as equal partners to the employers. In fact, the terms "employee" and "employer" have no part in the scheme of things; instead, all are supposed to join together in managing the business for the common good. Different interpretations are placed on what is meant by co-partnership and there is very little evidence to show that the idea in its fullest form is anything more than an idealistic notion. A few companies have claimed success, but there are so many practical difficulties which become apparent on studying the likely implications, that the method can be dismissed. A diluted form, such as the issue of shares or the payment of bonuses, is a more realistic approach. Employees should participate in policy-making and management, but only in a *consultative capacity*. The actual decisions must be made by those charged with the responsibility for the functions involved; management should be in the hands of managers, not those who are being managed.

From what has been said the reader will have gathered that policy 3 is the one which is recommended. After due consideration has been given to the factors such as legal requirements, agreements, Government policy, efficient management and cost, the *content* of the policy has to be determined. Some of the possibilities for inclusion are outlined in the next section.

CONTENT OF A PERSONNEL POLICY

The principal factors which should be considered when formulating a personnel policy are considered below:

1. Wage and salary structure

Selection of the most appropriate methods for calculating the wages or salaries due is vital to co-operation and high morale. Are time rates to be employed or is some incentive payment to be made? This question must be answered and the factors which influence the decision are considered in Chapter XVI.

2. Organisation and procedure

This factor is related to the section above but is often neglected: the organisation for setting wage and salary scales, and the procedures followed, should be clearly defined. Such matters as the following should be understood by all concerned:

(a) The department responsible for fixing the rates of pay.

(b) Machinery for negotiating pay increases or conditions of employment.

(c) Channels of communication for notifying employees on all matters affecting wages and salaries.

(d) Extent to which the personnel manager should be involved in wage negotiations.

These and related aspects should be looked into. It seems clear that the personnel manager can play a very important role in ensuring that *communication* on wage and salary practices is efficient. He can also advise line managers and workers on the likely effects of changes in rates or conditions. A great deal of industrial unrest is caused by actions which are not understood, especially those which affect wage payments.

3. Promotion

Not all employees wish to be promoted; nevertheless, for those who have the desire there should be an understanding of the policy adopted. This is not a straightforward issue for which simple rules can be laid down. To promise that a new recruit *will* be promoted is a very dangerous practice, yet to attract the right type of man or woman the prospect of promotion may have to be very real.

A positive policy is essential and this should be linked with the procedures for the training and education of employees. If examples of promotions which have taken place can be quoted, this is much safer than making definite promises. The recruit will see that there *is* a policy, and that provided he works hard and shows his worth he has a reasonable chance of success (*see* p. 231 for job evaluation).

4. Education and training

The extent to which the company is to involve itself in education and training, and the persons responsible for carrying out the policy, should be defined. Induction training should be an integral part of any education and training programme: an early introduction to the primary objectives of a company, and the means of achieving them, are very necessary.

5. Recruitment and selection

Attracting employees, recruiting them, placing them in appropriate jobs, and carrying out all the necessary procedures is an important part of the work of the personnel department (*see* Chapter XIV).

6. Health and safety

The need for adequate light, heating and ventilation is outlined in Chapter VII (p. 77). Provision of proper safety devices such as machine guards are required by law. The employer has a duty to perform in providing a safe working place. Similarly, employees are required to obey the regulations relating to safety.

7. Welfare facilities and fringe benefits

Provision of certain welfare facilities, such as a medical centre at a foundry where frequent accidents occur, is sound common sense. The directors have to decide what non-essential projects should be included as part of the personnel policy. Should a company have its own doctors? What medical services, if any, should be provided on the illness of an employee and his family? Is a social club necessary? These and similar questions have to be answered.

"Fringe benefits," the indirect payments made to employees in the form of welfare facilities, luncheon vouchers, payment during sickness, pension and life assurance, now form a substantial part of the total wage cost. Executives and other staff employees now regard fringe benefits as a natural part of their service contracts. There is a growing tendency to bring hourly paid workers into line with staff workers, although not on such generous scales.

8. Redundancy and downgrading

A personnel policy should recognise that redundancy may become necessary, and that downgrading, as well as promotion, is very much a possibility. As a man approaches retirement he may find difficulty in keeping up the speed expected of him. This applies particularly in heavy industries where some tasks require considerable physical strength. The transfer to lighter work, most likely at lower rates of pay, is a humane way of dealing with the slowing worker who can still play a useful part in an organisation.

Redundancy is inevitable in a rapidly changing, technological world. Fortunately, workers who become redundant can often be absorbed by transfer to similar work. Where this is not possible, severance pay should be made, thus allowing time for the employee to find employment.*

Those matters which require further explanation are covered in later chapters. In the sections below is a survey of what sort of attitudes and systems are likely to produce the motivation and morale necessary for achieving the primary objectives.

ACHIEVEMENT OF HARMONY OF OBJECTIVES

Some of the factors which are likely to affect the achievement of the *Harmony of Objectives* are discussed below.

SOUND ORGANISATION

An organisation which is efficient and is appropriate for the business concerned is essential. The requirements for such an organisation are given in Chapter V. However, it is also very necessary to recognise the *informal* relationships which exist as well as the *formal* organisation.

Workers placed together to perform tasks tend to form themselves into social groups. This leads to a variety of relationships being established rather as shown on page 40 where the *Graicunas Theorem* is explained. Whether the formal organisation and the informal relationships transpire to be one and the same thing is an open question. What is important to notice is that any manager who wishes to manage efficiently must quickly learn about the informal relationships which exist. He should find out the relationships within each primary working group and those which exist between the groups. It is no use relying upon the formal organisation when he knows quite well that the procedures implied have been modified by the informal relationships which exist. An efficient manager takes the two together and harmonises them so that they work to the common goal.

All aspects of managing are affected by the informal relationships, and here it is advisable to list some of the more important factors:

1. Leadership.—The departmental manager or foreman is the formal leader, but within each primary working group there will tend to be an unofficial leader. Whether the group will work in accordance with the written rules will depend very much on the attitude of the *unofficial* leader whose attitude to co-operation and work will tend to be followed.

2. Communication.—What is happening or supposed to be happening is quickly circulated through the multitude of channels of communication. If not properly handled the "grapevine" can become a monster which strangles all good personnel relations. An executive who must

* *Redundancy Payments Act, 1965*

confide in his subordinates immediately he is told a confidential fact, or a post-room supervisor who whispers the contents of letters received, can cause industrial unrest very quickly. If an incentive scheme is to be introduced, but the unions have not yet been consulted, and the news leaks out, then all kinds of rumours will probably circulate. This kind of situation leads the management into a position of weakness before the negotiations have commenced; the proposals may be turned down without even being studied and discussed.

3. *Unwritten rules.*—Within the framework of the informal relationships there tend to emerge the unwritten rules, the code of behaviour which must be followed by all rank and file employees. This may also occur at manager level, but not to the same extent.

Contravention of the unwritten rules can lead to serious trouble. A worker who pushes his output beyond that expected of him by his working group is likely to meet with disapproval. In one factory in which the author was employed each worker had a notebook in which he kept the times taken on the components produced. When he started on a batch of components, the worker would refer to his book and then make sure that he took a similar time to that recorded earlier. There was a fault in the *formal* organisation which allowed this practice to carry on; when this was remedied and job-time recorders were introduced all times showed a marked improvement, some being halved. The absence of the supervision given by an effective control system had allowed operators to manipulate times just as they pleased.

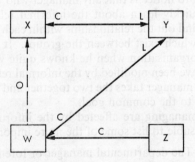

FIG. 31.—*Sociogram for a group of four workers*
L = Leader; O = Opposition; C = Co-operation.

Some writers have insisted that it is impossible to chart the informal relationships which exist. There is no doubt that this would be very difficult in a large business, viewed as a whole. However, there is nothing to prevent a supervisor from discovering the unofficial leader of a primary working group and to find out which workers communicate with each other and which do not. This kind of information may be shown on a diagram known as a sociogram (Fig. 31).

The sociogram shows that Y is accepted as a leader by X and W. Conversely, as denoted by the Cs, Y is willing to co-operate with X and W, and Z is willing to co-operate with W. There is opposition to X from W, which means that they do not communicate with each other if they can possibly avoid doing so, and they certainly resent working with each other.

From this very simple sociogram it is possible to see that Y is accepted as the unofficial leader. When planning how the work shall be carried out or when informing the group of any fact the supervisor should remember the informal relationships which exist.

EFFECTIVE LEADERSHIP

There should be effective leadership for a specific business and for each part of it. The qualities of leadership have to be *adapted* to meet particular situations and cannot be stereotyped to deal with all situations. A works manager who has been very successful at a non-union plant may find himself in very deep waters when transferred to a plant which is virtually controlled by unions and where the word of a shop steward has more weight than that of a supervisor.

Bearing this fact in mind it is possible to establish a general pattern of the qualities required for leadership which are summarised below:

1. High intelligence.—This does not mean the same thing as *superiority*. A leader should be able to come down to the level necessary for the employees he is leading.

2. Education: broad as well as technical.—A leader should have a wide knowledge of many fields as well as being master of his own speciality. The word "education" is used in a broad sense to include any process whereby a person can improve his knowledge, and not necessarily formal education. Getting a man to broaden his vision is far from easy. Experience in technical colleges has shown that many student engineers and scientists are against the introduction of liberal studies, especially if these take up time which could be used for the study of examination subjects. Nevertheless, there is fairly general acceptance among educationalists that the broadening of a man's outlook is vital.

3. Acceptability.—Some men are accepted as leaders without question; others have great difficulty in commanding the necessary respect. Much depends upon the confidence felt in a leader. An example of this was seen in August 1965, when almost 20,000 men were made idle by a strike at the Fisher and Ludlow car body plant at Llanelly, Wales. A welder was suspended because he refused to obey the instructions given by a foreman, on the grounds that the latter was *not a skilled craftsman who was competent to give instructions*. Because of the strike the British Motor Corporation's plant at Longbridge, Birmingham, was brought to a standstill.

4. Maturity.—A leader should have the maturity necessary for acceptability, coping with situations and making decisions. He should be emotionally stable and unlikely to break down with the frustrations and responsibilities which inevitably exist in a complex business.

5. *Drive.*—This should be present in sufficient quantity to achieve both personal and company objectives. Often this drive is provided by normal, healthy motives, but this is not always the case. Some men become leaders because they are obsessed with ideas which are regarded by an outsider as "eccentric" or "neurotic." The chief accountant who insists on auditing the petty cash even though the task has been assigned to one of his subordinates, or the sales manager who will never take a holiday for fear he is not in his office when an important customer wants him are examples. These may be signs that the managers just cannot delegate responsibilities. At the same time, this kind of neurosis may be the driving force behind a man.

When selecting managers it is important to remember that a man who is so very normal that he cannot be distinguished from any other man is unlikely to change when he becomes a manager. On the other hand, a man with character who has shown evidence of drive is likely to "expand" with added responsibilities.

Drive by itself is not enough for effective management. A leader must be able to inspire and motivate those under him. This motivation may take a *positive* form when a manager gives instructions, consults, assists with problems and reprimands, in order to achieve the desired objectives. For most purposes this is adequate and should be regarded as being effective management. It builds up valuable personnel relationships between a manager and his subordinates. Each individual is regarded as a separate problem who must be dealt with in the most appropriate manner: the aim is to try and satisfy his basic needs (*see* p. 193) and at the same time achieve the primary objectives of the business.

There are employees who do not want contact with a superior. A man may resent being overlooked for promotion and, therefore, will not want to be consulted or feel that he belongs to a team. Another person, skilled at his work, may resent being told what to do, but when left on his own, will do all that is necessary in his work. Yet another type of worker may have a "chip on his shoulder," and be constantly causing trouble; he is against all authority and managers generally. These types of personality are usually in the minority, but often provide a manager with his major problems. He cannot harmonise their basic needs with the primary objectives because they do not respond to normal behaviour. In extreme instances, dismissal is the only solution but with marginal cases the manager has to accept and make the best of the difficulties. He must rely on the *Law of the Situation* (*see* p. 36) and hope that *negative* motivation will produce the desired results.

Nor should drive be confused with the hard, blustering, whip-cracking force which characterised some of the early management of industrial companies. Leadership should imply democracy where all join in to achieve the objectives in a spirit of co-operation. There should be willingness, not forced labour. Firm discipline should be tempered with understanding or workers will resist.

6. *Management skills.*—A leader should be conversant with the techniques of management. He should be skilled in dealing with people and in the conditions necessary for maximum production. Techniques such as production control, management accountancy, cost control, ergonomics, cybernetics and network analysis should be familiar terms. The extent to which he requires knowledge *in depth* depends upon his responsibilities. A supervisor would not require the same knowledge as that required by a general manager.

7. *Loyalty.*—Loyalty to the business in which he is employed is an essential factor in good leadership.

This list should give an indication of what is required of a leader. Many do not possess these qualities and, therefore, do not always lead as they should. On the other hand, some leaders are egotistical and over-bearing, and yet have sufficient drive and confidence to carry all before them. When dealing with human beings it is impossible to formulate rules which show positively those who can lead and those who cannot. All that can be done is to indicate *likely qualities* required for leadership.

The term "leader" has been used to signify a manager at any level. A general manager and a foreman are both leaders; the difference lies in the area being managed and the related responsibilities. Each will require to possess the qualities listed to the appropriate degree for the work to be performed. This does not follow that a foreman would be capable of performing the work of general manager or vice versa. As stressed earlier, leadership is *for a situation,* and there is no positive way of telling how a man will react when he is placed in that situation: only when left to manage is an appraisal possible. The best that can be achieved is to assess character and to form an opinion on the likely chance of success.

Examination Questions on Chapter XIII are given at the end of Chapter XV.

CHAPTER XIV

THE PERSONNEL DEPARTMENT AND STAFF
RECRUITMENT

THERE are no positive guides available which indicate when a business should have a separate personnel department. In companies of equal size some will manage without one, while others find it quite indispensable.

The *functions* of a personnel department have to be carried out in any business, irrespective of its size, even though an executive may have to combine this work with other duties. Unfortunately, in these circumstances what usually happens is that employees are engaged and discharged, but there is no real effort made to follow a real personnel policy. A busy works manager, for example, should be concerned with getting the right people to fill his vacancies, but he should not be expected to deal with the necessary preliminary work and subsequent record keeping. If he spends too much time on *routine* personnel work his other duties will tend to be neglected.

Whether a personnel department can be justified, and its size, are dependent on a variety of factors: the size of the labour force, rate of turnover of workers, the extent and nature of the personnel policy, and problems being encountered from workers and unions all influence its existence and scope.

No absolute minimum size of labour force can be said to justify a personnel department. In one business 100 employees may be sufficient; in another a staff of 500 would call for the same facility. Generally, when a business employs around 250 people there appears to be justification for a full-time personnel man or woman. In a business of this size it is likely that a few people will come and go each week and there will be sufficient related work to justify the existence of a department, however small. There is no precise formula for determining the nature and scope of the functionings of a personnel department, though an indication of its possible organisation is shown below.

THE PERSONNEL MANAGER

A good personnel manager can more than earn his salary by advising the line and functional managers on personnel matters, and by letting employees see that he is actively concerned with their welfare. In addition, much valuable information can come from the records maintained in the department.

In Chapter V it was noted that a personnel manager was usually regarded as a "staff" man—one who advises but has no direct responsibility for the work of others (except, of course, those in his own department). In theory therefore a personnel manager is primarily an adviser who assists the other managers in their work of carrying out the personnel policy.

There is no doubt that the staff relationship attributed to a personnel manager can be justified in a great many cases. However, with the growth in importance of industrial relations it would seem he is becoming a negotiator as well as an organiser. His skill in this capacity can avert a strike and his hard bargaining can reduce a pay claim and save his company money. In these circumstances he is *acting*, not simply *advising*, and so is more of a functional manager—*i.e.* responsible for a particular function. Possibly this is the reason for some companies having separate industrial relations executives—and even separate departments for industrial relations work, and so the two functions are separated: in fact, although different, they are so inter-related that they should be under one command whether he be called Personnel Manager, Labour Officer, Personnel Director (possibly with a seat on the Board), or whatever other title is selected as being appropriate.

PERSONNEL FUNCTIONS

When a company has many divisions there may be a personnel department at each plant or factory and a personnel and industrial relations department at the head office. Industrial relations negotiations of a serious nature are then conducted by an expert based at the head office. The advantage of this practice is that a highly skilled negotiator can be employed by the company as a whole, though a possible disadvantage is that he may not understand local conditions at a particular plant. In this instance the local personnel officer is always available to advise him.

A study of the contents of a personnel policy such as that given on p. 199 will show the nature and extent of the personnel department's functions. The personnel manager (whether under this or another title) will be responsible for carrying out, or advising on, this policy. In more specific form he will have to deal with the following:

1. Provide the routine personnel services such as:

    (*a*) selection;
    (*b*) recruitment;
    (*c*) engagement;
    (*d*) induction and training;
    (*e*) wage and salary procedures;
    (*f*) record keeping.

2. Negotiate with workers and unions on working conditions and related matters.

3. Advise on, co-ordinate and control all the personnel functions, thereby obtaining and maintaining a high standard of morale. The co-ordination and control should be done in consultation with line and functional managers and should include observance of and reporting on significant trends in staff turnover, absenteeism, accidents and possibly working conditions.

ORGANISATION OF THE PERSONNEL DEPARTMENT

An organisation chart for a small company with a total of around 600 employees is shown in Fig. 32. It will be seen that the functions are of a basic nature. The welfare facilities, such as exist, are dealt with by the

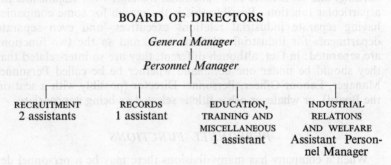

FIG. 32.—*Personnel organisation for a business with about 600 employees*

assistant personnel manager who is also the industrial relations adviser, a duty shared with the personnel manager. Social activities are dealt with by a staff association so that the personnel department acts as an intermediary whenever required, but does not have any active part in organising functions.

On the recruitment side are two assistants who are responsible for recruiting all weekly-paid employees. The personnel manager interviews all applicants for senior positions. A records clerk maintains all necessary records and presents statistics to the personnel manager and to line and functional managers.

Education and training involves oversight of an apprentice scheme and contact with various educational institutions, including schools and colleges of technology. The miscellaneous aspect includes liaison with the canteen manageress on requirements for the canteen and complaints and suggestions from employees.

This arrangement is not put forward as an ideal upon which future systems should be based: it is simply an example of the type of organisation which is found in practice.

In a large company a much more detailed departmental chart should be possible: the volume of work would be much larger, and the personnel staff would specialise to a greater extent.

Figure 33 indicates the type of organisation which may be found in a large business. In this diagram each factory has a personnel manager, but the detailed break-down has only been given for Factory *Y*. It will be seen that the personnel organisation is headed by a director and reporting to him is an industrial relations officer. The personnel managers are in direct contact with the industrial relations officer on all matters affecting industrial relations. He advises on the policy being followed.

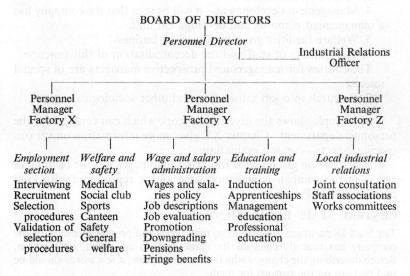

FIG. 33.—*Personnel organisation for a large business*

The Industrial Relations Officer acts in an advisory capacity to the Personnel Managers in Factories X, Y and Z.

The various sections have been made self-explanatory and no attempt has been made to show the number of personnel officers likely to be engaged in each. This will depend upon the size of the factory and the policy being adopted.

The accommodation of the personnel department should include private interviewing rooms and the siting of these is important so that interviews may not be disturbed by noise and interruptions. These rooms should be tastefully decorated and equipped with suitable chairs and desks. Another factor is convenience of access. The department should preferably be sited where present and prospective employees can gain access without difficulty. For this reason the department is often situated near the main gate of the works.

H

PERSONNEL DEPARTMENT—PRACTICAL ILLUSTRATION

A practical illustration of how the personnel department operates in a complex business is shown below. It is interesting for a number of reasons; in particular, the following should be noted:

1. The use of job descriptions and job evaluation (discussed later in this chapter and the next).
2. Salary and wages organisation.
3. Methods of recruitment.
4. Management development—it will be seen that the company has a management planning and development unit.
5. Welfare facilities given by a modern business.
6. The training of staff and the decentralisation of this function. The courses for managers and prospective managers are of special interest.
7. Research into job satisfaction and other sociological aspects.

This example shows the diversity of work which can come under the personnel department. Chapter XV gives more information on various specific aspects—*e.g.* job evaluation.

The description given on the following eight pages was the basis of an article in the company's staff magazine and is reproduced with kind permission of BP Ltd.

CENTRAL STAFF DEPARTMENT

THE Staff Department familiar to so many past and present members of the company has recently changed its name and, to an extent, its function. Before describing the changes which have taken place, a few words should be said perhaps on the reasons for them.

The rapid growth of the BP Group interests in recent years has brought about a substantial increase in the number of our staff; we now employ men and women of over 50 nationalities in as many different parts of the world. This is a far cry from the years, not so long gone, when the company's activities were largely concentrated in the Middle East. In these changing circumstances, the Staff Department's function has grown steadily. Another development, brought about by the increase in numbers, the complex mixture of the work and the location of our staff, has been the need to learn and develop a number of specialist techniques to help us in the staff management function.

Following a careful examination and analysis of Staff Department's responsibilities, it was decided in 1962 that the day-to-day management and administration of staff should be placed to a greater extent in the hands of general management. The growing isolation of the individual from those responsible for staff administration had to be overcome, and it was thought that this could best be achieved by placing much of Staff Department's work closer to the individual in his own departmental organisation. Altogether nine "Staff Units" (one in each major London Office department, one for the smaller departments and one at the Research Centre at Sunbury) have been created to assist and advise departments in the management and administration of their staff, whether in the United Kingdom or in centres overseas for which the department is operationally responsible. So far as associated companies are concerned, there is a close and regular interchange of ideas and experience, liaison being achieved in the first place through the London Office Departmental Staff Units.

With the creation of these Staff Units in the London Office, the Central Staff Department continued its responsibility for the formulation of general personnel policies and practices for all British staff, for providing specialist services required by departmental and company managements, for co-ordinating the activities of the various Staff Units, for providing management with a channel of communication where this is necessary for the staff and advising and assisting staff who seek guidance on personal matters.

This article describes the main functions of the Central Staff Department.

Employee relations division

Two things which interest most of us on and after joining a new enterprise are the job we do and the money we are paid for doing it. Employee Relations Division is responsible for formulating policy on the latter and on conditions of employment for staff, such as hours of work, leave and holiday entitlements; it is particularly concerned with the design of a salary structure that will enable managements to pay their staff fairly, both in relation to other staff and to those in other companies who are doing comparable jobs. This work, which is shared by Staff Relations and Job Evaluation Branches, entails frequent surveys of salary levels throughout industry, and over the years a close liaison has been developed with other employers. A large organisation like our own has to deal with salaries on a systematic basis and guides must be provided for managements, the design of which calls for specialist skill and practice.

Jobs in the company are graded, each within a distinct salary range. When a department creates a post, it suggests an appropriate grade for it and compiles a "job description" setting out the purpose and component duties of the post together with the skills, responsibilities and relationships associated with it. This "job description" is analysed by Job Evaluation Branch and a close comparison is made between the post in question and other similar posts in the company which have already been graded. A tentative grading is thus established, the salary range of which may then be checked against the "market rate" payable for a similar job by other companies with whom the Branch exchanges information. The resultant assessment is further checked by a broad survey within BP in order, so far as possible, to preclude anomalies. In all this, it is essential to evaluate the post and not its incumbent. The grade of a job is finally settled with the departmental management concerned.

Staff and industrial relations

Staff Relations Branch carries out surveys, keeps our salary structure under review and works out and proposes adjustments when necessary. It also establishes appropriate recruitment rates. The Branch is likewise responsible for working out salary levels for staff serving overseas. In doing this, it has to reconcile differences in local living costs, in taxes and in the circumstances or ways of life in the many and varied countries we work in, so that there is a reasonable comparison in expatriate standards of living wherever expatriates may serve. This has become increasingly complicated by such political considerations as the need to reconcile expatriate salaries (which quite properly include an element as an incentive to work abroad) with the salaries of overseas nationals who are doing the same work. The necessary balance to be achieved in such cases is an important part of salary determination.

Together with salaries, we have to consider wages. Industrial Relations Branch is responsible for providing advice to London Office departments and to managements at home and overseas on matters affecting wages and related conditions of employment. Usually, wages and basic conditions are negotiated with representative Trade Unions, and an important part of the Branch's work is to consider the nature of agreements and proposals for change. Negotiations are conducted by local managements themselves, the Branch assisting them with information and advice as necessary. The Branch exchanges views and information with other employers also, and is in close contact with Government departments: changes in labour law, particularly that part of it related to arbitration and conciliation, may have an important bearing on the way in which negotiations are conducted.

In order to anticipate and evaluate trends and to formulate policy for the future, the company's own position is continually reviewed; constant liaison is maintained with other organisations and detailed study and research are undertaken. This enables the Branch to pass on accumulated knowledge to those areas of the company which have need of it. During recent years, there has been a tendency for work in industrial relations to become increasingly specialised, so that another important activity of the Branch is to recruit and train industrial relations staff for the group's operations at home and abroad.

Recruitment and placement branch

Having, so to speak, set the stage for the employment of people, the next consideration is recruitment. After departmental managements have estimated the number and types of jobs which they require to be done each year, and for which they have no staff available within their departments, they apply to Recruitment and Placement Branch for candidates, giving full details of the job to be done and the qualifications of the person needed to do it. As it is the company's policy, whenever possible, to promote its own staff rather than to seek newcomers from outside, the small Placement Section of the Branch first ascertains whether there is, anywhere in the Group, any individual who could fill the vacancy. If there is such a person, the Section will negotiate with the departments concerned and will co-ordinate the ensuing transfer. If, after enquiries and internal advertising, it is found that there is no one suitable for the job in question, then outside recruitment is put in hand.

Successful recruitment implies more than the filling of newspapers with offers and having a chat with those who respond. Selection interviewing is a skilled job and recruiters are required to have specific training for this work, which includes the proper use and interpretation of aptitude tests. A long-term view of the company's staffing requirements has to be taken so that the right calibre of men and women are available to the Group in future years. Recruiters visit Universities and Technical Colleges to explain the company's activities and to give advice to students who may thus become attracted to a career with BP. Nor does this practice stop at the higher educational level. Although no positive attempt is made to attract younger people, visits are nonetheless made, on invitation, to schools and talks are given about the company, not only to boys and girls but to institutions and associations.

Representatives of the Branch attend careers exhibitions and conferences for school and university teachers; visits to such places as the Sunbury Research Centre are arranged for university professors and schools representatives. All this cannot be done unless recruiters themselves have an adequate knowledge of the group's operations which will enable them to reply to enquiries. Visits to United Kingdom and overseas centres are made from time to time by members of the Branch so that they can become fully acquainted at first hand with local conditions.

More will be said later of the Probationer Assistant and Apprentice Training Schemes, but here it should be mentioned that each year the company recruits a considerable number of young men into these schemes: selection for apprenticeships is rigorous and highly competitive, involving the testing of the candidates, the setting up of interview panels and (in the case of probationer assistants) the holding of two-day selection boards.

The day-to-day procedures for selecting staff to fill particular vacancies are something of which we have all had experience. The recruiter is responsible for every stage of an engagement—for advertising, sorting out applications, interviewing prospective staff, answering their queries, arranging for candidates to be interviewed by departments, making offers of employment, following up references, seeing the recruit on the first day of work, and thereafter following up an appointment with an interview after six months or so. There is in all this a two-fold responsibility; to the company for a correct selection of staff and to candidates for giving a good first impression of BP. The nature of the work is such as to require a helpful, objective and sympathetic approach, whether in a formal interview or in one of the discussions periodically undertaken with the parents of interested youngsters. Perhaps the most important feature of Recruitment and Placement Branch is the close and constant contact it maintains with departments. This is essential to the whole process of employing staff. At the moment, there are seven male and three female recruiters, the latter being concerned wholly with the engagement of women.

Female staff

Mention of female staff should remind us that approximately 40 per cent of all our staff in the United Kingdom are women and that their number has multiplied three-fold since the last war. Trends in female staff employment have changed greatly in the last few years for, among other things, there are ever-increasing opportunities for women outside the commercial field with which the company has to compete in securing staff for the forty or so different kinds of jobs it has to offer them.

It is continually necessary to study fresh approaches to the recruitment of women by keeping in touch with the changes taking place and by exchanging information and ideas with other organisations. New systems of employment which can lead to better control or efficiency are always being sought and, where practicable, introduced. Besides being concerned in all this, the adviser, Female Staff, assists the staff manager in the interpretation of staff policies as they affect women in the company and in maintaining a close liaison with departmental managements.

In addition to the female staff in the United Kingdom, a number of doctors, nursing sisters, teachers, secretaries, and shorthand and copy typists are employed in the company's centres overseas. The adviser, Female Staff, may be asked to assist in their recruitment and postings and, to help her in this, she pays periodical visits overseas.

Management development

Once a person has been engaged for a job, progress in his or her career must obviously hinge chiefly upon performance. Some staff will inevitably work better than others and this will be reported in the staff review forms, which are designed to evaluate an individual's performance and indicate his or her potential for the future. The best use of talent in the group can be assured if systematic arrangements are made to foresee both jobs and the people who will do them: whereas departments estimate their own particular needs and deploy their staff accordingly, the movement of people with high potential, wherever they may be employed, is a matter of vital interest to the group as a whole and this interest may transcend that of a particular department.

The need to provide a systematic review of talent has led to the recent creation of the Management Planning and Development Unit. The Unit is responsible, in conjunction with departmental managements, for establishing areas of the company in which future managers may be in short supply and, by forecasting such situations, help to avoid them.

Lists are compiled of staff whom departments consider, on review forms, are of outstanding ability, and plans for the future development of such individuals, by means of specialist training and experience, are then agreed with departments. Advice is also given, when requested, to associate companies in the preparation of their management succession plans. Lastly, this Unit is also responsible for the design of staff review forms and advising departmental managements as to how these forms can best be completed; this is desirable to ensure a uniform method of staff appraisal throughout all departments.

In regard to the movement of staff generally, there may be occasions when a department is unable, for one reason or another, to continue to employ certain of its staff. In this case, their names and particulars are referred to Placement Section, whose other activities have already been mentioned, so that efforts can be made to arrange a transfer of such individuals to a job elsewhere in the company.

Administration division

The welfare of all staff requires constant consideration and alertness, and BP can claim a reputation in this aspect of its staff management which is the envy of many organisations. A part of Administration Division's task is to promote and supervise schemes and policies which will help to keep serving staff of the company happily and usefully employed. The staff Housing Scheme, the special arrangements for medical insurance (BUPA), the organisation of social and sporting activities and travel arrangements are some aspects of the Division's contribution. Last year alone, Travel Section arranged over 6000 passages overseas for staff and their families on duty and, in addition, it helped in more than 3000 private journeys abroad. When one adds to this the 3000 rail journeys and 12,000 hotel reservations arranged in the same period, some idea of the magnitude of this work is revealed.

The Division is also concerned in the more general administration of staff; it is, in short, a custodian and arbitrator of all the staff administration policies that have been evolved over the years by men with much experience of a wide variety of situations and a very genuine understanding of the personal problems facing our staff at home and overseas.

The administration of large numbers of people these days often calls for statistical help. The Staff Information and Statistics Branch maintains records of all employees in the United Kingdom as well as of expatriate British staff serving overseas. By means of punched cards and other aids, the Branch can locate both past and present members of the company and can provide departments with essential statistical information on staff. Although personal files are now held by individual departments, it is this Branch that provides a staff statistical service to Central Staff and other departments.

Central Staff Administration Branch performs duties, similar to those of other Departmental Staff Units, on behalf of the smaller London Office departments.

Secretarial and typing services for the Department are provided by the Secretarial Services Section.

Training division

Training is usually necessary for all new recruits and for most people on transferring from one job to another; it is required when new jobs or functions grow or are created. Training is not something that just happens to a man and then is finished, for it has been said that all men are at all times under training. Central Staff Department does not train people. In BP, the responsibility for training an individual belongs to the individual's manager. The role of Training Division is to help managers throughout the company to fulfil their responsibilities in this field. That is a simple statement but it describes a complex operation.

The three branches of Training Division are designed to cope with the three main aspects which training can take. Apprentice Training Branch is responsible for overseeing the training of all young people from school or university who are equipping themselves with the basic skills and experience necessary to enter a profession or trade. In addition, the Branch deals with company information courses for new entrants and oversees the Further Education scheme by which the company assists its employees to add to their education.

Industrial Training Branch is responsible for seeing that skill training thoughout the company is adequately developed and maintained, and it gives professional appraisal, advice and help in this field wherever this appears to be necessary. For example, in commissioning a new refinery, help is given to local Management in the large-scale training effort which must be undertaken before commissioning is possible and this is a special problem where refineries are located in industrially under-developed countries. Similarly, when a new product is launched which calls for a co-ordinated campaign of training so that the sales force in each country is alerted and informed with precise knowledge, Industrial Training Branch is involved in the development and application of such a programme.

Management Training Branch seeks to help the company's managers and prospective managers develop the skills and attitudes which are necessary in their function. Management courses are currently run at three levels. Stage I is designed to give younger men an opportunity of broadening their outlook and to introduce them to management problems and techniques; Stage II is for older men but goes to greater depth and deals more with specialised subjects; Stage III gives an opportunity for senior managers to study some of the major problems facing the BP Group.

Each Branch has to fulfil its responsibilities in several different ways. Firstly, in co-operation with the major departments in London Office, it must take some executive responsibility for central action: for instance, the University Apprenticeships and the Probationer Assistantships are organised directly by the Apprentice Training Branch; central management courses are run by Management Training Branch and courses in technologies are organised by the Industrial Training Branch. But the major part of the work in each branch lies in visiting subsidiary and associate companies and, where necessary, advising them on training method and policy (and also in learning from them) and providing a co-ordinating link in this function throughout the Group.

The training officers in the various companies within the group co-operate with Training Division in this way and a group policy, based on practical experience, can thus evolve and be implemented. In addition, because BP is an international group, large numbers of men have to be moved around the world for special experience and training. This involves all three Branches. Under the wing of Apprentice Branch are young Adenis, Nigerians and West Indians training at various levels to become engineers, chemists and accountants, while in a year something like five hundred BP men from overseas Associates attend courses or undergo individual training arranged by Management Training and Industrial Training Branches.

Lastly, because of the experience of the educational system which their work gives them, Training Officers are able to act as a source of advice on personal educational problems to employees within the company.

Staff research

There is a growing understanding of the many factors which govern or can be made to influence staff management and there is increasing evidence that social sciences are proving to have practical application to the benefit of organisations like BP, but few of which have at present ventured into this new field of research. To examine this, a Staff Planning and Research Unit has recently been created. Studies are currently being undertaken by the Unit with a view to establishing those factors which lead to personal satisfaction with a job and therefore to greater individual productivity. This study calls for the detailed survey of existing communication in each group company, and the preliminary analysis of the data submitted indicates a need to reconsider some of our present staff practices.

In addition to the research into factors affecting staff productivity, the Unit is responsible for surveying the staff element of Marketing Company Three-Year Plans and for assisting in the preparation and analysis of all staff plans.

These, then, are the functions of Central Staff Department. The satisfactory fulfilment of them is of importance to our success as individuals and, thereby, as a company; it is for this reason that they come under the close personal direction of the chairman.

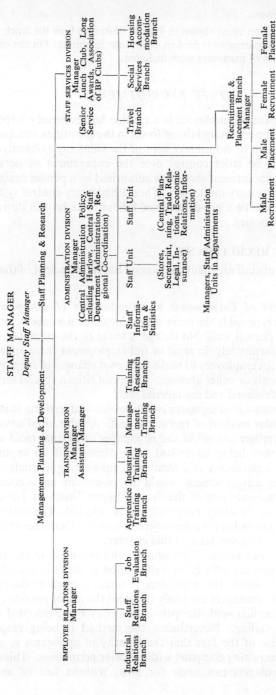

Fig. 34.—*Practical illustration—personnel department*
Courtesy of BP Ltd.

Organisation chart

The organisation chart shown in Fig. 34 illustrates how the work of the Central Staff Department is broken down into functions. On the original chart the names of managers were included.

STAFF RECRUITMENT

The recruitment of employees is a routine but extremely important task. Without the necessary labour force, in the quantities and qualities required, there can be no achievement of the company's objectives.

There should be strict control over the engagement of personnel and each new appointment should be authorised by a person designated as having the necessary authority. When a budgetary control system is operated there will be a pre-determined labour force broken down into the various categories.

SOURCES OF RECRUITMENT

The sources of staff are many and varied but the principal of these are as follows:

1. Department of Employment and Productivity (Employment Exchange).—This is possibly the main source for manual workers, machine operators and clerical staff. No charge is made to the employee or the employer. Unfortunately, in areas of full employment there appears to be a tendency for employees to make their own changes of employment via advertisements or other avenues. In certain cities a special service is offered for professional and managerial staff.

2. Advertisements in newspapers and journals.—Advertising is now an extremely popular method of recruiting staff. A substantial advantage is that the advertiser can select the newspaper or journal most appropriate to the post being advertised. For example, if an engineer is required there is the choice of a number of engineering journals; for an accountant the advertisement would be placed in an accountancy journal. Alternatively one of the "status papers" such as *The Times*, *The Guardian*, or the *Daily Telegraph* can be selected. The cost will be fairly high but justifiable for a managerial position. Examples of display advertisements are given later in this chapter.

3. Personnel consultants.—Consultants who specialise in the recruitment of managers are now being called upon to assist in the filling of senior posts. Whether this procedure is sound is open to debate and many personnel managers are likely to resent the use of outside experts who are not familiar with the personnel policy being adopted or the conditions prevailing. Nevertheless the method is being employed, possibly because of the fact that the identity of applicants is not revealed to the recruiting company without prior permission. This means that senior managers can apply for posts without fear of applying to their own company with its possible, unfortunate, consequences. The costs involved in this method are quite high to the company.

4. *Recommendations from existing employees.*—Because an employee has recommended a business there is generally a certain amount of confidence felt by the prospective employee and the person who is selecting.

5. *Notices exhibited in the works or at the main gate.*—This method has the advantage of showing what vacancies exist and can prevent the endless stream of enquiries which is possible in an area where there is a high rate of unemployment.

6. *Private employment bureaux.*—These bureaux are used mainly for clerical and secretarial staff. They are quite widespread in the London area, and both temporary and permanent staff may be contacted. A fee is charged for each employee supplied.

7. *Universities, colleges of technology and schools.*—All these are a very useful source of employees for a full range of jobs. The universities are used for recruiting graduates to train for positions of responsibility or for research posts. Colleges of technology also have students of graduate standard and, in addition, provide younger applicants for training as engineers, accountants, chemists, physicists and technicians.

8. *Professional bodies.*—Some professional bodies maintain an appointments register from which engineers, accountants and others can be recruited. However, this is not a service which is always available so its existence cannot be relied upon.

JOB DESCRIPTION AND ADVERTISING

Whatever sources are approached for staff a prime requisite is that details of the job are set out clearly so that the right type of applicant is likely to respond. A *job description* for this purpose falls into two parts: an assessment within the business of the qualifications and personality required, and the rationalisation of this information in the preparation of advertisements or letters to the various sources of recruitment listed above. A third use for the job description is in "job evaluation" which is discussed in Chapter XV, and where the specific headings are set out from which a complete job description can be produced.

Within the company many firms adopt a standardised form of labour requisition which incorporates a job description and the authority to engage staff. This should be completed by the appropriate line manager and be acted upon by the personnel department.

Job descriptions (also known as job specifications) can play a very important part in establishing a firm foundation for a personnel policy. Selection, training, promotions, wage and salary structure, and many other vital matters are affected by the nature of jobs being carried out. Full knowledge of what is involved is therefore a first requisite for knowing what to do when making personnel decisions. Provided an advertisement gives sufficient detail to attract the right type of people any deficiency in the job description can be put right by sending further particulars to applicants or by explaining to them at the interview. Once a full job description is available, a foreman or other line manager can use an agreed abbreviation, together with an appropriate reference number so that the Personnel Department can quickly trace their copy of the job description.

Study of advertisements in national newspapers will show the sort of compromise that is reached when describing jobs. Quite often, of course, the company responsible has not bothered to consider a full job description so the brief details are the only particulars available. However, it is now true to say that many progressive companies do employ properly trained and qualified personnel staff who develop sound management practices.

As examples of job descriptions and as indications of the different qualities required from employees for various levels of responsibilities copies of three advertisements which appeared in the *Daily Telegraph* are reproduced below with the kind permission of the publishers. They cover the following posts:

1. Senior electronics engineer (Fig. 35)

Study of this advertisement will show that the emphasis is on *technical* knowledge and skill. Clearly and concisely is shown: (a) the job; (b) location; and (c) possible salary. An attempt is made to match the job to the man, a procedure described later in this chapter. Reference

SENIOR ELECTRONICS ENGINEER

THE JOB Application of the latest digital techniques to the instrumentation and control of mechanical equipment.

LOCATION Birmingham area.

THE MAN Is of Higher National Certificate standard.
Has an industrial training/background.
Has several years' experience of semi-conductor switching circuit design.
Is keen to acquire responsibility in the application of electronics in an expanding industrial field.

SALARY Attractive starting salary and advancement for the go-ahead man.

Applicants should write details to:
S.E.17858, Daily Telegraph, E.C.4.

FIG. 35.—*Job description—electronics engineer*

to responsibility is to "the application of electronics" which is quite different from the other two job descriptions given below. This is an important consideration for any position: the nature of the *management content* of the job.

2. *Foreman for Welding Department* (*Fig. 36*)

The man required for this position was expected to have recent experience of welding techniques, once more emphasising the technical aspects. In addition he had to "possess organising ability, initiative, drive, and accept responsibility for control of a small number of personnel engaged on a specialised product."

THE BRITISH STEEL PILING CO. LTD.

require a

FOREMAN

FOR WELDING DEPT.

with up-to-date practical experience in submerged arc and other systems of welding and of weld testing techniques. Candidates, aged 30–40 years, must possess organising ability, initiative, drive, and accept responsibility for control of small number of personnel engaged on a specialised product.

Contributory Superannuation and Life Assurance Scheme. Good canteen facilities.

Apply giving full particulars of age, education, qualifications and experience, to:

The Personnel Officer,
Claydon, Ipswich, Suffolk.
Telephone Claydon 431.

FIG. 36.—*Job description—foreman*

Technical knowledge and skill are important, but there is emphasis on the management functions: (*a*) organising ability; (*b*) initiative; (*c*) drive; (*d*) control. If the reader turns back to Chapter III he will see that *organising* and *controlling* abilities are two of the three principal functions of management. The third is *planning* which is mainly the prerogative of higher level management. The requirements, initiative and drive, show that the company is looking for a man who can make decisions and obtain the expected output.

A criticism which could be levelled against this advertisement is the lack of information on salary. The previous example was not specific enough regarding this point, but at least it stipulated that an attractive starting salary was envisaged.

3. Works manager (Fig. 37)

With this advertisement most of the emphasis is given to the managerial content of the job. Production planning and leadership are specially mentioned and it is quite clear that these are of the utmost importance. Technical qualifications are also mentioned, but these are a background to the functions of management.

WORKS MANAGER

An old-established highly progressive Engineering Company in London, E.3 (20 minutes from Liverpool Street Station), having 100 employees working on semi-bulk production high quality light engineering speciality assemblies (unit weight 100 lbs. approx.) consisting of machined parts and welded fabrications, requires a Works Manager preferably between the age limits of 28 to 38.

He will have full responsibility for the efficient handling of production and workshop labour and be responsible direct to the Directors. In the initial stages detailed assistance will be given by the Works Director, whose retirement is due in 12 months.

Previous experience of management and production planning and leadership is essential.

Commencing salary will be £2,000 per annum with pension and other benefits and if in addition the applicant has the technical and other necessary qualifications, short term progression to the Board is open.

Applications, which will be treated in strict confidence, should include full details of experience, age and qualifications. Also the most convenient dates for an interview.

W.M.17844. Daily Telegraph, E.C.4.

FIG. 37.—*Job description—works manager*

APPLICATION FORMS

A standard form of application is an aid to marshalling all personal details in the order required. A serious criticism is that an applicant is not required to "sell himself" by being asked to apply in a letter. For some senior appointments a simple request for "proposals" is a much more realistic approach than a form of application. A good manager should be able to marshal his facts into a form which presents him in the best possible light.

The design of application forms should receive careful attention. In a large business there may be the need for one type of form for rank-

and-file positions and another for professional and/or managerial appointments. A typical form is shown in Figs. 38 *a* and *b*.

SCIENTIFIC SELECTION

If a number of applications are received for a post it is usual to draw up a short list. Around six is a normal number for this, and these candidates are invited to attend for interview.

Before an interview commences the interviewer should familiarise himself with all the pertinent facts: if an interview is to be effective it must be as a result of confidence on both sides, and this can be as much hindered by ignorance of relevant details by the interviewer as by any unsuitability in the candidate. Each applicant regards himself as unique and mistake of fact or confusion with other applicants often leads to annoyance.

Once confidential relations are established it is usual to allow applicants to ask questions or give opinions: these will aid the interviewer in making an assessment of personality. Further information can be obtained from details given on the application form. The word "scientific" is used in the title of this section to indicate that there is a *systematic approach* to the matter of selection.

Interviewing has many defects, but is still by far the most usual method of selecting personnel to fill positions of all levels and grades. For this reason an understanding of the technique is essential to all managers who are concerned with recruiting staff. Industrial psychologists have done more work on this subject than anyone else. A summary of a talk given by an industrial psychologist, Mrs J. Martin, B.A., A.M.I.P.M., is reproduced by her kind permission and constitutes the text of the following two pages.

INTERVIEWING—PROCEDURE AND TECHNIQUES

Most of us regard ourselves as shrewd judges of character. Other people are often incompetent in this respect, allowing themselves, when attempting to assess their fellows, to be misled by what is superficial or irrelevant. We, on the other hand, can size up a person accurately and objectively. It is mainly because this belief is so widespread and so well entrenched that the interview has been accepted for many years as a reliable means of assessing human personality for a variety of purposes. Evidence may be brought forward which casts doubt on the reliability of the interview as a method of appraisal, but this is readily shrugged aside as being applicable only to other people. You and I know a good man when we see one.

However, a considerable body of research evidence shows that a formidable case can be made against the use of interviews as a means of assessing an individual's character and potentialities. Investigations have been carried out to check the validity of selecting adults for posts of various kinds by means of interviews. The results are not very heartening. Marked differences have been found between the judgments formed by different interviewers, and follow-up studies have shown that decisions arrived at in this way do not provide a very

[*Continued on p. 226*

APPLICATION FOR EMPLOYMENT
(FACTORY)

Surname .... Date of Birth ....

Christian Name(s) .... Married or Single ....

Home Address .... No. of Children ....

.... Nationality ....

....

....

For what work are you applying? ....

Have you ever been employed by this Company? ....

If so, please state department ....and date from..........to..........

DETAILS OF DISABILITY OR SERIOUS ILLNESS

Registration Number .... Expiry Date....................

Office of Registration .... Nature of Disability ....

Nat. Insurance No. ....

Have you ever suffered from a serious illness? ....

For what period have you been absent through illness in the past 3 years?

....

EXPERIENCE IN INDUSTRY

Name and Address .... Date Joined....................

of present/last employer................ Date Left........................

.... Present Rate ....

Nature of Business........................ Nature of Job ....

Reason for Leaving ....

Name and Address .... Date Joined....................

of previous employer .... Date Left........................

.... Finishing Rate................

Nature of Business........................ Nature of Job ....

Reason for Leaving ....

OTHER INFORMATION

You may give details of any special experience

....

....

....

Signature of Applicant .... Date ....

FIG. 38 *a.—Employment application form for a factory worker (front)*

EMPLOYMENT SECTION

Classification ....

Hours ....

Rate—*basic* .... *job* ....

Remarks on suitability of applicant

Signed ....

MEDICAL DEPARTMENT

Examination:

X-Ray result:

Signed ....

FACTORY

Accepted YES/NO

Department or Section ....

To Commence on .... at ....

Remarks:

Signed ....

Engagement Letter and Note	Action taken	Induction
Handbook	Acknowledgment	Social Club
Confirmation	N.I. Card	
	P.45	
	References	
	E. of P. Permit	

FIG. 38 b.—*Employment application form for a factory worker* (back) satisfactory prediction of the extent to which a person is likely to succeed in a particular job.

The reasons for the inadequacy of the interview as a means of assessment are reasonably clear. Its chief deficiency no doubt lies in the fact that an interviewer's judgment is inevitably based on a small and often wholly unrepresentative sample of the behaviour of the individual who appears before him. The smaller any sample, the less likely is it to reflect adequately the whole from which it is drawn. Furthermore, a person's behaviour in an interview is likely to be unrepresentative for additional reasons. This situation is unreal and often stress-provoking, and a person's reactions in these circumstances are often uncharacteristic. Verbal facility is often mistaken for intelligence or reasoning power and a person's appearance can influence the assessments that are made of his intellect and character.

Despite this seemingly wholesale condemnation of the use of interviews and despite all the developments in scientific testing, *the interview has never lost ground and reigns supreme in methods of selection.* The world is full of bad interviewers because they do not have the aptitude for interviewing and are not aware of how to go about it. So let us now be a little more constructive by considering what an interview is and what procedures and techniques are involved.

What is an interview? It is a face-to-face encounter with a purpose: it employs conversation. The interview should aim to bring out *attitudes* rather than facts. *The key to finding this out is through people's sentiments and feelings rather than someone's knowledge.* Conversation is the means by which this is achieved.

There are two processes at work in an interview which can be elucidated:

    (*a*) stimulation;
    (*b*) cognition.

By stimulation we mean what the word implies—getting a person to "open up." This is vitally important to the success of an interview. Therefore, the interviewer must ensure that the interviewee is sufficiently stimulated. Sometimes the person being interviewed will be sufficiently "keyed up" and ready to talk—but occasionally stimulation is necessary.

The second process—cognition, involves the assessment of attitudes. It is essential to do this fairly and without personal prejudice. A good interviewer knows himself and his own weaknesses. We build up the assessment from the beginning of the interview until the end and even afterwards.

A man who is good at stimulation is not necessarily the good assessor of an attitude or situation. It is easier to teach assessment because the "knack" of stimulation is something which is extremely difficult to teach.

Starting at the beginning, let us take a look at the setting of an interview. A good waiting room for potential interviewees not only helps them but in doing so helps the person interviewing. A nervous person in a bad waiting room which is perhaps cold will often not do justice to himself. As for the interview itself, it is perhaps unnecessary to set the stage too much. It is perhaps better to have the candidate's chair at one side rather than have him facing opposite with the desk in between acting as a sort of barrier.

There are one or two *rules of behaviour* when interviewing of which we might remind ourselves. Do not loll back on an easy chair while the candidate is sitting upright: one should look alert in an interview. Mainly it can be said that behaviour should be left to social convention and the requirements of the particular situation. The interview can and should be allowed to follow the direction it takes naturally. A planned interview rarely runs exactly according to the scheme. *It is fundamental that the candidate should be put at his ease.*

The topics of conversation vary enormously. However, it is usually necessary to "warm up" a person with a few general topics of mutual concern, and immediately a social relationship is established. Try to cultivate ways of establishing a *rapport* or relationship.

We want to discover the interests and sentiments of the candidate, his social relationships, family and friends. Should one raise unpleasant topics? We should in fact raise them because otherwise the candidate may be on edge wondering if they will be asked. Should one criticise in an interview? If we completely limit criticism then it tends to become rather artificial but we should not be destructively critical. The interviewer should never argue or give advice.

The good interviewer avoids questions of a highly suggestive value such as "You wouldn't like canteen work, would you?"

He makes considerable use of indirect questions—particularly when he is dealing with matters such as family relationships on which reserve or evasion may be expected.

One can aid stimulation in an interview by certain tactics, *e.g. amplification by agreement* when the examiner takes up some remark of the candidate, develops it and tries to study the attitudes with which it is expressed. *Partial disagreement* will test the general attitude of the candidate; while *surprise* will induce the candidate to amplify his views. Interest is a very obvious tactic. Lack of interest on the part of the interviewer is suggested as the only way to get a person to stop.

Mention must be made of the *autobiographical history* interview, as it is one of the most successful techniques in interviewing. It is not so much what the person tells you but how he tells it.

The good interviewer obtrudes as little as possible into the conversation; he takes part only as far as it is necessary to give information or to elicit information from the candidate. The interviewer must play as passive a role as possible, concentrating on trying to interpret the facts of the candidate's experience in the light of the circumstances which have influenced his progress and of his own attitude to the events and achievements discussed.

Interviewing is an art rather than a science, but like most arts can be improved by closer study.

What form should the assessment of candidates take? Some people can classify types fairly easily, but often it takes practice to make a fair assessment. The Seven-Point Plan aims at providing us with a simple but scientifically-defensible assessment "system."

The plan, devised by the National Institute of Industrial Psychology, consists of a series of questions gathered together under seven headings. It should be regarded as a short list of items that seem to deserve consideration in any comprehensive investigation of a person's occupational assets and liabilities.

THE SEVEN-POINT PLAN

The National Institute of Industrial Psychology has pioneered work on employment selection, and the two men responsible for many developments in this field are Professor Alec Rodger and Mr John Munro Fraser.* The former was responsible for the Seven-Point Plan which is a systematic approach to describing a job and matching a worker to it, and which is reproduced by kind permission of Professor Rodger and the National Institute of Industrial Psychology.

1. Physical make-up.—Has he any defects of health or physique that may be of occupational importance? How agreeable are his appearance, his bearing and his speech?

2. Attainments.—What type of education has he had? How well has he done educationally? What occupational training and experience has he had already? How well has he done occupationally?

3. General intelligence.—How much general intelligence can he display? How much general intelligence does he ordinarily display?

4. Special aptitudes.—Has he any marked mechanical aptitude, manual dexterity; facility in the use of words or figures; talent for drawing or music?

5. Interests.—To what extent are his interests intellectual; practical-constructional; physical-active; social; artistic?

6. Disposition.—How acceptable does he make himself to other people? Does he influence others? Is he steady and dependable? Is he self-reliant?

7. Circumstances.—What are his domestic circumstances? What do the other members of the family do for a living? Are there any special openings available for him?

No claim is made for the infallibility of the scheme. Indeed, the author of the plan acknowledges a number of possible disadvantages which are shown below:

1. Individuals are not readily divided into seven neat parcels, each representing a particular quality.

2. Each person's qualities are in a continuous state of change so that the past, present and future developments should be assessed. The Seven-Point Plan gives the impression that the assessment is only concerned with the time when the interview takes place.

3. Judgment is still essential. Interviewers should not run away with the idea that the Plan selects the most suitable candidate quite automatically.

Allowing for these possible limitations, and used sensibly, the Plan can provide a foundation for effective selection procedures. Because of

* See the latest edition of this writer's standard work *Employment Interviewing*, Macdonald & Evans, 1966.

the systematic approach a much more objective assessment of a candidate can be compiled. A number of interviewers (*e.g.* a committee) can employ the same system and then compare the results.

The Plan is flexible so that it can be adapted to meet the requirements of any business. Any system should cover the following:

1. Job description (*see* pp. 219 and 231 for details and examples).
2. Job requirements based on the Seven-Point Plan.

Some schemes use points so each requirement is given a numerical value. For example, physical make-up for a job may be given six points as a maximum. Any candidate who possesses all the physical requirements can then be given six points, and other applicants fewer points dependent upon the assessment.

FINAL SELECTION

From a management theory standpoint it should be remembered that line and functional managers should have the final say as to who should be engaged. The management law *Parity of Authority and Responsibility*, explained on p. 35, states that authority and responsibility should go together. Accordingly, if a departmental manager is to be held responsible for the work of men in his department it is only right and proper that he selects them. There is then no excuse that the wrong personnel have been selected. The personnel department staff carry out all the routine work of advertising and sorting the completed application forms; they may also carry out preliminary interviews before the final selection is made.

In some businesses, the entire process of engaging employees is left to the personnel department. This is quite wrong and is in opposition to the idea behind the personnel function—namely, to advise on employee selection. Unfortunately, many line managers shirk their responsibilities by expecting workers to be engaged without any effort whatsoever on their part. A request is sent to the personnel department to the effect that an operator or other worker is required and the department is expected to produce the man without any more ado. This kind of arrangement is unfair to the personnel department who cannot be expected to know every requirement in detail. It is rather like a request from the maintenance department to the purchasing department for "mild steel for maintenance" to be obtained. Without knowledge of quality, size, shape and other particulars, no attempt to purchase would be made. The maintenance engineer would be expected to know precisely what he wanted and would take responsibility for suitability of the material once purchased according to his specification.

The engagement of employees is a much more serious matter than purchasing maintenance materials. If the latter are wrong, they can be returned to the supplier or used for some other purpose. This is not the case with a misfit employee who may be difficult to discharge, and even if he is dismissed eventually the costs of hiring, training and loss of production can be very high indeed.

In order to cut down the work of a line manager it is sometimes possible to come to a compromise arrangement, whereby he approves the final candidate who is selected by the personnel staff. Whether this can be a realistic practice depends upon the circumstances. What would happen if a number of "final" candidates were rejected by a fore-man is a matter for conjecture; yet this could happen and, if so, there would be the problem of deciding who had the last word.

A procedure which could be followed more often is for a line or functional manager to be present when interviews take place. He could then ask questions and form his opinion through the entire process, thus ensuring that the selected candidate would have his approval. The main difficulty is the fact that interviews can be very time-consuming. How-ever, properly time-arranged for a line manager's convenience, this system can work and can certainly speed up the process of recruitment. The method which calls for the personnel department to interview applicants who are later interviewed again by the manager for whose department they are being selected is long-winded and cumbersome.

Examination Questions on Chapter XIV are given at the end of Chapter XV.

CHAPTER XV

JOB EVALUATION AND WAGE STRUCTURE

As implied by the name, job evaluation is concerned with *placing a value on each job* and is not concerned with the efficiency of the people carrying out the work. The latter is more properly described as *merit rating* (*see* p. 239).

When used in connection with salaried staff (*e.g.* accountancy personnel) the description often used is *job grading*. However, this is still job evaluation, although a different approach for arriving at the grades may be adopted. A scheme developed by the Institute of Office Management for office staff is reproduced later in this section.

Basically, job evaluation involves the following steps:

1. Describing the requirements for each job.
2. Giving each requirement a value (usually on a "points" system).
3. Totalling the values given so as to arrive at a total value for the job.
4. Linking the values with the wage or salary structure, thereby paying for each job in terms of what it is worth.

The important feature of a system of job evaluation is that an attempt is made to be as objective as possible, and to disregard the qualities of the persons who are doing the jobs. Each time a job is considered the question asked is: how does this job compare with other jobs and what is its *relative* value?

Because judgment is involved it follows that absolute accuracy cannot be obtained. Nevertheless, the accuracy is sufficient for most practical purposes and, therefore, job evaluation is an extremely valuable tool of management.

PROCEDURE FOR JOB EVALUATION

There is no standardised procedure for planning, installing and operating a system of job evaluation. Each scheme should be tailored to meet the needs of the business concerned. Remembering this fact, an outline of the procedures involved in job evaluation is given below:

Describing jobs

Examples of the brief job descriptions used when advertising were given in the previous chapter. In job evaluation it is necessary to give attention to the following:

[*Continued on p. 233*

231

JOB DESCRIPTION FORM

Job Description Ref: J31

Job Title: Drill operator   *Department:* Machine-shop

                                      Sex: Male

Assessor: M. Jones   *Date:* 21/8/19..

1. Job Essentials

Sets up drill; studies production orders and drawings; drills holes in accordance with instructions; makes simple calculations when necessary.

2. Job Analysis

Receive components from internal transport man. Obtain production order from foreman and then clock on to job using Job Time Card. Put Material Requisition into Stores and then obtain necessary jig and other tools from Tool Store.

Commence drilling operations, and when batch completed place ready for collection by internal transport. Clock off job and then obtain a new production order and repeat process.

3. Job Requirements

SKILL

Training time: 3 weeks for simple operations and up to 12 weeks for difficult operations.

Dexterity: Essential for most of the work.

Complexity: Ability to read drawings and follow production orders essential. Work involves drilling small batches on a variety of components.

RESPONSIBILITY

Accurate reading of production orders/drawings.

Inaccurate drilling will lead to rejection of costly components.

Has responsibility for drilling on many expensive materials, including stainless steel.

Must ensure that drills are maintained in good condition by proper handling.

MENTAL EFFORT

Reasoning: Required to interpret instructions on drawings and production orders.

Concentration: Must be observant at all times when operating drill.

WORKING CONDITIONS

Conditions quite pleasant and clean.

Work fairly monotonous.

No heavy carrying or lifting involved.

No special hazards involved provided safety regulations are followed.

FIG. 39.—*Simplified job description form*

(*a*) Precise title of the job (*e.g.* drill operator, storekeeper, maintenance fitter, but *not* labourer or machine-shop operator because these are too general).

(*b*) Analyse the job into its constituent tasks and record *why, how* and *when* these are done.

(*c*) State what responsibilities are involved, including orders received and given, and contact with other people in the organisation. Linked with this would be the skill, knowledge and training required to carry out the work.

(*d*) Conditions of employment for each job should be recorded. This has an important bearing on evaluation. A man who re-lines a furnace with refractory material has to work under much more arduous conditions than, say, a tool maker.

These and related matters should be considered. The degree of analysis depends upon the nature of the job being described, and the opinions of those responsible for job evaluation (the assessors). An example of what is involved can be seen from the job description form (Fig. 39). This form only illustrates the principles involved, and should *not* be regarded as an accurate job description for a drill operator.

The information necessary for completing a job description form has to be obtained from observation, discussions with operators and supervisors, and consultation with work study or organisation and methods experts.

An important aspect of job evaluation is to *obtain agreement* on each job description. Usually this involves agreement by the operators who are actually carrying out the work. If an operator does not agree with a job description then he should be given an opportunity to appeal. This appeal is, in fact, more likely to come when a "value" has been placed on a job. If the value is linked with wage payments an operator is very much concerned with seeing that he gets the largest possible value assigned to his job. Some companies have a committee to deal with appeals; others obtain agreement through the trade unions which represent the workers.

Evaluating jobs

Once jobs have been described the evaluation process can begin. As a first step it is usual to select a number of "key jobs" which may be used as standards against which to compare others. These should be representative of the type of work carried on, and should be capable of being recognised as such by the personnel in the factory when job evaluation is being introduced. Skilled, semi-skilled and unskilled jobs should be included, and as many as twenty may be necessary to obtain a representative selection.

The "weights" to be employed should now be chosen. The most usual are "points," so many points being allotted to each main factor

JOB EVALUATION FORM

Job Description Ref: J31
Job Title: Drill operator *Department:* Machine-shop
 Sex: Male
Assessor: M. Jones *Date* 25/8/19. .

	Max	Notes	Points
SKILL			
Training time	12		6
Dexterity	30		25
Complexity	20		15
Basic knowledge	18		12
	80		58
RESPONSIBILITY			
Initiative required	5		3
Control over production	5		4
Control over costs	5		4
Care of tools	5		4
Quality control	5		4
	25		19
MENTAL EFFORT			
Dealing with situations	12		8
Concentration	13		6
	25		14
WORKING CONDITIONS			
Unpleasant working conditions	5		2
Monotony	5		4
Physical effort	5		3
Special hazards	5		2
	20		11
Maximum Grand Total	150		102

JOB CLASSIFICATION

Grade	A	B	C	D	E	F
Points possible	up to 100	101 to 110	111 to 120	121 to 130	131 to 140	141 to 150
Points awarded		102				

FIG. 40.—*Simplified job evaluation form*

contained in a job. Reference to the job description form (Fig. 39) will show that the job requirements are broken down into:

(a) Skill.
(b) Responsibility.
(c) Mental effort.
(d) Working conditions.

When points have been awarded there may be a position something like that shown below:

(a) Skill   80 points
(b) Responsibility   25   „
(c) Mental effort   25   „
(d) Working conditions   20   „

How the points are accumulated, from taking points awarded to each sub-division of a job requirement, is shown on the job evaluation form (Fig. 40). If the Seven-Point Plan is employed, described in the previous chapter, the breakdown of the job requirements could follow those given on p. 228.

There are other methods of job evaluation such as factor comparison, relative ranking of jobs in order of importance and job grading: an example of the latter for office workers is given on p. 237. Some plans adopt a combination of these methods, but for the rank-and-file factory employee the Points Method appears to be the most popular.* This method is easy to employ and understand. Moreover, there is a certain preciseness given from the use of numbers. This is not to say that any job evaluation can be 100% accurate, but numbers allow a more accurate assessment to be made than is possible from any method which uses a general approach such as "High," "Low" and "Medium."

If a points system is to be used, it is first applied to all the key jobs, and subsequently all other jobs are fitted into the pattern and evaluated by reference to the points given to the factors in the key jobs.

The example of a job evaluation form which is shown in Fig. 40 has been simplified to stress only the basic principles. In practice a much more detailed analysis of the job requirements would be necessary and points would be awarded to each. The "notes" column would be completed by the assessor to explain why points had been awarded. As in the case of the job description, the analysis and points awarded should not be regarded as indicative of the relative importance of operating a drilling machine.

* See, for example, *Job Evaluation, a practical guide*, p. 11, where this conclusion is reached. Published by the British Institute of Management, London, 1961.

DETERMINING THE WAGE STRUCTURE

Once job evaluations have been prepared for all the *key jobs* it should be possible to determine the wage structure. Taking a simple example, a situation similar to the following may emerge:

Job class	Average rate (pence per hour)
A	60
B	65
C	70
D	75
E	80
F	85

Referring to this table it is possible to see the hourly rate appropriate for any job. This is the foundation stone upon which the wage structure is built.

An alternative approach is to plot on a scatter diagram the hourly rates against the points for all the key jobs. The procedure is to place dots at the appropriate points and then to find an average by drawing a line in a way which shows an equal number of dots at each side. A simple scatter diagram is shown below:

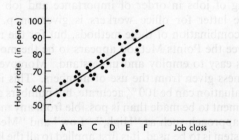

FIG. 41.—*Points system for evaluating average hourly rate*

Many refinements are possible in calculating the existing wage rates, and for details of these the reader is asked to consult a specialist book on job evaluation. Theoretically, *on average* the wages paid will be the same as when job evaluation was not employed. In practice, so that no worker may feel that he is being dealt with unfairly, a wage level may be fixed which is slightly above the average obtained from the existing scale.

The process of evaluating all jobs should continue until every job has been covered.

When dealing with clerical and other office work a different approach will be necessary. Instead of a points system it is generally advisable to use a scheme which employs grades. The work of the Institute of

Office Management is worthy of special mention. This is summarised in a book entitled *Clerical Job Grading and Merit Rating* and the reader is advised to refer to this for further details. A summary of the job grades is shown below.

JOB GRADES (INSTITUTE OF OFFICE MANAGEMENT)

The six job grades (A–F) used are defined as follows:

A grade.—Tasks which require no previous clerical experience; each individual task is allotted and is either very simple or closely directed.

B grade.—Tasks which, because of their simplicity, are carried out in accordance with a limited number of well-defined rules after a comparatively short period of training (a few weeks); these tasks are closely directed and checked, and are carried out in a daily routine covered by a time-table and short period control.

C grade.—Tasks which are of a routine character and follow well-defined rules, but which require either a reasonable degree of experience or a special aptitude for the task and which are carried out according to a daily routine covered by a time-table and subject to short period control.

D grade.—Tasks which require considerable experience but only a very limited degree of initiative and which are carried out according to a predetermined procedure and precise rules; the tasks are carried out according to a daily routine which varies but not sufficiently to necessitate any considerable direction.

E grade.—Tasks which require a significant, but not extensive, measure of discretion and initiative or which require a specialised knowledge and individual responsibility for the work.

F grade.—Tasks which necessitate exercising an extensive measure of responsibility and judgment or the application of a technique (legal, accounting, statistical, engineering).

Jobs are fitted into the appropriate grades and then paid on a scale which also coincides with the A–F scale. An allowance for merit is made by assessing a clerk's ability into "qualified," "experienced," "superior" and "superlative." An explanation of merit rating is given in a later section in this chapter.

BENEFITS FROM JOB EVALUATION

A number of advantages are claimed from the employment of job evaluation and these are summarised below:

1. It provides a systematic procedure for describing and placing a value on each job.

2. A man is paid for the work he performs so there is a tendency for him to be more satisfied than when job evaluation does not exist.

3. Arising from 2 above there should be more co-operation, higher morale, less absenteeism, reduced labour turnover and an overall improvement in efficiency.

4. The job descriptions can be employed in recruitment and selection.

There are some limitations and these are as follows:

1. Too much reliance may be placed on the "scientific assessment" of the jobs with the result that dissatisfaction is felt with the entire scheme. This emphasises the importance of consultation with employees and unions before a job description is settled.

2. No allowance is made for differences displayed in performing a job. Two men doing the same job will be paid the same wage even though one is much more experienced and produces a much higher output. This disadvantage can be overcome by paying a merit award or some form of incentive bonus.

3. Rates of pay are affected by the supply and demand for workers as well as the nature of the job.

If the job evaluation scheme is followed without regard to the conditions of the labour market there may be difficulty in obtaining the services of employees who are trained to perform certain jobs.

These limitations must be remembered and overcome by appropriate action. They are not insurmountable barriers, but rather difficulties of the kind normally encountered in the process of management. Properly handled they should not invalidate a job evaluation scheme.

A PRACTICAL SCHEME

The foundation for a practical scheme of job evaluation may be obtained from Tables V and VI (pp. 239–242) which are reproduced and adapted from *Time Study and Ratefixing* by courtesy of Sir Isaac Pitman & Sons Ltd. The points are shown as indications of the kind of analysis which may be used: the scheme can be adapted to meet specific requirements.

TABLE V.—BASIC FIGURES FOR POINT EVALUATION OF WORK

	Points		Points
A. PROFESSIONAL EXPERIENCE BASED ON TRAINING		**B. BODILY EFFORT FOR CONTINUOUS PERFORMANCE**	
(a) Work carried out by an unskilled worker according to instructions	1	(a) Light work, sedentary, manipulating work-pieces up to 1 lb per piece	1
(b) Work carried out by an unskilled worker independently ...	2	(b) Normal work, standing, manipulating work-pieces up to 11 lb per piece	2
(c) Work carried out by a semi-skilled worker according to instructions	3	(c) Heavy work, standing, manipulating work-pieces of 22 to 55 lb	3
(d) Work carried out by a semi-skilled worker independently...	4	(d) Hard work, standing and connected with trying rhythmic movements of work-pieces or tools up to 11 lb	4
(e) Skilled worker, at least three years of apprenticeship, during the first two years after finishing the apprenticeship	5	(e) Very hard work with trying and constantly repeating movements for mastering heavy loads	5
(f) As (e), but during third and fourth year after finishing the apprenticeship	6		
(g) As (e), but during the fifth year after finishing the apprenticeship and later	7		

TABLE V—*continued*

Points

C. INTELLIGENCE (PERCEPTIVE FACULTY)
(a) Below average 1
(b) Average 2
(c) Above average 3

D. SKILL AND EXPERIENCE
(a) Of low degree as required for A (a) (b) (c) 1
(b) Of normal degree as required for A (d) (e) (f) 2
(c) Of high degree as required for A (g) 3

E. ACCURACY AND QUALITY OF THE WORK
(a) Low quality plain fit, not below Fit 8 of ISA tolerances ... 1
(b) Normal quality, fine fit to 6 and 7 of ISA tolerances 2
(c) High quality, extra fine fit, to 5 of ISA tolerances 3
(d) First class quality, extra fine fits, adjusting, honing and lapping work 4

F. CONSCIENTIOUSNESS, RELIABILITY, SAFETY OF PERFORMANCE
(a) With usual work-pieces 1
(b) With valuable work-pieces ... 2

G. UNDERSTANDING OF THE NECESSITY OF ORDER AND CLEANLINESS
(a) Within the narrow limits of an individual work-place ... 1
(b) Within larger limits, for instance, common tool room, stores, etc. 2

Points

H. HONESTY
(a) Care of low values 1
(b) Care of high values 2

J. PRESENCE OF MIND
(a) When objects of low value are in danger 1
(b) When objects of high value are in danger 2

K. INDEPENDENT THINKING AND RESPONSIBILITY
(a) Simple thinking, e.g. for mechanical mass production ... 1
(b) Normal thinking, e.g. for changing series production ... 2
(c) Reflective thinking, e.g. for difficult work of a special character 3

L. ALLOWANCES FOR DIRT AND TROUBLE OF VARIOUS KINDS
(a) Cleaning of lavatories, bad conditions of dust, fumes, etc., without any effect dangerous to health ... ...
(b) Bad conditions, gauged by noise difficult to bear, excessive dirt, quick changes of temperature, fumes and gases occasionally dangerous in effect to health 2
(c) Bad conditions, due to excessive heat, noise, gases, etc., long continued exposure which may result in damage to health ... 3

M. DILIGENCE, ENERGY, EXERTION OF WILL
(a) For work defined under A (a) to A (g) 1
(b) For work defined under L (b) ... 2
(c) For work defined under L (c) ... 3

MERIT RATING

Reference to merit rating was made earlier in connection with the clerical grading plan created by the Institute of Office Management. Each person's ability in performing a particular job is assessed and, where warranted, an additional payment known as a "merit award" is made.

Unfortunately, there are difficulties encountered in deciding when a merit award should be made. A simple scheme for merit rating may take the following form:

(a) Basic rate per hour = Normal performance.
(b) Basic rate + £0·01 = Skilled performance.
(c) Basic rate + £0·02 = Very skilled performance.

TABLE VI.—POINT EVALUATION

TYPE OF PERFORMANCE	GROUP OF WORKERS	A	B	C	D	E	F	G	H	J	K	L	M	Total Points	£
						INDIVIDUAL POINTS ACCORDING TO TABLE V									
1. Messenger for non-confidential messages	Unskilled	a-1	a-1	a-1	a-1		a-1		a-1					6	0·30
2. Messenger for confidential messages	Unskilled	a-1	a-1	b-2	a-1		b-2		b-2					9	0·45
3. Easy work in the yard: clearing, cleaning, simple transport work under supervision	Unskilled	a-1	a-1	b-2	a-1		a-1					a-1		7	0·35
4. Heavy work in the yard: continuous loading and transporting in gangs; work of similar kind in the workshops	Unskilled	a-1	b-2	a-1	a-1		a-1	a-1	a-1			a-1		9	0·45
5. Crane driver	Semi-skilled, independent	a-1	c-3	b-2	a-1		a-1	b-2	a-1		a-1			12	0·60
6. Slinger of crane loads, charge hand of gangs, mentioned under 4	Semi-skilled, independent	d-4	b-2	b-2	a-1		b-2	b-2	a-1		a-1			15	0·75
7. Boiler and engine attendant (automatic stoking)	Semi-skilled, independent	d-4	b-2	b-2	a-1		b-2	b-2	a-1	b-2				16	0·80
8. Store room, drawing office, or tool room attendant (if several, each for a limited part of the work)	Unskilled	d-4	b-2	b-2	a-1		a-1		a-1					11	0·55
9. Ditto as 8, but only one person working in the room, responsible for the work, or if several persons working in one room, each responsible for his part and keeping a card index of his work	Semi-skilled	b-2	b-2	b-2	a-1	a-1	a-1	b-2	a-1		a-1			13	0·65
10. Tool room attendant, simultaneously repairing and maintaining tools, e.g. sharpening simple tools, whetting and setting reamers, adjusting jigs and fixtures, putting together tools for a particular job, etc.	Skilled, with limited ability of work, for instance in consequence of an accident in the shop	e-5	b-2	b-2	b-2	a-1	a-1	b-2	a-1					16	0·80
11. Machine work in cutting off and sawing shop (sawing and cutting off only)	Semi-skilled	c-3	c-3	b-2	a-1		a-1		a-1					11	0·55
12. Roughing on cutting off and drilling machines in cutting off shop, measuring by caliper slide accurate to 0·02 in.	Semi-skilled	c-3	c-3	b-2	a-1	a-1	a-1		a-1					12	0·60
13. Simple drilling, boring and facing work and the like without tolerances	Semi-skilled	c-3	c-3	b-2	a-1	a-1	a-1		a-1					12	0·60

AUTHOR'S NOTE: The rates of pay shown in the final column of Table VI require adjustment to present-day hourly rates before being used.

TABLE VI—*continued*

TYPE OF PERFORMANCE	GROUP OF WORKERS	A	B	C	D	E	F	G	H	J	K	L	M	Total Points	£
14. Drilling to tolerances ISA/H7, but with an accuracy of lengths and centre distances not below ISA quality 8	Semi-skilled, independent	d-4	c-3	b-2	a-1	a-1		a-1			b-2			14	0·70
15. Precision drilling with tolerances ISA/H7 and accuracy of lengths and centre distances according to ISA quality 7, required only on drilling	Semi-skilled, independent	d-4	c-3	b-2	b-2	b-2	a-1	a-1			b-2			17	0·85
16. Simple milling and planing work without adjustment to special accuracy measuring by caliper slide up to 0·008 in.	Semi-skilled	c-3	c-3	b-2	a-1	a-1		a-1			a-1			12	0·60
17. Milling and planing work to tolerances ISA quality 8 to 9 with accurate adjustment in two planes according to marking off or standard face	Semi-skilled, independent	d-4	c-3	b-2	a-1	a-1		a-1			b-2			14	0·70
18. Precision and planing work to tolerances of ISA quality 7 and with accurate adjustment in two planes according to marking off and standard faces, further more universal milling work (index head work) and difficult milling work on changing jobs of various kinds, including setting	Semi-skilled, independent	d-4	c-3	b-2	b-2	a-1	a-1	a-1			c-3			17	0·85
19. Jobs on horizontal boring and milling machines to tolerances ISA quality 7 and accuracy of lengths and centre distances, etc., not below ISA quality 8	Semi-skilled, independent	d-4	c-3	b-2	b-2	a-1	a-1	a-1			b-2			16	0·80
20. As 19 but also accuracy of lengths and centre distances to ISA quality 7	Semi-skilled, independent, sometimes even skilled	d-4	c-3	b-2	b-2	b-2	a-1	a-1			c-3			18	0·90
21. High precision boring work on special high class boring machines to tolerances ISA quality 6 to 5	Skilled	f-6	b-2	b-2	b-2	d-4	a-1	a-1			b-2			20	1·00
22. Work on capstan lathes without tolerances for external diameters, internal diameters with tolerances reamed, without setting	Semi-skilled	c-3	b-2	b-2	a-1	a-1		a-1			a-1			11	0·55
23. Work on capstan lathes with an accuracy of ISA quality 7 and 6, inclusive setting	Semi-skilled, independent	d-4	b-2	b-2	b-2	b-2		a-1			b-2			15	0·75
24. External, internal and surface grinding, roughing only, with an accuracy not closer than 0·002 in.	Semi-skilled	c-3	b-2	b-2	a-1	a-1		a-1			a-1			11	0·55

I

TABLE VI—continued

TYPE OF PERFORMANCE	GROUP OF WORKERS	INDIVIDUAL POINTS ACCORDING TO TABLE V												Total Points	£
		A	B	C	D	E	F	G	H	J	K	L	M		
25. As 23, but with an accuracy of ISA quality 7 to 6 and including setting	Semi-skilled, independent	d-4	b-2	b-2	b-2	b-2		a-1			b-2			15	0·75
26. Precision grinding work with an accuracy of ISA quality 5 and below 0·004 in., including setting	Semi-skilled, sometimes skilled, independent	d-4	b-2	b-2	b-2	d-4	a-1	a-1			b-2			18	0·90
27. Simple turning jobs, chuck and centre work, accuracy not below 0·02 (turning for grinding) bores, reaming to tolerances	Semi-skilled, sometimes skilled, independent	c-5	b-2	b-2	a-1	a-1	a-1	a-1			a-1			13	0·65
28. Turning work with accuracy of ISA quality 7 to 6; turning work of various kinds, for example, producing tools	Skilled	f-6	b-2	b-2	b-2	b-2	a-1	a-1			b-2			18	0·90
29. Difficult turning work with a degree of accuracy requiring highly developed sense of touch, e.g. measurement by large gauges, calipers, inside micrometers, etc., profiling work with high degree of accuracy, and turning work requiring special experience	Skilled	g-7	c-3	b-2	c-3	c-3	a-1	a-1			c-3			23	1·15
30. Setting of one-spindle automatics for single work pieces and of capstan lathes according to tool-plan with strictly ordered tools	Skilled	g-7	b-2	b-2	b-2	b-2	a-1	a-1			b-2			19	0·95
31. Setting of multi-spindle automatics, including all work required, as for instance, determination and combination of tools and appliances	Skilled	g-7	b-2	c-3	c-3	b-2	a-1	a-1			c-3			22	1·10
32. Fitter, working in gangs	Skilled	c-3	c-3	b-2	b-2	b-2	a-1	a-1			b-2			18	0·90
33. Fitter, working independently	Skilled	g-7	c-3	b-2	b-2	b-2	a-1	a-1			b-2			20	1·00
34. Maintenance fitter and tool maker for normal work	Skilled	g-7	c-3	b-2	b-2	b-2	a-1	a-1			b-2	a-1		21	1·05
35. Tool maker for tools of very high accuracy and gauges of accuracy according to ISA quality 6 to 5	Skilled	g-7	c-3	c-3	c-3	c-3	a-1	a-1			c-3			24	1·20
36. Independent fitters for assembly work, charge hands (working supervisors of gangs) and maintenance fitters for work of high responsibility	Skilled	g-7	c-3	c-3	c-3	b-2	b-2	b-2			c-3			25	1·25

There should be a clear indication from the personnel department, agreed with unions, how each category (*a*), (*b*) and (*c*) should be determined. The fitting of each employee into the appropriate category should be left to the responsible line manager.

In practice, there is a tendency for the merit award to become an automatic award after a certain period has passed; *e.g.* after twelve months' service. This is quite contrary to the purpose of the award and is often due to pressure from unions. The author has encountered cases in industry where the very fact that a man has been employed for a year without being dismissed (and dismissal would have been extremely difficult without strike action) is taken as justification for a merit award. Merit rating thus becomes a device for obtaining an amount above the basic rate with or without the existence of the necessary experience and skill.

Another form of merit rating, based on years of service, generally applies to clerical and administrative posts. An employee is appointed on a scale which ranges from a minimum to a maximum. The assumption made is that each year of experience counts for an increment until the maximum is reached. Some companies also pay long service awards in addition to the maximum for the grade. Thus a man may be paid an additional amount of, say, £40 after ten years' service. This system has the effect of reducing labour turnover, but whether it improves efficiency is open to doubt. A better way would be to encourage a man to aim for promotion; all too often when there is virtually no turnover of labour and no promotion, there comes a point when employees see themselves in a routine job, being paid much more than they are worth, and being quite happy to carry on without undue effort. All this leads to stagnation and inefficiency and encourages the operation of Parkinson's Law (*see* p. 59) to the fullest possible extent.

EXAMINATION QUESTIONS

Also includes Questions on Chapters XIII and XIV

1. Construct an executive rating scale which will indicate your view of the qualities to be considered in appraising an individual. For each trait on your scale, describe the several levels in such a way as will clearly convey a rating.

2. What techniques are available for management development purposes? List and briefly describe these techniques, giving in detail the advantages and limitations of one such technique. In the course of a management development programme what is the purpose of an appraisal interview?

3. What advantages are to be gained from a well-defined policy of industrial training and an effectively planned training programme? Describe briefly two methods for the training of semi-skilled workers on short-cycle repetition work.

4. The wages and working conditions of the workers in an industry are often governed by some form of agreement between organised bodies of employers on the one hand and employees on the other.

Tabulate the items which may be covered in the scope of such agreements and list the usual contents and terms contained in them. What effect will recent agreements on redundancy pay have on the management problem of planning employment?

5. How would you recruit and train foremen? Should a foreman be a member of a workmen's trade union and should his remuneration be related to the incentive earnings of the workpeople under his charge? State clearly the reasons for your views.

6. List and annotate the preparations for and the requirements of a good employment interview procedure for the recruitment of foremen. Outline a programme for the induction of the selected candidate.

7. Give a list of guiding principles and procedures which can be used to increase the effectiveness of employment interviews. Discuss the need for training interviewers to achieve effective selection.

8. Assume that a manufacturing company employing altogether about 1000 people is about to appoint for the first time a personnel manager. Tabulate (*i.e.* list one under the other) *ten* types of activity or service for which this personnel manager will probably be made responsible. Alongside each, indicate who is probably at present responsible for that service.

9. Draw a simple chart of the organisation of a Personnel Department for a company employing 2000 people and give a complete list of the staff of the department, indicating briefly the duties of each member of the staff.

10. Tabulate the duties and responsibilites of a personnel manager. In a medium-size company what are the advantages of employing such a specialist? What difficulties might be created in other management spheres?

CHAPTER XVI

PERSONNEL PROBLEMS: I

A FULL coverage of all matters affecting personnel is outside the scope of a general work of this type. A summary of the most important of these matters is given on pp. 199 to 201 in connection with personnel policy. Those which require further explanation are covered below.

INDUCTION

Induction ("indoctrination" or "orientation," as it is sometimes called) is the act of introducing a new employee to a business. It may be carried out by a member of the department in which a person is to work or by a training officer attached to the personnel department. The latter method is preferable; specialist knowledge and a planned programme are necessary for proper induction. In brief terms, induction training generally has the following objectives:

1. Introduction to the organisation, its objectives and its policies

There are many ways of accomplishing the introductory phases of an induction programme. Some companies rely on lectures and organised tours of the factory. Others, more ambitious, have films which tell the story of the company including its growth and achievements. One chemical manufacturing company known by the author has a coloured film which tells the story of the inventor of the basic chemical showing the discovery, the development, the present-day production processes, and the uses of the finished product.

Creating a favourable impression from the first day is vitally important. Care should be taken not to exaggerate what the company does or is likely to do for the welfare of its employees.

2. Explanation of the personnel policy

The likely contents of a personnel policy are outlined in an earlier chapter. A simple, practical guide to a company's policy and the regulations and conditions of employment may be included in an Employees' Handbook. Details of the social activities may also be published in the same book or in a separate booklet.

3. Introduction to the department

Once all general explanations have been made an employee can be shown his workplace and can meet his fellow workers. A foreman or chargehand can then explain the nature of the job and the procedures

245

followed within the department. Production orders, route cards, job cost cards and other forms should be explained so that an employee knows what is expected of him.

4. Induction audit

There is a danger that an employee may be given too much to learn in a very short period. For this reason some companies spread out the induction programme over a number of weeks, taking up one or two hours each week.

Irrespective of the method used for introducing employees to a business there should be an audit on the effectiveness of the induction programme. This can lead to improvements and, in addition, can act as revision for the employees who are given a "refresher course." The training department can organise short courses which cover all matters previously explained. Employees can then clear up any misunderstandings or difficulties they have encountered. Moreover, they can be encouraged to take a more active part in the social and sports activities. Sometimes a tour of the factory can be very valuable at this later stage, instead of when an employee first joins the company. When he has been working for a number of weeks he is able to appreciate the significance of what he sees much more than when he starts.

Because the process of induction gives an employee his first impressions of the organisation, it is vital that the task is carried out thoroughly and efficiently. An employee is made to feel welcome and is shown that he is to play an important part in the operations of the business. In addition, he is introduced to the company's objectives and conditions of employment. Once completed, the matter of giving formal training appropriate to the job can be given attention.

TRAINING

All employees have to receive some form of training. Even a skilled man joining a business has to be shown some aspects of his work. He may have to be instructed on how to operate a new machine; very likely he will have to receive training on the procedures relating to production control, cost accounting and other routines.

In addition to training a man or woman for some specific job, there is also a need to develop employees so that they become more skilled in a particular occupation or have wider general knowledge of techniques likely to be required in the future. When training potential managers it is necessary to broaden their outlook, rather than train them in a particular skill. The differences in approach at various employee levels should be clearer from a study of the training methods discussed later in this section.

Some companies leave the bulk of training to their rivals. They then pay attractive wages and salaries and recruit staff who have already received all formal education and training. However, this seems a very short-sighted policy. High morale and loyalty are not obtained merely by paying high wages. Furthermore, with a proper training programme there is more hope of obtaining the desired *quantities* and *qualities* of personnel. Some further advantages of an effective programme are as follows:

1. Training period reduced.—Left to haphazard, hit or miss methods an employee may take days, weeks or months to "pick up" the necessary skill. When the requirements for each job are understood and training tailored to those requirements it is possible for each employee to reach maximum output in the shortest possible time.

2. Can provide for succession.—As employees leave, whether by resignation, retirement or other reason, there is a need to ensure that other employees are available to carry on the work. This is especially important when considering the continuation of the established pattern of management.

3. Improvement of efficiency.—There is a definite correlation between training and efficiency. New methods, improved machines, better layout, more effective material utilisation and other matters can be covered by training to improve the efficiency of those who are already working at an efficient level.

4. Introduction of new techniques.—These can be introduced to employees by a company's own training officers or by sending them on courses at colleges of technology or similar institutions. Cost reduction, value analysis, ergonomics, net-work analysis and other techniques, described in other parts of this book, can be taught to employees so that they can be introduced into the company.

5. Developing a company image.—Internal training programmes can incorporate propaganda which puts forward the policy of the company. At the same time, by carefully prepared lectures, announcements in pay packets, notices, and other means of communication, a company image can be developed. Whether this is the correct image depends very much upon the success of the programme being followed.

Some will argue that the creation of a company image is far removed from training. Viewed in a narrow sense this is true. However, training should not be restricted to simply teaching a skill; there should always be the target of high morale with its resultant co-operation. In this way, both employees and the business can benefit.

6. Overcoming labour shortages.—Without an effective training programme many a business would have failed to expand. Faced with a shortage of skilled operators the only solution is often the training of unskilled labour. This has applied particularly in the development areas where there is often no legacy of trained workers.

7. Developing supervisors.—Many companies rely upon internal training or courses at colleges of technology to educate and train actual and potential supervisors. The National Examinations Board for Supervisory Studies is now responsible for many courses which are either company- or college-based. There is now recognition that much depends upon the effectiveness of supervisors in achieving co-operation and optimum output.

METHODS OF TRAINING

Where education ends and training begins is very often difficult to locate with precision. Training includes all the processes whereby employees are shown and taught the necessary skills for a particular job. Accordingly, any education which is technical in nature may be regarded as part of training. Broadly speaking, training should be comprehensive enough to allow an employee to understand the nature of the work he is performing.

The training given should be appropriate to the type of work to be performed. A potential manager will need a much different training from that given to a machine operator. Attempting to give everyone the most comprehensive training possible would be both wasteful and unnecessary. The main methods are as follows:

1. Apprentice training

Apprenticeships are still a recognised form of teaching a young man or woman a trade or profession. Whether the tying of a young person to a business for a term of years can be justified is a matter for debate. Certainly many apprenticeship schemes are worth while, but others are little more than a method of obtaining cheap labour.

Apprentices may be learning a trade (a trade apprentice) or a profession (a pupil apprentice or articled clerk). This applies in engineering, accountancy and other professions. With some apprenticeships, a small salary is paid; with others, such as accountancy, it may be necessary for the parent to pay a premium. Sometimes a salary is paid and this tendency has been on the increase in recent years. The growth of the importance of industrial accountancy has meant that a new approach to training has had to be devised. Practical experience and study for examinations is still the order of the day. However, the young man or woman now expects a progressive salary as well as facilities for training. Many companies now give day release (one day per week), block release (a number of weeks full time), or even send students to college or university for full-time courses extending over a period of years.

2. On-the-job training

This is one of the most important methods of training for all types of work, whether on the shop floor or in the office. The newcomer is asked to observe and then to carry out the work under supervision. If necessary, a job is broken down into elements and each of these is taught before the trainee is expected to take other work.

Although all types of work can be covered, the method is best when dealing with routine work which takes a relatively short time to learn. When a job is complex, and involves the exercise of judgment and making decisions, both theory and practice may be necessary. This is why professional specialists such as engineers and accountants have to pass examinations as well as obtain experience. A similar sort of training is also necessary for any managerial or supervisory posts.

With on-the-job training there is need for properly trained instructors; otherwise, an inefficient instructor can produce a number of inefficient "offspring." Bad habits, such as taking risks, may be imitated by trainees.

3. Vestibule training

A "vestibule" is a room or chamber and, therefore, *vestibule training* simply means training within a room. In practice, it means the setting aside of a special place where training can go on without interfering with normal production. Thus, for example, a company may have a model machine shop in which operators spend a number of weeks before commencing in the machine shop proper.

Many businesses now have training schools, management colleges and trained staff. Many thousands of pounds have been spent on developing training programmes; some of the aids employed include language laboratories, training manuals and programmed learning machines.

With the vestibule method there can be the correct blending of theory and practical work. However, there is no doubt that the method is expensive. Not many companies can really afford to attract and keep the men and women qualified in engineering, science and business studies which would be necessary to teach all the techniques and skills required to run a business. Making full use of local colleges of technology, in conjunction with vestibule training, is possibly the most effective method.

4. Classroom training

The classroom method is the most appropriate for teaching the principles and practice of many subjects. As many as 25 students can be in a group assigned to one lecturer and in appropriate circumstances many more students can be accommodated. Some universities are notorious for their large lecture theatres in which as many as 50 or more students sit and listen to a professor or lecturer read a paper. If discussion is to be encouraged—and this is very desirable—a maximum of 20 students is recommended.

If a lecture is to be effective, there should be a planned approach to covering the subject matter. A good lecturer covers his subject without appearing to rush and yet without wasting time. There should be ample time allowed for questions throughout the lecture and not just at the end.

In supervisory and managerial training there has been a good deal of stress given to discussion and seminar periods. There is no doubt that these are a very effective method of teaching a subject. However, they should not be relied upon entirely: a combination of lectures and discussions is likely to be the most effective.

Lectures can be long and boring. The use of visual aids can do much to relieve tedium and can increase the effectiveness of the teaching process. Overhead projectors, slides and films, television, charts, magnetic boards, statistical kits, accounting machines, machine tools, scale models and other devices are all examples. Last, but not least, is the use of chalk and blackboard, the backbone of all visual aids.

Other methods used in the classroom and worthy of special mention are the following:

1. Seminar groups.
2. Case studies.
3. Programmed learning.
4. Role playing.
5. Business games.

These are outlined below.

1. Seminar groups

There are two types of seminar. The first is that in which a *student* gives a lecture on some predetermined topic. The alternative is the discussion and exchange of ideas under a chairman. This method is also known as the discussion group or conference method.

Properly organised the seminar where all students participate can be a fruitful method of teaching principles of management and other topics. Ideas are sparked off and discussion follows, which in turn leads to further ideas. Those *participating*—and this is the key function —learn from the students within the group. A firm chairman is essential and where a number of seminar groups are operating on the same subject they may all meet and one member from each group can "report back" on the findings. The latter process is an extremely useful device at management conferences and courses.

2. Case studies

A case study is a problem used for discussion and, possibly, solution. The latter is not essential because many management case studies are capable of a number of solutions. Thus, for example, when dealing with a personnel problem the personnel policy being followed will affect the outcome.

With management case studies the usual procedure is to ask students to read a description relating to a business, its managers and a problem (or problems) being encountered. The situation presented is then analysed by asking and answering questions and/or discussing the facts. Finally, conclusions are reached.

This method is said to have been developed by the Harvard Graduate School of Business Administration. It has many followers, but suffers from a serious disadvantage if used by students who have an inadequate knowledge of basic principles. What is often overlooked in Great Britain is that management education is not as yet at the same standard as in the United States of America. In the latter, graduates in business administration are *normal*; in Britain the universities are only just developing courses which, to the present time, have not been very popular. Many of these, although supposed to be management courses, have been nothing more than courses in economics with mention of one or two management techniques.

The success of the U.S.A. case study method owes much to the fact that the managers do have the necessary basic knowledge needed to analyse the problems.

3. Programmed learning

Programmed learning may be tackled by the use of teaching machines or by providing students with specially prepared texts. Both methods break down the subject matter into easy stages; students then learn a stage at a time and test themselves at each stage before moving on to the next.

There is no doubt that programmed learning can be very successful for many subjects which can be broken down into a simple form. If a programme is followed in accordance with the instructions, each student is motivated to learn as quickly as possible.

The main disadvantage is the cost of preparing each programme, which may be immense. In addition, some subjects do not lend themselves easily to programming and, even when they do, take up far too much space. Thus, for example, a book which covers only a small part of the accounting field—company reports—has more than 100 pages. An ordinary textbook would cover the same topic in approximately one-quarter of the space.

4. Role playing

Role playing is an aspect of training which is often overlooked; yet the possibilities are immense, especially in the field of human relations.

Conducting interviews of all types, whether for selection, dealing with grievances or dismissal, can all be covered. The lecturer observes the students acting the part of interviewer and interviewee, and can then criticise and demonstrate how an interview should be conducted.

A similar example is to be found in the teaching of law. Students become the prosecution, plaintiff, judge and jury and try the case before them. Subsequently, lecturer and students can analyse and criticise the proceedings, thus learning from the process.

5. Business games

A business game is an extension of the role-playing method of training. A series of transactions are taken, representing the activities of a business, and students make decisions, the effects of which are calculated in terms of profits or loss.

The effectiveness of a business game depends very much upon its content and the way it is compiled. It should be as realistic as possible and yet not so complex as to make understanding impossible.

Calculation of the profit or loss may be done manually or by computer. Both methods can be successful, but delays may occur with the manual method, thus causing frustration.

For management training, business games can provide useful exercises in decision making. The main criticism levelled against them is that they are often artificial and do not represent conditions found in practice.

THE INDUSTRIAL TRAINING ACT, 1964

The brief survey of training would be quite incomplete without mention of the *Industrial Training Act, 1964*. Since then considerable progress has been made in some industries, but the full effects have not been felt.

A summary of the main provisions of the Act is given below:

1. Through industrial training boards, make further provision for industrial and commercial training.

2. Impose a levy on companies to meet the cost of training and operating the training boards.

3. Make grants to employers in respect of any approved training which is undertaken.

In order to make the description a little more complete, the work of the Engineering Industry Training Board is described below. This is done *very briefly*: employers who wish to pursue any matter which is mentioned should contact the Secretary of the appropriate Board.

ENGINEERING INDUSTRY TRAINING BOARD

The Board is responsible for training within the engineering industries and is charged with the following responsibilities:*

1. To ensure a good supply of properly trained men and women in industry.

2. To improve the quality and efficiency of industrial training and retraining.

3. To share the cost of training more evenly between firms.

* Quoted with kind permission from *Information Paper No. 1* (March 1965), issued by the Board.

These objectives are common to all the boards set up under the *Industrial Training Act.*

A register of approximately 27,000 establishments coming within the scope of the Board is maintained. From these companies the Board raises money by means of a levy which is calculated by reference to the total annual wages and salaries bill of each firm. In turn, the companies can claim back the levy in the form of a grant for training carried out provided this complies to a satisfactory standard.

As a guide to what constitutes good training the Board has issued *Information Paper No. 3* (September 1965). This is not only a valuable guide to what is expected, but it also provides a lesson on what kind of training should be incorporated into a firm's personnel policy. For these reasons the details are reproduced below.

THE PRINCIPLES OF GOOD TRAINING

Introduction

It is the Board's responsibility to see that training is fully adequate at all levels whether the people concerned are to become operatives, craftsmen, supervisors, sales, clerical or commercial staff, technicians, technologists or members of management. The success of a training scheme must depend largely on the selection of the most suitable people and on the foundation upon which training is built.

Planned schemes

The Board therefore attaches great importance to the planning of training schemes, the selection methods used, the control exercised throughout training, and the attainment of high standards of performance.

Whilst it is true that some first-class people have in the past received their training in companies which have no properly organised schemes, it is certain more people could be better trained by properly planned and controlled schemes. Schemes of training should be written down and available for inspection, and proper records of progress should be kept.

Induction courses and safety training

All new entrants should receive adequate induction training and it is essential that they be given instruction in safe working. Safety instruction is a continuing requirement throughout the whole period of training.

First-year off-the-job training for craftsmen and technicians

For training craftsmen and technicians, the first year of training is all-important. It should be spent off the job in an area used solely for training purposes, with instruction given by someone trained in methods of instruction. Some small firms, though not able to provide training schools, will be able to provide a special area for this purpose.

The first year of training provides the foundation from which later training develops, and should be broadly based so as to provide flexibility later on. The Board will shortly be publishing more detailed recommendations about first-year off-the-job training.

The Board is anxious to encourage the formation of group training schemes for those firms which cannot themselves provide this first-year off-the-job training.

Use may also be made of first-year training schemes for apprentices at technical colleges or Government Training Centres.

Assessments of progress should be made at regular intervals throughout the year, and records kept.

Further education of craftsmen and technicians

Attendance for an approved course at a technical college by day release or block release is an essential feature of good training schemes so that those under training shall have a full understanding of their skill and also develop their general education so as to realise their full potential.

It should be noted that the Board has decided as a matter of policy that from September 1966 onwards firms will not be eligible for grant unless day release or block release throughout the period of training is given where these facilities exist. The Minister of Labour* has also announced that he will not approve grant schemes for any of the training boards unless they comply with this provision.

Clerical and commercial training

The Central Training Council† is considering the schemes of training necessary for the clerical and commercial staff of firms covered by all the training boards. In the meantime, firms are expected to release their junior clerical and commercial staff for suitable courses at technical colleges.

Training for supervisors

In order that foremen and other supervisors may be equipped to carry out their duties effectively they should be trained in supervision. In addition, many supervisors play a vital part in training because they may have charge of trainees. Firms should give sound training both to existing untrained supervisors and potential supervisors either by mounting training programmes themselves or by releasing their supervisors for courses at technical colleges or other approved establishments.

Management training

The Board wishes to encourage management training and expects firms to prepare management succession carefully and see that the people concerned are adequately trained.

Operative training

The formal training of operators has often been neglected in the past and needs to be developed. Firms are requested to re-examine their programmes of training for operatives, taking particular account of the need to have a planned syllabus of training and of modern methods of training such as programmed instruction techniques.

---

* Now Secretary of State for Employment and Productivity.

† Responsible for co-ordinating the work of the industrial training boards.

Technologist training

Engineering technologists receive their education in universities or technical colleges and their associated practical training in industry. The Board gives particular approval to sandwich methods of training and education, whereby engineering students spend alternating periods in industry and in a college or university.

The Board and the Ministry of Labour* have announced details of grants which will be paid to firms towards the cost of the periods of industrial training forming part of sandwich courses leading to a Higher National Diploma or a degree at a technological university, or an award of the Council for National Academic Awards. These grants will be paid to a firm in respect of their own employees or in respect of college based students who are accepted by the firm for practical training. The grants are payable for courses which start from 1st September 1965.

Specialist training

Many firms have training needs of a specialist character and the Board recognises the need for these and wishes to encourage them. The Board's grant scheme has been framed to take account of such training.

Training officers

It is a management responsibility to concern itself with training. Each firm will need a member of management to be responsible for planning, organising and supervising its training.

A training officer with these responsibilities, whether full time or part time, whether working for one firm or for a group training scheme, will himself need a course of training. Short full-time courses of training for this purpose are available at some technical colleges, and the Board is proposing to pay special grants for attendance at such courses.

Instructors

Instructors, whether full- or part-time, should not only be carefully selected and well qualified in their technical field, but must also be trained to instruct. Courses are available for this purpose, particularly those at Ministry of Labour* Instructor Training Colleges.

Conclusion

Set out briefly in these paragraphs are those aspects of good training which the Board considers particularly important. The aim should be to specify each job with such care as to know exactly what skill is needed to perform it: to select and train people in the most effective and economical way to do their work, and to test and ensure that, in the end, they have learnt in all its stages to understand and to carry out the job that is required of them.

Employers who provide the facilities described will earn a higher grant payment. These facilities are not however an end in themselves. They merely provide a framework in which good training can be given. The real purpose of training should not be obscured: it is to ensure that manpower is used effectively and that a firm's performance reaches the highest possible level of efficiency.

* Now Department of Employment and Productivity.

WAGES AND SALARIES

One of the most important requirements for a man or woman is an adequate wage or salary which is commensurate with the responsibilities and duties involved. The distinction between wages and salaries is still preserved in industry and commerce, although this is not always clear cut. Basically, the difference lies in the type of work being done by the employees—administrative and clerical workers are paid salaries, whereas manual workers and machine operators receive wages. With the levelling up of wages with salaries and the tendency to give manual workers fringe and related benefits, many so-called salary earners are no better off, and are sometimes worse off, than manual workers. Indeed, I.C.I. Ltd now pays salaries to manual workers.

The organisation and administration for wages and salaries is far from standardised. In some companies, the accountant takes full responsibility; in others, the personnel department is involved. There is much to be said for dividing the work between the personnel manager and the accountant. The former would be involved in establishing a wages and salaries policy and would take part in negotiating scales. On the other hand, the accountant should have full responsibility for calculating and paying any sums due to employees.

When establishing an organisation for wages and salaries certain guides can be followed:

1. There should be an aim to pay wages and salaries at least equal to those paid for similar jobs in the area or in the industry.

2. Whenever possible, some form of job evaluation should be employed.

3. Employees should be rewarded for effort made. If one employee is more efficient than another then he should be paid more: incentive payments may be the solution.

4. Jobs of equal status should be paid the same wage or salary, irrespective of the person who performs the work. This is a general rule; it may be varied in managerial posts where the drive and initiative of the person holding the post can materially affect efficiency.

5. There should be full co-operation between unions and management. Each employee should know where he stands and should understand what he must do to obtain an increase in pay. In addition, there should be a clearly established system of communication for dealing with wage claims and grievances.

Essentially, there should be a *planned approach* to the determination of how employees' wages and salaries shall be calculated. Moreover, the policy followed should be flexible enough to cope with all changes in economic and related conditions.

Wages of manual workers, machine operators and similar employees may be calculated on the basis of time worked or work done. In Great

Britain the usual practice is to pay a guaranteed minimum wage and this, to some extent, reduces the possible harshness of any incentive scheme, but also reduces its effectiveness to stimulate production.

Much has been said and written in recent years on the desirability of obtaining a high level of morale from payment by results. There is no doubt that co-operation is an essential requisite of sound management. However, no positive proof is available to show that employees do co-operate when *no* incentive payment is made. On the other hand, there are many examples available to show that production has increased considerably after some form of payment. F. W. Taylor and others have shown what benefits can result from the introduction and operation of an appropriate incentive wages system.

TIME RATES

As the name implies, *time rates* are wages calculated by reference to the number of hours worked. How attendance times are calculated was shown in Chapter XV. The rate may be per hour or per day.

Some companies have consistently paid a rate above that ruling in the locality and/or industry: this is referred to as a time rate at a high wage level. It is hoped that by paying these higher rates there will be more co-operation and labour turnover will be reduced. In theory this seems sound, but in practice there is again no evidence that high wage rates *always* have the desired effects. In the motor industry, where the time rates at a high wage level are said to have originated, industrial disputes have been a characteristic of modern times.

There are no hard and fast rules regarding when a time rate method of calculating wages should be employed. The main considerations are as follows:

1. Type of work.—When high-quality work is required there may be need to pay time rates. Similarly, if spoilage would involve very heavy losses, skill rather than speed should be the order of the day.

2. Measurement of work.—In order to make a direct payment to individual workers, the work must be capable of precise measurement, either in units or standard hours. If of a general nature, such as maintenance, storekeeping, painting and tool-making, there may be great difficulty in measuring the output of each man. An alternative to paying time rates is to give some form of bonus (discussed in a later section).

3. Individuals cannot control output.—In some industries, such as chemical processing or flour milling, an individual may have little or no control over output. In these cases, a time rate is usually paid, although some form of incentive based on quality may be possible.

4. Output flow is erratic.—If a worker cannot be guaranteed a steady flow of work then he cannot really be expected to be paid on the basis of work done. When in these circumstances an incentive scheme has to be operated, some form of waiting time has to be paid, thus ensuring that there is a guaranteed minimum wage.

5. *Supervision.*—The payment of time rates usually means that there has to be very effective supervision. If not, the output per man will tend to be low.

6. *Relation between payment and output.*—Some form of incentive payment only becomes worth while if productivity increases as the amount paid out in wages increases. Another factor is the influence of output on overhead costs per unit produced. The larger the number of units produced in a period the smaller will tend to be the absorption of *fixed costs* per unit.

7. *Acceptance by trade unions.*—No trade union in Great Britain appears to have any objection to time rates, provided the hourly rate is at least that agreed between employees and unions. On the other hand, there is no such thing as a universal acceptance of all incentives. Many are still viewed with suspicion, no doubt due to the inefficient work measurement which prevailed in many industries when work study was first introduced.

The problem with any form of time rate payment is to stimulate workers so that each produces a fair day's work. If labour costs are too high (not enough work produced), then a business is likely to have difficulty in selling its products. When the market is favourable, high costs mean high prices, so that in the end the consumer has to meet the costs of inefficiency.

INCENTIVE PAYMENTS

There are a large number of incentive schemes, many effective, but probably just as many that suffer from some defect. Some are complicated and are not easily understood by either managers or workers; another failure is that there is no effective incentive to produce at the desired level of activity.

In brief terms, the requirements for an incentive scheme are as follows:

1. The scheme should be simple to understand and to operate.

2. Interests of the business and the workers must be considered (the *Principle of Harmony of Objectives*).

3. Where necessary, instructions should be issued or training given on the operation of the incentive scheme.

4. Standards should be based on carefully prepared estimates arrived at by the employment of work study.

5. A guaranteed minimum rate should be payable, thus giving an employee a sense of security. At the same time, this avoids injustice when the flow of work is delayed.

6. There should be consultation between employees and management before and after an incentive scheme is introduced.

7. Joint consultation should also be available for dealing with increases in rates or any grievances which may arise.

8. Payment for work done should be paid within a reasonable time. If the performance and the payment are separated by a lengthy period of time there is a danger that the incentive will be reduced and even lost.

Principal types of incentive scheme

The principal types of incentive scheme are as follows:

1. Piece rates.
2. Premium bonus or sharing plans.
3. Measured day work.
4. Group incentives.

These are discussed in turn.

1. Piece rates

As the name implies, a piece rate scheme rewards a worker according to the number of "pieces" he produces. The "piece" may be a single unit, a length of material (*e.g.* inch or foot), a number of components added to a unit, or some other measure. Generally, a piece rate scheme is simple to understand and operate. Moreover, there is a positive incentive for a man to work as hard as possible.

Some of the earlier schemes, such as the Taylor Differential Piece Rate Scheme, attempted to induce the worker to strive for a very high level of production. There was one rate for the employee who failed to achieve standard output and another—much higher—for *all* units once standard output had been produced. Differential schemes are little used now, and in the U.S.A., where they were invented, they are apparently out of favour.

Provided the rates are set by the most advanced methods available, making use of work measurement and other techniques, there is much to be said in favour of this method. A serious disadvantage is that if the work is of a varied nature, the number of rates may be considerable. Any change in wage rates in an industry will involve a considerable amount of clerical work to amend the piece rates.

2. Premium bonus or sharing plans

Pioneers of industrial efficiency such as Rowan* and F. A. Halsey, attempted to reward employees for working faster, and management for providing the necessary machines and facilities. Since, when the

* There appears to be doubt as to when this scheme was introduced and by whom. Some books name David Rowan (1901) and others James Rowan (1898)

times are set, the rate fixers usually consider the existing methods of production it seems strange that the creators of the premium bonus schemes should want to reward the employer. In fact, this sharing of time saved tends to cause resentment among employees.

The schemes vary according to the percentage taken by the employee. The Halsey 50:50 plan shared any time saved on the basis of half to employee and half to employer. Thus, for example, if a worker saves 30 minutes on the standard time, he then receives an extra 15 minutes' pay over and above the time taken on the job.

Example

Standard time for job = 2 hours
Actual time taken   = $1\frac{1}{2}$ hours
Time saved   = $\frac{1}{2}$ hour
Wage for the job:
 $1\frac{3}{4}$ hours × basic rate.

Because of the possible antagonism of employees there is likely to be difficulty in obtaining the necessary co-operation. Moreover, the incentive to work hard is not as great as some of the much more simple schemes. Although still employed, premium bonus schemes are becoming a thing of the past. An understanding of them is important because some modern methods have adopted the same principles for fixing standard times. In addition, when devising new techniques the lessons learnt from the premium bonus schemes can be put to good purpose.

3. Measured day work

There are different interpretations given to the term "measured day work." In all schemes it is usual to fix standard times by means of work study. The differences which exist are in the bases used for calculating the wage due.

One method pays a flat time rate and uses the standards as the means of control. If a worker does not reach the desired standard he is reprimanded. In very sophisticated systems, where assembly lines or conveyer working is employed, lights or other signals operate when standard output is not being maintained. Some companies pay time rates at a high level, thus giving employees the necessary incentive to work hard.

When dealing with individuals, as opposed to groups, there is much to be said for using standard times as a means of calculating wages due. If a worker produces the equivalent of 50 standard hours in a 40-hour week he is paid for 50 hours at the basic rate. There is thus a direct incentive for a man to work faster and produce as much as possible. Because there is no question of sharing with the employer more co-operation should be possible. Furthermore, the scheme is easy to follow and to operate. Where for any reason a worker cannot obtain work then he should be paid at the basic rate for the lost-time period.

4. Group incentive schemes

The schemes discussed so far are, in the main, for calculating each individual's wage separately. When employees work in a group and there is difficulty in measuring the contribution made by an individual, then any incentive scheme must consider the work of the group as a whole.

An obvious disadvantage of any group incentive scheme is that if the work assignments given to individuals are unequal, dissatisfaction may result. This can be aggravated still further if there are one or two employees in the group who are simply unwilling to co-operate. Reference to the social and working groups is made in other chapters. As shown there, unofficial leaders, including trouble-makers, can negate all efforts of managers to obtain co-operation.

The main argument for using a group incentive scheme is that it tends to induce a state of co-operation. Undoubtedly, in appropriate conditions, this is the case. That this is difficult to achieve has already been noted in the previous paragraph.

INCENTIVES FOR INDIRECT WORKERS

The incentive schemes so far explained have been for direct workers; *i.e.* those actually producing. In addition, there are schemes which cater for indirect workers, including executives and supervisors, as well as, in some instances, direct workers. An outline of these schemes is given below:

1. Bonuses for managers including supervisors.
2. Incentive payments for salesmen.
3. Bonuses for clerical staff.

1. Bonuses for managers

A major problem with all management positions is that there is no *positive* relationship between a manager's effort and the output in terms of saleable products or services. With a direct worker who is operating, say, a drilling machine, the output can be measured in terms of the number of units or standard hours. On the other hand, a works manager will have responsibility for a wide field of activities and there may be times when he is working extremely hard and yet total output may be quite low. The economic climate, labour conditions, material availability and other factors may influence output. These facts must be faced when devising a suitable scheme. Unfortunately they are not easily overcome, and so the tendency is to take output or profits as a basis for calculating any bonus paid to executives. This will probably mean that no bonuses are paid in a depression; to offset this fact it should be remembered that managers are usually kept on the payroll throughout difficult periods, so, in effect, bonuses are being paid.

Another problem with a manager's job is that there is often great difficulty in employing job evaluation. This does not mean that the task is impossible, but quite often job descriptions for managers are in such outline that they become almost meaningless for the purpose of fixing salaries or bonuses.

Some of the possible methods of rewarding managers are listed below:

(*a*) *Bonus based on the profits of the company.*—Besides providing an incentive for a manager to induce his subordinates to work harder, the bonus is intended to foster co-operation, loyalty and a high level of morale. The amount payable may be calculated by a variety of methods; a common method is to calculate a percentage on the salary paid in the past year. One company in which the author was employed paid a percentage on salary which was equivalent to the dividend paid to ordinary shareholders. If a 10% dividend was paid then the same percentage was added to salaries. A manager earning £2000 per annum received a £200 bonus.

Unfortunately, all cash payments are subject to income tax and, therefore, unless a bonus is substantial the net amount received by an employee may be too small to provide any incentive. For directors and top managers some companies provide for extremely large bonuses which can mean, in a boom period, payments in excess of the basic salary.

(*b*) *Issue of shares.*—Issuing shares to employees so that they become "partners" has been an ideal state in the opinion of theorists for many years. Unfortunately, this is one of the cases where theory and practice have not been matched. Many of the earlier schemes failed because neither employees nor managers really appreciated the motives behind the "co-partnership" scheme. The loyalty and co-operation expected often did not materialise.

In more modern times some of the industrial giants, such as I.C.I. Ltd, have introduced share bonus schemes and this has tended to make the schemes more noticed and respected. Whether they still have something to offer to *workers* generally is still a matter for debate; possibly an additional wage payment would be more appreciated.

When dealing with managers only, there seems considerable merit in making share issues. The number of shares would tend to be larger than that issued to ordinary workers and, in a few years, can build up to a substantial holding. Because managers can be more easily educated to understand the meaning of the issue, what it represents and the progress being made by a company, there seems more chance of success. Turnover of executives may be reduced and loyalty and co-operation should be encouraged.

A variation of the scheme outlined is one which gives top managers an *option* to purchase shares at a future date. A favourable price is established (it may be the current market price) and then the manager concerned is permitted to buy if he wishes. If the share price has risen considerably then the managers concerned make a nominal gain which may be realised by sale of the shares. A disadvantage is that the income from the sale is subject to Capital Gains Tax.

(*c*) *Bonus on output.*—Departmental managers and supervisors may be paid a bonus on the efficiency obtained within the departments for which they are responsible. This kind of scheme has the advantage of stimulating junior managers to greater effort and inducing workers under them to work as hard as possible. Some form of standard has to be established and then a bonus paid according to the actual achievement (*e.g.* 5% above standard results in 5% of salary as a bonus). Examples of bases upon which standards can be set are as follows:

1. Output in department in tons, units or standard hours.
2. Prime costs.
3. Overhead costs.
4. Quality.
5. Output of individual workers (*e.g.* under some premium bonus schemes a supervisor takes a share of the time saved).

There are many other possibilities, but enough has been indicated to show the nature of these schemes.

(*d*) *Fringe benefits.*—These are not limited to managers; they are applicable to all grades, but there is a *tendency* for office staff and managers to benefit more from these schemes.

There is no standardised pattern of benefits; nor is there universal adherence to the idea of paying fringe benefits. What does seem certain is that the amount paid in this way is on the increase. The heavy burden of taxes, the idea of the affluent society, the problems of attracting and keeping managers, and other factors have all contributed. A list of possible benefits is given below:

1. Sickness benefits.
2. Medical schemes.
3. Sick pay.
4. Bonuses.
5. Provision of car.
6. Provision of telephone at home.
7. House purchase.
8. Payment for education of children.
9. Purchases at special discount.
10. Financial assistance in times of difficulty; *e.g.* sickness of one of the employee's family.

The motives for paying fringe benefits may vary from one company to another. With some it is simply a matter of providing employees with as good as that obtainable from other companies. The payments may also be part of personnel policy and may have, as their object, the creation of a co-operative spirit by building up a reputation for being generous and for assisting employees over and above that required by law or trade unions.

2. Incentive payments for salesmen

Providing an incentive payments scheme for a sales force can be an extremely difficult assignment. Conditions vary from one area to another and even within the same area; setting an incentive which is fair to all, therefore, becomes very difficult.

In a general textbook, there is inadequate space to cover all facets of remuneration for salesmen. A summary of the possibilities are as follows:

  (a) Salary + bonus.
  (b) Salary + commission.
  (c) Salary + bonus and commission.

Generally speaking, the salary should be sufficient to provide a reasonable standard of living. The commission or bonus then gives the necessary stimulant to sell more.

A commission is related to the amount sold; e.g. 3% on all sales. On the other hand, a sales bonus is usually paid after a sales quota or other standard has been achieved. Thus, for example, a salesman may be expected to obtain a sales quota of £1500 per month; if he betters this he may be paid a bonus which is calculated by reference to the above target figure.

3. Bonuses for clerical staff

Incentive schemes for clerical staff may be similar to those described earlier for managers. Bonuses are probably the most appropriate form of incentive for all office workers whose effort and output cannot be measured with reasonable accuracy.

When dealing with routine jobs such as mechanical posting, invoice typing, envelope addressing, and pricing of orders some form of standard may be possible. More attention is now being paid to the application of work study to the office field. This also includes organisation and methods work by which methods and procedures are simplified and standardised, thus improving efficiency.

PRODUCTIVITY BARGAINING

Productivity bargaining and the subsequent agreements which have been made have received considerable attention in recent years. Since the much publicised Esso Petroleum agreement at the Fawley Refinery

(1960) many industries have become involved in bargaining of this type —where increased productivity was expected for an agreed rate of pay.

The earlier agreements, including the Fawley Agreement, have been restricted to a company or to a plant. They were not accepted for an industry as a whole. Because of this fact, employers' associations have not had any considerable influence in the negotiations. Generally, the bargaining has been between a company and the appropriate trade union. However, agreements at national level have been concluded which, although not strictly productivity agreements, have stressed that there must be *productivity commensurate with the wage-rates agreed upon.*

Definition

A *productivity agreement* (or *bargain*) is one which tries to link the basis for calculating wages with work done. The employer and employee negotiate on the basis of a fair wage for the work to be done. Usually, though not necessarily, the following aims are sought:

1. Greater efficiency and, therefore, a more effective use of manpower.
2. Reduced labour costs per unit produced.
3. Better utilisation of the plant and machinery.
4. Elimination of restrictive practices relating to methods of work and demarcation practices for different functions or operations.

There are two main features within the agreement. The *first* is the change in methods of performing the work. These can cover the use of work study and other management techniques, as well as changing manning arrangements (*e.g.* one man per machine instead of two) and organisational structures. The *second* feature is the method employed for calculating the wages, fringe benefits, or non-monetary rewards (*e.g.* shorter working hours).

With a productivity agreement *both sides* benefit from the changes made and, since the bargain is made on a mutual footing, there should be ready acceptance of its principles.

Problems

Although, as shown, the benefits of productivity bargaining can be considerable, there are difficulties, which are as follows:

1. Arriving at an accepted standard of efficiency.—This can be thought of in terms of "management objectives," "standard costs" or other yardstick. The maximum amount that can be paid out in wages should be determined before negotiations start. However, the problem is to decide what the costs will be for the products when the *new* methods have been agreed—this may be very difficult when they have not yet been employed.

2. Linking wages and work.—The principles of incentive schemes are outlined earlier in this chapter.

3. Getting managers to change.—One of the critical factors in British industry is the reluctance to agree to new methods. This is particularly the case with managers who have had no formal training in the newer techniques, and therefore are very loath to admit their ignorance.

4. Trade-union and employee attitudes.—Very often trade-union officials and employees are very suspicious of proposed changes. There has to be an appropriate environment and all necessary preparatory work has to be done beforehand.

5. Establishing effective control systems.—If an agreement cannot be effectively enforced then it is unlikely to be of value. Cases have been known where the definition of "productivity" has been so vague that no satisfactory measure was available. Just as important, when a yardstick is established, there should be adequate production and costing systems which enable control to be exercised. These are discussed in Part Four of this book.

Proper negotiating machinery and effective channels of communication are very essential to the success of productivity bargaining. Since the attitudes which stem from this approach can vitally affect *industrial relations*, there is a strong case for giving full consideration to this vital aspect of management. For further details of this important subject readers should refer to the Engineering Employers' Federation publication entitled *Productivity Bargaining and the Engineering Industry* (March 1968).

EXAMINATION QUESTIONS

1. Discuss in all aspects the relationship between a works manager and a personnel manager.

2. Give an outline of a management development scheme appropriate to a large and rapidly expanding company with many diverse divisions. The scheme should be designed to ensure effective recruitment, selection and use of management potential within the company.

3. You have been given the assignment of carrying out job methods training for supervisors; list the steps in job method analysis which would form the basis of such training.

4. Standards are important tools of the manager. Name:

   (*a*) two types of standard that could be used by a managing director;
   (*b*) two that a sales manager might use;
   (*c*) two that could serve a personnel manager.

   Show how *two* of these standards would be calculated.

5. What steps would a personnel officer take to ensure that the staff selection procedure operated by his department is efficient and effective?

6. Outline a comprehensive training scheme suitable for a large factory. The scheme should take into consideration all occupations, ranks, and ages.

7. Set out the various main functions for which a personnel department is responsible and under each function describe briefly the work carried out.

Note: Some questions are of a general nature so reference to other chapters will be necessary.

PERSONNEL PROBLEMS: I 267

7. Set out the various main functions for which a personnel department is responsible and under each function describe briefly the work carried out.

Note: Some questions are of a general nature, so reference to other chapters will be necessary.

CHAPTER XVII

PERSONNEL PROBLEMS: II

DISCIPLINE

ONE of the most difficult problems facing all managers is how to deal with the personnel under them. Only by adopting the correct approach to motivation, the giving of instructions, and finally, where necessary, reprimanding, will the required high level of co-operation be forthcoming. Only in the last resort should dismissal be contemplated, and yet this should be very much a part of a personnel policy.

References to motivation and to sound leadership are made on pp. 24 and 193. These are very essential as a basis for effective discipline.

There are two basic forms of discipline and these are as follows:

1. Positive or constructive discipline.
2. Negative discipline.

These are considered in turn. As a general rule, positive discipline should be employed as far as possible.

POSITIVE OR CONSTRUCTIVE DISCIPLINE

Positive discipline is not quite what it sounds. Indeed, "co-operative discipline" would be a much better term. It means the fostering of co-operation and a high level of morale so that the written and unwritten rules and conditions are obeyed willingly. An important requirement is to let an employee know as soon as possible what is expected of him. Effective communication is, therefore, a vital prerequisite.

The induction of employees was explained earlier. This is extremely important, for a good beginning encourages co-operation. Other matters to watch are as follows:

1. Instructions should be explained in such a way that they are readily understood. If in doubt, explain again.

2. Treat all employees fairly and without personal preference or prejudice.

3. Try to achieve *Harmony of Objectives* through careful study of each individual, attempting to harmonise the efforts of all employees for the common good.

4. Do not bully, show bad manners, shout or become impatient when matters are not proceeding according to expectations.

5. Encourage employees to ask questions and to show an interest in what is going on. At the same time be willing to help when problems are raised.

6. Consider the personalities who are to work in each group, and try to avoid putting together those who do not have the qualities required for co-operating with each other.

7. Set a good example by not breaking any rules. If there is a rule that no smoking is permitted then a supervisor should not smoke in the department. Only by showing that he follows the rules can a manager expect co-operation from his subordinates.

NEGATIVE DISCIPLINE

Negative discipline means control by force; by threats, and dismissal for the least diversion from complete submission: employees are made to "toe the line." Up to 1939, this was a common feature of management. (*See* p. 195 on "Autocratic Exploitation.")

With the growth of the trade union movement and, from 1945 onwards, the era of full employment, negative discipline has been replaced by a more constructive approach. Another factor which has contributed to the change is the growth of management education. The British Institute of Management has done much to stimulate and encourage both formal and informal courses. With the establishment of business schools in Manchester and London the facilities for advanced work in the management field are being greatly extended.

The basic failure of negative discipline is the assumption that harshness and maximum efficiency are compatible. What generally happens in practice is that the workers somehow comply with the rules and produce a reasonable output, often not very willingly. It therefore becomes a battle of wits between managers and employees; one side trying to outwit the other. This is certainly no way to obtain co-operation and is not a basis for sound management practice.

DISOBEDIENCE

When rules are not obeyed there should be appropriate action. There is no standard pattern for dealing with offenders; much depends upon the nature of the offence and the number of times an employee has digressed. For a first offence of a minor nature a warning may be sufficient, but more drastic action would be called for if there is a repetition. In the case of a serious offence, especially one which endangers life, immediate dismissal would be justified. Bearing these differences in mind a list of possible courses of action is given below:

1. Reprimand with no further action.—Suitable for minor offences which must nevertheless be dealt with formally.

2. Reprimand and an official record made on the employee's personnel card.—The reprimand may be by word of mouth or may be in writing. The latter is necessary when an employee has made himself such a nuisance that evidence is required to dismiss him.

3. Immediate suspension with or without a right of appeal.—Often this method leads to dismissal, but this is not necessarily the case. It is certainly better than immediate dismissal, where there is always a danger of strike action by the fellow workers of the man or woman dismissed. Even if there *is* justification for terminating a man's contract of employment, modern cases have illustrated all too well that many workers are willing to "come out" in support of a colleague whether or nor their action is fully justifiable.

4. *Downgrading or demotion.*—This course of action is often used when a man has reached an age where he loses his vigour or intellectual powers. In certain manual jobs, connected with steel-making, coal mining and other heavy industries, workers can stay in these highly paid posts for a relatively short period, say, 20 years. Similarly, in top-management posts, which require the exercise of considerable drive and initiative, a man may not be able to stand the pace. A company may find it necessary to transfer a manager to work which does not require him to exert himself too much. This applies especially when ill health accompanies a man's later years.

5. *Discharge of employee.*—Discharge of an employee should be used only as a last resort. Usually a threat is enough to bring an offender back into line. However, if, despite repeated warnings, there is no improvement the necessary action to discharge should be taken, no matter how unpleasant this is likely to prove. The procedures to follow when discharging an employee should be stated in writing and given to all managers, including supervisors. There should be no question of indiscriminate discharge, each manager making his own rules. The most serious penalty allowed to be imposed by a manager should be suspension, followed by a written report to his superior.

EXAMPLES OF OFFENCES

The offences which may be committed by an employee are summarised below:

1. Lateness—occasional lateness may be excused, but once it becomes habitual there should be prompt action.
2. Absence without good cause.
3. Wasting time.
4. Not obeying safety regulations.
5. Improper use of time recorders.
6. Malingering.
7. Excessive spoilage.
8. Fighting.
9. Smoking, when this is prohibited.
10. Absence from place of work.

These are offences for which a warning would be issued on a *first* offence. Repetition could lead to dismissal. More serious offences are as follows:

1. Pilfering.
2. Refusal to obey an instruction given by a superior.

3. Conduct of an indecent or immoral nature.

4. Incompetence which is so gross as to constitute a man being a liability to his company (*e.g.* spoilage of work valued at thousands of pounds).

5. Deliberate and malicious damage to property or harm to a person.

6. Mis-appropriation of company funds.

7. Any foolish or malicious act which is likely to lead to damage, loss of life, injury or other serious effect.

There is difficulty in generalising; much depends upon the circumstances, the consequences and the employee concerned. A new employee, who was unaware of certain facts, might be treated more lightly than one who has worked with the company for a number of years.

PROMOTION

Reference to a positive promotion policy was made earlier in Chapter XIII. This means that the act of giving a man greater responsibilities should be part of a definite plan or policy and not simply left to chance. Sound management should include provision for succession; whether positions should be filled from within an organisation by promotion, or by recruitment from outside, is a matter on which opinions vary. Generally, promotion means going to a different job with a higher salary. In practice, there may be some difficulty in distinguishing between *promotion* and *transfer* which means the movement of a man from one post to another at the same level. Sometimes an employee is given a substantial increase in salary, but keeps the same job; he may be given another title such as "production director" whereas he was previously "production manager."

Ignoring these anomalies it is necessary to consider how to deal with the matter of promotion: *i.e.* giving an employee greater responsibilities or improved status. The main question is whether seniority or ability should be considered. Some companies still follow a policy of promoting on the basis of seniority, but this is a very risky practice. Rewarding long-service employees is to be applauded provided this does not result in a reduction in efficiency. Unfortunately, all too often, the man who has waited years and years for another employee's job is so set in his ways as an assistant that he just cannot make decisions himself. This applies particularly at middle- and top-management levels.

The criterion in all cases should be ability to perform the work. If abilities of applicants *are equal*, then seniority should be considered. By "seniority" is usually meant the number of years' service with a company.

Not everyone agrees that *ability* should be the main consideration. There is a tendency for trade unions to favour promotion on the basis of seniority. Some of the arguments used to justify this line of thought are as follows:

1. Seniority and experience go hand-in-hand and, therefore, it is right and proper to promote on this basis.
2. There is less danger of personal preference being exercised. A manager may prefer a young man who has a pleasant outlook and who goes out of his way to please him. Yet the older man may be just as efficient or even more so.
3. Subordinates are more willing to work under an older man who has given many years of service to a company. This may or may not be true; much depends upon the circumstances.

What is vitally important is that the selection procedures should be so arranged that the best people are selected for promotion. Linking education, qualifications, ability and seniority, and matching these with the job requirements, should ensure that a fair and effective promotion policy is followed.

SAFETY

An employer is legally obliged to provide a safe working place, including any necessary guards on machines and equipment. In a large organisation it is quite usual to employ a full-time safety officer; in smaller concerns the post would only occupy part of a man's occupation.

The object of employing a safety officer is to give recognition to the importance of reducing accidents to an absolute minimum. It does *not* mean that safety should be the sole responsibility of the one officer. Safety constitutes an obligation on *all* employees, irrespective of job or status. The safety officer has to ensure that all possible steps are taken to train and educate everyone on the importance of safety and the avoidance of accidents. He should have the backing of all levels of management, including the board of directors.

Often the best results are obtained through a safety committee which has representatives from each main department. The safety officer may be the chairman of the committee. Some of the methods employed for eliminating accidents are summarised below:

1. Management should provide good working conditions: adequate lighting, heating and ventilation should be top priority.
2. Machines and equipment should be in a good state of repair.
3. Guards should never be removed except for maintenance, and then only when the machine is not running.
4. When purchasing new machines and equipment, management should buy those with a high standard of safety in their design.
5. Layout of factories and departments should be as safe as possible.

6. Train employees so that safe working methods are employed. Work study engineers should be used to study the methods employed and training should incorporate the procedures designed.

7. Employees should be instructed to wear clothes which do not increase the danger of accidents occurring. Where necessary, protective clothing, including goggles and gloves, should be provided. When a person's hair is long he or she should take steps to ensure that there is no danger of this being caught in a machine.

8. Ladders, components, materials, tools and other movable items should not be left on the floor or other place where they could cause danger.

9. Only qualified operators should be permitted to operate machines or drive trucks or other vehicles.

10. There should be rules and regulations which cover safety precautions.

11. Adequate publicity should be given to the prevention of accidents by means of film shows, display of posters, competitions, lectures and other methods.

12. Workers should report any unsafe machines or likely hazard so that corrective action can be taken.

13. Excessive overtime should be avoided.

14. If an accident does occur then there should be provision for treatment of the injuries. A first-aid box is the absolute minimum; with a medium or large company a medical centre with full-time staff is not unusual.

Once an accident occurs there should be a report made on the person involved, the nature of the accident, why it happened, and the steps taken to prevent a similar occurrence in the future. An analysis of all accidents should also be compiled revealing all relevant facts, as well as days lost as a result of the accidents.

LABOUR TURNOVER

"Labour turnover" is the term given to the measurement of employees leaving a company and their replacement. The more that leave and have to be replaced the greater tend to be the costs relating to the following:

1. Recruiting and engaging.
2. Training.
3. Spoilage.
4. Loss of production while learning.
5. Increased number of accidents.
6. Excessive wear and tear of machines from unskilled operators.
7. Failure to meet orders on time.
8. Payment of overtime in order to catch up on lost production.

K

These and other costs must be recovered in the costs of products. The effect may be a reduction in profit available for shareholders and for future growth.

REDUCING LABOUR TURNOVER

Because of the very high costs which may result from a high labour turnover, there should be a planned and continual effort to keep labour turnover to a minimum.

A personnel manager should supply a full analysis of labour turnover showing why employees are leaving the company. Some of the reasons may be quite unrelated to the policy being followed; e.g. women marrying or men transferring to lighter work because of ill health. Others will focus attention on the weaknesses of the personnel policy. There may be dissatisfaction at the rates of pay, working conditions, promotion prospects, or with the treatment from an employee's immediate superior.

Once an employee indicates that he wishes to leave, his superior may interview him and ask why; alternatively, he may be seen by a personnel officer and a discharge form completed showing the reasons. Unfortunately, the true reasons for leaving may not always be revealed.

MANAGEMENT BY PARTICIPATION

Modern management thought emphasises the need for *participation* by workers and managers in the task of finding the best solution to each problem which a business faces. This aspect is stressed in the chapters which deal with co-operation, morale and the achievement of the objectives of the business. The purpose of this section is to examine four important aspects, which are as follows:

1. Communication.
2. Committees in management.
3. Collective bargaining.
4. Suggestion schemes.

These are considered in turn. The survey is very brief and readers who wish to consider the topics in more detail are advised to consult one of the specialist books listed in the Bibliography.

COMMUNICATION

Communication means the transmission of information so that persons affected receive and understand it. The latter is vital, because, quite often, distorted versions of instructions have led to serious mistakes being made and strikes have been triggered off. Many employees spend a large part of their working period *communicating* by speaking to others. The more effective this function can be made, the more efficient become managers in dealing with the personnel under their command.

Effective communication is not achieved automatically or easily. The very fact that employees have different levels of education and abilities presents a problem. If instructions are to be given they should be capable of being understood by all concerned. The possibility that many words have many different meanings or interpretations complicates the matter still further.

Another desirable feature of any method of communication is that there should be "feedback"; that is to say, there should be replies from those who are given instructions. These may be *direct* or *indirect*, but so long as the replies are forthcoming the precise form they take is unimportant. The establishment of committees and suggestion schemes so that employees can participate indirectly in improving efficiency is an integral part of any communication system.

Reasons for communication

The reasons for effective communication within a business may be summarised as follows:

1. Transmission of information to employees.
2. Issue of orders or commands in such a way as to induce co-operation, motivation and high morale.
3. Behaviour patterns are established which help to build the form of informal organisation which achieves the *harmony of objectives*.
4. Induction training and other forms of training and education are made possible.

Methods of communication

Methods or systems of communication may be classified in a variety of ways:

1. Downward communication.—This means informing from top management downwards to the lowest-grade worker. As a general rule, any system should be designed so that information passes down the formal line as portrayed by an organisation chart. There should never be any question of informing the rank and file before notifying managers or supervisors. Examples are the spoken word, written instructions including notices, and informal or formal talks by all levels of management to employees.

2. Upward communication.—Although the reverse of downward communication, the two functions are very much related. A vital part of management is the encouragement of upward communication so that there is the necessary "feedback." The establishment of suitable procedures for dealing with complaints and for encouraging employees to take a pride in their work are essential. The value of committees and suggestion schemes are dealt with later in this chapter. Included in this category are joint consultative committee meetings, reports on production, performances and costs, suggestion schemes, listening to complaints and the views of supervisors.

3. Horizontal communication.—The two methods described act in a vertical manner, moving either upwards or downwards. Recognition must also be given that information should flow across the organisation chart between managers having the same level of authority. It would obviously be wrong for orders to be given by one supervisor to another, but co-operation between them should be encouraged as much as possible.

Unofficial communication

"Have you heard . . ." is a familar enough phrase to anyone who has worked on the shop floor or in an office. Sometimes the rumour may be correct; often the story is distorted or not even true. Equally often, rumours start because a decision has been made on an important matter and the personnel affected have not been told. There is, therefore, a state of expectancy and minds which are receptive to anything.

This unofficial channel of communication, or *grapevine* as it is called, is inevitable in any organisation. However, much can be done to reduce its damaging effects by having an effective, official communication system. If employees *know* that they are told when changes are to be made they will have confidence and trust: this leads to a high level of morale and more co-operation.

Committees and suggestion schemes are an integral part of any modern communication system and are discussed in the section which follows.

COMMITTEES IN MANAGEMENT

Committees are used for very many purposes. They represent a method of governing by democratic means. Representatives of all departments can be included on a committee so that no part of the business is ignored. In practice, of course, there is a danger that committees can become too large so that very rarely is anything constructive achieved. Yet if they are really small they cannot be said to be using the opinions of all interested parties. Somehow a compromise has to be reached and this can be a very difficult problem.

Advantages and disadvantages

There are many advantages and disadvantages associated with committees. The extent to which these are found depends very much upon the way committees are organised, their timing, and the character of the chairman. The latter is most important; unless there is a firm, yet fair and unbiased chairman, committee work can be reduced to a meaningless function.

The *advantages* claimed for the use of committees are as follows:

1. Useful as a method for co-ordinating the work of a number of related functions all working towards the same objectives.

2. Ideas can be pooled and used for the benefit of all who are on the committee and for the business as a whole.

3. Problems can be solved by discussion by the committee.

4. The sanction and authorisation of expenditure is best done by a committee which can consider the effects on all departments of the business.

5. A useful channel of communication, especially in the field of human relations. Individuals may be afraid of voicing opinions on conditions, but their feelings may be expressed by a representative on a committee. This is the basis of Joint Consultation.

6. Members of a committee are made to sit and face problems and, as a result, many new ideas are expressed and developed.

7. The responsibility for decisions is shared rather than borne by one man or woman. Any decisions become the prerogative of a group.

8. Full use can be made of specialisation. Committees can be composed of functional and line managers who represent each major division of the production, sales and accounting departments.

Possible *disadvantages* which, although fewer in number, can be very serious are as shown below:

1. Committees are very time consuming. Every executive must make the most effective use of his time.

2. Decisions may be taken because a committee wants to be unanimous, but these may not necessarily be for the benefit of the business as a whole.

3. The responsibility for decisions is on the committee and not on individuals. This may lead to some members voting for a decision which they would not favour if they had to decide separately.

4. Negotiations may be protracted and are often postponed indefinitely.

5. One member of a committee can prevent it operating efficiently by putting forward arguments which are irrelevant.

Types of committees

The types of committees found in practice are quite varied. Typical examples are given below and reference is made to some of them in other parts of the book:

1. Board of directors.—This is concerned with policy making and is the method used for directing the operations of a limited company.

2. Budget committee.—When budgetary control is in operation, any co-ordination of budgets, sanctioning of budgets and control of performances can be done through a committee.

3. Cost reduction committee.—Whether this is a normal cost reduction committee or a value analysis committee the object is the same: the reduction of costs generally on particular products or in specific departments. On these committees it is usual to have representatives from accounting, production, sales and one or two specialists, such as design engineers and methods experts.

4. *Works committees.*—These are formed to increase productivity in a business and to provide a means of dealing with problems. Other matters which may be dealt with are:

(*a*) Accidents and safety.
(*b*) Welfare.
(*c*) Social activities.

5. *Joint consultative committees.*—By the employment of committees a company can provide a method of dealing with grievances, conditions of employment, wages and salary negotiations and any other problem. In effect, a joint consultative committee is a means whereby workers and managers are brought together so that there can be created an atmosphere of co-operation and understanding.

COLLECTIVE BARGAINING

With some large companies, such as the Ford Motor Company, all matters which may be termed "collective bargaining" are dealt with by separate procedures. Some of these are listed below:

1. Recognition of the union and its rights within a business organisation.

2. Rights of the management in relation to workers. This is a very difficult problem. Managers should be permitted to *manage* without undue restrictions being imposed by trade unions. Yet the latter have to safeguard their members.

3. Conduct of union business. The times permitted for union business have to be clearly defined. Similarly, there should be provision for union notices and the activities of shop stewards.

4. Wages and other benefits. Rates of pay, job evaluation, merit grading, incentive schemes, shift differentials, work study and timekeeping are all examples of factors which influence wages.

5. Hours of employment including holidays, leave of absence, meal and break periods and other matters which affect hours.

6. Discipline and discharge of workers: the procedures to be followed.

7. Accidents and safety.

8. Promotions, transfers, redundancies and short-time working.

9. Pension and sickness rights.

Many of these are affected by law as well as by agreement with trade unions. The National Insurance scheme provides for sickness benefits, and the Graduated Pension scheme requires an employer to deduct contributions (or supply an alternative scheme) to provide for a retirement pension for each worker. The *Factories Act* gives minimum requirements on aspects affecting the health and safety of employees.

If negotiations between managers and unions fail then the dispute may go to arbitration or there may be a withdrawal of labour (a strike). The right to strike for a legitimate cause is the privilege of all employees. Unfortunately, in the post-war (1945 onwards) era there have been many wildcat strikes which have done considerable damage to the reputation of trade unions.

SUGGESTION SCHEMES

A suggestion scheme is a means whereby employees are given an opportunity to submit ideas on any matters which affect the efficiency of the business. Usually, when an idea is developed into a commercial proposition, such as an improved method, or the reduction of costs, the employee concerned is given an award in the form of a cash prize.

The most common method is to provide blank forms and suggestion boxes. Any ideas are outlined on a form and then dropped into one of the boxes. Subsequently, ideas are studied by an official or a suggestions committee. The size of the award may be determined by reference to the costs saved in a year; a suitable percentage should be predetermined, *e.g.* 10%, but this is not standardised.

A number of advantages have been claimed for the use of suggestion schemes. Unfortunately, there seem to be two lines of thought: one which believes wholeheartedly, and the other which will not use suggestion schemes under any circumstances. The success of a scheme often depends upon the enthusiasm of managers and the way in which it is organised.

Possible advantages are listed below:

1. Employees are allowed to participate in management through the suggestion of creative ideas.

2. The business gains from the ideas: in the short run employees are given awards, and over a long period they can enjoy the prosperity of the business.

3. Inventions and technical improvements, which may be of considerable value, can result from a scheme.

PERSONNEL STATISTICS

The personnel department should compile statistics so that information is available on any matter which is included, or could be included, in the personnel policy. This information may be classified as follows:

1. Individual statistics.
2. Group statistics.
3. National statistics.

The first two of these are considered below.

PERSONNEL RECORD

Surname		Christian name(s) ....
Address		Date of birth ....
		Married/single/widow/er ....
		Children ....
		Nationality ....
(Changes)		National insurance no. ....
		Pens/sup'n memb. no. ....
		Disabled person (Nature of disablement)

Date of start/ transfer/ promo- tion	Reason for award/ promo- tion	Department	Job	Clock No.	Consolidated salary						
					Weekly				Yearly £	Annual increases £	Total yearly £
					Basic rate	Job rate	Bonus	O/T rate			

Termination		Pay in lieu of notice
Date		Accrued holiday pay
Reason		Progress pay
		Gratuity

FIG. 42 *a.—Personnel record card* (front)

INDIVIDUAL STATISTICS

For each employee there is a need to compile a record of all significant events. These would include timekeeping, salary payments, absences, training received, qualifications obtained, progress made in jobs, promotions and transfers. Any special efforts made by an employee, or any reprimands of a serious nature, should also be recorded.

This information can be used when considering training, promotion,

PREVIOUS EMPLOYMENT RECORD

Previous employment with this Company:- ....
Department.. Date: from.............. to..............
Name and Address................................ Date Joined ....
of present/last employer .... Date Left ....
Present Rate ....
Nature of business .... Nature of job ....
Reason for leaving ....

Name and Address................................ Date Joined ....
of previous employer................................ Date Left ....
Finishing Rate ....
Nature of business .... Nature of job ....
Reason for leaving ....

ANNUAL HOLIDAYS				ANNUAL REPORT			
Date comm.	Days taken	Date comm.	Days taken	Date	Rating	Date	Rating

Training	Medical department

FIG. 42 b.—*Personnel record card* (back)

wage and salary awards, and any other change in the status of an individual. Some companies require an annual report to be made on each employee and this is filed, or summarised on his personnel record card. An example of the latter is shown in Figs. 42 *a* and *b*.

GROUP STATISTICS

Statistics for a business as a whole may often be regarded as measures of morale. If workers are not satisfied with their jobs they will not work as willingly as those who *want* to co-operate. There are two distinct types of information.

1. Statistics on output and costs.—High productivity and high morale usually go together. If production targets are being beaten and costs are kept within the predetermined standards there is evidence of sound management. Accountancy reports and statements on costs, output and quality can indicate the levels of achievement.

2. Personnel statistics.—Frequent absences, habitual lateness, large number of accidents, high rate of labour turnover and surveys on employee attitudes can all indicate the effectiveness of the policies being followed.

Some of the most usual indices which are calculated are as follows:

1. Labour turnover

The following formula is used to find out the percentage of labour turnover for a given period:

$$\frac{\text{Total number leaving} \times 100}{\text{Average number on payroll}} = \text{Percentage of labour turnover}$$

It is of course important that the numbers are both for the same period—which may be a month or a year. The figures should be compiled over a number of similar periods if they are to have significance: a single ratio is of very limited value.

The same method can be applied to show the progress in engaging additional staff to *increase* the labour force as distinct from only replacing those who leave.

2. Accident ratio

This may be expressed in a variety of ways. Two possibilities are:

(*a*) The number of accidents.
(*b*) The days lost as a result of accidents.

The ratio of accidents to hours of work may be calculated by the formula shown below:

$$\frac{\text{Number of accidents} \times 1,000,000}{\text{Total hours worked}} = \text{Accident ratio}$$

Total hours worked is for the total labour force, whereas the 1,000,000 is the standard number of hours used as a basis. A smaller figure could be used; *e.g.* 100,000 hours.

Again, a single ratio is of limited value and, to be significant, a comparison with the figures of other companies in the industry as a whole should be made.

Accidents may also be classified according to their nature, cause and consequence. This is generally done in official statistics.

3. Absence ratio

Loss of man hours or days can be very serious and is often an indication that there is something amiss with the personnel policy. A formula for calculating the ratio is as shown below:

$$\frac{\text{Man days lost} \times 100}{\text{Total possible man days}}$$

The calculations exclude any holiday periods. Care must be taken when employing the percentage. If a man has been ill it is clearly wrong for him to be criticised. On the other hand, a man who takes off two or three days per month without good cause should be reprimanded.

IMPROVEMENT OF MORALE

For details of how accidents may be prevented and labour turnover reduced the reader is referred to the sections dealing with these topics. Other sections in the book also deal with the achievement and maintenance of high morale.

EXAMINATION QUESTIONS

1. Chester Barnard said that "the first executive function is to develop and maintain a system of communications." Discuss this view, dealing in particular with:

(*a*) the common sins of communication;
(*b*) the guiding principles for a manager wishing to improve his communication skills;
(*c*) the nature of communication in a business environment.

2. What are the advantages and disadvantages of using committees as an integral part of the management of a business? In a business where you found the top executives were required to spend an excessive amount of time attending meetings, what steps would you take to reduce this requirement?

3. What are the functions of a *safety committee*? How should it be composed? What procedure would you advocate for co-ordination of such a committee's activities with those of the work study staff?

4. Absentees for the past ten weeks in one section of a works averaged 30% and, in another, 7%. Draft a report stating the causes of the absences and advising the action to be taken.

5. Outline some of the ways in which committees are used in business, making notes of the special features of each. Show how committees can be:

(*a*) effectively operated;
(*b*) misused in business practice.

6. What benefits can be expected from the operation of an employees' suggestion scheme in industry? Outline the method of operation of such a scheme giving a formula for the determination of the awards to be made. What difficulties would you expect to encounter arising from such a scheme?

7. Outline a programme of training and induction for the sales representatives of a large office machinery manufacturer. Would it be effective to

use the "case-study" method of training in this case? Give reasons for your answer.

8. Itemise the factors which need to be determined in laying down management policy on staff salaries. List the advantages and disadvantages of rewarding length of service by salary increases.

9. What action would you advise to be taken for introducing any system of payment by results in a factory which has been working entirely on day work rates?

10. State six main features of an employment policy and say how you would measure their effectiveness.

11. Supply one word or a short phrase to denote each of the following:

(a) The systematic presentation of the essence of many people's observation, experiment and experience.

(b) The process of classifying jobs according to the quality of skill and experience they require and the responsibility they entail.

(c) The attempt by a supervisor to assess the quality of an individual's performance in his job.

(d) The function performed by the board of directors of an undertaking.

(e) The department of a manufacturing company responsible for seeing that the goods made maintain the standards laid down.

12. What is the purpose of joint consultation? Describe the points to be observed in setting up a joint committee and enumerate the subjects normally discussed.

13. What action would you recommend to ensure adequate recruitment and retention of personnel in conditions of acute labour shortage?

14. Describe the main functions embodied in the general term "Industrial Relations."

15. Give your recommendations for setting up and operating a works safety organisation within a factory.

PART FOUR

FINANCIAL MANAGEMENT
AND STATISTICAL METHOD

Chapter XVIII

FINANCIAL MANAGEMENT

A BUSINESS may buy, manufacture, sell and distribute for the purpose of earning profit. When small in size the owner may calculate the profit earned or loss incurred on each transaction. He may carry the details in his mind and not keep any formal accounts or, alternatively, he may keep memorandum records in some form or other.

With growth the problems increase: there is a larger volume of buying and selling; the manufacturing units become larger and more complex; the number of employees multiply and organisational structures become more complicated. These and other factors all make a common recording language very essential.

This language should meet a number of requirements. It should not be verbose; profit and loss is concerned with £s and, therefore, words should be kept to a minimum. Another factor is the existence of sound, basic principles which can be followed so that the records kept are capable of being interpreted along similar lines by different people. Although scientific accuracy is impossible—because of the many variables—there is, nevertheless, a need for guide posts which ensure the realistic recording and valuation of transactions and assets and the ascertainment of profit or loss. A further consideration is the necessity for controlling expenditure on materials purchased and consumed, on personnel employed and on all fixed assets acquired and utilised.

Because of the rapidly changing state of the manufacturing organisation the accountant is faced with an extremely difficult task. Management should be made aware of these difficulties because the accounting records can only be accurate and useful when all personnel appreciate what is involved in record keeping, and the importance of following the procedures laid down. All too often there is contempt for the necessary timekeeping and recording on the shop floor with the result that the accounting data are vitiated from the start. If senior management appreciate what the accountant is trying to do they are likely to support him and make both the accounting function and their own much more efficient.

SCOPE OF ACCOUNTING

Accountancy is a wide and diverse subject which extends into all fields of activity. If a purchase is made, an expense is incurred, or wages are paid, each represents a transaction which must be recorded. There is a need to show the payments which have been made and the amounts which have been received. Ideally, the records should reflect sacrifice involved, but with changing price levels this is not easy and quite often the actual cost or purchase price is the only figure available.

The area of operation for accounting may be broken down into fairly distinct fields. However, some overlap is inevitable because the activities are related and there is no universally accepted definition for each of them. Bearing these facts in mind the topics will be covered in the following order:

1. Provision of finance.
2. Financial accounting (Chapter XIX).
3. Cost accounting (Chapter XX).
4. Management accountancy (Chapters XXI and XXII):

    (a) Budgetary control.
    (b) Standard costing.
    (c) Marginal costing.
    (d) Decision accounting.
    (e) Profit and loss measurement.

      (i) Return on capital employed.
      (ii) Revaluation accounting.

    (f) Capital expenditure decisions.

What is important to notice is that accountancy is a *tool* to be used by managers, employees, shareholders and, in appropriate circumstances, the general public at large.

PROVISION OF FINANCE

In order to produce and sell there must be adequate finance to acquire fixed assets, raw materials and other supplies. In addition, there should be enough cash or credit to meet obligations for wages, salaries, miscellaneous supplies and other necessities.

The problems of financing are present because there is an inevitable time lag between planning and the completion of a sale by the receipt of cash. In a new business a very *simplified* version of what may take place is shown below:

1. Idea for a product or service is conceived.
2. Finance is obtained. This can be cash and credit.
3. Fixed assets (*see* p. 306)—buildings, machinery, equipment— are purchased or hired.
4. Current assets (*see* p. 306)—items to be consumed such as raw materials, fuel and sundry supplies—are acquired.
5. Plans are made to produce and sell. Detailed drawings, specifications, bills of material, standard cost cards, production orders and other documents will have to be prepared.
6. Plans are put into operation. These would cover not only pro-

ducing and selling, but also the physical and financial controls such as production control and cost accounting.

7. Products are completed ready for sale.

8. Orders received from the salesmen are dealt with and the products are despatched.

9. Customers are invoiced and within a period, which can vary from seven days to twelve months (or even longer), payments are received.

10. *Throughout* the whole period, payments will have to be made to suppliers and employees. The finance required for this purpose is known as "working capital." Generally speaking, the longer the cycle involved in producing and selling, the larger the working capital which will be required.

In many cases, more than twelve months will elapse before any payment is received from the sale of the products or services. Even after cash starts to flow into the business a further considerable time may pass before receipts exceed payments.

SOURCES OF FINANCE

The types and sources of finance are many and varied. In the limited space available, it is only possible to give an outline of the main sources, distinguishing between (*a*) permanent or long-term capital, (*b*) medium and short-term capital, and (*c*) specialist institutions.

As a general rule, the bulk of the finance should be of a permanent nature. Temporary shortages in working capital can be met from borrowing and similar short-period funds. Although the concern here is with *external* finance there is also *internal* finance. The cheapest method of financing is that which comes from retention of earnings, *i.e.* ploughed back profits. Depreciation provisions and various forms of reserves (*see* pp. 304 and 310), all enable a business to grow without recourse to external borrowing.

Provided that ordinary shareholders are receiving a reasonable rate of return on the investment in a business, they do not generally object to profits being kept back. Indeed, if a company continues to grow and, as a result, earns more profit, the ordinary shareholders stand to gain from increased share prices as quoted on the Stock Exchange. This argument is affected by the taxation laws in existence at a particular time, but no Government is ever likely to impose such a burden that companies could not continue to develop.

As is shown from pp. 381 to 384, when calculating an adequate return on capital employed, there are problems connected with the risk involved in the type of business concerned and in the replacement of fixed assets in periods of rising prices. These matters also affect the earning and calculation of profit. Any student of management must try to appreciate that historical costs, *i.e.* prices paid in the past, do not always show an accurate picture of the affairs of a business. Adjustments may be necessary to convert the figures to present values.

In conclusion, it can be stated that a certain percentage of the profit earned should be retained in the business. The precise size will vary from one concern to another, but factors which influence this matter are: total profit earned; reasonable dividends having regard to the risk involved; plans for growth; and the nature of the business—some require a much larger investment in fixed assets than others.

The various methods available for obtaining *external* finance are now discussed.

PERMANENT CAPITAL

The types and sources of finance for permanent capital are as follows:

Savings and loans

These are generally appropriate when the business is in the very early stages of growth. The one-man business or partnership is appropriate for this type of finance. Usually a limited volume of fixed assets is employed and there are only a few employees. Once a large capital investment in fixed assets becomes necessary then the issue of shares on a "private" or "public" basis often becomes vital.

Share capital

The main division of share capital is into (*a*) ordinary shares and (*b*) preference shares. The latter are entitled to the first division of the profit earned, usually at a fixed rate. On the other hand, the ordinary shareholders are generally paid a higher rate of dividend, but they do carry greater risks.

Financial management is concerned with getting the correct balance between the value of ordinary shares (equity capital) and preference shares and debentures. This balance is known as the "capital gearing." When there is a small proportion of equity capital the structure is said to be highly geared. This may mean very high rewards for the ordinary shares in the good year and no dividends in the lean years. In short, the shares are speculative. Moreover, if the company encounters a difficult period and is unable to pay the dividends, there is always the danger that the preference shareholders will exert their powers and take over the control from ordinary shareholders. Quite often they are given this right when the preference dividends are in arrears.

If a private company is involved the shares cannot be the subject of a public issue. For a company to be classified as "private" there must be compliance with the relevant provisions of the *Companies Acts*. In particular the number of shareholders, excluding past and present employees, must not exceed fifty. Generally, the shareholders in such a company are of the same family or are friends. Some very large companies of international importance come into this category, the finance for growth coming from ploughed back profits. However, it is more usual for the large companies to be "public," *i.e.* having shares quoted on a stock exchange and permitted to issue them to the public by advertising or other means.

A public issue may be made by means of a "placing," when the shares are purchased by an issuing house or broker and then sold to selected clients such as insurance companies and other large investors. An alternative method is by an "offer for sale" whereby the issuing house buys the shares and then advertises them in an offer for sale document so that they can sell them to the public. Other methods are issue by tender, which employs a special way of determining the price of the shares (the shareholders bid); a rights issue where the shares are issued to existing shareholders; and bonus issues when a free issue of shares is made, also to shareholders. Very strict rules must be followed when making an issue of shares, these being stipulated by the *Companies Acts* and the regulations of the Stock Exchange.

Debentures—loan capital

If a company wishes to borrow money on a long-term basis then it is usual to acknowledge the loan on a formal document known as a "debenture." This may give a right against the company's assets so that failure to pay the interest due allows the debenture holders to be preferential creditors. When the debentures give no charges against assets they are said to be "naked" or "unsecured." Only companies with a very good profit record and a high financial standing can hope to make a successful issue of unsecured notes.

The debenture holders are creditors and not shareholders. They are paid interest and not dividends; accordingly, the payments are charged *against* profit whereas dividends are an *appropriation* of profit.

The issue of debentures can be a very useful method of obtaining finance at reasonable cost. However, the interest is a fixed charge which, if too heavy, can become a millstone which can strangle a company, especially in the early stages of development or when profits fluctuate from one year to another. If employed, then the proportion of debentures should be reasonable having regard to the ordinary and preference share capitals. A property company can generally borrow on long term more than a manufacturing company of a similar size. However, each company should be considered on its own merits and the capital structure designed accordingly.

MEDIUM-TERM CAPITAL

Medium-term capital is finance which is obtained for longer than one year, which is not intended to be of a permanent nature. Generally, five years is the maximum period, but there is no hard and fast rule. The main types of capital coming into this category are shown below:

Bank loans

Term loans are special loans for the purchase of fixed assets. British banks are now willing to lend money to industry for periods of up to ten years. The advantage of a loan is its certainty in terms of years. On the other hand, a bank overdraft may be withdrawn at very short notice.

This method is very suitable for small- and medium-size businesses, especially in the early stages of development. It is unlikely to be employed by large companies; indeed, the scheme organised by the main banks was never intended for this purpose.

Hire purchase

Hire purchase needs no introduction. The hirer pays a deposit and then a number of instalments have to be made; at the end of a period when a specified number of instalments have been paid the property in the goods passes to the hirer.

There is no doubt that this method of obtaining finance is convenient and quick without complicated, legal formalities. As a method of purchasing fixed assets it has few equals. Unfortunately, there is a major disadvantage in the form of high interest charges. Usually the rate is based on the total sum borrowed initially and, therefore, considering that instalments are paid from the very beginning, the *effective* rate of interest tends to be double the *nominal* rate. A 10% per annum rate for a period of two or three years can mean a charge of 20% or more.

Sale and lease back

A company which requires additional finance may sell some of its property to an investment company with a right to lease back at an agreed rental. For example, an engineering business may sell one of its office buildings and then take a lease on it for a number of years with a right to renew.

This method is likely to be useful when working capital has to be increased on a permanent basis. However, the investment company will obviously be out to make a profit which will be included in the rental. The latter will have to be met in lean years as well as good years and for some companies the financial strain may be very great. A more orthodox method of borrowing may be preferable.

Mortgages

Finance may be obtained by borrowing from a bank, insurance company, investment company or other similar institution. As security, the lender requires a charge against the borrowing company's property; this is known as a "mortgage."

For periods of 5, 10 or 20 years this method has some advantages. Generally up to two-thirds of the value of the property can be borrowed without complicated legal procedures. However, the annual interest may be so large that the company is burdened beyond what can be regarded as a reasonable limit.

Equipment leasing

Many types of fixed assets can now be obtained on lease. The property in the asset remains vested in the finance house, but the manufacturer is able to use the machine or other fixed asset so long as he pays the rental. Unlike hire purchase, the fixed asset never becomes the property of the hirer.

This method suffers from the same disadvantage as the earlier methods which require a fixed annual amount to be paid.

In its favour, the method is easy to understand and to use. A company short of cash can replace its fixed assets, thus remaining up to date in production methods with a good possibility of more than paying the rental from the increased profits.

SHORT-TERM CAPITAL

Capital coming under this heading is borrowed for a period not exceeding one year. As a general rule, short-term borrowing should be employed only to cover temporary fluctuations in working capital such as, for example, when trade is seasonal. At the period when sales are not producing revenue and stock-piling is taking place, short-term capital can bridge the gap.

The most usual methods available for raising short-term capital are borrowing from banks and accepting houses, and credit facilities from suppliers. These are dealt with below, credit facilities coming first.

Credit facilities

Obtaining goods and services on credit is an accepted method of transacting business. It is an important source of short-term finance and may vary from a few days up to a number of months. The most usual is one month after delivery of the goods.

A business with a quick turnover may sell the goods quickly enough to pay off the debt incurred. However, in a manufacturing industry the production cycle may cover many months and, therefore, there will always tend to be an interval between the purchase of materials and the sale of finished products. Nevertheless, obtaining credit for only one month can play an important part in the growth of business.

Borrowing from banks

Loans from banks are one of the most popular methods of obtaining short-term finance. The same applies to bank overdrafts. Both can generally be obtained at a reasonable rate of interest.

Bank loans tend to be more certain than the bank overdraft which may be withdrawn with little or no notice. On the other hand, the bank overdraft does permit a businessman to use a facility as a "buffer," borrowing when necessary and reducing or eliminating the overdrawn balance when cash is available.

A bank loan is generally for a definite period of time and there is not the same danger of withdrawal. On the other hand, the method does tend to be more expensive than the bank overdraft simply because interest has to be paid for the full period of the loan.

Before a bank manager allows money to be borrowed he will naturally wish to be satisfied that there is a reasonable expectancy that the interest will be paid and the principal will be repaid. He may ask for some form of collateral security to be given. In addition, he will want to know the *purpose* of the loan and will wish to study the past record of profits over a number of years.

Undoubtedly, loans and overdrafts are two of the most popular methods of obtaining short-term finance. A company of good standing can usually take advantage of this facility quickly and easily at reasonable cost. Moreover, there is no form of stigma attaching to dealings with banks. Financing by means of hire purchase, mortgages or some form of leasing does not always meet with approval.

Borrowing from accepting houses

A business may open an account with an accepting house. The latter is a merchant bank which specialises in "acceptance credits," a method whereby a borrower can obtain acceptance of bills of exchange which are payable three months after sight.

Once the bills have been accepted they become "prime bank bills," and can be discounted (*i.e.* cashed) with only a small charge being deducted from the face value.

There is no doubt that this method can be of great value to any business which wishes to finance a transaction or series of transactions, with the expectation of repaying when the goods are sold. This is known as a "self liquidating" transaction. Possibly the greatest use of this method will be in importing or exporting, where bills of exchange are still employed.

SPECIALIST INSTITUTIONS*

The role played by banks, discount houses, issuing houses and accepting houses has already been outlined. This brief description of the methods of financing would not be complete without reference to other specialist institutions which have been set up, mainly by the British Government or at least with its sponsorship.

A summary of the main institutions is given below:

Board of Trade Advisory Committee

Loans, provision of premises, and grants may be obtained from the Board of Trade for any company which proposes to establish itself in a *development area*, thus providing employment to workers.

* *See* also Chapter XXVII on the economic aspects of banking and finance.

A development area is an area which is designated as such by the Government, generally because of under- or unemployment. Examples may be found in Scotland, England and Wales where excessive specialisation, such as shipbuilding, has meant that the areas concerned have been the first to suffer from any trade depression and whose rate of unemployment tends to be above that for the national average.

An application for advice and assistance has to be made through the Secretary of the Board of Trade Advisory Committee.

The Export Credits Guarantee Department

In an effort to encourage exporting, the British Government has established the Export Credits Guarantee Department (known as E.C.G.D.). This department advises exporters and, through the provision of insurance, enables loans to be negotiated for all types of export business.

E.C.G.D. does not provide the finance, but, by covering the risks involved in exporting, and guaranteeing that loans will be repaid, it encourages banks and other institutions to provide loans which would not otherwise be available.

Finance Corporation for Industry Limited (F.C.I.)

This Corporation is willing to supply fixed capital where the sum required by a business is in excess of £200,000. Generally, it operates only when a company is not able to obtain funds from normal borrowing or the issue of share capital. This could arise when a business is developing a product which is not at a stage where commercial gain can be shown as being positive, and yet it is in the national interest that further work takes place.

The Corporation operates along normal commercial lines so the borrower must be able to justify the provision of the loan.

Industrial and Commercial Finance Corporation Limited (I.C.F.C.)

The amount of permanent capital which may be supplied may be between £5000 and £200,000. Shares or debentures may be taken up by the Corporation; alternatively, the assistance can take the form of a loan.

Each proposal for finance is taken on its merits, but, generally speaking, only soundly managed companies are assisted. The I.C.F.C. tends to specialise in assisting the small private company where expansion becomes very difficult due to lack of finance.

SELECTION AND ORGANISATION

A normal commercial business will use a *combination* of the methods outlined to obtain the correct amount and type of finance. As indicated, the bulk of the capital should be of a permanent nature, but this can be augmented with medium- or short-term finance. The appropriate sources or types of finance will vary from one period to another. Much depends upon the state of the money market, in particular the cost of borrowing and the availability of funds from the various sources. Taking into account all relevant factors at the particular time the most appropriate combination will be selected.

In financial planning much can be gained by an appropriate organisation structure and the employment of the appropriate tools of management. Management accountancy includes many techniques, including budgetary control, and these should be used to the fullest possible extent.

Examination Questions on Chapter XVIII are given at the end of Chapter XX.

CHAPTER XIX

OUTLINE OF FINANCIAL AND COST ACCOUNTING

THE conventional treatment of financial accounting and cost accounting has been to regard them as being quite separate subjects. However, in more recent times there is a strong body of opinion which favours integration, thus avoiding duplication of records and accounting personnel.

This chapter and the next are concerned with an *outline* of financial and cost accounting so that the reader who has had no formal training in accounting can at least obtain an appreciation of the main principles. As far as possible, the subjects are treated together, thus giving emphasis to the fact that in practice they should be integrated as far as possible.

DEFINITIONS

Both financial and cost accounting are concerned with the recording of transactions so as to be able to calculate profit (or loss) for one or more transactions and to show the assets and liabilities owned or incurred by the business.

Accounting uses words and figures to communicate the transactions which have been entered into. As far as possible, words are kept to a minimum and follow a standardised pattern, especially when recording in the books of account.

Financial accounting is concerned with the *external* transactions and, therefore, records all dealings with the outside world. Any purchase or sale of goods and services, and fixed assets, whether for cash or on credit are covered. The analysis of the accounts emphasises the purpose of conventional, financial accounting and this is shown on the chart in Fig. 43.

Cost accounting deals with the *internal* affairs of a business. It attempts to show the results of the operations carried out and emphasises throughout the measurement and achievement of efficiency. Fixed assets, workers and materials are brought together with the object of transforming the resources employed and thereby obtaining a saleable product or service. Generally special attention is paid to the *control aspect* of the quantities and prices of the resources necessary for the transformation.

This fact is shown in the analysis adopted (Fig. 43). From the diagram it will be seen that the business activities of manufacturing and selling are recorded by (*a*) financial accounting and (*b*) cost accounting. These have been shown separately so as to emphasise the nature of the two techniques. However, in practice they can be arranged so that the analysis follows that required for cost accounting, but separate accounts are kept for cash and for debtors and creditors. The latter are not shown in the purely cost accounting system.

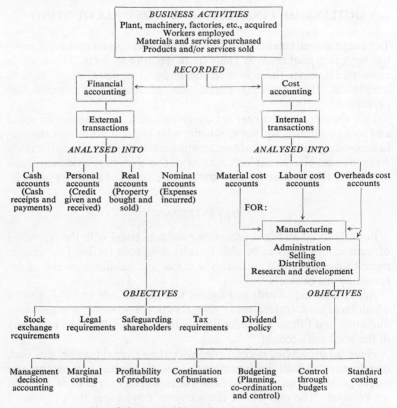

Note: Reference should be made to the explanatory text.

FIG. 43.—*Financial and cost accounting*

THE PURPOSES OF ACCOUNTING

ACCOUNTING AS A LEGAL NECESSITY

Financial accounting has grown into its present form to meet a number of requirements. Not least of these is the need to supply information required by law. The *Companies Acts, 1948* and *1967*, stipulate how the accounts of companies must be laid out and presented so as to show a true and fair view of the activities and state of affairs. The medium employed for presenting the information to shareholders is known collectively as the "final accounts," consisting of a profit and loss account, and a balance sheet. These are explained later in the chapter.

In addition, there is a necessity to supply accounts which are acceptable to the Commissioners of Inland Revenue for taxation purposes. Many critics of modern accounts have asserted that the form of the business records is being dictated not by management requirements, but on the basis of ascertaining how much tax should be paid. There is certainly a good deal of truth in this statement.

Accounts may have to be supplied for other reasons which originate from statutes, but space does not permit further coverage.

ACCOUNTING AS EVIDENCE OF DEBTS

Accounting information is vital for showing the indebtedness of a business. As noticed in the previous chapter, obtaining credit is a major source of finance. Indeed, it is true to say that for many companies the majority of transactions are on a credit basis.

The use of the terms *debit* and *credit* throughout accounting recognises the importance of credit transactions. Historically, *debit* means "he owes," whereas credit signifies "he trusts." Today a debit (abbreviated "Dr") is an entry made on the left hand of an account, and a credit (abbreviated "Cr") is a right-hand entry.

A fundamental rule of double-entry accounting is that for each debit entry in one account, there should be a credit entry in another account. Each transaction is viewed from a double aspect; on the one hand there is the company and on the other the debtor or creditor. Accordingly, each credit transaction involving an addition to an asset is shown on the debit side of the asset account, the credit entry being to the supplier's account (the creditor). A decrease in an asset is shown as a credit entry in the asset account. Not unnaturally this system is called "double-entry" accounting.

ACCOUNTING AS EVIDENCE OF CREDITWORTHINESS

Banks and other financial institutions which are concerned with lending can ascertain the likely risk involved in granting a loan. The profit trends, the fixed assets owned and the liabilities incurred can all be studied from the final accounts. In addition, credit ratings can be established and there are credit associations which specialise in doing this work. Some prepare a report on request, whereas others publish a ratings book and supplementary information to keep the ratings up to date.

ACCOUNTING AS A REPORT ON MANAGEMENT'S SOCIAL OBLIGATIONS

There are three social groups which management must serve:

1. Employees.   2. Shareholders.   3. Consumers.

In the interest of co-operation between *employees* and managers a sound system of communication is vital. An integral part of this system should be interim and final accounts which are informative on all matters which are of interest to employees and trade unions. These could include wages paid, materials consumed, overhead costs incurred and details of profit earned and its mode of distribution. A useful addition is a comparative statement of all the elements which go towards total cost incurred, often expressed as percentages, the total being 100%. The well-designed, informative company report can show that employees are being considered in a very material way by being given adequate remuneration, pension rights and various fringe benefits.

Reference to legal requirements has already been made. There are also the regulations which are required by the Council of the Stock Exchange. Any company which wishes to make a public issue of shares must comply with very strict rules and, among other things, must supply details of results for the past ten years. Protection of the *shareholder* is an extremely important aspect of accounting for public companies. This is rightly so, for management has a social obligation to share-holders just as much as to employees and consumers. With few exceptions the days of the supreme power of shareholders are now over. They are relegated to names on a share register, and very rarely do they become a collective body which has power to influence policy. Instead, the management of a business is left in the hands of experts. In fact, a modern tendency is to appoint executive directors who work in a full-time capacity.

Because of the diminishing influence of shareholders and the streng-thening of the ties with employees and consumers the idea that profit must always be *maximised* is no longer true. Today the emphasis tends to be on ensuring that all social groups receive an adequate reward. Moreover, this is aimed for a long period and is not taken on a year-to-year basis. In other words, there is emphasis upon long-term stability. Above all, there is an expectation of growth. Study of company reports shows that this is a very real issue. No chairman wishes to state that this was the year in which his company stood still or lost ground; in-stead he endeavours to show that the company has progressed. There is no better way for progressing than retained earnings and sound management.

How much an ordinary shareholder should receive in dividends is a matter which is open to debate. However, it is true to say that the rate should be at least that obtained elsewhere on an investment which is comparable in risk. In Britain the Bank Rate—the rate at which the Bank of England will discount first-class bills of exchange—is the key to other rates of interest. These undoubtedly affect what is a reasonable return to shareholders. It must not be forgotten that a shareholder will also be interested in *growth prospects*. The price of an ordinary share on the Stock Exchange is what is important when a shareholder wishes to sell: a £1 share may be priced at £2·50 which will be the market's valua-tion, after considering such matters as profit prospects, assets owned and the confidence felt for the board of directors and management. The relationships between the different elements on a balance sheet will be more apparent from a study of pp. 303 to 305.

Many *consumers* know little or nothing about the companies with which they trade. Yet in the interest of goodwill, without which profits cannot be optimised, it is vital for a company to present the correct image. Many company reports now show photographs of activities which are likely to be of interest to consumers. Descriptions of these activities are also included and appear in newspapers and journals in abridged form.

Even if consumers do not see the details from published company reports their interests may still be watched. Newspapers report all significant occurrences and any major developments may be the subject of news reports on television and radio. The matter does not end here. Any company which values its reputation must try to ensure that the methods employed or policy pursued meet with the approval of the Government of the day, and possibly some body such as the Monopolies Commission, the Prices and Incomes Board or a similar "watchdog."

From the brief outline given it should be apparent that published accounting reports are an important and vital link between the company and the inhabitants of the country (or world) within which it operates. In fulfilling its social obligations, management should ensure that the fullest possible disclosure is made in a way which is readily understood by all who may look at the information contained in the accounts.

ACCOUNTING AS AN AID TO MANAGEMENT

The purposes outlined in the previous sections show how the published accounts can be employed by interested parties. Collectively, they are known as the "stewardship of management." They are the legal and social obligations which should be fulfilled as part of the functions of management.

Unfortunately, showing other people what is being done is not necessarily the same as seeing that maximum efficiency is being achieved. The published accounts, or the purely book-keeping entries from which the final accounts have been compiled, often tell a manager little or nothing upon matters which are vital to sound management. Some of these are as follows:

1. What policy shall be followed in the future and what plans shall be made?

These require detailed information on the economy and the business operations. Cost accounting, budgetary control and other facets of management accountancy are essential tools of management for all planning activities (*see* Chapter XXII).

2. Which decision should be made when considering such matters as indicated below?

(*a*) The fixed asset to be purchased from a number of alternatives.

(*b*) Whether product X or product Y or both should be produced and at what price.

(c) Should a component or product be manufactured or purchased ready made from outside?

These and similar questions are the very essence of management.
Conventional accounting is often meaningless in solving these problems.
Instead, the management accountant must supply information in a form
which enables all *relevant factors* to be stressed. The exercise of initiative and judgment can then be carried out with a full knowledge of the
likely consequences. Other uses of accounting are as follows:

1. *Defining responsibilities.*—Budget and/or cost centres have to be
established so that departmental managers have clearly defined responsibilities.

2. *Controlling costs.*—Costs have to be controlled for cost centres and
for individual products. Budgetary control and standard costing,
explained later, enable this control to be exercised. The study of the
behaviour of costs and the division into "controllable" and "uncontrollable" help to locate the areas of responsibility. These matters
are covered further in Chapters XXI and XXII.

3. *Measuring the effectiveness of management.*—The overall yardstick
for measuring efficiency is the return on capital employed. Conventional
accounting very often adheres to the use of original costs for recording
the values of fixed assets. This in turn affects the calculation of the
"capital employed" and the "profit" earned. Recognition that prices
change is a vital part of management and the accounting methods
employed should reflect this fact (*see* Chapter XXII).

FUNDAMENTALS OF ACCOUNTING

The two-sided character of accounting was stressed above. Each
transaction, it was noted, is recorded twice; one entry is on the debit
side, whereas the other is on the credit side, of the appropriate accounts.

Because there are two sides to each transaction it follows that the
debit entries should be equal in value to the credit entries. Furthermore,
since any increase in an asset is debited and liabilities are credited,
there is a basic equation which can be applied throughout all accounting, irrespective of the business concerned. This equation is:

$$\text{Total assets} = \text{Total liabilities}$$

At any time the debits and credits should be equal in value. In
practice, because there may be many thousands of transactions in a
period the accountant takes only the *balances* (the differences between
the two sides) on each account and lists these in two columns (debit and
credit) and then totals them. This has the same effect as taking all the
entries because the two totals should be equal, thus showing the accuracy of the accounting. The name given to the list of balances is a
trial balance.

THE BALANCE SHEET

A statement which shows the assets owned and liabilities which are outstanding is known as a *balance sheet*. As will be appreciated from what has been stated in the previous section, the two sides should necessarily agree. However, this does not mean that the totals will remain static. Nothing could be further from the truth, for each transaction entered into will tend to affect the assets and liabilities.

A simple balance sheet is shown below:

X. Y. Co Ltd,
Balance Sheet
as at 1st January 19 . .

	£		£
Liabilities	1000	Assets	1000

Obviously, this is inadequate because no detail is shown. It is usual to specify the liabilities and assets. Before going on to a further example, it is necessary to notice that liabilities are shown on the left-hand side and assets are on the right-hand side. This is the opposite order to that given earlier for debits and credits in the accounts which appear in the main book of account (the ledger). What should be appreciated is that strictly speaking a balance sheet is not part of the double-entry system and, therefore, the entries are not debits and credits, but collectively represent a statement of affairs at a particular moment of time. Possibly to emphasise this fact the order is the reverse from that used throughout an accounting system. However, this does not seem to be an adequate reason for carrying out a practice which causes difficulty to students of accountancy and anyone else who wishes to understand the implications of a balance sheet. In an effort to eliminate the effects of a misleading convention many accountants now prefer a vertical balance sheet, an example of which is given later (Fig. 44).

A balance sheet which introduces more terms is now given:

X. Y. Co Ltd,
Balance Sheet
as at 1st January 19 . .

	£		£	£
Share Capital	1000	*Fixed Assets*		
Reserves	100	Buildings	800	
		Machinery	300	
Long-term Liabilities			——	1100
Loan from Bank	300	*Current Assets*		
Current Liabilities		Stocks	200	
Sundry Creditors	210	Debtors	100	
		Cash	210	
			——	510
	£1610			£1610

The vertical balance sheet

A more detailed, vertical balance sheet is given in Fig. 44. Figures have been omitted. In order to become more familiar with published accounts, readers are advised to study those issued by well-known companies.

ITEMS ON THE BALANCE SHEET

The most important of the new terms introduced on p. 303 are explained below:

Share capital

The share capital represents the money invested in the company by shareholders. In practice, this is divided into ordinary and preference shares and any sub-divisions of these. The price of the shares is also usually given, but this would be at their nominal value (*e.g.* £1), and not the price quoted on the Stock Exchange (*e.g.* £2·65).

An important principle of accounting is that any capital is viewed as a "liability" of the business (X.Y. Co Ltd). This is logical because if a company is liquidated the share capital must be paid back to shareholders. The word *liability* is used in a special sense because it is generally *only* on liquidation that the share capital would be returned. However, this possibility is a sound enough reason for the principle adopted. Once the principle is understood a more logical approach would be to think of the left-hand side of the balance sheet as "share capital and liabilities." Even this is subject to what is said in connection with reserves and equity capital in the next paragraph.

Reserves

Reserves on a balance sheet may be given many different titles. They may be for future taxation, for replacement of fixed assets in times of rising prices, redemption of loans or for some other reason. The essential characteristic of a reserve is that it is formed from *profit* which has been retained in the business.

Any profit which is transferred to a reserve and which is intended to be regarded as belonging to ordinary shareholders is known as "shareholders' equity." Generally speaking this figure is equal to the value of total assets *less* any other commitments such as long-term liabilities, current liabilities and preference shares. When these are deducted this shows the value of that part of the business which is owned by ordinary shareholders. If the figure is divided by the number of shares an approximate share valuation is obtained.

Long-term liabilities

Any loan which is obtained for longer than one year is regarded as a long-term liability. Mortgage debentures generally come under this heading.

BALANCE SHEET

CAPITAL EMPLOYED (Sources of funds)

	Authorised		This year Issued	Last year Issued
			£	£
Ordinary Share Capital	*This year*	*Last year*		
Full details to be shown of authorised and	£	£		
issued capital including numbers of shares and nominal values, whether fully paid or not, to be stated including amount				
Capital Reserves				
Share Premium Account	...	...	...	...
Capital Redemption Reserve Fund ...	...	...	...	...
Debenture Redemption Reserve	...	...	...	...
Fixed Assets Replacements Reserve ...	...	...	...	...
Preference Share Redemption Fund ...	...	...	...	...
Revenue Reserves				
Profit and Loss Balance	...	...	...	...
General Reserve	...	...	...	...
Taxation				
(Details to be given)	...	...	...	...
1. TOTAL EQUITY CAPITAL	...	...	£	£
Asset value of each Ordinary Share ...	...	...	...	

	Authorised			
Preference Share Capital	*This year*	*Last year*		
Full details to be shown of different classes of	£	£		
authorised and issued capital including numbers of shares and nominal values, whether fully paid or not, to be stated including amount				
	£	£		

			This year	Last year
2. PREFERENCE CAPITAL	...	...	£	£
Interest of Minority Shareholders				
(Details to be given)	...	...	...	
3. MINORITY INTEREST	...	...	£	£
4. LONG-TERM LIABILITIES	...	...		
Debentures and other long-term liabilities would be detailed				
TOTAL CAPITAL EMPLOYED (1 + 2 + 3 + 4)	...	...	£	£

EMPLOYMENT OF CAPITAL (How the funds are employed)

			This year	Last year
			£	£
CURRENT ASSETS				
Stocks (detailed)	...	...	...	...
Debtors	...	...	...	...
Marketable Securities (short-term investments)		...	...	...
Cash	...	...	...	...
Prepayments	...	...	...	...
1. TOTAL CURRENT ASSETS	...	...	£	£
CURRENT LIABILITIES				
Creditors	...	...	...	...
Overdraft at Bank	...	...	...	...
Taxation (detailed)	...	...	...	...
Final Dividends (net)(detailed) ...	...	...	...	...
2. TOTAL CURRENT LIABILITIES	...	...	£	£
3. NET CURRENT ASSETS (Working Capital) ...	...	...	£	£
(1 above less item 2)				

FIXED ASSETS	Cost	Aggregate Depreciation	Net (*This year*)	Net (*Last year*)
Land and Buildings				
Plant and Machinery				
(Other details to be given when necessary)				
4. TOTAL FIXED ASSETS			£	£
INVESTMENTS				
Details of investments to be given showing				
(i) trade investments	...	...	...	...
(ii) other investments	...	...	...	...
(a) quoted including market values	...	...	...	...
(b) unquoted	...	...	...	...
5. TOTAL INVESTMENTS	...	...	£	£
TOTAL CAPITAL EMPLOYED (3 + 4 + 5) ...	...	...		£

FIG. 44.—*Pro-forma vertical balance sheet*

L

Current liabilities

Debts which are expected to be settled fairly quickly (*e.g.* within one month) are shown as current liabilities. In theory any debt which is to be paid off within one year comes into this category. A bank overdraft is a good example. In actual practice, creditors expect to be paid well before one year has elapsed and bank overdrafts can be recalled at very short notice.

At all times there should be a healthy relationship between current liabilities and current assets, a matter which is considered below.

Fixed assets

Assets which are purchased for permanent use in a business are known as "fixed assets." Once acquired they are used to manufacture and sell the products which are the basis of the main objective of a business; *e.g.* land, buildings, tools, vehicles, are fixed assets. They are the means by which raw materials are transformed directly or indirectly into saleable products. The expenditure is known as "capital expenditure," but should not be confused with *share capital*.

Current assets

For most companies a current asset is one which is consumed and converted into cash within one year. Raw materials and other supplies are obtained; they are then worked on and converted to finished goods and then they are sold on cash or credit terms. Some companies may

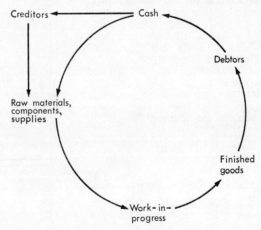

FIG. 45.—*Financial circle*

take longer than a year because of a long production cycle, *e.g.* when the business is to build bridges or ships. However, even in these circumstances it is quite usual for contracts to require payments to be received as the work proceeds. Figure 45 shows the operating cycle of a business.

The raw materials, etc., may be paid for immediately or at a later date. What should be apparent is that the current assets normally change their form time and time again during the course of a year.

A very useful measure of solvency is the ratio between current assets and current liabilities. This may be expressed as follows:

$$\text{Current ratio} = \frac{\text{Current assets}}{\text{Current liabilities}}$$

A general guide is that the ratio should be 2 to 1; that is to say, that current assets should be twice the current liabilities, thus leaving an adequate balance to pay for wages and other expenses which have to be met. The amount which is in excess of current liabilities is known as the "working capital."

Sometimes this ratio is called the *2 to 1 ratio*, but this is a misleading term. To imply that there can be an ideal ratio which will apply in all conditions and for all types of business is obviously quite nonsensical. A much different ratio (above or below the 2 to 1 ideal) can be quite satisfactory in appropriate circumstances.

What is more important is the nature of the items which go to make up the ratio. How much stock, the speed of turnover, period of credit given and received, and many other factors are more important than the *size* of the ratio.

A more precise measure is the quick or liquid ratio (known also as the *acid test* ratio). This is concerned with *liquid* assets and liabilities and may be expressed as follows:

$$\text{Quick or liquid ratio} = \frac{\text{Liquid assets}}{\text{Current liabilities}}$$

The ratio should be at least 1 to 1 so that liquid assets cover current liabilities. A lower figure *may* indicate financial difficulties.

THE PROFIT AND LOSS ACCOUNT

The second section of the company report is the profit and loss account. In practice this account is prepared before the balance sheet. Not until the profit earned is calculated and the profit appropriations have been made is the balance sheet compiled.

As implied by the name, the concern is with the result of operating a business for a period, the intention being to show whether a profit has been earned or a loss incurred.

The profit and loss account which must be prepared for the benefit of shareholders of public companies is very much a summarised version of the complete profit and loss account. Provided the requirements of the *Companies Acts* are complied with, there is no necessity to disclose all the vital information relating to a business. For example, as the law

PRO-FORMA PROFIT AND LOSS ACCOUNT
X Co Ltd, and Subsidiary Companies
for the year ended............

	This year	Last year
	£	£	£
Trading Profit before bringing into account the following (Note 1):		
Add:		
Income from Trade Investments ...		
Bank and other Interest		
Deduct:		
Depreciation		
Auditors' Remuneration and Expenses		
Pensions Contributions		
Additional Provision for Liabilities not yet ascertained		
Deduct:		
United Kingdom Taxation based on the Profit of the year:		
Corporation Tax		
Deduct:		
Proportion of Profit of a Subsidiary Company attributable to share-holders outside the Group (Note 2)		
CONSOLIDATED NET PROFIT OF THE YEAR (Note 3)		
Deduct:		
Preference Dividends for the year to 31st December		
Less Income Tax		
5% Preference Stock		
7% Preference Stock		
Proposed Ordinary Dividend for the yera		
Less Income Tax		
PROFIT OF THE YEAR RETAINED		
Add:		
Unappropriated Profits brought fwd.		
Transfer to:		
General Reserve		
Unappropriated Profits carried forward	£	£

1. In practice the Notes would be attached, but these have been omitted.
2. The *Companies Act, 1967*, requires disclosure of the *amount and basis of turnover* except for banking and discounting business (*see* text).

FIG. 46.—*Minimum requirements for profit and loss account*

stands, there is no compulsion to show the volume of sales if the company is not part of a group and its turnover does not exceed £50,000,* or the stocks on hand. Neither is it necessary to show the operating costs of the business although there are certain items which must be shown separately; *e.g.* charges for hire of plant and interest on loans.

PROFIT AND LOSS ACCOUNT

	This year (date to be given) £	Last year (date to be given) £
1. SALES FOR PERIOD		
Less Expenditure of Trading and Manufacture:		
Materials Consumed		
Wages and Salaries		
Overhead Costs (suitably detailed)		
2. TOTAL EXPENDITURE	£	£
3. GROSS PROFIT (1 above less item 2)		
4. *Less* Depreciation on *cost*		
5. TRADING PROFIT (3 above less item 4)	£	£
6. *Add* Gross Income from Investments (distinguishing between trade investments and others and income from quoted and unquoted investments)		
7. TOTAL GROSS PROFIT	£	£
Less Finance and Tax Charges:		
Interest on Debentures (other types also to be given in detail)		
Taxation (on present year's profits):		
(*a*) United Kingdom Corporation Tax		
(*b*) Overseas taxes on profits		
Less Proportion Attributable to outside shareholders in subsidiaries (shown "net" and distinguishing between paid and retained)		
8. TOTAL CHARGES: Finance, Taxation and Minority Interests ...	£	£
9. NET PROFIT FOR YEAR (7 above less item 8)	£	£
APPROPRIATION ACCOUNT showing how profit is appropriated to shareholders and retained in company		
10. BALANCE OF NET PROFIT (9 above)	£	£
Less Appropriations:		
(*a*) Transfer to Fixed Assets Replacements Reserve		
(*b*) Transfer to Debenture Redemption Reserve		
(*c*) Transfer to Preference Share Redemption Fund		
(*d*) Dividends (less tax)		
	£	£
Preference dividends		
Ordinary dividends		
(Distinguish between dividends paid and proposed.)		
(*e*) Other transfers to reserves (detailed)		
11. TOTAL APPROPRIATIONS	£	£
12. PROFIT AND LOSS BALANCE (10 above less item 11)		
Add Profit and Loss Balance from *Previous* Year		
BALANCE OF PROFIT CARRIED FORWARD	£	£

FIG. 47.—*Pro-forma example of profit and loss account*

A pro-forma example of a profit and loss account which gives the minimum details required by law is shown in Fig. 46. In comparison,

* *Companies Act, 1967.*

another example which illustrates how *full* disclosure can be made is shown in Fig. 47.

Management has an obligation to shareholders and other interested parties to disclose *fully* all relevant facts, not simply those which the law lays down as the bare minimum. Moreover, besides being *complete* the published accounts should be laid out so that they can be understood by anyone of average intelligence who wishes to study them.

It will be noted in both examples that two years' figures have to be given. This is to allow a comparison to be made of the two latest accounting periods. Many companies include a summary of the figures for five or even ten years, thus permitting the reader to see the *trend* over the whole period. When studying accounts or balance sheets it is the relative size of figures and the growth trend that are important. Single figures, taken in isolation, reveal very little.

SUPPLEMENTARY INFORMATION

When studying company reports full use should be made of the supplementary information which is often given. Graphs and diagrams which make for easy understanding are generally a feature of this information. From a study of the details it can be seen whether management is fulfilling adequately its stewardship function. The resources under its control should be used efficiently so that the business, shareholders, employees and the community as a whole can benefit.

Space does not permit a full coverage of all the possible aids to better understanding of the published accounts. However, Fig. 48 and Fig. 49 are typical of the aids being employed by the more enlightened companies. Figure 48 shows the return on total net assets (*i.e.* capital employed) and the return on sales. Chapter XXII deals with return on capital employed and reference should be made to the appropriate sections.

When dealing with return on sales it should be appreciated that *volume* of sales as well as the rate of return is important. Many companies are constantly striving to earn a larger profit by increasing volume and accept a lower profit margin per unit produced. Provided the increase in turnover is large enough, the additional revenue will more than offset the reduction in price. Furthermore, an increased volume of output may mean lower production costs per unit, so that can be a gain from this source.

TRANSITION FROM FINANCIAL TO COST ACCOUNTING

Integration of financial and cost accounting has already been stressed; this is the ideal. However, the growth of accounting generally commences with simple book-keeping, followed by a comprehensive system of accounting. As the complexity of manufacturing develops there is a need for cost accounting which may or may not be integrated

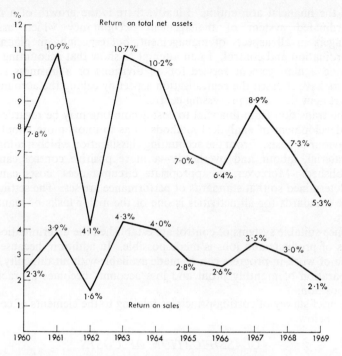

FIG. 48.—*Return on assets and sales*

The figures shown are related to profit before tax and before payment of debenture interest.

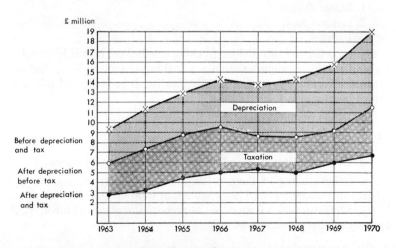

FIG. 49.—*Profits Graph*

with the financial accounting. Finally, there is the growth of a fully co-ordinated system of management accountancy which assists managers in all aspects of management, but especially in planning, co-ordination and control. In an attempt to show that accounting can provide a management service for all divisions of a business some writers have stressed the centralisation aspect by calling the accounting department the "data processing centre."

The transition from financial to cost accounting may be regarded as the development of analytical methods so as to know more about the behaviour of costs. From the accounting classification which is adopted —material, labour and overheads—a more positive control can be established. Moreover, in appropriate circumstances, costs can be predetermined so that standards of performance are set. The setting of these standards for all activities is one of the major tasks of management.

Once suitable systems of control are established the determination of costs of products and jobs is made possible. In addition, because the value of work-in-progress can be made available without difficulty, the preparation of monthly profit and loss accounts becomes a practical proposition.

A brief survey of costing principles relating to the elements of cost is given below.

CLASSIFICATION OF COSTS

Accountants classify costs in a way which emphasises the main elements which go to make a product. Briefly the classification employed is as follows:

1. Material cost.
2. Labour cost.
3. Expense.

These are further sub-divided to show whether the cost is incurred as a *direct result* of manufacturing a saleable product *or* is an indirect expense. Accordingly, a further classification is possible and this is as shown below:

1. Direct material cost ⎤
2. Direct labour cost ⎬ Prime costs.
3. Direct expense ⎦
4. Overhead costs (*i.e.* indirect material, labour and expense).

An understanding of these principles is *absolutely essential* to any student of management. They enable him to appreciate how costs are likely to behave, which is an essential prerequisite of cost control. Each element of cost is considered in turn.

1. Direct material cost

Any material which goes into a saleable product or its use is directly essential for the completion of that product is known as "direct material" and the amount paid is a "direct material cost."

The important fact is that the accountant is able to trace the material to a specific product or batch of products. There is no question of saying that the benefits from the material consumed have gone to a variety of jobs or products; if this were the case the material cost would be treated as overhead cost and would be apportioned on some equitable basis to *all* products.

In an engineering business the steel, brass, copper and other metals which go into the components made will be treated as direct materials. On the other hand, a strip of metal used to repair a machine tool or to build a shelf in the stores would be treated as indirect material.

From what has been said it should be apparent that direct material costs can be controlled in a positive manner. This is so because any material used can be authorised before an issue is actually made. Subsequently, the materials used can be traced to a specific job or product and the cost becomes part of the prime cost. How material costs are controlled is discussed in the next chapter.

2. Direct labour cost

The workers who convert the direct materials into saleable products are called "direct labour," and the direct wages are the "direct labour costs." Again there is a definite link between the incurring of expenditure and a benefit received by a specific product.

Just as with direct material, it is possible to control the direct labour cost. There are in fact two areas of control: (*a*) time spent in the factory or works; (*b*) time spent on individual jobs or products. The latter may be regarded as the *effective time* and, therefore, is a most important concept in the maximisation of efficiency. Generally speaking, the more positive the control over effective time, the greater will be the productivity per direct labour hour.

Examples of direct labour are such employees as machine operators, assembly workers and welders. Some workers are difficult to classify and should be treated in the most convenient manner bearing in mind the necessity for accurate costs and the expenses involved in tracing the direct costs. In some engineering works there is some difficulty in tracing the labour costs in the paint shop. Strictly speaking these costs are of a direct nature, but if a wide variety of components and jobs goes through the shop, there may be too much trouble involved in timing each one. Instead a compromise may be necessary, either treating the direct wages as indirect costs (overheads) or estimating the time spent on each from past experience. Much depends upon the circumstances and each case must be taken on its merits.

The control aspect is dealt with more fully on page 319.

3. Direct expense

Any costs, other than direct material and direct labour costs, the incurring of which results in a benefit which can be traced to a particular product or batch of products are "direct expenses." The naming of a number of these will clarify the definition.

The cost relating to patterns or drawings produced for a specific job may be treated as the direct expense of such a job, provided one of two conditions is satisfied. The first is that the patterns or drawings are totally consumed on the job; the second is that, though the patterns or drawings can be used again, there is no reasonable expectation that they will be used again.

Any additional payment for overtime (*overtime premiums*) may be treated as the direct expense of a particular job, provided that when the order was taken overtime working was anticipated, the overtime premium thus being expected. Overtime premiums arising from a request by the customer for overtime on a job to be worked can also be treated as a direct expense, provided the customer is to pay the extra cost. When the overtime premiums relate to general overtime, that is, overtime to meet normal production commitments, then the extra cost is usually treated as an overhead expense. Reference to the "benefit rule" will show why this is so.

Tools or equipment used for a specific job, and no other, may have their costs of purchase or hire charged to that job as direct expense.

Any costs incurred on experiments in connection with a specific job, and no other, could be treated in a similar manner. However, where benefit to the future is likely to accrue, the costs may be capitalised and charged to the jobs receiving the benefit.

PRIME COSTS

The prime cost of a product is made up of direct material, direct labour and direct expense. In some businesses, only the prime costs are ascertained. The main reason for this practice may be because of the original belief that only direct costs were "productive." These days, with mechanisation moving more and more towards automation, there is recognition that direct costs are not the only costs nor are they always the largest costs. Furthermore, because direct costs can be controlled quite effectively, the indirect costs should be given more attention, not less!

INDIRECT EXPENSES (OVERHEADS)

Any costs which cannot be classified under one of the direct categories given above are indirect expenses or overheads. They may be viewed under two headings:

1. Costs incurred whose benefits cannot be traced directly to a specific job or product. These are the most usual, and a list is given later.

2. Costs which are relatively small in size and, although strictly direct costs, the problem of tracing them to individual products is just not worth while. Examples are glue in box-making and small screws in large machines.

Because of the general nature of these costs the tracing of them to products has to be accomplished by some arbitrary means. There are, in fact, two schools of thought: (*a*) that which believes that all overhead costs should be recovered in the costs of products and (*b*) that which separates variable from fixed costs and does not recover the latter in the costs of products. The first approach is known as the *total cost* or *absorption method* whereas the second is called *marginal costing* or *direct costing*. The latter is discussed on p. 369.

Examples of overhead costs are given below under the following headings:

1. Manufacturing.
2. Administration.
3. Selling and distribution.
4. Research and development.

The lists are not intended to be exhaustive, but are given as illustrations of the main costs.

1. Manufacturing overhead costs

Manufacturing overhead costs are divided according to the elements of cost—materials, labour and expense.

All service department* costs are indirect costs. A service department is one directly connected with production yet not actually producing a product; from the cost accountant's point of view it is therefore a department which has no costs which can be associated directly with a product. The plant maintenance department is a typical example. The head of this department is charged with the responsibility of ensuring that all machinery and equipment used in production is regularly oiled and maintained and, in addition, he attends to other related matters. Not only the producing departments but also other service departments rely upon the efficient operation of the maintenance department.

All materials consumed by a service department are indirect materials, and all workers employed in a service department are indirect labour. Payments made for lighting, heating and insurance, on behalf of a service department, are indirect expenses.

---

* The description "department" is used here to describe a particular division of a business. The terms "cost centre" and "budget centre" used later generally have the same meaning.

A list of service departments usually found in a general engineering factory should make the definition clearer:

Name of service department	Principal functions
Tool room	The manufacture and repair of jigs, fixtures and small tools.
Inspection	The inspection of raw materials, components and finished products.
Internal transport	The transporting *within* the factory of materials, equipment and other items.
Receiving and stores	The receiving of raw materials and other items from outside suppliers and the correct storage of these once they have been entered on a goods received note or sheet and the stores bin card.
Works canteen	The preparation of meals and refreshments for the employees of the production departments.
First aid and welfare	The rendering of first aid and assistance with personnel problems: generally ensuring the wellbeing of employees.
Works office (*Note.* Normal office comes under *Administration.*)	Dealing with all clerical matters that must be carried out in the production departments.

In the producing departments, which are all departments where certain costs can be directly traced to a specific product or batch of products, all workers not actually engaged upon the conversion of the direct material are indirect labour. The payments made to these workers are indirect wages, and the materials they use are indirect materials. Taken from a general engineering factory, the following are examples of producing departments and indirect labour:

Producing Departments

Machine shop.	Finishing shop.
Welding shop.	Paint and spray shop.
Assembly shop.	

Indirect Labour

Supervisors, foremen and chargehands.
Machine setters.
General workers.
Apprentices and trainees.

If any of these workers should be connected with a particular process, or actually work on the conversion of direct materials to the finished product, they may be treated as direct labour.

Typical manufacturing overhead costs are as shown below:

Building expenses:

rent,	light and heat,
insurance,	depreciation,
rates,	miscellaneous.
repairs,	

Plant maintenance.
Plant depreciation.
Indirect labour.
Management and supervision (but *see* "Administration" below).
Tools.

Power expenses:

oil,	depreciation,
fuel,	insurance,
labour,	sundry expenses,
rent and rates,	stores.
water,	

The division shown can be varied to meet particular requirements. How these costs are recovered in the cost of each product or job is shown later in this chapter.

2. Administration costs

All *management expenses* which do not relate to the categories 1, 3 and 4 listed earlier are classified as administration costs. They are in effect the expenses of providing a general management and clerical service.

For each department in an office there will be such costs as those shown below:

Audit fees.	Postages.
Bank charges.	Printing and stationery.
Cleaning costs.	Rates and taxes.
Depreciation.	Rent.
Directors' fees.	Salaries.
Donations.	Supplies (sundry).
Insurance.	Telephones.
Legal costs.	Travelling expenses.

Many of these costs are of a fixed or semi-variable nature (defined below).

3. Selling and distribution costs

In some industries the major proportion of total cost derives from selling and distribution, and most businesses incur these costs to some degree. Unfortunately, they are often very difficult to control simply because the costs are extremely difficult to predetermine.

Selling costs are incurred in order to maintain and increase the volume of sales. They cover all expenses directly or indirectly necessary to persuade consumers to buy. A better idea of the nature of these costs can be seen from the list given below:

Salesmen's
    salaries,
    commissions,
    telephones,
    travelling,
    stationery,
    postage,
    bad debts.
Sales administration salaries.
Rent of sales office.
Rent of showrooms.
Depreciation.
Insurance.
Advertising.

The distribution function covers all activities connected with transporting products to customers and storing them when necessary. Besides the expenses of outside transport there will be the cost of the company's own vehicles, the salaries of clerks and managers, depreciation of equipment, repairs and maintenance, wages, stationery, insurance and other related expenditure.

4. Research and development costs

Research and development are grouped together because they are very much related. In practice difficulty is experienced in separating the two functions. When research results in a definite benefit which has commercial possibilities, then the development engineer takes over.

The costs will vary according to the extent and nature of the research and development which exists. Some companies have to provide large buildings with many research and development staff; others manage with few or no facilities. Much depends upon the nature of the product or service being produced. In the chemical industry, electronics, plastics and specialist machine manufacture the introduction of new ideas is vital. Innovation at the right time can be the main source of profit. The British economy has been built very largely on the inventiveness of its engineers, chemists and other professional men and women.

CONTROLLING COSTS

Costs for all the functions mentioned above can only be controlled by the watchfulness of managers and workers. There should be a positive effort at all times to ensure that waste and inefficiency are kept to a minimum.

The accountant, in co-operation with the managers responsible for the functional divisions, devises systems and methods which allow control to be exercised as part of the normal routine. Basically the following principles apply:

Division into cost centres

This division means that responsibilities are defined in terms of accountability. A machine shop may be a cost centre in itself or there may be a number of cost centres. Much depends upon the size of the machine shop and the nature of the operations being carried out. Being designated a cost centre means that costs for that section are to be accumulated separately. Only when it is worth while by results should the accountant introduce refinements such as additional cost centres. In appropriate circumstances a single machine tool could be treated as a cost centre.

When the costs ascertained relate only to a person or persons, then the cost centre is a "personal cost centre," otherwise it is an "impersonal cost centre."

The physical layout of the factory and the cost centres very often coincide, but such relationship is not essential; there may be one department which covers a particular function, but this may be divided into a number of cost centres. A single operation being performed by men and machines could be a cost centre.

Costs are predetermined

This predetermination may be on the basis of one or both of the following:

1. Functions and departments.—Budgetary control, as is explained in Chapter XXI, employs this basis. Costs are predetermined for a future period, usually a year.

2. Products and/or components.—When identical products and components are produced in large quantities it becomes worth while to determine in advance the best methods of production and, as a corollary, the standard costs. The latter represent what costs *should be* for stated conditions and a predetermined level of output. More details of standard costs are given in Chapter XXI.

Comparison of predetermined costs with actual costs

Unless some measure or yardstick is provided there is no way of telling the state of efficiency being achieved. Different men employed on producing the same product would tend to work at different speeds and levels of efficiency. To take an example:

Name	Average Time Taken
B. Barker	20 min
L. Lawrence	25 min
R. Rudd	28 min

Who can be regarded as working efficiently? Without a predetermined *standard time* it is only possible to hazard a guess. If this is 18 minutes then none of the men is doing well; on the other hand, if 30 minutes then all three are working very well.

The important fact which emerges is that pre-planning is an essential part of efficient management. Predetermination of costs should be part of this pre-planning and, subsequently, comparison of the plans (standards) with actual performances enables control to be exercised.

Variations between standard and actual costs

The accountant refers to these variations as *cost variances*. When their causes are determined they are presented to the appropriate managers so that corrective action can be taken.

Design of costing systems and methods for complete control

The basic costing systems are either job costing or process costing. They are described in Chapter XX. Within these two systems or variations of these are many systems or methods. For example, there are methods necessary for recording labour times and for paying wages. Direct materials and overhead costs have to be authorised and controlled and routine methods are necessary.

ABSORBING FACTORY OVERHEAD COSTS*

The factory overhead costs are usually apportioned to individual departments of production. This practice of departmentalisation is essential in all cases where it is necessary to trace responsibility for costs. The justification can be summarised as follows:

1. The total costs incurred by both service and producing departments can be ascertained. This is essential for cost control.

2. An overhead rate can be calculated for each department or cost centre. An average rate for the whole factory is very rarely acceptable for the differing conditions normally found. Overhead responsibility will vary between departments: some may have expensive

---

* In textbooks "recovering" and "absorbing" overhead costs are employed to indicate the use of overhead rates for charging indirect costs. The Institute of Cost and Works Accountants prefer "absorbing" or "absorption" on the grounds that "recovery" appears to imply recovery in the selling price, which is not necessarily the case.

machinery, others have very little machinery, *e.g.* a machine shop and an assembly department.

3. Departmental idle capacity can be measured much more easily.

Apart from these reasons is the fact that departmental profit and loss account preparation is greatly facilitated. Also decisions regarding the continuance of a department (when fixed cost will be excluded from the calculation) or the reasonableness of expenses incurred can be made.

To achieve these aims the cost accountant must clearly define the "cost centres" of a factory before going on to accumulate and attempt to control costs relating to such centres.

Methods of apportioning factory overhead costs to cost centres are covered in the next section. Whenever possible a direct charge should be made to the appropriate cost centre. The remaining overhead costs have to be apportioned to both service and producing cost centres. The service charges are then transferred to producing cost centres, so that all costs are absorbed by the products or jobs.

APPORTIONING FACTORY OVERHEADS

The principal methods used for apportioning factory overhead costs are as follows:

1. Square or cubic footage.
2. Capital values.
3. Number of employees.
4. Employees' wages.
5. Kilowatt-hour capacity.
6. Radiators; number or area.
7. Departmental direct charges.

1. Square or cubic footage

Building service and land costs can be apportioned on this basis. Thus, occupancy costs, such as depreciation on buildings, building repairs, heating, fire insurance on buildings and the upkeep of the grounds, can be charged to departments according to the square or cubic footage enjoyed by each department.

The method is generally satisfactory, but there may be some unfairness where some departments occupy preferential positions. Space in a certain part of a building, say, on the first floor, may be more valuable than in other parts. Some departments may have higher ceilings than others, and this fact may mean that a larger cubic volume is included.

Corridors and stairways may complicate matters, but this difficulty may be overcome in one of two ways. They may be excluded from the total area, but their costs included in the total costs; this automatically takes care of the apportionment. Alternatively, the cost of the corridors and stairways may be apportioned on the basis of the number of employees in each department.

2. Capital values

Depreciation of equipment and machinery, and insurance and repairs on machinery, may be apportioned on this basis.

Insurance is probably more accurately apportioned on the insurance values of the individual assets, and a better basis for repairs is by direct charge to each department, the amount calculated by reference to time sheets.

3. Number of employees

Canteen and first-aid costs may be apportioned according to the number of employees in each department. In the case of canteen costs this basis may not be very accurate, for not all employees may use the canteen. Those workers on the lowest rates of pay may be concentrated in certain departments; these workers may find canteen meals too expensive and adopt some other means, such as bringing their own lunches. If meals are free, apportionment according to the number of employees in a department should give reasonable results. Otherwise, unless the view that the charge should be shared according to service offered to departments (even though not used!) is adopted, the fairer basis is according to the number of employees actually using the canteen.

Supervision costs may be apportioned on the basis of number of employees or on a basis of the time spent in each department by the supervisor. The latter method is preferred when a supervisor has to give more attention to some workers than to others. The time spent in each department can be obtained for a limited period and an average basis determined for use in the future.

Cost accounting and statistical costs, especially those connected with timekeeping, may be equitably apportioned according to the number of employees in each department. In many cases the number of forms, statements or reports, or even the number of entries, may provide a better basis.

Where the number of tools supplied and repaired by the tool room is approximately the same for each worker, then the number of employees in a department should be a reasonable basis for charging tool room costs to other departments. Often an estimate of a department's usage is more accurate. This can be obtained by keeping a schedule of tools made and tools repaired, and detailing the time spent on each and materials used, and the department to which each tool is sent.

4. Employees' wages

Employers' liability insurance may be charged according to the total wages paid to the employees in each department. National insurance contributions paid by the employer may also be dealt with in this way unless workers of different ages and sexes work in the same department, when an analysis of actual payments made is much better. The reason for this is obviously the various rates payable; there is a rate for male and a rate for female, and these are further varied according to age.

5. Kilowatt-hour capacity

The lighting costs when lamps are of different sizes may be apportioned on this basis.

6. Number of radiators (or sizes of radiators)

Heating costs may be apportioned on this basis and reasonable results obtained. The method is suitable where temperatures differ greatly between departments or where heating losses vary widely. Where uniform heat has to be supplied under similar conditions in each department, the square or cubic footage basis will suffice.

7. Direct charges to departments

Bases are ascertained by study of time sheets, departmental meters, material requisitions, or other records. Thus, machinery maintenance and repairs may be traced by the use of time sheets and material requisitions. Indirect labour cost, such as supervision, may also use this basis. When the number of employees does not provide a suitable basis the tool room cost can also be charged in this way. When timekeeping and wages calculations are not proportionate to the number of employees—say, where different methods of payment are in force, piece-work in one department, time rates in another—a direct charge, where possible, will be more accurate. Power, light, water and steam, when directly metered, are also apportioned by this method.

METHODS OF ABSORBING OVERHEADS

When only one product is being produced a uniform charge for overhead may be possible. Total overhead cost for the factory or department is divided by the number of units to arrive at an absorption rate per unit of production. This method is unsuitable for job costing, and only in certain cases suitable for process costing.

Where a number of different commodities are being manufactured, some means must be found to charge each with a fair and reasonable share of the overhead cost. There is one of two factors to consider, depending upon whether an overhead is fixed or variable. Wherever possible, fixed costs are charged on a basis of relative benefit, and variable costs are charged according to responsibility. A method which covers both bases should be the aim. The modern method is to assign responsibility and relative benefit by reference to the time spent on each job or unit of production. The direct-labour hour rate and machine hour rate methods are typical examples. In most cases the recognition of time absorbed, it should be noticed, will refer only to departmental times; the tracing of responsibility or receipt of benefit may be achieved at the time departmentalisation of expenses is carried out. Thus, the relative benefits received by each department from the rent of the factory may be determined by comparing the space occupied: the appropriate charge could then be made to each department. If a department occupies one-quarter of total floor space, then it benefits accordingly and is charged with a quarter of the rent.

One method of apportioning overhead to products may not be suitable for general application even in the same factory or department. One department may employ highly specialised, expensive machinery when the machine hour basis will be the obvious choice; another may have no machine work, so a direct-labour hour basis will be appropriate.

The rates used to absorb overhead may be based upon actual expenditure or normal (estimated) expenditure. The latter is probably more usual under job order costing, but can also be used with a process costing system. With actual overhead there is a time lag before the rate can be calculated; the normal overhead rate avoids the necessity of waiting for overhead costs to be accumulated. The most important methods used to charge overhead to products are as follows.

1. Material cost percentage rate

The formula is as follows:

$$\frac{\text{Factory overhead for period}}{\text{Direct material cost for period}} \times \frac{100}{1} = \frac{\text{Percentage of direct}}{\text{material cost}}$$

If for a particular department direct material cost for a month is £8000 and factory overhead for the same month is £4000, then:

$$\frac{£4000}{£8000} \times \frac{100}{1} = 50\%$$

Thus if Job No. 22 has a direct material cost of £20, then £10 will be added for overhead.

In very few cases will overhead benefits or responsibilities vary in direct proportion to materials used. Where different types of materials go into a product, results which are nothing more than ludicrous may emerge. In the manufacture of industrial instruments a great variety of materials is used, including gold and platinum wire. Any instruments not requiring the incorporation of rare metals will obviously fare better than the others on the question of incurring overhead costs. The costs obtained will tend to be quite inaccurate. For this reason the method has limited use: an example where it may be used is in the production of bulk materials; e.g. cement, sugar, paint.

2. Wages percentage rate

A formula for determining the wages percentage rate is:

$$\frac{\text{Factory overhead for period}}{\text{Direct labour cost for period}} \times \frac{100}{1} = \frac{\text{Percentage of direct}}{\text{labour cost}}$$

Example. Dept "X"

Factory overhead for month = £2000
Direct labour cost for month = £6000
Job No. 36 direct labour cost = £30

$$\frac{£2000}{£6000} \times \frac{100}{1} = 33\tfrac{1}{3}\%$$

The overhead cost for Job No. 36 will be £10.

For some overhead costs, this method will give reasonable results; with others, there is little relation between direct labour and the overhead cost incurred. The lower-paid worker may occupy the same floor space as the higher-paid worker, yet the latter's products may be charged with more rent, rates, depreciation and other space costs. This inaccuracy may be mitigated if the higher wage is due to greater efficiency, for then more units per period will be produced by the higher-paid worker. When, in a department, expensive machines are used by some workers and others use hand tools, unfair overhead charges will be made; this is also the case when workers vary in ability—some working at an average rate, whereas others work at high speed.

The method is easy to apply, and reaches its highest degree of efficiency when there is uniformity in wage-rates, skill of workers, equipment used and work performed. When standard costing is used the wages percentage rate may be employed with advantage.

3. Prime cost percentage rate

The appropriate formula is:

$$\frac{\text{Factory overhead for period}}{\text{Prime cost for period}} \times \frac{100}{1} = \frac{\text{Percentage of prime}}{\text{cost}}$$

(*Note.* Direct expense is usually omitted from the calculation because it appears only in certain cases.)

This is similar to methods (1) and (2). Instead of taking a percentage on direct material or direct labour, the two are taken together and applied to each job. Thus, if the prime cost of Job No. 40 is £50 and the percentage of prime cost to factory overhead is 50%, then £25 will be added for overheads.

Because, like the other two methods, the time element is ignored, the weaknesses of those methods also apply to the prime cost method.

Recognition of the importance of time is shown in both the direct-labour hour method and the machine hour method. Time is the most important element in the incurring of overhead, and it is for this reason that methods which consider the productive time taken are the most equitable.

4. *Labour hour rate*

A formula for calculating the labour rate is:

$$\frac{\text{Factory overhead for period}}{\text{Direct labour hours for period}} = \text{Direct-labour hour rate}$$

Factory overhead would be applied to jobs by multiplying the number of direct labour hours on a job by the direct-labour hour rate. Thus if the total of factory overhead costs is £2000 and the number of direct labour hours is 10,000, then the direct-labour hour rate $= \dfrac{£2000}{10,000} = £0\cdot20$.

If a job takes 20 hours, then the overhead applied will be £4.

A disadvantage of the method sometimes alleged is the fact that additional clerical records are necessary. These should show:

(*a*) The number of direct labour hours spent on each production order or job.

(*b*) The total number of direct labour hours worked by the employees in each producing department.

However, this information should, strictly speaking, be kept so as to control costs; moreover, the information may be required for production control. Thus, where full use is made of the information the disadvantage becomes an advantage.

The method is suitable from the point of view of cost control where hand-labour methods exist and where uniformity of rates, workers and conditions is present. Where there is a predominance of machinery, however, the machine hour rate method is more suitable.

5. *Machine hour rate*

Again a formula can be employed, *i.e.*:

$$\frac{\text{Factory overhead for period}}{\text{Machine hours for period}} = \text{Machine hour rate}$$

This formula should be applied for each machine or group of similar machines. The latter avoids having too many rates and, accordingly, keeps clerical costs to a minimum.

The procedure followed for calculating the machine hour rate is to treat each machine or group of similar machines as a cost centre. Apportioning overhead costs to cost centres is dealt with earlier in this chapter. In the case of a machine cost centre the following costs would be apportioned to the individual machine (or appropriate group):

(*a*) *Operating expenses,* such as depreciation, insurance, maintenance, power and lighting.

(*b*) *General overhead expenses* not included in (*a*).

(*c*) *Cost of floor space occupied*—rent or depreciation of building and other occupancy costs not included in (*a*).

All these are added together and then divided by the machine hours to give a rate per hour. Products made on the machine are then charged at the hourly rate on the basis of machining time involved.

There is no doubt that the recognition of the machine as a vital factor in the apportionment and absorption of factory overhead costs can lead to greater accuracy. In the modern age of mechanisation and automation the factory overheads resulting from the use of machinery are far in excess of costs from other sources, and it is only right and proper that this fact should be considered.

When calculating the machine hour rate great care should be taken to avoid *excessive* refinements which would complicate the procedures and lead to high clerical costs.

Conclusion on methods

The methods which would normally be employed are as follows:

Wages percentage rate.
Labour hour rate.
Machine hour rate.

No method can give absolute accuracy, but carefully compiled and used in appropriate circumstances, one or more of these three should provide acceptable results.

MISCELLANEOUS OVERHEAD ABSORPTION

The absorption of *factory* overhead costs is covered above. This section is concerned with the principles involved in absorbing the remaining overhead costs.

RESEARCH AND DEVELOPMENT COSTS

Research and development costs may be absorbed on one or more of the following bases:

1. Treat in the same way as fixed assets, writing a proportion off each year, *i.e.* as depreciation. This can be included in the factory overhead costs.

2. In appropriate circumstances treat as a *direct expense* and charge to jobs or products involved.

3. Write off to profit and loss account in the period in which the expense is incurred. The products may be charged with an appropriate amount. Alternatively, any research expenditure which does not result in tangible benefits may simply be written off without any charge being made to individual jobs or products.

There is no general agreement on which method to employ. The circumstances should be allowed to determine the choice.

SELLING AND DISTRIBUTION COSTS

Selling and distribution costs are normally written off to cost of sales account in the period in which they are incurred. This is logical, because these costs arise from the sales in a period, and it would be quite wrong to defer the writing off to a future period. Advertising costs are a possible exception.

For effective control it is usual to apportion costs to sales areas, thus extending the principle of establishing cost centres to the areas of sales and distribution. Thus, for example, sales salaries may be absorbed on the basis of a direct charge. On the other hand, general advertising costs may be apportioned according to actual or estimated potential advertising. If advertising costs in one year are expected to result in benefits in future years the total cost is capitalised, a proportion being written off each year.

Analysis of selling and distribution costs is subdivided according to sales areas, salesmen, sizes of orders, methods of selling and delivery, and products or jobs. In the latter case, the absorption may be based on a percentage calculated by reference to factory cost or gross profit or selling price. Alternatively, a rate per product may be charged. Whether such apportionment to individual jobs or products is worth while is a debatable point on which different accountants hold opposing points of view. In any case, it will be difficult to obtain a reasonable standard of accuracy.

ADMINISTRATION COSTS

Administration costs may be treated as period costs, being written off to profit and loss account in the period in which they are incurred. Alternatively, they may be divided between work-in-progress (production) and cost of sales (selling). A further possible procedure is to treat the *total* administration costs as a charge to production. Charges to products or jobs may be made on the same bases shown above for selling and distribution costs.

When administrative functions are centralised an attempt is often made to charge the costs to area factories or branches. This may be done on the basis of turnover, total cost, or the total number of employees in each area.

THE OVERHEAD ABSORPTION "FALLACY"

In the previous section it was shown that manufacturing overhead costs are generally dealt with by charging them to cost centres and then absorbing them in the costs of products by an hourly rate or other basis.

One of the main advantages of this procedure is that a total unit cost can be ascertained, which in turn can be used for determining profit and loss on a job or product and for fixing prices to charge to customers.

Here it is necessary to notice that not all accountants agree with the absorption of *all* overhead costs. They argue that the *total cost method*, because it is based on estimates, can be misleading and can often lead to a wrong decision being made. Some have gone so far as to say that overhead absorption is simply a fallacy to give the impression of accuracy or preciseness.

There is no doubt that the accountant who faces up to the problem of the accurate absorption of fixed overhead costs has his hands full. Also, in certain circumstances, the allocation and apportionment of fixed overheads can be very misleading. However, this does not mean that anyone using total costing is wasting his time. When fixing prices it becomes very necessary to consider what fixed costs are involved in producing a job or product. Even if the figures are not 100% accurate they are better than nothing.

This matter is taken further in connection with marginal costing, discussed in Chapter XXI.

BEHAVIOUR OF OVERHEAD COSTS

The understanding of how costs *tend* to behave with changes in output or sales is a very important part of the management function. Costs may be classified as follows.

1. Fixed costs

Fixed costs are those which tend to remain constant irrespective of the volume of output or sales.

Sometimes these are called *policy costs* or *period costs*. Examples are given below:

Rent.	Subscriptions.
Rates.	Advertising.
Insurance.	Management salaries.
Clerical costs.	Supervision.

A word of caution is necessary. The classification is based on how costs *behave*, not what they are called. In one business a cost may be fixed, whereas in another it may be semi-variable or even variable (defined below). For example, the salaries of supervisors may be variable when they are dismissed with changes (reductions) in output. Once they become staff employees who are not usually discharged, then the supervisors' salaries may be viewed as being purely fixed. From this example it will be appreciated that the classification of these costs is very much affected by the policy being adopted—hence the term *policy costs*.

The period being considered is very important to an understanding of the definition. Over a long period (a number of years) the fixed costs will tend to change. The value of money is never constant so there is a certain inevitability for rent, rates, insurance and other costs to be increased or lowered.

Another important factor is the range of output being considered. When accountants speak of fixed costs they mean that the costs are expected to be constant over a limited range of output; *e.g.* between 90% and 110% of manufacturing capacity. If there is a substantial change in output so that capacity has to be, say, doubled, nobody can expect the fixed costs to be the same as for 90% to 110% of the original capacity. The new fixed costs will tend to remain constant for the *new output*.

2. Variable costs

Variable costs are those which tend to change with changes in output or sales.

For each unit produced or hour worked there is an assumption made that the variable cost *total* will increase by a definite amount; *e.g.* £1·00 per unit.

Examples are shown below:

Indirect materials.	Overtime premiums.
Spoilage.	Lost time.
Carriage inwards.	Repairs and maintenance.

Again, the examples should not be taken as indications that the costs concerned will always be variable. Much depends upon the nature of the business.

3. Semi-variable costs

Costs which are regarded as semi-variable are those which vary with changes in output but the variation is *irregular*. These costs contain a fixed element and a variable element. Many costs come into this category and the cost accountant has to determine which part is fixed and which is variable. For this purpose he may use statistical techniques: for details of these the reader is referred to *Management Accountancy* by J. Batty (Macdonald & Evans).

Costs which tend to exhibit semi-variable tendencies are as follows:

Depreciation.	Heat.
Insurance.	Water.
Coal.	Electricity.
Telephones.	

It will be noticed that some of these costs were also given under the variable category. The behaviour of the cost is the determining factor.

A better understanding of a semi-variable cost may be obtained from considering the normal telephone charge. This is made up of a quarterly rental plus a charge for calls made. A typical account may be as follows:

	£.
Rental	4·00
Local calls (charge per call)	3·50
Trunk calls	2·43
	£9·93

The fixed element is the £4 rental, whereas the variable element is the £5·93 which varies with the use made of the telephone.

IMPORTANCE OF THE DISTINCTION

Because fixed costs tend to remain constant in total, irrespective of the volume of output, certain "laws" may be stated and these are as follows:

1. The larger the volume of output produced, the lower will be the unit cost or hourly cost for fixed overheads.

2. If nothing is produced the total loss will be the fixed overhead costs.

3. In a period of depression, provided an order covers variable costs and some part of fixed costs, it will be an advantage for the manufacturer to continue producing.

This statement only applies to a limited extent. Wrongful adherence to this rule can lead to unprofitable operations. The important fact to remember is that in the *long run* a business must earn profits in order to survive.

These *tendencies* can be employed when making decisions on determination of prices, volume of output and control of costs.

When dealing with control the fixed costs, being the result of a management decision already made, are often outside the jurisdiction of departmental managers, foremen and supervisors. On the other hand, variable costs can best be controlled at the points at which they are incurred. The departmental manager is in a key position for exercising this control and this should be regarded as a very important part of his duties. As shown in Chapter XXI when compiling budgets there is a need to let responsible officials *participate*. This not only leads to more realistic budgets, but also aids cost control and improves efficiency.

GRAPHICAL PRESENTATION

How costs tend to behave is illustrated by the break-even chart shown in Fig. 61. The reader is advised to study this chart along with the relevant text in Chapter XXI (pp. 371–374).

Examination Questions on Chapter XIX are given at the end of Chapter XX.

COST ACCOUNTING SYSTEMS

THIS chapter is concerned with the systems employed by cost accountants to make management more effective. It is arranged in sections to cover the following topics:

1. Process costing.
2. Job costing.
3. Batch costing (and hybrid costing systems).
4. Organisation for labour costs.
5. Organisation for material costs.
6. Organisation for overhead costs.

Job costing, and its close relation batch costing, are of special importance to engineering industries and for this reason are given more emphasis than process costing.

PROCESS COSTING

Process costing is one of the two principal methods of cost accounting. It is generally employed when a standard product is being made which involves a number of distinct processes performed in a definite sequence. In oil refining, chemical manufacture, paper making, flour milling and cement manufacturing, as well as many other industries, this method is used. The object is to trace and record costs for each distinct stage. Here the concern is not with finding the costs for individual units as in job costing, but with obtaining the *average cost* per unit for each accounting period. Often by-products or joint products are produced and these have to be considered when calculating the average cost per unit.

The total time spent and materials used on each process, as well as services such as power, light and heating, are all charged. For this purpose a process cost sheet may be employed (Fig. 50).

The process cost sheet is a summary of all operations for the month. The current operating charges are entered on the sheet showing:

1. The transfer cost from the previous operation.
2. The costs incurred by each operation showing material, labour and overhead in separate columns.

This separation of transfer costs and conversion cost is extremely important, for the charges incurred by a department are its measure of efficiency. These are the responsibility of the head of the department, so it is readily apparent what has been incurred within that department and the cost is not distorted by charging costs in previous processes.

The sheet can be used as a basis for:

(a) Closing entries at the end of each month.

(b) Operating statements, without need to look up the ledger accounts.

					Cost Centre No. 1			Cost Centre No. 2		
Date	Ref.	Mat.	Labour	O/head	Mat.	Lab.	O/head	Mat.	Lab.	O/head

PROCESS COST SHEET
Accounting Period ....

Summary
Centre No. 1 £ £
Materials xxx
Labour xxx
Overhead xxx xxx

Centre No. 2
Materials xxx
Labour xxx
Overhead xxx xxx
£xxx

Production
No. of Units _____
Cost per Unit £ _____

FIG. 50.—*Process cost sheet*

Within the Cost Ledger an account is kept for each process. The direct material, direct labour, and factory overhead costs are transferred from the process cost sheet. These are debited to the process account, and then any completed units are credited to cover the transfer to the next process. The balance on the account represents the work-in-progress at the end of the period, which, of course, becomes the opening balance for the *next* period. An example of a process account is as follows:

Process Account I

	£		£
To Direct material	400	By Transfer to	
„ Direct labour	300	Process II	1100
„ Factory overhead	600	„ Balance c/d	200
	£1300		£1300
To Balance b/d	£200		

The units involved in each process may also be shown.

Because of the repetitive, standardised nature of the processes, units produced and conditions, it is possible to employ standard costing to its fullest extent. Calculation and analysis of cost variances allows costs to be controlled, and the yield variances show the efficiency obtained in converting the raw materials to the finished product.

JOB COSTING

As the name implies, job costing is concerned with finding the cost of each individual job or contract. Accordingly, this system is employed when the production cycle consists of separate jobs each made to a customer's special order or specification. Examples are to be found in general engineering, shipbuilding, furniture manufacture, building contractors and special order printing.

The main feature of the system is that each job has to be planned and costed separately. This means that detailed instructions have to be issued on the performance of the work. It also means that the organisation and its problems tend to be more complex then when process costing is employed.

Overhead costs may be absorbed on jobs on the basis of actual costs incurred or on predetermined costs. The latter method involves the estimation of overhead costs and production hours for each department: an overhead rate is then calculated and this is used to arrive at the cost of each job. Later, there will tend to be over- or under-absorption of overhead costs. However, as a general rule, the errors which occur are not great, and the fact that management is able to estimate the costs of jobs and ascertain their profitability without waiting until the actual overhead costs are known makes predetermined costs worth while.

ESTIMATING

The process of determining in advance what a job will cost is known as "estimating." It involves consideration of the following factors:

1. *Material content and prices.*—Material specifications should be prepared and then the expected prices used to arrive at the direct material cost.

2. *Labour hours and rates.*—Work study may be employed to arrive at the labour hours. In many engineering factories there are rate fixing departments, where synthetic times are compiled and recorded for use in incentive schemes and in estimating the costs of jobs. Once times are known, the wage rates expected to be paid in the period when the job would be done are used to convert the labour hours into costs.

3. *Overhead costs.*—The overhead costs expected to be incurred on a job would be added to the prime cost (direct material plus labour costs) to arrive at a total cost for the job. Opinions differ on which overheads should be included in an estimate. Some estimators include only factory

overheads and leave the research, development, distribution, selling and administration costs to be covered in a percentage which also includes profit. Others add these other costs according to the bases employed for absorbing overheads.

4. Percentage added to total cost.—What percentage to add to cover profit and contingencies depends upon the policy being followed and the degree of competition being experienced. It is often a policy decision to be determined by the board of directors. Direct expenses (*see* p. 312) may have to receive special attention. If they are to be incurred by a particular job then they should be included in the estimate.

Many accountants advocate the use of marginal costing techniques for estimating. The reader is advised to study the section which deals with this topic, remembering that this approach may be appropriate in suitable circumstances.

ACCUMULATION OF JOB COSTS

Job costs have to be accumulated by the use of suitably designed forms and procedures. These are discussed later in this chapter in connection with control. Here it is important to notice that the costs are transferred to a job cost sheet. Subsequently, the overall control over the profitability of jobs is exercised by comparing each element of actual cost with its estimated cost. Profit earned and profit expected are also compared, thus showing management the accuracy of the estimating and the success of the policy being followed.

BATCH COSTING

Batch costing is a form of job costing. Instead of costing each component separately, each batch of components is taken together and treated as a job. Thus, for example, if 200 units of component Part No. 100–32, a reflector, are to be manufactured, then the costing would be as for a single job. The unit price would be ascertained by dividing the costs by 200.

Besides maintaining job cost sheets it may also be necessary to keep summary sheets on which the cost of each component can be transferred and the cost of the finished product can then be calculated. This applies in general engineering where many hundreds of components may go towards making the finished machine or other "product." Often the components are made at intervals of months or even years so that there is an accumulation of costs over a period. In these circumstances the preparation of a comprehensive cost schedule for each machine can be a major task in itself.

Provided these differences are appreciated the basic principles for batch costing and job costing are virtually the same.

HYBRID COSTING SYSTEMS

Many costing systems do not fall neatly into the category of either job costing or process costing. Often systems use some features of both main costing systems. Many engineering companies use *batch costing*, which treats each batch of components as a job and then finds the average cost of a single unit. Another variation is *multiple costing*, used when many different finished products are made. Many components are made which are subsequently assembled into the completed article, which may be bicycles, cars or other products of a complex nature. Costs have to be ascertained for operations, processes, units and jobs, building together until the total cost is found.

Different names may be used to describe either process costing or job costing. Thus, for example, *unit costing* is the name given to one system where there is a natural unit, such as a sack of flour, a hundredweight of cement or a barrel of beer. *Operation costing* is a variation of unit costing, and is used when production is carried out on a large scale, popularly known as mass production. *Operating costing* is the term applied to describe the system used to find the cost of performing a service such as transport, gas or electricity. These are all variations of process costing. *Contract* or *terminal costing* is the name given to job costing employed by builders and constructional engineers.

All these methods ascertain the actual cost. In addition, as indicated earlier, there may be superimposed on a particular system standard costing and/or marginal costing, both of which are special techniques.

ORGANISATION FOR LABOUR COSTS

When dealing with labour costs it is usual to distinguish between direct labour and indirect labour (*see* p. 312). This division is for the purpose of control of costs, but it should not be forgotten that indirect workers also have to be engaged, paid and their costs controlled. Although what is stated below applies mainly to direct labour, it could equally apply to indirect labour where appropriate.

The basic principles are the same whether job or process costing is employed. With job costing there will generally be a need to use individual job cards for each worker, whereas with process costing the attendance cards or time sheets will suffice.

The principal functions relating to each employee are discussed below.

ENGAGEMENT OF EMPLOYEES

The procedures used for engaging workers are covered in Chapter XIV. Once engaged it is usual to assign a clock number to each man or woman. This may be preceded by a departmental code to show the department in which he or she is employed. This number becomes the identifying code and is used on clock cards, wage sheets, pay packets and all personnel records.

TIME RECORDING

With all workers it is usually necessary to have some form of time records to show and control the following:

1. Attendance time.—This is time spent at the factory and is often the basis of the wage calculation. Accuracy is, therefore, vital and some form of mechanical time recording is advised.

2. Effective time.—Time spent in a factory should be utilised as effectively as possible. This means that lost time should be kept to a minimum. In the majority of cases the lost time has to be included in the hours used for calculating the wages due. Accordingly, to a company this represents a definite loss which must be recouped from the effective time. Prevention is always better than cure and, therefore, if systems can be devised which eliminate lost time this should be the aim.

A very interesting analysis of lost time is given on p. 338 (Fig. 51). This was taken from an engineering works in a shop which produced heavy machinery. The figures are in minutes and the lost time is 8·3%. Facts relating to the example are that 6 days of 8 hours each were taken and the formula used for calculating the percentage was as follows:

$$\frac{\text{Compensated regular lost time} \times 100}{\text{Net working time allowed}}$$

$$= \frac{218 \times 100}{2627} = 8 \cdot 3\%$$

The net working time is calculated:

$$6 \times 8 \times 60 - (218 + 35) = 2880 - 253 = 2627 \text{ minutes.}$$

Experience has shown that time recorders are the most effective method of showing the times spent on jobs and the control over those times. All workers should be given a clock card so that comings and goings may be mechanically recorded by use of a time recorder. There are other methods, but these are now outmoded and, because of their inefficiencies, should not be tolerated. The advantages claimed for card time recorders may be summarised as follows:

1. The worker makes the record himself, so he cannot, afterwards, dispute its accuracy.

2. Time recorders can be operated quite rapidly, so delays are minimised.

3. Clerical work in the wages office is simplified. For example, there is no question of having to write up an attendance book, and any lateness or overtime may be shown automatically by the time

M

recorder printing in a different-coloured ink—say red instead of black.

4. In suitable cases the same clock card may be used to record both attendance time and times spent on operations (effective time).

5. There is greater accuracy and a much more legible record.

OBSERVATION OF LOST TIME IN MINUTES

Working Time: 7 a.m. to 9 a.m.   9.15 a.m. to 12 noon.   12.30 p.m. to 3.45 p.m.   Stops agreed upon: 9 a.m. to 9.15 a.m.   12 noon to 12.30 p.m.

Types of Lost Time	Day of Observation						Due for Compensation		Un-paid for
	Mon.	Tues.	Wed.	Thur.	Fri.	Sat.	Regular (a)	Irregular (b)	(c)
Waiting for instructions	—	3	—	—	—	2	5	—	—
Waiting for material	2	—	4	—	20	—	6	20	—
Waiting for transport or assistance	5	2	—	4	2	3·5	16·5	—	—
Getting out tools	2	3	2	1·5	2	1·5	12	—	—
Locking up tools	2	2	3	2·5	2	3	14·5	—	—
Exchanging used tools	—	—	6	—	—	—	6	—	—
Entering up figures for wage account	1	—	2	1	1	—	5	—	—
Receiving wages	—	—	—	4	—	—	4	—	—
Interruption by foreman	—	5	—	3	—	—	8	—	—
Interruption by other workmen ...	1	—	—	—	—	—	1	—	—
Personal needs	12	9	12	14	11	9	67	—	—
Fetching food and drink	3	4	4	3	3	3	20	—	—
Fetching oil and cleaning material	—	3	—	2	—	4	9	—	—
Minor faults in shop	—	—	—	—	15	—	—	15	—
Cleaning bench	4	5	3	4	3	10	29	—	—
Cleaning surface plate	—	—	—	—	—	15	15	—	—
Arriving late	5	—	—	2	—	—	—	—	7
Arbitrary stoppages	—	2	3	—	4	—	—	—	9
Personal conversation with other workers	3	—	—	2	—	1	—	—	6
Total lost time	40	38	39	43	63	52	218	35	22
Nett time for actual work ...	440	442	441	437	417	428	2605	—	—
Total working time	480	480	480	480	480	480	2880	—	—

FIG. 51.—*Example of a lost time record*

Reproduced from Time Study and Ratefixing, *edited by the Institute of Economic Engineering, London, 1945, by courtesy of Sir Isaac Pitman & Sons Ltd.*

Time recorders, at one time situated near the factory gates, are now often to be found in each department. This avoids time being lost between the gate and place of work.

At the end of a week the total time shown on an attendance card should be reconciled with the worker's total, effective time. When both times are collected on the one record, no difficulty should be experienced. When separate records are necessary, such as, for example, when a worker performs operations on batches of different types of components, the totals from the two records have to be brought together and compared.

Irrespective of the method used for recording times, it will be necessary to have idle or lost time segregated from normal production time and have it explained.

JOB TIMING EQUIPMENT

The job time card (Fig. 52) is very simple to prepare and operate. The clock number and name of the worker is placed on the top of the card and then as the work is issued the job number is inserted in the column shown. Any lost time can also be recorded on the card under an appropriate standing order number so that a foreman can initial the card to show that the reason given is quite legitimate.

If the times are added up at the end of each week, the reconciliation of effective time and attendance time is a very simple operation. Any discrepancy between the two can be investigated without delay.

CONTROL OF LABOUR COSTS

Direct labour costs may be controlled by a variety of methods, the best known of these being as follows:

1. Standard costing (*see* p. 364). This is difficult to employ when job costing is used.

2. Estimated times—comparing estimated with actual time.

3. Payment of some form of incentive. When an incentive scheme is in operation lost time may be negligible.

4. Effective supervision.

5. Control accounting whereby reports and statements are used to focus attention on any wasted or lost time.

6. Employment of the most efficient methods. If two men can do a job then it is clearly wrong to employ three: this fact is often hidden unless work study is employed.

7. All overtime working should be banned unless approved by a responsible manager.

ORGANISATION FOR MATERIAL COSTS

There should be effective control of all receipts and issues of materials and parts kept in a stores. This control, as far as possible, should be achieved automatically as part of a routine system.

It will be obvious that the initial planning of a system is of the utmost

No.............................. NAME			
JOB No.		**TIME**	**Time Clock Record**
	Off		
	On		
	Off		
	On		
	Off		
	On		
	Off		
	On		
	Off		
	On		
	Off		
	On		
	Off		
	On		
	Off		
	On		
	Off		
	On		
	Off		
	On		
	Off		
	On		
Grand total should agree with attendance time			

FIG. 52.—*Job time card*

Courtesy of International Time Recording Co Ltd

importance. The stages involved, and possible procedure, may be summarised:

1. Initiation of purchase order. This is done by:

(a) Purchase requisition from stores, or production planning (when a schedule programme is followed), *or*

(b) Purchase requisition from the department requiring material not normally stocked.

2. Preparation and issue to supplier of purchase order.
3. Receipt of materials into stores. The recording involved is:

(a) Entries on goods inwards sheet or note.

(b) After inspection, where necessary, the preparation of a returned to supplier form or rejection report which is sent to the purchasing department so that arrangements can be made for the return of the materials to the supplier.

4. Details of materials received are entered on bin cards held in the stores and/or on the stores record in the material control office. This is done from the stores copy of the goods inwards sheet.

5. Invoice received from supplier and passed for payment by the purchasing officer.

Before being certified, "in order for payment," the invoice is checked —quantities, prices, etc.—by reference to a copy of the purchase order, already entered up from the goods inwards sheet.

6. Invoice sent to accounts department for payment, being used as a medium for entering up the stores ledger.

ADMINISTRATION OF STORES

The principal departments concerned with the stores and stores records are:

1. Material control* department.
2. Purchasing department.
3. Accounts or costing department.

The functions of these, so far as they affect storekeeping, are now discussed.

Material control department

A modern practice, which recognises the importance of stores control, is the creation of an executive position to cover all the responsibilities which arise from the usage, in production, of large quantities of materials. The title is, appropriately, that of material controller. Often the responsibilities of this executive extend to being in charge of the administration of the stores, the section responsible for initiation of

---

* The term "material control" is also used to describe the planned flow of materials in a factory.

purchase requisitions (which may be done in the stores or in a material control office), and the purchasing department. In some organisations, however, the material controller may be nothing more than a stores manager, being in a junior capacity under the purchasing officer.

As will be apparent, irrespective of the exact extent of the material controller's duties he will normally be held responsible for the execution of the policy of the business as regards the extent to which stocks are to be carried. If the stock of each material is to be kept to an absolute

PURCHASE REQUISITION. No..........				
Date............				
To Purchasing Dept.		From.............................Dept.		
Code	Material Description	Quantity	Delivery Required	Remarks
Signed (Storekeeper) .... Authorised (Material Controller)				

Fig. 53.—*Purchase requisition*

NOTES

1. The purchase requisition will normally be completed by the stores clerk when stocks carried reach the re-order level. It may, however, be used by other departments when indirect materials, not held by the stores, are required.

2. Additional columns are often provided. There may be a column for the purchase order number and columns for price and value. The latter may be used to show the extent of future purchase commitments—essential for budgeting.

3. The purchasing department will order goods only when authorised by a purchase requisition.

minimum, without production stoppages, then a systematic procedure will be essential. Much of the skill of carrying minimum stocks may be regarded as the initiation of the purchase requisition at the correct time. If this is sent to the purchasing department too early, excess stocks may result; if too late, there may be a hold-up in production owing to a shortage of the material concerned. Obviously, a routine which enables purchase requisitions to be completed at the right time is essential: this can now be examined.

Initiation of purchase requisition (Fig. 53).—As already indicated, the purchase requisition may be initiated by the stores or by a material control office—depending on the particular organisational pattern adopted. In addition, materials and parts not normally held in stock may be requested on a purchase requisition by heads of departments, *e.g.* maintenance materials may be requisitioned by the maintenance engineer. This second method involves authorisation of the purchase by, say, the works manager, although for small purchases the maintenance engineer will normally have the necessary authority. If a maintenance stores, quite separate from the production materials stores, is considered necessary, records will normally have to be kept as for ordinary storekeeping, *i.e.* bin cards and stores ledger. The production planning department may also be concerned with requisitioning. An outline of the normal procedure will now be covered.

The two principal methods used to enable purchase requisitions to be initiated are as follows:

1. By schedule. Production requirements of materials are estimated and a "provisional schedule" drawn up. Possibly orders are placed on suppliers with a provisional delivery date stated. Later, when it is more apparent that the estimated materials *will* be required, a "frozen schedule" comes into operation. The delivery date then becomes quite positive and the supplier is notified to that effect. The system can be varied, of course, to suit the particular business concerned. What is essential is that there is a definite programme of production of a standardised product—usually on a large scale. The production planning department will often be responsible for notifying the purchasing department of schedule requirements.

2. By the minimum–maximum method. From a practical point of view this method has a wider application than the schedule system, and is, therefore, probably of greater importance.

This second method is now examined.

Minimum, maximum and re-order levels.—For each kind of raw material part or component it is possible to estimate a "maximum," and a "minimum," stock level; between these two will lie a level which, in practice, will tend to be the stock carried.

The maximum quantity will be fixed by taking into account such matters as those shown below:

(*a*) The storage facilities available and the physical nature of the product. Where deterioration takes place or there is danger of obsolescence, or space is limited, other things being equal, the smaller will be the stock carried.

(*b*) The ordering of economic quantities. An expensive special pattern or tool may be required for the production of a component and, if so, this fact will be reflected in the price quoted by the supplier. The practice usually followed by a manufacturer is to "cover" the special pattern or tool by including its cost in the quotation: obviously the larger the number of units included in a quotation, the smaller will be the share, *per unit*, of the fixed cost of the special pattern or tool. The greater this fixed cost, the larger will tend to be the economic ordering quantity, which, in turn, will be reflected in the maximum stock level.

(*c*) Possible price fluctuations. There will be a tendency to hold larger stocks when prices are rising or are likely to rise.

(*d*) The rate of consumption. Where 50 units are likely to meet production requirements for the next ten years there would be no justification for carrying 500 units, even if the ordering of such a quantity would mean some reduction in the initial cost per unit.

(*e*) Availability of cash to pay for purchases and, later, capital to be locked up in the form of stock. Excess stock carrying implies that the business is not making the most efficient use of its resources: cash should not be "frozen" in this way, especially if there are profitable outlets for its use.

All these factors require to be considered; the best solution of one may conflict with the best solution for another. Thus the storage space which could conveniently be made available may be sufficient to store only 1000 units of a certain product. Suppose the price to be paid for the 1000 units was £0·50 each, but that if a quantity of 4000 were to be purchased the price would be £0·25 each, then, provided 4000 units would be consumed within a reasonable period, a decision would have to be made which considered these two conflicting circumstances. Possibly a minor reorganisation of the stores would make available sufficient space to store the 3000 extra units. From this it will be clear that in fixing the maximum stock level no single factor will be considered, but all relevant matters will be taken into account and a compromise adopted. One factor may, needless to say, carry much greater weight than another, depending upon the circumstances; if there is a shortage in the supply of an *essential* material this fact, until the supply position improves, will tend to be the main influence in fixing the maximum stock level of such material. From what has been observed, it should be apparent that a maximum stock level cannot be fixed with any degree of permanency, for when circumstances change the level will probably need revising.

The minimum stock figure will normally be fixed after due regard has been given to the purchasing time-cycle; that is, the period normally taken to obtain a specified material, counting from the date of placing the purchase order to the expected date of the receipt of the material in the stores. The reliability of the supplier will have to be considered when arriving at the "normal period," due allowance being made for any likely delay. The rate of consumption is extremely important. In connection with maximum stock it was noted that supplies should not generally be carried for long periods. The minimum stock level, from the viewpoint of consumption, is set to ensure that production is never at a standstill. If average production is maintained and the purchase orders are placed in good time the stocks should not fall below the minimum level. A small margin of safety to cover normal fluctuation in usage should, of course, be allowed when making the calculations.

In addition to minima and maxima the question of the correct re-order levels should also be given attention. In some cases a re-order level will coincide with the minimum stock level, but this is not always the case. To ensure that the purchase order is initiated in good time a re-order level which is above minimum level may be fixed. This is likely to be so when the minimum level is at its lowest possible point, say to cover two weeks' production. Should there be an unexpected increase in the usage rate or an unforeseen delay in delivery, reliance on minimum stock level, to initiate a purchase order, may result in loss of production. To avoid this occurrence, a percentage, the size depending upon the circumstances, will be added to minimum stock level, to arrive at re-order level.

An example of the sort of calculation involved in arriving at the three stock levels, once the relevant details have been considered, can be given thus:

Data Relating to Part No. 400–201. Adjustment Wheel

Purchasing Time Cycle (*i.e.* period covered from date of order to delivery)	= 30 days
Average Daily Rate of Consumption	= 50 units per day
Maximum No. of Units Consumed during a 30-day period	= 2000 units
Minimum No. of Units Consumed during a 30-day period	= 1200 units
Standard Order Size (*i.e.* size of order: fixed after considering such factors as price, transport costs and storage space available)	= 3000 units

The above information may be obtained from the stock records, or be estimated by making trial production runs and referring to relevant production records. Minimum and maximum stock levels can be calculated as follows:

Minimum stock level

Largest number of units consumed during a 30-day period	= 2000
Less Average requirements for the Purchasing Time Cycle 30 × 50	= 1500
Minimum level is therefore:	500

Maximum stock level

Largest number of units consumed during a 30-day period	= 2000 (Re-order level)*
Less Minimum consumption for a 30-day period	= 1200
	800
Add Order to be received (Standard Quantity)	= 3000
Maximum level is therefore:	3800

This method of arriving at the three levels is not to be regarded as the only one used. There are others, some probably less accurate, some more "scientific." The object of showing the method in question is to illustrate the principles involved.

The purchasing department

The purchasing department is headed by the purchasing officer or buyer. Briefly, his routine work involves responsibility for the following functions:

1. Upon receipt of a purchase requisition to understand clearly what materials are required.

2. To be aware of possible sources of raw materials or supplies.

3. From the possible sources to obtain full details and prices of the items covered by the purchase requisition. Obviously, for items which are purchased regularly, it will be unnecessary to obtain a quotation for each new request. Instead, quotations may be obtained every few months, or other suitable period.

4. To select the supplier offering the best terms and conditions. Price will not be the only consideration in the choice, for often delivery is more important. However, other things being equal, price should be the deciding factor.

5. To place a purchase order with the supplier selected.

6. To obtain acknowledgment of the purchase order from the supplier.

7. To ensure that the delivery promise is kept. Normally a "progressing" or "follow-up" system is employed.

8. Upon receipt of the goods to receive a goods inwards sheet from the receiving department. Details of quantities received are entered on the copy purchase order. This is a duplicate of the one sent to the supplier with the addition of a printed "box," suitably ruled and headed, so that date of receipt, goods inwards sheet number, and

---

* *Re-order level.* Since there is a possibility of 2000 units being consumed within a period of 30 days—which is also the purchasing time-cycle—it will be clear that the re-order level is 2000 units. If an ordering point is fixed below 2000 units there will be a danger that stocks will be consumed before a replenishment is received.

quantities may be entered. Later, when the supplier's invoice is received, the price can be checked with the price originally quoted, and the quantities invoiced compared with those shown as having been received, before the invoice is passed for payment.

9. To return goods which are not according to specification or, alternatively, reach some agreement with the supplier on payment.

10. When an invoice is received to check quantities, prices and other relevant details, then authorise for payment.

11. To send the invoice, duly authorised and showing the account to be charged, to the accounts department.

The accounts or costing department

Payment for the goods is made within a reasonable time of receiving the approved invoice from the purchasing department. Details of those items which go into the stores have to be entered into the stores ledger, usually one sheet or card being reserved for each type or grade of material. At the end of each four-weekly accounting period the totals are posted to the stores control account in the cost ledger. The invoices are thus the principal source of debit entries in the stores ledger and stores control account.

The other key documents are material requisitions and material return notes. Each issue from stores must be authorised by a material requisition which has been signed by a responsible official. Similarly, any returns of materials to stores have to be covered by a material return note. Both are essential for effective control. The requisitions provide the credits and the notes the debits for the stores ledger and stores control account.

The method for pricing the materials, so that requisitions may be evaluated, is normally taken from the following:

1. Average price.—The most usual average adopted is that which, when being calculated, considers the quantities purchased, this being called the "weighted average price." After each new purchase is received the new average price is calculated by the formula:

$$\frac{\text{Stores ledger cost balance of material}}{\text{Total units in stock}}$$

Both the cost balance and the units will include the *new* purchases.

2. First in, first out price (FIFO).—For the purpose of pricing stores it is assumed that the materials received first are issued first. This conforms with what should, in practice, occur, for if the earliest purchases are used before later ones there will be less chance of deterioration. Needless to say, although this relation between actual usage and issue price is desirable, it may not always be achieved.

3. Last in, first out price (LIFO).—In this case the price paid for the last purchase is used until a quantity equal to that purchase has been issued, then the price is changed to the one paid for the most recent purchase. The price charged will tend, when prices are rising, to be equal to current price. Thus as much as possible of actual cost is being charged against production, and profit is kept as realistic as possible. Stock is valued at a low, conservative figure.

If controls are to be effective there must, obviously, be some means of ensuring that book figures and actual figures agree. Unless this is done, there will come a time when the records kept are valueless. A complete physical stocktaking may be accomplished only at considerable expense and, usually, when the producing departments are not operating. An alternative approach, which is now adopted by most progressive concerns, is discussed below.

PHYSICAL STOCKTAKING AND THE PERPETUAL INVENTORY SYSTEM

For a number of reasons it is usual to obtain detailed information on the quantities and values of stocks carried. From a purely financial point of view there is the necessity to calculate the values of stocks carried for the balance sheet and profit and loss account; to effect insurance covers; to calculate the rate of turnover of particular items and to ensure maximum economy in stock carrying.

Physical stocktaking has many disadvantages. Production may have to come to a standstill and, in addition, great expense may be involved in counting each class of stock, especially where overtime working is involved for a number of days. There are thus the extra expenses of carrying out the stocktaking and, also, the loss in production. The latter should not, however, be over-emphasised, for the period affords an opportunity for plant and machinery to be overhauled and cleaned.

To avoid *frequent* physical stocktakings the *perpetual inventory* system may be used. This is a method which uses planned procedures and specially designed forms to show, at any time, the stock on hand, both as to quantity and value, for each item of material or each part. If a stores control account is maintained in the factory or cost ledger it should be possible to furnish without delay the total value of the stocks carried. The system usually takes the following form:

1. Bin cards in the stores which show the volume or number of items on hand. One card is normally kept for each different type or size of material or part.

Some authorities, it should be noted, consider bin cards an unnecessary duplication of the stores ledger. There is much to be said for this view and, certainly, there is great difficulty in ensuring that the entries made on the cards are accurate and up to date, especially when the person handling the physical goods also maintains the records. However, the initiation of purchase requisitions usually requires that a record is kept in the stores or in a material control office. For this reason the extra record can be justified.

2. A stores ledger with an account for each size or quality of a particular material or part is kept in the accounts or costing department.

3. Control accounts are maintained in the factory ledger. The stores control account will show the value of the stocks held.

4. A number of items of stock are counted, weighed or gauged daily, and any discrepancies between the physical count and the figures shown by the bin cards and stores ledger are investigated. Some differences may be due to clerical errors, others to normal causes (losses in cutting or breaking bulk), whereas some may be a result of inefficient storekeeping (wrong quantities issued, wastage and breakage, pilfering and loss of items through wrong labelling or location).

The differences are written off, or brought on to, the records. Forms suitably ruled and put into pad form can be used both for the actual count and for adjusting the bin card, stores ledger and factory ledger. The counting can be done by stores auditors, and any discrepancies, once investigated, should be brought to the attention of the official in charge of the stores and appropriate records, who can then authorise the adjustments in the records to be made.

Wherever possible, each item of stock should be counted a number of times—generally speaking at least twice—each year, in addition to the annual physical stocktaking. The number of items of stock can be divided by the number of working days to give an average daily count. Provided the items do not differ considerably, as regards ease of counting, the average daily count should indicate the number of staff required to carry out the continuous stocktaking system. To minimise the work, items may be counted when the stock is low. The "requests" for stocktaking, by preparation of the form already mentioned for stock checking, may be carried out by the appropriate clerk who raises the purchase requisition; that is, when the stock is at re-order level.

Besides furnishing accurate records of stocks, which facilitates the preparation of monthly profit and loss statements, the perpetual inventory system linked with *continuous stocktaking* can claim the following advantages:

1. By adopting a system of checking items without notice an efficient control over stocks is exercised. Storekeepers will tend to take great care, and pilfering should be kept to a minimum.

2. Because stocks are counted by degrees, more time can be spent, and greater accuracy result, than when a complete physical stocktaking is carried out.

3. Incipient defects in the stores system can be rectified before much damage through loss or irregular practices has occurred.

4. Slow-moving stocks can be noted and, where necessary, action taken to prevent excessive accumulation of stocks. Possible action may be the amendment of re-order levels or the marking of the material requisitions to the effect that the oldest stock must be issued first, thus reducing the danger of deterioration.

ORGANISATION FOR OVERHEAD COSTS

The various types of overheads are described in Chapter XIX. Unfortunately, control over these costs is far from easy. There is no definite correlation between the volume of output and many of the overhead costs. Moreover, the services obtained from incurring these costs often may never be evaluated in terms of "are these really necessary?" Yet in comparison all *direct* costs are usually justified in the form of standard or estimated times and by compiling detailed specifications.

Some of the methods available for controlling overhead costs are as follows:

1. Budgets.—Budgets are prepared for each department (budget centre) to show the overhead costs to be incurred. Later the budgeted and actual costs are compared, generally on a monthly basis, and cumulative to date. These are shown on a departmental operating statement which is simply a list of the various overhead costs, showing the variances between actual and budgeted, and any action taken or to be taken.

2. Cost consciousness.—One of the most effective methods of controlling overhead costs is by the education and training of managers, supervisors and workers in the act of cost control. Wastage of material, leaving machines running, not bothering to turn off lights, making a number of journeys when one would do, and similar occurrences can often be prevented if the responsible employees are made aware of their significance in terms of cost. Sometimes a bonus is paid when costs are kept below a certain figure and this helps to instil cost consciousness into all concerned.

3. Voucher system.—The voucher system of control simply means that all expenditure must be authorised by a manager signing a voucher. If employed by managers who do expect that every expenditure should be justified, then quite good control can be exercised.

4. Value analysis.—This is a special form of cost reduction programme. A committee is established for investigating all aspects of design, production, materials used and so on. The basic aim is improvement and cost reduction. Although a very new technique, many thousands of pounds have already been saved by some companies who are employing value analysis.

5. Reports and statements so as to stimulate action (see p. 359).

TRANSITION TO MANAGEMENT ACCOUNTANCY

From cost accounting the natural development is to management accountancy which uses all facets of accountancy to assist managers in being more efficient. This subject is outlined in the next chapter.

EXAMINATION QUESTIONS

Also includes Questions on Chapters XVIII and XIX.

1. Describe fully the routine for control of the purchase and receipt of material from outside suppliers.

2. Outline the essential features of a perpetual inventory system of stock control.

3. Discuss the considerations that influence the setting of maximum and minimum stock levels and re-ordering levels.

4. In making a programme for production in a factory how would you allow for stoppages and loss of production caused by breakages, defectives, making samples and patterns, etc., in each operation or process? Taking as an example a factory with which you are acquainted, give a definite indication of the amount of the allowance you would make.

5. You are asked to consider the advisability of issuing stores of minor value in bulk to user departments in order to save expense in handling and accounting for individual stores requisitions of small value. List the factors you would take into account before giving your views.

6. What are the main steps in buying production materials? What essential information should be contained in a purchase requisition?

7. As general manager you have decided to set up a cost reduction committee with a maximum of five members. Suggest the composition of this committee and detail its terms of reference. What procedure would you advise the committee to follow in order to reach quick results? How would you measure the achievement of this committee?

8. What are the principal responsibilities of a purchasing department? Under what conditions should purchasing be centralised and what safeguards should be introduced to ensure complete co-operation with other departments?

9. What methods are available to decrease stock and stores inventories and to increase the rate of turnover? What training would you give storekeepers with this object in view?

10. Your company is considering the movement of part of its production to a Government development area. State the arguments in favour of this move and what difficulties might arise if the step were taken.

Chapter XXI

MANAGEMENT ACCOUNTANCY: METHODS OF COSTING AND CONTROL

DEFINITION

MANAGEMENT accountancy is concerned with the financial aspects and implications of management. Besides providing managers with information on the future, present and past operations of a business or on the likely effects of making a decision, the function operates in an advisory capacity on all problems which affect costs and/or profitability.

Used properly, management accountancy is a fully *integrated* system which embraces all methods concerned with financial planning, co-ordination and control. In effect, there is a welding together of all functions of management through the management accountancy system.

This is not to say that accounting data can replace sound judgment and the making of decisions. What is being stressed is the fact that figures may be employed to show what has happened or the likely consequences of any action to be taken. Without this information the management functions can only operate blindly and intuitively. No responsible manager can hope to carry out his work without guidance; management accountancy provides this guidance.

There follows in the sections given below an outline of some of the techniques employed as part of management accountancy. The provision of finance, financial accounting and cost accounting were covered in earlier chapters.

BUDGETARY CONTROL

One of the essential features of modern management is *planning* and control. Budgetary control recognises the importance of these functions and attempts to show the plans in financial terms. Subsequently the actual performances are compared with the plans and control is exercised.

A further essential feature of budgetary control is the *co-ordination* of all the management functions. Reference to the definitions given in Chapter III will show that co-ordination means the synchronisation of work and the dovetailing of all parts together. In particular there should be co-ordination of the sales and production functions so that what is produced is being sold and vice versa.

Some of the most important features of a budgetary control system are outlined below.

FORECASTS AND BUDGETS

As an initial step to operating a fully co-ordinated system of budgetary control it is usual to prepare *forecasts*. These are statements expressed in quantitative and/or financial terms and indicate *probable* production, sales, costs or other facts. They are tentative plans which are considered and compared before deciding upon which set of plans to adopt (Fig. 54).

Once alternative plans have been considered and resources are available for carrying them out, the detailed budgets are prepared. These are statements which show the financial implications of the plans made. They form an overall blueprint which reflects the policy and objectives for a future period, which is often twelve months.

Budgets are prepared for each functional division of a business and for budget centres. The functional divisions are as follows:

1. Sales.
2. Production.
3. Administration.
4. Research and development.
5. Distribution.

For these it is necessary to consider, where appropriate, the matters shown below:

1. Costs.
2. Capital expenditure.
3. Stocks.
4. Purchases.
5. Credit.

A budget centre is a section of a business which is treated separately for the purposes of cost control and for defining responsibilities. Costs are controlled best at the points at which they are incurred and when planning the organisation structure due regard should be paid to this principle. The span of control, explained in Chapter IV, should be limited. A budget for a budget centre is known as a "departmental budget."

The overall result, shown in terms of profit or loss, for each division of a company or for the company as a whole is summarised in a Master Budget which is, in effect, a planned profit and loss account and balance sheet, together with certain statistical information such as return on capital employed, current ratio and quick ratio (defined in Chapter XIX).

BUDGET PERIODS

Planning should be carried out in respect of convenient periods. As a general rule, budgets cover twelve months, though they may be for

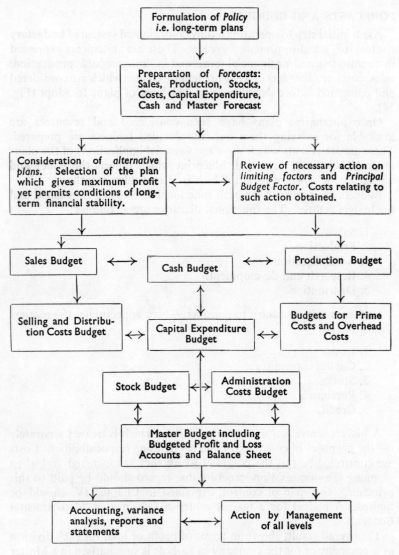

FIG. 54.—*Budgetary control: diagram of procedure*

NOTES

1. Only the functional breakdown has been shown. A budget will be required for each budget centre within each functional division.

2. Quite often the sales forecast will be the first step in budgeting. However, this will not necessarily be the case. In some businesses production capacity will be the principal budget factor and, therefore, the production forecast will be the starting point.

shorter periods such as three or six months. This applies particularly to the cash budget.

Forecasts usually cover a period of years from one to twenty. From research carried out by the author it was found that five years is the most usual period for long-term forecasting.

The budget period of twelve months is divided into "control periods." These are usually one calendar month or a month of four weeks. At the end of each control period the position is reviewed. Any adverse tendencies are investigated and management action is taken.

The corrective action may be stimulated by the employment of suitably drafted reports and statements. Alternatively, there may be a personal approach to the manager concerned. Some concerns prefer the committee form of organisation; they may hold monthly "production meetings" or they may have a *budget committee* through which all variations from standard performances are fed. The committee is composed of representatives from the functional divisions and any action to be taken can be suggested by the committee.

In the application of budgetary control the fullest use is made of the management law known as the *principle of exceptions*. This principle consists of a number of related parts which may be summarised as follows:

1. Each person performs the work allotted to him in the prescribed manner without infringement on the work of others.

2. The work is carried out with the minimum amount of instruction and supervision. As a corollary of this, a subordinate should only consult his superior when there are unusual occurrences or emergencies.

3. Matters which are not proceeding according to plan are reported upon so that corrective action can be taken. This allows managers to concentrate on important matters and disregard any others.

PREPARATION OF BUDGETS

There is now recognition that the opinions of all functional managers can be invaluable in the preparation of budgets. Production executives can give information on output and costs, and salesmen and sales managers can estimate demand from the information they gather from their contact with customers. Any estimates provided by this method can be adjusted to allow for the policy being followed or anticipated economic changes. Any adjustments made should be explained to the functional managers. Consulting those who are responsilbe for achieving the budgeted plans is good psychology; if employees participate in the preparation they will tend to feel that they are carrying out plans made by themselves. This fact alone should lead to ready co-operation which is an important aspect of achieving any goal.

Statistical techniques may also be employed in gathering the information required for forecasting the demand for products or costs.

Records of past achievements can also be utilised to show what might happen in the future. However, it is often stated that the *past is no guide to the future*. There is a great deal of truth in this assertion so the figures of previous years should not be used without considering the conditions which operated in the earlier periods and those which are expected to prevail in the future budget period.

STANDARDS OF PERFORMANCE

For effective management there must be clearly defined standards of performance. This can be regarded as the principle that business activities depend on standards. This means that *plans should be stated in terms of standards and made known to all concerned*. Study of the activities of any modern business will show that this is done at all stages; the formulation of policy; the purchase of materials and supplies; the engagement of employees; the manufacture of the product, and its subsequent sale. For materials the quality, quantities and prices have to be determined and this applies similarly for employees. When a business engages an employee a job specification has to be prepared (*see* Chapter XIV); this in itself is a form of standard.

Budgetary control is concerned with standards of performance for output and costs. The big question which must be answered when considering the effectiveness of budgetary control is: what do the standards represent in terms of efficiency? There are two possibilities with variations in between:

1. Budgeted costs quantities are what are expected, having regard to what has occurred in the past.

In other words, the budgets are primarily statements of expectations from existing or future facilities which are to be operated at the present level of efficiency, whether this is high or low.

2. Budgeted costs and quantities are what are expected after considering anticipated conditions, volume of output, replacement prices and the efficiency which can be achieved from the effective utilisation of the resources owned by the business.

This second approach is forward-looking and recognises that a business should aim at operating efficiently so as to produce the largest volume of output for the lowest possible cost. At the same time, all the social groups should be rewarded on a satisfactory basis (*see* p. 299).

DESIGN OF BUDGETS

The precise form the budgets will take depends upon the nature of the business and the designing skill of the accountant or organisation and methods expert. An appreciation of what is involved may be obtained from looking at the pro-forma example of a forecast given opposite (Fig. 55).

Study of the diagram of procedures (Fig. 54) will show that the sales budget and production budget are considered together. In practice, which comes first depends upon the business involved; some companies start off with the assumption that they are going to produce certain quantities of products which have to be sold; others decide what volume of demand exists and then produce the appropriate quantities. The important principle to be observed is that the two aspects are co-ordinated.

PRODUCTION FORECAST

Quarter: from.........................

to ....

Product	Budget Centre Producing X	Budget Centre Producing Y	Budget Centre Producing Z
	Units	Units	Units
A	4000	4000	4000
B	9000	—	9000
C	4000	4000	—

FIG. 55.—*Specimen production forecast*

NOTES

Where units are shown this indicates the forecast of work to be carried out in the budget centre indicated. Thus, for example, "4000" in column X in respect of product A indicates that material, labour and other requirements will be needed for operations to be covered in that centre. The same applies in columns Y and Z. It should be noted that these are the same units as in column X.

In the case of product B it will be apparent that no operations are involved in budget centre Y; this is also the case for product C in centre Z.

As noticed in Chapter XVIII the provision of finance is an important part of the management process. There will have to be adequate finance for any plans which are made. Similarly there must be adequate provision for material supplies and for labour required to carry out the work. If one factor (*e.g.* serious shortage of machine tool operators) predominates to such an extent that all budgets are influenced by it, this is known as the "principal budget factor." Before proceeding further with the plans it will be necessary to take action to overcome the major problem. When there are a *number* of problems to overcome such as shortage of cash, limited drilling capacity, and extreme competition in a particular market these factors are called "limiting factors."

FIXED AND FLEXIBLE BUDGETS

When considering budgets it is necessary to distinguish between two basic types:

1. Fixed budget which shows *one* volume of output or sales and the related costs.

2. Flexible budget which shows a *range* of volumes of output or sales and costs for each.

The flexible budget allows capacity achieved and budgeted capacity to be compared. For example, if 90% of production capacity is achieved then in order to compare the actual costs incurred with budgeted costs it will be necessary to look at the 90% column on the flexible budget. Only in this way can there be effective control of costs. How a flexible budget is compiled is shown in Fig. 56.

FLEXIBLE BUDGET								
	Month January				*Dept.* A.B.			
Overhead Cost Description	*Bases for calculating Total Cost*		*Output in Percentages*					
	Fixed	*Variable*	90%	95%	100%	105%	110%	115%
	£	Per Std. hr. £	£	£	£	£	£	£
Variable Costs:								
Spoilage		0·05	450	475	500	525	550	575
Indirect Materials		0·10	900	950	1,000	1,050	1,100	1,150
Semi-Variable Costs:								
Indirect Labour	500	0·25	2,750	2,875	3,000	3,125	3,250	3,375
Power and Light	400	0·10	1,300	1,350	1,400	1,450	1,500	1,550
Heat and Water	200	0·10	1,100	1,150	1,200	1,250	1,300	1,350
Insurance on Stocks	150	0·025	375	388	400	413	425	438
Repairs and Maintenance	600	0·25	2,850	2,975	3,100	3,225	3,350	3,475
Fixed Costs:								
Supervision	1000		1,000	1,000	1,000	1,000	1,000	1,000
Depreciation	4000		4,000	4,000	4,000	4,000	4,000	4,000
Rent Charges	1500		1,500	1,500	1,500	1,500	1,500	1,500
Other Space Charges	900		900	900	900	900	900	900
			£17,125	£17,563	£18,000	£18,438	£18,875	£19,313
Rate per Standard Hour			£1·90	£1·85	£1·80	£1·76	£1·72	£1·68

FIG. 56.—*Example of a flexible budget of manufacturing overhead costs*

NOTES

1. The figures used are purely hypothetical; total figures are taken to the nearest £1.
2. Output may be stated in terms of:
    (*a*) Percentages, when it is quite usual to state what "100%" represents (*e.g.* as in example, 10,000 standard hours or, say, 10,000 units of product *X*).
    (*b*) Units of output.
    (*c*) Sales values.
    (*d*) Standard hours.
3. The semi-variable costs will have been separated into their fixed and variable elements.
4. Costs for any output which is not an exact multiple of 5% may be found by interpolation.
5. The charge "per hour" is used for simplicity—in practice, for many costs, it would be unrealistic.

REGULATION THROUGH BUDGETARY CONTROL

Control of performances and costs is obtained from *comparison* of actual achievements and budgeted standards and then getting managers *to take action.*

Effective communication is an essential part of management. In budgetary control, standard costing and similar systems a good deal of reliance is placed on properly designed reports and statements. These are usually divided into:

1. *Special reports* which cover unusual occurrences such as those listed below:

(a) Production delays when considerable time has been lost.
(b) Machine breakdowns involving a large number of hours.
(c) The effects of labour disputes.
(d) Whether to make or buy components or products.
(e) Whether to purchase or hire fixed assets.
(f) Capital expenditure decision reports.
(g) Minimum price to charge in a trade recession.
(h) Whether to substitute machines for hand labour.
(i) Cost reduction recommendations.
(j) The most appropriate method of obtaining new funds.
(k) The best methods of investing cash which is surplus to present needs.
(l) Special investigations into particular systems employed.
(m) The feasibility of employing a computer.
(n) Study of effect of idle capacity on the profitability of the business.
(o) Effects of diversification or simplification of the product range.
(p) Market research projects.
(q) Study of the strength of competitors.
(r) Closing down of departments or plant.
(s) Costs of holding stocks of raw materials or finished goods.
(t) Significant developments which arise from time to time, whether due to political action or other reason: *e.g.* a Government credit squeeze, entry into a common market, removal or introduction of tariffs on particular products, cancellation of important contracts by an overseas buyer.

These twenty examples of matters which may be covered by special reports should serve to illustrate the nature of these reports.

2. *Routine reports* which deal with everyday matters and events.

For control within the budget centres (*i.e.* departments or sections), departmental operating statements are employed. An example of such a statement is shown in Fig. 57.

There are a number of rules which should be observed when preparing reports and statements. For convenience these are summarised below:

Consider the level of management

Reference to Chapter IV will show that the responsibilities of managers vary according to the nature and scope of their work. A simple breakdown will show what is meant:

1. Directors—concerned with policy.
2. General management—deal with the overall state of the business.

Both (1) and (2) will require reports on major matters such as those listed earlier in connection with special reports. In particular they will wish to be kept informed on the volume of production and sales and whether profit expectations are being realised. Any significant occurrence which affects industrial relations would also be brought to the notice of top management without delay.

3. Functional management—the production manager will want to know about production and related costs and the sales manager will have to be informed on deviations from the sales and selling cost standards.
4. Department managers, foremen and supervisors. They will have to be kept informed *in detail* of any matter which is affecting the efficiency of the particular department or section.

Follow the "principle of exceptions"

This principle is explained earlier in this chapter. The reports and statements should concentrate on *deviations* from standards and not report on all and sundry.

Understand the basic principles of report writing

The main principles are as follows:

1. Comparative statements should be used; *i.e.* showing what *has happened* against what *should have happened*.
2. Prepare for a definite purpose and not cover every possible contingency.
3. Employ simple language so that there will be no difficulty of understanding by the reader.
4. Make sure that the names or departments concerned with the report are clearly shown.
5. Distinguish between costs which are *controllable* and those which are *uncontrollable*.

All costs are controllable by someone, but when preparing reports it should be remembered that not all performances and costs are the

DEPARTMENTAL OPERATING STATEMENT

Department AB Period January 19...

Activity { Standard: 10,000 Standard Hours / Actual: 9,500 Hours

Overhead Cost	Actual	Budgeted for Actual Hours	Analysis of Variances			Remarks
			Favour-able	Un-favour-able	Con-troll-able	
	£	£	£	£	£	
Variable Costs:						
Spoilage	480	475		5	5	
Indirect Materials	975	950		25		Uncontrollable price increase
Semi-Variable Costs:						
Indirect Labour	3,000	2,875		125	125	Investigate
Power and Light	1,390	1,350		40	40	Investigate
Heat and Water	1,100	1,150	50		50*	Investigate
Insurance on Stocks	390	388		2	2	
Repairs and Maintenance	2,900	2,975	75		75*	Repairs kept to a minimum this period. Major break-down X Dept.
Fixed Costs:						
Supervision	1,000	1,000	—	—	—	
Depreciation	4,000	4,000	—	—	—	
Rent Charges	1,500	1,500	—	—	—	
Other Space Charges	900	900	—	—	—	
	£17,635	£17,563	£125	£197	£47	

* Favourable Variance deducted to arrive at total "Controllable."

FIG. 57.—*Example of a departmental operating statement*

NOTES

1. The budgeted costs refer to *actual* activity, thus making the Variance Analysis figures more realistic.

2. The insurance on stocks cost *may* be regarded as an uncontrollable cost, but in the illustration the variation between standard and actual is, in any event, too small to warrant any action being taken.

3. Whether or not any deviation from standard warrants investigation depends upon its size in relation to the standard cost. In practice, the cost analyst will know, from experience, which items require attention. Some businesses fix a percentage (*e.g.* 10%); any deviations from standard are converted to percentages, and those below the stated figure are ignored, whereas all others are investigated.

responsibility of the person for whom a report is intended. In particular, the following facts should be recognised when dealing with departmental operating statements:

1. Fixed costs are often the result of policy decisions. Accordingly, whether these should be included in routine reports has to be determined. Some accountants prefer to exclude them altogether.

2. Costs incurred in previous departments (A, B and C) in the production processes cannot be held to be the responsibility of a later department (D).

For these reasons, as a minimum requirement, the manager of a particular department should be given information on what is going wrong as regards prime costs (defined in Chapter XIX) and variable overhead costs incurred or to be incurred in that department. Any additional costs information would be supplementary and, therefore, should be kept to a minimum, being included only if it is felt that greater understanding and, therefore, co-operation would result.

VARIANCE ANALYSIS

The difference between a budgeted cost and an actual cost is known as a *cost variance*. Cost accountants have classified variances into a number of different categories and there is official terminology for these which has been suggested by the Institute of Cost and Works Accountants.

Basically the terms may be classified according to the elements of cost:

1. Material cost variances.
2. Labour cost variances.
3. Overhead cost variances.

They may be analysed daily, weekly or monthly. A simple form of analysis is used on the departmental operating statement shown in Fig. 57.

Budgetary control often adopts this general method of showing variances as the difference between actual and budgeted costs for a budget centre. This applies even for the direct material and labour costs.

When standard costing is employed, with or without budgetary control, a more detailed analysis of variances is possible. The formulae for calculating variances and their significance are given on p. 367.

RESPONSIBILITY FOR BUDGETS AND CONTROL

The responsibilities for setting budgeted costs and performances and later for controlling have to be clearly understood and stated. The precise responsibilities of a particular executive; *e.g.* the production engineer, will vary from one business to another. Nevertheless, the following list should act as a guide:

EXECUTIVE	BUDGET AND AREA OF CONTROL
Budget controller	*Administration budget**
	Cash budget†
	Capital budget†
	Master budget†

The budget controller will usually be directly responsible for collecting the facts and ensuring that all necessary steps are taken to compile the budgets stated. *In addition,* he will take all the necessary steps to ensure that all executives understand the part they have to play in setting up the budgets. Once the information has been collected and has been sifted by the budget controller's department and has been examined by the budget committee, the controller arranges for the interim and final budgets to be drafted. Successful launching of the system and its continued operation also come within the responsibility of the budget controller. He will provide all the facts needed for co-ordination and control, but he cannot *himself* ensure that co-ordination and control become realities and not merely plans. All executives, supervisors, and even the rank and file workers can contribute towards these achievements.

Buyer (or *purchasing agent*)	*Purchasing budget*

In conjunction with the budget controller or accountant the buyer establishes standard prices. Quantities of materials and supplies have to be estimated by the production engineer, the works (maintenance) engineer, and other departmental heads; the buyer integrates the information and supplies it to the budget controller so that the purchasing budget can be prepared.

Departmental managers or *foremen*	*Departmental budgets*

Each departmental manager is consulted by the budget controller and by the budget committee. In this way he is able to understand the nature of his budget and, because he takes part in its preparation, can accept it as a target which is capable of attainment.

Distribution manager	*Distribution budget*

This assumes that a separate distribution budget is compiled. This will cover all distribution costs—transport and storage costs and certain packing costs. Sometimes distribution costs are dealt with along with selling costs and included in the selling costs budget. They then become the responsibility of the sales manager, although, in this case, there may still be a distribution manager, who reports to the sales manager.

Research engineer, *research chemist,* or *development engineer*	*Research and development budget*
Sales manager	*Sales budget*

* Often the responsibility of the Office or Administrative Manager.
† Often dealt with by the Accountant.

ADVANTAGES OF BUDGETARY CONTROL

The principal advantages which may accrue from the employment of budgetary control are summarised below. Whether these benefits are realised, and to what extent, depends very much on the system and the attitude of management. Some systems are much more efficient than others; a costly and elaborate system is not necessarily the best because there is such a thing as "over control." If unnecessary refinements do not add to the usefulness of a management accountancy technique then they should not be employed.

Briefly, then, the possible advantages are as follows:

1. Policy, plans and action taken are all reflected in the budgetary control system. There is formal recognition of the targets which the business hopes to achieve (*see* p. 37 on primary objectives).

2. Everyone working in the business should know what is expected of him. One of the first essentials of sound management is to let each man know his responsibilities.

3. Deviations from the plans made are brought to light through variance analysis and corrective action is stimulated by reports, statements and personal contact.

4. Delegation of responsibilities is given positive recognition by the preparation of budgets for each budget centre.

5. Co-ordination is achieved by the interlocking of all the budgets: (*a*) through a master budget and (*b*) by the necessary control system which is watched over by the budget controller.

STANDARD COSTING

Standard costing is similar to the budgetary control explained in the previous section, except that the concern is with the detailed standard costs *for each product* and not simply for each department.

The processes involved are as follows:

1. Predetermination of standard costs in respect of labour, material and overhead for each product.

2. Comparison of actual costs with standard costs.

3. Analysing the cost variances so that the reasons for them can be ascertained.

4. Reporting daily, weekly or monthly to managers so that corrective action can be taken.

With standard costing there is a positive effort made to select the most effective methods of organising and producing *before* the standard costs are set. This is not necessarily the case with budgetary control. A standard cost is a reflection of what a cost *should be* and not what it is

STANDARD MATERIAL REQUISITION. No.............

Date............   Prod. Order No.............

                                    Part No.....................   No. Off.........

Code	Material Description	Quantity (Std.)

Issued (Stores) ....   Authorised ....

Rec'd by (Worker) ....   Stores Ledger Folio ....

FIG. 58.—*Standard material requisition*

NOTES

1. Because the price and value columns are omitted there can be a great saving in time and effort brought about because:

(*a*) Prices do not have to be entered on the requisitions.

(*b*) Values (prices × quantities) do not have to be calculated.

(*c*) Values of issues do not have to be entered in the stores ledger or on a materials issued analysis sheet to arrive at the totals for the month.

2. Offsetting the reduction in work are the following:

(*a*) Calculation of values, from a materials issued analysis sheet for month-end posting to stores control account and, from balance quantities, in the stores ledger, is necessary.

(*b*) Values must be entered in the stores ledger each month.

expected to be. This is the basic difference between setting standard costs and estimating.

For standard costing to be employed there must be standardisation of methods and products. If the business is producing to customers' specification, each job being *entirely different*, then there would be difficulty in setting standard costs and the benefits therefrom would be negligible. Generally the system is to be found where process costing is employed or where batch costing is in existence for ascertaining the cost of standard components. With job costing there is often difficulty experienced in employing standard costing. In these circumstances, budgetary control alone can be used.

EXCESS MATERIAL REQUISITION. No.............				Variance Calculation (unfavourable)
Date............ Prod. Order No.				
Part No. .... No. Off.				
Code	Material	Quantity	Price (Std.)	Value
				£

Issued (Stores) .... Authorised ....

Rec'd by (Worker) .... Stores Ledger Folio...........................

Variance Analysis Sheet Folio............

Reasons for Excess ....

....

FIG. 59.—*Excess material requisition*

NOTES

1. Only when the foreman is fully satisfied that the extra materials are warranted should he authorise the issue.

2. The reasons for requiring the extra materials should be stated.

3. Unfavourable variances can be calculated by reference to the excess material requisitions. These variances can then be summarised to arrive at total variances for each day, week, month, or other period.

CONTROLLING COSTS

There are two methods which may be used for detecting variances and these are as follows:

1. Use forms which automatically segregate the deviations from the set targets. This means:

(*a*) using standard forms for normal usage or prices (Fig. 58); and

(*b*) covering any exceptional (above standard) costs by specially designed authorisation forms, usually in a distinctive colour (Fig. 59).

Those coming into (*b*) can be segregated quite easily so that any excess costs can be seen as the work proceeds and not months afterwards. One example is given (Fig. 59). This relates to material issues and it will be seen that no prices are entered on the material requisition, which is a great saving in itself as compared with the conventional method where each requisition has to be priced separately.

2. Calculate cost variances for each element of cost. As will be apparent, the direct labour and direct material variances are very much the concern of production managers because they are responsible for these. The formulae for calculating the variances are shown below.

PRIME COST VARIANCES

Material variances show whether more or less than the standard price has been paid for material (material price variance) and whether a smaller or larger than standard quantity of material has been used (material usage variance). The labour variances are similar, the concern being with labour rates (labour rate variance) and labour hours (labour efficiency variance).

Management will be very concerned to know why there have been variations from standard and statements can be prepared to show the reasons.

Formulae for calculating the variances are as follows:

Material price variance:

$$\left(\begin{array}{l}\text{Actual} \\ \text{price}\end{array} - \begin{array}{l}\text{Standard} \\ \text{price}\end{array}\right) \times \text{Actual quantity}$$

Material usage variance:

$$\left(\begin{array}{l}\text{Actual} \\ \text{quantity}\end{array} - \begin{array}{l}\text{Standard} \\ \text{quantity}\end{array}\right) \times \text{Standard price}$$

Labour rate variance:

$$\left(\begin{array}{l}\text{Actual} \\ \text{rate}\end{array} - \begin{array}{l}\text{Standard} \\ \text{rate}\end{array}\right) \times \text{Actual hours}$$

Labour efficiency variance:

$$\left(\begin{array}{l}\text{Actual} \\ \text{hours}\end{array} - \begin{array}{l}\text{Standard} \\ \text{hours}\end{array}\right) \times \text{Standard rate}$$

OVERHEAD VARIANCES

For factory (manufacturing) overhead costs, the variances are calculated for the factory, as a whole, or separately, for each producing cost centre and service cost centre.

The *overhead cost variance*, which is a "total" variance—difference between total standard, and total actual overhead for the output achieved—can be subdivided into:

(a) *Overhead budget variance*, which is the difference between the budgeted overhead (total per budget) and actual overhead (total spent for period). This variance is a measure of efficiency in spending.

(b) *Overhead efficiency variance*, which attempts to measure efficiency for the output actually achieved. The standard efficiency (in terms of hours) is compared with actual efficiency (in terms of hours) multiplied by the standard overhead rate for the actual production, any difference being the efficiency variance.

(c) *Overhead volume variance*, which shows any idle hours, or overtime hours, evaluated by reference to the standard overhead rate. The variance is thus the difference between the actual level of activity, irrespective of actual output, valued at standard overhead rate, and the standard level of activity, valued at that rate.

(d) *Overhead calendar variance* (*or sub-variance*), which may be regarded as an "adjustment variance." When the standard costs are set, for each accounting period, a fixed number of working days will be anticipated. If, for example, a business has an accounting period which covers 22 working days (4 weeks $\times$ $5\frac{1}{2}$ days) and the standard costs are fixed with this number of days in mind, then, obviously, if this number is not worked, or is exceeded, the overhead charges will not be as expected. Moreover, because the length of the accounting period is different, the overhead volume variance will be affected and will require adjustment.

For examples of how these calculations are made the reader is referred to *Standard Costing* by J. Batty, published by Macdonald & Evans.

SETTING STANDARD COSTS

Very briefly the most favoured methods for setting standard costs are as follows:

1. *Direct materials.*—A standard material specification is compiled, and by reference to size, weight or other measure the standard quantity of material is determined. Due allowance should be made for normal waste or cutting losses.

The standard price is determined by the purchasing agent and accountant after due attention has been paid to possible increases or reductions in prices within the future period for which the standards are being set.

2. *Direct labour.*—For setting standard times it is advisable to employ work study. This means that there should be close co-operation between the cost accountants and work study engineers (*see* p. 115).

The principal stages involved are as follows:

(a) Selecting the best method of performing each operation and the tools to use.

(b) Recording each operation and making this standard practice.

(c) Determining how long an average worker should take to carry out each operation.

(d) Training each operator to carry out the work in the prescribed manner.

The wage-rates should be set after all work has been graded into different categories. Future trends have to be estimated before the standard rates can be set.

3. *Overhead costs.*—The procedures described for budgeting costs when a budgetary control system is being employed also apply to setting standard costs; *i.e.* from past experience, and with consideration of *future* conditions and prices, a careful assessment is made of each type of expense. This is so for *all* overhead costs, whether they are production, selling, distribution, research, development or administration.

ADVANTAGES OF STANDARD COSTING

Possible advantages from employing a system of standard costing are summarised below:

1. Standard costs are a yardstick which may be used for showing the state of efficiency achieved.

When actual costs only are recorded the process is known as "historical costing." This suffers from the grave disadvantage that no one is sure whether the costs reflect efficient performances.

2. Deviations from predetermined standard costs are located promptly and reported to management.

3. The *principle of exceptions* is followed so that managers can concentrate on matters not proceeding according to what has been planned.

4. Clerical costs can often be reduced because of (3) and the fact that material prices do not have to be entered on records and forms.

5. Interpretation of reports can be made much easier so that all levels of management can understand what is happening.

6. Cost control and cost reduction are greatly facilitated.

7. From the very inception of standard costing, there is a positive effort made to improve efficiency. All functions are examined and the best methods selected before setting standard costs.

8. Standard costs are a true reflection of sacrifices involved and, therefore, can be used with safety when formulating production and price policies.

9. Bonus payments and incentive schemes can be based on achievement of the standard costs.

10. Production and accounting staff co-operate in the setting of standards and control of costs.

MARGINAL COSTING

Marginal costing is a special technique of cost accounting which gives formal recognition to the behaviour of costs. The following principles apply:

1. All variable costs (defined on p. 330), *i.e.* prime costs and variable overheads, are designated "marginal costs."

N

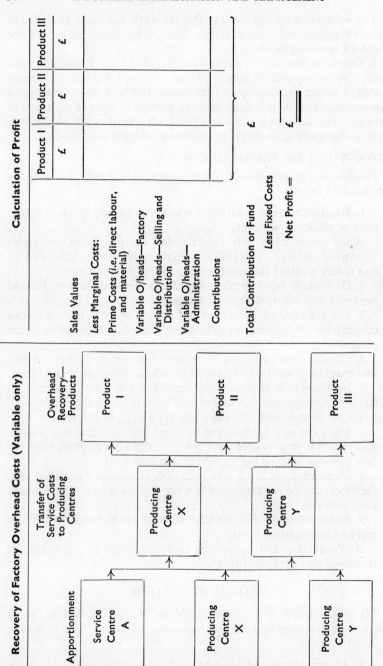

Fig. 60.—*Diagram to show marginal costing*

2. Fixed costs (defined on p. 329) are kept quite separate from the marginal costs and this fact is reflected in costs of production, statements employed, profit and loss accounts, and break-even charts.

The technique is also known as incremental costing, direct costing, and differential costing.

When considering the costs of products the fixed costs are disregarded. Instead these are kept in total to be met out of the difference between sales revenue and marginal costs: this difference is known as the "contribution." The allocation and apportionment of fixed costs, it is argued, are useless refinements which confuse rather than assist management: accordingly, marginal costing is the most useful technique for showing the appropriate choice from a number of alternatives. That there is some truth in this assertion is not denied. However, there are also dangers attaching to the indiscriminate use of marginal costing, and these are covered later.

A better idea of what is involved in the technique is shown by the diagram (Fig. 60). What should be emphasised is that marginal costing always exists with some form of system such as job or process costing. The same principles are followed as for orthodox costing described in Chapter XX except that the fixed costs are kept segregated.

BREAK-EVEN ANALYSIS

One of the most useful aids for showing at a glance useful information on important aspects relating to a business is the "break-even chart." This is a chart on which lines are drawn to represent:

(a) Fixed costs.
(b) Marginal or variable costs.
(c) Sales revenues.
(d) Total costs.

The point at which the total cost and sales lines meet is where a business is just paying its way; there is no profit being earned nor any loss being incurred. This fact gives the chart its name.

The most conventional type of break-even chart is that shown in Fig. 61. Special attention should be paid to the wedges which are formed by the total cost line and the sales revenue line. If the profit wedge is broad when considered vertically, then the rate of earning is quite good.

In order to make the principles understood, the reader is advised to study the figures given below, and then to see if he understands the method used by tracing the figures on the chart.

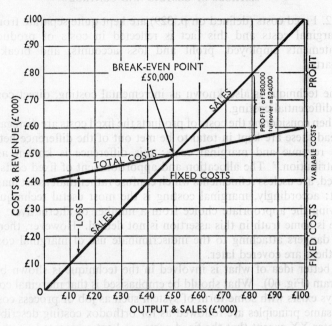

FIG. 61.—*Break-even chart*

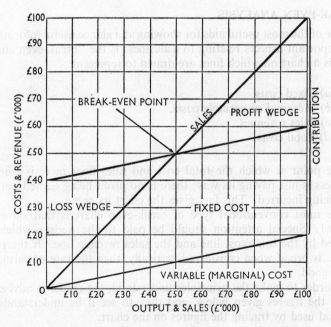

FIG. 62.—*Break-even chart (showing contribution)*

Management Problem

The fixed costs for the year are £40,000. Variable cost per unit for the single product being made is £2. Estimated sales for the period are valued at £100,000. The number of units involved coincides with the expected volume of output. Each unit sells at £10.

Required: The profit earned at a turnover of £80,000.

The variety of charts which may be prepared is numerous. In a general book of this type it is impossible to give examples of them all, but the following should indicate the possibilities:

Contribution break-even chart (*Fig. 62*)

The importance of this chart is based on the fact that the contribution earned by a business is shown without further calculation.

Profit appropriation break-even chart (*Fig. 63*)

In Chapter XXIII reference was made to capital structures and the issue of shares. In the profit appropriation chart it is possible to show the following facts:

A = Break-even point of £25,000.

B = Sales required to cover debenture interest; a true profit is not earned until this volume of sales is obtained.

C = Sales required to enable debenture interest and preference dividends of £10,000 to be paid.

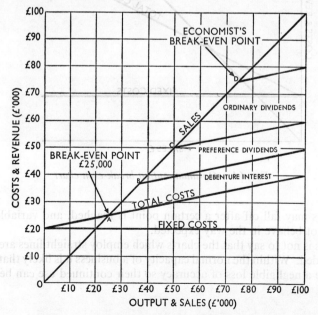

FIG. 63.—*Profit appropriation break-even chart*

D = Sales required to enable debenture interest, preference dividends and ordinary dividends (£20,000) to be paid. At this point the total capital employed is being paid—presumably—a reasonable return. Because economists take the view that all factors of production, including capital, must be paid an adequate return before it can be said that a profit has been earned, point D is sometimes called the "economist's break-even point."

Optimum output break-even chart

The break-even chart which employs straight lines to portray sales and costs is not strictly accurate. A more realistic situation is shown by the chart given in Fig. 64.

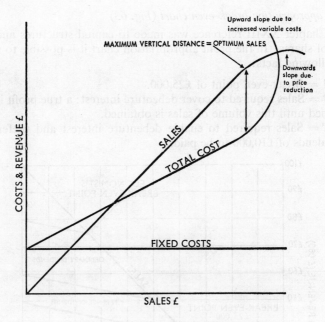

FIG. 64.—*Optimum output break-even chart*

Sales may fall off after a certain point is reached, and variable cost may not behave in the way expected.

This is not to say that the charts which employ straight lines are to be discarded. Within the normal capacity of a business it is likely that there will be a negligible loss of accuracy so their continued use can be justified.

ADVANTAGES OF MARGINAL COSTING

The advantages claimed for marginal costing are listed below:

1. The cost of a product does not vary from one period to another.
This assertion is based on the fact that the fixed cost *per unit* is greater for each reduction in the volume of output.

Example

Fixed costs £1000			
Month 1 output	.	.	. 2000 units
Month 2 output	.	.	. 1000 units

Fixed cost *per unit:*

Month 1	.	.	.	.	. £0·50
Month 2	.	.	.	.	. £1·00

2. Because of (1) sales managers and others who are concerned with justifying prices have more confidence in the marginal costing system.
They are not faced with different unit costs from one period to another.

3. Marginal costing avoids the under- or over-recovery of overhead costs.
This is only partly true because variable overhead costs also enter into any calculation of predetermined costs when job costing is used.

4. Problems connected with a greater or smaller volume of output tend to be simplified.

5. Cost control is greatly facilitated because due recognition is given to the way costs behave. There is still a need to predetermine costs to control effectively. For this reason, marginal costing without standard costing or budgetary control is likely to be of limited value.

6. Due recognition is given to the fact that a profit is not earned until products are sold.
When calculating profit only the relevant costs are deducted from the sales values (*see* Fig. 60).

POSSIBLE WEAKNESSES OF MARGINAL COSTING

While admitting that some of the arguments for marginal costing are sound, many accountants qualify the usefulness of the technique as follows:

1. In the long period a profit must be earned or the business will not survive.
If prices are based on marginal costs, without regard to the size and nature of fixed costs, there is a danger that they will not include a profit. For this reason, reliance on marginal costs alone can lead to unsound decisions and unprofitable orders.

2. The separation of fixed costs is important, but this act alone does not show managers what is happening. Calculation of the appropriate variances may give much more valuable information.

3. Many costs are semi-variable and the problem of ascertaining

which part is fixed and which is variable may be almost as bad as the process of apportioning these costs to products.

In addition, there is the question of the accuracy being attained. Some of the methods employed for separating the fixed and variable elements may give approximations only.

Conclusion

Although there can be great justification for employing marginal costing the manager who is not an accountant should not jump to the conclusion that the technique cures all ailments. The other systems and methods are just as useful in appropriate circumstances.

DECISION ACCOUNTING

Any accounting employed for assisting with the making of decisions is sometimes referred to as "decision accounting." Quite often marginal costing principles are followed, but this is not necessarily the case.

Examples of problems which confront managers quite regularly are shown below:

1. Should a department which appears to be unprofitable be closed?
2. How far can prices be reduced in order to obtain business?
3. In a trade depression should a plant be closed down?
4. Should a product be made or bought outside?
5. Which method of production should be employed—machinery or hand labour?
6. Should new funds be raised by issuing shares or debentures, and what terms should be offered so that the issue is a success?

There are many other problems which have to be solved, but enough has been shown to indicate that the field of operation is very wide indeed. Strictly speaking, decision accounting is not a separate system, but rather a recognition that accounting data can be used for comparing alternative courses of action.

Some authorities on management regard the most important attribute of a good manager as the ability to make decisions. These decisions must generally be correct or losses will result.

For the purposes of illustration typical problems and suggested solutions are given below. Space does not permit a comprehensive coverage of all possible problems and the reader who wishes to pursue the subject further should study a book on management accountancy.

PRICING OF PRODUCTS OR JOBS

The marginal costing approach to the pricing of products or jobs is based on the formula:

$$\text{Sales price} - \text{marginal cost} = \text{contribution}$$

If the price obtainable makes a contribution towards fixed cost and profit, the theory is that the products which make the largest contributions should be produced and sold first. A corollary to this is that in a trade recession any orders which cover marginal costs and some part of fixed costs should be accepted, thereby minimising losses.

Some accountants have gone further and suggested that in order to obtain additional business, over and above what is regarded as normal capacity, any jobs which cover more than marginal costs should be accepted. This is based on the assumption that fixed overhead costs will be absorbed by the products made as part of the normal capacity and, therefore, an additional product which makes any contribution—no matter how little—is a worthwhile proposition. Other accountants have criticised this procedure as being dangerous and unsound. There is always the danger that the marginal or "out-of-pocket" business will take the place of the ordinary business and thereby reduce profits instead of increasing them.

The principles involved in arriving at a decision on whether or not a job is worth while are illustrated below.

Question

Drake and Co Ltd is experiencing a difficult trading period and, as a result, is operating well below the normal capacity to produce and sell.

An enquiry has been received for 100 units of a product (X) and the directors are very anxious to obtain the order. The costing information relating to X is as follows:

Direct labour per unit: 2 hours at £0·25 per hour.

Direct material cost per unit: £0·50.

Overheads are recovered on the basis of £1·00 per direct labour hour for variable costs and £1·50 per direct labour hour for fixed costs.

Additional costs relate to special moulds which have to be purchased 1 per product at £0·10 each, and equipment costing £200. In both cases (moulds and equipment) there is no hope of the costs being recovered by other products.

Assuming that the order can be fitted into the existing capacity without difficulty you are required to calculate the *minimum price* which could be quoted.

Suggested solution

Statement of marginal costs for 100 units of product X

	£	£
Direct labour cost:		
200 hours at £0·25 per hour		50
Direct material cost:		
100 units at £0·50 per unit		50
Direct expense:		
100 moulds at £0·10 each	10	
Equipment	200	
		210
Variable overhead cost:		
200 hours at £1·00 per direct labour hour		200
		£510

The marginal cost shown by the statement is £510, so this is the absolute minimum price. However, this does not allow for any contribution towards fixed costs. Accordingly, it may be advisable to quote a higher figure. How much should be added to the figure of £510 depends on the urgency of obtaining the order. Clearly, an attempt should be made to cover some part of fixed costs; *i.e.* to earn a contribution.

DEPARTMENTAL (OR PRODUCT) PROFIT AND LOSS ACCOUNTS

The departmental (or product) profit and loss account in marginal costing form is very useful for determining whether or not a department should continue to operate or whether a product should be eliminated. In either case the decision can be determined by reference to the contribution made or loss incurred by the department or product.

An example of how a marginal profit and loss account is compiled is shown below. This is in the form of a question and suggested solution.

Question

The Arnold Co Ltd has three departments each of which makes a different product. Cost and related data for the past year—not expected to change very much in the next year—are as follows:

	Department		
	A	B	C
Sales revenue	80,000	40,000	60,000
Marginal costs:			
Direct material	10,000	5,000	10,000
Direct labour...	4,000	5,000	16,000
Variable overhead	10,000	5,000	20,000
Fixed overhead cost	20,000	10,000	20,000
Total costs	£44,000	25,000	66,000

The manager in charge of Department C is very perturbed by the results. The product being made has an assured market and there is no other product which could be substituted for the product already being made. Prime and variable overhead costs (marginal costs) are down to a low level and there is little hope of these being reduced further.

You are required to present the information in the most suitable manner, indicating as far as possible whether or not Department C should be closed down.

Suggested solution

The marginal costing approach to the question is shown below.

Marginal Profit and Loss Account of the Arnold Co Ltd

Department	Sales value	Marginal cost	Contribution	Loss
	£	£	£	
A	80,000	24,000	56,000	—
B	40,000	15,000	25,000	—
C	60,000	46,000	14,000	—
	180,000	85,000	95,000	—
Less Total fixed costs			50,000	
NET PROFIT =			£45,000	

Department C makes a contribution of £14,000 towards fixed costs. If this department is eliminated altogether the following applies:

Department	Sales value	Marginal cost	Contribution
	£	£	£
A	80,000	24,000	56,000
B	40,000	15,000	25,000
	120,000	39,000	81,000
Less Total fixed costs			50,000
NET PROFIT =			£31,000

The profit is reduced by £14,000, the contribution made by Department C.

Special note on method

The method of approach employed above assumes that fixed costs should not be allocated and/or apportioned to departments. However, in certain circumstances this may be quite illogical. If a department is entirely separate and self-contained it will incur its own fixed overhead costs which are traceable to that department and to no other. Accordingly, no amount of arguing is likely to convince management that fixed costs from a number of separate departments (or factories) should be lumped together in the manner suggested by the marginal costing approach. In these circumstances, each department should clearly cover its own fixed costs.

If all fixed costs cannot be traced to separate departments with certainty then, rather than put all fixed costs into a common pool, a different approach may give better results, *viz.*:

(*a*) Charge all fixed overhead costs which are incurred for a particular department to that department.

(*b*) Any fixed costs which are incurred on behalf of a number of departments go into a common pool.

This method (*a*) and (*b*) is likely to give more acceptable results than the pure form of marginal costing. This applies whether departments or *products* are being considered.

Examination Questions on Chapter XXI are given at the end of Chapter XXII.

MANAGEMENT ACCOUNTANCY: PROFIT AND EFFICIENCY

PROFIT AND LOSS MEASUREMENT

THE calculation of profit is briefly covered in Chapter XIX in connection with final accounts. Here the concern is with profit as a measure of the overall efficiency of a business, and the problems of calculating profit in a period of rising prices. These matters are discussed under the following headings:

1. Return on capital employed.
2. Revaluation accounting.

RETURN ON CAPITAL EMPLOYED

The "capital employed" in a business is the investment represented by the total assets used by the managers in order to earn profit. As a general rule all assets, whether fixed or current, should be considered when making the calculation. The term *capital employed* should not be confused with share capital which is the sum contributed by shareholders (*see* Chapter XVIII on issue of shares).

There are differences of opinion on the matter of definition, but basically there are two approaches:

1. Gross capital employed.—All assets are taken and no deduction is made except possibly assets *not* being employed due to, say, a trade depression.

2. Net capital employed.—This is the gross capital *minus* current liabilities.

Provided that the method selected is used consistently, either approach may be adopted. It should be remembered that the purpose is to measure the effectiveness of internal management.

The old idea that a business exists to earn a maximum profit has now been replaced by a broader concept. There is now recognition that the following matters should be considered:

(*a*) Wellbeing of employees (*see* p. 193).
(*b*) Satisfaction of the consumer.

Unless the consumer is satisfied it is very unlikely that a business will continue to earn a profit. The products sold must satisfy a need and must be priced at a realistic level. Although price increases may increase profit there is a limit to which consumers will go; once this is reached the fall off in sales will tend to reduce profits.

(c) Long-term stability.

No board of directors likes a policy which produces violent fluctuations in sales, production and profits. In times of full employment there is difficulty enough in maintaining a skilled labour force; if permanent employment cannot be offered by a business, employees will tend to move elsewhere. Furthermore, many shareholders and other investors will tend to view with great disfavour any instability in earning profits and paying dividends.

(d) Adequate profit to cover the following:

(i) dividends to shareholders which are adequate to compensate for risks involved and are at least equal to those being paid by similar concerns, and interest to debenture holders;

(ii) reserves for expansion and to ward off any difficult periods; and

(iii) reserves for maintaining intact the real capital of the business as reflected by the earning capacity of the assets employed (see revaluation accounting, below).

All these factors should be considered when determining what is an adequate return on capital employed. Besides being concerned with earning profit the directors must ensure adequate growth and the continuity of the business for the benefit of employees, shareholders and the economy at large.

THE MASTER BUDGET

Reference to the master budget is made in Chapter XXI on budgetary control. When determining the profit for management planning so that the master budget can be prepared, the factors considered in the previous section must all enter into the calculation. In looking at the problem of defining the profit target the directors may consider the following:

1. *Minimum rate of profit.*—This is the rate which is just worth while; if a lower rate is expected alternative investments should be considered. The rate paid on the *market price* of gilt-edged securities may be a guide to what is a minimum rate.

2. *Normal rate of profit.*—To the minimum rate of profit it is usual to add a percentage to cover the risk involved, bearing in mind the nature of the product or service being produced and sold. The rate would vary from, say, 2% in industries with stable demand to, say, 20% for ventures which are highly speculative.

3. *Target profit.*—This is the profit which will appear on the master budget and it is around this that all other budgets will be built. All the factors discussed in (d) above (adequate profit) will have to be taken into account.

The burden of taxation, future conditions and the policy being followed will have a considerable influence on the final figure.

An example of the calculation, which is very much simplified, is given below:

Calculation of target profit

The business concerned is a light engineering company with a specialised market in industrial instruments (automation). Trade is quite good and the present demand is expected to continue for a number of years provided prices are not increased too much. The directors are anxious to continue with a policy of steady expansion. Much of the machinery is old and needs replacing over the next ten years. A summarised version of the balance sheet is as follows:

Balance Sheet

Capital and liabilities	£	Fixed assets	£
Capital—Ordinary		Plant, machinery	480,000
Shares	500,000		
Reserves	18,000	Stocks	10,000
Creditors	2,000	Debtors	5,000
		Bank and cash	25,000
	£520,000		£520,000

Calculation

1. Minimum profit, say,		6%
2. Risk factor, say,		5%
3. Growth and dividend cover, say,		14%
	Target profit =	25%

The risk factor would be determined by considering the fact that the company is operating in a specialised market, but, by its progressive nature (automation), would be fairly competitive. Costs have to be controlled very severely in order to keep prices stable. This adds to the risk and calls for considerable managerial skill.

The fact that the machinery has to be replaced within the next ten years means that as much profit as possible should be retained in the business. This problem may be very acute if prices of replacement machines have risen considerably since the date of purchase of the old machines.

Viewed another way, the calculation may take the following form:

	%
Dividends	10
General reserve	5
Replacement reserve	10
	25

The figures used are purely hypothetical, many sweeping assumptions have been made, and many factors have been ignored altogether. Nevertheless, the principles underlying the example should have been made clear.

Calculation of the expected return (target profit)

Taking the gross capital employed concept as a basis the expected return on capital employed would be as shown below:

$$25\% \text{ of } £520,000 = £130,000$$

Measurement of top management effectiveness

In the preceding section was shown how to plan for a target profit. Whether this is done or not, there is still a need to measure the effectiveness of the overall policy, planning and execution of the business operations.

When a target profit is fixed, the return on capital employed can be calculated and a comparison made, thus arriving at a profit variance. If there is no target figure some assessment of what is reasonable will have to be made on the lines indicated above.

A formula for calculating the return on capital employed is:

$$\frac{\text{Profit}}{\text{Total assets}} \text{ expressed as a percentage.}$$

Some companies publish a graph to show the return on capital employed: an example is given in Fig. 48. It will be seen that the net capital employed is taken for the purpose of calculating the return.

REVALUATION ACCOUNTING

Revaluation accounting is concerned with two matters which are closely related:

1. Maintaining capital intact

The reference to capital is to *capital employed* as explained in the previous section. Top management has a duty to ensure that values of assets in terms of *purchasing power* and *earning capacity* are maintained intact in real terms. Fixed assets may be shown at £100,000 on a balance sheet, but to replace them might involve spending £200,000. This matter is discussed later in this section.

2. Calculating a realistic profit

In very simple terms the profit of a business may be expressed as follows:

$$\text{Sales revenue} - \text{Costs} = \text{Profit}$$

The big question centres around the word "costs." Basically a cost is a sacrifice, and the price paid is an expression of that sacrifice. For convenience no distinction is made between the sacrifice and the price: they are grouped together and called a "cost."

If a ton of material *A* is priced at £50 and a hundredweight of material *B* is priced £50, then the two materials for the quantities stated are assumed to cost the same. This is a fair assumption to make provided they are being considered at the same time. However, supposing the ton of material *A* was purchased two years ago for £50, and there has been a 100% increase in price since then, can it still be said that the hundredweight of material *B* at £50 is today equivalent to the ton of material *A*: surely the latter should now be priced at £100?

With orthodox accounting, material *A* would be charged at the original price paid, *i.e.* £50, and this is so despite the fact that a company would have to spend £100 to replace it.

A similar problem, though greatly magnified, occurs with fixed assets such as plant, machinery and buildings. A machine which cost £10,000 ten years ago may now cost £20,000; a building erected in 1938 for £10,000 may now cost £100,000 to replace. These are very real problems and it is necessary to consider how they should be dealt with. They involve policy decisions on two matters:

(*a*) Costs to be charged in the accounts and on jobs or products.
(*b*) Finding the necessary finance to replace the assets as they are consumed or are worn out.

The first refinement affects the calculation of profit. In a period of rising prices the charging of original costs (historical costing) leads to an overstatement of profit which may be paid out to shareholders, thereby reducing the real capital employed.

If the second matter is ignored a time will be reached when major items have to be replaced and no provision will have been made. This could lead to a very serious financial crisis which at the best would probably result in loss of earning power, and at the worst to liquidation of the company.

Some of the methods employed for dealing with replacement problems are as follows:

1. Revaluation of fixed assets periodically; *e.g.* every year or every few years.
2. Charging an extra amount for depreciation (*see below*) to cover replacement costs.
3. Pricing material requisitions at current replacement prices or standard costs so that realistic material costs are charged against jobs or products and in the profit and loss account.
4. Revalue fixed assets each year, calculate any loss in purchasing power of current assets when ascertaining profit, and charge depreciation on the basis of current replacement costs. This is *complete* revaluation accounting which is practised by a small minority of companies.

For revaluing fixed assets it is possible to use index numbers, or have a professional valuation made, or use insurance values, or take the market prices of similar assets.

As regards charging depreciation in the final accounts the reader is referred to pp. 307 to 310 (Fig. 46). An explanation of what is meant by depreciation is now given.

Depreciation

When fixed assets are purchased they are expected to be employed within the business for a number of years. Each year, through a combination of factors, each fixed asset generally falls in value; this natural reduction is known as "depreciation." It is brought about by wear and tear and the passing of time.

In order to cover the appropriate cost of the *proportion* of the fixed asset which has been used up, it is usual to include an amount in the overhead costs and in the financial accounts. *Depreciation*, therefore, has two meanings: the natural reduction in value, and the amount charged in costs to recover the cost of the fixed asset.

Generally the amount so recovered is based on the original cost of the asset, but as noticed earlier in this section, the replacement aspect of fixed assets should not be overlooked.

Depreciation may be calculated in a variety of ways, but basically they all have the same objective—the recovery of the total cost at the end of the serviceable life. An example should illustrate what is involved:

Machine tool cost	£5000
Residual value at the end of eight years	£1000
	£4000

From this it will be seen that £4000 has to be recovered over the eight years. This may be done on the basis of £500 per annum and it is known as the "straight line" or the "equal instalment" method. Alternatively, a percentage could be calculated which, when applied on the *reduced balance* of the cost, would write off the £4000 in eight years. For example, if 15% is chosen, £600 would be written off in the first year and £510 the second year. The 15% is used only for illustration and is not to be regarded as being the correct percentage for reducing the £4000 to nil at the end of eight years. This approach is known as the "reducing balance" method.

Many other variations exist, including one system being used for cost accounting and another for financial accounting. For details of these the reader is referred to a textbook on accounting.

What is important to notice is that the omission of depreciation from any calculation of profit or costs can have very serious consequences. Moreover, the charging of depreciation does have an important effect on the cash situation. How this is accomplished is shown by the example given below:

Example—Charging Depreciation

Company A

Balance Sheet year 1

	£		£
Share capital	2500	Fixed assets	2000
		Cash	500
	£2500		£2500

Profit and Loss Account
end of year 1

	£		£
Costs (excluding depreciation)	4000	Sales	5000
Profit	1000		
	£5000		£5000

If the company follows a policy of distributing all the profits to share-holders, the balance sheet at the beginning of the second year will be precisely the same as at the commencement of business. It will be noticed that no depreciation has been charged in the profit and loss account. If depreciation is charged the position would be as follows:

Profit and Loss Account
end of year 1

	£		£
Costs	4000	Sales	5000
Depreciation (say)	200		
Profit	800		
	£5000		£5000

The balance sheet at the beginning of the second year will now show a changed position.

Balance Sheet

	£		£	£
Share capital	2500	Fixed assets	2000	
		Less Depreciation	200	
				1800
		Cash		700
	£2500			£2500

In practice, such simplified conditions will not operate. Nevertheless, the principle will still apply even in the most complex organisation. Naturally the "cash released" does not usually stay in the form of cash. There will be stocks and debtors which will be converted into cash, then again back into stocks and debtors. So long as a business is in existence this process continues.

Advantages of concept—"return on capital employed"

The return on capital employed concept has many advantages over other methods of measuring efficiency. It is the only measure which can be said to show satisfactorily the benefits being obtained for the sacrifice involved, the latter being represented by capital invested. Some of the benefits and advantages of calculating the return on capital employed are summarised below:

1. Allows external comparisons to be made. The progress of one company or companies generally may be compared with the progress being made by the manager's own company.

Information on other companies may be obtained from newspapers, professional journals and published accounts. Earnings for different industries are published from time to time in *The Economist*. In addition, information may be obtained from the *Centre for Inter-firm Comparison*, an organisation which was set up by the British Institute of Management in association with the British Productivity Council. The ratio of operating profits to assets employed is taken by the Centre to reflect the earning power; it is a "primary ratio," which may be analysed into its constituent subsidiary ratios.

2. Internal comparisons can be made in respect of different divisions or departments of a business.

3. The relative profitability of different products may be illustrated by reference to the capital which is employed to produce and sell each product.

This advantage may not always be available to a business, for the simple reason that the assets employed produce and sell a large variety of products and there is no way of showing in accurate terms what value of the capital or what figure of profit relates to specific products. In such circumstances *estimated* figures of capital employed and profit for each product may be used to give a guide to the relative profitability.

4. The relative profitability of future courses of action may be obtained. Expansion of plant, introduction of a new product or other development, may be assessed in terms of profit through the estimated return on estimated capital to be employed.

5. When the return on capital employed is calculated any changes in circumstances, since the previous return was calculated, may be taken into consideration without difficulty. Increases in assets

employed and even changes in the value of money can be reflected in the calculations.

6. The return on capital employed can become an integral part of the budgetary control system. Significant percentages and ratios may be shown in the master budget. Subsequently any profit variances may be calculated so that management is able to follow progress being made and, if necessary, to take corrective action, such as changing the use to which capital is to be put.

7. If management ensures that an adequate return on capital is earned then many indirect benefits should accrue to the business concerned. Some of these are listed below:

(a) Regular and satisfactory dividends to shareholders.

(b) Adequate reserves allowing progress to be made, the company being able to grow at a rate which may be regarded as healthy.

(c) Because of (a) and (b) there may be no need to seek outside funds. If the latter have to be sought then, because of the financial standing of the company, there should be no difficulty in obtaining them.

(d) The business should be able to ward off any unexpected competition or other adversities without great difficulty.

(e) Because of the confidence and security which must inevitably arise from earning adequate profits the business will tend to have a good credit rating and to attract the best type of workers and management.

There is no doubt that a keen watchfulness, to ensure that all divisions of a company earn an adequate return, is likely to be of great value to any business. Efficiency will also be watched; every function which affects profit-earning will be under constant scrutiny. Accordingly, assets are used in the most effective way possible.

The next section deals with the acquisition of fixed assets which are regarded as a form of investment. Like any other investment they should yield an adequate return on the funds locked up.

CAPITAL EXPENDITURE DECISIONS

In accounting terminology any money spent on fixed assets is known as "capital expenditure." The distinguishing feature is the expectation that the assets purchased will be used for producing, selling or other functions, over a period exceeding one year. Thus, for example, the cost of a drilling machine to be used in a machine shop would be regarded as capital expenditure.

Selection of the most appropriate machine or other fixed assets is an extremely important matter, and is one requiring considerable knowledge as well as the exercise of judgment. The basic knowledge required can be broken down into:

1. Technical

Type of machine required for job, alternative machines available, their operating ability, reliability, and the feasibility of introducing the chosen machine into the existing plant, are all examples of the technical knowledge required. The list could be extended to cover many other aspects.

2. Financial

The *economics* of purchasing the machines which are best suited for the job would come under this heading. There are a number of aspects:

(a) Initial cost and useful life.
(b) Installation costs.
(c) Running costs.
(d) Expected revenue or expected reduction in costs.
(e) Profit expected.
(f) Cash available.

Each machine would be considered and the one likely to give (i) the highest rate of return and (ii) the most advantageous cash position, would be the one selected.

When considering the cash position it will be necessary to study the cash forecast and budget. The fact that cash will be received, as well as being paid, should not be overlooked. Ideally the asset to be purchased should enable cash to be received when there is likely to be a shortage as shown by the cash forecasts: similarly, payments should be planned for when cash is available. These aims are not easy to achieve, but should be attempted as part of the long-term planning and/or budgetary control system.

The methods used for assessing the profitability of capital projects have received a good deal of attention in recent years both in textbooks and in accountancy journals. Unfortunately, there appears to be no very strong evidence in Britain that the most suitable methods are used. Indeed, the intuitive approach to problems seems to be very common in spite of obvious drawbacks.

Since a man's judgment and opinions are influenced to a great extent by the information in his possession, it follows that the more facts that are available on a particular project the more accurate is likely to be the decision made, provided that there are not so many facts that there is confusion. Put another way, a manager's decision is likely to be only as good as the information he has available for comparing alternative courses of action. Intuition and judgment cannot be replaced by the collection of facts, but there is no doubt that the decision-making mechanism is likely to be strengthened materially by the systematic collection and analysis of relevant data.

Below are listed the principal methods used for assessing the profitability of each capital expenditure project. Clearly, not all projects may be capable of being assessed in terms of profitability; for example, pure research and welfare projects may not have to be justified in this way. The planning and laying out of beautiful gardens or playing fields in the grounds of a factory or works may also be difficult to justify in terms of profit. Many of these general, "unessential" projects may, of course, lead to better labour relations and, therefore, to an improvement in profit earning. However, actually showing that such projects *are* profitable would be extremely difficult and probably impossible.

Even on the capital expenditure projects which are expected to improve the volume of output or result in some other tangible benefit, not one of the methods explained below can give absolute accuracy. Each has its own peculiar advantages and disadvantages. The one likely to give the best results should be the one selected. Study of the theoretical principles will assist in selecting the best method. Practical experience will show what modifications or adjustments are necessary in order to employ the method to meet the needs of the particular business.

METHODS EMPLOYED

The principal methods employed for ascertaining the profitability of each project are as follows:

1. Pay-back method.
2. Return on investment method.
3. Present-value return on investment method.
4. Return on total capital employed.

This method approaches the problem by ensuring that the total capital employed earns an adequate return. Additional assets purchased should increase, or at least keep constant, the percentage rate of return on total capital employed.

5. Minimum total cost or unit cost.

All these methods can be used for comparing alternative investments. For all methods, but especially those using present-value techniques, it is better to use the expected cash flow (*i.e.* cash to be received or paid) rather than profit or gain computed by conventional accounting. The first three methods are explained in detail below.

1. Pay-back method

The "pay-back method" is concerned with equating the revenue and costs relating to a capital expenditure project over a period of time. Put another way the method attempts to determine the number of years in which the investment is expected to pay for itself. If a machine is to cost £5000 and extra revenue is expected to amount to £1000 the first year, £2000 the second year, and £2000 in the third year then the pay-back period is three years.

If a machine can be treated in isolation from other machines then the yearly sales value of the products from the machine *less* any running and maintenance costs shows the annual profit. A number of years are taken to calculate the pay-back period.

In practice a fixed asset cannot usually be treated as a separate entity. The introduction of a new machine often introduces problems. It may displace an older machine. There may have to be a rearrangement of duties between workers. Quite likely some costs may be reduced. Therefore, both the costs incurred and the costs saved will have to be taken into account.

When comparing alternative statements the one which pays for itself first is the one selected.

Advantages and limitations.—The pay-back method is simple to understand and operate. Furthermore, it shows how quickly the invest-ment will be recovered. This can be very important for a company short of cash. Normally, only investments with a short pay-back period are considered. No doubt the convention which lays down this rule arises from the fact that there is great difficulty in forecasting the sales, costs and serviceable life of a fixed asset for any period in excess of, say, five years. In an industry which is experiencing rapid technological development the limited pay-back period offers some protection from the danger of obsolescence. There is a quick recovery of the cash invested.

Although the method has many followers it also has many critics. Some accountants have rightly pointed out that the true profitability of investments cannot be determined merely by considering the pay-back period. Indeed, in that period only the recovery of costs is considered. The profit comes after all costs have been recovered and not before. Therefore, much better results would be obtained by considering the full serviceable life of each asset: only then can the total, expected profit be ascertained. A further possible disadvantage is the fact that limiting the investments to those with a short pay-back period (*e.g.* up to five years) may mean overlooking many profitable investments. A machine may have a serviceable life of twenty years and over that life may be quite profitable. However, if the pay-back period extends beyond that laid down by policy this means automatic exclusion from being con-sidered. A serious limitation is the ignoring of the time factor. Sums of money received at different times in the *future* have to be discounted to *present* value. Otherwise no true comparison of different investments can be made. The "present-value return method," discussed below, overcomes this obvious weakness of the pay-back method. A further criticism sometimes advanced against the pay-back method is that too much importance is attached to the quick recovery of cash. Investment in fixed assets must necessarily be a lengthy process. The artificial attempt to "shorten the period" may be useful when forecasting cash flows, but it should be remembered that the chief concern is with profitability. Accordingly, this should be the factor to determine the most suitable method.

A practical illustration of the method is shown later in this chapter.

2. Return on investment method

This method considers the rate of return likely to be obtained from the investment. When comparing alternative courses of action the investment which shows the highest return is the one normally selected.

The rate of return may be expressed as a *percentage* of the average amount of the investment. A simple method of obtaining the "average amount" is to divide the total investment by two. Thus, if the proposed investment is £10,000, then the average investment over the entire life, considering depreciation, is taken to be £5000. This assumes that the amount recovered in the form of depreciation will be used to purchase materials or other supplies or alternatively will be invested internally or externally, outside the business. Not all accountants agree with the view that half the investment should be taken for measuring the expected rate of return. When the investment is made the total amount has to be spent; this is the total sacrifice to be made. Accordingly, it can be argued that the total investment involved should be the amount taken.

Care has to be taken when considering "rate of return," to make sure that the precise rate being calculated is understood. The term may refer to total return obtained; *e.g.* in the illustration given below Machine X is shown to result in a £1 return for each £1 invested. Alternatively, "rate of return" may refer to "net return"; *i.e.* the net *profit* actually obtained. For Machine X in the example given there is no net return: each £1 results in £1 with no surplus for the purpose of comparison. Which definition is used does not really matter. However, it is very important to understand which definition *is* being used. Otherwise *actual* profitability will not be understood.

Other measures are the amount obtained per pound sterling invested and the *average* amount obtained each year per pound sterling invested. The former method involves dividing the total profit expected by the total investment. The latter—the average yearly calculation—involves finding the average annual profit and then dividing that by the total investment. A simple illustration is shown below.

Illustration

A company is considering the purchase of a new machine. There are two machines which will do the work, the details of which are as follows:

	Year	Machine X	Machine Y
Capital cost		£20,000	£24,000
Earnings	1	£10,000	£8,000
(or net cash flow)	2	£10,000	£8,000
	3	Nil	£20,000

Calculate the rate of return (*a*) per £1 invested and (*b*) per £1 invested on an average annual basis.

Suggested approach

(*a*) *Per £1 invested*

	Machine X	Machine Y
Earnings	£20,000	£36,000
Investment	£20,000	£24,000
Rate of return per £1 invested	£1	£1·5

(*b*) *Per £1 on annual basis*

	Machine X	Machine Y
Earnings	£20,000	£36,000
Average annual profit	£10,000	£12,000
Investment	£20,000	£24,000
Rate of return	£0·5	£0·5

From the examples given it will be evident that there are many weaknesses in both methods of expressing the rate of return per pound sterling. The straightforward rate per pound invested shows the apparent superiority of Machine *Y* and this result would have been shown even if the full £36,000 had been forthcoming in the third or even later years. In other words, the timing of the receipts is ignored—money to be received earlier is more valuable, yet the method ignores this fact completely. The second rate of return (the average method) ranks both machines as being equal, yet it is quite clear they are not equal. A much better result would have been obtained if the earning periods had been the same; *i.e.* both three years. This could be overcome to some extent by dividing the £20,000 for Machine *X* by 3 instead of 2. This would then give an average annual profit of £6666⅔ and a rate of return of £0·33 per annum. Even when this modified procedure is followed the timing of the receipts is not taken into account and for this reason the method is not to be recommended.

The percentage rate of return is probably the most satisfactory method, but even this has the definite weakness of ignoring the fact that receipts occur at different time intervals. If the earnings from the different investments do accrue at the same time then obviously this method can be used. If the timings are different then the present-value return method is much better. This is covered in the next section.

A further problem which may arise is connected with calculating a reasonable rate of return on investments. Some companies stipulate a minimum rate. Investments which do not show this rate are automatically excluded from consideration. The general procedures and pertinent considerations relating to determination of a reasonable rate of interest are most relevant to the profitable employment of capital, a topic which was considered earlier.

3. Present-value return on investment method

A person faced with the choice of having £100 now or in one year's time would normally elect to have it now. If he was offered £100 now, but £110 in a year then he may be tempted to wait for the £110, for quite clearly, unless the risk involved in waiting is very great, the £100 he is foregoing is going to earn him 10% which is quite a reasonable return.

This simple example should illustrate the present value concept of money. The £100 due in one year is not worth as much as £100 *now*. In fact if 10% is taken to be a normal rate of return for a particular type of investment the £100 due in one year is at present worth only £90·91. If it is necessary to wait two years for the £100, then taking compound interest at 10%, the present value is £82·64.

When considering different investments, with earning patterns which are not the same, it should be clear that only by discounting the earnings to present values can any valid comparisons be made. The timing of the receipts is thus taken into consideration. Similarly, when costs are incurred at different intervals they too can be converted into present values.

The object of all the methods being described is to arrive at the most profitable investment. The present-value return method is no exception. When this method is used there are two ways of tackling the problem of calculating profitability. These may be summarised as follows:

(a) Trial and error yield method.
(b) Net gain method.

In both cases the cost of the investment and the expected receipts have to be considered. As already mentioned earlier in the chapter, the expected *cash* payments and receipts, *not* the costs incurred and sales values as shown by the accounts, should be the figures taken. Clearly if a sale is expected to be made in one year, but is not expected to be paid for until the next, then it cannot be said that cash is to be received in the first year. The same applies to materials and services purchased. Fortunately in many businesses the regularity in each year of sales, stocks, and costs is such that costs and receipts tend to approximate to cash flows. When wide variations do occur so that the cash flows are different then adjustments of sales and costs will be necessary.

A problem which must inevitably arise is what points of time are to be used for assessing the present values. Cash from sales flows throughout a year. Similarly the costs incurred are paid for throughout a particular year. Therefore the question which must be answered is which date (or dates) can be taken for calculating present values. If six-monthly intervals are taken then a different result would be obtained from when yearly intervals were taken. Again, fortunately, a simplified approach can be taken, the cash being assumed to be received at the end of each year. The net cash flow is, therefore, sales *minus* costs bearing in mind the fact that the sales and costs should relate to cash to be received and to be paid. Adjustments may also have to be made to cover the effects of taxation, interest and any special working capital changes brought about by the investment.

The functions of the two different ways is described below:

(a) *Trial and error yield method.*—As the name suggests the object is to find the expected yield from the investment. This procedure involves a number of stages which may be summarised as follows:

1. List the annual sales and costs other than depreciation and, deducting the latter from the former, obtain the net cash flow.

2. Obtain the capital cost. Often this will already be at present value because the cash is spent *now*.

3. Calculate the present value of the net cash flow by using an appropriate rate of interest. This rate is found by trial and error from present-value tables. The object is to make the cash flow equal to the capital cost.

4. Carry out this procedure for each project being considered and then rank the projects in order of preference.

A simplified example now follows.

Example: trial and error yield method

A company is considering the purchase of a machine. The following data are available for two suitable machines.

	Machine X	Machine Y
Capital cost	£20,000	£24,000
Net cash flow: Year 1	£10,000	£8,000
2	£10,000	£8,000
3	Nil	£20,000

You are required to calculate the yield for each machine.

Suggested approach

	Machine X			Machine Y		
	Cash Flow	Conversion Factor	Present Value of Cash	Cash Flow	Conversion Factor	Present Value
Net cash flow	£	£	£	£	£	£
Year 1	10,000			8,000	0·8333	6,666
2	10,000	No differ-		8,000	0·6944	5,555
3	—	ence between cash flow and capital cost		20,000	0·5787	11,574
Capital cost	20,000			24,000		23,795
	Rate of return = 0% (There is actually a net loss)			Rate of return = Approximately 20%		

This method shows quite clearly that Machine Y is a much better investment than X. The rate of return method (the second method discussed) purported to show that Machine X investment would result in a definite return. In actual fact the investment cost is only just covered and when the receipts are discounted to present values (using *any* reasonable rate of interest) a loss is incurred.

For Machine X there is no need to convert the cash flow to present value because it is quite obvious that the former is smaller than the latter.

The rate of interest of 20% for Machine Y is found by referring to interest tables which are available in a comprehensive book on management accountancy. At this stage the trial and error procedure has to be adopted. A good plan is to use the conversion factor for each year at stages of 10%. The approximate point on the scale of interest rates can be located quickly and then the actual rate can be found.

When a number of alternatives are available the same procedure is followed. This will allow a table showing the relative profitability of all projects. Generally speaking the investment with the highest return is the one selected.

(*b*) *Net gain method.*—The net gain method attempts to arrive at the difference between the present value of receipts and payments. As with the previous method the *cash* flows should be taken.

One of the difficulties of this method is the selection of an appropriate rate of interest. One rate will give different results from another. The principal object should be to assess a return which reflects what can be expected from putting the money in alternative investments. This is a matter which is discussed later.

Example: net gain method

Taking the problem shown in the previous section the suggested approach is as shown below.

Net gain schedule

	Machine X £	Machine Y £
Capital cost (present value equals original cost)	20,000	24,000
Cash flow (present value converted by using 10% discount)	17,355	28,910
	£2,645 (loss)	£4,910 (gain)

Machine Y is clearly the more profitable investment. In fact, Machine X incurs a loss.

Expressing the return as a percentage

The return on the investment may be expressed as a percentage of the amount invested by the following formula:

$$\frac{\text{Average annual net profit*} \times 100}{\text{Average investment†}}$$

* Or net cash flow.　　　　† Or total investment.

This may be used with the present-value methods or the ordinary rate on investment methods which do not convert cash flow (receipts) to present values. Obviously the concern is with an average percentage which though suffering from the limitations of all averages should give a very good guide to profitability.

The fact that the average investment is obtained by dividing the total investment by two has already been noted.

Illustration of the principle

Taking the figures for Machine Y used in the previous example the percentage rate of return (net profit) is as follows:

Unadjusted figures: $\dfrac{£4,000}{£12,000} \times \dfrac{100}{1} = 33\%$ (approx.)

Figure adjusted to Present Values: $\dfrac{£3,005}{£12,000} \times \dfrac{100}{1} = 25\%$ (approx.)
(10% discount)

The average investment is the original cost of £24,000 divided by two, a principle already explained. The average net profit is found by dividing total net profit by three (the life of the machine). The simplest way is to take the £4000 and convert to the present value, assuming that the amount accrues at the end of the third year, but this method is rather artificial.

Pros and cons of present value. There is no doubt that the present-value concept has much to offer when attempting to assess profitability. Due recognition is given to risk and uncertainty and their corollary, the fact that money due in the future is not worth its face value in the present. In other words the timing of the expected receipts is given due recognition in the calculations.

In practice the methods explained would be broken down into standardised routines. For the present-value methods, tables can be employed so that the appropriate rates can be found without difficulty.

Any expenditure which is written off within the year in which it is incurred is known as *revenue expenditure* and is not generally subjected to these methods as described above (*see* Overhead Costs, p. 312).

EXAMINATION QUESTIONS

Also includes Questions on Chapter XXI.

1. Outline a cost reduction scheme concerned with the expense of sales representation. State what items need to be examined and the action necessary to effect cost reduction in this sphere.

2. A large order is received from a desirable customer by your sales department for one of your standard products to be delivered by a specified date. Your order book is, up to the time of delivery required for this order, already 90% filled, and this order, if accepted, would increase the load by one half during its period of manufacture. There is no indication that so large an order will be repeated.

Discuss the advisability of accepting the order and the means by which it could be fulfilled on the one hand, and of refusing it on the other hand, apart altogether from its effect upon the earnings of the business.

3. The cost of a job is presented to management in the following form:

	£	£
Direct materials		0·60
Direct wages—		
Department A	0·20	
Department B	0·30	
Department C	0·10	
		0·60
Factory overheads—		
Department A	0·25	
Department B	0·45	
Department C	0·10	
		0·80
Factory cost		£2·00
Administration, selling and distribution expenses ...		£0·40
Total cost		£2·40

The sales manager states that the highest price he can obtain for this job is £2·25, but that large orders can be obtained at this price.

Criticise the layout of the job cost, and, using any suitable additional figures, indicate how you would present the cost.

4. Write a short essay on the underlying principles of employee remuneration and incentives as they affect the employer, the employee and the national economy.

5. How does budgetary control facilitate the delegation of authority and yet act as an instrument of co-ordination?

6. In a certain business it has been the custom to absorb administration costs as a percentage of production costs. A customer buys otherwise identical products in different materials, one cheap, one expensive, and complains about the difference in the prices quoted, which he contends should amount to the difference in material price only. Give fully your views on the problem.

7. An expanding business, making modest profits, finds its bank overdraft to be increasing. The managing director states that this indicates a need for the introduction of further capital, but a study of the figures indicates to you that with more efficient management, ample capital actually exists in the business. Using suitable figures, prepare a report to the managing director, indicating how the necessary capital can be found within the business.

8. "Standard costing is always accompanied by a system of budgeting, but budgetary control may be operated in businesses where standard costing would be impracticable."

Discuss this statement, and indicate the method and use of budgetary control systems in the type of business mentioned in the latter part of the quotation.

9. Tabulate a profit and loss statement using the following income and expenditure groupings:

Sales: Material Cost: Wages Cost: Direct Expense:

Other Production Costs: Administration Costs.

Each of these six items may show variances. Specify what these variances may be in each case by inserting their names, with suitable figures for items and variances, in your tabulation. The tabulation should be in columnar form, *Actual* being compared with *Standard*, and variances being shown, for the current monthly period and for the total of five periods to date. Show final totals and profit.

10. It has been said that marginal costs are used primarily in guiding decisions yet to be made. Choose two examples, and tabulate specimen figures with details for each to illustrate the statement quoted.

11. The following is a summary of the trading accounts of a manufacturing company for the past three years:

	Year 1 £	Year 2 £	Year 3 £
Sales	25,000	24,000	20,000
Less cost of goods sold:			
Materials	8,000	7,700	6,100
Direct wages	7,000	6,700	5,200
Production overhead	5,450	5,400	5,250
Total production costs	20,450	19,800	16,550
Decrease in stocks of finished goods ...	150	50	50
Cost of goods sold	20,600	19,850	16,600
Gross profit	4,400	4,150	3,400
Selling and administrative costs	3,500	3,450	3,250
Net profit	900	700	150

In year 1 the factory operated at 80% of capacity, in year 2 at 75% of capacity, and in year 3 at 60% of capacity. Of the production overhead, £4500 was fixed, and of the selling and administrative costs, £2500 was fixed. Re-draft the above figures in order to bring out clearly the effect of diminishing output and diminishing volume of sales on the net profit.

12. A small jobbing foundry quotes for pattern equipment and castings on the basis of the following:

Pattern cost	£75.
Metal cost	£3·27 per cwt.
Labour cost	£0·75 per casting.
Variable overhead	£0·80 per casting.

Each casting weighs 84 lb and the price quoted is £7 per casting, to include the cost of pattern equipment.

From the foregoing information, prepare a break-even chart and determine from it at what sales level contribution to fixed overhead will begin.

13. Describe the stages in the creation of a sales budget for a company selling on a national basis through representatives.

State what analysis you consider is necessary in the build-up of a budget of sales expenses for such a company.

14. What procedure would you introduce to control the purchase of replacement and additional capital equipment?

CHAPTER XXIII

STATISTICAL METHOD

As industrial technology advances, new techniques are devised to cope with the increasing complexity of systems and controls. Many of these techniques are based on mathematical statistical concepts. New techniques bring new technicians who, in turn, produce more and more data, most of which are designed to assist the production manager and others in their task of making decisions.

In order that the manager may make full use of this information (and have the ability to discuss the results with the "experts" in their own language) it is becoming increasingly important that he has an appreciation and working knowledge of statistical method and the terms used in statistics. He should be able to read data presented in graphical form; understand how control lines on the quality control chart are adjusted to give the required level of control; and when the operational research team talk in terms of probability he should be able to follow the trend of the argument.

This chapter has been included to give an appreciation of the scope and uses of statistics in the field of industrial administration. In a work of this nature it is not possible to give more than a superficial coverage of the subject, but the chapter will direct the attention of the reader to the various aspects of statistics and serve as a basis on which he can build from further reading.

Statistics (singular noun), otherwise known as statistical method, makes use of statistics (plural) or data. Statistics may be descriptive (that is data presented as they stand, for information purposes) or mathematical. Statistical method performs certain operations on the data to enable conclusions to be drawn. These conclusions will usually include confidence limits which indicate the probability that the conclusions drawn are the correct ones.

Statistical method is an important management aid and some of the areas in which this tool is used are given below:

1. Business charts and graphs.—This is probably the most common area of the use of statistical method.

2. Statistical quality control.—The theory of probability is used in designing control charts and acceptance sampling schemes.

3. Designed experiments.—Rather than make haphazard tests, experiments should be conducted in a systematic way and the results similarly analysed.

4. Time series.—Time series, from which predictions such as sales

o   401

trends may be made, are most important for the future planning of production.

5. *Operational research.*—Operational research has already been discussed in a previous chapter. Again, probability plays its part in linear programming and stock control problems.

The above applications, with the exception of operational research, will be described in this chapter.

CHARTS AND GRAPHS

Charts and graphs offer a pictorial way of presenting data. A mass of data is meaningless until the details have been sorted out, and by that time the overall picture has been lost. When confronted with a large volume of information it is first necessary to see the general pattern at a glance. The chart or graph shows immediately the overall picture, and if more detailed information is required, reference may be made to the axes while still retaining the whole pattern.

Charts and graphs may be grouped under four headings:

1. *Pictorial charts*, such as pie charts and pictograms.
2. *Block charts*, such as bar charts and Gantt charts.
3. *Graphs*, including line graphs, rate of change graphs and cumulative percentage frequency curves.
4. *Distribution graphs*, plotted with the frequency of occurrence of the data on the vertical axis.

Although four main divisions are given, there is often no clear-cut boundary between any two.

PICTORIAL CHARTS

Pictorial charts are useful when presenting data of a technical nature to managers or to laymen or others not conversant with the particular data to be presented.

Pictograms (or ideographs) show the information in picture form by representing each fixed group of units by a small symbol. As long as the symbols are all the same size and only the number of symbols indicates the number of items no confusion should arise, but when, as in Fig. 65, size is used as a comparison, care must be taken to avoid misrepresentation. The oil drum in the figure is twice the height but *eight* times the volume. In three-dimensional figures the eye tends to see and compare the volumes rather than the heights. The same applies to areas.

When information is given as the breakdown of a total into its component parts, the *pie chart* can be used (Fig. 66). This chart shows the components as percentage "slices" of the whole pie and indicates changes in proportions but not in absolute totals. It is a very effective form of presentation, when the information concerns one period of

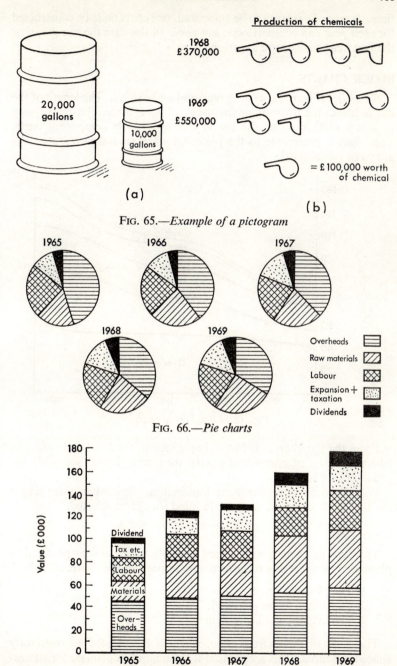

Production of chemicals

1968
£370,000

1969
£550,000

= £100,000 worth
of chemical

(a)

(b)

FIG. 65.—*Example of a pictogram*

1965   1966   1967

1968   1969

Overheads
Raw materials
Labour
Expansion +
taxation
Dividends

FIG. 66.—*Pie charts*

Value (£000)

Dividend
Tax etc.
Labour
Materials
Over-
heads

1965   1966   1967   1968   1969

FIG. 67.—*Bar chart* (compound)

time. If several years are to be compared, one chart must be constructed for each year and comparison is not easy. In this case the *line* graph or the band curve chart are superior.

BLOCK CHARTS

Bar charts (Fig. 67) are easily read and understood. The length of the bar indicates the quantity or frequency of occurrence. Bar charts may be compound, in which the bar is split up into its component parts. This chart is preferable to the pie chart when several years' statistics are to be represented.

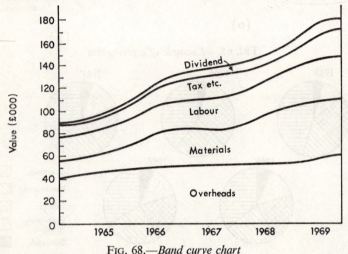

FIG. 68.—*Band curve chart*

From the bar chart it is but a simple step to the *band curve chart* in which the bars of compound charts are merely joined smoothly together (Fig. 68).

Figures 66–68 show the same information depicted in three ways; the best method for the purpose in mind should be selected.

Gantt charts

This type of chart is widely used in applications such as production planning and three sets of information appear on the chart:

1. The planned figure.
2. The actual figure achieved.
3. The actual cumulative figure.

The basis of the chart is time, which is represented by constantly spaced distances. This means that if the quantities planned for successive periods vary, then they must be plotted to different scales in order to be accommodated in the space provided. The quantity planned for the period is also represented by the distance period on the chart.

For example, if the periods are weekly, and each week occupies one inch on the chart, then planned output of 1200 will occupy one inch; and a planned output of 1600 the following week will also occupy one inch. The actual output is plotted within its period and, if it exceeds the planned amount, the excess is plotted on another line within the same period.

Period	Week 1	Week 2	Week 3	Week 4	Week 5	Week 6	Week 7
Planned / Actual	1200-1550	1600-1000	2000-1600	2000-2000	2000-2300	1600-2300	1400
Weekly Actual							
Cumulative		WK 1 WK 2	WK 3	WK 4	WK 5		WK 6

FIG. 69.—*Gantt chart*

The cumulative, however, *can* overlap into the next period, but upon entry into another area it must be plotted to the scale of that area. Figure 69 illustrates this chart. The figures for week 1 show an excess of output: the cumulative bar thus extends into week 2, and the amount of this extension is calculated as follows. The output is 1550 against 1200 planned. Out of the 1550 can be taken 1200 to complete the week's programme, leaving a balance of 350 as a start to the following week's programme. The planned amount for *this* week (week 2) is 1600 and 350 units is about 22% of 1600. The cumulative bar is therefore carried on into week 2's area to cover 22% of the distance. Week 2 required only $1600 - 350 = 1250$ units to complete its total requirement. If only 1000 units are produced, this, together with the 350 brought forward from week 1, represents 1350/1600ths of the planned output. Thus the cumulative moves forward 1350/1600ths or 84% of the way across the second week's space. The third week therefore starts off with a 250 unit deficiency. Thus, when the third week's figures are available, 250 must be deducted to make up the deficiency before the balance is plotted in week 3's cumulative area.

Gantt charts are simple to use and can incorporate elastic strings for the bars. Charts of this type can be purchased commercially.

GRAPHS

The graph is a more accurate way of presenting data than the pictorial chart. To the layman with only a passing interest in the information it is not as appealing or eye-catching as its pictorial counterpart.

The most common type is the *line graph* which is plotted against two axes, thus allowing two variables. There is the independent variable which is the chosen base, such as time in years, heights of people, etc., and the dependent variable which is the data that are dependent on the other chosen variable. For example, with a given set of height statistics, the number of people of a certain height depends on the particular height we choose. The independent variable is usually plotted on the *x* axis.

On one chart field several graphs may be plotted, superimposed for comparison purposes. This method may produce a confused graph which is hard to follow. The various lines can be in different colours, but the band curve chart in which the lines can never cross may be preferred.

These simple graphs have their limitations and in certain applications one of the specialist graphs may be required.

Rate of change graph

The majority of graphs in normal use indicate absolute changes—equal vertical increments representing equal amounts. In some cases it is necessary to make relative comparisons on a percentage basis. Thus if the departmental manager's profit rises from £800 in June to £880 in July, how does this compare with the total factory profit of £12,000 and £13,200 for the same months? The normal graph would show these as £80 increase and £1200 increase respectively. This graph would not indicate that in fact they had both risen by 10%.

To divide out the ratio $\frac{880}{800}$ the logs are subtracted:

Thus $$\log \frac{880}{800} = 2 \cdot 9445 - 2 \cdot 9031 = 0 \cdot 0414.$$

Similarly $$\log \frac{13200}{12000} = 4 \cdot 1206 - 4 \cdot 0792 = 0 \cdot 0414.$$

Therefore if the figures be plotted against a log scale on the *y* axis, the gradients will be equal. Graphs drawn on paper ruled in this way are called semi-log graphs, or rate of change graphs. Equal gradients anywhere on the graph indicate equal *rates* of change, not equal absolute changes.

Figure 70 illustrates the difference: Fig. 70 *a* shows the total sales compared with the sales of the western area, plotted on linear paper. It would appear that this area is lagging behind in its upward trend. Figure 70 *b* proves that in fact this area's sales are increasing at a faster rate than the total (or average),

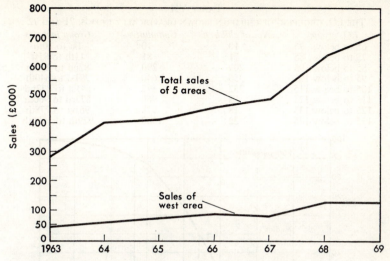

FIG. 70 *a.—Comparison of sales plotted to a linear scale*

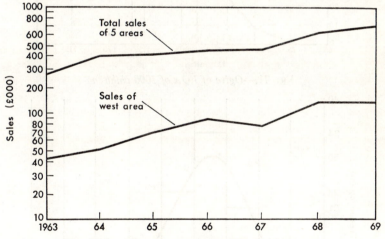

FIG. 70 *b.—The same comparison on semi-log paper*

The cumulative percentage frequency curve

This graph is illustrated in Fig. 71 and is sometimes called an ogive (pronounced *oh-jive*). The curve is useful in finding the median, quartiles, percentiles and deciles by graphical means. With grouped distributions the assumption is made that the items are evenly distributed within the groups so the points on the "curve" are joined by straight lines. The example shows the percentage of people below the respective I.Q.s plotted from Table VII.

TABLE VII

THE I.Q. GROUPING OF CHILDREN SHOWN GRAPHICALLY IN FIGS. 71 AND 72

I.Q. group	No. of children	Cumulative	Group includes
65 to below 75	10	10	1st to 10th
75 to below 85	71	81	11th to 81st
85 to below 95	209	290	82nd to 290th
95 to below 105	350	640	291st to 640th
105 to below 115	232	872	641st to 872nd
115 to below 125	88	960	873rd to 960th
125 to below 135	18	978	961st to 978th
135 to below 145	22	1000	979th to 1000th

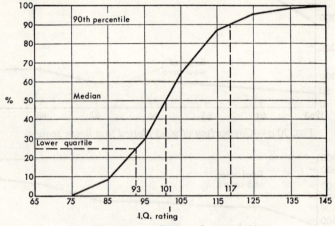

FIG. 71.—*Ogive of I.Q.s of 1000 children*

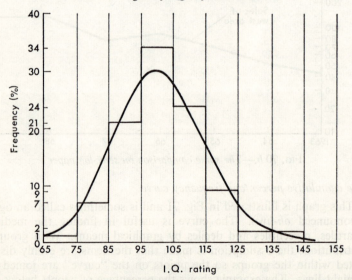

FIG. 72.—*A "normal" distribution (Histogram of the data from Table VII superimposed for comparison)*

Z chart

The Z chart is really a compound graph of three components on the same chart field. If the three graphs are to the same scale on the y axis the lines form a "Z."

The graphs forming the Z chart are plotted from readings of "current" or periodic (weekly, monthly, etc.) figures, the cumulative values of these figures, usually annually, and the moving annual total. This total is the sum of the preceding twelve months' values. Thus each moving annual total (M.A.T.) consists of the sum of twelve readings, and the line "moves" with these totals. The current total is often plotted on a different scale to emphasise the fluctuations.

In the example (Fig. 73) it will be seen that although the scales in the

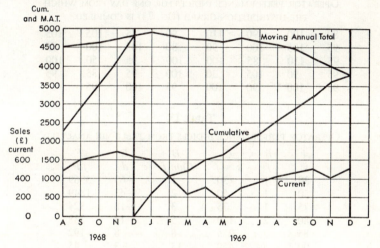

Fig. 73.—"Z" chart of sales

period August–December were higher than those during the preceding nine months the M.A.T. is still falling. This is due to the exceptionally high sales during the preceding September–December period. Thus the M.A.T. indicates an overall decrease in sales.

DISTRIBUTION GRAPHS

Consider the figures in Table VIII. Presented to a manager in this way they are just a forest of readings and one cannot see the wood for the trees. By constructing a distribution graph many of the parameters can be seen by inspection. The most usual forms of distribution graph are histograms and frequency curves. Figure 72 shows the figures from Table VII (the I.Q. grouping of children) in the form of a histogram as well as a frequency curve; Fig. 74 shows the figures from Tables VIII and IX as a distribution curve.

Some of the parameters immediately apparent are the *spread* of the figures, and the mode. These and others are discussed below.

Measures associated with distributions

Average or mean.—The average can be given in two ways:

(a) simple average in which each item is counted once only, *i.e.* is of equal significance with every other item, or
(b) weighted average in which each item is assigned a weight factor proportional to its importance in the group of items.

TABLE VIII

OPERATOR PERFORMANCE INDICES FOR ONE DAY FROM WHICH
THE DISTRIBUTION GRAPH (FIG. 74) IS COMPILED

80	100	90	110	90	85	105	105
95	105	100	90	80	105	100	75
95	110	85	100	100	95	50	100
95	90	105	30	100	95	85	95
95	100	90	100	95	100	95	

TABLE IX

OPERATOR PERFORMANCE INDICES FROM TABLE VIII ANALYSED

A	B	C	D	E	F
s	f	s × f	Cum.f.	d	fd²
30	1	30	1	−63	3969
50	1	50	2	−43	1849
75	1	75	3	−18	324
80	2	160	5	−13	338
85	3	255	8	−8	192
90	5	450	13	−3	45
95	9	855	22	+2	36
100	10	1000	32	+7	490
105	5	525	37	+12	720
110	2	220	39	+17	578
	39	3620			$\Sigma fd^2 = 8541$

KEY

s = speeds or performance indices
f = frequency of occurrence
Cum.f. = Cumulative frequency
d = deviations of s from the true mean

Table IX relates to the performance indices of a group of operators over one day, the figures being quoted to the nearest five, and ranging from 30 to 110. The simple average of this list is 820 ÷ 10 = 82·0, but it is the weighted average which must be used in this case because some of the speeds occur more often than others. The frequency of occurrence may be used as the weight factor. From Table IX the total of the performance speeds (column *C*) is 3620 and there are 39 readings. Thus the average is $3620 \div 39 = 92 \cdot 8$, or 93 approximately. The weighted average is obviously the same as the simple average of all 39 readings.

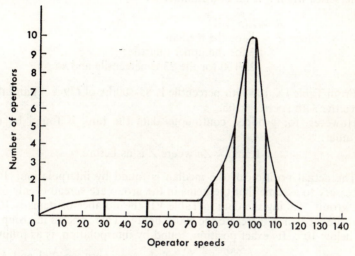

FIG. 74.—*Distribution from data in Table IX*

Median.—The median is the middle figure of data ranked in order of magnitude. If the variables are grouped (*e.g.* I.Q.s of children; 65 to below 75, 75 to below 85, etc., as in Table VII) the group in which the median occurs is found and the actual value located by interpolation. The example in Table IX, however, is a discrete series and the 20th term is the median. By reference to column *D* (cumulative frequency) all operators up to the 13th are working at 90 performance and below. Thus the 14th to 22nd operators inclusive are working at 95 performance. Thus the 20th operator also works at a speed of 95.

The formula for the median's position is $\dfrac{n+1}{2}$ for discrete series.

Mode.—In the example the speeds 30 and 50 have reduced the mean to 92·8 which is neither (*a*) representative bulk of the readings nor (*b*) one of the specified speeds. It is obvious that most of the readings are clustered around 100. Now the mode is the value in a series at which the greatest number of cases is observed. In this case it is 100 and therefore is more representative than the average. (It is the mode which is used by the "off-the-peg" manufacturer.)

Quartiles.—The upper quartile is the figure midway between the median and the top of the series and the lower quartile midway between the median and the bottom.

Percentiles.—Just as the quartiles divide the series into four parts, the percentiles divide it into 100 parts.

The general formula for finding the rank of these measures in a discrete series when *n* is an odd number is:

$$R = Z(n + 1)$$

where $Z = \frac{1}{2}$ for the median
$\frac{3}{4}$ for the upper quartile
23/100 for the 23rd percentile and so on.

From Table IX, the 85th percentile is 85/100ths of (39 + 1) and this gives the 34th speed = 105.

However, for grouped continuous data the rank is found by the formula:

$$\text{Rank} = Zn \text{ where } Z \text{ is as before.}$$

The actual position of the median is found by interpolation. It is necessary to assume that the items in the group are spread evenly over the group. Taking the data in Table VII the number of items is 1000 and the median is therefore the 500th figure. This appears in group 95 to below 105. Its exact position, found by interpolation, is as follows. The 500th figure is $\left(\dfrac{500 - 290}{350}\right)$ of the way between 290 and 640. Therefore the median is also three-fifths of the way between the extremes of the group, 95 and 105. Thus its value is:

$$95 + \left(\frac{3 \times 10}{5}\right) = 101$$

All the above measures may be found graphically from the ogive as illustrated in Fig. 70.

Dispersion.—The mean of the distribution will fix its position on a chart, but will not say much about the curve, even though the shape may be fixed. If the width is also known the curve is defined more precisely.

Dispersion indicates how the items are distributed around the mean. Some measures of dispersion are:

1. *Range.* This is the distance between the extreme readings (*i.e.* highest minus lowest) and, because it is so easy to calculate, this is the measure used by factory personnel in their control records (*see* p. 416).

2. *Mean deviation.* This is the sum of the deviations from the mean, divided by the number of readings. In Table IX, columns *B* and *E*, the total, or weighted, deviations are 371 (neglect signs) which, divided by 39, gives 9·5.

3. *Quartile deviation* is given by the formula:

$$Q.D. = \left(\frac{\text{upper quartile} - \text{lower quartile}}{2} \right)$$

This measure gives the spread but not with reference to the mean.

4. *Standard deviation.* This is more difficult to calculate but gives far more information. The formula is: $\sigma = \sqrt{\dfrac{\Sigma f d^2}{n}}$

where σ = standard deviation
n = number of readings
d = deviations of readings from the mean
f = frequency of each reading.

Using Table IX, the calculation is carried out as follows: column *E* gives values of the deviations of the performances from the average, and column *F* gives the squares of these values multiplied by their respective frequencies of occurrence. The sum of these values represents $\Sigma f d^2$ which in this case is 8541. The standard deviation, by the formula, is therefore:

$$\sigma = \sqrt{\frac{8541}{39}} = 14 \cdot 8$$

Comparisons.—If these measures of dispersion are now compared the differences between them are apparent:

Range	Mean deviation	Quartile deviation	Standard deviation
80	9·8	5	14·9

The bulk of the readings lie between 85 and 105, *i.e.* 95 ± 10. The range gives a spread of 80 due to the extreme figure 30 and is not representative of the bulk of the distribution. The mean deviation however gives 9·8 (approximately 10) and the standard deviation approximately 15. Thus these two measures are more representative of the bulk of the readings. It will be seen later that on a roughly "normal" distribution, as is the one under consideration, six standard deviations (three each side of the mean) will take in nearly all the readings.

Normal distributions

Some data, especially natural statistics such as heights and weights of people, form a bell-shaped curve obeying a fixed mathematical formula. Figure 72 shows this normal curve. It is symmetrical, and mean, median and mode coincide.

In industry the normal distribution is important because much of the data when plotted as frequency distributions approximate to this shape. All processes work to fixed limits or tolerances and a high proportion of machining processes turn out components whose sizes are distributed in this way.

STATISTICAL QUALITY CONTROL

In order to understand the operation of the charts used in statistical quality control it is necessary to appreciate the theory of probability on which they are based. The distribution graphs mentioned earlier— normal and binomial—will be reintroduced in this section.

PROBABILITY

The probability of certain events occurring or not occurring in a given situation may be predicted with predetermined confidence by applying the appropriate reasoning and statistical theory.

If r be the number of ways a specific event can occur and n represents the total of equally likely results, the probability of this specific event occurring is given by the ratio $r : n$.

Example

A die is thrown. What is the probability of it falling with an even number showing?

Total number of equally likely results $(n) = 6$ (any 1 of 6)

Number of ways specified event can occur $(r) = 3$ (3 sides are even)

Thus the probability $= \dfrac{r}{n} = \dfrac{3}{6} = 0.5$

The above example is a case of the *addition rule*. This rule is used when events are mutually exclusive (*i.e.* only one event can occur and the others are excluded). In this example if the 4 turned up then the other five sides cannot. Thus the probability of a 4 turning up is one chance in six, or $\dfrac{1}{6}$. Similarly the probabilities for the 2 and the 6 are all $\dfrac{1}{6}$. The total probability is therefore $\dfrac{1}{6} + \dfrac{1}{6} + \dfrac{1}{6} = 0.5$ as before.

Another rule is used when the events are not mutually exclusive, as when more than one dice are thrown.

Example

Three dice are thrown. What is the probability that all will show even numbers?

This time if a 4 turns up then there is nothing to prevent a 4 occurring on another die or even on *all* dice. In this case the *multiplication rule* is used:

$$0.5 \times 0.5 \times 0.5 = 0.125$$

or one chance in eight.

Normal distribution and probability

The normal distribution graph, outlined earlier in this chapter (Fig. 72), may be used for purposes of prediction in cases where the data fall into this pattern. If the standard deviation lines are calculated and inserted above and below the mean, it is found that within the 1σ,

2σ, and 3σ limits, the numbers of items included between these lines are, respectively, 68, 95·5 and 99·7%. To put it another way the chance of a single item being within, say, ±2σ of the mean is 95·5% or 19 in 20. As 99·7% of items lie within ±3σ, 6σ can be taken to include virtually all the items. These probabilities are used in fixing control lines on charts.

CONTROL CHARTS

In Chapter IX an account was given of quality control as applied to the various inspection centres.

In order to control the quality effectively it is necessary to keep a running record of the quality level. It is impossible to eliminate all variation in a process and for this reason working limits or tolerances are placed on specifications. These variations are due either to random effects known as chance variations, or to such things as tool wear, setting changes, material changes, etc., which are known assignable causes. As 3σ includes nearly all the items (99·7%) this 6σ spread is called the Basic Spread. To take in 99·8% of the items we use 3·09σ limits. The basic spread should be within the design tolerance. If it is equal to this tolerance there will be no room for variation, that is, if the spread should increase or the mean alter, rejects will occur as the tail of the distribution falls outside the tolerance. Again if the basic spread increases to more than the tolerance the tails will always be over the tolerances and rejects will *always* be present.

The control chart is a means of presenting the collected information in graphical form. The mean of the specification can be plotted as a target and lines at distances equal to plus and minus 3·09σ from the mean also inserted on the chart. The chance of an item falling outside either line is one in 1000, thus with odds as great as this, when the readings of five samples are plotted on the chart and one falls outside the lines, it is more than likely that the reject is due to assignable causes, and action should be taken to remedy the defect. These lines are therefore known as control or "action" lines.

Instead of plotting all the samples on the chart, the averages only can be plotted on a "means chart" (or "average chart") (Fig. 75). On the individuals chart, if the mean remains fairly constant and the spread increases, some readings fall outside the control lines, but these same readings, plotted on a means chart as averages, will be plotted as points falling on or very near to the mean line and none will be anywhere near to the control lines. It is obvious therefore that on the means chart different control lines must be set. The standard deviation (and hence spread) of means of samples (σ_n) and the standard deviation of the individuals are connected by the formula:

$$\sigma_n = \frac{\sigma_p}{\sqrt{n}} \text{ where } n = \text{the sample size.}$$

Thus action lines are set at plus and minus 3·09 σ_n or $\frac{3\cdot09\sigma_p}{\sqrt{n}}$.

These charts usually show the range in addition to the mean in a combined "average (or means) and range chart."

In addition to the "action" lines some charts show "warning lines" which are intended to inform the user when samples are approaching the danger level. These lines are spaced so that they are only reached once in 40 times by chance (*i.e.* 2σ). Thus if one sample average falls

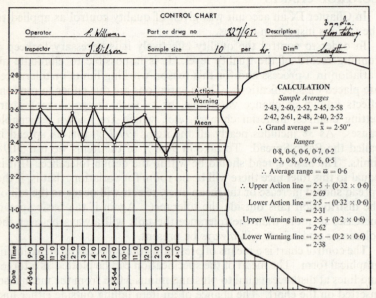

CONTROL CHART

Operator *P. Williams*   Part or drwg no *327/9T.*   Description *Glass tubing* $\frac{3}{4}$ *in dia.*

Inspector *J. Wilson*   Sample size *10* per *hr.*   Dimⁿ *Length*

CALCULATION

Sample Averages
2·43, 2·60, 2·52, 2·45, 2·58
2·42, 2·61, 2·48, 2·40, 2·52
∴ Grand average = $\bar{\bar{x}}$ = 2·50″

Ranges
0·8, 0·6, 0·6, 0·7, 0·2
0·3, 0·8, 0·9, 0·6, 0·5
∴ Average range = $\bar{w}$ = 0·6

∴ Upper Action line = 2·5 + (0·32 × 0·6)
= 2·69
Lower Action line = 2·5 − (0·32 × 0·6)
= 2·31
Upper Warning line = 2·5 + (0·2 × 0·6)
= 2·62
Lower Warning line = 2·5 − (0·2 × 0·6)
= 2·38

Fig. 75.—*Average and range chart*

between the warning and action lines the probability of this happening by chance is greater than 1 in 40. If the next sample average also falls in this area of the chart the odds against this happening by chance are so great that the operator would be justified in taking action.

To design a control chart for a particular process it is necessary to obtain data from which to compute the standard deviation of the process. About twenty samples are taken from the process when it is fairly stable. From these samples the sample averages are calculated and then the grand average ($\bar{\bar{x}}$). The average range is also found ($\bar{w}$). From the formulae below and tables of A and D factors the positions of the control lines are found.

Formulae:
$$\text{Upper action line} = \bar{\bar{x}} + A\bar{w}$$
$$\text{Upper warning line} = \bar{\bar{x}} + A'\bar{w}$$
$$\text{Lower action line} = \bar{\bar{x}} - A\bar{w}$$
$$\text{Lower warning line} = \bar{\bar{x}} - A'\bar{w}$$
$$\text{Range action line} = D\bar{w}$$
$$\text{Range warning line} = D'\bar{w}$$

A and *D* factor tables can be found in any standard textbook on statistical method.

ATTRIBUTES CHART

Although controlling quality by actual measurements (variables) is the most satisfactory way since it provides the most information, it is not always possible to obtain these figures. The check may be a visual

---

QUALITY CONTROL SAMPLING CHART

Dept. *Spray Shop*   Sample 25 per 200
Description *Cabinet*   Code number B 382/C1   Inspector *F.B.J.*

Reject

Uneven spray			1		1					3		3	4				
Blemishes	2			2		1	2					1	3	1			
Rough weld			1														
Paint runs			1	3	1	1				1			1				

Number defective

12																	
11																	
10																	
9																	
8																	
7																	
6												X	X		ACTION		
5			X														
4														WARNING			
3					X				X								
2	X		X			X											
1		X		X					X	X							
0		X				X	X	X									

Time

Date	6/5			5/5			6/5			7/5								
Result	P	P	P	P	P	P	P	P	P	P	P	P	P	P	F	F		
Result of 100% test													42 Rej	56 Rej				

DETAILS OF TEST to be carried out.

Inspect spray for quality and rough welds showing after spraying.

FIG. 76.—*Control chart for attributes*

---

one for damage or for colour which cannot easily be measured. Again it may be cheaper to use a "go : no-go" gauge and sort the products into "good" and "bad." In these cases (checking by "attributes") the *number* of rejects is used instead of actual dimensions. The type of chart used is shown in Fig. 76. As in the case of the average and range chart, data are required from which to make calculations.

The rejects from twenty samples are counted and expressed as a percentage of the total items in the samples. This gives the expected level of rejects. The probability of obtaining the various levels of rejects can be calculated from the corresponding terms of the binomial expansion of the appropriate equation. The control lines can again be set at $1 \cdot 96\sigma$ and $3 \cdot 09\sigma$. To simplify the calculations, graphs have been compiled using Poisson probability paper from which the positions of the control lines can be read.

BINOMIAL DISTRIBUTION AND ACCEPTANCE SAMPLING

The multiplication rule gives the probability of dice showing three even sides, but does not indicate the probability of finding, say, two even and one odd or one even and two odd. In industry an inspector may take a sample of five parts from a batch. The multiplication rule allows him to calculate the probability of all being bad or all being good, but not the probability of, say, two bad and three good. The binomial expansion helps him here.

Suppose the batch is 10% defective and the inspector takes a sample (at random) of 5. By usual convention the 10% or $\frac{1}{10}$ is assigned the symbol p. The other 90% or $\frac{9}{10}$ must be good, and these are q. Now $\frac{1}{10} + \frac{9}{10} = 1$ and $p + q = 1$. Similarly $(p + q)^2 = 1$, $(p + q)^3 = 1$ and so on, or in general terms $(p + q)^n = 1$.

Now in the case specified where the sample size is 5 $(p + q)^5 = 1$. The mathematical expansion of a binomial series can be performed on this expression and the successive terms will give the probabilities of obtaining the required number of rejects.

In the example quoted:

$$(p + q)^n = (0 \cdot 1 + 0 \cdot 9)^5$$
$$= (0 \cdot 1)^5 + 5(0 \cdot 1)^4(0 \cdot 9) + 10(0 \cdot 1)^3(0 \cdot 9)^2 + 10(0 \cdot 1)^2(0 \cdot 9)^3 + 5(0 \cdot 1)(0 \cdot 9)^4 + (0 \cdot 9)^5$$

If this expansion is analysed it will be seen that the power to which p is raised decreases from n to 0 in successive terms, similarly the power of q increases from 0 to n. The coefficients (i.e. 1, 5, 10, 10, 5, 1) are found either from Pascal's Triangle or from the combination ^nC_r where r is the term in question, less 1. (Thus for the first term, $r = 0$.)

This theory is used in statistical quality control to design sampling plans for *acceptance sampling* (*see* Chapter IX). To use the expansion obtained for the purposes of probability of obtaining x rejects in a sample, the term whose power of p is x is calculated.

Example

What is the chance of picking 3 bad and 2 good in a sample of 5?

Now p represents rejects and q represents good items. Thus we look for the term in the expansion whose power of p is 3 and of q is 2. This is the third term ($r = 2$), *i.e.* $10(0 \cdot 1)^3(0 \cdot 9)^2 = 10 \times 0 \cdot 1 \times 0 \cdot 1 \times 0 \cdot 1 \times 0 \cdot 9 \times 0 \cdot 9$

$$= 0 \cdot 0081$$

This is approximately eight chances in 1000 or one in 125.

Obviously the inspector does not calculate these odds himself, but he is given pre-calculated sampling plans such as DEF 131A (published by H.M.S.O.).

DESIGNING EXPERIMENTS

When production is being carried on the flow-line principle, or by some other form of continuous processing, it is often found necessary to carry out tests in order to improve on the quality produced by the existing methods, or perhaps to improve the yield. For example, in the manufacture of certain types of radio valves it is necessary to process the cathode by causing chemical changes to take place in its surface. These changes are brought about by the passage of an electric current through the cathode. The conditions necessary to obtain optimum activity in the cathode depend on the time of application and on the strength of the current. The present production may be producing an average activity of, say, 15 mA, whereas by altering the processing conditions it may be possible to increase this to a higher figure. In order to investigate this theory an experiment which will take into account both of these factors can be planned.

By varying the processing time and activating current, the optimum activity for a given time may be found. But the best activity level may not be given by combining the optimum time at a given current with the optimum current at a fixed time. Therefore the two factors must be varied together. The usual way to carry out experiments of this type is to select settings above and below those in use and combinations of the sets of factors. For example in the case under discussion the currents may be 80 mA and the time 20 seconds. The levels chosen could be 60, 70, 80, 90 and 100 mA and 16, 18, 20, 22 and 24 seconds respectively. Each set consists of 5 levels and if these are combined 25 tests (*i.e.* 5×5) must be made. If each test consists of 20 valves, then 500 valves would be needed. After being processed to the above conditions the 25 batches are tested and the results analysed.

The analysis is made by finding the average activity of all the 100 valves made at the 60-mA level (regardless of the times), the average of the 100 made at the 80-mA level and so on.

The figures are then rearranged to find the average of the 100 valves made at the 16-second level, then the mean of those at the 18-second test and so on. The current which gives the best average, and the time which produces the best average, are used for the new processing. The result may not coincide with the best individual batch, but it is these conditions which are used nevertheless.

The above statement may be qualified by the addition of the phrase "provided that the test result is *significantly different* from the normal production." The implications of this statement are examined below.

SIGNIFICANCE

If samples are taken from a batch of work or "parent population," and the means of these samples plotted on a frequency distribution, comparatively few of these means will coincide with the mean of the parent population. The distribution formed by plotting these mean values will take the shape of a "normal" distribution. This is so even when the parent population is not normal (provided enough samples are taken).

The standard deviations of this distribution and of the population distribution are connected by the formula:

$$\sigma_n = \frac{\sigma_p}{\sqrt{n}}$$

where σ_n is the standard deviation of the means and n is the sample size. This was discussed on p. 415.

Thus sample means have their own standard deviation when plotted and can be treated in the same way statistically as can individuals. It is possible therefore to estimate the probability of a sample mean being, say, any number of standard deviations away from the population mean by the method used on p. 414.

When a test batch is made as in the experiment just discussed, it is necessary to determine whether the result is really different from the usual production or whether it is just one of these wandering samples, in which case it is merely part of the usual production and further tests made at these conditions will give results whose means are grouped around the usual production mean. By the argument used on p. 414 it is apparent that the further the sample or test mean is from the normal production mean, the less is the probability that this is due to chance, or in other words, the more likely that it is not part of the parent distribution at all but part of a separate distribution (*i.e.* the more significant is the difference). Thus we have a method of determining the probability that a test is really better than normal production.

There are four cases to consider: where it is desired to test the difference between the sample mean and:

(i) the population or true mean using large samples (say greater than 30);

(ii) the population or true mean using small samples;

(iii) another sample mean from another parent source using large samples;

(iv) another sample mean from another parent source using small samples.

The factors affecting this measure of probability are obviously (*a*) the separation of the means and (*b*) a measure of the distance each side of the parent mean a sample mean may move by chance.

Combining these a formula is obtained as follows:

$$t = \frac{\bar{X} - \bar{x}}{\frac{\sigma}{\sqrt{n}}}$$

where $\bar{X}$ = population mean, $\bar{x}$ = sample mean, $\frac{\sigma}{\sqrt{n}}$ = standard error of mean (σ_n).

The above formula is used when considering case (i).

The value of *t* indicates the significance level. For example if $t = 2$, from p. 471 it will be seen that the chance of a sample being outside the 2σ limits is $(100\% - 95\cdot5\% = 4\cdot5\%)$. Therefore when $t = 2$ the $4\cdot5\%$ is reached and this indicates that the result is "just significant." A level of 1% however would be "very significant" whereas $0\cdot1\%$ would indicate "highly significant." In practice the level of 5% ($1\cdot96\sigma$) is regarded as "just significant."

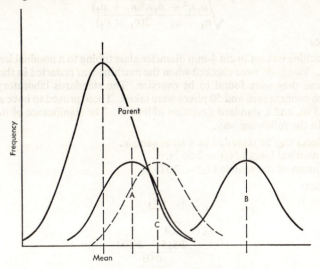

FIG. 77.—*Significance*

Figure 77 shows three sample distributions in relation to a population distribution. Distribution *A* is so near to the parent population mean that there is little doubt that it comes from this population. Distribution *B* is so remote from the population distribution that it almost certainly is part of another distribution. Distribution *C* is a borderline case and there *is* doubt whether it is significantly different from the parent distribution.

When the samples are small, case (ii), as frequently occurs in industry, the above method is invalid and the formula used is as before, but the standard deviation is estimated from the sample standard deviation by applying the Bessel Correction:

$$\sigma = s\sqrt{\frac{n}{n-1}}$$

In the case of small samples the significance levels for given values of t must be obtained from tables published in most textbooks dealing with statistical method.

The formula used in case (iii) is:

$$t = \frac{\bar{x}_1 - \bar{x}_2}{\sqrt{\frac{s_2{}^2}{n_1} + \frac{s_2{}^2}{n_2}}}$$

The suffixes 1 and 2 relate to the two samples.

In the case of small samples, case (iv), the formula is modified accordingly and the significance levels are again found from tables.

$$t = \frac{x_1 - x_2}{\sqrt{\frac{n_1 s_1{}^2 + n_1 s_2{}^2(n_1 + n_2)}{n_1 + n_2 - 2(n_1 \times n_2)}}}$$

Example

A machine was set to cut 4-mm diameter glass tubing to a nominal length of 2·50 in. Two rods were checked when the machine was restarted in the afternoon and they were found to be oversize. The standards laboratory were asked to confirm this, and 50 pieces were taken. These proved to have a mean of 2·515 in. and a standard deviation of 0·03 in. The significance of this was tested in the following way.

50 pieces can be regarded as a large sample.
The nominal length $(\bar{x}_2) = 2·50$ in.
The mean of the sample $(\bar{x}_1) = 2·515$.

Thus:

$$t = \frac{\bar{x}_1 - \bar{x}_2}{\frac{\sigma}{\sqrt{n}}}$$

$$= \frac{2·515 - 2·500}{\frac{0·03}{\sqrt{50}}}$$

$$= \frac{0·015 \times \sqrt{50}}{0·03}$$

$$= 3·5 \text{ approx.}$$

Now $t = 1·96$ indicates a level of "probably significant."
$t = 3·09$ indicates a level of "very significant."
Thus $t = 3·5$ indicates a level of "highly significant."

The complaint that the rods were oversize is therefore justified.

TIME SERIES

Important in business, particularly in the production and sales fields, is the study of trends. Data can be collected over a period of years and when plotted on a graph show upward or downward trends. A trend over a long term can give an indication of future sales movements and serve as a basis upon which production may be planned. The trend will, however, only *indicate* the future movement and will not replace a

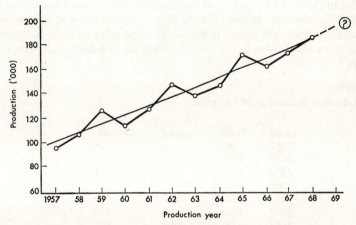

FIG. 78.—*Time series showing production for year*

genuine crystal ball. Seasonal fluctuations (*e.g.* the large toy sales at Christmas) may be taken into account and due allowance made as with cyclical fluctuations. The things which upset the predictions are catastrophic happenings such as long strikes which may stop production, or people may suddenly decide to abandon their television sets in favour of the cinema to the detriment of the former's sales. Moral: do not extrapolate too far ahead.

A time series is made up of three parts as follows:

1. The basic trend which will indicate the movement of the data.
2. The fluctuations mentioned above.
3. The residual variations including chance variations not covered by the above.

There are a number of methods which may be used to separate the trend, some of which are:

(*a*) A smooth curve or line of best fit sketched through the points in the graphed data (Fig. 78).
(*b*) The moving annual total such as in the "Z" chart may be used.
(*c*) A regression line may be computed and fitted to the figures.
(*d*) The moving average may be calculated and used as the trend,

MOVING AVERAGE METHOD

The moving average of a set of figures is the arithmetic mean of the figures taken n at a time consecutively. The number of periods (n) chosen will depend on such factors as the periods of the cyclic fluctuations, etc. Where n is an odd number of periods (a five-year moving average for example) a straight average is taken and the figure obtained placed against the middle or $\frac{n+1}{2}$ th figure. However, when n is even (twelve months or four quarters) there is no middle figure against which to place the average. In this case the figures are totalled n at a time and consecutive totals are added in pairs. To obtain the average the sums of the pairs are divided by $2n$. To illustrate the two cases examples are given.

Example

Production figures (in '000 of crates)

Year	Prod.	Five year total	Moving av. trend ($\div 5$)
1957	96		
1958	106		
1959	124		113
1960	114		123
1961	126	566	130
1962	146	616	134
1963	138	648	145
1964	146	670	152
1965	168	724	156
1966	160	758	166
1967	170	782	
1968	186	830	

Question: Will the increase be maintained in 1969? If so the moving average will be about 172 and production for 1969 about 176.

The case where n *is even:*

Year	prod.	Four year total	Sum in pairs	trend ($\div 8$)	Deviation of production from trend
1957	96				
1958	106				
1959	124			114	+10
1960	114	440		123	−9
1961	126	470	910	129	−3
1962	146	510	980	135	+11
1963	138	524	1034	144	−6
1964	146	556	1080	151	−5
1965	168	598	1154	157	+11
1966	160	612	1210	166	−6
1967	170	644	1256		
1968	186	684	1328		

To obtain the above moving average when $n = 4$ years the 1957, '58 '59 and '60 production figures are added to the 1958, '59, '60 and '61 figures (sum in pairs column) and this gives a total sum of 8 years' figures (although 1958, 1959 and 1960 are counted twice). To obtain the trend the total is divided by 8 and the quotient is placed beside the middle year of the years taken. In the case above, the middle year is between 1957 and 1961 *i.e.* 1959. The procedure is repeated for each moving average.

The above figures for the four year moving average have been plotted in Fig. 79 and the trend superimposed.

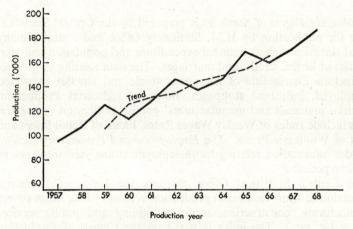

FIG. 79.—*Production year showing trend*

The fluctuations or deviations from the trend may now be determined by subtracting the trend from the actual production figures. From the last column in the above table the deviations show a three-year repeating cycle.

Where the fluctuations are seasonal the original figures may be "de-seasonalised" by subtracting the average deviations algebraically from the original figures.

PUBLISHED STATISTICS

In carrying out their various functions the departments in a factory or business are continually collecting data. Some data, as in the case for example of absentees' records, quality control charts and time sheets, are used for the firm's information and for control purposes. Data such as this, which is "first hand" information, are known as Primary Data. Secondary Data, however, are those data which can be regarded as "second hand" and are used for purposes other than that for which they were collected.

Secondary data or statistics may be published in journals or Government reports and the information contained in these can often be of use to businessman and worker alike. Some of the more important and better-known sources of secondary data are:

> The *Monthly Digest of Statistics,*
> *Economic Trends,*
> The *Board of Trade Journal,*
> The *Economist,*
> The *Financial Times,*
> The *Abstract of Statistics.*

The *Monthly Digest of Statistics* is prepared by the Central Statistical Office for publication by H.M. Stationery Office and contains many official statistics such as national expenditure and population and vital statistics of births, deaths and marriages. The data relating to production include distribution of manpower (male and female), registered unemployed, industrial stoppages, Index of Industrial Production, industrial materials and manufacturers' goods. Indices on wages and prices include Index of Weekly Wages Rates, Index of Retail Prices and Index of Wholesale Prices. The *Employment and Productivity Gazette* provides information relating to unemployment analysed into regions and time periods.

The Central Statistical Office prepares the Index of Industrial Production to show changes in production volumes. This Index covers manufacturing, construction, servicing, mining and public services (gas, water, etc.). The index is based on the Census of Production provided for by the *Statistics of Trade Act, 1947.*

EXAMINATION QUESTIONS

1. The following information relates to the sales, and cost of sales per unit of a particular concern. What ways are there of expressing these figures graphically? Illustrate them. (Absolute accuracy in the illustrations is not required.) What method is recommended in this case, and why?

	1966 £	1967 £	1968 £	1969 £
Cost of Sales—				
Direct labour	40	45	50	53
Overheads	40	46	53	61
Materials	20	24	37	38
Total...	100	115	140	152
Profit	20	16	25	28
Sales	£120	£131	£165	£180

2. Give a brief explanatory note on *each* of the following:

(*a*) chain index;
(*b*) ogive;
(*c*) ratio scale graph;
(*d*) scatter diagram.

3. What do you understand by a moving annual total? Illustrate by example the use of moving annual totals in a sales chart and explain the significance of the trend.

4. The manufacturers of brand "X" margarine held a tasting test to determine whether people could distinguish between their product and butter. Each subject was presented with 6 biscuits, 5 of which were spread with butter and one with brand "X" margarine, and asked to pick out the margarine.

Of 1680 people tested, 345 picked out the margarine-spread biscuit correctly.

(*a*) What proportion of people would you expect to pick out the odd biscuit, if their choice were purely random?

(*b*) Could the results given above be purely due to chance or could some people tell brand "X" margarine from butter?

(*c*) How does the theory of the normal curve help in assessing the results?

5. The table below represents extracts from a (fictitious) survey conducted two years ago by a professional organisation.

Analysis of salaries in the 30 to 35 age group

Annual salary £					Number of engineers
less than 750	...	...	...	...	83
750 and less than 1000	...	...	...	...	120
1000 ,, ,, ,, 1250	...	...	...	...	201
1250 ,, ,, ,, 1500	...	...	...	...	232
1500 ,, ,, ,, 1750	...	...	...	...	197
1750 ,, ,, ,, 2000	...	...	...	...	112
2000 ,, ,, ,, 2250	...	...	...	...	96
2250 ,, ,, ,, 2500	...	...	...	...	63
2500 to 2750	...	...	...	...	36

(*a*) Plot these figures on a cumulative frequency graph and from this find the values of the median and of all the deciles.

(*b*) Show how you would use these deciles to determine whether £1700 per annum is a reasonable starting salary for an engineer aged 30, assuming that his qualifications are the same as those of the engineers in the survey.

(*c*) What allowances would you need to make before using the survey for this purpose?

6. The following chart is for the use of the foreman. Enumerate its faults as a method of presentation of this information.

TYPE No. 3412.   Date presented: 5th July 19...

PRODUCTION MADE GOOD, 994.

MATERIAL LOSSES FOR MONTH ENDING 30th April 19...

PROCESS 1 3·38%	PROCESS 2 14·56%	PROCESS 3 0·77%	PROCESS 4 6·65%
Cause A. 0·5%	Cause A. 0·65%	Cause A. 0·2%	Cause A. 4·28%
„ B. 0·4%	„ B. 1·26%	„ B. 0·32%	„ B. 1·45%
„ C. 2·04%	„ C. 1·79%	„ C. 0·25%	„ C. 0·71%
„ D. 0·25%	„ D. 4·78%		
„ E. 0·1%	„ E. 1·87%		
	„ F. 2·99%		
	„ G. 0·31%		
	„ H. 0·37%		
	„ I. 0·13%		

7. The following figures were obtained by measuring the hardness of components selected at random from an assembly line:

93	80	100	84	53	104	94	96	88	98
85	95	110	117	75	77	82	102	81	65
77	100	70	91	101	83	90	79	103	104
108	92	83	84	64	99	105	76	87	57
63	69	126	75	72	65	75	85	95	112
115	103	95	90	89	88	75	81	86	87
93	90	89	102	90	99	91	98	93	100

Group the figures into a suitable frequency distribution and from this calculate the mean hardness found and the standard deviation of the distribution.

8. Describe, with the help of sketches, *four* different types of statistical graph or diagram and state the particular advantages of each of the methods of presentation.

9. The mean weight of a large loaf produced at a bakery was found in a series of quality control checks to be 30 ounces, with a standard deviation of 1 ounce.

Sample batches of 4 loaves were then taken from the travelling oven at 2-hourly intervals and the following are the averages of the last 6 consecutive sample batches:

$$29·6, 29·4, 29·9, 30·2, 30·3, 30·1$$

(a) Draw up a control chart for these averages and enter the figures on the chart.

(b) What proportion of loaves would you expect to fall below the legal minimum weight of 28 ounces?

PART FIVE

THE INDUSTRIAL ENVIRONMENT

Chapter XXIV

THE RISE OF INDUSTRIALISATION

The nation arising in these small islands off the Eurasian land-mass has had unprecedented responsibilities and opportunities in the growth of material and social progress during the past 300 years. In particular, the great and accelerating economic changes of the so-called Industrial Revolution led to wealth at home and confirmed the development of the Empire overseas. The prestige, prosperity and voluntary Commonwealth association now resulting have today given Britain a respected position at the world's conference tables.

In the early stages of industrial development the lack of scientific knowledge and the backward state of public conscience inflicted harsh conditions on the many; at the same time new opportunities came to the comparatively few to gain wealth and power, a philosophy which could at last be practised beyond its traditional stronghold of the landed aristocracy and one which, owing to its immediacy, had little room for philanthropism.

This twofold division of interest between employers and employed is still the basic phenomenon of modern industrial organisation. Much has been achieved by voluntary and Government action to eliminate bitterness resulting from past memories, but the responsibility of management remains and is increasingly onerous. On the one hand, the employer becomes less of a personality owing either to the increasingly diffuse or to the monolithic nature of ownership; on the other hand, the employee has become better educated and more articulate.

A brief survey of the growth of industry is given below.

THE MIDDLE AGES TO THE EIGHTEENTH CENTURY

THE FEUDAL SYSTEM

The main unit of economic life in the eleventh to the fourteenth centuries was the manor, based on agricultural self-sufficiency and a pyramidal structure of personal rights and duties. Though the feudal system is sometimes thought to have been imposed by William the Conqueror, in fact he gave rigidity to a concept which already existed.

The famous Domesday Book surveyed the manors and the 80 townships of the new kingdom. The population at this time was about 1·8 million of whom about two-fifths were villeins, who obtained protection and a piece of land from the manorial lords in return for regular weekly work and occasional extra duties as required: they were the virtual equivalent of the tied agricultural labourer of more recent times. Roughly another two-fifths of the population had similar obligations, but general economic inferiority to the villeins. The two other main classes of people of the manor were the superior "freemen" and organising officials. The former did not have to perform "week-work," and the latter controlled the running of the manor, based on custom. The little industry that did take place usually involved the blacksmith— mainly for the primitive agricultural implements—the miller, the brewer, and perhaps an armourer and mason.

THE GROWTH OF TRADING AND TOWNS

Though self-sufficiency was the keynote of the feudal system, some trade did take place. Cloth, nails, weapons and salt were traded for locally-produced farming surpluses at markets and fairs in the towns growing up near route- and river-crossings or at ecclesiastical centres. Barter had been adequate for the self-contained manorial economy, but outside trading pointed the need for some kind of money. In addition, the necessary rental services from the manorial lords (which required them to join the King's army with a retinue of men each year) and from the villeins (of working specified duties for the lord) were gradually being commuted to definite money payments. The lords wanted money to pay their annual dues to the King (in lieu of actual service) and money allowed both men and towns on the manor to purchase their freedom.

The growth of towns both indicated and caused the breakdown of the inward-looking manorial system. The lords' desire for money and the townsmen's desire for a strong measure of self-government led to the institution of a borough charter in return for an annual lump sum, especially in the thirteenth and fourteenth centuries. The town was allowed its own court, market (usually weekly) and fair (usually annually). Perhaps most important of all in its emancipation was the permission to create a merchant gild to virtually monopolise local trading—often this was later sub-divided into craft gilds, or associations of masters, journeymen and apprentices in one trade.

The main objects of the gilds were to establish and maintain standards of workmanship, apprenticeship and behaviour, and to establish funds to protect members and their families from hardships arising from ill health or death. It is sometimes thought (erroneously) that modern trade unions originated from these craft gilds. More likely, however, the gildsmen foreshadowed the development of a commercial middle class which was destined to play a dominant role later in industrialising England.

Nevertheless, farming was still the principal occupation of thirteenth-century England and was destined to remain so for another 500 years. Baronial power was strong and increased with the enclosure movements for sheep-rearing in the late Middle Ages, especially after the Black Death of 1348–49 had killed at least one-third of the labouring population. This gave a fillip to the principal manufacturing industry of the age—the cottage-weaving of wool, especially in eastern England. At first the raw product only was exported, mainly to the weaving centres in Flanders. By the mid-thirteenth century the domestic coarse-weaving industry had become sufficiently established in rural areas to facilitate an important cloth-exporting trade as well. Near the end of the century Edward III induced the skilled Flemish weavers to settle in England, safe from religious persecution, and fine-quality cloth manufacture arose.

Metal-working was perhaps the only other noteworthy industry of these times, primarily for weapons of war rather than implements of peace—reflecting the unsettled nature of the times. Iron-smelting, using wood as fuel, was located mainly in forested areas such as the Weald and Gloucestershire. Other industries, of less importance, included the production of glass, and salt, shipbuilding and the mining of lead and coal.

THE WIDENING OF TRADE

Just as the manorial system had been weakened by outward-looking influences earlier, so the towns suffered from the restrictionist grip of the gilds in local trading in the late fifteenth century. The masters had become self-centred and monopolistic, often adopting very high entry standards and liveries which could only be afforded by the wealthiest. The idea of free association for commercial purposes was being stifled in older towns and, anyway, trading was becoming more nationalistic in character. On the one hand this led to the growth of crafts in newer towns, or outside the walls of the older ones: on the other, it led to growing State regulation of commerce to promote increased national strength. Both developments superseded the narrow trading concepts of the gilds, though the wealthier Livery Companies of the City of London maintained a strong general influence until the late eighteenth century.

In late-mediaeval England the location of wool manufacture moved from the plains of the east to the higher lands in the rural west and north, with its domestic and part-time nature emphasised. In "home industry" the women and children carded and spun, and the men wove the yarn. Merchant capitalists, using pack-horse transport, delivered the raw material and collected the finished product. Production was cheaper and less restricted than in the old gild-dominated towns and facilitated the use of local water supplies for power and for fulling (the cleansing and shrinking of cloth); but by the nature of production the work could not be closely supervised and losses of cloth and time had to be tolerated by the travelling merchants.

At this time, exports of raw wool, hides, leather and tin from England were controlled by the Merchant Staplers and woollen cloth primarily by the Merchant Adventurers. The country had been a late starter in

P

international trading owing to her position on the fringe of the Old
World. The Mediterranean had maintained its position as the centre
of exchange, dominated by Venetians and Genoese; trading in Northern
Europe involved continental merchants such as the Hansards of
Germany and Scandinavia, who largely provided the initial impetus and
enterprise which brought English traders wider markets.

During the reign of Elizabeth I England emerged from being a
subordinate fringe of Europe, spiritually dominated by the Papacy, into
an independent island ruling its own Empire. Economically this was
due mainly to three phenomena: first, the great geographical discoveries
of the fifteenth and sixteenth centuries which converted England (and
Spain) into a spring-board towards the New World; second, to the
growth of Crown-chartered companies monopolising trade in developing areas* and, finally, to the increase in mercantilism to strengthen the
home country.

It is not necessary in this brief survey to discuss at length the economic fallacies behind a policy which negates the advantages of international specialisation. It is more important to consider the effects of
mercantilism and the opening-up of the New World on British industry.
The need for ships for trading and naval purposes combined with iron
(wood-smelted) for armaments in these troubled times created a boom
in these industries, but led to Acts limiting the number and position of
ironworks to preserve forests for shipbuilding. The Gild system was even
more firmly replaced by the Domestic, which itself lasted until the
Factory system arose. There were no notable mechanical improvements
in textiles, except the stocking frame in the newly-arising hosiery trade
in Nottingham and Leicester during the seventeenth century.

On the land the enclosure movements had continued to cause much
poverty in the labouring classes and the great Elizabethan Poor Law of
1601 reflected this condition. By 1700 these movements had slackened
in pace and scarcely more than half the rural areas had been enclosed.
But in the first half of the eighteenth century most of the remaining
common land was involved, the process being confirmed between 1770
and 1820 by the application of science to drainage, ploughing, sowing,
stock-rearing and crop rotations.

THE INDUSTRIAL REVOLUTION FROM THE
MID-EIGHTEENTH CENTURY

SETTING AND STIMULI

From the time of Elizabeth I to 1750, the population of England and
Wales increased from 5 to 6·5 million, accompanied by improving living
standards and the development of pottery and hardware in the Midlands,
cutlery in Sheffield and the growing concentration of domestic woollen-

* *E.g.* Muscovy Company (1555), Levant Company (1579) and East India Company (1600).

manufacturing in Yorkshire and cottons in Lancashire. But the country was still primarily agricultural, only one-fifth of the population living in towns.

The tempo of economic change accelerated in the mid-eighteenth century and was associated with the beginnings of modern industrialisation; only since that time has a general expansion of goods and services been a regular occurrence. In the last two centuries, the population has become seven times more dense and the average real income has become unrecognisably greater and more varied. In that time the unit of economic activity has become the Company in an urbanised society, involving complex and impersonal relationships.

Britain had a number of strong geographic and commercial advantages enabling her to be the leader of the so-called Industrial Revolution. She had a commanding position to trade with North America and Europe, as well as good coal and iron resources. She had built up a strong banking and credit system at home and commercial contacts overseas. Above all she had evolved a social, economic and political climate providing internal stability as a background for personal freedom and the acceptance of industrial change. Holland was perhaps more commercially advanced, while France and Germany (then a series of empires) were as well favoured with natural resources; but none of these countries had as sound a commercial and geographical base, combined with a lack of military involvement between 1815 (Napoleonic Wars) and 1899 (Boer War) as did Britain. Her only military campaign in the period was the excursion in the distant Crimea (1854–56).

The student is directed to Mrs L. C. A. Knowles's book, *The Industrial and Commercial Revolutions in Great Britain during the Nineteenth Century*, for a more lengthy analysis of the distinctive features which stimulated the transformation of the economy. Personal freedom permitted mobility from the land to the industrialising coalfield-based towns and led to the national spirit of *laissez-faire*, later succeeded by the safeguarding of markets and raw materials by colonial expansion. The application of steam to land and sea transport further increased the mobility of labour, bulky and perishable materials and industrial location. It vitalised the developments in the iron-founding, engineering, coal, textiles and chemicals industries.

THE GROWTH-SPURT TO 1875

Though the start of the Industrial Revolution was probably in the middle-late eighteenth century, and economic change was accelerated by the pressure of the Napoleonic Wars, the most marked period of industrialisation was between 1815 and 1875. The rate of expansion was 3–4% per year, or twice the average of the previous century, and by 1860 Britain supplied half the world's coal and manufactured goods.

Up to 1850, industrial growth was mainly associated with cottons in

Lancashire, a prolonged depression in farming and harsh conditions in the newer factory towns. During the third quarter of the century the relative importance of the still-expanding textile industries declined owing to the rapid expansion of the metallurgical trades, associated with the development of railways, steamships, free trade and the *Limited Liability Acts* of 1855 (re-enacted in 1856) and 1862.

The general importance of the railway (from the 1830s) can hardly be over-emphasised. The new form of cheap, rapid, bulk transport rapidly superseded the much slower canals and meant that industrial location was no longer dominated by the need for immediate proximity to producing or importing areas of raw materials. Perishable foods could be transported further and more quickly to the rapidly-expanding town populations. Socially, the railways enabled associations of employees to be formed more easily and workers to spend week-ends and holidays away from the industrial towns. In association with the steamship the New World was opened up both as a market and as a source of food and raw materials for Britain and, later, Europe. Business concerns with world-wide interests arose and the concept of world economic and commercial interdependence became a reality.

GROWING INTERNATIONAL COMPETITION 1875–1914

In the last quarter of the nineteenth century there was a general reaction against *laissez-faire*, except in Britain. Nationalism and the desire for economic self-sufficiency developed abroad as the industrialising countries emerged from political and military upheaval—for example the Franco-Prussian war, involving the two main potential European competitors, and the Civil War in North America. State-sponsored tariffs were raised against British manufactured goods, once the required items of British capital equipment had been imported.

Intensive international competition for overseas markets and raw materials developed, reflecting the active pursuit by States of uncommitted territories or "spheres of influence." Thus, while industrialisation was binding countries in economic ties, colonial aspirations tended to form separate trading units.

British farmers were also in difficulties in face of huge cheap imports of agricultural and then (after refrigeration) animal products from the New World. The Government did not waver in its maintenance of free trade, however, because industrial towns needed the food and Britain could not hope to maintain or increase her manufactured exports by checking the only means by which the new primary-producing countries could pay for them.

Until the First World War the United Kingdom's industrial structure was dominated by small and independent business units. The ideal of competition still prevailed and the so-called staple industries (coal, iron-and-steel, heavy engineering and textiles) were composed largely of highly individualistic family or partnership enterprises. Two reasons were that free trade would render ineffective any form of monopolistic agreement and that British firms served export markets of widely-differing specifications: but the most important explanation was that in the majority of industries the level of technology was such that the optimum scale of production was relatively small and new competitors could enter fairly easily. Loans for business operations could be obtained from banks and merchants, while re-invested profits provided sufficient funds to allow an increase of fixed capital.

Nevertheless, there was a movement towards larger units of production and a greater concentration of output, especially in the public utilities (to avoid wasteful duplication) and the newer highly-capitalised industries (e.g. chemicals and electrical engineering). Technological advance in iron-and-steel, paper and match-making tended to exceed market-growth, inducing amalgamation and the squeezing-out or absorption of weaker firms. The movement was initially towards horizontal agreements between firms making similar products to avoid cut-throat competition in depressed market conditions; e.g. J. and P. Coats in 1890, and the Imperial Tobacco Co in 1901. Then, especially in the heavier industries, came the development of vertical integration (backward and forward) to give firms guaranteed sources of materials and markets for their products: in the 1890s, Lever Brothers (chemicals) and John Brown (steel and shipbuilding) were two outstanding examples.

Combination had proceeded much further in the U.S.A. and in Germany by 1914 and most of the international agreements existing at the outbreak of the First World War were American-inspired.

DEVELOPMENT OF LARGE-SCALE AND NEW TECHNOLOGIES SINCE 1914

At the outbreak of the First World War Britain was still a major industrial power, but maladjusted structurally in relation to the world economic trends of centralised business organisations, tariff protection and new technologies, such as mass production. The industrial history of the last half-century has been one of increasing size of firm and product-sophistication, partly in response to technical development and partly to external economic pressure.

The past 50 years have also seen the rise of lighter, consumer industries, making use of the modern, flexible road-transport system and of gas, oil or electric power to move from traditional coalfield locations and set up near the conurbations these new trades serve. Nevertheless, the main manufacturing areas are still (except for London and Belfast) in the region of the coalfields which came into prominence at the start of Britain's industrial greatness. The economic and social vulnerability of congested single-product manufacturing areas has been reduced by regional diversification and *Town and Country Planning Acts* since the 1930s.

Between 1911 and 1961 the proportion of the labour force in manu-facturing has risen from one-third to two-fifths of the total and there has been a steady decline in the importance of industries with a relatively low product per worker (*e.g.* clothing and textiles) and an expansion in those with a relatively high average product-value (*e.g.* chemicals and engineering).

The suppression of competition in the national interest in the First World War gave a further impetus to the growth of industrial combines. Official Government support was given to the movement towards uni-fication and product-standardisation in chemicals and engineering. More efficient firms gradually enlarged their size and percentage share of the market. In 1919 the Report on Trusts by a Standing Committee, set up by the Ministry of Reconstruction one year earlier, listed 93 varieties of combination and concluded that trade associations were tending to increase.

The difficulties of the basic industries in the inter-war depression were aggravated by extreme specialisation and stubborn individualism. Inadequate financial reserves prevented reorganisation and re-equip-ment, so the trend towards rationalisation was defensive rather than offensive. It tended to raise industrial efficiency by systematic elimina-tion of excess capacity in production, distribution, management and research rather than conferring monopolistic powers. Most schemes for industrial streamlining in the 1930s were at least indirectly supported by the Government; they were primarily horizontal and terminable in character, and attempted to regulate output, prices and channels of distribution. The role of the specialist manager became increasingly distinct from the owner-manager and family businessman who domin-ated the British industrial scene up to the First World War.

Movement towards concentration was also evident in the newer technological industries. Between 1922 and 1939 the number of motor-vehicle manufacturers fell from 88 to 33, and between 1928 and 1939 the number of rayon suppliers fell from twenty to eleven. In 1926 I.C.I. was formed by the pooling of resources, organisation, knowledge and research facilities by a number of former competitors to control more than one-third of the output of chemicals. As well as these formalised structures, the general growth of trade associations was apparent.

The effect of the Second World War, like the First, was a pooling of industrial knowledge and resources as a means to a joint national effort. The economic situation since 1945 has been one of almost-continuous inflation and rising prosperity. Though the muting of competition seems more likely to occur during periods of general econo-mic difficulty, in fact the need to increase exports into mountingly competitive overseas markets has led to firms seeking greater domestic security, especially since the early 1950s. (The mergers of Austin and Morris in 1952 and Courtaulds and British Celanese in 1957 took place when their respective sectors of the economy were under pressure.) In addition, many of the newer and technologically-advanced products have been developed as off-shoots from established firms in peripheral industries: for example, electronics from the radio industry and man-made fibres from the petro-chemical industries.

It is possible to distinguish three structural types of firm within modern British manufacturing industry: one or more dominant firms producing more than one-third of the total output among a number of smaller ones, as in the vehicle, aircraft or tobacco industries; second, many firms of similar size as in footwear, pottery and building; and lastly, but most important, several dominant firms with many far smaller ones, as in iron-and-steel, drugs and radio equipment.

In most industries it is possible to identify a typical size of plant, even though individual ones may vary greatly. The optimum plant-size has tended to increase with developing technology, and horizontal or vertical integrations have enlarged the average size of firms. Larger business-units are better able to finance and use technical developments which in themselves often lead to larger scale by standardising and simplifying production. The greatest impetus towards company co-operation or combination seems to occur from mutual apprehension of external economic conditions or (more recently) the domination and perhaps take-over of the weaker by the stronger.

History of industrial relations

For a survey of the historical growth of industrial relations, the reader is referred back to Chapter XII. It was felt that students would prefer to have all aspects relating to Personnel Management in the same section.

Examination Questions on Chapter XXIV are given at the end of Chapter XXV.

CHAPTER XXV

PRINCIPAL DEVELOPMENTS IN SOME MAJOR INDUSTRIES

GREAT transitions have taken place in industrial technology in the last 200 years. This chapter may be looked on as a supplement to the previous one dealing with the growth and effects of industrialisation. The elaboration of the notable developments within the major industries should enable the student to realise how dependent progress has often been on the enterprise of the individual (initially) and the pressure of world industrialisation (latterly).

Just as Mrs L. C. A. Knowles's book, *Industrial and Commercial Revolutions in Great Britain during the Nineteenth Century*, was recommended for study concerning that period of the Industrial Revolution in general, so Prof. G. C. Allen's book, *British Industries and their Organisation*, is an excellent source of more detailed information of specific industries in this century. For current information on the major industries the student is directed to the *Annual Abstract of Statistics* and the *Official Handbook of Britain*, produced by H.M.S.O., as well as the various publications by the Boards, Federations and Institutes of the particular industries. The value of balanced and reputable newspapers and magazines must also be emphasised: the stuff of which tomorrow's history books are largely compiled. From what has been stated in this section, it should be apparent that the survey which follows covers only the main developments in the industries concerned. Nevertheless, this should be sufficient as a background to a study of modern industrial administration.

COAL

The output of coal was about $2\frac{1}{2}$ million tons a year in 1700, mainly from small surface pits with rarely more than a dozen mines. By 1800 annual production had quadrupled, largely owing to the growing demands of the iron, textiles, pottery and glass industries. The problem of drainage had been solved by Thomas Newcomen's steam-pump, invented by the Dartmouth blacksmith in the first decade of the eighteenth century, but it was not until virtually the last decade that James Watt's steam engine was used to provide power for raising coal from the pits. In 1815 the safety lamp was invented by Sir Humphry Davy and the first efficient coal-hauling locomotive was constructed by George Stephenson—thus the safer mining of deeper seams and the more rapid surface movement of coal to markets were foreshadowed. By the mid-nineteenth century an iron- (then steel-) wire rope had been introduced to haul coal-buckets and worker-cages to the surface, the Fourness exhaust fan (1837) had greatly improved mine ventilation, compressed air was being used for coal-cutting machinery and railways had largely superseded canals for bulk-movement.

Perhaps of equal importance in the growth of the coal industry was the more stringent Government legislation to ease the harsh conditions which initially arose from labour shortages. The 1842 Report of a Royal Commission on young labour in the mines disclosed that children were ordinarily employed at eight years old, working 12 to 16 hours in a normal working day, moving coal by trolley and on their backs or operating ventilation doors and miners' cages on which the colliers' lives depended. In that same year, the first of the *Coal Mines Acts* forbade the employment underground of women and boys under ten years old and in 1850 Government inspection was introduced. From 1855 to 1911 a succession of Acts imposed safety regulations; in particular the compulsory provision of two shafts for better ventilation and as an alternative escape route if needed.

By 1854 coal production had reached nearly 65 million tons a year and expanded rapidly to a record 287 million tons in 1913, when onetenth of the employed male population was engaged in the industry. This high rate of growth resulted partly from the application of the coal-powered steam engine to basic industries and as a means of transport, and was emphasised by the development of gas, electricity and chemicals. The expansion was however mainly due to a greatly increased export trade—from 10 million tons a year in the late 1860s to 98 million tons (including bunker) in 1913; this both aided the industrialisation of other countries and provided an exchange cargo for the increased number and size of ships carrying Britain's imported commodities (so reducing the all-round freight-rates likely with a return cargo of mere ballast).

But mining is essentially a robber industry and the more accessible seams were inevitably exploited first. The average annual output per head was maximised a full quarter-century before the highest annual total in 1913, achieved under conditions of increasing cost. The First World War and its after-effects accelerated the changes affecting the industry and led to its decline.

During the war, manpower and equipment in the mines were strictly economised at home and reduced exports overseas encouraged foreign customers to develop their own resources. In the immediate post-war period the Government fixed home prices and licensed exports in the face of huge demands, but several factors reducing long-term demands were coming into play. Improved efficiency in the use of coal in boilers and furnaces aggravated the effects of strong competition from the growing use of electric power in industry and oil-fuel firing in ships, while the internal-combustion engine enabled road transport to rival the railways.

The 1925 Royal Commission on the Coal Industry indicated that high costs resulted from the use of old machinery, the unco-ordinated diversity of privately-owned producing units and non-standardised channels of distribution. In 1924 there were 2480 mines owned by 1400 undertakings which varied in size from small pits with a dozen miners to large companies employing several thousand. All but 2% of the 1923 output came from just over half the number of undertakings (715), each employing at least 100 persons. Mines employing 500 or more persons averaged 51 years of working life and only 19% of coal was mechanically cut. Generally the cost advantage seemed to lie with the larger undertakings where output per man-shift tended to be higher, even though smaller groupings were often nearer the market and produced a higher grade of coal. The Commission broadly recommended a more rapid extension of mechanisation and a rationalisation of marketing agencies.

There were two temporary stimuli to coal exports in the early 1920s: the four-month strike in the U.S. industry in 1922 and the French occupation of the Ruhr in the following year. A Government subsidy to mine-owners from August 1925 to May 1926 led to a further short-lived revival of coal exports, but a seven-month strike concerning wages and hours from May 1926 worsened the general position. Thus it was not until almost ten years after the end of the war that the coal industry could squarely face the rapidly-changing world without transient stimuli or setbacks. In 1929 Britain's coal output was only 4% less than the average of 1909–13 (with exports 16% below the 1913 figure), but the industry was about to become a heavy sufferer in the world depression which began that autumn. Output declined generally by one-fifth and in the depth of the depression (July 1932) two-fifths of the labour force were unemployed. Even the best production year of the 'thirties (1937: 240 million tons) had an output 7% below 1929—principally owing to the continuing increased efficiency in the use of coal, its replacement by oil-fuel, gas and electric heating at home and the decline of export markets overseas.

In the late 1920s private cartels for price- and output-regulation arose. The *Coal Mines Act, 1930,* enabled the Government to impose its own overall control of production and minimum prices (according to district and quality). The Act also established a Reorganisation Commission to encourage colliery amalgamations for efficiency. Further Government measures before and during the war gave closer supervisory control over the industry. In 1945 the Reid Technical Advisory Committee recommended the creation of a central authority to stimulate the reorganisation of the industry on a regional basis; one year later the post-war Labour Government, with general approval, nationalised the whole industry owing to its vital importance to the country's economy, the great variations in size and efficiency of its component parts and the general need to modernise equipment and improve labour relations.

The *Coal Industry Nationalisation Act, 1946,* brought all assets under public control vested in the National Coal Board as from 1st January 1947. Previous private owners were compensated and the N.C.B. has grouped the (present) 600 collieries into 43 areas within nine regional divisions. Though the Board has a complete monopoly to mine coal in Great Britain, most retail distribution is in the hands of private organisations.

The N.C.B. has invested heavily in the mechanisation of mining, conveying and cleaning operations to offset the decline in manpower and extraction of coal from inferior and less accessible seams.

The discovery of natural gas in the North Sea, following upon the coming of age of nuclear power as a potential source of energy, has led to a re-examination of overall fuel policy by the Government. A new assessment of the balance among the available primary fuels (coal, oil, nuclear power and natural gas) has been made in the White Paper (Cmnd 3438) of November 1967.

IRON AND STEEL

The development of iron and steel is a characteristic feature of a modern industrially-advanced country and was a necessary concomitant with engineering in Britain's nineteenth-century mechanisation. Iron had been produced in the country from the Roman era. Until the mid-eighteenth century it was smelted in charcoal-fired furnaces in the forested areas of the Weald, Gloucester and Staffordshire and used mainly for purposes of war or in specialist workshops, such as those producing ironmongery in the Midlands and cutlery in Sheffield. By this time the growing shortage of timber had been holding back the iron-making industry, causing a tendency to move to newer supplies in South Wales. But as knowledge spread of the process using coke for iron-smelting (employed by three generations of the Darbys in Shropshire after its discovery in 1709), so the centres of iron-production moved, especially after 1750, from the woods to the coalfields in the Black Country, Yorkshire, South Wales and the Clyde Valley.

About 1740 Benjamin Huntsman in Sheffield succeeded in making cast steel by melting Swedish iron (which was more pure than British) in a clay crucible. The local cutlers did not make use of the process until about 30 years later, by which time it had become very successful abroad.

In the early 1780s Henry Cort perfected his puddling furnace (patented 1784) and rolling mill (1783): pig-iron was stirred and melted with clinker rich in iron-oxide and the resulting carbon-purified "blooms" (or loops) were fed through rollers to remove the remaining dross. The replacement of charcoal had speeded up the beating process of conversion fifteen times.

Cort's and Darby's work led to the malleable-iron period 1784–1875, when Britain was the main producing country. The use, from 1800 onwards, of Watt's steam engine to provide the furnace-blast and milling power, combined with Neilson's hot-blast smelting process (1828), emphasised this position. The annual output of iron expanded rapidly from 68,000 tons in 1788 to $1\frac{1}{2}$ million tons in 1840 and to over 3 million tons by 1854, three years after the opening-up of the Cleveland Hills ore deposits. It reached $6\frac{1}{2}$ million tons just after the Franco-Prussian War when both these countries had temporarily high demands. The mid-nineteenth-century growth in production was principally associated with and used for developments in domestic and foreign transport—particularly for railways and iron steamships.

In 1856 Henry Bessemer outlined in a paper to the British Association that molten pig-iron could be cheaply converted into steel by oxidising the impurities and adding the appropriate proportion of hardening and toughening materials. The resulting steel was stronger and cheaper and could be produced in greater quantities than the malleable iron previously used for girders and rails. But, unlike those of Spain and Sweden, British ores contained phosphorus which the Bessemer converter was unable to remove. So both this and the 1868 William Siemens–Pierre Martin open-hearth process (which used iron and steel scrap rather than iron-ore) could not be fully utilised until, in 1879, the Sidney Thomas–Percy Gilchrist cousins introduced their technique of lining converters and open-hearth furnaces with phosphorus-absorbing basic materials.

At first, prejudice existed against basic or mild steel but its cheapness and easier manipulation than acid (phosphoric) steel in marine, railway and constructional engineering made it more popular. By 1913 nearly two-fifths of Britain's steel output of $7\frac{1}{2}$ million tons was basic, by which time alloy steels for specialist purposes were being processed.

Two main trends in production began in the 30 years or so before the First World War. First there was a strong move towards vertical integration—that is, successive processes under a unifying organisation. The trend was both backward and forward in that steel producers gained control of the sources of raw materials, such as coal, iron-ore and limestone, and the ultimate market, by acquiring shipyards, engineering and armaments plants. As well as effecting technical economies in time, fuel, transport and stocks, integration gave greater stability in periods of declining business activity. It is also important to note that with a growing dependence on imported high-quality iron-ores the newer, integrated iron-and-steel works were sited nearer the coast. Access to local coal supplies (as in South Wales, the Clyde valley, Northumberland and Durham) was preferable, but not essential, owing to increased efficiency in its use.

The second trend in production arose from the rapid development of the industry in the U.S.A. and Germany. In 1890 the former country overtook Britain in the output of iron and steel: thirteen years afterwards so did the latter. By 1913 Britain's annual total of 10 million tons of pig-iron was one-third that of the U.S.A. and two-thirds that of Germany. From 1910–13 iron and steel exports from Britain averaged $4\frac{3}{4}$ million tons a year (or roughly one-quarter the total weight of exports), but from the 1870s growing competition from the Continental pig-iron and basic-steel makers led to an increased concentration on the production of high-quality tubing, sheeting, tin-plate and also steel bars and sections. The principal trade-conference associations within the Iron and Steel Federation reflected this, though only limited co-ordination and planning resulted.

After the boom period during and just following the First World War the industry in Britain suffered because of growing pig-iron capacity abroad and mounting costs at home, so that a further concentration on sheets, plates and tubes occurred. The Depression hit the industry hard, annual production virtually halving to 5 million tons between 1929 and 1932. The Government imposed a $33\frac{1}{3}\%$ protective tariff to enable the newly re-formed Iron and Steel Federation to rationalise the industry. It is significant that the only two important new steelworks established in the 1930s were at Corby and Ebbw Vale, which illustrate respectively the locational attraction of low-quality iron-ore deposits (and thus expensively moved) and Government in-fluence to ameliorate unemployment conditions in severely depressed areas. Revival in the middle and late 'thirties was linked particularly with the recovery of structural engineering followed by rearmament, and by 1937 steel output was nearly 13 million tons—almost one-tenth that of the world. But exports did not show a corresponding revival, reflecting the slow recovery in international trade in general.

During the Second World War the Government exercised strong control over this strategic industry and maximum production was encouraged, both imports of scrap and high-cost producers being subsidised. By 1945 heavy capital investment for re-equipment and reorganisation was necessary and technical advance led to still-further concentration of the industry into very few hands. Steel production topped 16 million tons in 1950, just before its short-lived nationalisation by the outgoing Labour Government in February 1951. The return of the Conservatives in October led to a reversal in the 1953 Act, which offered the industry back to private enterprise and set up a new Iron and Steel Board for the general supervision of prices, efficiency and capital investment. In April 1965 the re-elected Labour Government issued a White Paper on its intention to re-nationalise 90% of the industry's productive capacity. This has now been done. Blast furnaces are larger and more efficient and experiments are being carried out on improving fuel injection and enrichening the oxygen-blast. The two most important steel-producing regions are South Wales and north-east England; this reflects the growing importance of deep-water coastal locations near coalfields and the easy marriage of domestic fuel with imported iron-ore and scrap.

ENGINEERING

This industry has grown almost entirely since 1750 and was both a consequence of and necessary requirement for the Industrial Revolution. By the mid-nineteenth century the development of precision machine-tools had enabled the creation of factory machinery for techniques of mass-production. It is not today a single industry but rather a number of trades; nevertheless all the branches of industrial, agricultural and transport engineering owe their origin to the basic application of steam-power to production in the eighteenth century or its replacement by gas, electricity and the internal-combustion engine in the last hundred years.

Steam-power was first used for the pumping of water from mines at the beginning of the eighteenth century. The early inventions by Thomas Savery (1698) and Thomas Newcomen (1705) were unsatisfactory and wasteful of fuel. James Watt's improved engine was first used in the Cornish tin-mines in 1776, though he had proved the principle on a working model eleven years earlier. In 1782 Watt adapted his engine to a rotary movement, extending its use from simply pumping to that of driving machinery.

Development took place slowly owing to the dearth of skilled engineers, but Matthew Boulton was able to bore cylinders accurately and produce equipment to match Watt's genius.* Similarly the workmanship of Henry Maudslay in the 1790s facilitated the making of Bramah's improved lock (patented 1784) and hydraulic press. Maudslay set up in partnership with Joshua Field in 1805 and they developed accurate screw-cutting and slide-rest devices on the lathe. Joseph Clement and Joseph Whitworth further improved and standardised the cutting of screw-threads in the mid-nineteenth century.

As well as its general use in textile and flour mills the rise of the precision steam engine in the first quarter of the last century paved the way for the means of transport which were to become vital to Britain's industrial strength—railways and steamships. The former enabled the establishment of the factory system on the coalfields while the latter increased the speed and capacity of merchant and passenger ships.

The ever-increasing rate of growth in engineering is closely associated with the progress of invention, specialisation and standardisation in the industries which it serves or on which it relies. In the last hundred years, for example, the cycle industry grew partly from the making of rifles and sewing-machines, which in its turn gave rise to the motor-car

* Watt, a former instrument-maker in Glasgow, devised his engine when repairing the University's model of Newcomen's. He joined John Roebuck in an ill-fated partnership which went bankrupt in 1773 and Boulton, a creditor, took over Roebuck's interest in Watt's engine as part-payment of the debts owing. One of the earliest engines made by the new partnership at Soho, Birmingham, was purchased by John Wilkinson, an iron-master who subsequently bored many cylinders for the new steam engine.

manufacturing industry. Developments were especially marked in the last quarter of the nineteenth century owing to the rise of many new trades such as machine-tooling, electrical and motor engineering. More recent improvements in alloy-metals and their working have enabled the production of high-speed tools on the one hand and supersonic air- and space-craft on the other.

In the 30 years before the First World War annual exports of machinery virtually trebled (the volume rivalling that of Germany but well ahead of the U.S.A.), and in 1913 $1\frac{1}{4}$ million people were employed in engineering occupations. After the immediate post-war boom of domestic recapitalisation Britain's former markets were better placed to produce machinery and machine-tools for themselves as well as compete with other British industries in mass-produced manufactures. Nevertheless the country's engineering production rose by one-fifth from 1924 to 1929, especially as the new lighter industries expanded.

The Great Depression led to a brief but drastic decline in output and, as the 1934 recovery of production to its former level showed, accelerated both the decline of the traditional industries of shipbuilding and railway equipment and the rise of electrical engineering, motor vehicles and aircraft, which were more flexible in locational requirements. The areas of heavy industry on the north and east coalfields had become depressed while the growing and strongly urban population of the Midlands and south-east England presented a strong dual attraction of market and labour force to new industries capable of using road transport and gas, oil or electric-power. Nevertheless the rises in foreign sales from the newer branches of engineering were generally insufficient to offset the decline in those from the longer-established ones. By 1937 U.K. engineering exports were about 15% less than Germany's, but only just over one-half those from the U.S.A.

During the Second World War the industry was again stimulated, especially in the production of armoured vehicles, aircraft and electronic equipment; the decline in shipbuilding was temporarily arrested. The post-war boom arising from capital investment (postponed during the war) has persisted with the continued growth of demand for household durables, vehicles and aircraft as well as provoking activity in chemical and now atomic engineering, automation and the persistent export and defence programmes. In real terms the annual output of the industry as a whole is about $2\frac{1}{2}$ times the 1939 total. During the mid-'thirties engineering was responsible for about a quarter of the net manufacturing output and about one-fifth of visible exports; by the early 'sixties engineering output represented over two-fifths of both by volume.

A brief survey of two engineering industries concerned with transport—shipbuilding and motor vehicles—is of particular benefit in illustrating the changing emphasis within the wide field of the industry in response to technological advance and demand.

SHIPBUILDING

This was one of the staple British industries of the nineteenth century. By 1850 Britain was easily the most advanced iron-manufacturing and engineering country, and in the following twenty years developed rapidly her iron-built and steam-powered shipping. Even so the tonnage of sailing ships constructed in that period was slightly greater, while in 1870 four-fifths of operating tonnage was still under sail. By the turn of the century the displacement of iron by steel and improvements in engine and boiler design accelerated the decline of sail; the steam-turbine and reciprocating engines of the early twentieth century further improved efficiency in coal consumption, so that by 1913 virtually all the ships constructed in British yards were steam-powered.

The years 1850–1913 were outstandingly successful for British shipbuilding, which became focused on the north-east coast and the Clyde. As the "Workshop of the World," in the first part of that period Britain had supremacy in metallurgical and engineering industries as well as cheap coal, a skilful labour force and, not least, free trade which developed her merchant trade fully and gave access to cheap food and raw materials. Inevitably other countries expanded their shipping trades and shipbuilding industries so that Britain's proportion of the world total gross merchant tonnage constructed annually dropped from four-fifths in 1892–94 to three-fifths in 1910–14. Nevertheless, the absolute British tonnage launched increased by two-thirds in the period, indicating a rapid growth of world trading. Just before the First World War over one-fifth of the merchant tonnage built in British yards was for foreign owners.

Production in the First World War was greatly stimulated by the destruction of merchant and naval shipping, but severely hampered by the shortage of manpower and steel. By 1919 Britain's merchant fleet was 14% below the 1913 total and represented one-third (instead of two-fifths) of total world tonnage. In the post-war boom, particularly in passenger and cargo liners, over 2 million tons were launched from her yards—two-fifths on foreign account—and by 1921 Britain's merchant fleet had recovered to her pre-war size.

But the volume of international trade between 1921 and 1925 was less than pre-war and larger, faster vessels were preferred. Comparatively few new merchant ships and virtually no warships were required. Britain's proportion of total world construction dropped below one-half in 1922–25, recovering slightly in the late 'twenties with temporarily-enlarged demands from international trade.

Though Britain's shipbuilding output was still easily the greatest in the world, her companies were slow to change from coal-burning steam-propulsion to oil-using internal-combustion and diesel-turbine engines, both of which were more convenient and less costly. The industry was suffering an absolute and relative decline, and unemployment in the 'twenties was rarely less than one-fifth of the labour force. It suffered badly in the Great Depression and in 1933 production was one-tenth that of 1930 with almost two-thirds of the labour laid off. In 1930 a Shipbuilding Conference had tried to alleviate competition by minimum tenders, rationalisation and the removal of excess capacity, but imposed the cost of compensation on operating yards.

Recovery from the Depression was slow and in 1937–38 output was still only two-thirds the 1929–30 level. Exports were one-sixth of their previous tonnage, mainly as a result of the growth of subsidised and tariff-protected industries abroad. The rearmament programme in the late 'thirties created a demand for warships and stimulated the introduction of more efficient engine design. Yet at the outbreak of the Second World War Britain had a smaller capacity than in 1914 with a more onerous task of construction and repair ahead. The country used specialist skill to develop new warship building techniques while the U.S.A. mass-produced her standard ships, using pre-fabrication where appropriate (a system also used in smaller re-opened British yards).

In 1945 British mercantile tonnage was almost one-quarter less than 1939, and for the first five post-war years the industry was kept very busy with domestic and foreign orders, especially as the potential competition from Germany and Japan was absent during their period of reconstruction. Even when these countries began to compete seriously the boom was perpetuated by the outbreak of the Korean War in June 1950, which averted the threatened decline in shipping orders. Oil tankers were in special demand, making up two-fifths of the tonnage launched from British yards in the 'fifties. But on the one hand there was a persistent rise in the cost of labour and raw materials; on the other, new and efficient post-war yards using prefabricated techniques in West Germany and Japan have supplied increasingly strong competition—particularly in the construction of super-tankers. Between 1949 and 1956 the British proportion of world tonnage launched dropped from two-fifths to one-fifth and is now about one-sixth.

The industry has maintained its traditional concentration in the Clyde and north-east England, additional important areas being north-west England and Belfast. Much of Britain's tramp tonnage is pre-war and will provide repair and rebuilding work for smaller yards; the bigger yards produce super-tankers, dry-cargo bulk carriers and the larger periodic naval requirements of the defence programme. The future depends largely on the state of international trade, the extent of Government subsidies abroad and new technological developments (*e.g.* nuclear power). The Government has offered over £40 million in loans and grants to stimulate the reorganisation of the industry into four or five large groups to improve Britain's position as a main shipbuilding country.

MOTOR VEHICLES

The rise of this industry has had a profound effect on British (and indeed world) life in the twentieth century, not only providing the mass of the population with a more useful and flexible means of transport than the railways, but also helping to free the location of new industries from the coalfields to the larger urban groupings. Its development hinged on the perfection of the internal-combustion engine for vehicle propulsion.

The first basic invention was the gas-driven model by Lenoir in 1860 and a coal-gas propelled road vehicle three years later. But the dominant problem of fuel-provision was solved by the use of a product distilled from the newly-opened oil supplies in North America—namely, petrol. In the twenty years from 1865 Markus, Otto, Benz and then Daimler produced successively-improved petrol engines. In the middle 'eighties the Daimler Co began producing cars in Germany and in 1889 and 1896 respectively French and English companies using the Daimler principle were established.

Another step forward was the patenting of the pneumatic tyre by Dunlop in 1888. This was taken out primarily for the growing cycle industry, but the Clincher patent applied it to motor-vehicle tyres. The demand for alloy-steels greatly increased since an engine had to be light in proportion to its power. Improvements in suspension, the chassis and electrical ignition also arose from (and helped to develop) the industry.

The U.S.A. introduced the principle of standardisation and interchangeability to the vehicle industry more rapidly than most European countries owing to a vast domestic demand and the great number of specialised component-making firms. The country deliberately set out to produce a cheap standardised motor vehicle and in 1912 half the output of half-a-million vehicles came from seven firms. In contrast the market served by the British vehicle industry was more diversified at home—and roughly one-quarter dependent on a large number of different demands overseas—with a large number of producers each manufacturing a small number of cars with frequent design-changes and little standardisation. In 1912 vehicle production amounted to one-twentieth that of the U.S.A. and the middle-class market had hardly been touched. The centre of the industry became the west Midlands, near Birmingham, Coventry and Wolverhampton, owing to the diversified light engineering industries of the region.

During the First World War the majority of British car plants turned to manufacturing aero-engines and shells, most new vehicles required in these four years being imported from the U.S.A. A post-war boom led to the doubling of Britain's 1912 car output by 1923. By 1929 the country produced nearly a quarter-of-a-million vehicles, just less than Canada or France but well below the U.S.A.'s output of over 5 million (four-fifths of the world total). Britain's share in world trade was very small, while in 1929 the U.S.A. exported the equivalent of twice the British total output. However, the U.S. vehicle industry was very hard hit in the Great Depression and even in its best production year in the 'thirties (1937) output was still 10% below 1929. By the same year British production had steadily advanced to double its 1929 output with growing Empire markets—though largely at the expense of a declining motor-cycle industry.

In the Second World War the car industry was again required to produce armoured vehicles and munitions, necessitating re-tooling and reorganisation to meet post-war domestic and overseas demands. The export drive given priority by the Government meant that between 1948 and 1950 less than one-third of the cars and less than one-half of the commercial vehicles manufactured were sold on the home market. The feared drop in domestic and overseas sales after the early post-war period has not materialised and the annual production of vehicles has trebled its immediate post-war figure. In particular, there has been a remarkable growth in exports to Europe and North America, especially of sports and quality cars. This boom seems likely to continue into the foreseeable future.

The industry is dominated by *four* organisations—British Leyland Motor Corporation, Ford, Rootes and Vauxhall—which supply about nine-tenths of the present annual capacity of 3 million cars, commercial and agricultural vehicles: the balance of one-tenth is made up by specialist manufacturers of heavy and public-service vehicles and luxury cars. Though the industry has been traditionally located in the west Midlands and (later) near London, large plants have been established recently in Merseyside, Wales and Scotland.

TEXTILES

COTTON

This was the first industry to become mechanised since, unlike wool, it did not have to resist the strong traditional practices of an old-established domestic industry. The introduction of East Indian cottons had stimulated a demand which encouraged the development of mechanised production in Britain. Nevertheless, it was not until the beginning of the nineteenth century that steam largely replaced water-power and, even then, the hand-loom weaver remained dominant for a further 50 years.

Mechanised improvements in the processes of carding and spinning, involving the twisting of pre-straightened fibres into thread, were applied more generally before those in weaving. A carding machine invented in 1748 was brought into wide use after its improvement by Richard Arkwright in 1775. In 1767 Hargreaves invented the hand-operated jenny to spin ten and later 100 threads simultaneously. Before this invention six to eight spinners could supply enough thread for only one weaver.

In 1768 Arkwright introduced his water frame. This water-powered machine produced stronger threads than the jenny for use as warp threads in weaving and when it came into general use, from 1785, it made factory industry essential. Nevertheless, the frequent location of suitable streams away from the labour supply, combined with unwillingness to go into factories and the lack of machine-training on the part of individuals, meant that the domestic jenny was widely used until the end of the century.

In 1775 Crompton invented his famous hybrid "mule"—a combination of the jenny and water frame. It could spin very fine threads and facilitated the development of muslin manufacture in England. Though essentially hand-operated it was adapted for water-power within 20 years and developed for steam-powered operation by the second quarter of the nineteenth century. Its later extension, the ring-spinning machine, came into general use in the 1880s and foreshadowed the use of female operatives in factory-spinning.

On the weaving side of the industry the first machine was invented by John Kay in 1733. This was a loom employing a flying shuttle, but was extremely unpopular with skilled hand-weavers since they believed it threatened their livelihood. An improved version was created by Kay's son in 1760 but did not come into general use until the turn of the century. So the first real step towards mechanisation was in 1784 when Edmund Cartwright invented his power-loom, seventeen years after the jenny and nine years after the mule. It was adapted for steam-power in 1789, but was not entirely satisfactory.

By the turn of the eighteenth century the efficiency of yarn production so far exceeded that of weaving that much was exported—almost £1 million in 1804 and 1805, mainly to the Near, Middle and Far East. This was considered a dangerous aid to competitive weaving abroad and when a successful power-loom was evolved by Horrocks in 1813 it was rapidly applied in the factories, though hand-looms held their own for almost another half-century.

The water-powered factories on the south Lancashire rivers became the chief cotton-spinning areas, with the added advantages of the proximity of Atlantic-facing Liverpool (for importing raw cotton and exporting finished cloth), coupled with the humid atmosphere to preserve the threads during spinning. The possession of coal when steam-power replaced water further emphasised the region's predominance, especially when the Clyde Valley with similar all-round advantages concentrated on heavy industry and shipbuilding. The Census of 1921 recorded that five in every six persons engaged in the British cotton industry were in Lancashire and adjacent areas of Cheshire and Derbyshire, the remainder being largely in the West Riding and Scotland. This distribution is still very largely evident, though the industry as a whole has declined in importance.

During the nineteenth century improved technical application of the main inventions led to a rapid increase in the quantity and quality of yarn produced. Owing to the complete dependence of the industry on imported raw cotton, this increase is reflected in the fact that between the beginning and end of the century the annual average weight of retained imports increased over 27-fold; and this total (1580 million pounds) rose by another one-third by 1910–13. The enforced import of raw cotton from other sources during the American Civil War (1861–65) led to a greater use of long-stapled Egyptian supplies, particularly suited to Lancashire cotton manufacture.

The industry remained very important in foreign trade until 1914, though exports underwent great changes in both composition and the markets involved. The proportion of yarns exported annually in relation to piece-goods dropped from between one-third and one-half up to 1850 down to just over one-sixth just before the First World War (having reached a record total weight 25 years earlier). This decrease in the percentage importance of yarn exports reflects the rise of a machine-spinning industry in Europe (1820–40) and subsequently the Near, Middle and Far East (after 1880). As this trend developed, yarn exporters concentrated more on fine materials for use in the hosiery trades of Europe. Thus, while at the beginning of the nineteenth century Europe took nearly all exported British yarn and (with the Americas) piece-goods, by 1913 Europe still took over one-half of the now fine yarn exports, but the piece-goods went mainly to British India, China, Japan and South and Central America.

Though her absolute production had risen greatly by 1913, Britain's share of total world cotton output was declining as the industry grew in other countries. Nevertheless, her share in world trade dropped little in the first decade of the twentieth century and was still 65% in 1909–13. But continued success was at the cost of excessive specialisation into (mainly) private weaving firms in north-east Lancashire and joint-stock spinning firms in the south-east of the country—this was to rebound catastrophically in the inter-war period.

During the First World War the industry ceased to expand owing partly to a slight decline in the labour force, though mainly to shortage of shipping-space for imported raw cotton. There was a short-lived boom in eastern markets until 1920, but from 1925 until (in reality) the Second World War, Lancashire was "under the hammer" as a new hostile atmosphere developed.

First, tariffs were raised against imported cottons in the U.S.A., Brazil and India, to enable these countries to set up their own plants. Then India and Japan used modern machinery, organisation and marketing to emphasise the advantages of cheaper raw materials and labour to compete in Britain's overseas markets. By 1928–29 her share in the international trade in piece-goods had dropped to 44% and nine years later to under 26%.

In the face of this decline, superimposed on the general world depression, cotton manufacturers attempted to band together for protection. In 1928 large-scale amalgamations for standardisation and bulk-trading were proposed. One year later, the Lancashire Cotton Corporation was created to implement these and rationalise the industry, in the face of surplus capacity and unprofitable trade. It certainly had an effect in reducing capacity, but the hard-hit industry recovered relatively slowly in the middle 'thirties.

At the beginning of the Second World War the bulk-buying of raw cotton was taken over by the Government and in fact not released completely until 1954. Production was curtailed (to three-fifths of the 1941 capacity) to save shipping space and free labour for more direct occupations of war. Post-war trends were both anticipated and inspired by the 1944 Platt Report of the Cotton Textile Mission to the U.S.A. This stated that the higher productivity of the American industry was due to greater mechanical efficiency and modernisation; the basic recommendations to reduce costs of production were the application of scientific method by standardisation, specialisation and better technical equipment on the one hand and scientific management to improve plant utilisation, labour productivity, wages, working conditions and spinner-weaver co-operation on the other.

In 1945 there was a great domestic and foreign demand for cotton goods, but the labour force, reduced by the war, was ageing and totally inadequate, while plant and equipment was in need of modernisation. Clothing rationing until 1949 diverted output abroad but the U.S.A. had greatly enlarged her export trade, war-devastated Europe and Japan were recovering their capacity and, as after the First World War, former importing countries were more self-contained. By 1951, though world production exceeded the immediate pre-war levels, exports were only four-fifths their former total—Britain again suffering most.

In 1951 there was a temporary boom, but the growth of synthetics and Far Eastern competition led to pressure on the Government to reduce imports from Hong Kong, India and Pakistan. Such action would have been contrary to the spirit of G.A.T.T. and Commonwealth trade, though mutual pacts were agreed to limit cotton exports from these countries to Britain. The Government also placed a series of contracts to help relieve problems of the industry, but the main action resulted from the *Cotton Industry Act* of 1959. This Act was passed five years after the Monopolies Commission had condemned the Calico Printers' Federation scheme of allotting trade to member firms at suggested prices. The scheme also included provision for levy on member firms to cover reduction in capacity. The Act provided for Government aid to the extent of two-thirds compensation for scrapping redundant plant and one-quarter the cost of re-equipment and modernisation. This scheme was administered by a Cotton Board under the Board of Trade. Automated looms now comprise one-third of the total installed productive capacity and the proportion is likely to rise in the near future.

The principal export markets in recent years have been South Africa, Australia, New Zealand and the Irish Republic. The E.F.T.A. market is half as large as that in the U.K., while the European Common Market is virtually three times the size. However, the burden of climbing the tariff walls of the latter, combined with generally lower capital costs in the Continental cotton industries and the anticipated liberalising against Far Eastern exports in the future, will require increased domestic efficiency and a likely rationalisation into fewer, larger and vertically-organised groupings.

WOOL

This is the oldest of Britain's staple industries. By the late sixteenth century a substantial domestic manufacture of, and foreign trade in, woollen cloth had already developed along streams in East Anglia, the west of England and west Yorkshire. The scattered domestic nature of the industry kept it a local one, dominated by capitalist merchant clothiers, well into the eighteenth century. The strength of the merchants and skilled cottage craftsmen is illustrated by the fact that even in west Yorkshire, with the advantage of abundant coal and Pennine streams, the occupation did not become a definite or complete factory industry until the 1850s. An additional technical reason was the comparative softness of the wool-fibre, though this was less marked with the longer-stapled worsted. The availability of greatly increased wool supplies from Australasia in the 1830s gave the industry a strong impetus.

By the beginning of the nineteenth century power-combing and -spinning had been developed—mainly by the application of machinery invented for the cotton industry. However, hand-weaving was not finally displaced until mid-century. About 1800 Benjamin Law discovered the basic process of the "shoddy" trade, or the disintegration and re-spinning of old woollen cloths into a cheaper and weaker one.

During the nineteenth century the volume of woollen and worsted exports grew rapidly until the early 1870s and then dropped sharply, though fine-quality woollens did recover just before the First World War. As with cotton, the industry remained stationary during 1914–18, since the emphasis was on munitions and restricting less essential imports, and former cloth-importing and raw-wool-exporting countries began manufacturing for themselves. In the post-war period Britain discovered that she had lost Far Eastern markets to local suppliers, but (unlike other staple industries) falling export markets were offset largely by rising home demand.

The Second World War again restricted domestic and export production and post-1945 development has been hampered by labour shortages. The tendency has been for the demand for fine worsteds to grow at the expense of that for woollens, with a rapid rise in the addition of man-made fibres for cheapness, price-stability and special qualities. Foreign trade has been rather more prosperous than in the cotton industry and Britain has largely retained her position as chief source of woollen and worsted goods in the Americas and western Europe despite former and new rivals building up their own production.

The British woollen industry has retained its traditional and individualistic structure without the need for the reorganisation required in cotton. There are over 1400 firms and two-fifths of the output is produced by 600 enterprises with fewer than 300 employees. There are no "futures" dealings as in the Liverpool Cotton Association and, owing to the difficulties of grading and the consequent need for inspection of lots, auctions or direct shipments of raw wool are usual. The worsted trade is horizontally organised, mainly due to its early industrial development—though holding companies are now common. Woollen firms are more vertically organised to control the process from fibre-blending to finished piece-goods.

CHEMICALS AND ARTIFICIAL FIBRES

Though chemists are employed in nearly all industries, the collective term "the chemical industry" implies one which supplies such materials to other sectors of the economy and the development of which depends on chemical research and knowledge. There is often a strong overlap with other industries, as in the case of petro-chemicals, photography, refrigeration and steel-hardening processes, or an even more direct connection as in paints, pharmaceuticals, plastics, fertilisers and artificial fibres.

CHEMICALS

The industry developed from the late eighteenth century when the discovery of laws of physics and new substances fostered the growth of textile-finishing and agriculture in particular. The discovery of chlorine by Berthollet provided for improved bleaching, and was followed by developments in the printing and dyeing processes; in Germany, Liebig pioneered the application of fertilisers to farming.

In Britain the heavy chemical industry was focused on the salt-deposits of Cheshire and subsequently Tees-side. Late-nineteenth-century amalgamations into the two large alkali-producing firms of Brunner Mond and Co (1881) and the United Alkali Co (1891) foreshadowed their uniting with other firms in the trade to form Imperial Chemical Industries Ltd in 1926. The bulk gas-making processes of the 1880s onwards created economically-usable supplies of sulphate of ammonia and coal-tar. In 1909 a Belgian, Baekeland, produced resins from processed coal, from which was developed Bakelite and the modern plastics industry.

It is impossible in a brief treatment to more than mention the principal lines of development of this many-sided sector of the economy, but it is worth outlining the most important area of contact between chemicals and textiles industries—namely, artificial fibres.

ARTIFICIAL FIBRES

Synthetic fibres all result from the application of chemical discoveries. By far the most important and longest established is cellulose-derived rayon (or artificial silk), with protein-based nylon and Terylene as more recent products. In 1890 de Chardonnet established his nitro-cellulose process of rayon-making on a commercial basis in a Besançon factory. Within a decade the cupra-ammonium and viscose processes were being developed in advanced industrial countries and, just after the First World War, the cellulose-acetate process became established. The main stimulus to development was the desire of textile-producing countries to be less dependent on imported natural fibres.

Though the main systems of rayon manufacture vary in the raw materials used and the qualities of the end-product, the basic process is common to all. Cellulose (derived from wood pulp or cotton linters) is chemically treated and squirted through small jets into a spinneret before solidifying into a continuous filament or being cut into lengths of staple fibre. Not only has viscose rayon helped to transform the clothing industry, but fibres have been processed for use in tyres, fan belts, blankets, carpets and surgical dressings. Nine-tenths of the total output comes from three (of nine) firms, each employing over 3000 workers in heavily-capitalised plants.

During and since the Second World War synthetic fibres have been developed from mineral sources as well. From 1941 nylon has been used in stockings, clothing and fabrics. More recently Terylene has been blended with wool to improve resistance to fading and soft, warm Courtelle and Acrilan have come into prominence. When blended with natural fibres these synthetic materials have given fabrics improved qualities of finish, colour, texture and strength and introduced much-valued properties of drip-dryness and crease-resistance. Artificial fibres have become an important export industry, especially to Australasia, other E.F.T.A. countries, South Africa and Eire.

SCIENTIFIC RESEARCH

NEED FOR RESEARCH

In an increasingly technological age it is obvious that Britain can maintain and improve her standing as an industrial country only by devoting a greater proportion of her annual production to research in this field. Official estimates* state that between 1955–56 and 1961–62 the total U.K. expenditure on research and development rose from 1·7% to 2·7% of the (rising) gross national product. In 1961–62 private industry carried out nearly three-fifths of all research (mostly by larger firms and especially those in the aircraft, chemicals and electrical engineering industries) and provided one-third of all funds; Government departments carried out just over one-quarter of all research and supplied three-fifths of all funds.

IMPORTANT INSTITUTIONS

In 1900 the National Physical Laboratory was set up for precise measurements in physics and engineering. It was controlled by the Royal Society, with a small Treasury grant towards equipment and annual upkeep. Government recognition of the importance of research and development in the First World War led to the setting up of the *Department of Scientific and Industrial Research* (*D.S.I.R.*) in 1916 which then took over from the Royal Society financial, but not policy, control of the National Physical Laboratory.

The D.S.I.R. was the Government's main co-ordinating body in the field of research and development by industrial, academic and its own institutions for 50 years until it was replaced by the *Science Research Council* on the 1st April 1965. The D.S.I.R. had basically three functional categories: firstly, those concerned with public hygiene, health, welfare and safety, such as the road research, water pollution and fire centres; secondly, those concerned with research applicable to specific industries, such as forest products, building and radio research stations; finally, those concerned with applied science, such as the National Physical, Engineering and Chemical Laboratories. Many of these research institutions have been transferred to the new *Ministry of Technology* and for a more detailed list of locations and functions of these establishments, the student is directed to the *Official Handbook of Britain.*

EXAMINATION QUESTIONS

Also includes Questions on Chapters XXIII and XXIV.

1. Do you think that people can be trained to be good managers, or that good management can be learned only by experience?

2. What do you understand by the Industrial Revolution? Examine its significance from the point of view of an industry with which you are familiar.

3. Give an outline of the development of either:

    (*a*) the coal industry, or

    (*b*) the steel industry.

* Report of the Advisory Committee on Scientific Policy, 1961–62.

4. What were the factors which caused the Industrial Revolution, what course did it follow, and why did it occur first in Great Britain?

5. State what you consider to be the main results of the development of coal, iron and steam-power after 1780.

6. Trace the evolution of Britain's trade with Europe and the rest of the world during the period 1850–1939.

7. Give details of the development of transport over the last 150 years.

8. Compare and contrast the developments in industry in the nineteenth century with those of this century.

9. Describe the main changes in the methods of commerce between 1700 and 1900.

10. State what you understand by the term *evolution of industry*.

11. Give an account of the development of roads and canals during the period 1700–1850.

12. Discuss the growth of monopoly during the twentieth century.

13. Write notes on *two* of the following:

    (*a*) mercantilism;

    (*b*) domestic system;

    (*c*) craft and merchant gilds.

14. "The lot of the factory worker now is immeasurably better than it was in the first half of the nineteenth century." Examine this statement.

15. Give an account of the effects of the development of the internal combustion engine.

CHAPTER XXVI

THE ECONOMIC ENVIRONMENT

DEMAND AND SUPPLY

ALL goods must be produced ahead of demand, and demand is dependent upon the economic situation. It is, therefore, very desirable that the administrator in industry should know something about the economic factors that determine the demand for his product and the price he will receive. The more he knows about these factors the better should be his forecasts of future demand on which his present-day production must be based.

DEMAND

The demand for a commodity is determined by the utility or satisfaction that it gives to the buyer at the time of purchase. In spending his income each individual will have a scale of preferences; *i.e.* a different degree of priority will be given to the purchase of each type of commodity, and the price will be influenced by this scale of priorities—the greater the satisfaction or utility derived from a purchase the greater will be the price that the buyer will be willing to pay. Having purchased one unit of a commodity the satisfaction derived from the purchase of a second will be less than that of the first, so that the purchaser would be willing to pay less for the second unit than he was willing to pay for the first. The following example illustrates this economic law, called the *Law of Diminishing Marginal Utility*.

TABLE X.—DEMAND FOR BALL-POINT PENS

	Units of utility	*Willing to pay**
1st pen	16	£0·16
2nd pen	14	£0·14
3rd pen	10	£0·10
4th pen	7	£0·07
5th pen	4	£0·04

* Assuming that a unit of utility is worth £0·01

From Table X it can be seen that if the market price is £0·16 this particular purchaser would be willing to buy only one pen, but at a price of £0·14 he would be prepared to buy two, and at £0·10 three pens. In diagrammatic form his demand for the pen at various prices would appear as shown in Fig. 80.

This is, of course, the demand curve for ball-point pens of a particular type by a particular individual at a particular time. Time is important,

460

for the satisfaction derived from purchasing a unit of a commodity can vary a great deal from one occasion to another. If a car runs out of petrol in some isolated part of the countryside the driver might give, say, £2 for a gallon of petrol from a passing motorist with a full petrol can and an eye for business. But if the dilemma occurred within a stone's throw of a petrol pump the driver would pay no more than the market price and would be in a position to choose from the various grades available.

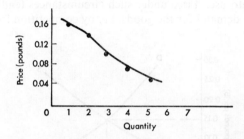

FIG. 80.—*Demand for ball-point pens: price/sales graph*

The total demand for a commodity can be calculated by adding together the demand schedules of the individual purchasers, and as the demand of the individual changes over time so will total demand change. There are a number of factors which cause the total demand to change. For instance, as our incomes change so does the pattern of our expenditure; increasing affluence leads us into buying those goods which we could not previously afford and into buying less of some commodities. Alternatively, the change in demand might be the result of a change in fashion or taste; or a new product may be put on the market which is a close substitute for a commodity we would otherwise buy. Taxation, in that it brings about a redistribution of wealth, may be a contributing factor to changes in demand, and changes in the prices of other goods may cause a change in price; *e.g.* a rise in the price of beef would tend to cause a rise in the price of lamb.

The extent to which the demand for a commodity changes in response to a change in price is known as *elasticity of demand*. If a fall in price brings about a less than proportionate increase in the quantity demanded then demand is said to be inelastic. If the increase in demand is greater proportionately than the fall in price, then the demand is said to be elastic. Those commodities for which there is no substitute tend to have an inelastic demand while those goods for which there are close substitutes have an elastic demand.

SUPPLY

The price which the producer receives for his commodity is determined by both demand and supply. The factors which affect the demand for goods have been considered and it is now necessary to look at those which affect supply. In the short period, the producer may be content to sell his goods at a price which does not cover all his costs of production if he can foresee the possibility of recouping all his costs in the future. In the long term, however, he will not produce his goods unless his costs will be covered: therefore, in the long term, supply tends to predominate in the determination of price. In the short term, supply cannot be changed to any great extent because it takes time to bring new plant and equipment into use. Price under such circumstances tends to be determined by the demand for the goods, *i.e.* by competition for the existing supply.

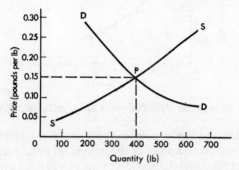

FIG. 81.—*The interaction of supply and demand*

The graph in Fig. 81 illustrates how price is determined by the interaction of supply and demand. The demand curve *DD* shows the quantity demanded at each price while the supply curve *SS* shows the quantity that the producer is willing to supply at each price. The market price is *P* where the two curves intersect—at this price both demand and supply are equal: in this example 400 are demanded and 400 supplied at £0·15 per lb.

COSTS OF PRODUCTION

The definitions which follow are those adopted by economists and are not necessarily the same as those used by accountants (*see* pp. 312 to 331). The producer's costs of production are of two types, *fixed costs* and *variable costs*. In the first category are those which do not vary over a wide range of output, such as rent, rates and the costs of administration. These costs have to be met whether the factory is working at full capacity or below it. Variable costs, as their name suggests, vary with output: *e.g.* wages and raw materials. These costs have to be met even if trade is poor and they, plus the costs of administration (clerical labour, etc.), are often referred to as *prime costs*. The fixed costs (other than those of administration) can be postponed in the short period and are known as *supplementary costs*.

The costs of production vary with the size of output. To produce one pen, for example, may cost £10, but if a million are produced the cost of production of the millionth pen may be only £0·01. Here the concept of *marginal cost* must be considered, *i.e.* the cost of producing one more unit. If 999,999 units have been produced then the marginal cost is the addition to total cost of producing the millionth unit. As a firm expands in size it stands to benefit from the economies of large-scale production; for example, it may be able to buy its raw materials in bulk at more favourable prices, or warrant the employment of its own transport, and the marginal cost would fall as output rose. This is the *law of increasing marginal returns*. But after a certain point is reached further expansion of output may be costly because the existing factors of production are being fully exploited and additional plant and equipment may have to be used. From that point the *law of diminishing marginal returns* will apply and the marginal cost will be rising.

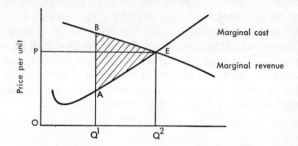

FIG. 82.—*Equilibrium of the firm*

Even though marginal cost is rising it will still be worth while producing the goods, provided that the marginal cost does not exceed the *marginal revenue* (the addition to total revenue from selling one further unit) and the producer will, in fact, maximise his profits by expanding production to the point where marginal cost equals marginal revenue. Consider Fig. 82, in which it can be seen that the marginal cost curve is falling at first (because of increasing returns) and then starts to rise. The gap between marginal cost and marginal revenue represents the producer's profit. At first glance it might appear that the most desirable output would be Q^1 because at that point the profit margin is at a maximum (the difference between marginal cost and marginal revenue— AB). However, if the producer restricted his output to Q^1 he would not be maximising his profits because he would be denying himself the further profits represented by the shaded area in the diagram. By expanding output to Q^2 he would obtain these profits and reach the point (E) where marginal cost equals marginal revenue and any further units produced would cost more than the revenue received for them.

TYPES OF COMPETITION

Assuming that all producers are rational human beings, they will strive to achieve the point of equilibrium where marginal cost equals marginal revenue. Just where this point lies depends a great deal upon the environment in which the goods are manufactured and sold. To the economist there are three different types of market, two of which are only notional in that they do not occur in practice; these are *perfect competition* and *monopoly*. However, these concepts do help in understanding the type of market which does exist; *i.e. imperfect competition.*

PERFECT COMPETITION

Under conditions of perfect competition it is assumed that there are many firms producing an identical commodity under identical conditions. Each firm produces only a small proportion of the total output and, therefore, is unable to influence the price by changing its output. Firms are free to enter or leave the industry as they please. Competition will ensure that there would be only one price for the commodity and the producer would, therefore, know that he could sell all he produced at a set price. If the market price was £0·10 then the marginal revenue would be £0·10 whatever the level of output, and the average revenue would also be £0·10. The point of equilibrium for the producer under such conditions can be illustrated as shown in Fig. 83.

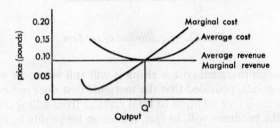

FIG. 83.—*Equilibrium under "perfect competition"*

At output Q^1 marginal cost is equal to marginal revenue and therefore profits are maximised. The least efficient (or marginal) firm will make only normal profits, *i.e.* just sufficient profits to keep it in business and, as normal profits are included in the cost of production, the marginal firm's average costs will equal marginal cost at the output Q^1. Even under conditions of perfect competition, however, there will be some firms which, through better management, have costs that are lower than those of the marginal firm. For such a firm the average cost curve would be lower than average revenue at the output Q^1, indicating profits above normal.

MONOPOLY

At the other extreme to perfect competition lies monopoly. Under this concept it is assumed that a particular industry is in the hands of only one producer and that there is no substitute for the commodity produced. In practice, there is no such thing as an absolute monopoly —as already mentioned, it is only a theoretical concept. The gas industry for instance is not a true monopoly because electricity is a substitute for gas.

A monopolist can charge what price he likes for his commodity, but he cannot control both the price and the output; he can determine only one or the other. For the commodity concerned there will be a normal downward-sloping demand curve, increasingly more of the commodity being demanded as the price falls (Fig. 84).

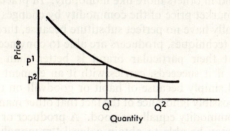

FIG. 84.—*The monopolist's demand curve*

If the producer decides that he will fix the price at P^1 then the quantity demanded will be Q^1. If he decides that he will produce quantity Q^2 then he must accept a price of P^2.

Whether it is worth while from the producer's point of view to change the price or the quantity will depend upon the elasticity of demand. If the demand is inelastic then an increase in price reduces the quantity demanded to a less than proportionate extent and his total revenue will go up. If demand is elastic, on the other hand, an increase in price will cause a more than proportionate drop in demand. It might be worth while, therefore, if demand is elastic, to reduce the price as this would result in a more than proportionate increase in the quantity demanded.

The monopolist, like other producers, will maximise his profits where marginal cost equals marginal revenue and he will endeavour to achieve that output of production at which this point of equilibrium is reached.

As in perfect competition, there is one market price for the monopolist's commodity. Unlike the producer under perfect competition, however, the monopolist cannot increase his output in the knowledge that he will be able to dispose of the additional goods at the present market price. As has been shown, in the diagram above, he must allow

Q

his price to fall if he wishes to increase his sales. This also means that his marginal revenue will not be equal to price as it is in perfect competition. If, for instance, he sells 1000 units of his commodity at £10 each and finds that to sell 1001 units he must lower his price (for all the units) to £9·995, the marginal revenue of the 1001st unit will not be £9·995 but £4·995. He receives £0·005 less for each of the 1000 units which could have been sold for £10, so that £5 must be taken from the £9·995 received for the 1001st unit to arrive at the marginal revenue.

IMPERFECT COMPETITION

In actual practice market conditions are imperfect, being somewhere between the two notional extremes of perfect competition and monopoly. Imperfect competition shares the features of both perfect competition and monopoly, in some instances being more like perfect competition, and in others more like monopoly. In practice a producer can affect the market price of the commodity by changes in his output, and goods usually have no perfect substitute because, through advertising and selling techniques, producers are able to convince at least some consumers that their particular brand is better than others. Such differentiation, if it succeeds, carries with it an element of monopoly. It may succeed simply because of habit or goodwill on the part of the consumer, or possibly ignorance of the fact that other manufacturers are producing a commodity equally as good. A producer or distributor of a commodity may be able to obtain a local "monopoly" price for a commodity because the local consumers are prepared to pay more for the commodity locally, rather than face the trouble and expense of travelling into a neighbouring town where prices are lower.

It is often claimed that imperfect competition causes waste because resources are expended on advertising and other selling techniques in an attempt to influence the consumer away from competing brands, even though such brands may be basically the same. The consumer suffers because the selling costs must be covered in the price he has to pay. Against this argument it can be claimed that advertising and other sales techniques increase the demand for a commodity and this may enable the producer to enjoy the benefits of the economies of large-scale production, which will reduce his production costs. These benefits may be passed on to the consumer in the form of lower prices. Furthermore, advertising is informative and helps the consumer in making his choice.

Imperfect competition may also be wasteful through permitting excess capacity in some firms. Industries tend to comprise more companies than would be permitted by economic forces under perfect competition, and consequently some firms do not make full use of their resources and costs of production are high. Having a large number of firms in an industry, each with its own brand name, does, however, give the consumer a wider choice. Mergers of firms tend to reduce this choice, and there is always the danger of a virtual monopoly arising in which there would be no choice at all. The consumer might, therefore, prefer to pay the higher costs of production of an imperfect market in order to retain variety. In any case, if the industry falls into the hands of a monopolist he may raise prices by restricting output.

MONOPOLY IN PRACTICE

A true monopoly, as shown above, does not exist, but the term is used quite commonly to mean a firm or combination of firms which account for a large part of an industry's output. The term *oligopoly* is used to describe the situation in which an industry is in the hands of a small number of large firms which by their concerted action can act as a monopoly.

It would be wrong to suggest that all monopolies and oligopolies are undesirable. Indeed such firms, through economies of large-scale production, may cheapen the product. They are more able to carry out research and avoid duplication of resources and excess capacity. But the absence of competition may result in some wastage of resources and a lack of choice of brands for the consumer. Obviously, as such concerns have the power to enforce high prices (though as shown above they can fix *either* the price *or* the quantity, but not both), some control over them is desirable, but it should be flexible. Monopoly legislation in Britain since the Second World War has recognised this need, acknowledging the fact that the mere size of a firm is not a criterion, and provides that each case should be considered on its merits.

The *Monopolies Act, 1948,* laid down four principles of efficiency: that large corporations should produce at prices meeting the requirements of domestic and overseas markets; that new enterprises should be encouraged; that there must exist both the fullest use and best distribution of men, materials and industrial capacity; and that technological improvements must be developed and markets expanded. The Monopolies Commission was given power to investigate the activities of virtual monopolies to discover whether or not they were in the public interest. From the detailed reports published by the Commission it is clear that restrictive practices existed in many industries and trades, varying from informal agreements to written contracts. The most common types of agreement were for price fixing and the imposition of conditions of sale, while others included the practice of "level tendering" (as in the building trade), zoning and exclusive dealing. Unfortunately, the Monopolies Commission has, as yet, no power to enforce firms to discontinue any of these practices, and legislation would be required in each case.

The *Restrictive Trade Practices Act, 1956,* provides for the compulsory registration of a wide range of agreements relating to the production and sale of goods. After registration such agreements can be brought before the Restrictive Practices Courts, and may be prohibited by law if they are found to be contrary to the national interest. The majority of the restrictive practices brought before the courts have in fact been declared to be against the public interest. But perhaps the most useful effect of the 1956 Act has been that after registration more than half of the agreements were abandoned. Persuading *entrepreneurs* to abandon or abstain from those monopolistic practices which are undesirable is more important than a number of prosecutions in the courts.

The *Monopolies and Mergers Act* of 1965 empowered the Board of Trade to refer to a strengthened Monopolies Commission any mergers which "appear to be against the public interest."

This blanket phrase has proved to be a difficult and intangible concept and, at present, the Board of Trade is conducting a full-scale review of policy on mergers, monopolies and restrictive practices. A White Paper is expected to follow.

Evidence of further new thinking on the subject of the "optimum" size of firms has emerged with the formation of the *Industrial Reorganisation Corporation*. This new body, backed by Government funds, seeks to encourage more concentration and rationalisation aimed at promoting the *international* competitiveness of British industry. To this end, the I.R.C. takes the initiative in the encouragement of desirable industrial regroupings. In this, it co-operates with the Ministry of Technology and the National Research Development Corporation.

RESALE PRICE MAINTENANCE

As far as price fixing is concerned the *Restrictive Trade Practices Act* provided for the registration of collective agreements—*i.e.* where two or more firms get together and fix a price for their commodity. Upon individual price maintenance, on the other hand, the Act gave its blessing, and in most trades with the exception of food, manufacturers have been able to insist that their products are sold by retailers at fixed prices. This was the situation up to July 1964 when, with the passing of the *Resale Prices Act*, resale price maintenance by manufacturers was made illegal. Like the *Monopolies Act*, however, the *Resale Prices Act* allows for flexibility. All price fixing arrangements must be abandoned or registered. If they are registered then they will be brought before the Restrictive Trade Practices Courts as are collective price agreements. It is then up to the manufacturers to convince the courts that it is in the public's interest that they should fix the prices at which their goods must be sold to the consumer.

There will be many economic consequences of the abolition of resale price maintenance. One of these is certain to be that retailing will pass more and more into the hands of the larger firms which, through competitive price reductions, will be able to draw customers away from the small store. This tendency should in some ways be to the advantage of the economy as a whole for the resources employed in distribution will be used more efficiently. The proportion of the working population employed in the distributive trades has been increasing year by year and, if the number employed in these trades can be reduced, there would be more workers available for employment in manufacturing industry, making possible increased output.

The tendency towards larger retail units, if it is not controlled, might eventually place the large firms in the position of being able to raise their prices rather than reduce them.

THE GENERAL ECONOMIC SITUATION

Whatever the type of competitive conditions in which the manufacturer produces and sells his goods, he must concern himself with the general economic situation. If the country is about to pass through a recession he may find that the demand for his product will fall off. On the other hand, a boom will stimulate demand. In the post-war years the U.K. has been very fortunate in that the extremes of deflation and hyper-inflation (severe inflation) have been avoided and the trade cycle has become much less obvious, governments having adopted alternative policies of disinflation and reflation. The four economic terms *inflation*, *deflation*, *reflation* and *disinflation* are explained below.

Inflation means a state of affairs in which the demand for goods and services exceeds the supply—the purchasing power of the community is too great—and unless something is done to combat this situation prices will rise. The term deflation implies just the opposite; *i.e.* where purchasing power is less than is required for the amount of goods and services available. This leads to a falling off of industrial activity and to unemployment. Reflation and disinflation are rather like mild forms of inflation and deflation respectively. When a government carries out a reflationary policy it deliberately brings about an increase in purchasing power in order to stimulate production of goods and services. This is the type of monetary policy pursued in the years 1958–60 and 1962–64. When such reflationary policies get out of hand, *i.e.* develop into inflation, then it is necessary to adopt a disinflationary policy. This amounts to combating inflation by reducing the amount of purchasing power or, alternatively, stopping incomes from increasing more rapidly than productivity. In much of the post-war period we have had to combat inflation. The major credit squeeze (a term used to cover all disinflationary measures) of 1955–58 may be said to have brought supply and demand into equilibrium, and since then the alternative policies of disinflation and reflation have been sufficient to keep the economy on a fairly even keel. These "stop–go" policies, as they are called, have come in for much criticism as they slow down the rate of economic growth. Industrial production rises quite rapidly during periods of reflation (as in 1963), but when it becomes necessary to dampen down demand because it is becoming excessive, producers are discouraged by the falling demand and output tends to level off. The national cake must increase in size to give everyone a bigger slice of it, but this can only be achieved if industrial production increases. During recent years the national income has grown, but not as rapidly as it would have done if the stop–go policies had been replaced by policies that would have enabled industry to maintain a steady rate of growth. This is, however, not so easy, for there is an important missing link—an effective *incomes policy*. Given full employment (*i.e.* an unemployment rate of no more than 1–2%), and strong trade unions, the pressure of demand for labour during periods of reflation causes incomes to rise more rapidly than productivity, and thus the demand for goods exceeds the supply. If the incomes policy could be more effective and severely restrict both wages and profits then it might be possible to ensure that incomes do not grow more rapidly than output, so that it is not necessary to bring to a halt an expansion of the economy achieved by a policy of reflation.

Another aspect of our economy with which the industrialist must concern himself is the external situation. Britain is an island which must export in order to import. About half of the nation's food requirements, and the majority of raw materials, are imported and must be paid for by selling goods overseas. Apart from 1956 and 1958, Britain has imported more goods each year this century than she has exported, in other words we have had an unfavourable *balance of trade*. But foreign trade consists of invisible items, such as our shipping services, earnings of British companies overseas, insurance and banking services, as well as visible items; when these are taken into account Britain has a favourable balance in most years. This balance is called the *balance of payments*.

The financing of two world wars during this century has necessitated the sale of many of our overseas investments. The loss of the relative interest and dividends has drastically reduced our "invisible exports," which had helped to meet the deficit in our *balance of trade*.

One cause of an unfavourable balance of payments is excessive demand for goods on the home market. If this exists then imports of foreign goods will rise and some goods which might have been exported will be used at home instead. It is not surprising, therefore, that periods of credit restraint, designed to dampen down demand, have occurred in the years immediately following those in which the balance of payments has been adverse. An unfavourable swing in the balance of payments should, therefore, be taken as a warning that credit controls may have to be imposed.*

London is the hub of the Sterling Area and nearly half of world trade is financed in sterling. Furthermore, sterling is a reserve currency; that

* *See* Chapter V for comment on the types of controls which may be used by the Bank of England to carry out the Government's economic policy.

is, a currency kept by other countries as part of their gold and currency reserves. Any lack of confidence in sterling can, therefore, have severe repercussions in the foreign exchange market; with so much sterling in use in the world its value can change quite rapidly in response to rumours. If it is feared that sterling will have to be devalued (maybe because of severe inflation in the U.K.), then holders of sterling will want to switch into another currency as soon as possible, and the consequent increase in the supply of sterling on the foreign exchange market will depress the value of the pound.

There are several ways in which sterling can be defended from such a turn of events. In the first place the Exchange Equalisation Account can be used to "mop up" any surplus sterling and so keep up its value. This Account holds the U.K.'s reserves of gold and convertible currencies, which it can use as the need arises. When sterling is weak it sells gold and foreign currencies in exchange for sterling and when sterling is strong it uses sterling to buy foreign currencies to build up the reserves. Most countries have adopted the system of fixed exchange rates laid down by the International Monetary Fund. On joining the Fund member countries have to declare a gold value for their currencies and from this it is possible to calculate a rate of exchange between any two currencies. Between the U.S. dollar and the pound sterling, for instance, there is a fixed rate of exchange of $2·40 = £1. There is some degree of flexibility in that there may be day-to-day fluctuations of up to 1 % either side of the fixed parities, but to all intents and purposes the rates are fixed not floating. If the U.S. dollar/sterling rate falls to around $2·38 = £1 then the Exchange Equalisation Account is certain to be operating in the market to keep up the rate, while if it goes up to nearly $2·42 then the Account will be buying foreign currencies with sterling in order to keep the rate down to within the agreed margin.

Another way in which sterling can be defended is by borrowing from the International Monetary Fund. All the member countries subscribe gold and their own currencies up to a stipulated quota, and they are permitted to borrow foreign currencies in exchange for their own, subject to certain formalities and limits. Britain has used the Fund on four occasions since it was formed in 1946 and on each occasion the currencies borrowed were incorporated into our reserves, thus helping to substantiate the apparent ability of Britain to withstand a run on the reserves, resulting from a balance of payments deficit and/or a weakness of sterling in the foreign exchange market.

In 1961 and in 1964–65 another device was used to defend the pound. This was the Basle Agreement whereby countries in Western Europe "stock-piled" sterling in order to keep up its value in the foreign exchange market. What this amounted to was that the countries concerned instead of selling their receipts of sterling for other currencies, held them apart from the market, thus keeping down the supply of sterling and avoiding a further fall in its value.

Another device for defending currencies is the "swap agreement." This is an arrangement whereby the Federal Reserve Bank of New York agrees to credit the account of a central bank in another country with a certain sum in dollars in exchange for an equivalent credit in the currency of the country concerned. For instance, the Federal Reserve Bank would credit the account of the Bank of France with $50 million and the Bank of France would credit the Federal Reserve Bank of New York with the equivalent of $50 million in French francs. The Bank of England has an arrangement such as this with the Federal Reserve Bank and this was extensively used in the 1964–65 crisis.

Stable exchange rates are vital to foreign trade, for unless the exporter can be reasonably sure of how much he will receive in sterling for the foreign currency that is to be paid for his goods he will not export them, and if he cannot be sure how much he will have to pay in sterling for the goods he is importing he will be reluctant to import them.

The United Kingdom Government devalued by some 14% in November 1967. The new dollar/sterling rate of exchange is $2·40 = £1.

At present the whole system of international exchange rates is under reconsideration.

EXAMINATION QUESTIONS

1. Distinguish between the *balance of trade* and the *balance of payments*. Can a country have an adverse balance of trade and yet a favourable balance of payments?

2. Explain the measures a country can adopt to maintain the external value of its currency.

3. What would be the probable effects on the United Kingdom's balance of payments of a rise in the level of internal prices?

4. Define elasticity of demand and describe the factors which determine it. Illustrate your answer with diagrams.

5. Define the terms *marginal utility, marginal cost* and *marginal revenue* and explain how the economist uses these concepts in analysing the formation of prices under perfect competition.

6. How far can economics be of service to the manager?

7. Explain how a business is affected by:

(a) rising prices;
(b) falling prices.

8. Explain the significance of the terms "marginal cost" and "marginal utility" in the determination of prices.

9. "Prices are no longer fixed by Supply and Demand: they are determined by the dominant firms in each industry."
Discuss this statement.

10. What factors, other than a change in the price of the commodity, may cause the demand for a commodity to change? Show, by a diagram, how such a change would affect the demand curve.

PART SIX

GENERAL PRINCIPLES OF FINANCE, AND BUSINESS LAW

Chapter XXVII

BANKING AND FINANCE

THERE is a vital relationship between the business unit and the sources of finance. Without the services which the financial institutions provide, industry would be unable to operate on anything like its present scale and technological progress would be impeded. On the banking system in particular rests a tremendous responsibility to industry and the community; not only does it provide essential services but it is also the medium through which the Government employs monetary controls to influence the level of economic activity. Those who are, or hope to be, in positions of responsibility in industry must therefore make themselves as well informed as possible about our financial system.

This chapter is concerned with finance in relation to the economy. Chapter XVIII also covers some of the same ground, but deals with finance from the point of view of financial planning. The slight repetition is felt justified in the interests of clarity.

The object of this chapter is to describe how money and credit is made available, and to show how the total of money and credit influences the whole economic situation and, therefore, the level of industrial activity.

TRADE CREDIT

Credit enables enterprises to produce goods in anticipation of demand and of revenue. The term *credit* embraces the borrowing of money from the banks and other financial institutions, as well as delaying payment of debts incurred. Thus, the manufacturer may purchase his raw materials with money that he has borrowed, or he arranges with his supplier to settle his account in, say, three months' time, by which time he hopes to have produced and sold his goods. The distributor of goods, *i.e.* the wholesaler or the retailer, may also seek credit in either of these two ways. Trade credit plays an important part in the availability of credit as a whole, as has been shown in the Report of the Committee on the Working of the Monetary System (Cmnd 827):

> "Trade credit figures in the balance sheet of the average business in the form of a credit item for amounts owing to it for past sales and a debit item for amounts outstanding to its suppliers. Both items are usually large in relation to other current assets and liabilities (such as bank credit); and the willingness of businesses to see either of them grow or diminish has an important influence on the availability of credit in the economic system. . . . In conditions of boom it [trade credit] can be used to finance a continuing expansion, even when bank credit is being contracted, so long as business

expectations remain sanguine. . . . Moreover, trade credit is so large in relation to bank credit that a comparatively small lengthening of trade credit would normally offset quite a large proportionate reduction in bank credit."

THE COMMERCIAL BANKS

The main source of institutional finance, as distinct from trade credit, is the commercial banking system. As its name suggests, the commercial banking system is that which provides services primarily, though by no means entirely, to industry and commerce. This is distinct from the network of savings banks which are concerned in the main with the safekeeping of the savings of the individual.

Nearly all the commercial banking business in England and Wales is in the hands of the ten Clearing Banks who jointly run the London Bankers' Clearing House. Of these, Barclays, Lloyds, Midland, National Westminster, commonly known as the "Big Four," account for the major part of the resources and business of the system. The other six are the District, Martins, Williams Deacon's, Glyn Mills, Coutts and the National Bank.

The main functions of the commercial banks are threefold; these are as follows:

1. The acceptance of deposits.
2. The provision of the means with which to transfer deposits.
3. The provision of credit.

The first two of these functions, that is the acceptance of deposits and the ways in which they can be drawn upon or transferred, can conveniently be dealt with together.

The banks will accept two types of deposits: those on current account (which amount to about two-thirds of total deposits), and those on deposit account. On current account no interest is paid, but the depositor has the advantages of immediate accessibility to his deposit and of being able to draw cheques on his account. To the businessman and to a large proportion of private individuals this last advantage is essential, for all the larger transactions and many of the smaller ones in the ordinary business of life are settled by way of cheque.

Of growing importance, too, is the credit transfer system through which any person, whether a customer of a bank or not, can transfer payments through the banking system for the credit of the account of a customer of one of the banks. Customers can also draw upon their balances in cash, of course, but in the case of deposit accounts the banks can technically insist upon seven days' notice being given.

The banks accept the responsibility of ensuring that cash drawings are made up in the right denominations of notes and coin to meet the needs of the customer (for making up wage packets for instance), and this often necessitates transporting notes and coin from one area to another, which is both a costly and risky business. One other way in which bank deposits can be transferred should also be mentioned. This is the banker's standing order whereby the bank is entrusted with the task of making payments on behalf of its customer on the day on which they fall due to be made. All the customer has to do is to sign an order requesting the bank to make the regular payments and then, of course, make sure that he has a balance on his account sufficient to meet them.

Bank balances whether on current or deposit account are an alternative to notes and coin as a means of settling transactions. They are, therefore, part of our money supply—the major part in fact—and as such they play a vital role, as we shall see later, in the determination of the level of economic activity.

The first two functions of the banks have now been considered. These are to accept deposits and to provide the means by which to withdraw and transfer deposits. The third essential function is the provision of credit. To appreciate what precisely is meant by this it would be as well at this stage briefly to examine a typical balance sheet of a "Big Four" bank (Fig. 85). This has been simplified and rounded off to make the task easier, but it nevertheless contains the items in the right proportions—proportions that are vital to a bank and two of which are rather rigidly adhered to.

A bank has responsibilities both to its shareholders and to its depositors. These are shown on the liabilities side of the balance sheet as *capital* and *deposits* respectively. For the shareholders the bank must make as large a profit as possible, and for the depositors it must maintain its assets in a sufficiently liquid form to ensure that it is able to meet depositors' demands for repayment. The way in which a bank strikes a balance between these rather conflicting responsibilities of profitability and liquidity is shown on the assets side of the balance sheet.

The first asset, *cash on hand and balances with the Bank of England*, is the most liquid, and the assets become increasingly less liquid lower down the balance sheet. Since 1946, the banks have by convention maintained a minimum *cash ratio* of 8%; *i.e.* cash on hand and with the Bank of England as a percentage of deposits. This ratio ensures that at any time the banks have sufficient cash to meet their depositors' needs—in practice the banks are being very conservative for it is very unlikely that at any one time repayment of as much as 8% of deposits would be demanded.

The next item, *cheques in course of collection and balances with other banks*, is a liquid item, but at any one time it must be assumed that other banks would hold cheques, which, if they were cleared, would approximately offset this item. It is not, therefore, extended as a percentage of deposits.

Call money is money lent overnight, or for a maximum of fourteen days, to the Discount Houses. It could therefore be called in quite quickly if the need arose. This usually amounts to about 8 or 9% of deposits.

BALANCE SHEET

Liabilities	£m.	Assets	£m.	% of Deposits
Capital	25	Cash on hand and with		
Reserve	25	Bank of England	85	8·5
Deposits	1000	Cheques in course of col-		
Acceptances	160	lection and balances		
		with other banks	60	—
		Call money	85	8·5
		Treasury bills	70	7·0
		Other bills	40	4·0
		LIQUIDITY RATIO		28·0*
		Special deposits	20	2·0
		Investments	175	17·5
		Investments in subsidiary		
		companies	5	
		Advances	500	50·0
		Premises	10	
		Acceptances	160	
	£1210 m.		£1210 m.	

FIG. 85.—*Typical balance sheet of a "Big Four" bank*

* The traditional minimum ratio of 30% was reduced to 28% in 1963. In practice the liquidity ratio is usually above the minimum, reaching a peak at the end of the calendar year when the Government's deficit (and hence the need to borrow by way of Treasury bills) is at its highest.

Treasury bills are bills of exchange drawn upon H.M. Treasury which are in effect documents undertaking to repay in 91 days (possibly 63 days) a sum of money borrowed by the Treasury. In practice the banks do not buy these bills until they have been issued for at least a week so that they will all mature within twelve weeks at the most. They yield interest at about $\frac{1}{4} - \frac{3}{4}\%$ below the Bank Rate.

Other bills of exchange are those drawn upon, or accepted by, banks or are commercial bills drawn by or on first-class trading firms. In the main they are for periods up to three months, though they may be for longer periods.

All the assets so far described, with the exception of *cheques in course of collection*, comprise the liquid assets of the bank. Again, by convention rather than law, these must not fall below a minimum of 28% of deposits. This ratio is important, for it is through restricting the supply of liquid assets to the banking system that the authorities can best control the creation of credit by the banks, a process which we must consider later in this chapter.

These liquid assets produce only a modest rate of interest (cash on hand produces no income at all, of course), and it is through the less liquid assets, *investments* and *advances*, that the banks earn the majority of their income. The item *investments* consists entirely of gilt-edged securities, half of which have less than five years to maturity and the other half more than five years. By the term *advances* is meant both loans and overdrafts; *i.e.* money lent to institutions, firms and private individuals. The difference between a loan and an overdraft is that in the case of a loan the bank opens a loan account for the sum that is to be borrowed and credits the customer's current account with that sum, whereas if the money is to be borrowed by way of overdraft the customer draws cheques in excess of his credit balance putting his account "in the red" to the extent of the overdraft limit arranged. A loan is repaid by occasional payments from the customer's current account and interest is charged on the outstanding balance on the loan account. Interest on an overdraft is also payable on the outstanding balance but the borrower has the advantage that credits to the account, such as salary payments, will reduce the interest that has to be paid to the extent that they remain undrawn upon. Into the item *advances* the banks will invest as much as possible of their customers' deposits, for this is the most profitable asset, but it is unlikely that the proportion of *advances* to *deposits*, which already exceeds 50%, will be raised much further. The *advances* ratio has never exceeded 60%, and it is extremely unlikely that the banks would now want to have as large a slice of their deposits as that invested in the non-government sector of the community; unless, therefore, bank deposits increase, advances are not likely to rise.

Having thus worked the way through a typical bank balance sheet it should be easier to see how banks create credit, and the extent to which they can do so. Every time a bank makes a loan it creates a deposit, because the money that is lent will be used by the customer of the bank to settle some transaction and the recipient (or some later recipient) of the cash will pay it into his account. But if the cash that is lent by the bank was originally paid in in the form of a cheque drawn on another bank (thus decreasing that bank's deposits) then the net effect of the process will be neither to increase nor to decrease bank deposits as a whole. In other words, no credit has been created. The creation of credit requires a fresh inflow of cash into the banking system, which usually means that the public sector of the community (the Government, local government and the nationalised industries) must be spending money which will then come into the private sector (the non-government sector) of the community, whose bankers are the commercial banks. Take a situation, therefore, where a cheque for £1,000,000, drawn on the Bank of England, is received by a customer of a commercial bank, the Allied Bank. He pays the cheque into his account and the bank's balance sheet will change as follows:

ALLIED BANK

Deposits + £1,000,000	Cash on hand + £1,000,000

The Allied Bank would not want to keep this deposit in the form of cash as cash earns no income. If, for instance, the bank must keep 10% in cash then there will be 90% (£900,000) available for lending. The Allied Bank's balance sheet will now appear as follows:

Deposits + £1,000,000	Cash on hand	+ £100,000
	Advances	+ £900,000
+ £1,000,000		+ £1,000,000

If the £900,000 that is lent by the Allied Bank is used by the customer to pay for some transaction with a customer of the Beaver Bank then Beaver Bank's deposits will increase by £900,000 and so will its cash on hand. If only 10% need be kept in cash, £810,000 (90%) will be available for lending. These changes will be reflected in Beaver Bank's balance sheet as follows:

Deposits + £900,000	Cash on hand	+ £90,000
	Advances	+ £810,000
+ £900,000		+ £900,000

The £810,000 lent will, of course, come back into the banking system as a deposit with, say, the Cornhill Bank, and the deposits of the banks as a whole will then have risen by £2,710,000 (£1,000,000 + £900,000 + £810,000). The process will continue until the original £1,000,000 has been whittled down to such a small sum that it will not be worth while converting it from cash to other assets. The overall effect of the original inflow of £1,000,000 of fresh cash to the banking system will be to increase bank deposits by several times this amount. In other words there is a credit-creation "multiplier."

The size of the "multiplier" must depend upon a number of factors.

For instance, upon the extent to which a bank buys such assets as Treasury bills and Government stocks instead of using all of the 90% of each instalment of "fresh cash" to make advances. Cash used to buy these securities might flow back into the public sector and to some extent offset the original inflow of fresh cash into the banking system. Another determining factor is the public's desire to hold deposits with financial institutions other than the banks. Money lent by a bank may not come back into the banking system. It may instead be paid as a deposit into one of these other institutions and be used to buy Government securities.

The commercial banks, as has now been demonstrated, can create credit if they come into the possession of fresh cash and to an extent several times as great as the amount of the cash inflow. But this assumes that the Government sits back and allows the banks to create credit. If it is contrary to the Government's monetary policy to allow the money supply to be increased (and it is necessary to remember that bank deposits account for three-quarters of the money supply), then the Bank of England will step in and "mop-up" any fresh cash. This would be done by *open market operations, i.e.* selling securities to firms and individuals thus reducing their bank balances, or by *special deposits*, whereby the banks would be instructed to pay over a certain proportion of their deposits to the Bank of England to be frozen until such times as the Government chooses to see them repaid. Another device which could be used would be to raise Bank Rate (the Bank of England's rate of interest for discounting bills of exchange for the Discount Houses) to which other market rates of interest are linked. Higher interest rates discourage borrowing, but it is unlikely that the banks would find it difficult to increase their advances despite the higher "price" that has to be paid for them.

THE BANK OF ENGLAND

The measures mentioned above that can be taken to control the credit-creating process of the commercial banks are all weapons of the Bank of England, the central bank. When the Bank of England was founded in 1694 it was established as a commercial bank. There was no such thing as a central bank in those days. Gradually the Bank of England took on the functions which are now recognised as being essential to a central bank, and the Bank was nationalised in 1946 when it was given broad powers of control over the commercial banks. It is the Government's bank, having the accounts of the Government departments, and is also the bankers' bank. The banks keep approximately half of their 8% cash ratio in the form of a current account balance with the Bank of England, and by means of these accounts the banks are able to draw additional notes and coin, whenever they are required, and to settle their day-to-day balances with the Bankers' Clearing House.

As central bank, the Bank of England is responsible for the note issue. All the Bank of England notes at present in circulation are fiduciary (not backed by gold), apart from some £300,000 which are issued in addition, being backed by the small amount of gold coin which the Bank still holds. The fiduciary issue has increased year by year to meet the needs of the community (for instance, bank depositors who quite naturally expect to be able to draw their balances in cash if they so require), and is also varied seasonally to meet the community's needs at holiday times and at Christmas.

The central bank of a country must act as "Lender of Last Resort" to the financial institutions which are unable to borrow sufficient from other sources. This the Bank of England does for the twelve Discount Houses who receive this concession as a *quid pro quo* for tendering for all the Treasury bills put up for tender every Friday. The Government is thus assured that it will get the day-to-day finance it wants in order to meet its expenditure, and the Discount Houses are assured that if all else fails they can balance their books by borrowing from the Bank of England.

This borrowing can take one of two forms. A Discount House can discount bills with the Bank at Bank Rate (this is the meaning of Bank Rate—the rate at which the Bank of England will discount first-class bills), or it can borrow from the Bank for a minimum of seven days at Bank Rate or possibly up to 1% above Bank Rate. The Discount Houses act as a buffer between the Bank of England and the commercial banks enabling the latter to maintain a steady cash ratio despite the rather violent day-to-day fluctuations in the flow of funds between the Government (*i.e.* the public sector) and the private sector of the community.

The country's reserves of gold and foreign currencies are held by the Bank of England, and the Bank operates the Exchange Equalisation Account through which, by buying and selling foreign currencies, fairly stable exchange rates are maintained. Limitations in the supply of foreign currencies to residents of the United Kingdom trading and travelling abroad are also the province of the Bank.

Management of the national debt, *i.e.* paying interest on Government stocks and issuing and redeeming stocks, is also a task of the Bank. In managing the debt the Bank of England is able to manipulate long-term interest rates as a deliberate part of the Government's monetary policy.

This is one of the ways in which the Bank of England carries out one of its principal functions: as agent for the Government in carrying out its monetary policy. The Bank has several monetary weapons in its armoury with which to influence the level of economic activity. Bank Rate, which, as has already been mentioned, is the rate of interest at which the Bank will discount first-class bills, can be used to discourage or encourage borrowing. There are several links between Bank Rate and other market rates of interest so that an increase in Bank Rate will result in an increase in the general level of interest rates. Bank Rate is sometimes described as a blunt weapon of control in that it only discourages or encourages; it does not reduce or increase borrowing by any set sum. It is nevertheless a useful control in that it has very strong psychological effects. A rise in the Rate is taken as a warning signal that credit is going to be made scarcer, and a reduction in the Rate as a "green light" to economic expansion. The external effects of a change in the Bank Rate are also important. An increase in the general level of interest rates will attract an inflow of short-term capital to London from overseas investors who foresee an opportunity to receive a higher yield on their capital than they can earn in their own countries. Just the opposite would, of course, occur if the level of interest rates was lowered. Both movements are very important from the point of view of the balance of payments.

By buying and selling Government securities to the private sector the Bank carries out open-market operations. If it is necessary to reduce the spending power of the community it will sell securities receiving cheques drawn on the commercial banks in payment, and if it is desirable to stimulate the economy then the Bank will buy Government stocks and inject cash into the community. The movements of cash affect the credit-creating ability of the banks.

Depending, too, upon the state of the economy, the Bank will either call for or repay special deposits. These are a given proportion of the banks' deposits which are frozen at the Bank of England for an indefinite period. If, for instance, the banks are instructed to pay over 2% of their deposits then they must do so in cash, and if their liquidity ratios are down to the bare minimum then they will have to either sell some of their investments or call in some of their advances. The ultimate repayment of the 2% will enable them to expand their advances and hence their deposits.

If the measures so far described are insufficient to bring about a required contraction in the money supply, the Government, through the medium of the Bank of England, can issue directives to the banks. These are of two kinds, quantitative and qualitative. Quantitative directives are in the nature of instructions to either freeze or reduce the level of advances while qualitative directives require the banks to give priority in their lending to particular industries such as those concerned with exports or defence.

By funding operations the Bank of England can also affect the credit-creating powers of the banks. These operations take the form of replacing a short-term security with a longer-dated security. For instance, in 1951, when the banks' liquidity ratios were well above the minimum (they stood on average at 39%), the Bank of England was responsible for the issue of £1000 million of Serial Funding Stock. These were issued in place of Treasury bills and, in that the banks took up some £500 million of the total, their liquidity ratios were reduced to an average of 32%. At this lower ratio the Government was in a much better position to control the creation of credit.

In addition to the commercial banks and the central banks there are several other types of financial institutions whose functions need to be understood. These institutions are discussed below.

THE MERCHANT BANKS AND ISSUING HOUSES

The term *merchant banks* is loosely applied to a number of financial firms in the City of London which originated as businesses that bought and sold goods and later started to provide a range of financial services for their customers. Some of the merchant banks still do some marketing, but in general their present-day functions consist of the ordinary banking services which the commercial banks provide, plus acting as accepting houses and in some cases as issuing houses. As accepting houses these institutions have an important role in the system of bill finance. By "accepting" a bill of exchange these houses undertake to pay it on behalf of their customer. This confers on the drawer of the bill the ability to discount the bill at a fine rate of interest, for such a bill is a "bank bill" and as such is eligible for discount by the Bank of England as lender of last resort. This type of bill is thus sought after by the commercial banks and discount houses to form part of their liquid assets.

From the point of view of the trader who has drawn a bill of exchange upon a debtor, obtaining the acceptance of a merchant bank enables him to obtain his money immediately instead of at the date of maturity of the bill, and at the lowest possible rate of discount.

Issuing houses provide an invaluable service to firms that seek additional capital by issuing shares. Not all of the merchant banks are issuing houses nor are all of the issuing houses merchant banks, but it is convenient to deal with the two types of institutions together.

As sponsors and underwriters for new issues, the issuing houses make it easier for the borrower to raise money through the Stock Exchange. The fact that an issuing house is prepared to undertake the issue encourages investors to take up the shares. With the assistance of the firm of stockbrokers who are to act for the issue, the terms of the issue will be agreed and underwriters found. The latter are in the main insurance companies which, for payment of a commission, will commit themselves to subscribe for the shares if they are not taken up by the public.

In addition to arranging the actual issue of shares, the issuing houses act as advisers on the practice and law concerning new issues, and on a variety of other financial matters such as amalgamations, acquiring subsidiary firms and reorganisations, as well as the possible sources of finance. They also act as trustees and advisers for pension funds, and trust funds of various kinds.

HIRE PURCHASE FINANCE HOUSES

The hire purchase and credit instalment debt in the U.K. amounts to more than £1200 million and the major part of this is owed to hire purchase houses. These institutions accept deposits from the public (from firms as well as private individuals), at rates of interest quite favourable to the depositor, but usually requiring three or six months' notice for withdrawals. They also borrow from the banks and accepting houses. There are a large number of small finance houses, but the major part of the total hire purchase debt is due to the larger houses which are members of the Finance Houses Association. The commercial banks have interests in the larger finance houses by owning all or part of the share capital.

The hire purchase companies provide finance for a number of purposes. The purchase of motor vehicles accounts for more than half of the debt, while such items as furniture, radios and television sets, domestic appliances and industrial and farm equipment account for most of the remainder. Hire purchase is normally extended for a one-, two- or three-year period but some of this credit is for four years and, in addition, the finance houses do extend straightforward loans to firms for business purposes over five years or more, but only in exceptional circumstances.

As has been indicated, hire purchase debt takes two forms: hire purchase and credit instalment. The essential difference between the two types of credit is that under hire purchase agreements the goods remain the property of the seller until payment has been completed, while under credit-instalment selling the ownership of the property passes to the buyer on payment of the first instalment.

INDUSTRIAL AND COMMERCIAL FINANCE CORPORATION AND FINANCE CORPORATION FOR INDUSTRY

The I.C.F.C. provides finance for the relatively small business concern which wants to borrow on long term rather than borrow from a bank on short term, and which is too small to be able to issue shares to the general public through the New Issues market. This institution thus fills to some extent the so-called Macmillan Gap—the *Macmillan Report on Finance and Industry* of 1931 drew attention to the difficulties of smaller industrial and commercial enterprises in obtaining finance and recommended that a company should be formed to devote itself to the needs of such concerns.

To assist in fulfilling this need another corporation, the Finance

Corporation for Industry, was established at the end of the Second World War. The shareholders are the Bank of England, and some insurance companies and trust companies, and like the I.C.F.C. the Corporation can borrow on the market. F.C.I. provides capital for the purpose of the re-equipment and development of industry to assist it to increase its efficiency and so help towards the maintenance and extension of employment. It provides assistance when bank finance is not forthcoming or a public issue cannot be arranged. For further details, the reader is referred back to p. 295.

NEGOTIABLE INSTRUMENTS

To complete this chapter it is appropriate to examine briefly the principal negotiable instruments used in business.

The majority of business transactions in Britain are carried out with cheques and to some extent banknotes are used. For foreign transactions the principal instrument is the bill of exchange. All these instruments are negotiable which means that all rights under them are transferred either by mere delivery or by delivery accompanied by endorsement. The person in *bona fide* possession of a negotiable instrument is presumed to be the lawful owner of it.

A Bank of England note is a promissory note in which the Bank undertakes to pay a stated sum to the bearer of the note. Anyone who takes a note in good faith, unaware that it has been stolen, has a right to the note.

A bill of exchange is defined by the *Bills of Exchange Act, 1882*, as:

an unconditional order in writing, addressed by one person to another, signed by the person giving it, requiring the person to whom it is addressed to pay on demand, or at a fixed or determinable future time, a sum certain in money to or to the order of a specified person, or to bearer.

In practice, a bill is drawn by a creditor upon his debtor and will be made payable on demand or at some determinable future date such as 30, 60 or possibly 90 days after the date of the bill. Alternatively, it may be payable one month, two months or three months after the date of the bill—a month being taken as a calendar month. The debtor is allowed three days of grace so that a bill that is due on 1st June need not be paid until 4th June, unless that day is a Sunday or Bank Holiday, in which case it is payable on the previous day.

A creditor, after he has drawn a bill, will send it to his debtor who must signify his acceptance of the bill before it becomes a contract. He does so by writing the word "accepted" across the face of the bill followed by his signature. Usually he will indicate where the bill is to be paid by writing, for instance, "accepted payable at XYZ Bank, Littletown," but this is not essential. Having received back the accepted bill, the creditor can, if he wishes, discount the bill with his bank, or alternatively hold the bill until maturity and then present it to the debtor for payment.

A cheque is a bill of exchange, drawn on a banker, payable on demand. As it is payable on demand it needs no acceptance. By virtue of the *Cheques Act, 1957*, a cheque need no longer be endorsed, provided that it is paid into the account of the payee. If it is a third party cheque then the payee must endorse it before it is paid into an account. Cheques payable to bearer do not need to be endorsed.

THE NATIONAL GIRO SERVICE

The Government already has considerable influence on the banking system. It controls the amount of cash and credit available by the means explained in this chapter. However, the normal banking system has tended to be in the hands of the commercial banks, which are limited companies operating to earn profits. The Post Office savings account system could not be regarded as a competitor, because transfers between customers' accounts were not possible.

From the autumn of 1968 the National Giro Service was introduced. This is in direct competition with the banks and is operated by the Post Office. Customers keep accounts and are able to transfer payments to other account holders by completing transfer instructions. The important feature of the system is that cheques as such are not required.

Other important aspects of the Giro Service are as follows:

1. All payments into accounts and transfers are cleared centrally by means of a computer.

2. Payments can be made by the service instead of by sending postal orders or other means. A person not having an account simply pays in the amount due and completes the transfer form (these can be preprinted by the creditor).

3. "Standing orders" can be completed whereby specific payments can be made each week or month quite automatically, *e.g.* hire-purchase instalments.

4. Salaries, wages and pensions can be paid through the system by transfer to the appropriate employees' accounts.

5. The charges for the service are as stipulated in the details which are issued by the Post Office.

The advantages claimed for the Giro service are as follows:

1. Daily accounting.

2. Statements which show debit and credit items separately, subdivided by categories.

3. Easy identification of each item on the statement.

4. The incorporation in the statement of the account holder's own reference information.

5. The integration of Giro with the customer's own accounting and billing system.

6. Payment of wages and pensions by transfer, or payment order encashable at a post office.

7. An automatic payment system without the need for supporting vouchers.

8. Rapid transfers to and from bank accounts.

9. Ready access to the international Giro payments network.

10. Ready acceptance of a Post Office service by the general public.

Source: *National Giro for the Businessman*, published by the G.P.O.

EXAMINATION QUESTIONS

1. Outline the functions of the Bank of England, commenting upon their relative importance.

2. Explain how the banks create credit. Are there any limitations on their ability to do this?

3. Define the functions of the merchant banks and issuing houses.

4. Give an account of the measures which a central bank might adopt to arrest inflationary tendencies.

5. What steps can a country which lives by trading take to ensure that its economy remains prosperous?

6. Explain the meaning of devaluation, and consider the economic effects of a devaluation of the pound sterling.

7. Define the functions of I.C.F.C. and F.C.I. Why were they established?

8. Define *bill of exchange*. What is meant by "acceptance" of a bill?

CHAPTER XXVIII

GOVERNMENT AND INDUSTRY

INTRODUCTION

THE purpose of this chapter is to give an *outline* of how the British Government functions. In addition, the role of the Government, and its relations with industry, are examined. This short chapter cannot do full justice to what is a detailed subject; moreover, government should be concerned with *current* happenings. Students requiring further information are advised to study the books recommended at the end of the chapter and to read national newspapers which give details of Government procedures and policy decisions.

DEVELOPMENT OF GOVERNMENT

The British Government is elected by a majority of the people voting according to democratic principles. It is a body charged with the responsibilities for determining the policy of the State and for ensuring that the laws are carried out and upheld. This is a general statement. Strictly speaking the "Government" is chosen by the party in power and the administration of law is not a function of government (*see* below).

In Britain the evolution to the present-day practices has extended over hundreds of years. From the time of William I (1066 onwards) there has been a monarchy, and the systems and procedures have been affected by this characteristic. While there was a break in the normal practice from 1649 to 1660, this was only short lived.

From early times to the end of the seventeenth century there was conflict between the monarchy and Parliament. Important landmarks can be seen from statutes which gave Parliament increased power:

1. *Magna Carta, 1215.*—This Charter gave many rights to the barons which were previously at the discretion of the monarchy. It freed the Church and established that justice should be meted out by the law of the land. Although government as known today was not yet in existence, the Magna Carta may be regarded as a most important step in its establishment.

2. *Petition of Right, 1628.*—Again, this was a measure to obtain greater rights. In particular, there was a move made which required Parliament to consent to the levying of taxes. It also dealt with the billeting of soldiers, martial law and illegal imprisonment.

3. *Bill of Rights, 1689.*—The Bill of Rights is regarded by many authorities as the major step towards modern government, whereby the country is ruled by the elected representatives of the people for the

benefit of the latter. In effect, this Bill made illegal the passing of laws, collection of taxes, keeping of a standing army and related matters *unless* any such act was given prior consent by Parliament. This meant that considerable power had passed from the monarch to Parliament.

4. *Act of Settlement, 1701.*—This Act is related to the *Bill of Rights* and consolidated still further the rights of Parliament. Besides laying down conditions relating to the title to the crown (*e.g.* the monarch must be a member of the Church of England) the Act also determines the succession to the throne.

5. *Other Acts.*—Many other acts have been passed by Parliament thus establishing the principle that it alone possesses absolute power for making law—known as the "sovereignty of Parliament." Examples are the *Parliament Acts, 1911* and *1949*, which reduced the powers of the House of Lords, and *His Majesty's Declaration of Abdication Act, 1936*, which amended the terms of the *Act of Settlement* by varying the right of succession.

6. *Common Law.*—Decisions made by the law courts become a part of the law of the land, and therefore affect the manner in which people may behave. Many law cases affect companies and trade unions, and so have a direct bearing upon their activities. Thus, for example, in the case of *Salomon* v. *Salomon & Co Ltd* (1897) AC 22 it was confirmed that a company was a legal person which could own property and was quite separate in identity from the shareholders.

In addition to decisions on cases there is also the *interpretation* of the laws made by Parliament, *i.e.* the statute law. Judges are often called upon to determine what is intended by statutes. For this reason the careful drafting of Bills is essential, *i.e.* documents which have not been approved by Parliament, and therefore are not yet part of the law.

The matters 1 to 6 may be classified in a different way:

(*a*) *Rules of law.* All laws which are derived from statute or common law come under this heading. These should not be confused with the *Rule of Law* (*see* below).

(*b*) *Conventions.* These are rules which are followed primarily because they help to ensure political stability. If they were disregarded there is a serious danger that the party concerned would invoke disfavour (*see* below).

RULE OF LAW

An important principle of the British legal system is that *all* people are subject to the law and, if they do wrong, must be punished. This concept is known as the *Rule of Law.*

Persons "in authority" must operate within the law or they must answer to a court of law. This means that the law operates the same for the rich as for the poor. Moreover, the Constitution upon which the country is governed is derived from the law.

Although these basic principles are the same since they were first formulated by A. V. Dicey in 1895, there have been modifications in their interpretation. The modern State requires very wide powers, and therefore there has been an inevitable encroachment upon what were formerly regarded as "private rights." In particular, industry and commerce are subject to many regulations which are aimed at giving greater safety to individuals or other protection.

Nevertheless, even admitting the need for a more liberal view of what is meant by *freedom* of action within the law, care has to be taken to ensure that those in authority do not exceed their powers. Public opinion is a safeguard, but often actions do not receive enough attention, especially if those who are being suppressed do not know their rights.

Since April 1967 there has been a Parliamentary Commissioner or *Ombudsman*, who has authority to investigate any complaints of maladministration, especially where there is a misuse of powers.

THE CONSTITUTION

Because of its gradual evolution the British form of government may be said to be unique. Much of what takes place is determined not by written rules or regulations but by convention. This is the reason for the assertion that the *rules of conduct* in Britain are based on an *unwritten Constitution*. Nevertheless, there is an expectation that the *conventions* will be followed, and so they are in effect the code of behaviour, *i.e.* the laws.

In addition, statutes and case law, mentioned earlier, become embodied in the Constitution. How the conventions should be interpreted has been the subject of works by eminent authorities, *e.g.* A. V. Dicey, Walter Bagehot and Erskine May. All these sources of law become "intertwined" so as to form a workable Constitution which *is flexible*. This is in contrast to the *written* Constitution of the United States of America, where precise procedures have to be followed to pass a law.

Examples of conventions are as follows:

1. If a Government is defeated in the House of Commons on a measure which is regarded as being of major significance, then it should resign.

2. The Queen is required to give her assent to Bills and act according to the wishes of her Ministers.

3. The Cabinet is based on convention, and so is its mode of operation. It is primarily concerned with key issues, many of which have to be determined by committees.

ORGANISATION OF GOVERNMENT

Although there is some overlap of duties, it is usual to divide the functions under three main headings:

1. Legislature—the section which deals with making the laws.

2. Executive—concerned with administration, *i.e.* the practical application of the laws and also their initiation.

3. Judiciary—made up of the courts of law and concerned with the interpretation of the laws.

These three are explained in more detail below.

THE LEGISLATURE

Parliament

The *House of Commons*, in which Members of Parliament sit, is the main part of the Legislature. There is also the *House of Lords*, which can also initiate Bills, except Money Bills. Matters contained in the Bills are debated by both Houses and then sent to the Queen or a Commission acting on her behalf for the Royal Assent. They then become Acts of Parliament or statutes.

Theoretically, the Legislature is controlled by the Queen-in-Parliament, but, in fact, it is a convention that the Queen always gives her Royal Assent to Bills. The Queen has other functions:

(*a*) *She opens Parliament.* This takes place at the beginning of each session and includes the delivery of a speech from the Throne, prepared by the Ministers, indicating forthcoming legislation.

(*b*) *Selection of Prime Minister.*

(*c*) *Dissolution of Parliament.* The maximum life of a Government is five years, after which re-election is necessary. However, dissolution may take place at any time on the *advice* of the Prime Minister.

For (*b*) and (*c*) it is clear that usually the Queen must act in accordance with the wishes of her advisers.

Today the term "Queen-in-Parliament" refers to the Queen and both Houses, the three collectively being *Parliament*.

The *House of Lords* is unlikely to succeed with any Bills which are of a controversial nature. Moreover, although Bills, other than Money Bills, can be delayed up to one year, in practice the Lords' powers are not very great. An extremely useful service is provided through the detailed consideration of Bills which the House of Commons has not been able to examine fully.

Parliamentary privileges

Both Houses enjoy certain privileges which guard their members. They cannot be sued for slander on words spoken in either House, and any member or person outside Parliament may be punished or imprisoned for "breach of privilege," *i.e.* making statements or acting in a manner which affects the reputation of the House. The Speaker, *i.e.* chairman of the House of Commons, can decide whether there is a possible breach of privilege when the case is referred to the *Committee of Privileges.* In addition to *freedom of speech* there is also the privilege of deciding how proceedings shall be conducted—this applies to the House of Commons, for the powers of the House of Lords may be varied in the Commons.

Access to the Queen is also a privilege—this is a collective right for the House of Commons as a whole through the Speaker, and an individual right for each member of the House of Lords.

Procedure

Bills introduced into Parliament have to follow set procedures. In the case of Public Bills (*see* below), these may be summarised as follows:

1. Preparatory stage, when the details are examined by a Cabinet Legislative Committee and then drafted into legal form. When outside interests are affected the appropriate bodies have to be consulted, *e.g.* local authorities. Finally, a date for introducing the Bill into the appropriate House has to be settled.

2. Reading or debating stages, for giving the House an opportunity to examine each Bill. It is made up of the following:

(*a*) *First reading*, when the Bill is introduced to the House.

(*b*) *Second reading*, when the Bill is debated, possibly over a number of days. A Bill may be defeated by the party in opposition by voting on a motion. Defeat is unusual, because the officials known as the *Whips* ensure that Notices are given to members on how they have to vote; to ignore a "three-line whip" is to risk expulsion from the party.

(*c*) *Committee stage*, when the Bill is given a detailed examination by a standing committee.

(*d*) *Report stage*, which is referring back to the House so that any amendments proposed by the committee can be approved.

(*e*) *Third reading*, when the Bill is approved and sent to the House of Lords (or Commons depending upon where the Bill was initiated). A Money Bill would not be sent to the House of Lords.

This process (*a*) to (*e*) is then repeated in the House concerned.
Note: The procedures may be varied according to the nature of the Bill, but the essential steps are the same for all Public Bills.

3. Royal Assent. This is the formal approval of the Bill. It now becomes part of the law as an Act of Parliament.

Types of bills

Bills may be classified as shown below:

1. Public Bills, which deal with matters likely to affect the community as a whole. Often they are concerned with putting into legal form the policy being pursued by the Government in office.

A subdivision is as follows:

(*a*) *Money Bills*, which deal with spending or obtaining finance and have to be approved by the House of Commons. The *Cabinet* decides the content of a Money Bill after the following procedures have been carried out:

(*i*) Estimates are prepared by departments in December which are considered by the Treasury.

(*ii*) The *Committee of Supply* considers each departmental estimate.

(*iii*) Following the Budget Speech in April (details of which are the responsibility of the Chancellor of the Exchequer), the details are approved by resolutions passed by the *Committee of Ways and Means*. These become the Finance Bill and then the Finance Act.

(*iv*) *Consolidated Fund (Appropriation) Bills* are incorporated into the *Appropriation Act* which shows how the money can be spent.

Notes: The Committees of Supply and Ways and Means are "Committees of the whole House."

Safeguards against misuse or excessive spending of public funds are available through the Public Accounts Committee (financial investigations) and the Comptroller and Auditor General who is responsible for approving payments from the Consolidated Fund (the Government's banking account) and also for auditing the Accounts from Government departments.

(*b*) *General Public Bills* dealing with Government proposals.

(*c*) *Private Members' Bills* which are public bills initiated by a member, not necessarily with Government support.

2. *Private Bills* are initiated with the hope of giving benefit to private individuals or corporate bodies, such as local authorities.

The principal differences in procedure between private and public bills are as follows:

(*a*) There are seven stages to pass, as opposed to eleven for a public bill.

(*b*) A private bill has to be submitted through Parliamentary agents to Examiners of Petitions for Private Bills. Any views of parties who oppose a Bill have to be considered before it can be taken further. Because of the heavy expenses involved in this method there is a tendency to ask for permission to carry out an act by applying for a "provisional order" or a "special procedure order." Both of these can give the required powers without the complexity and expense involved in the procedures for private bills.

3. *Hybrid Bills*, which have the characteristics of a public bill, but affect only a particular party. These are comparatively rare.

THE EXECUTIVE

The parties involved in administering the laws are primarily the same as those who have the legislative powers. The executive responsibilities are in the hands of the leaders of the political party in power. There is the Prime Minister and his Ministers, some of whom will be members of the Cabinet, as well as the Law Officers of the Crown. These are known collectively as the "Government."

In addition, there is the *Privy Council*, which has around 300 members who are eminent persons, including present and past Cabinet Ministers. The full Council does not meet regularly, but a small committee meet, consisting of four to six members who are Cabinet Ministers, together with the Queen. Proclamations *or* Orders in Council are made, thus complying with the decisions of the Cabinet.

The most important person in the Government is the leader, *i.e.* the Prime Minister. He decides the membership of the Cabinet and acts as its Chairman. In times of crisis he is able to make decisions without consulting the Ministers involved, although obviously consultation is to be preferred.

Next in order of importance are the Ministers, who, with the Prime Minister, make up the Cabinet, which has considerable legislative and executive power. It is backed by a Secretariat and can call on advisers who are full-time civil servants or are persons appointed full-time or part-time for a specific purpose.

The Attorney General and Solicitor General and, in Scotland, the Lord Advocate and Solicitor General for Scotland, are the law officers of the Crown. These are political appointments, *i.e.* Members of Parliament of the party in power for the time being.

THE JUDICIARY

The Judiciary consists of the House of Lords, the courts of law, the judges, police forces and other officials who are concerned with interpreting and carrying out the law. Chapters XXIX–XXXI explain how the laws of England and Wales are administered.

GOVERNMENT CONTROL OF THE ECONOMY

INTRODUCTION

Today, the influence of the Government on the economy is extremely far reaching. Indeed, there is no area where the effects are not felt. In this section it would be futile to consider more than an outline of the main provisions and, even then, only so far as they have an impact on the growth and development of industry and commerce. Some of these major developments are considered below.

CONTROL OF VITAL INDUSTRIES

Avoidance of duplication and the provision of a vital service which is not likely to earn a profit are the main reasons for central control of an industry. There is also the possibility of industries being acquired by the Government in the national interest. Examples of the types of organisation which may be created are as follows:

1. Public boards and corporations

Such boards as the Marketing, Water Resources, and Hospital Boards provide illustrations of statutory organisations which are created to deal with specific functions. Some of these, particularly those concerned with marketing, have met with considerable resistance from the suppliers of the commodity to be marketed. The Egg Marketing Board and the "Lion" brand met with strong resistance until the scheme was modified quite drastically.

Public corporations are bodies created for the purpose of owning assets and operating a business enterprise. There are two forms—those created by Royal Charter, such as the B.B.C., and others which are given legal recognition by Act of Parliament. The nationalised industries cover a wide range of activities which include the Bank of England, electricity, gas, part of the transport industry, and coal.

2. Location and planning of industry

Under various Acts development areas have been created in which companies are given preferential treatment primarily in financial assistance or taxation concessions. The Treasury, Board of Trade, Department of Economic Affairs (D.E.A.) and National Economic Development Council (Neddy) all have an influence on the development of companies. Some of their activities are outlined in subsequent sections.

Some industries are given subsidies on a general basis. In others, aid is given to build essential projects such as the new liner the *Queen Elizabeth II* for which a special loan of £20 million was given.

3. Financial regulation

Through the Treasury and the Bank of England the Government is able to control lending to industry by raising the rate of interest (the Bank Rate, *see* p. 182) and by giving specific instructions on the rate of borrowing that can be permitted.

In addition, the rate of income tax and corporation tax tends to influence the attitudes of employees, managers and directors towards the achievement of the personal and company objectives. A high rate of taxation reduces the incentive to work harder and thereby affects the rate of growth.

The Budget is now a political and economic device for stimulating or discouraging activity in industries or areas. Spending can be curbed by modifying purchase tax on certain goods; licences and road taxes can be increased; import or export duties can be varied. These measures are not limited to an annual review. In the case of an economic crisis or emergency the so-called "little Budgets" can be introduced to permit changes to be made without delay.

Differential rates of tax on profits according to whether or not they are distributed as dividends can also have an influence on the policy adopted by a business. Similarly, the practice of charging interest on debentures *before* arriving at the profit figure has had a marked effect upon the capital structures developed by companies. These are devices which have been used in the past which have tended to encourage particular actions to be followed by businessmen. For details of methods of taxation in force at the present time students are advised to refer to a recent book on the subject.

ECONOMIC STABILITY

The Treasury is concerned with all financial matters of the country, and therefore plays a major role in the policy being followed in relation to taxation, providing funds for running the country, controlling expenditure and keeping a watch on currency, banking and related matters. Through the Budget proposals, and measures such as credit squeezes, hire-purchase restrictions, and changes in direct and indirect taxation, the economy can be made to operate according to the wishes of the Government. This is very much the *short-term* control of the economy. Over a longer period it has now become usual for a Government to consider the long-term National Plan whereby expansion rates are suggested, and the ways and means of achieving the targets are also indicated. The Treasury is also involved in long-term planning, but the prime responsibility for this work rests with the Department of Economic Affairs along with the National Economic Development Council.

Through regional planning boards and other committees the plans are considered and then implemented. The Department of Employment and Productivity is also involved in this planning and control. One of the most difficult tasks has been the attempt to control prices and incomes. A *norm* has been established beyond which prices and incomes will not be permitted to rise unless there are exceptional circumstances. This has meant a tremendous volume of work because all significant changes have had to be referred to the Prices and Incomes Board. In effect, Government control is being exercised over the supply and demand for products and for employees. While there is no denying that some degree of control is necessary, there are those who would argue that some of the restraints have gone too far. However, on the other side, there is no doubt that some parties—companies, employees, and trade unions—had developed a "free for all" which could have resulted in disastrous consequences for an economy which has to rely on exporting for survival.

Moves towards integration by agreement between two companies or by a *take over* of one by the other are also subject to control. Any development which is likely to lead to creating a virtual monopoly in an area where this is undesirable may not be approved by the *Monopolies Commission*. At the same time there has been encouragement towards more concentration and rationalisation of companies by the formation of the *Industrial Reorganisation Corporation* (*see* p. 468).

R

SELECTIVE ENCOURAGEMENT

The policy pursued by Governments in recent times has been to encourage the growth of specific types of business and to discourage others. This is an attempt to give priority to those industries likely to increase exports and, thereby, strengthen the balance-of-payments position.

Many examples can be quoted, but, since new measures are introduced from time to time, the reader is advised to keep abreast by reading of the latest developments in newspapers and journals. The selective employment tax whereby "service industries" are taxed at a higher rate than manufacturing industry is an illustration of a discriminatory tax. Concessions in the tax allowances for entertaining when foreign buyers are involved is another form of encouragement for exporting companies. The imposition of purchase tax at high rates on specific products can have the effect of curbing spending on the home market.

When necessary, for health reasons, a Government may publicise the ill effects of a commodity, as occurred with cigarettes when even television advertising was banned.

SAFEGUARDING EMPLOYEES

From the first *Factories Act* there has been a steady stream of legislation which has affected the employer and the employed. Successive Governments have also widened the social services, so that sickness, industrial injuries and retirement benefits have been extended. Medical services are also included in the services now controlled by the State. A further move towards giving safeguards to employees is the *Redundancy Payments Act, 1965*, which requires a sum to be paid to any person who becomes unemployed by virtue of redundancy.

As shown elsewhere in this book, even the training and education activities have not escaped attention. Under the *Industrial Training Act* training boards have now been established for most industries. Whether full value for money is being obtained has been doubted by some employers. However, this is largely in their own hands. If they wish to train their employees, then facilities can be provided. Unfortunately, many are still content to pay lip service to the idea, but do not have a comprehensive programme for education and training.

Much of the legislation has been concerned with improving the conditions of employees (*see* Chapter XXXI). However, under the requirements of the *Companies Acts* directors and managers have to observe strict regulations in the raising of finance and in the use of shareholders' funds. While there is no denying the need for safeguards, there are some who consider that not enough attention has been paid to controlling the activities of trade unions, and particularly those union members responsible for unofficial strikes. In the future it seems likely that the legislation in this area will be strengthened so that fewer production hours will be lost.

NECESSITY FOR GOVERNMENT CONTROL

There is now general acceptance that legislation is necessary to ensure that the resources of a country are used to the best advantage. Where there is disagreement is how the desired level of control can be achieved without stifling initiative.

As shown in other parts of the book, a company has to establish *objectives* which earn an adequate profit when translated into a percentage return on capital employed. The question is how to watch "public interest" and yet provide the environment for competitive enterprise—true free enterprise or *laissez-faire* is an artificial concept which cannot exist in modern conditions.

Regulations should be framed so that they interfere as little as possible with the efficient operation of a business and yet ensure the appropriate conditions of employment. In addition, the production of dangerous drugs and obnoxious products must be controlled. As regards "public interest" there seems little doubt that over a long period the normal operation of supply and demand will provide the goods and services required by consumers. Inevitably, mistakes will be made, but over the long period any commodities not sold will no longer be produced. In effect, therefore, the public interest is being pursued as part of normal business practice. Enlightened boards of directors do more than rely upon supply and demand. They create a *company image* quite deliberately so that the products made are accepted by the consumers; needless to say, these products have to be of the type which satisfy the demand at reasonable prices.

One of the big problems with the increased control of industry by government is the expenditure necessary for carrying out the work. Economic planning, social services, public corporations, granting subsidies to some industries and not to others, and generally taking an active part in directing business affairs, requires a tremendous organisation. Looking after the affairs of State is itself a complex task, and yet the problems multiply when measures have to be considered for separate industries and even individual companies. The high costs of carrying out the operations have to be met from direct or indirect taxes. Unfortunately, if taken too far there comes a stage where incentives do not exist. No amount of economic planning can replace the need for sound management and the will to work at a high level of efficiency. Monetary and non-monetary rewards should be adequate enough to stimulate industrial development.

Recommended Reading

F. J. Wright, *British Constitution and Government*, Macdonald & Evans, London.

K. B. Marder, *British Government*, Macdonald & Evans, London.

E. C. S. Wade and G. Godfrey Phillips, *Constitutional Law*, Longmans, Green & Co Ltd, London.

EXAMINATION QUESTIONS

1. Consider the statement that "free enterprise and public interest rarely coincide so some form of nationalisation of essential industries is inevitable." Examine the economic and social implications.

2. Give an explanation of the main stages involved in creating an Act of Parliament.

3. What is an "unwritten constitution"? Consider the main elements of the British Constitution.

4. Can conventions play a useful part in governing a country, or are statutory laws to be preferred? Examine the position in Britain as compared with the United States of America.

5. There are three main powers exercised as part of government:

    (a) legislative;
    (b) executive;
    (c) judicial.

Explain how these are organised.

6. Distinguish between the "rules of law" and the "Rule of Law." What importance may be attached to each?

7. Explain the role of the Prime Minister and the Cabinet within the British Government.

8. "Profit must remain the prime motive for business enterprise." How can this concept be maintained if Government control is exercised?

CHAPTER XXIX

ELEMENTS OF THE LEGAL SYSTEM

THIS section is concerned with giving an appreciation of the law so far as it is likely to affect managers. Cases and other references have been omitted, but students who wish to obtain more details should refer to specialist books on law.

THE LAW IN MODERN COMMUNITIES

DEFINITION

In a study concerned with the outline of the legal system it may suffice to say that the law is a *rule of conduct supported by sanctions administered by the State.* There are other rules of conduct, such as moral and social ones, but these depend largely for their enforcement on the strength of public opinion, and this may well vary from generation to generation. For that matter, ideas about what the law should be also change from age to age, but it is recognised in most civilised states that such changes should take place in accordance with some recognised constitutional procedure.

CLASSIFICATION OF LAW

Law may be classified as follows:

    1. International law.
    2. Public law.
    3. Private law.

    1(*a*). *Public international law* is concerned with the relationship between States as separate legal entities. Its weakness lies in the difficulty of enforcing the legal rules involved.

    1(*b*). *Private international law*, often called *Conflict of Laws*, tackles the problem of deciding which legal system should be applied in a case involving the nationals of more than one country.

    2. *Public law* concerns the State. It includes: (*a*) constitutional law, which deals with the functions of the State, and (*b*) criminal law, which deals with the punishment of crime at the instance of and by the State.

    3. *Private law* is concerned with actions between private individuals and has many divisions; these include the law of contract, the law of tort, the law of property and the law of succession. It is inevitably enforceable at the instance of the individual, not the State. Many of its aspects are covered in subsequent chapters.

SOURCES OF LAW

English law has several sources: legislation, the common law, judicial precedent and equity are the most important and are examined below.

Custom, and certain authoritative textbooks, are regarded as minor sources of the law.

LEGISLATION

Parliament is the supreme legislative body of the United Kingdom, and can make any law it wishes. Should a statute passed by Parliament prove to be ambiguous, it is the duty of the Courts to interpret it according to certain accepted principles of interpretation. Parliament alone may alter the statute.

Acts of Parliament represent what is described as original legislation. However, such is the pressure on Parliamentary time that in the course of the last few decades it has become customary for Parliament to authorise Ministers, public bodies and the like to issue orders or to make bye-laws, all of which have the force of law. This is known as *delegated legislation*, because the power behind such measures emanates from Parliament. Nevertheless, the fact that such legislation is not discussed in the same manner as original legislation, highly technical though it may often be, is a matter of some concern.

COMMON LAW

Common law was so called because it was the "unwritten law," which gradually became common to the whole of England and Wales after the Norman Conquest. This common law was certainly superior to the varying and often conflicting local customs which it supplanted, but it too had its defects and some of these were rectified by the growth of a supplementary body of law known as *equity* and applied in the Court of Chancery, but more will be said of that later.

JUDICIAL PRECEDENT

Judicial precedent refers to what is often called *case law*, as contrasted with the statute law, already mentioned. Over the centuries a principle known as *stare decisis* (to stand on the decisions) has become established, whereby a decision by a judge on a point of law is a "precedent" binding all judges in a court of inferior authority (and in some instances in the same court as well) to decide the same question in the same way, and this precedent forms another important source of law. Judges are only bound to follow precedents when the essential points of the case in hand match exactly the earlier decision. The cases are then said to be "on all fours." All this presupposes that information is readily available about such previous cases and, although the invention of printing made this possible, it was only in the eighteenth century that the publication of reports of decisions in both the common law courts and the Chancery Court became a matter of regular occurrence.

Incidentally, barristers in their court pleadings often quote cases from other courts when the circumstances of the case being heard are similar to those in previously decided cases. This may be particularly useful when the law in another country, usually a member of the British Commonwealth, is similar to that in the United Kingdom. In such instances, too, precedent applies but only on what is known as a persuasive basis; it is not binding.

GROWTH OF EQUITY

As already mentioned, the common law courts had their defects. In particular, there was an element of rigidity in the way such courts interpreted the law. By the fifteenth century there were various matters, such as breach of trust, for which no remedy was available at all; while in other spheres the remedy was quite inadequate.

Petitions about these defects reached the King, the fountain of justice, and he passed them on to the Lord Chancellor, who, as principal officer of state, and a clergyman, was said to be "keeper of the King's conscience." He dealt with these petitions,' and this was the origin of the Chancellor's Court of Equity, or of Chancery, as it became known. In time this Court developed its own rules, particularly with regard to trusts, and its special remedies. Equity as a system of law expanded alongside and often in rivalry with the common law, eventually becoming as rigid as the latter.

JUDICATURE ACTS, 1873–75

From early times the English legal system was overburdened by too many courts, giving rise to confusion and duplication of judicial work. The *Judicature Acts* swept away the old abuses, fusing the administration of the law. Details of the reorganisation are set out in the next section.

THE JUDICIAL SYSTEM OF ENGLAND AND WALES
SUPREME COURT OF JUDICATURE

The Supreme Court of Judicature was set up by the *Judicature Acts* to consist of two main sections: the High Court of Justice and the Court of Appeal.

At one time, the High Court had five divisions but now has only three: the busiest is probably the Queen's Bench Division—the name changes according to whether the sovereign is male or female—because it deals with all civil actions other than those specifically assigned to another division and because contracts and torts give rise to plenty of litigation anyway.

Another division is the Chancery Division which deals with many of the matters which, before 1873, were dealt with by the old Court of Chancery. Bankruptcy, mortgage and trust matters, as well as the wardship of infants, constitute a few well-known examples.

The third is the Probate, Divorce and Admiralty Division. This deals with those matters specifically mentioned in its name: the probate of wills (this in effect means the acceptance of a particular will as valid), the annulment and dissolution of marriages and legal disputes arising out of such things as collisions and salvage at sea.

Here it is appropriate to mention the assize courts. For historical reasons England and Wales are grouped into seven circuits and three (sometimes four) assizes a year are held in the principal towns of each circuit. The assizes exercise a certain amount of divorce and other civil jurisdiction, but their main function is to try cases of serious crime. The judges who go on circuit are nearly all from the High Court, but assize work is not a fourth division of the High Court and the origin of such work is in fact of considerable antiquity. London's Assize Court is the Old Bailey, but it has only a criminal jurisdiction. On the criminal side an appeal may be submitted from the assize to the Court of Criminal Appeal.

Finally, there is the Court of Appeal. This hears appeals on questions of fact and of law in the majority of civil matters with which the High Court deals.

House of Lords

The House of Lords, when sitting as a court, consists of nine Law Lords, that is judges who have been made life peers as Lords of Appeal in Ordinary with others who have held high judicial office. The House of Lords is the ultimate appellate body in both civil and criminal cases for England and Wales. Subject to leave from the appeal courts or the House itself, appeals are heard from both the Court of Appeal and the Court of Criminal Appeal.

SUBORDINATE COURTS

The subordinate courts deal with a considerable amount of legal work. On the civil side there are about 400 county courts in England and Wales which provide cheap and speedy justice in a variety of cases ranging from breach of contract to bankruptcy, although cases where a large sum is at stake may have to go to the High Court in London.

On the criminal side, magistrates' courts deal with minor crimes of all kinds as well as the preliminary investigation of serious crime. These courts have a limited amount of civil jurisdiction, such as bastardy proceedings and the payment of small debts.

ADMINISTRATIVE TRIBUNALS

Administrative tribunals, which are set up by statute, have proliferated in the course of the last 40 years because of the increasing complexity of modern life. These are not courts of law in the strict sense but they often function like a court, although with less formality. They are usually staffed by persons with a special knowledge of the problems involved, particularly if these relate to social legislation.

A typical example of an administrative tribunal is the local appeal tribunal set up under the all-embracing national insurance scheme that came into force in this country in 1948. The Traffic Commissioners who license goods and passenger vehicles constitute another example. From certain tribunals an appeal lies to the courts; from others, to higher tribunals, or even to the Minister of the department concerned.

The growth of such tribunals is understandable but, as with delegated legislation, is a matter of some anxiety. From time to time Parliament has been concerned about the working of these tribunals and, in 1958, a Council on Tribunals was set up to review their working and in particular to recommend changes in the law so as to make provision for an appeal to the High Court against any decision involving a point of law should this not be already possible.

DOMESTIC TRIBUNALS

Domestic tribunals are analogous to, but not identical with, administrative tribunals and mainly exist in the trade association and trade union spheres. Indeed, as the idea of the "closed shop" spreads, election to, or dismissal from, a union may be a matter of work or unemployment. In the professional sphere, examples are the Benchers of the Inns of Court, the Disciplinary Committee of the Law Society, and the Medical Disciplinary Committee of the General Medical Council.

As a basic rule, the courts do not interfere in the functioning of these domestic tribunals so long as they do not exceed their jurisdiction as laid down in the rules by which they were set up. Moreover, they must follow the rules of natural justice, but these "rules" are not laid down in any statute. Various authorities do, however, suggest that the most important of these "rules" may be the necessity to give a fair hearing to both sides, while no man should be a judge in his own cause. Some writers go so far as to suggest that when such matters as expulsion from a club or a union are concerned there should be a right of appeal from whatever body hears the case in the first instance.

LEGAL PERSONS

A legal person has duties and rights which the law will recognise although, as will be seen later, there are legal limitations upon the contractual capacity of various people. Nevertheless, legal personality is not confined to human beings, because the law gives other things "the breath of life."

CORPORATIONS

Most corporations consist of a number of people acting together to form an entity which has a legal existence of its own, quite distinct and separate from that of its members. Corporations come into being by Royal Charter or by Act of Parliament or, as in the case of the majority of commercial concerns, by registration in accordance with the provisions of such a measure as the *Companies Act, 1948*.

The fact that a corporation is a legal person means that it can trade in its own right, apart from possible exceptions which need not be mentioned here, and that it can sue and be sued. It has what is called *perpetual succession* which means, in effect, that its existence is not affected by the death of any, or indeed all, of its members, and that it goes on for ever unless, and until, steps are taken to bring its life to an end by due process of law. In practice, of course, a corporation must act through properly constituted agents: its directors, managers and its staff generally.

UNINCORPORATED ASSOCIATIONS

Unincorporated associations come into being when groups of people act together for some legal purpose without such associations becoming legal entities. Some such associations are of a special kind and are, in the words of one judge, "near-corporations," simply because various statutes have given them a special standing in the eyes of the law. Perhaps the most important examples of this special category are *partnerships* and *trade unions*.

The latter have certain privileges. Their property is protected by the criminal law, and they may bring and defend actions in their own name, provided they have registered with the Registrar of Friendly Societies.

The legal position of partnerships is governed by the *Partnership Act, 1890*, and of trade unions by the *Trade Union Act, 1871*, the *Conspiracy and Protection of Property Act, 1875*, the *Trade Disputes Act, 1906* and *1965*, and the *Trade Union Act, 1913*.

There are other groupings, such as local church and social clubs, which are unincorporated associations pure and simple. Banks and traders may recognise these as separate entities, but not the law. In practice many so arrange their affairs that property is owned on behalf of members by trustees, while contracts are entered into by various officials with both they, and those authorising them, jointly liable for such contracts.

INFANTS

As a result of a whole series of statutes, infants—that is, those under 21 years of age—have a somewhat special status in the eyes of the law.

So far as their contracts are concerned, the *Infants Relief Act, 1874,* applies, although the Report of the Committee on the Age of Majority, 1967, has recommended its repeal. They are fully liable for most torts (or civil wrongs), although an action is less likely to succeed against a very young child than against an older one. They may now vote, both in central or in local government elections, at the age of eighteen, and they may marry at sixteen provided consent is obtained from either their guardians or their parents. However, apart from exceptions, they are not entitled to make a will. They may not own land in an absolute sense, but trustees can hold it on their behalf so that it enures to the benefit of the infants.

THE IDEA OF PROPERTY

The whole subject of the law of property is both broad and complex and, therefore, it is only possible to make some very general comments. At one time all land belonged to the Crown and different people ranging from barons to serfs had varying rights and duties under a series of tenancies. Over the centuries the position changed and a really large-scale overhaul and simplification of the law of property took place in 1925. That year saw the passing of many measures to reform property law, the most important being the *Law of Property Act.*

OWNERSHIP AND POSSESSION

One thing that was not changed in 1925 was the old historical contrast between ownership and possession. The distinction is as valid as ever and can be of great practical importance.

Ownership is essentially a legal concept, a matter of right, and refers to the legal entitlement of an owner to do what he likes with his own property, subject to restrictions imposed by the State.

Possession, on the other hand, is essentially a matter of fact and refers to the ability of the possessor to exercise control over the property possessed, as well as his intention to exert exclusive control. In the majority of cases ownership and possession go together, but it is possible for these to be separated, as in the cases of the borrowing of a book or the leasing of land, to give but two examples.

Two types of *possession* should be recognised:

1. *Possession in fact,* which involves physical control as a matter of fact without involving any claim of right by possession; *e.g.* a porter carrying one's luggage has possession in fact but not in law.

2. *Legal possession,* which exists "when a person exercises effective control over a thing coupled with an intent, on his own behalf, to exclude others from the use and enjoyment of the thing either permanently or temporarily."

Thus legal possession need not be actual physical possession. The porter has actual physical possession of your baggage, but you still have legal possession.

A person in possession has a good title against all the world except the true owner.

CHOSE IN ACTION OR CHOSE IN POSSESSION

Most legal textbooks analyse at some length and with varying degrees of complexity the difference between a *chose in action* and a *chose in possession*. All that is proposed here is to explain the two in fairly general terms.

A *chose* is a thing and a *chose in possession* is, therefore, a tangible thing capable of physical possession and covers what are known as chattels—in effect moveable items such as a car and furniture—as well as land. The owner may be said to be capable of deriving the full range of benefits from his chose in possession.

A *chose in action*, on the other hand, is an intangible thing which is not capable of physical possession, but which represents a right which may be enforced at law if necessary. Choses in action comprise: (*a*) money recoverable under a contract or as damages for breach of contract; (*b*) money recoverable under a judgment already obtained; (*c*) in the extended application of the term: shares and stock in companies, patents, copyrights and other personal property of an intangible nature. Most of these are evidenced by a mere piece of paper, but such paper represents rights with a monetary value. The owner may be said to be capable of deriving the full range of benefits from his chose in action, other than the right of physical possession.

In conclusion, it could be mentioned that when it comes to buying or selling, or making a gift of choses, it is usually a simpler process in the case of a chose in possession than in the case of a chose in action.

PROPERTY AS SECURITY FOR A LOAN

Property in one form or another is the only really acceptable form of security and, as often as not, this involves a mortgage. A mortgage is the transfer of or the creation of an interest in real or personal property (*i.e.* land or moveables) by a borrower, called the mortgager, in favour of a lender, called the mortgagee, by way of security for the repayment of money borrowed together with interest. By various legal processes the lender obtains an interest in the borrower's property without normally going so far as to take over either ownership or possession, and once the loan is repaid that interest is given up. If, however, the loan is not repaid the lender can, again by due legal process, take steps to strengthen his grip on the property and, in the ultimate, use it in such a way as to enable him to get his money back. There are various ways of doing this, but in the usual run of cases the result is a sale of the security.

Land is the commonest form of property offered as security for a loan, but life insurance policies and stocks and shares are among things which are also used a good deal.

Finally, brief mention might be made of what the lawyers call a pledge, the classic example of which is the pawning of an article as security for a loan, the article to be returned upon repayment. Here the borrower not only has to give the lender rights over the security, but he has actually to hand it over.

Examination Questions on Chapter XXIX are given at the end of Chapter XXX.

CHAPTER XXX

GENERAL PRINCIPLES OF CONTRACT AND COMMERCIAL LAW

CONTRACTS

A definition.—A contract is an agreement between two or more parties which is intended by them to be legally binding.

Thus every contract is an agreement, but every agreement is not a contract. In particular mere domestic or social agreements are rarely contracts, simply because they are not intended to have legal consequences. It may be bad manners to fail to keep a luncheon appointment, but it is most unlikely to be a breach of contract.

Consent—or *consensus ad idem* to quote the Latin phrase—is the most important characteristic of contract, and this is usually evidenced by a definite offer on the one side, and by its unqualified acceptance on the other. Indeed, offer and acceptance are so fundamental to a contract that their essential characteristics are analysed below.

PRINCIPLES OF A CONTRACT

Essentials of an offer

An offer is made when it is communicated by one party, the offeror, to another, the offeree. It may be made by writing or orally, or it may be implied by conduct—for example, a bus running in accordance with a timetable and showing the required destination on its indicator. The offer may be made to: (*a*) a particular person; (*b*) to any person belonging to a particular class or answering to a particular class; or (*c*) to the public generally.

The offer must be one which is capable of creating legal relations. In particular, it must be distinguished from a mere invitation to make an offer, which, in fact, is the case with goods on display in a shop. An article with a price on it in a shop window is *not* an offer to sell at the price on the ticket but *an invitation* to enter the shop and make an offer to buy. The price ticket indicates the price at which the shopkeeper will consider the offer but not necessarily accept it.

An offer may lapse before acceptance and this usually happens in one of three ways: (*a*) on the death of the offeror or the offeree; (*b*) if a *stated time* is given the offer lapses at the end of that time if not accepted; (*c*) where no time limit is fixed, the offer lapses if not accepted within a *reasonable time*. The law does not define "reasonable" and every dispute will be decided in the light of its own circumstances.

The offeror may withdraw or revoke an offer at any time before acceptance unless he has validly promised by means of what is commonly called an "option" to keep it open for a particular period. Once an offer has been accepted it is generally regarded as irrevocable. As a general rule an offer is made by an offeror to a specific offeree but a famous case, *Carlill* v. *Carbolic Smoke Ball Co Ltd*, showed that an offer may be made to the world at large, although a particular person has to accept it and fulfil the conditions set out in the offer before a contract can come into being.

Essentials of an acceptance

Acceptance, like offer, must be communicated in one way or another and although this is usually made either in writing or verbally it could also be by implication. A simple example of the latter might be the purchase of a newspaper at the station each morning, the passenger putting down a sum of money and the kiosk attendant handing over a particular paper without a word being spoken. The acceptance must correspond in all essential particulars with the offer. An "acceptance" subject to conditions is not legally an acceptance at all, but is a *counter-offer*. If a counter-offer is made, it amounts to a new offer, which must, in turn, be accepted by the original offeror.

The acceptance of an offer subject to various conditions generally means that the offeree accepts such conditions, provided that reasonable steps have been taken to bring these conditions to the notice of the offeree. No more is required than that; provided an offeree knew that there were conditions it makes no difference that he had not studied them.

Contracts by post

The method of concluding contracts is essentially a matter for the parties themselves to decide, but the post is often used. In such cases the law presumes that a contract is completed the moment a letter accepting an offer *is posted*, and this presumption applies even though the acceptance is delayed in the post or even if it never reaches its destination. It is, of course, open to the parties to agree if they so wish that this presumption should not apply.

In the case of the postal revocation of an offer, on the other hand, the law does not hold this to be effective until it actually reaches the offeree.

Consideration

Consideration is a doctrine of the English law which in essence means that there must be an element of *quid pro quo* in the normal contract; there must be something given for something. Usually one party gives goods or services in exchange for money, but such things as forbearance and trouble could also amount to consideration.

Provided some consideration, however small, is present the law does not as a rule enquire into its adequacy. However, consideration that is already past is not usually adequate and, therefore, the promise of a reward for services already performed on a voluntary basis is not binding in law even though the normal person would naturally honour such a promise. Furthermore, consideration must be *real*; that is, it must be something beyond what the person giving it is already bound to give.

KINDS OF CONTRACT

There are two main kinds of contracts: contracts by deed and simple contracts. A third class, *contracts of record*, are the obligations imposed by the entry of the proceedings in a Court of Record in its Parchment Rolls. Courts of Record include the High Court, Courts of Assize, Quarter Sessions and County Courts.

A contract by deed is often known as a specialty contract. It must be made in writing, and the writing must be signed by the party making the promise, then sealed and delivered It applies on various formal occasions, as in certain types of contract which are not supported by consideration, and contracts for the sale of freehold land. In these cases, and certain others, a deed is essential if contracts are to have legal validity.

The exceptions that require a written contract fall into two categories. One is where it is laid down by statute that writing is essential for that particular type of contract. The more important of these are contracts dealing with the carriage of goods, hire purchase, marine insurance, money lending and the transfer of shares in a limited liability company.

The other category deals with contracts such as those relating to a guarantee (in the sense of one person being responsible for another's debts) and the sale of land, which although basically perfectly valid without writing, cannot be made the subject of a successful action at law unless evidenced by writing.

A simple contract covers every type of contract other than a specialty contract and a contract of record. It may be made in writing, by spoken words or by conduct.

The general rule to remember is that a contract need not be in writing apart from the exceptions noted above.

CONTRACTUAL CAPACITY

It is a cardinal principle of English law that all persons are equal before the law. Thus, apart from certain exceptions, all possess the capacity to enter into contracts.

Infants (*i.e.* persons under 21) constitute the most important exception, and their contractual capacity is governed by the *Infants Relief Act, 1874.* In essence that Act states that some contracts, in particular loans of money, the supply of goods other than necessaries, and contracts which could not fail to operate to the infant's prejudice are "absolutely void" if entered into by an infant. As a matter of judicial interpretation "absolutely void" means that no such contract can be enforced in a court of law against an infant, whereas the infant might be able to bring an action for breach of contract.

Some contracts are held to be binding upon an infant, thus placing him on exactly the same footing as an adult. Apart from the contract of marriage—under English law the earliest this can be entered into is at the age of sixteen—the two most important contracts in such a category are those relating to apprenticeship or employment with an element of training, and contracts for "necessaries." These have been defined as "goods suitable to the condition in life of such infants and to his actual requirements at the time of the sale and delivery." The obligation here is that the infant pay a *reasonable* price for the necessaries, not necessarily the contract price.

Several other contracts entered into by an infant, particularly those of a beneficial and continuing nature such as partnership or the holding of shares in a company, fall into what is called the *voidable* category, that is they can be avoided if an infant so wishes, but upon the infant's majority they become binding, unless repudiated then or within a reasonable time afterwards. The Report of the Committee on the Age of Majority, 1967, has recommended the repeal of the *Infants Relief Act, 1874*. It suggests that full contractual capacity should be attained at eighteen, and that infants should be known as "minors."

Contracts made by persons of unsound mind are, on the face of it, perfectly valid. Should the other party know of the mental incapacity, the contract is voidable at the instance of the insane person during a lucid interval, or at the instance of a person appointed by the court to act on his behalf. The crucial question is "Was advantage taken of this person's mental condition?" If the answer is in the affirmative the contract is voidable.

If a person contracts under the influence of drink, and his mind cannot grasp the significance of his act, and this fact is taken advantage of by the other party, the contract is voidable.

VALIDITY OF CONTRACTS

The majority of contracts are carried out to the mutual satisfaction of all parties and cause no legal argument. From time to time, however, disputes do arise. Sometimes a contract proves less advantageous than one of the parties had expected, but this of itself would be no ground for either party repudiating the contract. Nevertheless there are some well-recognised factors which do affect the validity of contracts and these will now be briefly analysed.

1. Misrepresentation.—This is an untrue statement made by one party to a contract which induces the other party to enter the agreement. It may be (*a*) *innocent misrepresentation*, where a misstatement of fact is made without knowledge of its untruth and without intention to deceive, or (*b*) *fraudulent misrepresentation*, which has been defined as "a false representation of fact made with a knowledge of its falseness, or recklessly without belief in its truth, with the intention that it be acted upon by the complaining party, and actually inducing him to act upon it." In both cases the party misled may normally repudiate the contract, but in the case of fraud that party may claim damages as well. Under the *Misrepresentation Act, 1967*, a contract may be rescinded because of an innocent misrepresentation, even though the contract has been performed, or even though the misrepresentation has become a term of the contract. It is not misrepresentation to "puff up" one's own goods; extravagant praise should be accepted with a pinch of salt, and it would only be misrepresentation if "supported" by false facts and figures.

2. Duress.—Duress is actual or threatened interference with the personal liberty of one of the parties to a contract: the presence of duress enables the party affected to repudiate the contract. Thus if a person is forced at the point of a pistol to enter into a contract, the contract can always be set aside later. It is voidable at the instance of the party to whom the duress is applied.

3. Undue influence.—Undue influence represents mental or moral persuasion, but here too the party affected may repudiate the contract.

The influence must be proved by the party seeking to set aside the contract. Undue influence is presumed to exist unless the contrary is proved where a contract is between parties who are within a fairly close relationship, such as doctor and patient, parent and child or solicitor and client, but in other cases it must of course be proved to the satisfaction of a court.

4. Mistake.—The law on this point is somewhat complex, but it is probably correct to say that a party cannot avoid a contract merely by saying that he only entered into it as a result of a mistake. However, some mistakes are so fundamental as to strike at the root of a contract: such as a mistake concerning the existence or identity of the subject matter of the contract, or a mistake concerning the identity of the other contracting party when such identity is important. In all these instances the contract is not voidable, as in the cases previously studied, but *void* which means in effect that the law considers that a contract never existed at all.

5. Illegality.—Certain contracts are illegal, and, as such, are void. They may be *illegal by statute*, or *illegal at common law*. Examples of the latter include agreements to commit a crime or a tort, to defraud shareholders or to defraud the revenue. Agreements contrary to sexual morality are also illegal at common law, as are those which are contrary to public policy.

Under the last heading there is a whole host of agreements which the law considers to be contrary to public policy because they may injure the due administration of justice, the public safety and either economic or social welfare. Public policy is of course apt to change as trends of public opinion change on economic, moral and social issues.

The only one that warrants further analysis is that example of the agreement injurious to economic welfare known as *an agreement in restraint of trade*. Such an agreement is one that imposes an unreasonable restraint upon an individual's right to earn his livelihood in his chosen way and is void, but if a restraint is reasonable in all the circumstances it will be upheld. Thus, where a business is being sold it would in general be reasonable to restrain the seller from opening up a similar business in the same locality but, special circumstances apart, any wider restraint would be unreasonable. Again, in the case of an employer and an employee, a restraint upon the activities of such employee upon his leaving would only be upheld if reasonably necessary to protect the former employer's business connections or trade secrets, and provided it be reasonable as regards both area and duration.

DISCHARGE OF CONTRACTS

The termination of a contract discharges the parties from their obligations, and is achieved in the following ways:

1. Agreement.—Both parties may agree to release each other from the obligations of a contract, while the contract itself may contain an agreed clause that, after a certain time and upon the happening of a particular event, the contract shall be discharged.

2. Performance.—Most contracts are discharged by due performance of the agreed obligations by all the parties concerned. In the majority of commercial contracts today, payment is made by cheque, but as a matter of strict legal theory a person to whom money is owed may claim to be paid in legal tender—that type of money which the law recognises as being appropriate for the payment of debts. At the time of writing, Bank of England notes may be used up to any amount, silver or cupro-nickel coins up to 40*s*. and copper up to a maximum of 1*s*., apart from the twelve-sided threepenny pieces where the maximum is 2*s*.

3. Frustration.—A contract which was capable of being performed when entered into may become frustrated before performance and, in such an event, it will be discharged. The courts have been reluctant to accept this as a valid ground for discharge, but by now it is recognised that frustration applies where performance becomes illegal or impossible as the result of a change in the law, or a change in circumstances so fundamental as to warrant discharge because this change was entirely beyond the contemplation of the parties when they entered into the agreement. An unexpected turn of events which merely makes performance more difficult or more expensive would not be regarded as "fundamental."

4. Breach.—There is said to be a breach of contract whenever a party does not perform his promise in the manner and at the time agreed. Breaches are of two kinds: (*a*) *actual breach*, which consists in not performing the promise and (*b*) *breach by renunciation*, often referred to as *anticipatory breach*. This occurs when, prior to the time for performance of the contract, one party renounces the contract by refusing or rendering himself unable to perform. The remedies for breach of contract will be studied next, but it should be noted that if a breach concerns a fundamental part of the contract the injured party has the option to treat it as a discharged contract.

REMEDIES FOR BREACH OF CONTRACT

Leaving aside discharge, already mentioned, there are various well-known remedies for breach of contract and these will be studied now.

1. Damages.—The large majority of successful civil actions end in the award of damages which may be defined as a sum of money designed to compensate the innocent party for the loss suffered. The case of *Hadley* v. *Baxendale* (1854) established the rule that compensation must represent the loss which is the natural and probable consequence of the breach, and anything beyond that would be considered too remote unless the parties had or should have envisaged such further damage at the time the contract was made. The person claiming upon a breach must take all reasonable steps to mitigate the loss.

2. Specific performance.—In some exceptional cases, damages may not be an adequate remedy and the court may, at its discretion, issue a decree known as *specific performance*, whereby the person in breach of contract is ordered, on pain of being held in contempt of court, to carry out his promise. This remedy is only rarely sought, and still more rarely granted, simply because with the majority of commercial contracts the goods concerned may easily be got elsewhere. It is only in the case of articles of peculiar rarity, or possibly of sentimental value, that this order is likely to be made.

3. Injunction.—An injunction is also a decree of the court of a purely discretionary nature which is only issued on comparatively rare occasions. It could be an order that something arising out of a contractual agreement should be done, or it could equally be an order that something should not be done. If, for example, an employee broke an agreement to sing for a particular theatre and not to sing for any other theatre, the court would not attempt to enforce the agreement to sing for the old employer, but might issue an injunction to restrain such employee from singing for any other employer.

Specific performance and injunction are known as *equitable remedies*.

4. Lapse of time.—Failure to take action without undue delay, over such a thing as a breach of contract, may mean that the right to bring an action will be lost. The law on this subject is contained in the *Limitation Act, 1939*, as amended by the *Law Reform (Limitation of Actions) Act, 1954*, and the *Limitation Act, 1963*. Under the *Limitation Act, 1939*, an action arising out of a simple contract has to be brought within six years of the cause of action or not at all; with specialty contracts the period is twelve years. This merely means that the debt cannot be enforced at law, not that it has been completely wiped out, although in most cases that would mean the same thing. The right to enforce an old debt of this kind will however revive (for another six or twelve years) if any part payment is made, or if the party responsible makes a written acknowledgment of liability, or if it is discovered that the loss of such right was due to fraud. Under the 1954 Act, actions in respect of personal injuries arising out of breach of contract must be brought within three years. The 1963 Act extended the period of limitation from three years in certain circumstances.

TORT
GENERAL PRINCIPLES OF TORT

A tort is a civil wrong amounting *in essence* to breach of duty for which the remedy is a common law action for damages. It must be distinguished from both a breach of contract and a crime. Negligence, nuisance and trespass are some of the more important torts that will be studied in this section, but purely personal torts such as defamation (libel and slander) are outside the scope of this work.

As a general rule, all persons, even infants, are responsible for the torts which they commit, but in some instances a person may also be responsible for the torts of another. This is known as the *doctrine of vicarious liability* and the best example is that of an employer being liable for the torts of his employee if they arise in the course of employment. Vicarious liability has given rise to many cases, and the doctrine not only covers torts authorised by the employer but also torts which represent an unauthorised manner of doing something authorised. The doctrine is perhaps understandable to the extent that the employer is far better able than the employee to pay damages and because the whole machinery of employment from which the tort arises has been set in motion by the employer. Nevertheless, the burden would be almost intolerable were it not for the fact that practically all employers now cover this risk by insurance.

DEFENCES

Different torts have different defences which may be put forward, and some of these will now be briefly analysed:

1. Consent.—If a person either expressly or by implication accepts the risk of incurring an injury, as in the case of a contestant in a boxing bout or spectators at a sporting event, consent may operate as a defence. This is known as *volenti non fit injuria* (that to which a person consents cannot be complained of by him as an injury).

2. Inevitable accident.—One example of an inevitable accident is "Act of God," *i.e.* damage caused by the operation of natural causes (such as earthquakes and hurricanes) so unforeseeable that the ordinary person could not be expected to guard against them. It therefore operates as a defence in tort. Another example is for the defendant to prove that the damage complained of was caused by some happening over which he had no control, so that it was not the result of any voluntary act of negligence on his part.

3. Necessity.—In some instances a person may feel compelled to commit a tort to prevent a greater evil, as in the case of the jettisoning of a ship's cargo in a storm. The defence of necessity will only succeed, however, if it was reasonable in all the circumstances and the party claiming it as a defence must not himself have caused the hazard that is sought to be avoided.

4. Statutory authority.—If a tort is committed by virtue of authority conferred by statute such authority serves in general as a defence. Everything depends on the words of the statute. The authority granted may only be *conditional* on the exercise of the act so as not to interfere with the rights of others.

TYPES OF TORT

Trespass

This tort covers trespass to the person, trespass to goods and trespass to land. It is not proposed to say more about trespass to the person other than that it includes assault, battery and false imprisonment.

Trespass to goods may be defined as an unjustified interference with goods in the possession of another. It has given rise to two derivative torts known as *conversion* and *detinue*. Conversion is intentional interference without lawful justification with goods in someone's possession. It would, for example, be conversion for a person buying an article on hire purchase to sell such an article at a time when he is still paying for it and ownership of it has not passed to him. The normal remedy is one for damages.

Detinue is the wrongful detention of goods belonging to another and could arise, for example, where a person who has borrowed an article refuses to return it on a promised date. The remedy will be for the recovery of the goods, or, if that is not possible, for damages.

Trespass to land arises where a person enters or remains without lawful justification on, over or under land in the possession of another. It could cover dumping rubbish or even sitting on a fence, but as a result of the *Civil Aviation Act, 1949*, it is not trespass for aircraft to fly over land at a reasonable height. Moreover, what would otherwise be trespass is not trespass if permission is granted. It should be noted that trespass to land includes trespass on the highway, trespass in the air and cattle trespass.

An occupier of land may, of course, ask a trespasser to leave and, if the trespasser fails to do so, he may be warned that he is liable to be forcefully evicted. If he still does not leave the occupier would be justified in using force, but it is important to remember that the law only condones the use of that degree of force which is necessary in all the circumstances.

Nuisance

Nuisance is a tort quite commonly met in everyday life and in the main it arises from the use of one's own property in such a way as to cause damage to another person's property, as in the case of diesel exhaust injuring vegetation, or the enjoyment of such property, as in the case of excessive noise. There must be damage which is more than trifling and the act complained of must have been unreasonable in all the circumstances of a modern society. Even locality is important— what is reasonable in one district may be unreasonable in another— but the peculiar sensitivity of a particular individual is not.

There is a particular kind of nuisance first established in the case of *Rylands* v. *Fletcher* (1868). If a person brings on to his land anything which is not there naturally, then that person is strictly liable if it escapes and causes damage. There are some defences, such as Act of God, but responsibility is much more likely to arise than in the escape of something naturally on the land. Various cases suggest that dangerous "things" include an artificial lake, electricity and yew trees.

Negligence

In simple terms, negligence may be defined as failure to take proper care in one's conduct. The degree of care necessary varies with the circumstances. For liability to arise there must be a legal duty to take care —every user of the highway owes a duty of care towards other users, to give but one example—and there must be a breach of such duty with ensuing damage. In dealing with a case of negligence, a court would always consider whether or not a person has behaved reasonably and with ordinary prudence in the circumstances concerned.

As usual in the law, the burden of proof will lie upon a person bringing an action, but as an exception to this rule negligence will be assumed— unless it can be proved otherwise—in the sort of case where a bag of flour falls on a passer-by.

From time to time an accident occurs where two parties have been negligent, one to a greater extent than the other perhaps. If the one were to be held liable the damages of the other would be reduced as a result of the *Law Reform* (*Contributary Negligence*) *Act, 1945*. The court will apportion the respective responsibility of the parties concerned.

Interference with contract

An intentional interference with a valid contract, resulting in damage to one of the parties, is a tort. It would be tortious to bribe or even to persuade a person to break a contract ("Give up your job and start with us tomorrow"), but it might be in order to induce a person to bring a contract to an end legitimately ("Why not give your present employers a calendar month's notice and start with us on the first of the month after next?").

A possible defence for this tort is the lawful justification argument; a person may claim that there was a duty to interfere with the particular contract on either legal or moral or social grounds. In one case, a union official's plea that he had a duty to persuade chorus girls at a certain establishment to break their contract of employment was successful because their pay was so unreasonably low as to conduce to their seeking immoral earnings to supplement such pay.

Malicious falsehood

Malicious falsehood is the tort of publishing a false statement about a person or his property which causes, or is reasonably likely to cause, damage. It may, or may not, amount to the tort of defamation (which covers libel and slander) as well.

There must, however, be a false statement of fact not opinion. It is not a tort to say that one's own sausages are the best in the town, but it would be to say that a rival's are full of bread—unless, of course, they were so in fact!

LIABILITY FOR DANGEROUS PREMISES

The liability of the occupier of dangerous premises is, in many ways, akin to that of a negligent person, but the subject warrants separate treatment, particularly with the passing of the *Occupiers Liability Act, 1957*. This Act requires the occupier of premises to take such care, as in all the circumstances of the case is reasonable, to see that a visitor will be reasonably safe in using the premises for the purposes for which he has been permitted to use them. A higher standard of care is required towards children than towards adults, although this is subject to the general rule that parents are the persons primarily responsible for the safety of their own children.

A trespasser must take premises as he finds them and he is not protected by the *Occupiers Liability Act*, although an occupier should not do any act which is calculated to injure the trespasser, *i.e.* he should have no concealed trap on his premises. An occupier is not bound to look out for the possibility of a trespasser being on his land, but if he does know he must make due allowance.

Incidentally, a trespasser is not easy to define and, although a simple definition, like a person on premises without permission, may be usually adequate, there is a possibility that people technically in such a category, but over whose presence there has been a degree of acquiescence, would not be trespassers in the eyes of the law. An example is where children are allowed to play on factory premises.

AGENCY

A contract of agency is formed when one person, known as the principal, employs another, known as the agent, to bring him into contractual relationship with a third party or to perform various acts in law on his behalf.

FORMATION OF AGENCY

There is in general no particular method of forming an agency but the most usual means are as follows:

Agency by express agreement

1. Word of mouth.
2. Simple writing.
3. Deed.—An agent who is to have power to sign deeds on behalf of his principal must himself be appointed by deed. This is called a *power of attorney.*

Agency without express agreement

1. *Implication.*—Here the agency arises as the result of the conduct of the parties and the common examples are children acting on behalf of parents, or employees acting on behalf of employers.
2. *Necessity.*—A person looking after the goods of another may, in an emergency, become an agent of necessity, if he is unable to communicate with the principal. A deserted wife not maintained by her husband may, in some cases, become her husband's agent so far as necessaries are concerned. In all cases, a pre-existing contractual relationship must exist between the parties, resulting in the property being already in the hands of the agent of necessity.
3. *Ratification.*—An agent may only validly act within the authority given to him, but even though this authority be exceeded the principal may approve of the transaction and this is known as *ratification.* However, for this to arise, the agent must have contracted as an agent and not as a principal, the principal must have been in existence when the contract was concluded, and the contract must be one which the principal is competent to make.

DUTIES OF AGENT

The agent has many duties towards his principal, but put in summary form the following are the most important:

1. He must carry out his mandate with reasonable care, diligence and skill. An agent cannot rely upon want of ability as an excuse for improper performance.
2. He must carry out the instructions given to him.
3. He must act for the benefit of his principal and he should not let such duty conflict with his own personal interests. It would be highly improper of an agent to make a secret profit out of his principal because the relationship is meant to be one of the utmost good faith.

If such a secret profit were made by the agent, not only could the principal recover it, but he could also repudiate the whole contract.

4. He must not delegate his duties except in an emergency, or when the usage of trade permits this.

DUTIES OF PRINCIPAL

The duties of a principal towards his agent may be summarised in the following manner:

1. He must pay the agent the agreed remuneration or, if none is agreed, a reasonable remuneration for that type of work. In addition, the principal must see that the agent is duly reimbursed in respect of all necessary expenses which the agent has incurred.

2. He must indemnify the agent against any liabilities or losses incurred by the agent in the due performance of his task.

No such liability arises where the agent acts outside his authority.

3. He must indemnify third parties suffering loss as a result of the agent's fraud, provided the agent was acting within the scope of his authority.

TERMINATION OF AGENCY

There are various ways in which an agency may be terminated. If an agency is formed, either for the completion of a certain task or for a particular period of time, then once such task has been done or the time has elapsed, the agency is at an end.

If the principal and the agent agree that the agency should be terminated then this must be so. If, however, one party wishes to give notice to the other—revocation by the principal and renunciation by the agent are the technical phrases—termination is by no means automatic unless of course the relevant agreement provides for termination in such an event. Indeed, unilateral termination might amount to a breach of contract and involve the one party compensating the other.

Finally an agency may be terminated because some law or other provides for this in certain circumstances. The most important circumstances are either death or insanity of either agent or principal. Termination by operation of the law also applies in the event of the principal being adjudicated bankrupt, but bankruptcy of the agent does not have such effect.

SALE OF GOODS

DEFINITIONS

The law relating to the sale of goods is codified in the *Sale of Goods Act, 1893.* Nevertheless, contracts for the sale of goods, although subject to the 1893 Act, are also subject to the general principles of contract already studied.

A contract for the sale of goods is one whereby the seller transfers, or agrees to transfer, the *property in the goods*—meaning here *ownership* as distinct from possession—to the buyer for a money consideration called the price. If, under the relevant contract, the property in goods passes from the seller to the buyer immediately, the transaction is termed a *sale*, but if the transfer is to take place at some time in the future the transaction is an *agreement to sell*.

Goods other than land may be defined as *choses in possession*. The difference between a chose in action and a chose in possession is indicated on p. 508. Choses in action are not goods, since goods mean moveable and tangible property. Growing crops are goods provided that they are planted and gathered within a year, and so are growing trees provided that under the contract they are to be severed before sale.

Goods clearly identified when the contract was drawn up are called specific goods, while those which have to be acquired or made are future goods.

TRANSFER OF PROPERTY

Property in goods refers to the ownership as opposed to possession which could be merely the temporary holding of the goods of another. The distinction between ownership and possession has already been studied under property, but it is now necessary to consider the precise moment at which the transfer of property takes place, because the person in whom the goods vest is normally the person who has to stand any loss that may arise from such things as fire and theft.

The basic rule on this point is that *property passes at the time which the parties intend it to pass*, and it does not necessarily have to be either at the time of delivery or at the time of payment. If, as is often the case, the intention of the parties is by no means clear, various circumstances have to be considered. In an unconditional contract for specific goods ready for delivery, property passes from buyer to seller when the contract is made. If such goods are not ready for delivery because the seller has to do something to get them ready for delivery, or has to carry out some act such as testing and weighing the goods, property does not pass to the buyer until the seller has done what is necessary and notified the buyer of this.

Where goods are delivered to the buyer "on approval" or on a "sale or return" basis, property passes as soon as the buyer approves of them, or deals with them in a way which shows his intention to accept them. Keeping the goods for an unnecessarily long time would, in fact, be evidence of an intention to accept them, but if a time limit is set for approval or return the recipient must ordinarily notify his intention within that time.

In the case of future goods, property only passes to the buyer when goods answering the description and fit for delivery have been unconditionally appropriated to the contract, and both buyer and seller have consented to the appropriation.

TRANSFER OF TITLE OTHER THAN BY RIGHTFUL OWNER

It is a basic rule of English law that a buyer can only acquire a good title to goods if the seller was the owner of the goods or was acting under the owner's authority. Thus a thief, not being a rightful owner, is unable to give a buyer a good title in any stolen goods and the fact that the buyer might have had no knowledge of the theft will make no difference.

However, there are a number of exceptions to the above rule and some of these are rather technical—such as a landlord seizing and selling the goods of a tenant by way of what is called "distress" for overdue rent.

One exception in particular, the picturesque *market overt*, warrants further study. This refers to any open and regular public market carried on in a particular place on given days, as well as to all shops in the City of London where goods are displayed and sold in the ordinary course of business. A purchaser in market overt who acts in good faith will acquire a good title to the goods even though they are stolen. If, however, the thief is prosecuted and convicted, the goods will revest in the person from whom they were stolen.

IMPLIED CONDITIONS

A *condition* is a term in a contract which is a vital one and failure to observe it by one party will not only entitle the other party to claim damages for any loss suffered, but also to treat the contract as discharged. It is, of course, up to the parties to decide upon the terms of a contract, but some conditions are deemed to be present by law.

It is an implied condition that the seller has the right to sell the goods. Furthermore, where goods are sold by description they should correspond with the description and be of merchantable quality, although the latter requirement does not apply where the buyer has examined the goods and failed to discover defects which his examination should have revealed.

Where goods are sold by sample there is an implied condition that the bulk shall correspond with the sample and be free from defect not apparent upon a reasonable examination of the sample, while the buyer should have an opportunity of checking the bulk against the sample.

Finally, there is an implied condition that the goods shall be fit for a particular purpose, where the buyer expressly or by implication makes known to the seller the purpose for which the goods are required, and that he is relying on the seller's skill and judgment, the goods being of a kind ordinarily supplied by the seller. This implied condition does not apply where the goods are sold under a patent or trade name.

IMPLIED WARRANTIES

A *warranty* is a term in a contract which is not a vital one and which is said to be collateral to the main purpose. Failure to observe a warranty merely entitles the other party to claim damages, but not to have the contract set aside.

In every contract of sale there are implied warranties: (*a*) that the buyer should have and enjoy quiet possession of the goods; and (*b*) that the goods shall be free from any charge or incumbrance in favour of any third party not disclosed to the buyer at the time of sale.

Many students consider that because the implied conditions and warranties already studied are in the Act they must be absolutely binding. However, the parties may by some agreement exclude these terms and although this would seem ill-advised the law would uphold any such agreement if the exclusion were in express terms.

DUTIES OF THE BUYER AND THE SELLER

In brief, the duty of the buyer of the goods is to accept and pay for them, according to the terms of the contract, and the duty of the seller is to deliver the goods.

In many cases, delivery and payment go together, but the parties can, of course, agree on all sorts of variations, such as delivery by instalments and payment after the expiry of credit.

RIGHTS OF THE SELLER

If a seller has not been paid for goods and the time for payment is due he is entitled to sue the buyer for the price, provided that the goods have already been accepted by the buyer. If, however, the buyer has wrongfully refused to take delivery, the seller may bring an action for damages in respect of any loss which he may have to suffer through having to sell elsewhere.

Neither of the above remedies is of any real value if the buyer is impecunious, and it is important to know of two other rights of the seller which are contained in the *Sale of Goods Act*. One is called a *lien*, and it refers to the right of an unpaid seller who is still in possession of goods, to keep them and refuse to hand them over to the buyer until the buyer has paid for them. The right of *lien* does not enable the unpaid seller to sell such goods unless they are perishable. Resale would also apply if the contract provided for this or if the seller gave notice to the buyer that he would resell the goods unless these were paid for within a reasonable time.

Another remedy is called *stoppage in transitu*, and this applies where the buyer is unable to pay his debts and the goods are on their way from the seller to the buyer, being in the possession of an intermediary such as British Rail. The unpaid seller may instruct the carrier not to deliver the goods to the buyer, but to return them instead to him. The seller must give appropriate notice to the carrier and he will, of course, have to pay the return freight.

RIGHTS OF THE BUYER

The buyer has a right to reject goods which do not comply with the contract although it must be remembered that phrases like "about" or "more or less"—these are purposely inserted in many contracts—allow the seller reasonable variation between the contract quantity and the actual quantity delivered.

The buyer may sue for damages when the seller wrongfully refuses to make delivery, although in the usual run of circumstances these damages are unlikely to be substantial because of the ease with which most goods can be got in an alternative market. If, of course, the goods were required by the seller for a special purpose—for use in the completion of a particularly lucrative contract for example—and that purpose was known to the seller then such damages could well be a good deal higher.

He may also bring an action for specific performance of the contract by the delivery of specific goods.

HIRE PURCHASE CONTRACTS

In a hire purchase contract goods are delivered to the hirer who agrees to make periodical payments for them. After the stated instalments are paid up he has an option to buy them. There is no agreement to buy the goods until this option has been exercised.

Hire purchase contracts thus protect the seller against losing ownership of the goods. While the contract is in force, the hirer could not pass a good title to a third party, should he attempt to sell the latter the goods.

The *Hire Purchase Act, 1965*, consolidated the statutory law on hire purchase. Its main provisions are as follows:

1. The Act covers transactions of up to £2000.
2. The terms of every hire purchase contract must be set out fully in writing and must be signed by the hirer in person. The contract must include a statement of the hire purchase or total purchase price, the cash price, the amount of each instalment and the date when each instalment is due.
3. A list of the goods must be included, sufficient to identify them.
4. The hirer must be informed of his rights under the Act in nontechnical language.

The Act gives the hirer the right to cancel the agreement within four days of receiving a copy of the agreement, which the seller is bound by statute to send him. This is the famous "cooling-off" period, designed to protect the housewife from over persuasive door-to-door salesmen.

RESALE PRICE MAINTENANCE

The *Resale Prices Act, 1964*, was designed to prevent manufacturers and suppliers of goods from imposing conditions for maintaining a minimum price at which the goods are to be resold.

Certain goods may be exempt from this provision, provided their suppliers can satisfy the Restrictive Practices Court that, if maintained minimum resale prices were ended, consumers would suffer some detriment.

MISCELLANEOUS COMMERCIAL LAW MATTERS

ARBITRATION

As an alternative to litigation, arbitration is growing in commercial importance. Arbitration may be defined as the determination of commercial disputes by the decision of one or more persons called arbitrators who are neither judges nor officers of any court. Any person may be appointed as an arbitrator and the *Arbitration Act, 1950*, which now governs the whole subject, does not lay down any special qualification. In practice, professional accountants are often appointed where the dispute has a predominantly financial flavour whereas in technical matters, covering such things as quality and specification, architects, chemists, engineers, surveyors and the like are appointed according to the nature of the dispute. Barristers are also often appointed mainly because their legal training enables them to weigh the evidence and to get to the root of a dispute.

It is usual whenever a contract makes a provision for arbitration to say who the arbitrator should be. Occasionally the arbitrator may be named, but more likely he would be a person to be nominated by, for example, the secretary of a particular Chamber of Commerce or the president of a certain professional institute. The court can appoint an arbitrator in certain circumstances.

In the hearing, ordinary rules of law and evidence apply, although there is less formality than in a court. If an arbitrator, after considering the evidence, feels that it is desirable to get a ruling on an involved point of law, he can submit the matter—"state a case" is the technical phrase —to the court for opinion.

The arbitrator's decision is known as an *award* and is binding on the parties; it can be enforced in the same way as a judgment of the court. There is no right of appeal as such, but the court may set an award aside if it is based on any serious error of law, or if there should be evidence that the arbitrator has been guilty of misconduct such as the taking of a bribe. The arbitrator himself may ask the court to set the award aside where, for example, he realises that he has made a serious mistake, or where additional evidence is discovered after the making of the award.

The growing popularity of arbitration is understandable. Not only is it often cheaper and quicker than litigation but, more important from the businessman's point of view, it is held in private so that publicity is avoided; it can also usually be arranged at a time and place to suit the parties.

COPYRIGHT

Literally, copyright is the right to copy, but it may be defined as the *exclusive right* of the author of a book or other composition (such as a drama, a lecture, a map, an opera or a photograph) to publish that work or to make copies of it or to perform it in public. The law regards such an author as a creator and under various statutes protects his "property," the current codification being the *Copyright Act, 1956*. The Act was passed to consolidate the law in the face of modern technological developments, in such fields as sound recording, films and television, for example, which had caused the previous Act, passed in 1911, to become outmoded. The author does not have to claim copyright because it is his property from the moment the work comes into being. No artistic or literary merit is required.

Infringement consists in doing anything which contravenes the sole right conferred upon the owner of the copyright. The normal course of action taken by a copyright holder in the case of infringement is to seek an injunction which, once granted, would make any further infringement a contempt of court.

There is no infringement if the holder of the copyright consents to a performance or publication, while any infringement, to be actionable must concern "a substantial part" of the relevant work, a phrase which rather naturally has given rise to a good deal of litigation. Moreover, what might otherwise be a breach of copyright may well not be a breach if the purpose of the apparent breach is research or private study.

There is no copyright in *facts* and news may, therefore, be repeated. Moreover, there is no copyright in law, but there would be in the arrangement and explanation in some legal commentary.

The *Copyright Act* set up the Performing Rights Tribunal to safeguard the holder's copyright in various works and to grant individual "performing right" licences or payment of such fees subject to such conditions as it thinks reasonable.

Copyright does not last for ever, but only for the life of the author and for fifty years after his death. If, however, a particular work is only published (or broadcast or performed in public) after the holder's death, then the fifty-year period stretches from the date of publication.

The guiding principle of copyright law can be summed up in the phrase, "what is worth copying is worth protecting."

PATENTS

A patent in an invention is a monopoly granted by the Crown for a limited period. It takes the form of letters patent and awards the exclusive right of making, selling or using an invention, thus it is thought, stimulating inventive genius. The maximum period concerned is usually sixteen years, with possible renewal requirements in earlier years, though the term could be longer in special circumstances. The law on the subject is to be found in the *Patents Acts, 1949* to *1961*, and a register of all patents granted is kept at the Patent Office.

Any person who claims to be the "true and first inventor" of an invention may send an application to the Patent Office, accompanied by the appropriate "specification," which describes the nature of the invention, but in practice the work is so involved that it is advisable to use the services of a Chartered Patent Agent. Problems have arisen as to who is the "true and first inventor," particularly where employer and employee are concerned. Where the latter has used the materials or the time of the former, patentable inventions are usually regarded as belonging to the employer.

Before any claim is accepted, the applicant will have to show that his invention is new in the sense that it has not been made known to the public within the United Kingdom; it must be useful and also be a contrivance or manufactured article. Thus a mere discovery, not linked with manufacture, cannot be patented, unless it is possible to put the discovery into effect. This may be achieved by the production of an old thing in a new or improved way, or by producing something both new and useful.

Four or five years may elapse between the application for a patent and ultimate grant.

If the grant of a patent is refused the inventor may appeal to the Comptroller of Patents and to the Patents Appeal Tribunal, presided over by a High Court judge.

The owner of a patent may assign it to another person, usually by deed, in which case that person takes over all the patentee's rights, or may permit others to use the patent by granting them a licence and this would normally involve the payment of royalties to the patentee. Use without permission would, of course, amount to infringement and the patentee could seek an injunction to restrain future use as well as damages for past use.

While discussing patents, it may be worth mentioning that there is kept at the Patent Office a Register of Designs under the provisions of the *Registered Designs Act, 1949*. The purpose of this provision is to protect novelties of an industrial nature which do not involve the invention required for the grant of a patent.

To be registered, a design must be new, a question of fact although often a question of degree as well, and be applicable to an article of manufacture or substance, whether natural or artificial.

Any application for registration must be accompanied by representations or specimens of the design. Acceptance or rejection of a design is a matter for decision by the Comptroller of Patents, but an appeal

s

against refusal may be made to the Board of Trade. Registration is granted in the first instance for five years, but after this it may be extended for up to ten years.

TRADE MARKS

The law in relation to trade marks is set out in the *Trade Marks Act, 1938.*

A trade mark is a mark used by a trader in relation to goods, and indicating a connection in the course of trade between the goods and some person having the right either as proprietor or as registered user, to use the mark. Such a mark could be a brand, device, label, name or word, or a combination of these things. The relationship between *goods* and trade marks must be stressed. It is not possible to register a trade mark if it relates merely to a process or a method, even if these are given a name.

A successful application for registration means an entry on the Register of Trade Marks—this too is kept at the Patent Office—and it gives the person concerned the exclusive right to the use of the trade mark upon, or in connection with, the goods for which it is registered. The register has two parts, A and B. Registration in A involves severer tests of distinction, and registration here gives the owner exclusive use of the trade mark. Any trade mark may be registered in Part B if it is capable of distinguishing the owner's goods from other goods. It is usual to register a trade mark in both parts. A person whose application is rejected by the Registrar may appeal either to the Board of Trade or to the court. Registration remains effective for seven years, but can be renewed from time to time by paying fees.

The registered owner of a trade mark may bring an action for damages as well as seek an injunction in respect of any infringement of his mark. The *Merchandise Acts, 1887, 1926* and *1953*, have introduced various criminal offences with regard to the improper use of trade marks. Such things as forging and falsely applying a trade mark or using marks "calculated to deceive" constitute a criminal offence.

EXAMINATION QUESTIONS

1. Discuss the legal position of the parties and the principles of law involved in the following circumstances:

(*a*) Robinson wrote to Smith, ordering certain goods. Smith, in the belief that the order was from Robertson, a firm of repute, despatched the goods to Robinson. The latter sold to Jones, left the country, and cannot now be found.

(*b*) Smart sold Slow a second-hand lorry. Smart knew that it had a defective gear box, but remained silent as to this while praising its other features. Slow has now discovered this defect.

2. (*a*) In what circumstances may a principal be liable on a contract made by a person purporting to act as his agent?

(b) Bigwoods Ltd, who own a chain of retail shops, authorise the manager of each shop to order goods for his shop to an amount not exceeding £500 in value. If a manager orders goods to the value of £1000 without further sanction, will the Company be liable?

3. Sparks is employed by Power & Co as an electrician. While carrying out certain repairs at the department store of Harridges, Sparks lights a cigarette and throws away the lighted match. This badly damages the fur coat of Mrs Lamb, a customer. Can Mrs Lamb sue Sparks, or Power & Co, or Harridges? Would your answer be different if Sparks had been forbidden to smoke during the course of his work?

4. Stubbs entered an antique shop and asked the price of a Regency work-table in the window. On being told that it was offered at £20, he said he would call back later. On his return he saw the table still in the window but marked at £25. He entered the shop and told the dealer that he would take the table at £20, "as previously offered." The dealer replied that the table had just been sold for £25.

Has Stubbs any (and, if so, what) remedy?

5. Jones and Smith agreed for the sale and purchase of a house "subject to contract." The form of contract was subsequently agreed between their respective solicitors and counterparts prepared for signature. Smith duly signed his part and posted it to Jones, but Jones did not sign or post his part and refused to proceed with the sale.

Discuss the legal position.

6. (a) How does the contract arise when goods are bought at auction?

(b) At a sale of goods by auction, Roland makes a bid of £25, which is followed by a bid of £30 by Oliver. Before the goods are knocked down, Oliver withdraws his bid, whereupon the auctioneer immediately knocks down the goods to Roland for £25. Is Roland bound to accept and pay for the goods?

Chapter XXXI

ELEMENTS OF INDUSTRIAL LAW

INDUSTRIAL law is in essence concerned with what is still quaintly called the Law of Master and Servant or, as recent writers have put it, the law of employer and employee. It covers not only the special features of the contract of employment itself, but also such connected matters as the law concerning conditions of places of work as well as social insurance. It is, therefore, quite a wide topic and only some of its more essential features will be analysed.

APPRENTICESHIP

Apprenticeship is a special type of contract of employment with the main, although not necessarily the exclusive, emphasis on teaching the apprentice skill in a craft or trade. An apprenticeship agreement has to be evidenced by a written agreement, commonly known as an *indenture,* and it is usual, although not essential, for a parent or guardian to sign such a document.

Misconduct by an apprentice does not entitle an employer to dismiss the apprentice, but only to complain to the local magistrates who could order the apprentice to carry out his agreement, failing which the magistrates could declare the apprenticeship to be at an end. A similar result might also arise as a result of really serious misconduct on the part of the apprentice; that is, misconduct which caused actual injury to the employer and which amounts to a refusal to be taught.

At one time it was customary for the apprentice to pay a premium for his tuition, but now that full employment is fairly general it is very much the exception for a premium to be paid.

CONTRACTS OF EMPLOYMENT

Until the passing of the *Contracts of Employment Act, 1963,* a contract of employment was merely a matter of agreement between employer and employee with no writing necessary as a general rule. In many cases some of the obligations between the parties were regulated by general contracts formed between the trade unions and federations of employers or large corporate employers.

The above Act affects the large majority of employers and workers and prescribes the minimum periods of notice which must be given by either an employer or an employee to terminate employment. In the case of the employer giving notice to an employee it varies from not less than one week for those with 26 weeks' or more, but less than two years' service, to not less than four weeks in the case of those with five years' or more continuous service, whilst an employee who has held a job for more than 26 weeks continuously must give the employer at least one week's notice, but the parties may of course agree on any longer period. There are complex rules about payment during notice, but the broad effect is to provide for normal pay to be given.

The other main provision of the Act is to require that certain conditions of employment must be given in writing to an employee. In essence such a statement must mention the date when the employment began, the rate of pay, the intervals at which remuneration is paid, the hours of work, holidays and holiday pay arrangements, sick leave and sick pay arrangements, details of pension scheme and length of notice which the employer must give and receive. If an already existing contract between an employer and an employee contains at least all these particulars, a further written statement in the form laid down by the Act need not be given. If the terms of employment are altered the employee must be informed of this within one month, by means of a written statement.

The Act has not affected some older features of employment law, such as summary dismissal. In the main an employer may only dismiss an employee on the spot where the employee has been guilty of serious misconduct. This must be more than an isolated act of insolence, and should be such as to interfere either with the business of the employer or with the ability of the employee to perform his duties. The acceptance of bribes, betrayal of an employer's secrets or drunkenness at work would be suitable examples.

On the other side of the coin, an employee may leave his employment without giving notice if the employer has been responsible for what amounts to a total breach of the contract of employment.

There are a few other instances where dismissal without notice might be justified, but it would probably be correct to say that the general tendency in business is to terminate employment with due notice and, if thought desirable, to pay wages in lieu of notice. Incidentally, the employee has no right to bring the contract to an end by repaying his own wages to the employer in lieu of notice.

REDUNDANCY

The coming of automation brought with it the need for fewer jobs. From the early 1950s Parliament debated the question of redundancy, but repeated attempts by M.P.s to introduce legislation for severance pay in redundancy met with defeat. By 1964 both employers and the T.U.C. were in favour of higher unemployment benefit as compared with severance pay.

Notwithstanding, the *Redundancy Payments Act* was passed in 1965 and is applicable to both manual and clerical workers. Certain persons, however, are excepted from the provisions of the Act; these include employees with less than 104 weeks' continuous service; part timers, relatives of the employer in certain circumstances; and those who have been dismissed on grounds of misconduct, or on grounds of ill health.

An employee is regarded as having been dismissed because of redundancy if the reason for his dismissal is that his employer's requirements for employees to do work of a particular kind have grown less, or stopped altogether.

This may be due to a variety of reasons. The employer may be going out of business; going over to automation; or reorganising various departments, or there may be a trade recession in the area. The crucial question is—"Does the employer need fewer men to do work of a particular kind?"

The Act schedules the methods of calculating the redundancy pay entitlement—up to a maximum of £1200.

Should any dispute arise between employer and employee over the provisions of the Act; *i.e.* in determining whether the employee's service was continuous or not—such disputes go before the Redundancy Payments Tribunal. The tribunal is composed of a permanent chairman who is a lawyer, a representative of the employers and a representative of the employees. The latter is normally a trade union official.

DUTIES OF THE EMPLOYER

The duties of the employer depend largely upon the relevant contract of employment. Those listed below do, however, represent duties which the law would deem to arise out of the normal contract of employment:

1. The employer must pay his employees either the wages agreed upon in the relevant contract or at least the wages directed to be paid by statute, whenever any such statute applies.

2. The employer must indemnify the employee for all expenses and liabilities properly incurred in doing his work.

3. For so long as an employee is paid the agreed or prescribed remuneration he cannot require the employer to provide him with work, apart from exceptions such as where commission is an essential feature of the remuneration or where publicity is important as, for example, in the case of actresses.

4. The employer must provide a reasonably safe system of work and this principle covers not only plant and premises but also such things as management and supervision. Thus, under this heading, adequate inter-departmental co-ordination is necessary.

References

Many people are under the impression that an employer is bound to give a reference (or a "character" as this is occasionally called), but that is not so, irrespective of the unwarranted assumptions which some people might make as a result.

If an employer does give a reference he must not state anything other than that which he honestly believes to be true and, if this is the case, the employee may well have no action even if the reference contains some uncomplimentary remarks about him. In legal language, the *doctrine of qualified privilege* might act as a shield against any action for defamation which the employee might be tempted to bring.

Payment of wages

In Britain the amount and manner of payment of wages are essentially a matter of agreement between the parties; such agreement may be either an individual one or the result of a collective bargain between a particular employer or a group of employers and a trade union. In that circumstance, evidence is necessary to show that such collective agreement was intended to apply in the particular case.

Over the years Parliament has, to some extent, circumscribed individual freedom over wage agreements, and various statutes now prescribe what the minimum rate should be. The majority of such instances arise under the *Wages Councils Acts, 1945–48*, but their origin goes back to the *Trade Boards Act* of 1909 set up to make statutory provision for minimum wages in what were called "sweated industries" where trade unionism was weak or non-existent and wages very low. The Secretary of State for Employment and Productivity (who superseded the Minister of Labour) may now set up a *wages council* whenever he or she is of the opinion that machinery in a particular trade for the regulation of wages is not adequate or is likely to cease. Once established, such council will consist of an equal number of representatives of employers and employees together with not less than one nor more than three "independents" who are often barristers and one of whom acts as chairman. The secretary makes all the appointments, but he would usually seek advice from such representative bodies as he may deem appropriate to consult.

A wages council has power to prepare what are known as "wages regulation proposals" and when made, usually after considerable review in draft form, the secretary would normally give effect to them with the result that such rates become the statutory minimum, failure to pay which would amount to a criminal offence. As an alternative, the Secretary has power to refer the proposals back for reconsideration and resubmission, but he has no power to vary them.

Regulation of a similar nature to that contained in the *Wages Councils Acts* may be found in the *Road Haulage Wages Act, 1938*, the *Catering Wages Act, 1943*, and various *Agricultural Wages (Regulation) Acts*.

Parliament has also intervened to control the manner in which wages should be paid. During the early years of the Industrial Revolution a practice grew up of paying wages in kind (or in truck), instead of in cash and, although this was understandable in certain circumstances, the idea was susceptible of considerable abuse in the hands of unscrupulous employers. To deal with such abuse, the *Truck Acts, 1831–1940*, were passed, to protect the worker in the free enjoyment of his earnings, prescribing that the wages payable to "workmen"—that is employees engaged in manual labour—should be actually paid in the current coin of the realm and any contract for payment in any other form was declared void. Moreover, any contract purporting to regulate the place where, or the manner in which, or the person with whom, any part of the wages should be expended was also void. Furthermore, no deductions were to be made from the wages of manual labourers except as authorised by law. Authorised deductions cover such things as income tax, national insurance and superannuation payments. Deductions may also be made for goods to be used by the employee in his work as well as for bad or negligent work, and even for fines, but all these are hedged in by various conditions such as consent of the worker and reasonableness of the deductions. Finally, deductions may be made for such things as the rent of a house let by the employer as well as payments to third parties authorised in writing by the employee.

In recent years, the *Truck Acts* have become something of an anachronism not only because strong unionism could soon deal with the evils against which the Acts were passed, but also because many manual workers now have bank accounts. The *Payment of Wages Act, 1960*, was passed authorising employers upon written request by an employee to pay wages other than in the current coin of the realm. Various methods of doing this have been authorised: payment into a bank account, payment by money and postal order and payment by cheque made payable to the worker. If such a system is used the employee must be given a statement in writing showing how his net wages have been calculated.

If a manual worker is unable to collect his wages because of illness, the employer may send the wages either by money order or by postal order and here no prior written permission from the employee is necessary. The precise definition of a manual worker has rather naturally given rise to a fair amount of litigation, but it is perhaps not necessary to try to analyse that here.

DUTIES OF EMPLOYEE

The duties of an employee also depend on the relevant contract of employment. Those listed below represent some general duties which the law would deem to apply in most cases:

1. The employee must obey his employer's lawful orders within the scope of the service undertaken by him. Such orders could lawfully cover both the nature of the work and the manner of performance, but an employee is not expected to expose himself to personal danger arising out of the employment other than that which he has agreed to accept.

2. The employee must use reasonable care not only in looking after

his employer's property, but also generally in the conduct of the employer's affairs so as not to involve the employer in loss.

3. The employee should be loyal to his employer and not abuse the employer's confidence. This duty connotes not only absolute financial honesty and secrecy over confidential information, but also refusal, even in his spare time, to assist his employer's competitors.

4. He must not absent himself without leave during working hours.

5. The employee must also abide by such restraint of trade clauses as may be reasonably necessary to protect the employer's trade connections or trade secrets, but in practice the number of employees thus affected is comparatively small. The restraint of trade doctrine has already been touched upon under contracts, but the point to remember here is that within limits it could bind an employee even after he has left a particular job.

FACTORIES ACTS

GENERAL PROVISIONS

Most students will have studied the advantages and disadvantages of the factory system and will have read of the decline of *laissez-faire* which militated against the reform of many of the employment abuses that arose out of the Industrial Revolution. But many a decade before the modern Welfare State came into being the social conscience had been awakened and, slowly but surely, the worst abuses were compulsorily cured. At first the reformers concentrated on limiting the hours of work of young people, but later various measures which came to be known as the *Factories Acts* tried to establish what might be described as the bare minimum of reasonably satisfactory working conditions. From time to time *Factories Acts* were codified and the *Factories Act, 1961*, consolidates all existing factory legislation. In this book there is only scope for the barest outline of this Act and any reader who has responsibilities under the Act should, of course, consult the Act itself and any regulations which may have been made thereunder to cover a particular trade. A few of the more essential features are analysed below.

Administration

The administration of the Act is in the hands of Factory Inspectors, appointed by the Secretary of State for Employment and Productivity (formerly the Minister of Labour). They have powers to grant a number of exemptions from the provisions of the Act if they see fit.

Definition

The full definition of a factory is contained in Sections 175 and 176 of the Act.

A factory includes any premises where one or more persons are employed in manual labour for the purposes of making articles, altering, repairing or adapting them for sale. These manufacturing processes must be carried on by way of trade, or for the purposes of gain, and the employer has a right of access to or control over the premises.

HEALTH PROVISIONS

The factory should be kept clean. Accumulations of dirt and refuse must be removed daily from benches and floors while the floor of every workroom must be washed or otherwise suitably cleaned at least once a week. All ceilings, inside walls and partitions with an impervious and smooth surface must be washed with hot water and soap or cleaned by other approved methods every fourteen months. If the surface is kept painted then repainting at intervals of not more than seven years is necessary, in addition to the washing. If the surfaces are whitewashed then these must be renewed every fourteen months.

A factory must not be overcrowded and, according to one test, there must be in each workroom at least 400 cubic feet of space for every person employed, not counting space more than 14 ft from the floor.

In each workroom a "reasonable" temperature must be maintained by non-injurious methods, but what is reasonable may vary according to the nature of the work done. In any room where a substantial proportion of the work is done sitting, and does not involve serious physical effort, the temperature must not be less than 60° F (15° C) after the first hour. A thermometer must be kept in a suitable position in each workroom.

Adequate ventilation of workrooms must be secured by the circulation of fresh air. Serious diseases can be caused by abrasive dust and poisonous fumes and steps to render these harmless may have to be taken not only under the general requirement of the *Factories Act*, but also under some detailed and technical regulations made on such subject.

There must be sufficient and suitable lighting (artificial or natural) in every part of the factory in which persons are working or passing. Where wet processes are carried on adequate means for draining the floors must be provided. Sufficient and suitable sanitary conveniences, separate for each sex, must be provided for persons employed in the factory. They must be kept clean, properly lighted and ventilated.

The Act contains various provisions requiring workers in certain dangerous trades to take their meals in places other than workrooms.

SAFETY PROVISIONS

The main safety provisions of the Act cover the fencing of machinery. Every part of transmission machinery and every dangerous part of other machinery and all parts of electric generators, motors, rotary convertors and flywheels directly connected to them must be securely fenced, unless in such a position or of such construction as to be safe to every person employed as if they were securely fenced. All fencing must be of sub-stantial construction and be maintained in an efficient state. Devices or appliances for promptly cutting off the power from the transmission machinery must be provided in every room or place where work is carried on. There have been a number of cases on this requirement and the general conclusion seems to be that the duty is an absolute obliga-tion, whatever the practical difficulties may be. Nevertheless, the Act does not protect against injury caused by a breakage in the machine itself, nor is there in general any liability for materials processed in the machine or for any machine sent to a factory for repair.

The Act also places restrictions on the cleaning of machinery in motion by women or young persons. Furthermore, restrictions are placed on young persons working without training on any machine specified by the Minister to be dangerous.

Lifting appliances must be securely constructed and properly main-tained and must be subject to period examination by a competent per-son. There are additional requirements in the case of passenger hoists and lifts.

Floors, passages and stairs must be of sound construction and properly maintained and must, as far as reasonably practical, be kept free from any obstruction and from any substance likely to cause per-sons to slip. Every staircase must have a handrail.

Safe access to work must as far as is reasonably practical be provided to any workplace. If a person works at a place where he has not a secure foothold or handhold and is liable to fall more than ten feet such a place must be secured by fencing or otherwise.

Special precautions are laid down for work in confined spaces where men are liable to be overcome by dangerous fumes. Steam boilers must have certain gauges and valves and must, of course, be properly main-tained and periodically examined by a competent person.

Goggles or screens must be used in industrial processes where there is risk of injury to the eyes.

A fire escape is obviously very important and all factories other than small ones must hold a certificate from the local authority that the means of escape from a fire are such as may be reasonably required. These means must be properly maintained and kept free from obstruc-tion. While any person is in the factory for the purpose of employment or meals, doors must not be so fastened or locked that they cannot be easily and immediately opened from the inside. All doors other than those of the sliding kind must open outwards. Fire exits must be marked by notices printed in red letters of adequate size. In certain factories provision for giving warning in the case of fire must be made, and effective steps taken to ensure that the workers are familiar with the means of escape, their use and the routine to be followed in case of fire. Appropriate fire-fighting equipment, placed in such a way as to be readily available, must be provided in every factory.

WELFARE PROVISIONS

An adequate supply of wholesome drinking water, with an upturned jet convenient for drinking or suitable drinking vessels with facilities for rinsing them, must be provided at suitable points throughout the factory, conveniently accessible to all workers.

Adequate and suitable washing facilities, including soap and clean towels or other suitable means of cleaning or drying, must be provided and maintained for all workers. There must be provision for adequate and suitable accommodation for clothing not worn during working hours, as well as such arrangements as are reasonably practicable for drying such clothing.

Where any employed persons have in the course of their employment reasonable opportunity for sitting without detriment to their work, there must be provided for their use suitable facilities for sitting, sufficient to enable them to take advantage of such opportunities. The facilities must include a foot rest with the seat.

In every factory there must be provided a first-aid box or cupboard of the prescribed standard—which varies with the number of persons employed—to be in the charge of a responsible person who must always be available during working hours. In every workroom a notice must be affixed stating the name of the person in charge of the box in respect of that room.

DANGEROUS TRADE REGULATIONS

The Minister has power to certify any process or work to be dangerous and to make special regulations. In essence, "dangerous" means a risk of bodily injury to the persons employed. Of many trades already regulated, chemical works, the manufacture of cinematograph films and the painting of vehicles, will serve as examples of the type of trades involved.

NOTIFICATION OF ACCIDENTS AND INDUSTRIAL DISEASES

Written notice must be sent forthwith to the district inspector of factories of all fatal accidents and of all accidents causing an employee more than three days' disablement from earning full wages. Where death occurs after this notice has been given, the inspector must immediately be notified of the death.

The Minister has power to extend the notification requirement to cover other accidents, while notice of certain dangerous occurrences— the collapse of a crane, to give but one example—must be sent irrespective of whether or not disablement is caused

Certain industrial diseases such as lead poisoning occurring in a factory must also be reported.

EMPLOYMENT OF WOMEN AND YOUNG PERSONS

The Act does not limit the hours of work of adult men, but does control those of women and young persons (those of either sex under eighteen years old).

In what follows it is important to differentiate between "working hours" and "hours of employment"; the latter includes time for meal breaks which are usually assessed at a minimum of half-an-hour for each meal. The limitations, in general terms, for women (over eighteen years of age) are:

1. The maximum normal working hours in a day may not exceed nine, or in a week 48.

2. Work may not commence before 7 a.m. nor finish later than 8 p.m. (1 p.m. on Saturdays); no Sunday working is allowed, and no spell of work may exceed four and a half hours without an interval of at least half an hour. The work spell, however, may be extended to five hours if this includes an interval of at least ten minutes.

3. Overtime is permitted for dealing with pressure of work, though fairly strictly limited when applied to factories. The maximum is 100 hours in a year and six hours in any one week. In addition overtime may not be worked during more than 25 weeks in a year. The total hours of work, including overtime, may not exceed ten in a day (or ten and a half where a five-day week is in operation) and the total hours of employment must not exceed twelve in a day. The details in (2) above also apply to overtime working, but the Minister has considerable powers to vary the rules, particularly in factories using electricity.

For young persons the general limitations are:

1. Young persons (of either sex) over the age of 16 and under 18 may work the same hours and with the same restrictions as women.

2. For those under 16, eleven hours' employment in a day is the maximum allowed, and work may not commence before 7 a.m. nor end after 6 p.m. Apart from this restrictions are again usually the same as for women, though certain exceptions may be permitted (especially for young men), provided that notices in the prescribed form are sent to the District Inspector of Factories and posted in the factory.

3. No young person may remain in employment in a factory for longer than the prescribed period without examination and a certificate of fitness for the work involved from the appointed factory doctor. This is valid for one year, after which further examination is necessary.

NOTICES AND RECORDS

Under the Act every factory occupier has, before starting occupation, to submit a return giving various particulars about the factory, while a notice in the prescribed form has to be posted at the factory entrance giving certain information such as an abstract from the *Factories Act*, and a notice of the clock by which the work period and meal times are regulated. Each factory must maintain a "general register" recording all important matters concerning the factory, to include, for example, particulars about young persons employed, the washing of the factory and notifiable accidents.

OFFICES, SHOPS AND RAILWAY PREMISES ACT, 1963

The provisions of the *Offices, Shops and Railway Premises Acts* are similar to the health, safety and welfare measures of the 1961 *Factories Act*. Details as to space per person, cleanliness of the premises, regulations as to temperature, lighting, ventilation, sanitary conveniences, washing facilities, drinking water, cloakroom accommodation, sitting accommodation, the fencing of dangerous machinery and first aid are all virtually the same as those contained in the 1961 Act.

Premises to which the Act relates must be registered with the local authority, whose duty it is to see that the regulations laid down in the Act are observed.

If more than 20 persons are employed, or 10 other than on the ground floor, it is the duty of the local authority to see that fire precautions are adequate by ascertaining that there is a means of escape and adequate fire-fighting equipment. Only then will the necessary fire certificate be granted.

SOCIAL INSURANCE

The law with regard to social security is to be found principally in the *National Insurance Act, 1965*, as amended by the *National Insurance Acts, 1966* and *1967*. The 1965 Act consolidated the *National Insurance Acts, 1946–64*.

These Acts consolidated and extended various earlier schemes of insurance against such contingencies as old age, sickness and unemployment with the result that practically all citizens are now covered from school leaving age until retirement. In fact, the Act forms part of the cradle-to-the-grave security of the Welfare State. However, national insurance providing benefits for certain contingencies, on what from an accountancy point of view is a more or less self-balancing basis, must be distinguished from the national health service providing free medical attention and treatment for all, whether insured or not, and with the bulk of the service's revenues coming from general taxation.

National insurance used to be administered by the Ministry of Pensions and National Insurance. In 1966, however, by the *Ministry of Social Security Act*, the Ministry of Pensions and National Insurance was abolished and its place taken by the Ministry of Social Security. The National Assistance Board was supplanted, by the same Act, by the Supplementary Benefits Commission. Should anyone query the benefit awarded they may appeal against the decision of their local social security officers to a local tribunal. It will consist of an independent chairman, one member selected from a panel of representatives of employers and one member selected from a panel of employed persons. Members are usually chosen for their knowledge of social problems. The final appeal is to the Commissioner.

National Insurance contributors—which, as a general rule, includes everyone between school leaving age and pension age—fall into three classes: employed persons who pay class 1 contributions (employers also pay at this rate); self-employed persons who pay class 2 contributions; non-employed persons and those who are not gainfully employed, who pay class 3 contributions. Class 1 contributors, taking employers and employees together, pay the most; class 2 a lower amount, and class 3 the lowest, but the range of benefits varies as well. To get any of the benefits in full a contributor must have satisfied what are known as "contribution conditions," which in essence involves the payment of a certain minimum number of contributions over a given period of time. The conditions vary for different benefits, but it is not proposed to go into these in any greater detail, nor is it proposed to quote the current benefit rates because these change from time to time. It is perhaps worth remembering that when a person is drawing sickness or unemployment benefit no contribution is then payable by him and he will, in fact, get a credit in his national insurance account, thus putting him on the same basis as if he had in fact paid contributions. It should also be noted that married women who are employed may choose to pay contributions and so get all benefits in their own right or not to pay and rely on contributions made by their husbands. Although a choice is not irrevocable a married woman asked to exercise such choice should give the matter very careful thought.

The funds necessary to pay the various benefits are raised by the contributions of insured persons, by the employers, and certain sums are also allocated by Parliament.

Contributions by insured persons and employers are paid weekly by stamp, and, as well as national insurance, cover contributions to the Redundancy Payments Fund, and the Selective Employment Tax, both payable by the employer, the National Health Service Contribution and Industrial Injuries Insurance.

The Ministry has issued a whole series of most useful leaflets explaining the various benefits and students who have occasion to study any of these further might ask for a copy of the relevant leaflet at the nearest Ministry office.

From an industrial administration point of view perhaps the most important benefits are retirement, sickness and unemployment benefits. At the time of writing, retirement benefit may normally be claimed at the age of 65 in the case of men and 60 in the case of women, but it is a condition precedent that any applicant should have retired from regular employment. This condition is quite separate from what has become known as the "earnings rule" which limits the amount a person drawing retirement benefit can earn from casual work before the pension is liable to be reduced. Once a man has reached 70 and a woman 65 none of these limitations applies. Pensions can be paid in any part of the world.

Sickness benefit is payable when a person is incapable of work through illness, mental or physical, provided he is not disqualified. A person may be disqualified for up to six weeks if his incapacity is due to his own misconduct, or if he fails without good cause to undergo a medical or other examination or such treatment as may be required, or to follow any prescribed rules concerning sickness.

Unemployment benefit is payable when a person is unemployed, provided this is not the result of a stoppage of work due to a trade dispute at his place of employment. Such restriction does not apply when a person has permanently changed his job since becoming unemployed, nor where he is not in effect directly involved in the trade dispute. Disqualification for up to six weeks may apply when a person has lost his employment through his own misconduct or has left his employment voluntarily without just cause. It also applies when the unemployed person has refused suitable employment or training and this includes neglecting a reasonable opportunity of seeking such employment and refusing to carry out any reasonable written recommendations from an employment exchange.

Other benefits under the Act are maternity benefit, both the grant and the weekly allowance, widow's benefit, guardian's allowance, death grant and child's special allowance.

INDUSTRIAL INJURIES

The law regarding industrial injuries can be found in the *National Insurance (Industrial Injuries) Acts, 1965 to 1967*. The 1965 Act is the principal piece of legislation.

These Acts lay down a compulsory insurance system and, apart from various exceptions set out in the Acts, all persons employed in insurable employment must be insured. No one can opt out of contributing and there is no age limit.

Two different types of injury are covered:

1. that caused by an accident *arising out of and in the course of the insured* person's employment; and
2. certain specified diseases and injuries due to the nature of the insured person's employment.

The phrase "out of and in the course of employment" dates back to an earlier statute, the *Workmen's Compensation Act, 1897*, and, as a result, a substantial number of decisions exist which interpret the phrase.

In general, the phrase covers periods at work but not, apart from exceptions applying to such people as representatives, time spent travelling to and from work. Employment is not interrupted when an employee does something he is not employed to do, but which is reasonably incidental to his work, such as having a meal in the canteen. Even accidents resulting from a breach of regulations may be covered if done for the purpose of, or in connection with, the employer's business. Most accidents occurring while meeting an "emergency" are also covered, the emphasis here being on saving life or property.

Conversely, there have been many decisions where certain accidents have been held not to have arisen out of the employment. This occurs if the injured person is doing work different from that for which he was engaged. Examples include accidents to drivers who deviate to see a friend; accidents to persons cleaning machinery when this is no part of the job; accidents caused solely by the worker's drunken state or his indulgence in horseplay.

Three basic benefits are payable. These are industrial injury, disablement and death benefits. *Industrial injury* benefit is paid out for incapacity during the first 26 weeks after the accident. In most cases this covers the period during which injured persons are unable to work. The benefit is paid weekly, with increases for dependants.

Disablement benefit is payable when industrial injury benefit ceases, if the injured person has suffered any *loss of physical or mental faculty* as a result of the accident or disease.

Under the 1965 Act an injured person is entitled to disablement benefit if the loss of mental and physical capacity is 1% or over. If the disablement is assessed at less than 20% a disablement *gratuity* is paid; if more, a disablement pension is paid. The assessment varies from 100% for the loss of sight or very severe facial disfigurement, for example, to 14% for the loss of an index finger. If disablement is assessed at 20% or more, a weekly pension is payable according to a prescribed scale, but if it is less than 20% there is a gratuity which is generally paid as a lump sum. "Disablement questions" are decided by medical boards—there is provision for appeal to a medical appeal tribunal—but decisions may be reviewed on evidence of non-disclosure or misrepresentation or that there has been an unforeseen and substantial aggravation of the result of the relevant injury. Disablement benefit may be supplemented by various benefits which apply when there are special circumstances. A special hardship allowance may be paid when a person is unable to follow his regular occupation or to do work of an equivalent standard, bearing in mind the prospects of advancement as well as the rate of remuneration. Unemployability supplement may be claimed if a person is permanently incapable of work. Constant attendance allowance may be paid where a person is so seriously handicapped as to need help with the ordinary necessities of life every day. If a beneficiary enters a hospital to receive approved hospital treatment his pension, if assessed at less than 100%, will be regarded as if it had been assessed at 100% for the period of treatment.

Industrial *death benefit* is the third main type of industrial injury benefit. This takes the form of a pension payable to the widow of an insured person who has died as a result of accident at work or prescribed industrial disease, but in order to get more than a nominal pension the widow must satisfy certain conditions such as being over 50 years of age or having responsibility for dependants.

As in the case of social insurance, the Ministry publishes some leaflets giving further useful information about industrial injury benefits. There is also a leaflet on prescribed industrial diseases.

Claims for benefit and any questions arising from an award are determined by an insurance officer, a local appeal tribunal or the Industrial Injuries Commissioners appointed under the Act.

The insurance officers, are the first "tribunal" to which claims are presented, while the ultimate appeal lies from the local appeal tribunal of three members to the Commissioner. It should be noted that an injured person is not restricted for a remedy to the *National Insurance (Industrial Injuries) Acts, 1965* to *1967*. If the injury is the result of the employer's negligence the employee may sue for damages at common law. The employee must then prove that the employer has failed to carry out his common law duties. These are a duty to provide a safe place to work in, safe plant and appliances and a safe system of work.

An employer has certain defences against an action. He may argue that the injured employee not only knew of the risk but also consented to incur the risk of injury. However, this agreement *cannot* be cancelled where there has been a breach of statutory duty. The employer may also argue that any award to an employee should be reduced because the employee was partly to blame.

INDUSTRIAL ARBITRATION

Industrial arbitration is quite separate from the commercial arbitration already studied, and refers to some legal problems arising out of the settlement of industrial disputes. One way of settling such a dispute is to refer the matter to an independent arbitrator, but this is a matter upon which all parties must agree because compulsory arbitration by law has not been tried out in Britain except in a somewhat half-hearted manner during war-time.

Under the *Industrial Courts Act, 1919*, the Industrial Court was set up as a standing body for the settlement of trade disputes. Its members were appointed by the Minister of Labour (now Secretary of State for Employment and Productivity) and operate under an independent chairman appointed by the Crown and with the status of a High Court judge, but it is not subject to Government control nor is it part of the country's judicial system. There is no means of compelling an unwilling party to have recourse to the Industrial Court nor are its decisions enforceable, but when acted upon by the parties they will become implied terms in the relevant contracts of employment.

Under the *Industrial Courts Act* the Secretary may set up a court of inquiry into any trade dispute and, although any recommendation has no legal enforceability, the reports of such courts often help to settle a dispute.

The *Terms and Conditions of Employment Act, 1959* provides that wherever in a particular industry "recognised terms and conditions of employment" have become established, whether as a result of a particular arbitration or of trade union activity or otherwise, any organisation of employers or workers may submit a "claim" to the Secretary for Employment and Productivity requesting that such terms and conditions should be compulsorily extended to a particular employer not already abiding by such terms and conditions. The Secretary may refer the matter to the Industrial Court, who after enquiry could make an award as a result of which the employer concerned would, in effect, be legally bound to adopt the "code of industrial relations" under reference.

EXAMINATION QUESTIONS

1. X, who has only one arm, is injured when unroping a load of timber which has been delivered to his employer's factory. When sued for damages by X, the employer pleads:

(*a*) that X was negligent in not waiting for an inspection by a competent person to see that the load was safe;

(*b*) that X willingly accepted what he knew to be a dangerous job; and

(*c*) that, but for X's disability, he could have prevented the timber from falling upon him.

Discuss the validity of each of these defences.

2. (*a*) Summarise the particulars that an occupier of a factory must enter in the general register in order to comply with the *Factories Act, 1961.*

(*b*) Under what circumstances must the district inspector of factories be informed of accidents and industrial diseases?

3. Summarise the general provisions as to welfare contained in the *Factories Act.*

4. A contract of service between an employer and an employee provides that the employee shall not, within a specified number of years after the termination of his service, engage in any kind of business carried on by the employer within a specified area.

Discuss the extent to which such a provision may (if at all) be enforceable against the employee.

5. The *National Insurance (Industrial Injuries) Act, 1965*, provides for

548 INDUSTRIAL ADMINISTRATION AND MANAGEMENT

insurance against personal injury by accident arising out of and in the course of insurable employment.

(a) Explain and illustrate the meaning of the expression "out of and in the course of insurable employment."

(b) State your opinion (with reasons) whether a bus conductor, who has been attacked and seriously injured by a gang of disorderly youths while in the course of his employment, will *prima facie* be eligible for disablement benefit.

6. What do you understand by a *period of interruption* of employment for the purposes of the *National Insurance Act, 1965*? In what circumstances, if any, are two such periods treated as one period?

7. (a) Give a concise account of the powers and duties of the Minister of Labour with regard to the prevention and settlement of trade disputes.

(b) Explain briefly what you understand by the following terms:

(i) conciliation;
(ii) voluntary arbitration;
(iii) compulsory arbitration.

8. (a) What length of notice should be given by an employer to terminate an employee's contract of service?

(b) In what circumstances has an employer the right to dismiss an employee without notice?

9. State with reasons your opinion as to whether a person insured under the *National Insurance (Industrial Injuries) Act, 1965*, would be entitled to benefit in the following circumstances:

(a) being a factory employee, he is injured in an accident while on his way home from work;

(b) being a foreman, he is assaulted and injured by an insubordinate workman during a meal break.

10. Captain Foulenough, then engaged to be married, recently commissioned Reynolds, an artist, to paint a portrait of his fiancée, and orally agreed to pay £250 as the artist's fee. The engagement having been broken off, Foulenough now refuses to accept or pay for the finished portrait. Advise Reynolds.

11. Discuss the exceptions to the principle of the *Truck Acts* that manual workers must receive their wages in full without deductions, stating in each case any conditions necessary to enable an employer to take advantage of the exception.

12. (a) Explain the meaning of *valuable consideration*, and its importance in the Law of Contract.

(b) Jones lent £1000 to Smith, who is not at present able to repay. Jones accordingly offers to accept £900 in settlement if that sum is paid at once. Upon payment of £900 to him, Jones gives Smith a receipt "in full settlement" of the debt, but subsequently claims the balance of £100.

Discuss the validity of this claim.

13. State, with reasons, your opinion as to whether a person insured under

the *National Insurance (Industrial Injuries) Act, 1965*, would be entitled to benefit in the following circumstances:

(*a*) being a locomotive driver, he is injured while driving a train by a pellet from a shotgun fired by a sportsman whose land adjoins the railway line;

(*b*) being a railway porter, whose duty it is to proceed to a certain station, he walks along the line in breach of regulations, and is injured by a passing train.

BIBLIOGRAPHY

For the benefit of those who want further reading material a list of books is given below. This is not intended to be exhaustive.

Accountancy

Batty, J., *Management Accountancy*, Macdonald & Evans, London.
Hartley, W. C. F., *An Introduction to Business Accounting for Managers*, Pergamon Press, Oxford.
Taylor, A. H. and Shearing, H., *Financial and Cost Accounting for Management*, Macdonald & Evans, London.

Economics

Hanson, J. L., *Textbook of Economics*, Macdonald & Evans, London.

Economic History

Wright, F. J., *The Evolution of Modern Industrial Organisation*, Macdonald & Evans, London.

Law

Frank, W. F., *Legal Aspects of Industry and Commerce*, Harrap, London.

Management

Branton, N., *Introduction to the Theory and Practice of Management*, Chatto and Windus, London.
Brech, E. F. L., *The Principles and Practice of Management*, Longmans London.
Drucker, P. F., *The Practice of Management*, Heinemann, London.
Stewart, R., *The Reality of Management*, Heinemann, London.

Marketing

Bolling, C. L., *Sales Management*, Pitman, London.
Giles, G. B., *Marketing Management*, Macdonald & Evans, London.
McIver, C., *Marketing*, Business Publications, London.

Office Management

Denyer, J. C., *Office Management*, Macdonald & Evans, London.
Symes, M., *Office Procedures and Management*, Heinemann, London.

Personnel Management

I.C.W.A., *Employee Remuneration and Incentives*, Gee, London.
McGregor, D., *The Human Side of Enterprise*, McGraw-Hill, New York.
Northcott, C. H., *Personnel Management*, Pitman, London.

Production Management

Radford, J. D. and Richardson, D. B., *Management of Production*, Cleaver-Hume Press/Macmillan.

International Labour Office, *Introduction to Work Study*, I.L.O.
Quick, J. H., Duncan, J. H. and Malcolm, J. A., Jr., *Work-Factor Time Standards*, McGraw-Hill, New York.
Rissik, H., *Quality Control in Production*, Pitman, London.
H.M.S.O., *Sampling Procedures and Tables for Inspection by Attributes*, Defence Specification (DEF 131A).
Sargeaunt, M. J., *Operational Research for Management*, Heinemann, London.
Burbidge, John L., *The Principles of Production Control*, Macdonald & Evans, London.
Better Ways, British Productivity Council, London.

Statistical Method

Moroney, M. J., *Facts from Figures*, Penguin Books Ltd, London.
Thirkettle, G. L., *Wheldon's Business Statistics and Statistical Method*, Macdonald & Evans, London.

INDEX